◄NEOS►
G U I D E

INDONESIA

handwritten notes:

WEST JA
KARTA &
INDONESIA
(O21

JIH·KP·BARU
BLK·MUSHOLA
ATAQWA.

Jimmy Sulaiman
536-77938 - Home.
Mosque.

MICHELIN
Travel Publications

Note to readers

Due to the current climate of insecurity prevalent in parts of Indonesia, certain islands, such as Timor and Kalimantan, do not feature in this guide. Those islands which are covered – Sumatra, Java, Sulawesi, Bali, Lombok, Sumbawa, Komodo and Flores – are highlighted in red on the map of Indonesia on the inside front cover.

To see how the guide is organised, turn to the table of contents on the following pages.

Practical information – The chapter entitled "Practical Information" gives general information to help you prepare for your trip and get by once there. In the section entitled "Exploring Indonesia", after each description of a town or site, there is a practical section (eg p 410 "Making the most of Ubud") giving information about the place in question: access, useful addresses, accommodation, eating out, shopping, and so on. Because of Indonesia's rampant inflation, rather than giving specific prices, hotels and restaurants have been classed by category to help you plan your budget. An explanation of these categories can be found on the inside back cover. However, we are obliged to point out that addresses and opening hours may change, and that certain pieces of practical information may have changed since publication.

Maps and plans – Place names and landscape features are given in the local language (usually Indonesian). However, on town plans, certain sites and landmarks (square, museum, etc) are referred to in English. A glossary of Indonesian words used in the text and on the maps can be found on the inside back cover (a full glossary is on p 111). The tour itineraries described and shown on the maps give ideas for excursions off the beaten track; ■ indicates possible overnight halts. Due to the often unreliable nature of Indonesian maps, as well as the difficult terrain evident in parts of the country, certain scales are approximate.

Michelin Travel Publications
Published in 2001

◁NE⊙S▷

N ew – In the NEOS guides emphasis is placed on the discovery and enjoyment of a new destination through meeting the people, tasting the food and absorbing the exotic atmosphere. In addition to recommendations on which sights to see, we give details on the most suitable places to stay and eat, on what to look out for in traditional markets and where to go in search of the hidden character of the region, its crafts and its dancing rhythms. For those keen to explore places on foot, we provide guidelines and useful addresses in order to help organise walks to suit all tastes.

E xpert – The NEOS guides are written by people who have travelled in the country and researched the sites before recommending them by the allocation of stars. Accommodation and restaurants are similarly recommended by a 🏠 on the grounds of quality and value for money. Cartographers have drawn easy-to-use maps with clearly marked itineraries, as well as detailed plans of towns, archeological sites and large museums.

⊙ pen to all cultures, the NEOS guides provide an insight into the daily lives of the local people. In a world that is becoming ever more accessible, it is vital that religious practices, regional etiquette, traditional customs and languages be understood and respected by all travellers. Equipped with this knowledge, visitors can seek to share and enjoy with confidence the best of the local cuisine, musical harmonies and the skills involved in the production of arts and crafts.

S ensitive to the atmosphere and heritage of a foreign land, the NEOS guides encourage travellers to see, hear, smell and feel a country, through words and images. Take inspiration from the enthusiasm of our experienced travel writers and make this a journey full of discovery and enchantment.

INDONESIA

Official name: Republic of Indonesia
Land area: 1 919 317 sqkm
Population: 210 000 000
Capital: Jakarta (Island of Java)
Currency: the rupiah (Rp)

Setting the scene

Volcanoes mirrored
in the rice fields
(Lombok)

"TANAH AIR KITA"
OUR LAND, OUR WATERS

The name that Indonesia has chosen for itself refers to a land of oceans and seas, with a necklace of islands, islets, reefs and volcanoes, a vast garland stretching along the equator on the borders of Asia and Australia, the Indian and the Pacific oceans. No fewer than 17 500 islands fan out, covering 5 000km from east to west and over 2 000km from north to south, making up the **largest archipelago in the world**. All these plots of land set end to end would make up an area some nine times larger than Great Britain, or just over a fifth of the size of the USA. Indonesia is like the separate pieces of a jigsaw puzzle, a dazzling mosaic of landscapes, some of it unexplored: several thousand of these islands are still un-named, and remain uninhabited, *terra incognita* covered in forest or ringed with coral, forgotten by time.

Twin curves across the sea

The map of Indonesia shows a double arc of islands standing out clearly, like two sets of stepping-stones that link the southern tip of the Malay Peninsula with the north coast of Australia. The more distinct of the pair, the outer arc of Sunda to the south, forms a perfect concave line. A little less clearly defined, the inner arc stretches out just above it, with three of the five largest islands in the archipelago: Kalimantan (the Indonesian portion of the island of Borneo), Sulawesi (formerly the Celebes) and Papua (formerly Irian Jaya, the western part of New Guinea), together with Maluku (the Moluccas).

Shifting plates

A region of continual evolution, this fragile string of islands scattered across the ocean is the result of intense pressure within the earth's crust. Three tectonic plates meet here: the Australian plate, which is moving northward, the Pacific plate, which is sliding to the southeast, and both pressing hard against the Eurasian continental plate.

As part of these movements, the **Sunda plateau** probably broke away from continental Asia during the secondary evolutionary era. Lying not far beneath the surface (the sea here is rarely more than 55m deep), this plateau underlies Borneo, the northeast part of Sumatra, the little islands of Bangka and Belitun and the Riau group of islands, as well as southern Thailand, Malaya and Cambodia: a stable zone where volcanic activity has largely died away. In its Indonesian regions, the generally low-lying landscape of Kalimantan stands out from the vast alluvial plains, similar to the landscape of eastern Sumatra.

The pattern changes round the edges of this tectonic platform, along the **arc of Sunda** (from southwest Sumatra to the Philippines, via Java, Bali and the Lesser Sunda Islands). Created by more recent tectonic activity, it presents a craggy ridge bristling with high summits, the dramatic peaks of gigantic and mostly submarine mountains, most of them volcanoes. The sea reaches unfathomable depths here (over 6 000m), and many of the mountain tops are lost in the clouds at heights of over 3 000m. The permanent snow-fields on the 5 030m summit of **Puncak Jaya** (Papua) stand out as the highest point in the whole of Indonesia.

Fiery mountains

With no fewer than 500 volcanoes – *gunung api* ("mountains of fire") in the national language – of which 128 remain active, Indonesia is the largest volcanic zone in the world. Activity is concentrated along a geological fracture line running from south-western Sumatra to Flores and then up towards Sulawesi and Maluku. Java alone has 33 volcanoes, 17 of them active. Sumatra has 21, while the Lesser Sunda Islands add to the total with the mountain peaks of Agung and Batur on Bali, Rinjani on Lombok and Kelimutu on Flores. Despite the danger, which may threaten anyone who approaches these monsters, climbing them is an unforgettable experience.

Murderous demons ...

Vulcanologists record at least one eruption every year in the archipelago, a very high average. Although many of the volcanoes merely grumble or spit out dense black clouds of smoke, their rage can also be extremely violent. One such episode was the explosion of **Tambora**, in Sumbawa (1815), probably the most deadly that the region has ever seen: hurling out tonnes of ash and stone for many kilometres around, the explosion killed some 42 000 people. **Krakatau** (Krakatoa), lying off the west coast of Java, was not far behind when it exploded in 1883: it caused a tidal wave worldwide and killed 36 000 people *(see sidebar p 236)*. Among the most impressive eruptions that marked the 20C, those of **Merapi**, Java, (1934), **Agung** in Bali (1963), and Semeru, Java (1978 and 1979), remain sharply etched in the memory.

... or kindly gods

In Java, Bali or elsewhere it is impossible to list all the gods dedicated to volcanoes. Simultaneously feared and venerated, their turbulence is responsible for the destruction of whole villages – but the cataclysms also fertilise the soil and are essential for the crops. Each eruption spreads a thick layer of ash rich in mineral salts, an unequalled natural fertiliser. Without this natural blessing the land would soon be impoverished, leached of all its goodness by the torrential rains. Thus endowed, the soil may yield up to three harvests a year in some regions, an advantage that explains the stubborn insistence on living in these dangerous zones where survival depends partly on the caprice of the volcanoes.

As a further benefit of the intense tectonic and volcanic activity, Indonesia possesses abundant mineral resources. As it surges up from the entrails of the earth, the molten magma brings enormous quantities of **minerals** to the surface – copper, sulphur, diamonds – wealth buried some 200km deep under the rocks that would remain unknown and inaccessible without the eruptions. The movement of the earth's plates also brings **rare metals** up to the surface, such as uranium, mercury and tungsten, together with gold and silver.

Equatorial climate, monsoons

Barely out of the airport, after long hours in an air conditioned plane, the warm humidity and stifling atmosphere are overwhelming. Rainfall here is calculated in metres, and the humidity content is around 80 %!

A monsoon region, Indonesia also experiences extremely varied climatic conditions from one part of the archipelago to another. The year is shaped by the reversal of winds that to varying degrees define the alternating pattern of dry and

The misdeeds of El Niño

This climatic phenomenon disrupts the entire global weather system, affecting ocean currents, and weakening and reversing the trade winds. Long restricted to the coast of Peru (where it was named "the child", meaning the Christ-child, because it appeared around Christmas time), El Niño shifted in the early 1980s away from South America and across the Pacific Ocean, to reach Asia and even Africa. By interrupting the pattern of the winds that regulate the monsoons of Southeast Asia, El Niño has brought drought to the area, with dramatic consequences. There is also the unwelcome effect of La Niña, a more localised phenomenon that occasionally follows, bringing incessant torrential rain in the midst of the dry season.

rainy seasons. The **northern trade winds** (from the northeast) bring torrential rain and prevail between October-November and April-May, while from June to September the **southern trade winds** (from the southeast) bring in drier and fresher air.

Other factors also affect the climate. The nearer to the equator, in particular, the more constant the humidity; the further away, the more perceptible the seasonal contrasts. The landscape relief also affects the rainfall; it is lower in eastern Bali and Lombok, from Sumbawa to Timor, where the dry season may last more than six months.

Tropical heat

With a relatively stable average temperature throughout the year, close to 26°C, Indonesia enjoys a perfect, mild climate. The air is naturally cooler in higher regions, and particularly at night, but the variation remains very slight. Above 1 000m the temperature drops noticeably: at around 20°C, Westerners revive while Indonesians feel cold, pulling on layers of warm clothing! Above 3 000m (only encountered when climbing some of the volcanoes), it becomes really cold and everyone needs heavy sweaters.

Luxuriant nature

Fertile farm plains and terraced rice fields in Java and Bali, dense luxuriant forests in Kalimantan, Sumatra, Sulawesi and Maluku, dry savannahs in Nusa Tenggara – the unique vegetation that covers the Indonesian islands is largely the result of the archipelago's geological and climatic contrasts. The country can take pride in having the richest and most varied flora in Asia or even the world. This tropical Eden contains a profusion of rare species, fragrant spices, medicinal plants, tempting fruit and shimmering flowers.

Protected by its island isolation, the **indigenous vegetation** (predating the arrival of mankind) has largely survived the centuries, despite the disturbances caused by human colonisation (hasty ground clearance, intensive farming, rapid urbanisation, the introduction of alien species from other countries) and natural disasters (volcanic, geological – earthquakes – or climatic). Some species have also evolved over time, adapting to a new ecosystem, and have even developed into **endemic** species, specific to a single island.

P Boursellier/Hoaqui

The impressive Mount Merapi, Java

The Wallace Line, a broken bridge between Asia and Australia

During a voyage of exploration which led him to all parts of the Indonesian islands, the British naturalist **Alfred Russel Wallace** (1823-1913) – a great admirer of his contemporary, Darwin – noted with astonishment the remarkable differences between the fauna and flora of the western islands, similar to those found in Asia, and the types found in the eastern islands, nearer to Australia. From this he inferred the existence of two distinct biological areas, marked off by a line through the **Strait of Makassar** between Borneo and Sulawesi and extending southwards between Bali and Lombok. In the scientist's opinion, a natural break occurred between Borneo, Sumatra, Java and Bali – formerly part of the continental mass of Asia – on one side, and the islands of Sulawesi, Sunda, Maluku and New Guinea, an offshoot of the Australian continent, on the other.

In modern times the Wallace Line has been challenged. It does not appear to be as clearly marked as its author asserted, and although the east-west demarcation shows up clearly, it appears in a more gradual and blurred form. Thus there is a very large transitional area of uncertain outline (Sulawesi, Maluku, and the Lesser Sunda Islands) known as **Wallacea**, where eastern and western influences are mingled. In this area the large number of islands encouraged the evolution of new original species.

One of the last primary forests

Predominating nearly two-thirds of the archipelago, on both sides of the equator (essentially Kalimantan, Sumatra, Sulawesi and Papua), the Indonesian tropical **rain forest** remains one of the largest in the world. More than 2 000 different plant species have been recorded here, most of them growing to dizzy heights. Their canopy, the leafy vault of tree-tops, is so dense that light can barely pierce it. In this warm, damp obscurity – a climate particularly favourable for small palm species, all varieties of fig, and wild orchids – many plants grow in symbiosis. Some, the **climbers** or lianas, grow by clinging on to the tree trunks or branches which act as support, while others, the **epiphytes**, grow on the highest trees to benefit from the sunlight and in their turn provide a home for lichens, mosses and heather. **Parasites** are not satisfied with clinging on to other plants; they also draw their nourishment from them, like the **rafflesia** *(see sidebar p 126)*, a giant orchid which absorbs sap through the roots of its creepers. Still more harmful, the **stranglers** (which include many fig species) spring out of the forks of great trees, sending long roots down to the ground and wrapping themselves round their host and stifling it. After this they develop into tree form, leaving only a long hollow column at the centre in the place of the original trunk.

The banyan, a sacred fig tree

A shaded place for meeting, the banyan stands at the heart of the village and also in front of the temples of the Hindu community, for whom it is a sacred tree. Unexpectedly, this immense tree (which belongs to the fig family) develops an aerial network of intertwining roots which, like enlaced lianas, hang down to the ground where they take root. They multiply indefinitely until they form a vault – the ideal shelter for an altar laden with offerings.

Mountain forests

A natural barrier to human activity, mountain escarpments and waterfalls still protect the mountain forests. These grow above an altitude of 1 000m, gradually giving way to more open and lower-growing vegetation. Many **tropical conifers**

Croton

Flamboyant

Poinsettia

Banyan

Jackfruit

Tree fern

H. Choimet

(different varieties of pine and araucarias) grow alongside relatives of the oak and chestnut tree, pink-flowering rhododendrons, rainbow-coloured and orange-tinted **crotons** and dazzling red **poinsettias**. Bathed in cool damp mist, the forest is also the terrain for **orchids**, tucked away in the dim shadows beneath **tree ferns** and **giant bamboos**. A convoluted labyrinth of green, blanketed with mosses and creepers which, in the shifting patterns of light and shade, can take on fantastical forms.

Impenetrable mangroves

Hundreds of thousands of hectares of mangrove swamp form fringes along the coasts of Indonesia, particularly on the southeast shores of Sumatra and Kalimantan. Made up of **mangroves**, this amphibious forest grows in salty locations, on the expanses of alluvial mud that build up in the estuaries. Exploited to excess for their timber – used to make charcoal – the mangroves present an extraordinary network of aerial roots, like stilts, which provide anchorage in the soft ground. Withstanding the tidal forces, they take in oxygen at the surface and draw on the sediments that are essential to their survival.

Monsoon forests

To the south of the equator, in the eastern part of the Sunda Isles with their more clearly defined dry season, the flora lives partly according to the changing seasons. This **tropical forest**, known as "the monsoon forest", has a mixture of deciduous and evergreen trees. Lower than the rain forest, the plant covering is also less dense. Depending on altitude and rainfall, several species of acacia, **eucalyptus**, valuable **teak**, and the famous sandalwood with its delicate scent have been recorded here.

The dry plains

In some areas the devastating effect of deforestation undertaken by humans has created sterile land where the forest no longer protects the ground from erosion. Invaded by grasses, this poor-quality land spreads out in vast stretches of grass and dry **brushwood**, sometimes dotted with clumps of traveller's tree shrubs (recognisable by their fantail fronds) *lontar* palms or succulents.

Island flowers

Overflowing all along the roads, crowding down to the shore or tucked away in some secret garden space, trees beyond number and clumps of flowers (more than 35 000 species!) display their harmonious, dazzling finery as far as the eye can see. Most of them are in flower throughout the year – light yellow **allamandas**, short-lived **hibiscus** with their long pistils, luminous **bougainvillaeas** with their diaphanous petals – except for the **flamboyant or coral tree,** whose dazzling red flowers appear only in the dry season. In contrast to these many-coloured flowers, the white flowers, tinged with pink or yellow, of the **frangipani** breathe out their delicate scents around temples and cemeteries. **Gardenias** stand out with their immaculate whiteness, and **cempakas**, delicate subtly-perfumed white flowers, accompany Hindu prayer and gift rituals. This is also true of **jasmine**, which is used in the kitchen for its strong scent. Finally, with flowers like pink or white stars springing from their rounded leaves, lilies carpet every pool of water, particularly the **lotus** that for Buddhists and Hindus has become a sacred symbol.

Orchid

Torch Ginger

Hibiscus

Allamanda

Bougainvillaea

Heliconia

Frangipani

H. Choimet

19

Tempting fruit

An extraordinary variety of fruit and vegetables and, of course, aromatic **spices** are spread out on the market stalls. These coveted objects that affected the history of the islands – pepper, cloves, cinnamon, nutmeg, cardamom and saffron – are all used to flavour Indonesian cuisine.

Generous palms

King of the tropical islands, the coconut palm is simply one type of palm among many others (nearly 150 types have been recorded in the archipelago). Producing sugar, copra oil, alcohol, building timber, basketry, roofing or household utensils, the trees are an inexhaustible resource which the Indonesians make great use of, from the roots (medicinal extracts) to the leaves (like those of the lontar palm, traditionally used for writing) and the fruit (delicious coconuts), not to mention the sap (palm wine, tuak) etc.

Whether you are an expert or simply curious, you should try the **exotic fruit**. You will be surprised by the strong flavour, even of familiar fruit – pineapples, all kinds of banana, mangoes and coconuts.

The prize for originality surely goes to the **avocado**, widely consumed in the form of juice mixed with sweetened, chocolate-flavoured condensed milk and seasoned with pimento! Sweeter fruit, such as guavas, papaya or star-shaped Chinese gooseberries, will please your palate. Some will overwhelm delicate taste buds: passion fruit, bristly-skinned rambutans, snake-skinned salak, and **mangosteens –** not to be missed under any circumstances. Others, finally, can only be described as "an experience", both indescribable and unforgettable: the smell (for which it is banned from the underground system in Singapore!), the consistency and the taste of the **durian** – highly valued as a fruit by the Indonesians – arouses extreme reactions. The choice is yours.

A unique fauna

Whether it lives in the rain forests, the dry grassy plains or the muddy labyrinths of the mangrove swamps, the fauna of Indonesia displays remarkable diversity. Bursting with abundant food sources throughout the year, the tropical flora creates an ideal habitat. But in this luxuriant tropical setting it may be essential to be capable of climbing or flying up to the top of the trees, either to feed (when food supplies are inadequate at ground level) or to escape from danger. Apart from birds and monkeys, there are many animals provided by nature with features, as original as they are effective, to make up for their lack of wings.

Flight without wings

Kingdom of the birds, the thick forest foliage also conceals astonishing flying reptiles and mammals that are better adapted to getting around in the air than on the ground. Endowed with lateral membranes which operate as a sort of parachute, or with palmate (hand-like) paws, all kinds of creatures move with agility from tree to tree, jumping, falling, gliding, making use in some cases of a prehensile tail like a fifth limb, steely claws or clasping fingers, to seize the branches. Among these unexpected competitors of the birds are the flying lemur (a small marsupial), the tarsier (a lemur-type creature with long clinging fingers, or tarsals, a nocturnal rat-sized primate capable of 2-metre leaps using its long tail for balance) the flying dragon (a winged lizard) the flying squirrel, the flying fox (a giant bat) and even the flying frog. Lacking any of the above features, the paradise snake whips through the air, bending its body into a flying U-shape.

Birds in their thousands

With several thousand species, nearly 400 of them native, Indonesia (particularly Sumatra and Papua) can satisfy the requirements of the most demanding ornithologist. Herons, egrets, frigate-birds, eagles, storks, ibises, cockatoos and parrots – the list of birds in the forests, along the waterways and on the island shores is endless.

Some will seem familiar, such as the **cocks** with red plumage, shimmering with shades of blue-green, or the brown chickens, wild ancestors of most of the domestic poultry in our farmyards and hen-houses. Introduced into Europe several hundred years ago to embellish gardens and parks, **peacocks** and **pheasants** have also spread overseas. You may see them, their heads adorned with silky feathers, spreading their tails to majestic fans to seduce females. More astonishing, the **brush turkey** (like the **maleo**, a native of Sulawesi, one of the fifteen recorded in the archipelago) has the distinctive feature of incubating its eggs for two or three months by burying them in the warm sands of beaches or volcanoes. There are also at least ten species of **hornbill**, numerous in the humid forests of Kalimantan, more rare in those of Sumatra or Sulawesi (native home of the red-humped hornbill). Easily identifiable by their impressive beak with its horned protuberance, they are also distinguished by their style of nest-building: the female settles in a hollow tree-trunk which she seals up, leaving only a narrow opening that enables the male to bring her food.

As you cross between the Lesser Sunda Islands, keep your eyes open to spot the **sea birds** that glide over the waves ready to plunge in and seize a fish. At the crossroads between the Indian and Pacific oceans, these islands lie conveniently along the route of many **migratory birds** such as petrels, terns, seagulls and **pelicans**. You will need far more patience and good fortune to see the **Bali starling**, the last native species of the island, which now only survives in the national park of Bali Barat. Among the most fascinating creatures of this rich birdlife are **birds of paradise**. Papua still provides shelter for some of them. Their tapering and temptingly coloured feathers made them the object of a lucrative trade for a very long period.

Monkeys, jungle acrobats

Indonesia has innumerable varieties of **primates**, particularly well acclimatised to the damp forests of Kalimantan and Sumatra, but also present on other islands. They generally live in colonies, perched high up in the trees where they find their food. Although they are tree-dwellers, the most common **macaques** also live contentedly near rivers or coasts. Some chase the little crabs teeming among the mangroves, or snatch mangrove leaves, like the **proboscis monkey** on Kalimantan, a swimming monkey with a large and distinctive muzzle that has earned it the nickname, "the Dutch monkey". But you are more likely to meet the monkeys that have been introduced into temple surroundings. Considered sacred by the Hindus, their familiar appearance should not deceive you: organised in close-knit and extremely hierarchical groups, these residents are skilful thieves and often aggressive.

The more peaceful **orang-utan** (literally "man of the woods") prefers the solitude of the lower forests, a setting that seems to reflect its gentle and melancholy expression. Tailless and capable of walking on its hind legs, this is one of mankind's closest relatives – although this does not prevent it from climbing trees and sleeping in them. Now diminishing in numbers, the species barely survives except in Kalimantan

A unique fauna

21

and Sumatra, where the last individuals are protected (particularly in the Gunung Leuser National Park, *see p 138*), but the destruction of the forest is accelerating their path to extinction. Their much smaller cousin the **gibbon** is also capable of standing upright, but it is above all an outstanding acrobat, swinging from branch to branch on its long arms with astonishing dexterity and speed.

Plant-eating creatures ...

Fruit, flowers, leaves, branches: for plant feeders, everything makes a good meal. The clearings in the tropical woodlands of Sumatra, Java and Kalimantan are a paradise for the many **deer species** such as the great **sambar**, the **muntjac** and the tiny mouse deer. They also provide shelter for various types of cattle, such as buffalo and the **banteng** (an enormous ox, native to Kalimantan and Java) and, more rare, the **anoa** or water buffalo (a dwarf wild buffalo, native to Sulawesi). Highly prized by apothecaries for the medicinal (and supposedly aphrodisiac) virtues of its horns, the **rhinoceros** is cruelly threatened. The last survivors are in Sumatra (with two horns) and in western Java (single horns). Their cousin the long-nosed **tapir** still lives in Sumatra, close to waterways. Another endangered species, the **elephant** virtually only survives now in the Sumatra forest.

Although mainly herbivorous, various species of pig and boar complement their diet with insects and small animals. The strangest of them is the **horned hog** (babiroussa) a type of boar, which lives in Sulawesi (*see also p 556*).

... and meat-eaters

Under the harsh law of the jungle, most of these animals fall prey to one of the **cat family**, although the latter are generally modest in size. These skilled hunters watch until they identify an appetising victim – then, crawling along the ground or lying low in a tree, they launch themselves into a frantic chase or leap out suddenly to bring down their victim. The most widely present species – various forms of wild cat – also fish for their meals. Extinct in Java and Bali, the last surviving **tigers** live reclusively in Sumatra. The rare panthers are now protected in Sumatra and West Java.

Other small predators prefer to attack rodents, reptiles, birds and insects. They include the **civet cat**, a curious animal that looks like a weasel, the **pangolin** (which digs out ant-heaps and termite nests), and the ferret-badger with its black and white head.

Little lizards and giant dragons

Snakes beyond number also live in the forests and the rice fields (*enquire locally about poisonous varieties*). But don't worry – the chances of coming face to face with a **reticulate python** (at 10m long, the longest snake in the world) are not great. Another giant, the impressive **Komodo dragon**, may reach 3m in length. Protected on the islands of Komodo and Rinca, the largest lizard in the world looks like a dragon, straight out of prehistoric times (*see p 514*).

Less dramatically, in the evenings you can sit back and watch the frantic dance of the **geckos** (*toke*), the tiny lizards that run up and down house walls, using the suckers on their feet. Don't chase them away: they snap up the mosquitoes and flying insects that are drawn to the lights. Every fly they swallow is downed with a series of little cries of satisfaction – "gec-kooo, gec-kooo". In their dash for food they sometimes take unwise risks, suddenly dropping down from the ceiling with a ridiculous "plif". Irritated or obstinate, the little creatures immediately clamber up again to renew the chase. A private circus that never fails to amuse.

The secret world of insects

Insects, lovers of humid heat, swarm in the muggy forests, above the stagnant waters of the mangrove swamps and flooded rice fields, with a distinct preference for the rainy season. As numerous as they are strange, many "borrow" shapes or colours, imitating and blending in with the bark of a tree, the green of a leaf, or the form of an orchid. Among the most attractive – but more rare, as a consequence of the greed of collectors – are the many delicate and vivid **butterflies** fluttering among the flowers that provide their food.

Treasures of the sea

More than three million square kilometres of inner seas lie between the Pacific and Indian oceans. Washing along more than 80 000km of coastline, these waters are the setting for sumptuous submarine gardens, crowded with creatures that are as varied as they are numerous.

Peaceful aquariums

See also the illustrations on p 24-25. Usually protected from major predators by impenetrable coral reefs, the **lagoons** and coastal waters provide a warm shallow habitat for an unusually diverse range of fauna. Infinitely complex, labyrinthine mazes of sharp-edged structures, plateaux of impenetrable crevices, the corals create a multifaceted aquarium with a population of wonderfully colourful tropical fish – as well as polyps, sponges, starfish, crustaceans, octopuses, shellfish and other molluscs. Take an oxygen cylinder or simply a mask and snorkel, and plunge down to discover this fascinating world: it offers inexhaustible visual delights. (*Be careful of coral and fish that are unfamiliar – many may cause rashes or even be poisonous*). Lit by the slanting rays of the sun, an astonishing moving palette displays all the shades of bright or pastel colours, whether varied or monochrome, striped or spotted. Follow the graceful **butterfly fish**, Moorish idols

Life and death of corals

Corals (which are animals and not plants) flourish exclusively in warm waters (at least 20°C) with high levels of light, and which are therefore shallow, not more than 50m deep. Microscopic creatures, generally with tentacles that can cause rashes, these innumerable polyps (from the Latin for "foot") multiply through arborescence (tree-like growth) at the rate of 1cm per year. New growth gradually takes over the calcified skeletons of dead corals. Depending on the species, this may become an isolated structure or a massed group, forming mysterious submarine forests coloured brown or pink, sulphur yellow, sky blue or pillar-box red. The three main types of reef can all be seen in Indonesia: fringe reefs which run along the coasts, barrier reefs which encircle the islands a few kilometres out to sea, and atolls which are formed when an island sinks and disappears. The coral reefs that once surrounded the islands form the outline of large lagoons of turquoise water in the midst of the sea.

and bannerfish (yellow, white and black) which explore the tiniest crannies with their long narrow muzzle, the **emperor angelfish** (yellow and blue), **damselfish** (cobalt blue) and the **parrot fish** (shimmering green and blue) which forage for food with their tiny teeth. Near the surface of the water you will also see large groups of slender **razor fish** swimming vertically, head down; above all there are the delicate white-striped and orange **clownfish** which quiver in the depths of anemones and approach the swimmer, curious or playful, if you tempt them gently

TROPICAL FISH

Sea snake
(Laticanda colubrina)

Longfin Bannerfish
(Heniochus acuminatus)

Clown Triggerfish
(Balistides
conspicillum)

Teardrop Butterflyfish
(Chaethodon unimaculatus)

Parrot fish
(Scarus)

Emperor Angelfish
(Pomacanthus imperator)

H. Choimet

Napoleon Wrasse
(Cheilinus undulatus)

Meyer's Butterflyfish
(Chaetodon meyeri)

Lionfish or Turkeyfish
(Pterois volitans)

Clownfish or Anemone fish
(Amphiprion percula)

Moorish Idol
(Zanclus cornutus)

H. Choimet

25

with a bit of bread. You will find yourself amongst a horde of creatures with evocative names, large and small, with regular or uneven shapes, some solitary, others moving round in tight groups, spinning with the waves or more cautiously hiding in hollows, flashing like arrows, or lazily swallowing the careless prey that venture near.

You may also come across some reptile surfacing to breathe. The waters of Indonesia are home to supple **sea snakes**, striped with dark and pale bands that sparkle as the body undulates. Admire them – but keep your distance, for although they rarely attack anything bigger than themselves (they measure between 1 and 3m in length but their mouths are so small that they can barely swallow anything more than the smaller fish, or nibble the lobe of your ear), they are nonetheless extremely poisonous.

Defence and camouflage
Often bristling with poisonous dorsal spines, the most dangerous fish are unfortunately particularly skilled at camouflage, either to escape predators or to provide cover when approaching their victims. Difficult to identify, most are easily overlooked, as they resemble the seabed. Take care, therefore, before setting foot on the bottom! Take particular care to avoid lion-fish or scorpion fish (like the majestic flying scorpion fish) which may be invisible among the algae, coral or rocks, and the stonefish with its treacherous appearance of a fixed stone.

Turtles, on the other hand, are entirely harmless. Unfortunately they have suffered severely from human predation; now protected, they are still highly prized both for the value of their shell and for their tasty flesh.

The savage world of the ocean

Further out to sea, before the sea bed drops down to shadowy depths, great predators pass by in fleeting disturbing shapes. More impressive species can be seen near sharp drops, notched with crevasses and caves, or above sandy slopes: **tuna**, swordfish (with their long armed jaw, narrow as a sword), night-hunting morays or the more redoubtable white, tiger and hammer sharks and the greedy **barracuda**. **Rays** glide gracefully past on their great fins, like the manta ray that can grow to 6m in breadth, or the eagle or electric ray that discharges electric shocks. Finally, as you travel from one island to another, watch the surface carefully: you may find yourself in the midst of a school of **dolphins** lightly skimming the waves or leaping energetically out of the water. More rarely, some whales survive in certain areas, as is the case with the astonishing **dugong** (sea cow).

A threatened Eden

Common practice in Java from colonial times, **massive deforestation** has taken an alarming turn in the long-protected islands. In Kalimantan, Sumatra, Sulawesi and to a lesser extent Papua, the final bastions of virgin forest have in effect been transformed into pasture-land, at the mercy of local and foreign timber and oil industries (particularly Japanese but also Malaysian and European). In the hope of attracting further foreign capital investment to make up the national deficit, the Indonesian government has granted concessions to more than 500 companies for several tens of millions of hectares of forest that are being transformed into large plantations (palm-oil, coffee, latex, cocoa, etc) or sliced open for mine-shafts (metals, oil).

Launched in 1935 and intensified since 1967, the policy of **transmigration** (*see p 202*) has not improved matters. In order to relieve the burden of overcrowding in Java, part of the population was moved to the underpopulated forest regions, where the jungle was cleared for agricultural purposes. And wherever a clearing appeared, roads and villages soon followed, bringing in fresh settlers in their wake. Savagely deforested and laid bare, the land quickly fell victim to erosion, a process of implacable scouring which within two or three years at most, defeats agricultural efforts as well as any regrowth of wild plant life.

Finally, this hasty destruction of plant cover tends to affect climatic conditions (a noticeable rise in temperatures and alarmingly longer periods of drought), encouraging the development of brushwood which, baked by the sun, proves easily combustible. And when the flora disappears the whole **animal kingdom** is threatened, forced to flee and frequently condemned to death. Java today has only 10% of its forest cover, while Sumatra lost one-third of its cover between 1982 and 1990, and the terrible fires of 1997 have made the situation worse.

Indonesia's forests are being destroyed at the rate of 1.5 – 2 million hectares each year, victims of human carelessness and, mainly, of the greed of managers guided only by financial interests. As a result, while a handful of people become wealthy, the inhabitants of these islands are gradually being dispossessed of their only capital possession: the nourishing jungle, the guarantee of Indonesian and global ecological balance.

Fire!

In August 1997 massive fires devoured the forests of Sumatra, Kalimantan and Papua. In scarcely three months, more than a million hectares went up in smoke. It was an ecological disaster of global significance. Visible from outer space, the noxious black clouds of smoke spread as far as Malaysia, Thailand and the Philippines, a radius of more than 1 500km, polluting the atmosphere, asphyxiating neighbouring countries, and interfering heavily with air and sea traffic throughout the region. The cause of this disaster was primarily human invasion of the jungle, slashing and burning with unpredictable consequences. Long held responsible by their local authorities, the native populations used to follow traditional techniques of perfectly controlled burning which fertilised the soil and regenerated the forest. The El Niño effect undoubtedly made a disastrous situation worse; but the satellite pictures prove irrefutably that more than 90% of the fires actually broke out on the land of industrial companies.

Protecting the environment

In these unhappy circumstances, the preservation of the natural heritage received considerable attention during the 1990s as part of a sustained policy. The government in effect implemented a vast programme designed to convert nearly 10% of the national territory (on land and at sea) into **nature reserves and national parks**. It is not simply a matter of assessing, regenerating or replanting plant and animal species threatened with extinction but also of establishing a system of regulation to protect the natural environment. These are useful measures, but not yet adequate: law-breaking remains the norm and, more disturbingly, we are still far from seeing a general awareness among the people as a whole, who are more concerned with their daily existence than with the national ecological future of their land.

The essential task of consciousness-raising will no doubt take several years to achieve.

Chronological table

Our land, our waters

Dates	Events	Places
1 million years BC	Java Man	*Trinil (Central Java)*
3000-500 BC	Austronesian migration to the archipelago	
300 BC	Penetration of the Dongson civilisation	
4-5C AD	Early Indianised kingdoms	*Kalimantan, West Java*
7-13C	Srivijaya Empire	*Palembang (Sumatra)*
8-10C	First Mataram kingdom	*Central Java*
778-824	Sailendra dynasty	*Borobudur (Central Java)*
732-919	Sanjaya dynasty	*Prambanan, Dieng (Central Java)*
919	End of the kingdom of Mataram	
1019-1049	Kingdom of Airlangga	*East Java*
11-13C	Kingdoms of Kediri and Janggala	*East Java*
1222	Ken Angrok founds the kingdom of Singosari	*East Java*
1292	Death of Kertanegara, last king of Singosari	
1293	The Mongol emperor Kublai Khan launches his fleet against Java	
1294	Raden Wijaya founds the Majapahit Empire	*Trowulan (East Java)*
1350-1389	Peak of Majapahit Empire under Hayam Wuruk	
Late 15C	Decline of the Majapahit Empire	
15-16C	Islam expands locally. Javanese sultanates	
1511	The Portuguese capture Malacca	*Malaya*
1527	The sultan of Demak takes the Majapahit capital	
Late 16C	The second kingdom of Mataram emerges	*Central Java*
1596	First Dutch expedition	*Banten (West Java)*
1602	Creation of the Dutch East India Company	
1619	Jayakarta (future Jakarta) renamed Batavia	
1641	The Dutch take Malacca. End of Portuguese presence	
1669	The Dutch take Makassar	
1740-1755	Mataram war of succession, partition	*Java*
1799	Collapse of the Dutch East India Company	
1808-1811	Willem Daendels (Dutch) governor	
1811-1815	Thomas Stamford Raffles (British) governor	
1824	East Indies divided between England (Malaya) and the Netherlands (Indonesia)	
1825-1830	Rebellion of Prince Diponegoro. Java War	
1873-1903	Aceh Wars	*Northern Sumatra*
1906	The Dutch take Bali	
1908	First nationalist movement	
1927	Sukarno creates the Indonesian National Party	
1942-1945	Japanese occupation	
1945	Sukarno proclaims the independence of the Republic of Indonesia	
1949	Recognition of the Indonesian state at The Hague	
1955	Bandung Afro-Asian conference	
1965	Failed coup d'état. Massacre of Communists, pogroms of Chinese	
1967	Sukarno cedes power to General Suharto	
1975	Invasion of East Timor	
1997	Forest fires, economic crisis begins	
1998	Student demonstrations, riots in Jakarta, Suharto resigns, replaced by Habibie	
1999	First free elections since 1955. East Timor gains independence	
2000	Separatist movements and religious unrest	

A FRAGMENTED HISTORY

In many respects the unity of the vast archipelago of Indonesia – a mosaic of 17 000 islands, 500 languages and five religions – has an element of the miraculous. Getting a firm grasp of the history of such a varied country, shaped by a colonial power less than a hundred years ago, would seem impossible – yet down the centuries various poles of power have emerged and have imposed their culture. In the west, Sumatra and above all Java served as bridgeheads for major external influences: Indian, Chinese, Islamic and then Western. In the east, the Maluku (Molucca) island group and its proliferation of rare spices was the setting for one of the greatest commercial struggles that the world has ever seen. And for a lengthy period the Lesser Sunda Islands (East Lombok, Sumbawa and Flores) were ruled by the sultans of Makassar. The dynamics that enabled this unlikely ensemble to develop were varied. External influences initially introduced their religions (Hinduism, Buddhism, then Islam and Christianity) through the channels opened up by trade – which also introduced a common language, Malay. The penetration and assimilation of these two factors, religion and language, were encouraged by ancient rivalries, particularly in Java, between the trading cities on the coast and the agrarian kingdoms of the interior. Over and above historical events, nature – vast stretches of sea, impenetrable tropical forests – played a crucial role and shaped the course of human lives. More than a frontier, however, the sea proved to be a unifying element, bringing all these peoples together round an "Asian Mediterranean sea" which extended far beyond the frontiers of modern Indonesia.

The earliest ages

It is in the paleontologists' paradise of Java that one of the longest periods of human occupation has been identified. The earliest humans probably came from Asia in the Ice Age, via the Malacca Peninsula, more than a million years ago. Frequently seen as the "missing link" between primates and the first *Homo sapiens*, "Java Man", or **Pithecanthropus erectus** (literally "upright human-monkey") lived peacefully in the Solo region of Sangiram. The Eastern branch of the great family of the earliest *Homo erectus*, "Java Man" developed like his distant African cousin Lucy 3 million years ago.

Fishermen and hunter-gatherers, the first **Homo sapiens** of the archipelago (around 40 000 years ago) represented the **Australoid** type: dark skin, fuzzy hair, small in height, similar to the Melanesian Papuans of Papua or the Negritos who were to populate the forests of Malaysia, the Andaman Islands (India), Borneo and some of the Philippine Islands. This period left substantial quantities of tools, particularly at Pacitan (East Java) and Sunga Mas (Sumatra), sites of the discovery of objects from the Middle and Late Paleolithic Ages (around 50 000 years ago). This does not, however, apply to the islands lying to the east of the **Wallace**

Java Man

The late 19C discovery, at Trinil (East Java), of human remains dating from the middle of the Pliocene Age (500000 BC) gave Darwin one of the first confirmations of his theories on the origins of mankind. It was however in Sangiran (near Solo) that the finest skeleton specimens were found. In 1936 Ralph von Koenigswald discovered the remains of a "Homo erectus" from nearly one million years ago. This skeleton, the oldest found outside Africa, gave credence for a time to the theory that Southeast Asia was the cradle of mankind. Other discoveries followed, in particular enormous mastodon tusks (4m long) and fossils dating back 500 000 – 1 200 000 years. Research continues at the site, where a museum has been set up, largely containing copies of bone remains.

Line *(see p 16)* which, unlike Sumatra, Java and Bali, never formed part of continental Asia: very ancient industrial activity has been recorded in Sumbawa and Flores, but the oldest tools discovered on Sulawesi date no further back than 29000-27000 BC.

Some populations, however, were very early in developing forms of agriculture and bronze-working, indications of advanced forms of society. Cave paintings have been discovered in Sulawesi and Papua, made by stencilling, and showing amputated fingers, a sign of mourning still current in some Papuan societies.

A language for two oceans

Divided into several groups, the family of Austronesian languages includes the largest geographical grouping in the world, stretching from Madagascar to Hawaii. Originating in Taiwan, the peoples who spoke them crossed the Pacific and Indian oceans. How? On board simple catamarans, like the "prahu" of Polynesian and Indonesian fishermen! At the farthest point of their advance in the Pacific, they landed on Easter Island in 500 AD, before reaching New Zealand to the south (around 900) and Hawaii in the north. To the west they colonised Indonesia, Malaysia, the Philippines and Thailand (2000-1500 BC), and pushed ahead as far as Madagascar. Apart from a few Papuan idioms from Papua, Ternate and the Lesser Sunda Islands, all the Indonesian languages therefore stem from the same Austronesian group. From archeology to linguistics, and even using DNA studies, sciences have shown characteristics shared by the former inhabitants of Hawaii, Easter Island, Madagascar and Indonesia. For example, in the original language of Taiwan as in Java and in Fiji, the same word – "mata" – means "eye".

"The Tree of Life", a stencilled group of hands discovered in Kalimantan in 1999 (possibly dating back between 20 000 and 60 000 years)

L-H Fage/Ed Spéléo

Austronesians and the beginning of the Neolithic Age

Between 3000 and 500 BC (some authorities suggest an even earlier date), Southeast Asia witnessed substantial human migration, spreading out in several waves from Taiwan. Heading south in their boats past the Philippines, the Austronesians dispersed across the archipelago to the west (Borneo, Java, Sumatra, Malaysia) and the east (Sulawesi, Moluccas, Oceania), assimilating the Australoid populations or pushing them back inland. This was when many of the characteristics of today's Indonesian peoples became established, and in certain populations, such as the **Dayaks** (Kalimantan), this Austronesian substratum survives almost intact.

The arrival of the Austronesians marked the spread of **agriculture**, animal husbandry (chickens, pigs), pottery and a settled communal way of life and habitat. As in all the Pacific islands, the basic food was taro, a tuber that was later replaced by rice. The Austronesians introduced the foundations of hierarchical societies (2nd millennium BC), of which the **megaliths** linked to ancestor worship are the most moving evidence.

The Bronze Age and the Dongson civilisation

The Dongson culture, the final phase of the Bronze Age civilisation that developed in northern Vietnam (between 800 and 300 BC) appears to have spread during the 3C BC throughout the whole of Southeast Asia. Although bronze was undoubtedly used earlier than this in the archipelago, the Dongson contribution seems to have been an essential element in Indonesia,

Silent drums

Wonderful artistic examples of a lost civilisation, the bronze Dongson drums were imported from Vietnam and then made in the islands at the beginning of the modern era. A wax model was first created on a clay base, and then a decorative design was carved into the wax before the bronze was applied. Among the various types of design noted by Heger, the star surrounded by tiny frogs, set in relief on the flat surface, is the most widely known. On the sides, animals and scenes of daily life are shown within geometric friezes, making up an ensemble of great elegance. Symbols of the power of some petty king anxious to gain the blessing of a distant authority, or instruments linked to funerary ritual, their function is still debated. Whatever the truth may be, specimens have been discovered in nearly all the islands from Sumatra to Papua, via the Lesser Sunda Islands, along a route which recalls that of the trade with India.

where many traces have been found: ceremonial axes and receptacles, and above all large drums. From the beginning of the modern era the many swallow-tail axes from Java and the superb flasks from Sumatra and Madura probably came from the workshops of Java and Bali. Gradually a recognisable local style developed, most impressively of all in the famous 2m-high **Pejeng gongs** of Bali.

The age of Indianised kingdoms (5-16C)

The oldest trace of the links between the Indian subcontinent and the East Indies survives in the work of the Greek writer **Ptolemy**, who mentions the distant islands of Sabadiba (Sumatra) and Labadium (Java) in the 1C AD. The famous geographer no doubt gained his information from merchants who knew the Indian kingdoms, then at the centre of a vast intercontinental trade network. Heavy consumers of gold and silver, they paid the Romans with spices bartered in Indonesia for pearls and precious stones. The dynamism of the East Indies nations, who explored as far as Madagascar at the beginning of the modern era, is also confirmed, and some even consider them the initiators of this trade. But the Indians were not alone in focusing on the spices of the archipelago, as can be seen in the well-established tradition in the Han court of chewing cloves before meeting the emperor (could this have been to avoid contaminating his surroundings with bad breath?) and in nutmeg, which has been discovered beside an Egyptian mummy.

Whatever the truth of such rumours, the links that developed at this time opened the way for Indian culture, which was to have a profound effect on the religions, myths and arts of the archipelago for over a thousand years. Javanese legend maintains that the Hindu gods settled in the east of the island, bringing Mount Meru with them on the back of the mythical bird **garuda**. Hinduism and Buddhism flourished in the archipelago, which over the centuries became one of the great centres of expansion for both these religions from the banks of the Ganges. The exuberant iconography of the temples of Prambanan and Borobudur draws heavily on the great Indian epics absorbed by the Indonesians, the *Ramayana* and the *Mahabharata*. But their contribution extended further than stone, and nourished equally the vigorous arts of *wayang kulit* and dance, as well as local myths of the god-king and the sacred mountain.

The early Indianised kingdoms

It was during the 4 and 5C that the Indian Gupta kingdom emerged. The oldest written Indonesian text (4C), discovered in Kalimantan, mentions a buffalo sacrifice undertaken in the name of a king whom we know only by his name, **Mulavaraman**. Above all, the choice of Sanskrit, the language of Indian scholars and priests, indicates that the integration of this foreign culture – the ideal vector for joining a commercial culture in full expansion – was prompted by local princes and did not evolve through contact with merchants or a military venture.

Another text, also in Sanskrit, carved on the 5C **stone of Tarumanegara**, discovered in West Java, recounts the great deeds of **Purnavarman**, king of **Taruma**, the oldest kingdom known in Java. The footprints of the king carved here have been compared with those of the Hindu god Vishnu.

The maritime empire of Srivijaya (7-13C)

In the 6 and 7C the expansion of trade between the Indian Ocean, the China Sea and the Spice Islands brought profound disturbance to the region. It was a Buddhist state, Srivijaya, that was to profit from events by seizing control of the Straits of Malacca, through which passed the trade in pepper, spices, camphor and benzene. Known to the Chinese as Shi-li-fo-shih, the empire sent ambassadors to the Tang court until the 8C. It was also recognised as a major religious centre, where, in the **I Ching**, a famous Chinese *bonze* (priest) listed over a thousand of his co-religionists versed in written documents at the end of the 7C. Established in southern Sumatra, Srivijaya also dominated western Java and sustained an episodic rivalry with the kingdoms in the centre of the island. Its influence spread much further than this, however, across the whole of Southeast Asia: traces have even been found of trade links with the Arabian peninsula. The peak of the maharajas of Srivijaya, in the 10C, is confirmed by Arab chroniclers who were astonished by their seafaring power.

This prosperity attracted envy, however, and in the 11C the Indian kingdom of Chola sent in frequent raids, while the Javanese took hold in southern Sumatra. In addition, the Chinese built a powerful commercial fleet to compete. In short, by the end of the 11C, when the capital shifted to Jambi, Srivijaya had had its hour of glory.

Prambanan (Candi Plaosan), detail of a frieze

The golden age of Javanese kingdoms (8-10C)

During the 8C two dynasties emerged in central Java, already the richest and most densely populated island: the Buddhist **Sailendra** and the Hindu **Sanjaya,** which became head of the agrarian kingdom of **Mataram**. A brilliant civilisation was born, with the Buddhist mandala at Borobudur and the temples of Prambanan as its finest features. Mataram was also an early model of a concentric kingdom, under the aegis of a god-king, which would reappear in Indonesian history.

The rivalry that sprang up between the two dynasties occasionally led to conflict, as for example in the late 8C when the Sanjaya heirs became vassals of the Sailendra. Only for a time: in 832 the Hindu dynasty took the lead by means of a marriage between a Sailendra queen and a Sanjaya king. Forced to flee after an uprising, the Buddhist prince Balaputra took refuge in Sumatra, where he managed to take the throne of the Srivijaya Empire, the sworn enemies of Mataram.

The sudden collapse of Mataram in 919 remains a mystery to historians, who suggest the possibility of an epidemic or an eruption of Merapi. Whatever the facts, the focus of power henceforward lay in eastern Java for several centuries.

The eastern kingdoms

In 929 King **Sindok** founded a dynasty near Surabaya, which expanded to dominate Bali and which even threatened Srivijaya in 990. However, 25 years later its capital was destroyed in a rebellion, forcing the young prince **Airlangga** to flee. A hero of Indonesian history, this great ruler of Balinese origin managed to reconquer the lost territories over several decades. An ascetic, and a great patron, it is to him that we owe the translation of the Indian classics into Javanese, an amazing cultural feat. On his death in 1049 his possessions were divided between his two sons, who founded the kingdoms of **Janggala** (near Malang) and **Kadiri** (further west, in the Brantas valley); in the end, Kediri annexed Janggala in 1150.

This marks the beginning of the history of **Singosari**, narrated in the 16C *Pararaton*, or "Book of Kings". It begins in blood with the epic of the bloodthirsty **Ken Angrok**, legendary son of the god Brahma. In 1222 he overthrew the king of Kediri, reunited the ancient lands of Airlangga and established his capital at Singosari (near Malang). Under his successors the kingdom took the name of the city and filled with temples. A devoted Buddhist and well-read in sciences and philosophy, **Kertanegara** (1268-92) became the greatest Singosari king and the first to have sought to unite the archipelago. He extended his rule to Java, Sumatra and into the Malay Peninsula, but his dream was broken by the Emperor of China, the Mongol leader **Kublai Khan**, who despatched his fleet to Java in 1293.

The Majapahit Empire (13-16C)

Assassinated during a palace rebellion, Kertanegara had no opportunity to confront the Mongol armada. The young prince **Raden Wijaya** preferred to come to terms with the invaders in order to take back his usurped throne: a skilful tactician, he even managed to get rid of his embarrassing ally without having to pay homage to him. In 1294 Raden Wijaya moved his capital further north to **Majapahit** (the present-day Trowulan), where he laid the foundations for one of the most powerful states that the archipelago has ever seen. This marked the beginning of a long era of prosperity, based on agriculture, maritime trade and a new architectural style characterised by the famous red-brick temples with split gates still current in Bali, used to celebrate a syncretic Hindu-Buddhist religion.

The empire reached its peak during the reign of **Hayam Wuruk** (1350-89) and his prime minister **Gajah Mada**, but a dynastic dispute after Wuruk's death marked the beginning of a civil war (1403-06). By the time they reunited in 1429 the Majapahit had lost their maritime supremacy to Malacca, and began a long decline.

Thus it was that, after a thousand years of expansion, the Indian religions found a refuge in Bali, marking the end of the classical period, which some historians have called the Indonesian Middle Ages.

Enterprising Islam (15-16C)

Contacts between the East Indies and the Arab world date back to the 7C, but it was only in the 13C that Islam spread out into the Malayan world, by means of **merchants from Gujarat** (India), Persia and Arabia. They promoted a tolerant faith, suffused with cultural features absorbed along the maritime routes of the Indian Ocean and the China Sea, which was unlike the missionary zeal of the Soldiers of God. After spreading along the north and east coasts of Sumatra in the late 13C, the faith took hold in Molucca and Java in the 15C, Lombok (1525), Sulawesi (1600) and finally Kalimantan (1605). In the 17C the Islamisation of the archipelago reached its limits, taking in the whole of the "Indonesian Mediterranean" except for Flores, Timor and part of the Moluccas.

An egalitarian religion, Islam offered the advantage of abolishing caste and ethnic restrictions. Further, adopting the religion that was born in Arabia meant joining a flourishing and expanding commercial network. In the 15C the Muslim dynasties controlled vast territories that extended from the Atlantic to the Indus.

The mass arrival of **Chinese merchants** at the same period was also to have profound repercussions on the history of the archipelago.

The day of the sultanates

The ports and great merchant cities became propagators of the word of the Prophet. Their prosperity, in contrast with the declining power of the old Indianised agrarian states, encouraged them to claim their independence and then to extend their domination further into the plains of the interior.

Lying on a very busy commercial corridor, which controlled the spice trade, **Malacca** (on the Malay Peninsula) also owed its wealth to its location near the pepper plantations of Sumatra. This was the first great city of Southeast Asia to adopt Islam, in 1419. In the 15C nutmeg and cloves, which grew only in the **Moluccas** aroused the envy of all the great powers. Muslims were the winners in this frantic race and, in 1480, the sultanate of Ternate was established.

But, as always, it was in **Java** that the fate of the archipelago was played out during the first half of the 16C. According to legend it was the **Wali Songo**, the nine apostles of Islam on the north coast (*Pasisir*), who were responsible for the expansion of the sultanates of Gresik, Tuban, Demak, Jepara, Cirebon and Banten. Historians have also confirmed the leading role of Muslim Chinese merchants in this process. The new faith expanded in the Sundanese territory (the west of the island) where power had always been lax. And it was the **Demak sultanate** that was responsible for firing the final shot at the Majapahit Empire (1527).

It was to vanish in its turn in the following century, in its struggle against Blambangan, the last Indianised kingdom in the east of the island. But in the early 17C a new Muslim power emerged: **Mataram**, the second to carry the same name.

The Portuguese era

From the early 16C the spread of Islam clashed with the arrival of the Portuguese, who also coveted the productive trade in spices. The capture of Malacca in 1511 by Alfonso de Albuquerque overthrew the Arab and Chinese-dominated commercial networks, and was a prelude to European colonisation. Muslim merchants withdrew to **Aceh**, on the northern tip of Sumatra, where a new sultanate developed which, helped by the distant Ottoman Empire, was to push back the Portuguese persistently. This was finally achieved in 1641 – but by a different European power, the **Dutch**.

In Java the Portuguese established short-lived contacts with the **kingdom of Pajajaran** (1522), but it was in the Spice Islands of the **Moluccas** (Ambon, Ternate and Banda) and the **Lesser Sunda Islands** (Flores, Solor and Timor) that they firmly established their hold. Through the efforts of Alfonso de Albuquerque, who encouraged his soldiers to marry local women, some sections of the population even adopted the Catholic religion. In the face of attacks by the sultans of **Makassar** (Ujung Pandang in Sulawesi), and then the Dutch, however, the Portuguese were driven out of the archipelago early in the 17C, retaining power only in the eastern part of Timor.

The Dutch East India Company (17-18C)

The arrival of **Cornelis van Houtman** in the great pepper-trading port of **Banten** in western Java (1596) marked the opening of the Batavian venture in Indonesia. The expedition aroused French and English interest in the Spice Islands, but it was the Dutch who, in less than fifty years, asserted themselves by force as the leading power in the archipelago.

Spices bought with blood
The Dutch East India Company (Vereenigde Oostindische Cie) was created in 1602, one of the first companies in history to be established on a multiple capital basis and skilled at negotiating treaties, raising an army, building forts and even declaring war in the name of the United Provinces. The company very rapidly seized control of the Moluccas, particularly the island of Banda, where the population was massacred or reduced to slavery.

As part of the project the Company managed to establish a strong bridgehead by 1614, under the wing of the young **Jan Pieterszoon Coen**, in **Jayakarta** (now Jakarta) near the Sumatra pepper plantations and the Sunda Strait. Coen's pragmatism knew no limits: in 1618, under the pretext of expanding the post, he built a full-scale fortress. Prince Wijayakrama responded promptly, but despite their smaller numbers the Dutch inflicted a stinging defeat on his forces. In 1619 they flattened the town and built a new one – **Batavia** – with Amsterdam as their model.

Their capture of Malacca from the Portuguese in 1641 confirmed Dutch control of the spice trade. Convinced that they were making a good bargain, they bartered a few islands with the English in exchange for a useless island in the New World – Manhattan!

The Java wars
Benefiting from the decline of Aceh and Malacca, Batavia became the archipelago's main trading centre, but the little colony was cut off from the inland areas. Twice, in 1628 and 1629, it nearly fell to assaults by the kingdom of Mataram. From then on the Dutch played assiduously on the division within the Javanese communities, in order to weaken them. In 1639 the Dutch East India Company signed a peace treaty with the little sultanate of Banten, then made overtures to **Sultan Agung** who ruled Mataram between 1613 and 1645. Since succeeding Senopati he had already conquered eastern Java, Madura and Bali, in the hope of reviving the glory of the Majahapit Empire. With their hopes of expansion in Java frustrated, the Dutch made a significant gain in 1669 by taking **Makassar**, an important staging post on the spice route. In the late 17C the Company benefited from the dynastic quarrels that were tearing the two sultanates apart. First came the surrender of Banten, in 1682, following a brief war. Then the revolts of the Madurese prince Trunajaya (1677-80) and the Balinese slave **Surapati** (1686-1703) gave them an opportunity to plunge into the interior affairs of Mataram. In the 18C, by the end of the **Wars of Javanese Succession** (see p 200), the Dutch had conquered a large part of Mataram, where the kings, divided and weakened, went on to establish themselves as patrons and benefactors.

These long years of disturbance had ruined the Dutch East India Company, however, at a time when the spice trade itself was in decline, and the Batavians lost their trading monopoly in Asia. In 1799 the company was faced with bankruptcy.

The Dutch East Indies (1800-1949)

The colony had barely become a crown possession before it changed hands during the Napoleonic wars. Appointed governor of the Dutch East Indies in 1808 by Louis Bonaparte, King of the Netherlands, **Herman Willem Daendels** hoisted the French flag in Batavia. Forced labour was introduced, the peasants suffered extortion, and part of the territory was taken over. His ambitious plan for a "trans-Java" transport road enabled him to open up the island but cost the lives of many workmen.

In 1811 the English captured Batavia and installed **Thomas Stamford Raffles**, with considerable knowledge of the Malayan world, as governor. Attentive to profits, the new governor introduced a system of land-rent which required farmers to pay over a third or even half of their harvest as rent. At the same time a small group benefited from his efforts to establish large plantations. At the end of the Napoleonic wars, however, the English restored the colony to the Dutch.

A profitable colony

It was a gloomy picture: coffee production was languishing and the land taxes brought in little. Above all, revolts were breaking out almost everywhere. In western Sumatra the Minangkabau region and its people were destroyed in a religious conflict, the **Padri war** (1815-24), in which the **imam Bonjol** (*see sidebar p 125*) distinguished himself. Next came the **Java War** (1825-30), led by Prince **Diponegoro**, which left the island exhausted and bled dry.

Once peace returned, the Governor General **Johannes Van den Bosch** established the *Kultuurstelsel*, a system of forced agriculture that was to make the Netherlands' fortune and enable it to finance its industrial revolution. From then on Java became a vast plantation producing coffee, sugar-cane, tea, tobacco etc, rather than food crops for local consumption.

Java in the 19C: the house of a Dutch resident (engraving by Van de Velde)

P Bénet

The system had its limits, however, and in 1860 the book *Max Havelaar*, which denounced its abuses, created an immense furore in the Netherlands. After 1870 the great state farms gave way to private plantations controlled by a handful of land-owners. Between 1850 and 1905 the European community expanded from 22 000 to 80 000 settlers. Factories and shops flourished, while electricity and the railway (1894) were introduced.

Yet this progress was of little use to the local population. **Raden Adjeng Kartini** (1879-1904), a young Javanese aristocrat later honoured as a national heroine, was the first to denounce both the colonial system, which deprived local populations of access to education, and the tradition that kept women under male control. Conquest continued at the same time: in 1903, after thirty years of conflict, the sultanate of Aceh capitulated, followed by the sultanate of Jambi and the kingdom of Batak. To the east Lombok (1894), Sulawesi (1905), Bali (1906) and Flores (1907-08) fell one after the other. With the capture of the western half of New Guinea (Irian Jaya, now Papua) in 1928, the Dutch achieved the unification of the archipelago, drawing up the outline of the future Republic of Indonesia (with the exception of East Timor).

National revival

In Java there were mutterings of discontent. In 1908 an anti-colonial student society, **Budi Utomo,** was founded. Next came **Sarekat Islam**, originally a straightforward corporation of Muslim batik manufacturers. In 1912 it became a nationalist organ-isation and seven years later claimed a membership of two million. Next, in 1920, the **Indonesian Communist Party (PKI)**, the first of its kind in Asia, was founded. Strikes, demonstrations and confrontations followed, with the colonial government responding by banning the PKI in 1927 and arresting the principal nationalist leaders. Among them was a certain **Sukarno**, who founded the **Indonesian National Party (PNI)** in 1927. The concept of a nation took hold in 1928 during the Medan rally, where a group of students proclaimed the **Youth Pledge** and adopted Malay as their common language.

In February 1942 the Dutch collapse (within barely ten days) under **Japanese** assaults was a major upheaval for the Indonesians. Welcomed as liberators, the new occupiers were quick to introduce their own forms of exploitation: labour camps, plundering and famine leading to revolts, which were ferociously put down – Indonesia suffered one of the darkest periods in its history. When in 1943 the Japanese attempted to win over the Indonesian nationalists, the latter therefore pre-ferred to follow their own line.

The war of liberation

On 17 August 1945, two days after the Japanese surrender, Sukarno and Mohammed Hatta proclaimed Indonesian independence, in which they became respectively President and Vice-President. A constitution was drawn up the next day. There were clashes with the Japanese and then the English, who were responsible for main-taining order. On their return, the Dutch embarked on a fierce struggle against the forces of the young republic, commanded by the charismatic **General Sudirman**. At the same time they sought to maintain their influence by creating a state in the eastern islands, which supported them.

The international scene had shifted, however, and the Americans no longer toler-ated the existence of great colonial empires. Threatened with being deprived of the funds promised by the Marshall Plan, The Hague finally yielded and recognised Indonesian **independence**, in December 1949. The only question that remained out-standing was the status of the western half of New Guinea. After a presence lasting 330 years the Dutch, who had never attempted to promote their language or culture, departed without a trace.

The Indonesian Republic

The task facing the new regime was clearly daunting. The economy was devastated by the years of war and there was the threat of a lack of rice, aggravated by the population explosion. The government first undertook to overcome the **secession of the Moluccas** (1950), and the armed rebellion of the Muslim movement **Darul Islam** in Aceh, the Celebes and West Java (1949-62). Having adopted a parliamentary form of government, Indonesia sank into the instability of coalitions dominated by the conservative Muslim Masyumi party and the Socialist party.

Controlled democracy

Sustained by Communists and nationalists, in 1953 Sukarno imposed the "Indonesianisation" of the economy. Externally, he encouraged *rapprochement* with the socialist group and set up the **Bandung conference** (1955), the founding act of the movement of non-aligned nations. Elsewhere, anxious to settle the **Papua** question, he confiscated the possessions of the Dutch, who were expelled, and took the matter to the United Nations, where he finally won his case in 1963.

Undermined by political instability, economic problems and military rebellions in Sumatra, Borneo and Sulawesi, the country was plunged into crisis. Sukarno had to attempt a difficult balancing act between two unyielding enemies, the PKI and the army. Repressed by General Nasution, the attempt at **secession in Sumatra** (1958-61) was to become a pretext for Sukarno to take control of the regime. He restored the constitution of 1945 and introduced a **"directed democracy"**. Invoking the ideals of the revolution, the president drew closer to the Communists and adopted an interventionist and anti-liberal policy. Unfortunately, agrarian reform and the attempt to establish worker councils aggravated the economic situation and clashed with business circles and the army. In 1963, concerned about the British project to set up a "greater Malaysia" – taking in Malaya, Singapore and northern Borneo – Sukarno chose confrontation **(konfrontasi)** with the West and drew closer to Communist China. The army was unhappy at this turn of affairs and it was in this tense atmosphere, with Sukarno still retaining immense prestige, that the 1965 *coup d'état* took place.

A monument to the Indonesian nation: Jalan Proklamasi (Jakarta)

P. Bénet

The "New Order"

Few events in recent history have had such an impact on the fate of so many while still retaining such a cloud of mystery. The immediate consequence of the failed *coup d'état* in 1965 was the elimination of the PKI, accused of being the instigator of the putsch. The price was fierce repression, with between 500 000 and 1 000 000 dead, and the Sino-Indonesian community bearing the brunt. In the following years the struggle for power was to turn to the advantage of **Suharto**, supported by the army, students and Muslim institutions. Dismissed by the Assembly in March 1967, Sukarno was placed under house arrest until his death in 1970.

At home, the new regime emphasised **economic growth,** literacy and birth control, all of which met with genuine success. Modern ideas took hold in Indonesian life, the capital filled up with new buildings, and a middle class emerged.

The *coup d'état* of 1965

During the night of 30 September, six members of the army headquarters staff were arrested and executed by "progressive officers". The high command was beheaded, apart from General Nasution, and Suharto, an obscure general in command of the elite Kostrad corps. The authors of the coup asserted their wish to save Sukarno's regime from a threatened plot controlled from afar by the CIA. The first hours of the event were to prove crucial in Indonesia's future, as Suharto swiftly won back control of the capital and thwarted the attempt. Many points remain obscure, concerning both the role of the Communist Party, which approved this "internal army action" without taking part itself, and that of President Sukarno, who condemned it.

For 32 years the political scene was to remain dominated by the controlling party, **Golkar**, supported by the army. This pattern remained very unequal, however, and the crisis that broke out in 1997 showed the structural weakness of an economy that was rotten with corruption at all levels. Further, the regime proved unyielding in its attitude to opposition, whether religious (massacre of the Muslims of Tanjung Priok in 1984), ethnic (Aceh and Papua) or political (press censorship and imprisonment). Externally, Indonesia contributed to the creation of **ASEAN** (1967), bringing together all the nations of the region with the aim of promoting economic growth and blocking Communist expansion. Suharto moved closer to the United States and broke with China, although relations were to be re-established early in the 1990s. In 1975 he invaded **East Timor**, the former Portuguese possession, which had just proclaimed its independence. However, the "27th province" made life difficult for the Indonesian army, which failed to defeat the guerrilla war of the Fretilin front after twenty years of armed conflict that caused the death of 200 000 people – one-third of the population.

Suharto in 1996

V. Miladinovic/Sygma

AT THE CROSSROADS

After its brutal introduction to the era of modernity and globalisation, Indonesia today stands at a turning point. Having gathered the fruits of growth and an improved standard of living, the spectacular collapse of the economy has undermined its legendary optimism. This stagnation, intensified by an unprecedented political crisis, has underlined the limits of a strategy, which has by-passed the modernisation of structures and above all of attitudes. Suddenly the contrast between the centre and the fringes stands out too strongly as does that between the newly prosperous and those left behind by progress, between economic liberalism and political authoritarianism, between tradition and modernity. During this period of uncertainty, Indonesians are now looking for a path to harmonious development.

Institutions inherited through independence

Although Indonesian political life is still regulated by the **1945 Constitution**, since the fall of Suharto strong pressure has been developed to adopt a genuinely democratic system. Various reforms have already been introduced.

The all-powerful figure of the **president** is elected by Parliament every five years, at the same time as a **vice-president** without powers but who may be called on to replace the president – as happened in 1998 when Habibie took over after Suharto's resignation.

Restricted under Suharto to a simple role as records office, the Chamber of Representatives of the People **(DPR)** has 462 members elected by universal suffrage (proportional voting) for a mandate of five years. At its side the **army** (TNI, formerly ABRI), controls 38 seats, compared with 85 in the old assembly. The recent suppression of the army's dual function (*dwifonkti*) has been one of the main demands of the students and reformers. The People's Congress **(MPR)**, which elects the president and vice-president, consists of 500 members of the DPR to which are added 135 provincial delegates and 65 representatives of religions and the various social groupings.

From the administrative point of view, the country is divided into **27 provinces** led by local parliaments elected under universal suffrage, and governors named by the central power. At a time when centrifugal forces are intensifying, increasing numbers of voices are calling for a federal system that would grant greater power to the

The five principles of the Pancasila

Aware of the extremely wide range of ethnic, religious and social elements in this growing country, Sukarno, the founding father of the Republic of Indonesia, decided to endow it with a common set of beliefs. On 1 June 1945, therefore, even ahead of the proclamation of independence, the Pancasila ("five principles") was pronounced, a genuine state ideology which all individuals and institutions were expected to uphold. The Pancasila, which was the focus for many speeches and celebrations, appears in the form of a set of five symbols in all the badges of the nation, beside the national emblem, the mythical eagle Garuda. Its five principles are belief in a single deity (star), a just and civilised humanity (chain), the unity of Indonesia (head of a banteng buffalo), popular sovereignty governed by the wisdom of deliberation and representation (the sacred banyan tree), and finally social justice (rice and cotton). Thus defined, the Indonesian project displays a will for federation, that is both tolerant and restraining, to promote religious, ethnic and social peace through consensual democracy.

The five symbols of the Pancasila R. Marca

provinces. At the next level down the scale there are the **kacamatan** – either municipalities (*kotamadya*), or districts (*kabupaten*) – which have a local parliament and a regent (*bupati*). This layer is itself divided into urban and rural **sub districts**. Lastly, **62 000 villages** (*desa*) – evidence of the scale of the rural areas – form the base of the administrative pyramid.

The uncertain future of the "Reformasi"

The colossal fires that destroyed millions of hectares of forest in Sumatra and Kalimantan in 1997 (*see p 27*) now appear to have been forewarnings of the collapse of the Indonesian economy and the fall of Suharto, who had been in power for 32 years. Supported by a large majority of the population, who were weary of the regime's corruption and social injustice, students were the spearhead for **Reformasi** (reform). The bloody riots in Jakarta (1 200 dead), which specifically targeted the Sino-Indonesian community, followed by the students' occupation of Parliament, forced the old dictator to hand over to his successor, **Habibie**, on 21 May 1998.

Although the new president made gestures of openness (liberation of political prisoners, the end of censorship, and multi-party rule), the opposition reproached the army and the "Suhartists" for retaining their control over key positions. In the free elections of June 1999 (the first since 1955), **48 parties** confronted each other, compared with three in Suharto's time. The victory of the opposition, represented by the PDI-P party of **Megawati Sukarnoputri** (33.7 %), Sukarno's daughter, was to open the way to the first democratic change of power in Indonesian history. Whatever happens, however, the new president will have to manage a large number of redhot issues: restructuring the banking system, growth in unemployment, the struggle against corruption, relations with the army, rebellions in Aceh and Papua, and the rise in religious and social tensions. Further, the new power will be particularly keenly watched by the international community on the question of East Timor, whose annexation by force has never been recognised by the United Nations. As a result of a referendum on self-determination in 1999, East Timor has now acquired independence, and United Nations troops have been monitoring the region. The year 2000 has seen continued unrest in Indonesia, with separatist movements in Aceh and religious differences in the Moluccas.

A demographic giant

With nearly 210 million inhabitants, Indonesia is the world's fourth most populous nation. As a result of the family planning policy introduced under the New Order, annual growth dropped from 3 % in the 1960s to 2 % in the 1990s.

However, one of the main concerns of the authorities remains the very **unequal demographic distribution**, between the overpopulated regions such as Java, and others such as Papua, Kalimantan and central Sulawesi, where the density is less than 30 inhabitants per square kilometre. Of the 17 500 islands that make up the archipelago, less than half are inhabited. Indonesia has undergone substantial internal migration, in particular to Java, which exercises a strong economic attraction. Although it contributes to social mixing, this **rural exodus** poses insoluble problems in the cities, particularly in Jakarta, where great numbers of people live in wretched conditions. However, in the early 20C, a policy of **transmigrasi** was introduced, designed to encourage the people of Java and Bali to settle in the underpopulated regions. Its impact on the settlement patterns of the population remains marginal, however.

From the ethnic point of view, the archipelago thus retains the appearance of an extraordinary **mosaic**, with hundreds of different peoples cohabiting *(see the introductory pages on the various islands)*. The motto of the Republic, *"Bhinneka Tunggal Ika"* ("Unity in Diversity") takes on its full meaning when you realise that nearly 600 languages and five religions are practised between one end of the country and the other.

The land of rice and spices

As in the whole of Southeast Asia, Indonesia is a land of **rice**, grown in fields that may be dry *(ladong)* or irrigated *(sawah)*, depending on traditional practice. The techniques of irrigation, on the other hand, are particularly sophisticated, and make it possible to follow a cycle of harvesting the rice every four months in the richest soils. The basic form of nourishment for the population, rice occupies millions of hands that carve out the rich landscapes of terraced rice fields from one end of the archipelago to the other. However, although it ranks third in terms of world production (48 million tonnes in 1999, half of it in Java) this is not always enough to feed the nation. Internal distribution is managed by an official agency, Bulog, which sets the price, but its role has been challenged in the wake of the economic crisis. In comparison, other **subsistence crops** (maize, soya, cassava, sweet potatoes etc) form a marginal element in the food supply.

Inherited from the colonial era, the **plantation crops** provide the nation with a substantial income (hevea, from which rubber is derived, palm oil, copra, coffee, sugar-cane, cocoa and tea), that places it among the leaders of world producers. The plantations, nationalised in Sukarno's time, now belong to large public or private cultivators.

But Indonesia is also the land of **spices** and medicinal plants (pepper, cardamom, nutmeg, betel nut, camphor, cashew nuts, cloves and aloes) as well as valuable timber (teak, sandalwood etc). Unfortunately, the large-scale deforestation of the forests of Kalimantan and Sumatra, together with intensive farming in some regions, are serious threats to the ecosystem.

An overpopulated land, Indonesia has little room for **livestock rearing**, which requires too much space. Further, pigs, which are banned under Islam, are barely present except in the Christian or animist islands (Flores, Sumba and certain regions of Sumatra, Sulawesi and the Moluccas). **Fishing**, on the other hand, despite its inten-

Rice threshing

R. Marca

sive nature, is difficult to assess. The hauls of foreign trawlers are substantially under-estimated and those of traditional fishing remain unquantifiable. Industrial **prawn-farming**, which is prospering at Cirebon (northern Java) and other locations, appears to offer a valuable future.

Mineral treasures

Rich in natural resources (the result in particular of volcanic activity, see *p 13*), Indonesia nonetheless undertakes virtually no systematic exploitation of its terrain. **Oil deposits** (the Java Sea, Kalimantan and Papua) and **natural gas** (Aceh, eastern Sumatra and the Natuna isles) have played a significant role in the expansion of the economy and continue to supply a noticeable share of export revenue (Jakarta is a member of OPEC). Since the 1980s, however, the government has been trying to reduce their share so that the economy does not suffer the devastating effects of a fall in rates. Apart from oil products, the island soils contain tin (Bangka and Belitung, in eastern Sumatra), nickel (Sulawesi), copper (Papua), bauxite (the Riau islands), gold (Papua, Sumbawa), and sulphur (Java).

Far from matching its mining resources, Indonesian **industry** suffers from many shortages (the nation provides for only half of its own steel requirements). Until the mid-1980s, the few activities inherited from the colonial era benefited from protectionist measures. Then the government adopted a series of measures designed to favour exports in particular: reduction in taxes, purchase of licences, detachment of the state from certain sectors, and encouragement to foreign investment. Metallurgy, chemicals, mechanical and electrical engineering as well as paper production and the assembling of electronic parts, all benefited from this encouragement, but it is undoubtedly the **textiles** sector which has shown the greatest success. This policy is based primarily on a network of small businesses with low bank input and little capital funding, but which create employment. Favoured by low labour costs, the policy has been very effective: 14 % of the active population are now employed in the secondary sector, which brings in 20 % of the GNP. In the end, however, industry remains handicapped by the lack of qualified staff, the absence of skills in advanced technology, the lack of transport infrastructures and **corruption,** which removes considerable amounts of money from the productive sector.

Over the same period **tourism** has seen exponential growth (nearly five million foreigners visited the archipelago in 1996), and now constitutes the third largest source of foreign currency (excluding oil products).

A ravaged economy

After a decade of economic growth at 8 % per year, Indonesia, which already saw itself as a new economic tiger, was hard hit by the financial crisis that began in Bangkok in the summer of 1997. There was a particularly brutal awakening in Jakarta, where the currency lost 80 % of its value in January 1998 (it has improved since then) and where the GNP dropped by 15 % in the same year. With colossal foreign debt, the collapse of the banking system, the flight of capital, unemployment (23 % of the active population), inflation (60 %), bankruptcies and a falling standard of living, the picture at the end of 1998 was very dark. The uncontrolled growth in an expansionary spiral corrupted by widespread dishonesty partly explains this phenomenon. With colossal loans granted without other surety than the guarantee of someone close to power, and long-term investments financed by short-term loans, the bases for growth were fragile and, when the crisis broke out, political uncertainty merely made matters worse. Henceforward the main task of the leaders will be to rebuild the confidence of economic players and foreign investors.

May 1998: when students took to the streets of Jakarta

Meeting the people

Smiles and delicacies
in Indonesia

RELIGIONS AND BELIEF SYSTEMS

Its number of believers makes Indonesia the world's leading Muslim nation, but this does not eliminate variety, and the country contains an amazingly diverse range of beliefs. Along with Islam, Catholicism, Protestantism, Hinduism, Buddhism and animist cults make up a mosaic of extraordinary complexity. A deeply religious nation, where every citizen is required to belong to one of the officially recognised religions, Indonesia represents a rare example of tolerance and harmonious cohabitation. This picture has sadly been overshadowed in recent years by the tensions that have developed in some regions.

The other characteristic feature of Indonesians, frequently displayed down the centuries, is their capacity to assimilate imported religions and integrate them into local beliefs. This unconcealed syncretism, which has flourished from one end of the country to the other, is undoubtedly the finest illustration of the spirit of the nation.

A deeply religious nation

Whatever form it takes, religious belief appears as the common denominator throughout the archipelago, with no fewer than 600 000 mosques, 31 000 Protestant churches, 14 000 Catholic churches, 23 700 Hindu temples and 3 900 Buddhist temples.

"Belief in one god" is the first of the five principles of the **Pancasila**, the official doctrine of the Republic that all its citizens are required to observe. Alongside the five official religions that fall within the concerns of the Ministry of Faiths (Islam, Protestantism, Catholicism, Hinduism and Mahayana Buddhism), certain traditional beliefs are still tolerated, such as *kejawen* (Javanese mysticism) or animism (in the most isolated regions), and are the responsibility of the Ministry of Culture. Since the late 1970s, on the other hand, the Confucianism practised by part of the Sino-Indonesian community has no longer been recognised.

Neither secular nor religious, the Indonesian Republic can be defined as a theistic state. The Ministry of Faiths helps with the construction of religious buildings, oversees public Muslim education (the primary *madrasah ibtidaiyah* schools and the IAIN universities), and has a monopoly in organising pilgrimages to Mecca. The guarantor of peace between the various religions, the state is expected to discourage evangelism and missionaries because they are a threat to the status quo (the same applies to inter-faith marriages). The ministers and priests of the various faiths must therefore be content with spreading the good word (*dakwah*) within their own communities. It is against this background that the last few years have witnessed a "revival" of Islam, visible in the number of mosques currently being built, the current practice of prayer at the workplace and the increasingly widespread custom for young Muslim women to wear the veil (*jilbab*).

In this context, asserting that one is an atheist may appear provocative to an Indonesian. Since the 1960s the term has even become synonymous with "Communism", viewed as the worst form of subversion and liable to imprisonment. Few indeed are those who dare to proclaim themselves "*muslim/katolik KTP*" ("Muslim/Catholic according to my identity card"), a subtle way of expressing a purely formal membership of one of the official religions (an obligatory category of the identity card).

Animism, tradition and syncretic belief

Hinduism, Buddhism, Islam, Christianity – all the major official Indonesian faiths are, paradoxically, imported beliefs. In taking root in the archipelago they have undergone profound changes through contact with local beliefs and cultures. Thus the

Agama anda apa?

What is your religion? For any Indonesian, belief in a god is something obvious, equally applicable to the foreign visitor, who will inevitably be asked the ritual question. Any negative response will almost certainly lead the questioner to express either his puzzlement or his pity, and make you an immediate offer to lead you into the ways of righteousness. Despite this, tolerance is always in evidence. This spirituality, profound and universal, regulates the high points in life and daily activity (circumcision, fasting, marriage, burial, pilgrimages, etc), but the many ceremonies are also an occasion to emphasise the importance of belonging to a community.

basis of traditions – **adat** – which have developed down the ages around the original Austronesian kernel *(see p 31)* permeates the way of life (the sense of welcome and hospitality, the feeling of community spirit and mutual aid) as well as the multifaceted beliefs and rituals (ancestor worship, propitiatory ceremonies, two-stage burials etc). In certain areas, such as among the Dayaks of Kalimantan or in Sumba, animist practices survive almost unchanged.

The result of a thousand years of syncretic belief, Indonesian society can be seen as a layered territory where religions have followed one upon another without ever being eliminated. For the local genius dwells in the capacity to assimilate and combine features introduced from outside, which bring added wealth to the original elements. In this way the Indian religions have taken over the cult of the sacred mountain, while Balinese Hinduism has moderated the caste system. Javanese Hinduism, meanwhile, offers innumerable examples of fusion with local tradition *(see p 204)* and some of its focal sites are former Hindu locations. Finally, the Christianity of the Toraja lives comfortably with buffalo sacrifice, and Flores has whip competitions to celebrate the ordination of priests.

Dominant Islam

Indonesia's overwhelmingly majority religion is Sunni Islam, practised by 87% of the population. Distance, however, explains the distinctive features that mark it out from its original source. And although the call of the muezzin, the minarets and the observance of fasting and daily prayer are widespread and familiar features, Indonesian Islam stands out in its spirit of tolerance, an expression in keeping with this friendly nation and bountiful land.

In its expansion *(see p 35)*, the religion of the Prophet Muhammad has based itself on pre-existing social structures (notably the Indo-Javanese mandalas, *see "Borobudur" p 302)* to establish its own network, in particular with the religious brotherhoods *(tarekat)* and the Islamic schools *(pesantren)* that are still numerous (with some 40 000 institutions for 8 million pupils throughout the country).

Indonesians make a distinction between *santri* Muslims (devout) and *priyayi* or *abangan* believers (whose faith is imbued with traditional beliefs). The great range of practices should be seen in

The five pillars of Islam

The essence of Islamic belief, the "shahada" is a profession of faith ("There is no god but Allah" and "Muhammad is his Prophet") that is recited by the faithful at each "salat", the five daily prayers. Proclaimed by the call of the muezzin, which sounds across the whole city (with Fridays the most important day), the "salat" is performed by prostrating oneself on the ground, facing towards Mecca ("Kiblat"). The third great principle of Islam, charity, ("zakat") is practised through gifts to Muslim institutions. A period for contemplation and piety, the fasting ("puasa") of the month of Ramadan enables the faithful to purify the spirit. No food, drink or smoking is allowed between sunrise and sunset, except for the sick, children and menstruating women. Lastly, Muslims are expected to undertake the pilgrimage to Mecca (the "haj") once in their lives.

the light of this historic process. In Java, for example, Islam first took root in the 16C on the north coast, where it remains universal, as in Madura. The faith then expanded to the west, to Sundanese territory, without encountering any great resistance on the part of the existing local powers. Today, the observance of Islam is still more orthodox here than in Central Java where tradition has had a profound effect on the Muslim faith. In the same way, the deep religious piety of Aceh, in northern Sumatra, contrasts strongly with the more flexible style in Java. And in Lombok, the **Wetu Telu Islam** (*see p 470*), despite being very marginalised, has retained its animist roots. Finally, in eastern Sumbawa, a famously orthodox island, all the women wear the veil – but it is in the form of silky sarongs draped over their heads.

Islam, a way of life

Like Muslims throughout the world, Indonesians adhere to the Koran, the words of Muhammad, and the histories of the life and works of the Prophet. An *imam* heads the mosque, the centre of religious life.

The edicts of the faith are observed in various ways, depending on the region. Charity, for example, is a matter of conscience and is subject to no legal obligation (unlike the custom in certain Arab countries). In Madura, requests are organised by the road on the way into each town. The **pilgrimage to Mecca,** on the other hand, is a heavy duty because of cost and distance, and the departure of a group of the faithful is an occasion for splendid celebrations in the countryside (200 000 people undertook the voyage in 1996). A strong tradition holds that seven pilgrimages to the tomb of Sheikh Durhanuddin at Ulakan (West Sumatra) are the equivalent of the journey to Mecca. However, the prestige gained from the *haj* is such that some farmers willingly sell their land to pay for the expedition. In the case of fasting, where observance also relates to a certain degree of social pressure, it is not as scrupulously observed as in the Arab countries, apart from the regions of great piety such as Aceh (you should not expect to find a restaurant open there at midday during Ramadan!).

Apart from the ban on eating pork, the other precepts of the Koran are also interpreted in a relaxed fashion, particularly the prohibition of usury, betting and alcohol. For women, wearing the **veil**

The Istiqlal Mosque, Jakarta: the right scale for the world's largest Muslim nation

T. Renaut/Tony Stone

– which isn't mentioned in the Koran – is undergoing a distinct revival among the younger generation; but, in general, women enjoy a far more liberal status than in Arab countries. This also applies to polygamy, which is forbidden for officials. It is subject to the approval of the first wife, and is in any case tending to disappear. In Sumatra, the Minangkabau even display a very rare example of a matriarchal Muslim culture in which land ownership passes through the female line.

Islam and politics

Although the concept of an Islamic state was set aside with the founding of the Indonesian Republic, the important place of this religion in the political system has remained an awkward question for the nation's governments. Until the beginning of the 1960s, certain regions (Aceh and West Java) suffered from disturbances stirred up by the Darul Islam movement. A significant factor under Sukarno, the **Masyumi Parti** never achieved its aim of imposing a state with an established official faith. Then, under the "New Order", Islam became marginalised in political terms despite the existence of a small party that lacked strong autonomy, the PPP (Party of Unified Development). This past explains the feelings of many Muslims, of being wronged and under-represented, even though they occupied all the key posts of the State, beginning with the presidency. In 1990 the creation of the Association of Muslim Intellectuals **(ICMI)**, under the direction of Habibie, answered Suharto's concern about dealing with these anxieties.

However, independent Islam has possessed powerful networks, in particular the **Nahdlatul Ulama**, the world's leading Muslim organisation (35 million members). It has benefited from the aura surrounding its leader, the highly respected Abdurrahman Wahid (alias Gus Dur), credited with the creation of the PKB (National Party of Awakening). The modernist option is represented by the **Muhammadiyah** (with 25 million members), whose former leader Amien Rais, founder of PAN (Party of National Mandate) is one of the figures in the opposition. Alongside them, around twenty parties proclaiming their Islamic faith have arisen since Suharto's fall.

A sprinkling of Christianity

The archipelago's second most important religion, Christianity, took root in the islands soon after Islam. The scale of its support has grown substantially in recent decades, from 2.8% of the population in 1933 to 9% in 1995. Within the Christian communities, two-thirds are **Protestants** (*protestan*, or more frequently *kristen*), the religion of the former Dutch colonisers, and one third **Catholics** (*katolik*). Introduced by the Portuguese early in the 16C, Catholicism was ignored by the Dutch over a long period. It was not until much later, at the end of the 19C, that the colonial powers undertook to evangelise the animist peoples of Sumatra and the Indonesian "Far East". Inspired missionaries, those who spread the word took great care not to offend the local populations, and compromised with tradition without trying to supplant or destroy it. Later, the visit of John Paul II to Flores in 1989 was a highly emotional experience for these Christians living at the ends of the earth.

A minority element at national level, Christianity nonetheless occupies a large area on the map of the archipelago, for in the "Far East" it is the majority religion. But although Flores and East Timor are Catholic lands, the south of the Moluccas (Ambon), the west of Papua and part of Sulawesi (Torajas and Minhasans) are Protestant. Elsewhere, the establishment of Protestantism marks a dotted line through northern Sumatra (Bataks), Central Java (in Salatiga and Gunung Kidul) and Kalimantan (Dayaks). Among all these peoples, Christianity is seen as a constituent element of their culture and a fixed point of their identity within the immense Muslim archipelago.

Religions and belief systems

Circumstances differ among the **Sino-Indonesians**, who only adopted Christianity *en masse* after the massacres of 1965-66, to avoid being accused of being Communists. This conversion, however, reinforced their image as a privileged and non-integrated minority, for many of them live in the mainly Muslim urban areas of Java and Sumatra. Tensions developed from 1992, with the burning of churches, and turned violent in 1999 as a consequence of the economic crisis, particularly in the Moluccas.

The Buddhist-Hindu foundation

Introduced early in the 5C by Indian merchants, for many centuries **Hinduism** was the dominant religion throughout the islands. Today, however, with the exception of Bali and some isolated pockets in Java (the Tengger lands, *see p 341*), this ancient faith is no more than a memory in stone, with Borobudur and Prambanan as impressive evidence for modern eyes. Barely 2% of the population of Indonesia claim adherence to Hinduism (*for more information, see the introduction to "Bali", p 354*).

Founded in India in the 6C BC by Prince Siddhartha Gautama (Buddha), **Buddhism** is not, strictly speaking, a religion, but a school of thought. It has many points in common with Hinduism, as can be seen in certain temples in Prambanan. According to this doctrine, human existence is a painful time and man can only obtain release by leading a life of asceticism and by observing a rigorous moral code made up of meditation. Only this can help him approach the state of Buddha, the first "enlightened" being to have reached the state of Nirvana, that of knowledge and liberation from desires and passions. During his life Buddha established a community of *bonzes* or *sanaa* (priests) and codified his discipline in the *vinaya*.

Appearing at the beginning of the Christian era, **Mahayana Buddhism** (from "Great Vehicle") promotes a concept of the Buddha's compassion and rejects the idea of individual salvation (contrasting with the "Little Vehicle"). For its model it takes the bodhisattvas, wise men who have passed the seven first stages, out of eight, that lead to Enlightenment, and are sometimes the object of a veritable cult. Beginning in the 7C **Tantric Buddhism**, which draws on magic ritual and refers to the world and its forces, enjoyed great expansion, particularly in Java.

Introduced soon after Hinduism, Buddhism spread remarkably in Indonesia under the aegis of the Srivijaya kingdom (7-13C), with its capital in Sumatra. From the 8 to the 9C, under the Sailendra dynasty, the centre of Java even took the lead as one of the main artistic and esoteric centres of Mahayana Buddhism.

Today, Buddhism only represents 1% of the population and most of its believers are Sino-Indonesians. Borobudur is clearly the central site of this religion: during the celebration of the *Waicak* (the anniversary of the birth and death of the Buddha), a procession of *bonzes* goes from the monastery of Mendut to the great mandala of Borobudur.

The Indian branch

In addition to its effect on the landscapes of Central Java, Indianisation continues to have a profound effect on Indonesian behaviour, political life and culture. Despite the centuries of Islamisation, therefore, the ethos of the priyayi (the former Javanese nobility), consisting of conformity and discipline, still prevails. Similarly, the country's political structure is based on the concentric model (the mandala) of the Indianised kingdoms: the centre of the country (Meru) lies at the heart of the capital, in Merdeka Square, where the Monas, the monument devoted to national independence in the form of a linga (the phallic symbol of Shiva), stands imposingly. From here it radiates out over the whole of Java, and then, in a second circle, over the rest of the archipelago. On the cultural level, although the use of Javanese and levels of speech which belong to it are increasingly giving way to Bahasa Indonesia, Javanese cultural life, in particular shadow theatre (wayang kulit), remains largely imbued with the great epics of the Ramayana and the Mahabharata (see p 58).

"BAHASA INDONESIA"
THE NATIONAL LANGUAGE

Spoken by more than 200 million people in the archipelago itself – to which should be added expatriate Indonesians, particularly in Singapore and the Netherlands – *Bahasa Indonesia* ranks sixth in the world's languages.

Developed by the **Dutch** in 1920 as a single language – in particular for colonial administration and educational needs – it was imposed throughout the country and became the **official language** of the Republic of Indonesia in 1928. It was also used for nationalist ventures, very active at the time, by favouring national integration.

Rather than using their own language, the colonists adopted **Malay** *(see sidebar p 30)*, already used since the 8C in the islands as the *lingua franca*. It was also used as a Muslim language from the time when Arab writing replaced the original Sanskrit, in the 14 or 15C. The working language for Indian, Chinese, Bugis and Javanese merchants – as well as for the Portuguese, English and Dutch in the coastal trading posts – Malay also offered the major advantage of not being a dominant language, such as Javanese.

Under the wing of the Dutch, the **Latin alphabet** replaced Arab characters to create an Indonesian language directly adapted from Malay and enriched with words borrowed from Sanskrit, Arabic, Persian and Chinese, as well as Dutch, Portuguese, English and French. Apart from these foreign languages, some local additions – Javanese, Sundanese, Minangkabau, Bugis, Toraja and others – have also influenced the new language, a **syncretism** that underlies regional divergences in pronunciation, intonation and spelling.

Languages in daily life
In parallel with this national language, which is used in education, official administration, the media, and by around three-quarters of the population, most Indonesians continue to speak a multitude of island languages or regional **dialects** at home and between members of the same ethnic group. Several hundred of these have been identified, most of which remain the mother tongue and the only language used in daily life.

Speaking Indonesian
You will find it relatively easy to learn some *Bahasa Indonesia* with a small handbook *(see also "Useful words and expressions", p 111)*, and you will soon be capable of using it to bargain for your purchases or to get around, particularly if you go off the beaten track. In tourist centres, on the other hand, you will be able to communicate in **English**, for the growing expansion of tourism is encouraging more and more Indonesians to learn it. Many people have taught themselves and, not having had an opportunity to attend school regularly, use their contacts with foreign visitors to learn new languages or perfect their understanding of them. In some regions, such as Bali, Yogyakarta or the Toraja area of Sulawesi, you may be surprised to hear guides or young students speaking **French** or even a little Italian, **Dutch,** German or Japanese, but their knowledge is usually limited to the most basic elements of conversation.

LITERATURE

A rich body of work consisting of long mystical epics read out loud, 15-19C Malayan literature was entirely transcribed in the Arab alphabet. The oral tradition was maintained until modern times in some regions such as in Sumatra and in Sundanese territory through the *pantun* (a long poem, recitations of which may last for a whole night). In the 20C, however, the choice of Malay as the national language meant that writers from Java were eclipsed. This meant that the leading "Indonesian" novelists almost always had Malay as their mother tongue, or a language very similar to Malay, in particular the Sumatrans from the Minangkabau area. It took nearly two generations for the Javanese and other peoples of the archipelago to absorb and use *Bahasa Indonesia*. Some ancient and modern bodies of literature have however survived in local languages, particularly Javanese, Sundanese, Balinese and Bugis.

The emergence of modern literature

Stories appeared in the press in the 19C using the old names *hikayat* (edifying prose narratives) and *syair* (a narrative poem consisting of single-rhyme quatrains), but which were devoid of mystical or supernatural elements. The abundant work in Malay by the Sino-Indonesians, and then the popular literature and novels with political material in the early 20C, paved the way for modern literature.

To control publication, the Dutch set up the **Balai Pustaka** publishing house in the 1920s. The characteristic traits of Indonesian literature were already appearing, including the use of high "Malay", realism, and the frequent use of the first person narrative. Urban culture came to be used as a background, but the theme of the difficult compromise between Western and traditional values preoccupied all minds. From the 1930s a fresh national awareness found expression in the review **Pujangga Baru**, which published work by **Amir Hamzah**, a poet with great religious spirituality. **Armijn Pane** wrote *Belenggu* ("The Chains"), the first psychological Indonesian novel. Among other writers for the review mention should be made of **Sutan Takdir Alisjahbana**, who enjoyed success with "Sails in the wind", and the poet JE Tatengkeng.

The "1945 generation"

The period between 1942 and 1965 was one of great flowering, in which the themes of advancing revolution and the emergence of new forces facing up to the West occupied a central place. A great figure of the post-war years, the poet **Chairil Anwar** was influenced in his writing by European poets, particularly Rilke. At the same time, other people writing for the *Gelanggang* review aimed for universal humanism. In the late 1950s, however, as in the political world, division in the literary world intensified between the writers of the **Institute of National Culture**, who supported the government, and those of the **Lekra**, Marxist writers producing politically committed work.

The leaden years

Following the events of 1965 Lekra members were executed or imprisoned and their writing banned. The dominant figure among this group, **Pramoedya Ananta Toer** (1925-) is a prolific writer whose novels, poetry, short stories and historical essays show striking psychological and social analysis.

A native of Sumatra, **Mochtar Lubis** (1922-) is the other great figure of contemporary literature. A journalist, he roams the world and publishes pro-Western articles which have earned him imprisonment under Sukarno. He is the author of numerous essays, short stories and novels *(The Outlaw, Road With No End)*, and his masterwork, *Twilight in Jakarta*, was first published in English.

A new generation emerged in the late 1960s, including one of its great figures the Sundanese poet, novelist and essayist **Ajip Rosidi**, who writes in both Indonesian and

PA Toer, an untamed pen

Written in Dutch prisons, the early novels by Pramoedya ("Guerrilla Family", "Dawn", "Sparks of Revolution") were an immediate success. After leaving prison he continued to work ("Stories from Blora") and travelled in the West, then visited Communist China in 1956, a journey which was to mark his thinking. Later, the military repression of Sino-Indonesians inspired an essay in which he threw light on the importance of the community in national history. Imprisoned once more under Suharto, he spent more than ten years in the island-prison of Buru, where he wrote a tetralogy, which was to be published abroad. Pramoedya is in fact one of the rare Indonesian writers to have been translated into numerous languages. His political commitment has never faltered and he continues to call for a democracy without compromise.

Sundanese. Another poet, but also songwriter, actor and stage director, **Rendra** (1935-) also enjoys immense popularity as a result of his texts denouncing social injustice. Not without humour, his rhythmical, egocentric style has been highly influential, notably for the poets **Darmanto** and **Sutardji Calzoum Bachro**. Others follow a different path, such as **Sapardi** and **Abdul Hadi**, whose work shows an introspective melancholy.

To avoid censorship, novels and drama also turn to the narrator's inner world, as in the novels by **Simaputang**. There is also the short-story writer **Danarto** and the playwright **Arifin C Noer**, who both examine the unconscious.

The fall of Suharto and the 1998 riots have inspired a quantity of prose, published in the review *Horison*. The great success of the year, however, was the novel *Saman*, by the young journalist **Ayu Utami**, presenting correspondence by lovers written with great freedom of tone. Unfortunately, despite the relaxation of censorship, the economic crisis and low print-runs remain a threat to publishing.

"Hello, Mister!"

M. Lemerle

Literature

THE DRAMATIC ARTS

"Created for ceremonial occasions or to entertain princes, the art of stage productions undoubtedly owes much to the privileged elite. The kings of Java and Bali and the sultans of the coastal principalities have always sought to encourage artistic life and to be artists themselves. Their subjects, meanwhile, have cultivated the arts in less sophisticated ways, keeping them more spontaneous and closer to witchcraft or magical practices."

When the French historian Marcel Bonneff emphasised in this way the twin aspects of the arts in Indonesian drama, he also pointed out the continual interchange between these two creative springs. Puppet shows, dance, drama, song, music – Indonesians love to see themselves represented on stage and to take part in the performance. For this nation which is always aware of social form but which dislikes removing its veil, the stage is the place where myths, taboos, beliefs and disputes can be aired, and where body and soul can reach the highest levels of spiritual and aesthetic achievement. Imagination, feeling, laughter – Indonesians know what they are looking for in the *wayang* performances (shadow theatre), even though the barriers are often kept up between these performances and straightforward secular entertainment.

"Wayang" in all its forms

All forms of *wayang* include a sacred and religious dimension, such as the Balinese ceremonies in which young dancing girls, intermediaries for the divine, perform in a trance, or performances of *wayang kulit* that are part of exorcism ceremonies.

As a backdrop to the psychic world of Indonesians, ancestral myths were reworked and assimilated through the **Indianised repertory** of the *lakon* (stories and narratives): in these accounts, deified ancestors acquired the features of Hindu hero-gods, accompanied by other Javanese characters such as the **Punokawan** *(see sidebar p 208)*. Extraordinarily varied, the *lakon* present gods and demons engaged in a struggle that forms the theme of the tale, and in which human characters can take sides.

In Java the Indian repertoire – chiefly the great epics of the *Mahabharata* and the *Ramayana (see below)* – is by far the most widely used in *wayang kulit* and dance performances. This repertoire was later enriched with the addition of *wayang madya* (the tale of King Joyoboyo) and, under the Majapahits, the adventures of Prince **Panji**. New themes appeared around this period for **wayang klitik** performances (with flat wooden shadow-puppets), which recount the struggle between Damar Wulan and Menakjinggo *(wayang wasana)*. **Wayang golek** puppets (made of wood carved in

B. Brillion/Michelin

The dramatic arts

the round) perform the exploits of Hamzah (*wayang Menak*), whose combats paved the way for the coming of the Prophet. Lastly, in modern times, the war of independence (*wayang perjuangan*) and the founding of the Republic (*wayang pancasila*) inspired new episodes for shadow theatre.

Puppet theatre...

Few of the world's arts show such a close intertwining of a nation's life and mystique as the **wayang kulit** of Java. Probably appearing at the time of the first Indianised kingdoms, this tradition of shadow theatre has survived setbacks of all kinds and become part of the cultural landscape created by Islamisation. Simultaneously picture and shadow, it blurs the distinction between the real world and the world of the imagination. As a psychic channel between man and the sacred (the root *yang* evokes the supernatural), it arouses the imagination and the mystical that lurks in every Javanese. In simpler terms, *wayang* remains the supreme form of entertainment. Genuine works of art, its puppets are carefully cut out of buffalo hide ("*kulit*" means leather) and then

B. Brillon/Michel n

"Wayang kulit" puppet (Java)

pierced with a mass of holes and painted in bright colours, often further enlivened with gold leaf. Certain figures, particularly the **gunungan**, the tree that symbolises the universe, demand infinite patience. Heavily stylised, the various characters are identified by their clothing, their shape and above all their behaviour – like the truculent **Semar** (*see sidebar p 208*).

The great director of the show, the **dalang** (puppeteer-narrator) holds the audience transfixed and fascinated as they sit on the ground without shifting until the first light of dawn. In Java the presentation has no sacred status and the audience can explore behind the stage when they wish, to observe the *dalang* as he crouches in the middle of the gamelan orchestra. Capable of controlling some forty puppets single-handedly for several hours, he has mastered a vast repertoire. His talent lies as much in his virtuosity as in his capacity to bring characters to life with a fresh intonation for each one and each occasion. Overflowing with imagination, he embroiders on the main theme with a never-ending range of variations, and spices his story with local or contemporary references. From time to time the pace quickens and the narrator adopts a serious tone to tell the story of the battle between the spirits of Good and Evil. The greatest *dalang* charge high fees for their performances, which are sometimes shown on television.

... and dance

Performed virtually throughout the archipelago in various forms, **masked dances** call on the oldest popular traditions. Actors are no more than supports for the spirit of the character, which they adopt for the length of the performance. For this purpose they wear a mask which often has an animal face, such as the Balinese *barong* (monster) or the east Javanese *reog* (tiger). At the time of the Indianised kingdoms court performances drew on these popular dances and refined the symbolism of the

"Wayang" in all its forms

mask to adapt it to *wayang*. This tradition is still very much alive in some regions, particularly Jakarta (*topeng betawi*), Cirebon (*tari topeng*), West Java (*topeng banjet*), Madura (*topeng dalang*) and Bali (masked *wayang wong*, and *jauk*).

In the centre of Java, on the other hand, *wayang topeng* has given way to **wayang wong** (or *wayang orang*), a form of danced drama in which the actors take on the jerky movements of the *wayang kulit* puppets, and where the action is sustained by sung dialogue using poetic language. Created in the 19C in the royal courts of Yogyakarta and Solo, these performances are sometimes described as "Javanese opera". In Bali, an older tradition is maintained in the 16C **gambuh** and the 17C **arja**, which presents the hero-prince **Panji**.

With their great sophistication the Javanese dances remained the prerogative of the aristocracy for a long period before attracting a wider audience through the troupes in Solo, Semarang and Jakarta – but without arousing the same popular enthusiasm as the Balinese dances. Western influence can be seen in these performances, with the use of a stage, stage sets and an orchestra pit. Good quality performances are also put on for tourists, with the most famous of them being the **Sendratari** in Prambanan (*see p 311*), in which the spectacular drama of the setting makes up for the language barrier.

The great Indian epics

A vast epic tale of 120 000 couplets, written between the Vedic era and the 5C AD, the **Mahabharata** tells how the Ganges basin was invaded and settled by Indo-European tribes. The extraordinarily rich text teems with philosophical digressions and legends, forming an anthology of both the sacred and the profane knowledge of the period. The story is about the rivalry between the **Pandawa** brothers and their cousins, the **Korawa**, for control of the kingdom, which was founded by their common ancestor Bharata. Dispossessed of their rights after a game of loaded dice, the five Pandawa are forced to go into exile in the forest for thirteen years. On their return they win back their kingdom at the end of a murderous battle lasting 18 days. The sinister figure in the tale is **Duryodhana**, son of Dhrtarastra, who has such a malevolent nature that his father decides to present the kingdom to his cousin and sworn enemy, Yudistira. The ill will of this unjust and violent character, and of his 99 brothers, sets up the intense rivalry between the two clans.

A crowded gallery of characters accompanies him and enlivens the epic – firstly, the three eldest Pandawa sons, all of divine descent. The eldest, the virtuous **Yudhisthira**, the incarnation of justice, is the son of the god Dharma; the impetuous giant **Bhima** has the god of the wind, Vayu, as his father; and the archer **Arjuna**, the most handsome of the three, is the son of none other than Indra, leader of the gods. His charioteer is **Krishna** himself, who is also counsellor to the Pandawa. The last two of the line, the twins **Nakula** and **Sahadeva**, sons by a different mother, hold only a secondary role.

There is also the beautiful **Draupadi**, whose hand is won by Arjuna in an archery competition. But an unwise remark by the young man's mother (words are all-powerful in the Indian context) overturns his idyll. Unaware of the nature of her son's prize, the mother urges her son to share it with his brothers, and Draupadi becomes the shared wife of all the Pandawa.

Probably written at the beginning of the modern era and based on earlier texts, the **Ramayana** (48 000 lines) also spread widely through India and Southeast Asia. Additions introduced a religious and devotional note that intended to deify Rama. The work of a single author, **Valmiki**, the tale picks up some of the themes of the

Mahabharata, but the central story is that of Rama, who sets out to search for his wife Sita, abducted by the demon Ravana. Son of King Dasaratha, **Rama** is in fact a manifestation of Vishnu, possessing every virtue as well as outstanding strength. However, following the intrigues of his mother-in-law Kaikeyi, he loses the kingdom of Ayodhya and departs to live in the forest for fourteen years. With his wife **Sita** and his brother **Laskhmana**, he carries on a merciless struggle against the demons (*raksasa*). To get his revenge, their leader **Ravana** adopts the features of a beggar-monk, abducts Sita and takes her overseas to his domain, Lanka. Rama forms an alliance with **Sugriva**, the king of the monkeys, and helps him to recover his kingdom. To thank him, Sugriva lends him his army, commanded by **Hanuman**, to fight against Ravana. Turned into a monkey, the brave warrior goes to Lanka where he sees Sita, then returns to his army and has a bridge built to invade Lanka. The terrible battle ends in a duel in which Rama runs Ravana through with his javelin. Husband and wife are reunited, but Rama repudiates his wife on the pretext that she followed Ravana. To prove her purity, Sita submits to trial by fire and comes through it unharmed. With his period of exile ended, Rama then returns with her to Ayodhya, where he is consecrated king.

Brilliant harmonies

The bright tinklings of the xylophone, the heavy vibration of a gong, the ripple of a flute, the strange echoes of the *angklung* bamboos – in palaces or village festivities, music accompanies every moment in the life of the Indonesians. Far more than a simple feature of tradition, it is an integral part of their culture, like *wayang* or dance, and it is closely linked to both.

Although each region has its own form of music, Java and Bali have raised the art to great heights with the **gamelan**. Created – according to legend – by a Javanese king in the 3C, the gamelan is a group made up essentially of percussion instruments, which alternate lively, piercing rhythms. Although it has retained its ceremonial status at the royal courts of Java and Bali, the gamelan has also developed a popular style; but it is still generally limited to its role as an accompaniment to *wayang*.

Gong music

A spectacular dazzle of brass and painted wood, the gamelan has a multitude of instruments. Hanging on a frame, the "gong ageng" closes each melodic phrase, while the "kenong", a large horizontal gong, marks out the different sections. The little "gong ketuk", with its sharp dry sound, follows a tighter rhythm. The great "kendang gending" drum merely marks the tempo of the piece, but it is the group of "saron" (metallophones) which gives the gamelan its distinctive sonority and melody. Major features of the ensemble, the "gender" (metallophone with strips hanging on bamboo tubes) and the "gambang" (xylophone) are sometimes accompanied by "bonang" (rows of small gongs set on a wooden frame). The sight of the musicians striking the bronze or metal strips with a small hammer, then pinching them immediately to halt the resonance is in itself almost like watching a dance. A little cello with two or three strings, the "rebab" creates its own melodic line and, sometimes, a flute ("suling") accompanies the group.

Ever since the descriptions by Sir Francis Drake, who visited Java in 1580, this instrumental ensemble has always fascinated and surprised Westerners by its structural formation and sounds. In the 20C some trends in European music, following the example of Debussy, have even attempted to assimilate it in order to extend the frontiers of harmonics. Its musical structure has no modulation, and the keynotes are not always sustained by a perceptible melody. Its polyphonic nature tolerates a multiplicity of secondary variations around the main theme, following a structure that is much freer than the Western equivalent. Gamelan music includes two pentatonic scales: the *slendro*, which is used to express vigour or solemnity, and the *pelog*, which evokes melancholy. Each is subdivided into instrumental and vocal scales.

In Sundanese territory certain dances are accompanied by an **angklung**, a strange object made of bamboo stems of varying lengths hanging on a frame, which are struck together by the musician. The great musical wealth of Sumatra reveals Arab influence in its instruments – such as the *serunai*, a kind of pipe, and the *rebana*, or tambourine – and in its song. On the other hand, its instrumental music reveals the influence of China and Indochina. The island of Nias also owes much to Java, apart from a form of native organ made of bamboo. The same applies to the Batak region, where the two-stringed lute is king. Another type of **lute**, played with a bow, is widespread in southern Sulawesi, together with the *rebana* and various wind instruments, while the bamboo transverse flute, originally from the Moluccas, can be heard in the Christianised parts of the island.

The arts in modern life

Modern dance

Detached from courtly art, modern Indonesian choreography is turning to the new urban middle classes in cities such as Jakarta, Yogyakarta, Solo, Denpasar and Padang. While it often draws on traditional forms and repertoires, it is also capable of considerable innovation. Some performers of the old guard, from the 1960s and 1970s, are still active, including **Edi Sedyawati**, the Balinese star dancer **I Wayan Diya** and the Javanese **Kardjono**, who favour the traditional style, while among those with a more modernistic approach are **Farida Oetoyo**, **Yulianti Parani** and **Sardono Kusumo**.

Among currently active choreographers, **Retno Maruti** goes beyond the *Mahabharata* to deliver a modern message that is addressed to multicultural Indonesia. In *Ciptoning*, for example, the words of Arjuna are reinterpreted as a call for the emancipation of women.

Didik, the dancer with two faces

Singer, mime artist, dancer, choreographer, actor, experimental artist – Didik Nini Thowok performs with happy eclecticism and innovation. Originally from Central Java, he undertook a classical training from the age of 5 before turning to popular and then Western dance. His irreverent approach has developed a confirmed taste for transvestite characters – following a long-standing Javanese tradition. One of his creations, the "Dwimuka" dance, depicts a character torn by inner struggles between Good and Evil. Dressed up with a mask on the back of his head, he acts either facing the audience or, in turn, with his back to it, inspiring irresistible laughter. Helmut Kohl, Bill Clinton and the Emperor of Japan have all enjoyed his talented performances from their visits. Didik celebrated the fall of Suharto in his own way, by dancing through the streets of Yogyakarta to the gates of the kraton.

The Gumarang Sakti troupe, led by **Gusmiati,** draws on *pencak silat* and the traditional Minangkabau dances of Sumatra in a production showing the talents of Gusmiati's son **Boi G Sakti**, himself a choreographer. Another representative of the rising generation, **Muhammad Ikhlas,** who is also a choreographer and dancer, directs the Cilai troupe. The son of Hoeriah Adams, one of Indonesia's most famous dancers, he blends traditional and modernistic styles. His productions *Transformator*, *Coda* and *Ambek* draw on the Minangkabau tradition but have been directed in a Western style. And the ballet *Ken Dedes*, created by **Rusdi Rukmarata**, presents an innovative and harmonious blend of traditional and modern dance.

The gamelan, or gong orchestra

P. Bourseiller/Hoaqui

The dramatic arts

Contemporary theatre

A deliberately national theatre that wanted to go beyond particular regional characteristics developed early in the 20C. It was created outside the world of the traditional elite, used the Malay language, was secular and based itself on the Western model. In this way **komedie Stamboel**, which flourished in East Java in the first half of the 20C, marked a turning point. The many written texts at that time borrowed substantially from Sino-Malay literature, before an original home-grown repertoire appeared through allegorical and historical verse dramas, comedies of manners and, during the Japanese occupation, texts praising national feeling.

The most famous popular drama, however, remains beyond doubt **ketoprak** (*see p 209*), which appeared in Java in the early 20C. Many troupes perform its repertoire, which draws on *lakon* narratives, Java's recent political history, Islamic and Western tales, and even comic strips! The scenes, which alternate battle action with long dialogue, are accompanied by gamelan music. *Ketoprak* is also well suited to social criticism, through the voice of the Punokawan. Its East Java offshoot, **ludruk** (*see p 209*) presents the vicissitudes and dramas of everyday life. Here too humour is important, with female roles being played by men.

Since the 1970s drama has shown intense creativity, particularly thanks to the **Taman Ismail Marzuki** centre in Jakarta, which continues to be Indonesia's main theatre for contemporary work. In the last years of the Suharto era drama became one of the main focal points of protest, despite censorship. Apart from **Putu Wijaya** (Teater Mandiri) and **Rendra**, the leading figures in independent drama, there are the **Teater Koma**, created in the late 1970s and directed by Nano Riantiarno, and the **Bengkel Theater** company run by his wife Ratna. Occasionally accused of vulgarity and commercialisation, the Teater Koma has had the immense virtue of bringing contemporary drama out of its closed circle of initiates, through its sense of entertainment. The same concern lies behind the works of the **Teater Lembaga Stage**, which staged Shakespeare's *Julius Caesar*, one of the largest productions ever seen in Indonesia (1997). Rendra has even acted in an adaptation of Ionesco's *The Chairs*. **Ratna,** who is also an actress, has written *Marsinah Menggugat* ("Marsinah accuses"), the true story of a female activist who was raped and murdered in 1993 for having organised a strike. The play was banned by Suharto after a few performances.

A remarkable phenomenon is the "worker theatre" that was invented in Indonesia, with clearly stated militancy. One of its companies, the **Teater Abu**, consisting almost entirely of workers, performed in Rendra's theatre. An ecological awareness is also developing, as in *Kok Bisanya Sih Kau Bakar Hutan Itu?* ("How could you have burned the forests?"), by the Teater Kecil, which has survived the death of its founder **Arifin C Noer**.

Pop, between conformity and wistful song

Throughout the archipelago, using highly varied voices, a vast number of local groups are working hard to present their faith, their misery, the beauty of nature or the disappointments of love. This provides the background music for your endless coach journeys.

One style is **kroncong** – a group of strings, flute and solo female voice – with a Portuguese influence, dating back to the 16C. Formerly relating to "low life" characters, *kroncong* was rehabilitated late in the day but now suffers from lack of interest among the young, who consider it boring and old-fashioned.

The dramatic arts

The leading form of popular music, heard in every minibus or karaoke bar, is without a doubt **dangdut**. It is based on *orkes melayu*, a style that combines elements of Malay, Western rock, Indian film music and Arab-style modern pop. The success of *dangdut*, often accused of vulgarity, lies partly in the performances by sensual singers wearing sequinned dresses. Although love takes first place in the repertoire, the tone sometimes veers towards humour, as in the song *Mabuk lagi* ("Drunk again"), in which a young woman complains of her companion's debauchery. The greatest hit is still *Kopi Dangdut*.

Dangdut's only serious competitor is **Jaipongan**, which was invented by **Gugum Gubira** in West Java in the 1970s, and based on a ritual village dance, the **Ketuk Tilu**. Gugum's main contribution was to revitalise the percussion section and opt for a real singer instead of the traditional *ronggeng* (singer-dancer, sometimes a prostitute). In its present form the *Jaipongan* alternates song passages using a gong for rhythm, with frenetic drum passages and shouts. The choreography, inspired by *Pencak Silat* – a martial art that advocates restraint in movement – shows a skilful combination of constraint and free individual expression. Breaking with the traditional Sundanese languor, the dynamic dance met with immediate success as it appealed to the spirit of the young people of the time who were frustrated by the ban on Western music. Forbidden for a time because of its "erotic" nature, *Jaipongan* is now a full-scale industry that brings in millions of rupiah.

In other respects, **Indonesian pop music** is slow to break away from Western influence. In turn it has explored jazz-fusion, punk, reggae, grunge, techno and more recently electronic music. Yet it is still dominated by a collection of rock groups, some hard rock, and by quantities of variety singers who follow the route marked out by the long-lived **Titiek Puspa**. In another style, the very popular rock group of the veteran **Iwan Fals** has added its voice to the anti-establishment poems by Rendra. A few rare groups escape conformism, such as *Potret* with its minimalist sound, or *Dewa 19*, whose original albums have found a very wide public. Among the largest sales for 1997 (750 000 albums) were the engaging variety duo **Anang-Krisdayanti** and the singer **Anggun**, who was a great commercial success when she appeared in France. Overall, however, the local music industry remains undermined by pirate recordings, a widespread problem.

Film, an embryonic art form

Held back by censorship, lack of money and the undeveloped distribution circuit, Indonesian cinema has seen its production fall heavily since the 1970s, when 150 films were produced every year. Since then, the air-conditioned cinemas of the large cities play safe with American blockbusters, while television screens are full of ultra-violent films from Hong-Kong, or Indian "Bollywood" musical comedies with their baroque kitsch. With a few exceptions, such as **Teguk Karya**, the genre of *auteur* film is struggling to emerge. In 1990 **Slamet Rahardjo** won praise from the critics for "My Sky, My Home". The film's themes of social inequality and the permanence of traditional forms of solidarity were examined through the friendship of two children from different backgrounds. Screened at Cannes in the "Un certain regard" section in 1998, "Leaf on a Pillow" by **Garin Nugroho** with the actress Christine Hakim has since been shown internationally. Performed by children from the streets of Yogyakarta, who play themselves, it draws an unrelenting picture of the wretchedness of city life.

CRAFTS

What other nation has such a wide range of arts and traditional crafts? Sculpture, painting and fabrics, right down to the most modest wicker basket delicately decorated with a wooden gecko – each object, however banal, seems to reveal an innate talent, evidence of the original artistic refinement of the archipelago's hundred peoples. Heavily influenced by the various cultural and religious trends that have marked the history of Indonesia, Indonesian handicrafts have nonetheless preserved the features that make them distinctive. Firmly anchored in the minds of most of the population since the most distant times, **animist traditions** continue to predominate, enriched to varying degrees by elements introduced by Buddhist, Hindu, Islamic, Chinese or European civilisations. Syncretism, the intermingling of beliefs into a single religion, has been strongest in Java and Bali, the result primarily of the assimilation of significant **Hindu-Buddhist** features, such as the great Indian epics. On the other hand, the censorship imposed by **Islam** on showing human and animal images has restricted artistic expression to some extent. This rigidity has also introduced a taste for stylised ornamentation.

The sacred, the useful and the beautiful

With a legacy of primitive traditions, Indonesian arts and crafts are largely inseparable from religion. Figurative and decorative interpretations draw largely on beliefs of a magical or spiritual nature, on forms of worship and ceremonial and social functions (ancestor or spirit worship, and marriage, burial and dance ceremonies).

Much of today's creativity has lost its religious or symbolic dimension, turning instead to values that are aesthetic or commercial. Many craftspeople have thus directed their skills towards the **tourist market**, adapting to Western expectations and tastes. This tendency is evolving towards mass production and profit making, to the detriment – occasionally – of quality and inventiveness.

Island fabrics

The skill of Indonesian artists flourishes in all its splendour in the making of textiles, a tradition that dates back to earliest history. Whether they were used as clothing for grand ceremonial occasions or for everyday use, fabrics once held great social and religious significance. This has either survived or is gradually dying away, depending on the region. The weaving method, the colours, patterns and style of a fabric – all show the ethnic origin and social status of the wearer, and indicate the **ritual or ceremonial function** for which it was designed. They may also point to sacred or magical powers.

Despite the introduction of industrial thread and chemical dyes, the ancestral methods continue, particularly in rural areas, demonstrating the use of a broad range of **materials** (generally fibres made of cotton, more rarely of bamboo, banana, sisal or other plants), **colours** (from natural colourings derived from plants or minerals such as *kombu* or *soga* for an orange-brown shade and indigo for blue, the two being used one after the other to produce brown shades), **patterns** (geometric or figurative) and **techniques** (ikat, batik and *songket*, to name only the best known).

Batik, or Javanese style clothes

Batik uses a system of resist printing for colouring the designs, alternating wax applications with dye baths. First sketched out on cotton or silk fabric, the designs then have wax applied on both sides, to prevent the dye from reaching specific areas. The operation is repeated for each successive shade, starting with the palest. At each new stage, the parts already coloured must therefore be covered with wax, and wax must be scraped off the sections to be exposed in the next colour dip. Once the work is complete, all traces of wax are removed in boiling water.

Traditionally, the craftsman applies the melted wax by hand with the help of his *canting*, a small container which enables him to mark out a delicate and precise line. The creation of a batik by this method, known as **batik tulis** ("written"), may take several months. Much quicker, but not so delicate in its end result, **batik cap**, applied with a metal stamp (*cap*), reduces the design to the repetition of simple motifs. There are also false batiks, **printed** industrially without wax: they are recognisable by their designs that have outlines that are too perfect and too-sharp, and usually appear only on the outer surface of the fabric.

The infinitely rich range of iconographic designs is a mixture of **geometric motifs** (rosettes, diamonds, stars, interlaced circles, and check patterns) which are an old tradition, and more recent **figurative images** (flowers, leaves, animals, and symbolic or stylised objects). The very elaborate composition is sometimes structured by straight or oblique lines which frame the motifs. The original natural colours (indigo, brown and white) have gradually given way to a brighter and more varied range of shades.

The origins of batik in Indonesia remain unclear. Probably made in **Java** for many centuries, it made lightning progress in the second half of the 19C. Restricted for a long period to the royal courts of Central Java (Yogyakarta and Solo), where it won acclaim, the art of batik was exported to other regions such as the north coast of Java, Madura, **Bali**, Sumatra and Sulawesi. In addition to these new centres of production, tourism and, in its wake, the global market have contributed to the explosion of styles, a trend that continues to stimulate contemporary creation in domains as diverse as art, fashion and furniture.

Island fabrics

The art of choosing ikat

P. de 'Wilde/Hoaqui

Ikat, or the colours of Sunda

Another expression of the weaver's art, and no less impressive than batik, ikat (literally "knotting, binding") is different in its technique, which requires the threads to be coloured before they are woven. Before each dye bath, therefore, protective fibres are knotted round the threads that are to be kept from the colour, depending on the intended design. Traditionally women's responsibility, this meticulous work generally takes a year, from the planting of the cotton to the final weaving.

Probably introduced more than 2 000 years ago, ikat owes its fame above all to the **Lesser Sunda Islands**, where it is still an integral part of daily life. The process can however be seen throughout the archipelago, with innumerable regional variations depending on the island and the village. Animals and individuals are depicted in Sumba, for instance, while geometric or floral designs (stars, keys, curves and spirals) feature in Flores. The Aga community in the village of Tenganan, **Bali**, makes double ikats known as *geringsing*, by dyeing the threads of both warp and weft before weaving (*see p 426*). Depending on shape and size, ikats can be used as sarongs or wraps, covers, hangings, or shrouds. Colours and designs vary infinitely, and you will find it difficult to choose.

Songket, shot silk

This less well-known name belongs to a delicate fabric, generally made of brightly coloured silk decorated with gilded or silver motifs in light relief. To achieve these designs the weaver applies **gold or silver thread** to the lighter, finer weft so that both silk and metal thread are woven together. Depending on the effect sought, the design may either be spread through the whole surface or threads may be made to stand out brilliantly to enhance the whole. The most luxurious *songket* come from the looms in northern **Bali**, southern **Sulawesi**, and some areas of **Sumatra** and Kalimantan. Highly coloured silk or cotton thread, or gilded or silvered metal thread may replace the pure gold and silver.

Basketwork

An ancestral tradition handed down from mother to daughter through the generations, basketwork has always formed part of everyday life in rural areas. One of the women's prerogatives, it makes good use of the abundant resources of plant fibre (reeds, bamboo, rattan, pandanus, raffia, *lontar* and other palms) available on all the islands. The mats, baskets, bags, boxes and hats

R. Marca

Ikat weavers

created by these skilled hands use materials, techniques, shapes, colours and patterns of great variety. Like the fabrics, models vary from one region to another, but also depend on the practical or ritual purpose for which they are intended. The aesthetic considerations of these items have also encouraged the expansion of production for the tourist trade and export, sometimes adapting traditional styles to modern taste.

Among the most sophisticated products are those from **Lombok** (baskets and boxes made of rattan woven in spiral patterns), **Sumatra** (bags and purses made of palm-leaves woven by the Minangkabau), **Kalimantan** (Dayak baskets and bags with handles and straps, made of woven rattan decorated with traditional motifs), and the *lontar* palm creations from the **Lesser Sunda Islands**.

Painting and sculpture

In Indonesian tradition painting is not an art in itself: it is a complement to other creative arts. For instance, it may serve as colouring for a carved wooden panel that will be part of the ornamentation for a temple or a palace, or it may be used to bring masks and puppets to life. It was only in the 1930s, with the encouragement of Westerners who settled in **Bali**, that painting came to be seen as a distinct art form *(see p 363)*.

As widespread as it is diverse, the art of sculpture plays a fundamental role – as decorative as it is religious – in the everyday life of the Indonesians. It must be said that they have an infinite variety of local materials at their disposal: jackfruit wood (abundant, cheap, but poor in quality), **teak**, sandalwood, mahogany and ebony (durable but expensive) as well as the ubiquitous **bamboo**.

Some communities – such as the Toraja in Sulawesi and the Minangkabau in Sumatra – carve the decoration of their traditional **houses** in wood.

Whether they are statues, masks or puppets – which take part in certain funerary rites in the outlying islands but above all in the dances in Java and Bali – or simply practical objects (sword handles, shields, canoes, gamelan chests, coffins, etc), the main figures are carved to honour an **ancestor**, venerate a protective divinity or appease a fearsome devil. Their decorative role is less important than their ritual function, and they have spiritual and symbolic value. Some are even considered to have supernatural powers, which give their sculptors special status. In **Bali** and Java sculpture has developed in similar ways to painting, and its artistic contribution is now more clearly recognised *(see p 363)*.

Gold and silver

Many of the archipelago's different peoples make jewellery and other fine metalwork (such as table silver), using gold, silver, and other metals found locally. Concentrated in **Bali** (at Celuk) and in **Central Java** (at Kota Gede, near Yogyakarta), the craft is also highly renowned in the north and west of **Sumatra** (Banda Aceh and Kota Gadang) and in southeast **Sulawesi** (Kendari).

Depending on the design that they wish to execute, the craftsmen carve and hammer the metal or create moulds, using the method known as **lost wax**. The patterns are taken from old traditional models as well as from more modern Western work. Drawing on the Hindu and Buddhist repertory (flowers, birds, reptiles, etc), or inspired by Islam (arabesques, stars and crescent moons), they are delicately engraved and may have relief elements added by an oxidation process. The most original technique, however, is that of **filigree** ornaments made of very fine strips of gold or silver that are arranged decoratively and then flattened with great care before being soldered with the use of a heat-sensitive powder. The figures created in this way, which are extremely delicate, are then mounted as jewellery or other objects.

The kris, the mystical weapon

Halfway between sword and dagger, the kris is above all a mystical object. Once the prerogative of Javanese and Balinese aristocrats who, in accordance with the *adat* (customary law) passed it on from father to son, it was an integral part of the ceremonial costume worn by men, indicating their social rank. Endowed with magic power, the kris generally held a spiritual power that protected its owner from danger through vibrations that were perceptible only to him. It also protected him by repelling evil influences. Sacred and regarded as possessing a soul, the knife was even capable of representing its noble owner in places that he could not reach in person. This attribute conferred a social and spiritual aura on the armourer *(empu)* who forged the kris and endowed him with a sacred quality, his skill being considered a gift from the gods.

The symbolic significance of the kris lies essentially in the way in which the blade is curved and wrought. Asymmetric, straight or curved (always an odd number of curves), the kris features a **naga** – the mythical snake that possesses magic powers – either at rest or active.

The finest specimens are made by using the **damascene** technique, which consists in encrusting fine strips of gold, nickel or iron to create contrasting designs. Carved of wood, ivory or bone, more rarely wrought of gold or silver, the handles are sometimes highly worked. Sculpted, engraved, even set with precious stones, they represent mythical beings of Hindu inspiration, such as Garuda, the eagle of Vishnu, and **raksasa** characters supposed to chase away evil spirits – themes which have survived Muslim censorship by means of stylisation.

The symbolism of the kris – still very much alive in the beliefs of the Javanese and Balinese, as well as among Indonesians of other islands – probably originated in Java, during the **Majapahit** period. In Sulawesi, Sumatra and Kalimantan, where they vary in size, shape and decoration and are often simpler, the daggers have also acquired very specific meanings.

Masks for every occasion (Ubud, Bali)

P. Bénet

DAILY LIFE

From one end of the country to the other, workers hidden under their wide conical hats made of palm-leaf are active in the **rice fields**, their backs bent to the task, leading their buffaloes to the fields for ploughing, pricking out the seedlings and scything the ripe crop. In striking contrast, the **large cities** appear to be resolutely directed towards modernity. Mixing extremes, they juxtapose glass towers and their air-conditioned offices with shanty towns and their dilapidated hovels, modern shopping centres with street vendors in search of a few thousand rupiah and, in the traffic jams, dazzling cars with shabby *becak*: outward signs of wealth unblushingly co-existing with the harshest misery. Between tradition and modernism, wealth and poverty, century-old customs still continue to regulate the daily life of Indonesians, going beyond social, ethnic and religious differences.

Immutable values

In Indonesia individuals are only defined according the groups to which they belong (family, community, clan, tribe, village and religion), all of which provide frameworks for the way in which life proceeds. Pillars of society, **family** and religion remain the fundamental values. Ancestor worship is still strong in many areas and, everywhere, the head of the family and older people are held in great respect. These values are expressed through the **village** community, the leading social and religious unit. Even city-dwellers continue to join in the life of the village where they were born and to follow the **customary law** (*adat*) handed down by the elders. Whatever their ethnic, religious or social origins, Indonesians remain faithful to the great community principles laid down by tradition, which guide them in all aspects of daily life. These are founded on mutual help and **solidarity**, consultation, debate and consensual decision-making. Guarantor of a certain stability in society, this unshakeable loyalty is also based on strictly hierarchical networks of **consanguinity**, with degrees of relationship dictating the privileges, rights and duties of everyone within the group.

The traditional house preserved

In towns as in the country, contemporary architecture responds above all to practical needs and, in overall terms, is singularly lacking in appeal. Fortunately the traditional style of house which gives so many villages their old-world charm still survives on all the islands, with regional features but also many shared traits.

Perfectly adapted to the Indonesian climate, the abundant **natural materials** – wood, bamboo and palm – provide the houses with pleasant natural ventilation. From simple huts to more elaborate dwellings, built on wooden or stone foundations, houses are always set up on **piles**, which preserve them from rain or flood waters, as well as from wild animals, rodents and harmful reptiles. The main architectural differences can be seen in the shape of the **roof** – whether it is straight or convex, or jutting out to varying degrees and pointing skywards (as with the Toraja in Sulawesi, *see p 579*, and the Batak and the Minangkabau in Sumatra, *see p 166 and 172*) – and the ornamentation of the **façades**. Whether they consist of simple bamboo lattice or panels of plaited palms, perhaps decorated with geometric or figurative designs, the façades may have sculptures, buffalo horns or stylised motifs carved into the timber and delicately coloured.

The living house

However decorative it may be, the traditional dwelling, which is sometimes confused with customary housing (*rumah adat*), above all has symbolic value. In the regions where animist beliefs are the most deeply rooted, the house is seen as a living being, animated by its own spirit. It is divided into three levels: on the lower storey (between the piles) and shaded by the building itself, are the **animals** – pigs, buffaloes, chickens, goats, dogs etc – together with tools and agricultural supplies. Certain domestic activities are also carried out here, and you will see women weaving ikats, plaiting baskets or sifting coffee beans. Several steps lead up to the intermediary level – the floor – which often opens onto a **verandah** where the men go out for fresh air and a chat. Inside, near the door, the fire is lit from dawn to boil the water and the rice for the day. With few partitions, the main section of the **living area** houses an extended family, with at least three generations living together under the same roof. Once married, the young men settle here with their wives, while the young women generally go to live with their husband's family. Used to living out of doors, the Indonesians are satisfied with a standard of comfort which is often limited, without running water or electricity, sleeping on the floor on matting or makeshift beds, in an atmosphere that does little to foster intimacy. From the small openings that serve as doors and windows pop up the little faces of small giggling, inquisitive children, greeting foreigners with a friendly "Hello misterrrr!"

Lastly, the roof is considered to be the most sacred area of the house, where **ancestors** are sometimes honoured with ritual offerings. It may also be used as storage space for food supplies.

Education for the elite

Rarely does a day go by without your seeing a string of schoolchildren in two-colour uniform, with little satchels in hand, engulfing a *bemo* or walking along beside the road. Indeed, even the tiniest village appears to have its own little school. However, in this relatively poor country where education is **neither compulsory nor free** (without considering the cost of books and uniforms), some parents do not hesitate to set their children to work in the fields, the house or in shops. Many young people also leave to try their luck elsewhere, attracted by job opportunities in the cities or tourist destinations. School attendance is therefore limited in practice to the increasingly privileged classes of the population, from primary school (6-12-year-olds) to secondary school (12-15-year-olds) and then the more academic high-school (15-18-year-olds). Only a prosperous minority goes to university.

Another major obstacle is that lessons are taught in *Bahasa Indonesia*, the national language, which many families do not use in their daily life, and which the children from remote districts or underprivileged backgrounds do not always understand.

Jeans or sarongs?

Although the Indonesians have generally adopted Western styles, traditional clothing remains widespread, particularly in the rural world. Regional variations show contrasts mainly in the fabrics, with **batiks** dominating in the west and **ikats** in the eastern islands (Nusa Tenggara). Directly linked to **religion** and ceremonial occasions, the style of clothing is also strictly regulated by the code laid down in the *adat*. Subtle details, invisible to the foreigner, can indicate the individual's social standing and the community to which he or she belongs.

More flexible than in other countries, Koranic precepts nonetheless encourage Muslim **women** to cover their heads with a *gilbab* veil. With it they wear a long tunic over loose trousers. Others wear a *kebaya*, a long-sleeved close-fitting bodice with a band of fabric (*setagen*) to outline the waist, and a long **sarong**, a large piece of fabric wound round the waist like a skirt which covers the legs. **Men** also wear the sarong, but knot it differently. A batik shirt or dark waistcoat complete the outfit, together with the *pici*, a black velvet cap traditionally worn by nationalists and Muslims.

SOCIAL ETIQUETTE

"Hello Mister!" is addressed with equal confidence to men or women. This enthusiastic greeting can be heard everywhere, the moment you leave the tourist areas. It is often the only English phrase known to Indonesians, and it has become their form of polite greeting for foreigners. In remote places you will also hear cries of **"Blanda!"** ("Dutch!"). People utter this in a tone of amusement blended with curiosity, taking all Westerners to be Dutch.

Meeting the Indonesians

This simple greeting leads to an avalanche of questions; contact with the Indonesians is immediate. In the street or in a *warung*, in a bus or at the station, they will speak to you at the slightest opportunity and in all circumstances. If you can manage the basic rudiments of *Bahasa Indonesia*, discussion will follow without delay, turning inevitably into a kind of cross-examination.

Every encounter brings its quota of questions, which are always the same. This repeated experience eventually wearies or irritates many visitors, particularly since the personal nature of the queries often appears intrusive to Westerners. You will always be asked, for instance, where you are going, where you have come from, what you do, whether you have eaten, had a siesta or taken a shower, how much you paid for your sarong, where your companion is, and so on. For the Indonesians this natural and friendly way of showing interest in you and opening up a conversation, a spontaneous way of being polite, does not necessarily require precise and specific answers.

Outdoor life in Indonesia

Bowman/Scope

Next, without warning, you will be asked your name, nationality, age, family circumstances, professional life, religious beliefs, etc. If this intrusion into your private life upsets you and you wish to cut the conversation short, there is nothing to stop you being evasive or enjoying yourself by inventing a life. And remember that you can always escape by making a joke or putting on a broad smile! But these encounters are also an opportunity to discover the Indonesians themselves, to make acquaintances, to practice your *Bahasa Indonesia* and, with careful use of boldness, politeness, calm and patience, there is every chance that sooner or later you will be invited into a private house or to attend a ceremony.

A few guidelines to avoid embarrassment

Although Indonesians show remarkable tolerance – particularly in tourist areas, where they have become used to certain "eccentricities" among Westerners – it is the responsibility of the foreign visitor to respect various conventions and so avoid shocking or upsetting others.

Appropriate dress – Take care to dress properly, avoiding clothes that are too revealing or transparent. Indonesians consider shorts and T-shirts to be indoor clothes and only wear them in private, or on the beach, and, by force of circumstance, at certain tourist sites. Elsewhere, in towns or offices and of course in religious places, trousers, or skirts below the knee, are essential, together with long sleeves and clothing that covers the shoulders.

Feet ... – Do not forget to take off your shoes before going into a house or a mosque. It is rude to raise or point your feet towards someone, or to make the soles of your feet conspicuous.

... and hands – Since the left hand is considered impure, using it for anything other than personal washing needs may be taken as an insult. Always use only your right hand to greet or touch others, receive or offer something, or for eating.

Greetings – Greeting usually consists of a handshake, bending the head slightly and, in some cases, introducing yourself. Muslims then touch their heart with their right hand, as a sign of goodwill. However, it is considered unacceptable to touch anyone else's head (avoid any affectionate little pats on children's heads, in particular), or to pat someone on the back as a sign of friendship.

The rule of hospitality – Blessed with a keen sense of hospitality, Indonesians may one day invite you to visit them at home, have a coffee, share their meal or attend a ceremony. It should be recognised that some invitations are not meant to be taken literally, particularly when you are offered a bath or asked to stay the night. To be clear about the situation, wait until the suggestion is repeated.

When you go in, greet the master of the house first, before other members of the family. Don't forget to offer your hosts a small **present** (particularly on a festive occasion), and do not take offence if they do not open the package in front of you. Politeness requires you to wait until you are invited (with a *"Silakan! "*, "Please!") to enter, sit down, or start eating or drinking. You risk offending your hosts if you refuse what you are offered: take at least a small amount to honour the occasion. It is important to remember that finishing what is on your plate or in your glass means a request for more: if you have had enough, leave a little. Otherwise, wait until you are asked if you would like more before helping yourself. To leave, explain where you are going but do not say that you *ought* to leave.

Physical contact – You will often see two men or two women holding hands or hugging each other: these gestures of friendship have no homosexual connotation.

On the other hand, you will never see the slightest physical contact between a man and a woman, and it is wholly improper for a couple to kiss or embrace in public.

A cool head – Traffic jams, tiresome police checks, slow administrative contacts and interminable journeys in overcrowded buses are all circumstances in which you will never see an Indonesian raise his voice or show the slightest sign of discontent, irritability or impatience. This impassiveness in the face of any ordeal sometimes ends up by disarming travellers, who interpret such excessive nonchalance as a lack of concern, or resignation. In fact it reflects the self-control that should regulate every attitude, whatever the circumstances – a fundamental character trait shared by most Asian peoples. It should also be noted that any public demonstration of emotion (shouting, sudden movements or agitation) is seen as an incomprehensible infringement of the code of good behaviour. It arouses only scorn, mockery or fear, and may even be taken for madness. Patience, discretion and calmness are the golden rule.

Neither yes nor no – Respectful and immensely courteous, the Indonesians are not by nature inclined to criticise or offend others, or even to disagree with or contradict them. Hence their custom of agreeing politely to any suggestion. Concerned in addition about never losing face, they take a high stance which will lead them into the most far-fetched replies rather than admitting ignorance with a frank "I don't know". When you need information, therefore – particularly if you are asking your way or enquiring about a bus time – be careful to phrase your question in such a way that it is impossible to answer with a simple Yes or No, and listen to several opinions – very often contradictory! – to get the facts.

Laughter and smiles – With unruffled tempers and an unbounded sense of humour, Indonesians always appear full of cheerfulness, and are inclined to laugh and smile. These universal expressions, however, have infinitely subtle nuances: a smile may express joy, pleasure, goodwill, personal attention to an individual, or may be used to overcome linguistic differences when greeting. But like laughter, it may also conceal embarrassment, uneasiness, dismay, fear, or any other emotion.

Time is elastic – It will not take you long to discover how incredibly elastic time is in Indonesia. *"Jam karet!"* is what you will hear if you appear hurried, or show impatience with a slow bus or are surprised when a friend is late. Here, there is time – and everyone takes it. And you will no doubt get the impression that Indonesians remain impervious to all notions relating to time – timetables, punctuality, hurrying, or running. In fact it is often better to refer to the different times of day (*pagi pagi, pagi, siang, sore* and *malam*), than to the hands of a clock (*see "Useful words and expressions", p 111*).

Religion – Inconceivable for Indonesians, being an **atheist** means for them having no ethnic or cultural identity. For this reason, when you are asked about your religion you can avoid interminable and pointless discussions by claiming to be, for instance, Catholic or Protestant (answers which they expect from Westerners).

"Mandi" – At home or by a river, sometimes even beside rice fields Indonesians wash themselves at least twice a day – at sunrise, late in the afternoon, and generally before religious ceremonies. They will therefore be surprised if you do not do the same. So, do not be surprised or offended if you are asked: *"Sudah mandi?"* ("Have you washed?"). It is in effect almost the same as saying "Good evening". Out of regard for modesty, never take a photograph of anyone washing (in public baths, beside the road or at a river).

The family – Indonesians marry and have a family when they are fairly young, and you will always intrigue them if you say that at the age of more than 25 you are unmarried and have no children. You can therefore reassure your questioners by referring to your little family (even if it is imaginary), but you will lay yourself open to inevitable questions on the names and ages of each one.

Rain and shine – The weather is not as frequent a topic of conversation as in the West, but Indonesians complain all the time about the heat, or about the cold as soon as the air gets a little cool, and flooding is also a popular topic. They will also ask you about the weather in your own country, and are always intrigued by strong seasonal contrasts – above all by snow.

Body language

Whether or not you master *Bahasa Indonesia* (see "Useful words and expressions", p 111), body language is very useful, and sometimes more effective than words. A complete form of communication in its own right, it is useful to know in certain circumstances to avoid misunderstandings.

● A little tilt of the chin or head upwards, with a friendly look, expresses goodwill or agreement.

● An almost imperceptible movement of the head or the gaze downwards often indicates consent. But be careful: it is also a way of saying that you have understood – even if this is not the case – so as not to offend. Hence the occasional misunderstanding.

● A gesture with the right hand, palm facing down, enables you to summon someone, or especially to stop a *bemo*, a bus or a taxi or, alternatively, to slow down traffic to cross the street. When this gesture is not acknowledged (particularly for getting off a bus), you can also clap your hands.

● To avoid appearing rude, disdainful or aggressive, use your thumb and not your finger to point something out. Do not point at people, rather make a sign with your head. Do not stand with your hands on your hips or your arms crossed when you are talking to someone.

● Among Muslims (although others do this too), putting your right hand over your heart after a greeting or handshake indicates respect. This can also indicate a polite refusal.

● When the person you are talking to rubs his two index fingers together while nodding his head at you slightly, he is enquiring if the person with you is your spouse or friend.

● Slanting the index finger across the middle of the forehead means *"Gila!"* ("Mad!"). Indonesians often do this when they are joking.

THE CUISINE OF THE ISLES

Indonesia's ethnic syncretism is reflected in the range of its cuisine – colourful, spicy, aromatic – which blends together the influences of the many nations that have marked its history. Arab and Indian merchants introduced the use of delicate **spices** (cardamom, cinnamon, coriander, cumin, turmeric, and pepper) and various dishes (such as the Indian *martabak*), while the Spanish introduced **peppers** as part of the ingredients for or accompaniments to many different dishes. During the colonial period the Dutch developed extensive market-garden crops (carrots, potatoes, cabbages and tomatoes). But it is the **Chinese** who have made the greatest contribution: noodles, soy sauce (*kecap*, which the Indonesians have adapted to their taste by adding a sweet element, *manis*), soya-bean cake (*tahu* or *tofu*), soya-bean curd (*tempe*), while vegetables crisply stir-fried in a *wok* (*cap cai*, a mixture of sautéed vegetables), now form part of the daily meal for millions of Indonesians.

Informal meals

From first light the mistress of the house is busy at her oven. Meals are usually very informal and more likely to be individual than taken with the family. Rice and its accompaniments are prepared for the day, and everyone eats when hungry. Only religious or family festivities are an occasion for collective meals. All the dishes are elegantly laid out on a table or a simple rush mat on the floor, and everyone takes what they want. If you are one of the party, you should observe **etiquette**. Begin by filling your plate with moderation: you will have plenty of opportunity to return for more. Next, wait until your hostess gives permission to begin with the phrase *"Silakan makan!"* (literally: "I beg you, eat!"). And remember to use your right hand – the left is considered unclean – having first washed in the pot of water provided for this purpose.

Lunch at the "warung"

B. Erillon/Michelin

Rice with every kind of sauce

In modest households or in dry districts where supplies are short, the basic staple food, **rice** is sometimes replaced by or "cut" with sweet potatoes, tapioca (cassava flour), maize or sago. Depending on the region and the family's standard of living, an assortment of small dishes embellishes the fare, forming an expert combination of flavours and complementary consistencies: vegetables (water spinach or *kangkung*, French beans, aubergine, pumpkin, cucumber, cabbage, breadfruit, jackfruit), **tahu** and **tempe** (soya curd and soya-bean cake), and fish, meat or eggs, served fried, grilled or simmered in coconut milk with a peanut sauce or a **sambal** (a chutney-style condiment based on red peppers) and accompanied by crusty **krupuk** (wafers of tapioca flour flavoured with fish or shrimps). In restaurants, if you try the **rijstaffel** ("rice table"), a Dutch innovation consisting of a large number of dishes, you will be able to enjoy a wide range of the country's culinary skills, and taste the subtle refinement of the blended flavours and the power of the spices.

For gourmets

The great number of regional styles of cuisine makes it difficult to speak of "Indonesian gastronomy" as such. In addition, the supremacy of the cuisine of **Java** and Madura (which many emigrants use to seek work in the other islands) and of Sumatra **(Padang)**, present in all the restaurants and *warung* of the archipelago, tend to push the innumerable local dishes into the background. You will, however, be able to try local fare during your travels, particularly if you are invited to a feast (such as a Toraja funeral ceremony) or to a private house (for a rite of passage ceremony, for instance, in Bali).

The main **local delicacies** are listed in the "Eating out" section for each town or region presented.

Snacks along the way

In the street, outside markets, mosques or temples, in buses, boats or trains you will always find something to eat, whether you are looking for a quick snack or something purely indulgent. From dawn to nightfall, street vendors patrol the roads pushing their wheeled food carts, announcing their arrival with blasts on an improvised horn. On their menu you may find: **sate ayam** (small chicken brochettes seasoned with a spicy peanut sauce), *mie bakso* (noodle soup with meat balls), **soto ayam** (chicken soup), *gado-gado* (a mixture of crisp vegetables coated with spicy peanut sauce), *nasi campur* ("mixed rice", generally an assortment of five or six ingredients: vegetables, *tahu* or *tempe*, meat, fish or eggs), *mie* or **nasi goreng** (noodles or rice sautéed with little pieces of vegetables and egg), **martabak** (thick savoury pancakes stuffed with egg or meat, or sweet pancakes with peanuts or coconut) and cakes (*kue*) of all kinds (based on tapioca, sticky rice, coconut, banana etc).

Located in pedestrian sites, the *warung* eateries are generally lively in the late afternoon. As well as the dishes described above, this is where you will find local specialities and, sometimes, grilled chicken or fish, served with rice and *sambal* (hot peppery sauce).

Finally, even the smallest town will offer Minang cuisine – usually called **"makanan Padang"** – originally from Sumatra: particularly spicy dishes, in most cases cooked in coconut milk, for those who love strong flavours.

Colourful drinks

Indonesians are always happy to sip tea or coffee, to which they almost always add very sweet milk. If you prefer these drinks plain, do not forget to specify *"pahit"* ("bitter"). Plain weak **tea** often accompanies meals. If you choose **coffee** (prepared "Turkish style"), wait for the grounds to settle in the bottom of the glass before drinking.

More unusual are the pink, yellow or fluorescent green drinks that may be syrupy, thick, hot or cold, and as surprising in their colours as in their consistency. There is a vast range of drinks that are a special treat for Indonesians – and for the curious: a base of crushed ice is sprinkled with rose-water syrup, palm sugar or sweetened concentrated milk, and further adorned with coloured jelly **(es campur)**, fruit, coconut **(es kelapa muda)**, or perhaps beans, maize, fermented rice or cassava flour. They make thirst-quenching and often very nourishing refreshments.

In non-Muslim regions you will also find local alcoholic drinks: light beers (*Bintang* or *Angker*), **tuak** (fermented palm-tree sap), **arak** (distilled spirits made from rice or palm, with an alcohol content of 60°), or **brem** (fermented and lightly sweetened rice wine). *See also "Eating out", p 98*.

R. Marca

"Krupuk", or Sumatran-style potato chips in the market

Practical Information

Indonesia:
a giant spice market

Before going

• Time difference

The Indonesian Archipelago stretches from east to west over three time zones (the further east you go, the later it gets). There is a one-hour time difference between the islands furthest to the west (Sumatra, Java, and western and central Kalimantan), those in the middle (Bali, the Lesser Sunda Islands, Sulawesi, and southern and eastern Kalimantan), and those furthest to the east (Maluku and Papua). At noon GMT during **daylight-saving time**, it is 6pm in Java, 7pm in Bali, and 8pm in Maluku. Outside **daylight-saving time**, it is 7pm in Java, 8pm in Bali, and 9pm in Maluku.

• International dialling

To call Indonesia from abroad, dial your country's international access code, then 62 + area code (without the 0) + your correspondent's number.

Main area codes

Sumatra

Bukittinggi	0752
Medan	061
Nias (Gunung Sitoli)	0639
Nias (Teluk Dalam)	0630
Padang	0751
Prapat	0622/0625
Sibolga	0631

Java

Bandung	022
Bogor	0251
Bromo	0335
Cirebon	0231
Jakarta	021
Malang	0341
Pangandaran	0265
Surabaya	031
Surakarta (Solo)	0271
Yogyakarta	0274

Madura

Pamekasa	0324
Sumenep	0328

Bali

Bedugul	0368
Candi Dasa, Tirtagangga, Padangbai	0363

Denpasar, Sanur, Kuta, Ubud	0361
Klungkung	0366
Lovina Beach	0362

Lombok

Ampenan, Mataram, Batu Bolong, Suranadi	0364
Senggigi, Kuta	0370

Sumbawa

Bima, Labuhan Sape	0374
Sumbawa Besar	0371

Flores

Bajawa	0384
Ende	0381
Labuhanbajo	0385
Maumere	0382

Sulawesi

Gorontalo	0435
Manado	0431
Palopo	0471
Poso	0452
Rantepao	0423
Sengkang	0485
Tentena	0458
Ujung Pandang	0411

• When to go

The best time to go to Indonesia is during the dry season in **May-June** or in **September-October** to avoid the busiest months; but no time of year should be ruled out.

Climate

Traversed by the equator, the archipelago boasts a consistently warm and humid climate. **Precipitation** varies according to the region and season. Rainfall is more plentiful and constant throughout the year as you approach the equator. Climatic differences are much more extreme in the southern islands (Java, Bali and the Lesser Sunda Islands). It rains almost every afternoon during the **rainy season** from

November to April. Precipitation reaches its peak in January-February, when the humidity content rises up to 100%. Even during the **dry season** from May to October, there are often tropical showers at the end of the day. The **temperature** varies relatively little, staying a pleasant 22°C-32°C throughout the year, thanks to the proximity to the equator and maritime influences. However, it can drop at higher altitudes where nights are chilly. July and August are usually the coolest months, while temperatures reach their highest levels in February and March.

At this latitude the **sun** rises between 5.30 and 6.30am and sets between 5.30 and 6.30pm, always very fast.

Busy periods

European vacationers arrive in droves in July and August. Prices go up, and it is hard to find hotel rooms and flights – especially domestic ones. Many **Australians** go at Christmas and in January. As for the **Indonesians**, they visit the tourist sites – Bali in particular – during school holidays (mid-June to mid-July as a rule) and for Idul Fitri at the end of Ramadan (for which the dates vary from year to year). Hotel rooms and bus seats are hard to come by during such times. In certain areas, finding a restaurant that is open in the daytime during the Ramadan fast can be a problem.

● Packing list

Clothing

Take light clothing, preferably **cotton**. Bring along a **cardigan** and a pair of trousers to keep warm in mountainous areas where temperatures drop noticeably in the evening. Elsewhere these clothes will protect you from mosquitoes, and could come in handy in air-conditioned hotels, buses and aeroplanes. Avoid wearing bathing suits, shorts, short skirts and low necklines outside of the few seaside tourist resorts. You must wear clothing that covers shoulders and knees when entering places of worship. **Sarongs** (required for visiting Hindu temples in Bali, and useful in numerous circumstances) can be purchased everywhere. Taking your shoes on and off when entering mosques and houses is a lot easier if you buy a pair of **thongs**, which are sold at every market and are well-adapted to the hot, humid climate. Don't forget that you are in a country that is quite attached to its traditions and is predominantly Muslim too; so be careful not to offend people. Out of respect for the Indonesians, dress properly, avoiding clothing that is too short, tight or low-cut. In places with many tourists (such as Kuta in Bali), some Westerners see nothing wrong in being scantily dressed, walking around town in bathing suits and basking on the beach topless. The locals are tolerant and have grown accustomed to such "eccentricities", but it still gets their tongues wagging!

Accessories

Don't forget sun hats, sunglasses and extra-strength sunscreen. **Earplugs** are also very handy to have around for dealing with the morning call to prayer, night-time cockfights and the music at full blast on buses! Remember to bring along a **torch** (a headlamp if possible) in case of a power cut, for night-time volcano climbs and to make up for the dim light from kerosene lamps in outlying regions. If you have an appliance that needs to be plugged in (video camera battery, electric razor etc), bring along an adaptor, as some rooms only have one socket, which is usually used for the fan. Lastly, if you're planning to travel by bus and *bemo*, take a sturdy waterproof bag (luggage is often stowed on the roof) that can be locked with a small padlock.

Before going

Gifts to bring with you

Indonesians are curious by nature. Many will ask questions about your family and country and will be delighted to look at **snapshots**. Bring along some small gifts – post cards, lapel badges, key rings, **lighters**, **perfume** samples, music cassettes and other items from your country – to thank your hosts for their hospitality and generosity. They are great **football** buffs and will be proud to wear a T-shirt or insignia from your favourite team. Advertising gadgets sold at the World Cup are a guaranteed success. Indonesians are dyed-in-the-wool smokers (the men anyway) and will enjoy trying your Western **cigarettes**. But they often prefer *kretek* (clove cigarettes) and even if you don't smoke, it's a good idea to have a pack with you. That way you can reciprocate if an Indonesian invites you home for coffee, if you want to thank a trek guide or driver, or simply to start up a conversation in a bus or *warung*. Avoid giving children candy, pens and money, however, as in some areas they have adopted the bad habit of always asking foreigners for them.

• All travellers

Travelling with children

Indonesians are fond of children and are very welcoming towards them. In seaside resorts with many tourists (such as in Bali), some hotels offer day-care services. Since your toddlers are less immune than you, the recommendations in the "Health and Safety" section *(see p 103)* apply doubly to them. Pay close attention to what they eat, protect them from the sun and give them plenty of water to drink. Bring along all the nappies, powdered milk and baby food they'll need, as such items can be found in big cities but less commonly outside them. Look into transport and lodging conditions before heading off the beaten track.

Single women

You can travel alone without any problem. Indeed, you won't be alone for long. Indonesians are open and curious by nature, and they are bound to approach you for a chat – tirelessly asking you the same questions – or to help you find your way. While you will be sought after, you will rarely be bothered. You will constantly be asked if you're married, so don't hesitate to reply in the affirmative! Usually a bit shyer, Indonesian women may occasionally approach you too. If you know some basic *Bahasa Indonesia*, they might invite you to their home for a chat, a cup of coffee or even to share a meal with their family.

Senior travellers

Elderly people can travel in Bali and Java with no worries. Elsewhere, it's advisable to enquire about transport and lodging conditions, which are not always terribly comfortable, as well as health facilities, which are often rudimentary. One should also be wary of the sun and drink plenty of mineral water to avoid dehydration.

Disabled persons

Unfortunately, there are no facilities designed for the disabled, but you can usually count on spontaneous help from Indonesians. However, some tourist sites will be inaccessible (volcanoes to climb, temples sitting at the top of long flights of steps, etc).

• Address book

Tourist information

There are a few Indonesian Tourist Promotion Offices overseas. Most can be contacted through the Indonesian **Embassies**, which will only provide you with scant information. Check out the **Garuda** airline offices *(see p 86)* and special interest tour agencies.

Indonesian embassies and consulates abroad

Australia – Australian Embassy, 8 Darwin Avenue, Yarralumla, Canberra, ACT 2600, ☎ 61/2 6250 8600.
Australian Consulate, Piccadilly Court, 3rd floor, 222 Pitt St, Sydney, NSW 2000, ☎ 61/2 9344 9933

Canada – Canadian Embassy, 287 Maclaren St, Ottawa, Ontario, K2P OL9, ☎ 1/613 236 7403.
Canadian Consulate, 129 Jarvis St, Toronto, Ontario, M56 1T6, ☎ 1/416 360 4020.

United Kingdom – British Embassy, 38 Grosvenor Square, London, WIX 9AD, UK, ☎ 020 7499 7661.

USA – Embassy of the United States of America, 2020 Massachussetts Avenue N.W., Washington D.C., 20036, USA, ☎ 1/202 775 5200.
Consulates: 5 E. 68th St, New York, N.Y. 1 ☎ 1/212 879 0600. 1111 Columbus Ave, San Francisco, CA. 94133, USA, ☎ 1/415 474 9571

Web sites

Art & Culture:

ArchipelaGo – www.goarchi.com The magazine section features interesting articles on Indonesian culture.

Indonesian homepage – http://indonesia.elga.net.id History, culture, lifestyles, economy, etc.

Press:

Time Asia Online – www.cnn.com/ASIANOW/time

Far Eastern Economic Review – www.feer.com

National Geographic – www.nationalgeographic.com

Travel & Tourism:

www.tourismindonesia.com Indonesia Tourism's official site.
www.traveljakarta.com Travel and tourism information concerning Jakarta .
www.bali.com A good source of information on Bali.
catcha.co.id Catcha Indonesia, a local search engine.

Volcanoes – www.volcanoes.com A wealth of information for volcano buffs.

Yahoo – http://dir.yahoo.com/Regional/Countries/Indonesia Touches on a variety of topics relating to Indonesia.

• Documents required

ID, visas

British, American, Australian and Canadian nationals will be given a 60-day tourist **visa** on arrival in Indonesia. Your **passport** must be valid for another six months after your date of departure, and you must have a **return ticket**. Trying to prolong your visa once there is a veritable obstacle course that will ruin your holiday, and get you nowhere! Your visa could possibly be extended a day or two past the expiry date in a case of absolute necessity (enquire at the nearest immigration office) in return for a daily fine, but it's advisable to avoid doing business with the local immigration services! If you plan on spending more than two months in Indonesia, the only solution is to leave the country on the expiry date on your visa (for Singapore, Malaysia or the Philippines), then return to obtain a new one. It shouldn't be a problem, but be sure to show your credentials and wear a big smile on your face! For other nationalities, enquire at your embassy. Young people under the age of 26 carrying an **international student card (ISIC)** are eligible for reductions on some domestic flights.

Customs

There are no restrictions on importing foreign currencies. You may even be asked to prove that you have enough resources to provide for your needs during your stay. You are allowed to import 2 litres of alcohol, 200 cigarettes, 50 cigars or 100g of tobacco, and a "reasonable quantity" of perfume.

It is strictly prohibited to import narcotics, firearms or ammunition, pornographic material, or Chinese printed matter or medicine. If you're carrying a recently acquired device (mobile telephone, camera, video camera, laptop, etc), bring along the invoice to avoid problems at customs when leaving.

Health regulations

There are no particular health regulations for entering Indonesia.

Vaccinations

No vaccinations are required to enter the country, but it is essential to be protected against diphtheria, tetanus and polio, and it is highly recommended to get vaccinated against typhoid, and hepatitis A and B. Ask your doctor for advice about vaccinations against Japanese encephalitis, rabies and meningitis. For malaria prevention, *see the "Health and Safety" section, p 103.* People who have been in a country where there is yellow fever within six days prior to their arrival in Indonesia must provide a vaccination certificate against all diseases.

WHO – For vaccination information, consult the World Health Organisation's International Travel and Health web site at: www.who.int/ith/english

Driver's licence

An **international** driver's licence is required for renting a car, but rarely for renting a motorcycle. Enquire at a local driver's association before leaving. *See also "Getting around", p 92.*

• Local currency

Cash

The **rupiah** (Rp) is the Indonesian currency. It has no subdivisions. Notes come in denominations of Rp100, 500, 1 000, 5 000, 10 000, 20 000, 50 000 and 100 000, and coins in Rp50, 100, 500 and 1 000. With galloping inflation in the country, it's not easy to give an accurate exchange rate. Between April and May 2000, the rate for 1US$ jumped from about Rp7 000 to Rp8 500. So it can change very quickly! At the time of publication, 1US$ was quoted at Rp 8 905 and 1 Aus$ at Rp 4 640.

Currency exchange

You cannot buy rupiah until you are in Indonesia. There are banks and money-changers at the airport, in tourist spots, cities and at most hotels. In addition to inflation, exchange rates vary considerably from one bank, moneychanger, city or island to another. The best rates to be found are in Bali and Java. Rates in hotels are often very bad. Moneychangers, however, usually quote much better rates than banks. The **American dollar** is still the best currency to have, and you'll get a better rate with large notes ($100). Other foreign currencies are only accepted in tourist areas. In more out-of-the-way places (Flores, Central Sulawesi, Sumbawa etc), bring along plenty of rupiah as it's almost impossible to change money there.

Be sure your bank notes are in good condition, otherwise they may be refused. And don't accept any torn notes, which you might have trouble getting rid of (especially in remote areas). Bring along a wad of small notes (*uang kecil*) as soon as you leave tourist areas and cities, or when travelling via *bemo*, taxi or *becak*, as it's often hard to get change – even for a Rp10 000 note!

Travellers' Cheques

These are mainly for use in large cities and tourist areas. But travellers' cheques in **dollars** are usually accepted elsewhere. Rates aren't as good as for bank notes, and there is a commission.

Credit Cards

Large hotels, some restaurants, department stores, travel agencies and airline companies accept **Visa** and **MasterCard**, and far more rarely American Express, in exchange for a 3% surcharge. Rupiah can be withdrawn with a credit card and passport at some banks in major cities and tourist resorts. **ATM**s can only be found in large cities and some tourist areas (Visa and MasterCard).

In case of loss or theft of your Visa card: ☎ 001/803 1933 6294.

● Spending money

Indonesia is very inexpensive. However, prices tend to rise the further you go from tourist areas. They go up considerably in July and August, the busy season, when it gets harder to bargain.

The range of prices for accommodation is particularly wide. Lodging for two in a family guesthouse can be as low as US$3 per **night**, or US$300 at a luxury hotel! A **meal** at a restaurant costs between US$1.50 and US$7.50 per person, and less than 75 cents in a *warung*. **Domestic transport** costs vary considerably depending on the level of comfort. For example, a small trip in a *bemo* costs around Rp1 000; a ride in a *becak* starts at Rp2 000, and a taxi costs a minimum of Rp1 500 per kilometre. The train trip from Jakarta to Yogyakarta costs Rp50 000 in economy; the flight from Denpasar (Bali) to Ujung Pandang (Sulawesi) is Rp1 500 000; the boat crossing from Sumatra to Java costs Rp300 000 in economy. In Bali, count on US$20 per day for renting a car, and around US$10 for a motorcycle; in the Toraja region (Sulawesi) you can have a car with a driver and guide for US$35.

Tack on **miscellaneous costs** such as visits to museums and temples, dance performances, hiking guides, water sports and, above all, purchases. Temptations abound and the prices will make you want to spend!

In short, two people can have a nice holiday on a **daily budget of US$40 per person** on average. If you have a tight budget, under US$9 will suffice if you use public transport, eat at the markets or *warung,* and stay at the most modest *losmen*.

● Booking in advance

Unless you like playing it by ear, it's wise to do some basic planning for your trip – a few weeks or months in advance depending on the season and your journey. During the low season you can pick your room on site at the last minute, but reservations are highly recommended in July-August and during the Christmas-New Year holidays. If you plan to go to Flores or Sulawesi by air, you must buy your ticket in advance as the planes are small and seats are often grabbed by tour operators (*see* "Getting around", p 92). To place a call to Indonesia, *see p 80.*

● Travel/Health Insurance

Remember to take out insurance if you aren't already covered. Enquire at your bank, as some credit cards include travel insurance (by paying for your plane ticket with a **Visa** card for instance). Otherwise, you will probably be offered the chance to take out insurance when buying your plane ticket through a travel agent. Insurance is usually included in the price of a package deal.

Travel Insurance Agency, Suite 2, Percy Mews, 755B High Rd, North Finchley, London, N12 8JY, UK, ☎ 020 8446 5414, Fax 020 8446 5417, info@travelinsurers.com

Travel Insurance Services, 2930 Camino Diablo, Suite 200, PO Box 299, Walnut Creek, CA 94596, USA, ☎ 800 937 1387, Fax 925 932 0442, webinfo@travelinsure.com

Mondial Assistance affiliates:
Australia: Worldcare Assist, ☎ 61-7-3371 0144, assist@worldcare.com.au
Canada: World Access Canada, ☎ (519) 742 2800, ext. 234, www.worldaccess.com
UK: ☎020 8666 9352, www.mondial-assistance.co.uk
USA: World Access Travel Care, ☎ (305) 535 7380, www.worldaccess.com

GETTING THERE

• By air

A number of airline companies fly to Indonesia (see in particular Air France, British Airways, Cathay Pacific, Garuda Indonesia, Japan Airlines, KLM, Lufthansa, Qantas, Singapore Airlines and Thai International). Most flights have at least one stopover in the company's country, which can prolong the trip by several hours.

Scheduled flights

Garuda The national airline offers several flights per week from London, Frankfurt and Amsterdam to Jakarta or Denpasar, as well as connecting flights between Jakarta and major cities in Asia. Garuda doesn't fly from the US or Canada; but there are many regular flights from cities throughout Australia. If you fly with Garuda, you will be eligible for a 50% discount on domestic flights.

Garuda Indonesia, www.garuda-indonesia.com
London: ☎ 020 7486 3011/7935 3780   Sydney: ☎ 2 9334 9901
Los Angeles: ☎ 310 348 9923   Toronto: ☎ 416 441 1448

Charter flights

Keep in mind that major airlines offer charter rates on their regular flights. Compare prices at various agencies.

International Airports

International flights land in **Jakarta**, Bandung, Surabaya (Java), **Denpasar** (Bali), **Medan**, Padang, Pekanbaru (Sumatra), Batam (Riau archipelago), Ujung Pandang, and Manado (Sulawesi). There are usually a few (expensive) shops, bars and restaurants, banks for changing money and sometimes a post office, as well as counters for major car rental companies. Taxis wait at the flight arrival area, and a (fixed price) ticket usually has to be bought at a special counter. Some city centres can be reached on very inexpensive public buses, but this often involves walking to the road outside the airport area (refer to the "Coming and Going" section for the desired city).

Reconfirming

Your return flight must be confirmed 72hr in advance. Rather than going in person, just call your airline company or ask your hotel or travel agent to confirm for you (for a small fee).

Airport taxes

Count on Rp50 000 for the airport tax when you leave Indonesia.

• By boat

Entry into Indonesia is authorised at the following ports: Jakarta, Semarang, Surabaya (Java), Benoa, Padangbai (Bali), Belawan / Medan, Dumai (Sumatra), Batam, Tanjung Pinang (Riau archipelago), Ujung Pandang, and Manado (Sulawesi).

From Malaysia – A fast hydroplane (a 4-5hr crossing) links Penang (Malaysia) to Medan (Sumatra) every day except Sunday; a twice-weekly ferry makes the same crossing in 14 hours! Other, less regular boats go from Lumut and Port Kelang, the port for Kuala Lumpur (Malaysia,) to Medan, as well as from Melaka (Malaysia) to Dumai (Sumatra).
From Singapore – Ferries run on a regular basis from Batam (Riau archipelago) in 40min. From there you can embark for Pekanbaru (Sumatra).
From The Philippines – The link between Davao and Manado has been discontinued until further notice.

• Travel agents and tour operators
Holidays in Indonesia are organised by all major tour operators (basic flights, stays and tours), who often feature worthwhile "plane + hotel" package deals. You might also check out the following organisations.

Special interest:

Adventures Abroad, 2148-20800 Westminster Hwy, Richmond, BC V6V 2W3, Canada. ☎ 800/665 3998, 604/303-1099 www.adventures-abroad.com Cultural tours for small groups.

Escapes Unlimited, 17842 Irvine Blvd, Suite 232, Tustin, CA 92780-3244, USA ☎ 714 508 0170, 800 243 7227, Fax 714 508 8474, escapesltd@aol.com Features a range of tours, from hiking and cultural experiences in Bali to sailing trips to Komodo, as well as a unique adventure tour at Camp Leakey in Kalimantan where you can interact with orang-utans in the rainforest.

Earthwatch Institute, Oxford, UK ☎ 01865 311 600, info@uk.earthwatch.org; Melbourne, Australia. ☎ 03/9600 9100; Massachussetts, USA ☎ 617 926-8200, www.earthwatch.org Offers a chance to do valuable volunteer work helping on a variety of projects, from wildlife studies with biologists to archeological surveys and community work.

Explore, 1 Frederick St, Aldershot, GU11 1LQ, UK ☎ 01252 319 448, www.explore.co.uk Adventure and sailing trips around the archipelago.

Footprint Adventures, 5 Malham Drive, Lincoln, LN6 OXD, UK ☎ 01522 690 852, www.footventure.co.uk Specialise in trekking and wildlife tours.

Pro Dive Travel, Dymocks Building, 428 George St, Sydney, Australia. ☎ 02/9232 5733 Organises diving tours from A to Z.

San Michele Travel, 81 York St, Sydney, Australia ☎ 1800/222 244. An Indonesian specialist offering a variety of adventure tours and packages.

Silverbird, 4 Northfields Prospect, Putney Bridge Rd, London, SW18 1PE, UK ☎ 020 875 9090. Tailor-made trips and special deals are offered by this Far East specialist.

Surf Travel Company, 12 Cronulla Plaza, Cronulla Beach, Sydney, Australia. ☎ 02/9527 4722, www.surftravel.com.au Surfing and yachting packages to Bali and other destinations.

Wildnerness Travel, 1102 9th St, Berkeley, CA, 94710-1211, USA ☎ 800/368-2794, 510/558-2488 690852, www.wildernesstravel.com Offering cruises, cultural adventures, and hiking on several islands.

On Site:

Bali Adventure Tours, ☎ 62-361 721 480, baliadventuretours.com
Pacto/AmEx, The Grand Bali Beach Hotel, Sanur, ☎ 62-361 288 247, Fax 62-361 288 240.
Orient Express Tours and Travel, Bali, ☎ 62-361 759 595, Fax 62-361 759 696, www.bali-holiday.com

Andikha Travel, Sanur, Bali, ☎ 62-361 287 376.

Indonesia Volcanoes Tour, www.geocities.com/thetropics/lagoon/1489 For those who want to explore Indonesia's jungles and volcanoes.

Mesra Tours and Travel, www.mesra.co.id/mesra/tour Adventure and eco tours, including Rain Forest & Mahakam River Hinterland.

Indonesia Adventure and Hotel Reservation Center, www.komodotours. com Offer affordable and flexible tours.

Carstenz Pyramid Expedition Specialist, www.puncakjaya.co.id Specialise in adventure tours.

Sasak Tours and Travel, www.sasaklombok.com Travel agent in Lombok specialising in nature, trekking and diving tours.

Other:

Asia Travel Mart, Malaysia ☎ 60/3 8996 8000; Fax numbers: Sydney 61/2 9475 1329; London 020 7681 3853; Massachussetts 1/413 215 1345, asiatravelmart.com

Asia Travel Network, Joondalup, Australia. ☎ 08 9301 2756, Fax 08 9301 2759, www.asiatravel.com

Travel.com, www.travel.com On-line travel agent.

A directory of travel agencies in Indonesia can also be found at www.travelmart.co.id
Bali Paradise Online is another good source of information at www.bali-paradise.com

"Selamat Datang": welcome to our country

R Marca

THE BASICS

• **Address book**

Tourist Information

Most cities have a tourist office (*dinas pariwisata*), which can help to varying degrees depending on the place. In tourist spots, the offices are likely to have a mediocre map of the city and one for the island or the surrounding area, as well as a programme of cultural events and a calendar of holidays. For more detailed information, enquire at a travel agency or at your hotel.

Embassies and Consulates

Australia – Australian Embassy, Jl Rasuna Said Kav C-15-16, Jakarta 12940, ☎ (62-21) 522-7111, www. austembjak.or.id

Canada – Canadian Embassy, Wisma Metropolitan I, 29 Jalan Jend Sudirma, Jakarta 12920, ☎ (62-21) 525-0709, www. dfait-maeci.gc.ca/jakarta

UK – British Embassy, Jl Thamrin 75, Jakarta Pusat, ☎ (62-21) 315-6264, www.britain-in-indonesia. or.id

USA – Embassy of the United States of America, Jl Merdeka Selatan 4-5, Jakarta 10110, ☎ (62-21) 344-2211, www.usembassyjakarta.org
Addresses for **consulates** in the main cities can be found in the corresponding "Making the most of..." sections in the "Exploring Indonesia" chapter. In some cities (such as Yogyakarta), cultural centres act as consular agents.

● Opening and closing times
Business hours for administrative offices, shops and services vary a great deal from place to place, and are thus only given as a general indication. As a rule, places close on Friday afternoons and Sundays.

Banks
For changing money: Monday-Friday, 8am-12noon or 2pm; sometimes on Saturdays until 11am. Currency exchanges in major tourist areas stay open all day, every day.

Post Offices
Monday-Thursday, 8am-2 or 4pm; Fridays until 11am and Saturdays until 1pm. Main post offices in large cities usually close at 6 or 8pm and are often open on Sunday mornings.

Telephone Offices
Telkom offices usually run 24hr a day. Private agencies such as **Wartel** close between 8pm and midnight depending on the place. Beware of doors closing at 10pm even though a sign may say the office is open 24hr a day (*24 jam*)!

Shops
Most shops stay open continuously from 9am to 6 or 8pm. Most usually close on Sundays, except tourist shops which are normally open seven days a week.

Markets
Some markets are held daily, others less frequently (every 3 days in Bali, every 5 days in Java, and every 6 days in the Toraja region) Enquire for each specific case.

Restaurants
Most are open all day, every day. Closing times depend on how busy they are (rarely later than 9 or 10pm outside the tourist areas).

Offices (administrative, etc)
Monday-Thursday, 8am-2 or 4pm; Fridays, 8am-11am (closed for the main prayer); Saturdays, 8am-12noon or 2pm.

● Museums, Monuments and Archeological Sites
Opening and closing times
Most tourist sites are open from 8 or 9am to 2 or 5pm; Fridays until 11am; Saturday and (sometimes) Sunday until 1 or 2pm. Many museums are closed on Mondays. Don't enter a mosque at prayer time.

Fees
In most cases you'll have to pay a very modest entrance fee.

● Mail
Stamps can be bought at post offices and postal agencies, as well as in some shops and big hotels. Count on 1-3 weeks for mail to reach Europe. Send your mail from a post office, rather than from an isolated mailbox or a *losmen*, preferably in a major city (it's faster), and have the stamps postmarked in front of you (postal workers have been known to keep stamps for their own use!). Main post offices have a **Poste Restante** service. Have anyone sending you mail write your surname in underlined capital letters, followed by the words "Poste Restante" and "kantor pos" and the name of the city. If your mail can't be found under your surname, try your first name as it may have been sorted incorrectly.

Sending a package

Small packages can be sent from post offices, which sometimes also have a service for sending big parcels (in Yogyakarta for instance). For larger packages, there are a number of reputable air and maritime freight companies, particularly in Bali and Yogyakarta. For a 10kg parcel, count on Rp1 500 000 **by air** (about 2 weeks) and over Rp400 000 **by boat** (2-3 months). For urgent parcels, **Express Mail Service** guarantees delivery in 3 days, for a high price (Rp436 000 per kg).

• Telephone, fax and telegram

The telephone network has been modernised in recent years and now covers most of the archipelago. In major cities you can make telephone calls, and send faxes and telegrams at offices of the state-run company, **Telkom** (in theory the cheapest). There are also many private companies such as **Wartel**. Calls can be made from **public phone booths** in major cities using coins or phone cards (on sale in *Telkom* and *Wartel* offices and in some shops and supermarkets).

There are two kinds of cards (pliable or hard) depending on the type of phone. Calling rates are much higher in hotels, almost all of which have faxes. *Indosat*, another telephone company, sells a prepaid card, **Pre Card**, that can be used in public phone booths or with a private telephone. The cost of the call is deducted from the card.

International calls

International calls can be made at most telephone offices, hotels and in booths that use phone cards.

Area codes

Domestic calls – *See the list of area codes, p 80.* Dial 0 before the number.

Javanese phone booth

Calling Indonesia from abroad – Dial international access code, then 62 + area code (without the 0) + your correspondent's number.

International calls from Indonesia – Dial 001 + country code + your correspondent's number.

Country codes – 44 for the UK; 1 for the US and Canada; 61 for Australia.

Collect calls

Collect calls can be made at some telephone offices in exchange for a small fee. Sometimes they can be made from a private phone by dialling 001 + 801 + the collect call code for the country (16 for Canada). An operator from the country you dialled will then put you through to the number you're trying to reach. **Home Country Direct** phones are becoming increasingly common in cities and tourist areas (*refer to the corresponding "Making the most of...").*

R. Marca

National – Dial 108 (local) or 106 (regional).
International – Dial 102.
Rates
A call to the UK costs about **Rp8 000** per minute. Rates are **25%** lower on Saturdays and Sundays.

• Internet
There are **Cybercafés** *(warung Internet)* and Internet centres at major tourist sites in Bali, Java and Sumatra. More and more **post offices** and some **Wartel** offices also provide Internet services, particularly in major cities in Java, Bali, Sumatra and Sulawesi. *Refer to the corresponding "Making the most of…" section for each city or region.*

• Festivals and public holidays
With so many ethnic and religious communities, Indonesia celebrates a multitude of festivals and public holidays. Hindu and Muslim festivals follow the lunar calendar. Get a copy of the *Indonesia Calendar of Events* available in the main tourist offices. For the meaning of the festivals and a description of certain celebrations, refer to the chapter on religion *(p 48)* and to the introductions for each island. More specific regional events are mentioned in the corresponding pages. All of the following national festivals are public holidays.

Fixed holidays

Tahun Baru (1 January)	New Year's Day
Hari Merdeka (17 August)	Independence Day celebration. Sports and cultural events start in early August
Hari Natal (25 December)	Christmas, celebrated by Christians

Changing holidays
Muslim holy days

Lebaran/Idul Fitri	The end of Ramadan, celebrated for 2 days
Idul Adha	Commemorates Abraham's sacrifice of his son Isaac. Involves prayers and goat sacrifices
Awal Muharram/ Tahun Baru Hijriyah	Muslim New Year
Garebeg Maulud/ Maulud Nabi Muhammed	Birth of the Prophet Muhammad
Al Miraj/ Isra Miraj Nabi Muhammed	Ascension of the Prophet Muhammad

Christian holy days

Good Friday	
Ascension	Ascension of Christ

Hindu holy days

Nyepi	Hindu New Year in Bali. Everything is closed and it is strictly forbidden to leave your house or hotel

Buddhist holy days

Waicak	Birth, enlightenment and death of Buddha

The basics

GETTING AROUND

Travelling in Indonesia is easy and cheap, but often long and uncomfortable, almost always involving heat, cigarette smoke, dust, crowds and delays! If you're on a short holiday, stick with rental cars and planes – the only rapid means of transport. For those with plenty of time, buses and minibuses (*bemo*) are the best way of criss-crossing the islands, with the exception of Bali where taking a *bemo* can be long and complicated (stopovers in Denpasar or Batubulan are common). Trains – more restful but no faster – run across the whole of Java. Elsewhere, don't even think about it: the railway network is practically non-existent. As for travel between islands, the national company's ships provide good service at a much lower cost than by air, but you can't be in any hurry.

• By bus

This is the most widely used and cheapest means of transport (there are a number of competing bus companies). **Tickets** are usually bought at bus terminals, but it's often easier to go through a travel agent, or even a hotel, especially in big cities. It is wise to **reserve** the previous day for a long haul, and several days in advance at certain times of year (Ramadan). Sometimes bus companies offer to pick you up at your hotel.

Prices vary considerably depending on comfort and speed. In the best category, the buses are modern, air-conditioned (sometimes overly so!) and comfortable, and have reserved seats (*VIP*). In the worst category the buses have hard benches with 5 people sometimes squeezing onto 3 seats, and they stop whenever anyone wants to get on or off (*ekonomi*). Whatever the category, the bus will be filled with smoke from *kretek* (clove cigarettes) throughout the trip. If you don't like the smell, take a bus equipped with **windows** that can be opened, and get there early enough to find a seat near one of them. Indonesians seem to fear draughts and have an amazing capacity for travelling with all the windows closed even during a heat wave! Bring along some **earplugs** as well, as drivers have the unfortunate habit of turning up the radio full blast when their favourite tunes come on, particularly on night buses.

If you are not worried about comfort, it's worth riding on an *ekonomi* bus. Loading, stopovers at bus terminals and mosques, and animated discussions with rooster's crowing in the background will afford you some unforgettable memories. As a rule, bus drivers drive fast, honk readily, and every trip is full of thrills.

Shuttle bus

Several companies, such as **Perama**, run daily shuttles between the main tourist sites in Bali and Java, as well as inter-island services (Java-Bali-Lombok). They are comfortable, fast and cheap and will make your life easier, but you'll only mix with other tourists. *For details, refer to the "Making the most of..." sections in the "Exploring Indonesia" chapters.*

Roads

While the roads are in relatively good shape on major routes through Java, Bali and Lombok, they are rather bad on the other islands on the whole. Twisting mountain roads, potholes and landslides turn some routes into real obstacle courses.

• By train

While slower than buses, trains are safer and less trying. The only decent railway network linking all the big cities is in **Java**. **Sumatra** has two small sections in the north and south of the island. More than a simple means of transport, trains are a pleasant and fun way to explore superb landscapes that are not very well known. The other islands have no railways. Most trains have **three classes**: first class (*eksekutif*) is air-conditioned, second class (*bisnis*) is comfortable and has fans, and third class (*ekonomi*) is crowded but a lot livelier. It's wise to **reserve** tickets in advance at a station or through a travel agent. Enquire about timetables (quite reliable) at each station.

• By boat

Although boat travel is rather slow, it will spare you some long, unpleasant bus trips. It is far cheaper than flying and links up the various islands – provided that you have enough time. The national company, **Pelni**, serves the archipelago's main islands on a daily, weekly and monthly or (more often) twice-monthly basis depending on the line. In all, there are **five classes**, from a basic seat or mattress in a large communal room or on the deck to an air-conditioned cabin with bunks and bathroom. Don't forget to bring along a cardigan, as it's usually very chilly (due to the air conditioning). There's no need to bring food, however, since you can dine on the boat (meals are theoretically included in the price of a ticket in the top four classes). Timetables (which change every month) and tickets (reservations open one week in advance) are available at Pelni offices and in local travel agencies. **Other companies** schedule shorter, more frequent (and usually daily) crossings linking Sumatra, Java, Bali and Nusa Tenggara.

• By air

When going long distances, air travel is less tiring and faster. However, with the economic crisis a number of routes have been phased out, and flights are frequently cancelled due to lack of passengers or for technical reasons. You should also be aware that there is an increasing tendency towards a disturbing carelessness with regard to the maintenance of the aircraft.

If you are going in July-August, during the Christmas-New Year period or at the end of Ramadan, **reserve** your tickets before leaving, particularly for links to Bali, Lombok, Sulawesi and Flores. You can always change the dates when you get there, as long as seats are available. Rates are, however, much better on the spot. For all domestic flights, even those you reserved a long time ago, **reconfirm** your ticket 3 days before and get to the airport early to be sure to get a seat, as overbooking is common. Have some rupiah handy for the airport tax (around Rp10-15 000). Many **travel agencies** offer reduced price tickets (up to 25% less than prices quoted by the airlines). Moreover, some airlines have **student** discounts for those with an international student card (ISIC).

Major airlines:

Garuda flies to Sumatra, Java, Bali and Sulawesi. It is the most reliable company. It offers passengers on its international flights a 50% reduction on domestic flights.
Merpati flies to the main destinations on the archipelago.
Bouraq flies mainly to Sulawesi, the Lesser Sunda Islands and Maluku.
Mandala flies mainly to Java, Sumatra, Sulawesi and Maluku.

• By car

While hiring a car is the best way to explore Bali on your own, in other areas it is more expensive and thus preferable – even mandatory – to hire a **driver**. In any case, you're sure to save time and avoid tiring bus trips; and you can stop whenever you like in a village or to admire the landscape. If the trip lasts several days, the driver's (inexpensive) room and board will be at your charge. Negotiate rates and specify exactly what route you want to take.

Car rental

Several big international agencies (Avis, Europcar, Hertz etc) have counters at airports, in major cities and big hotels; but the smaller local agencies offer very competitive rates. Check the condition of the car carefully (brakes, horn, headlights, windscreen wipers, tyres and air conditioning) as well as insurance coverage. The latter usually includes quite a high excess. Insist on a contract with third party insurance. You must have an international driver's licence and be over 18 years old. Seat belts are now mandatory, but they rarely work. Lastly, it is forbidden to leave Bali by car (but you may do so from other places).

Count on a minimum of Rp60 000 per day for a **Suzuki Jimny Jeep** (not recommended for more than 2 passengers as the back seats are often uncomfortable and have locked tinted-glass windows), Rp70 000-100 000 for a **Toyota Kijang minibus** (5-7 seats). Rates vary depending on the place, the agency and the length of the rental (negotiate a lower rate if you're renting the vehicle for several days).

Highway code

Driving is **on the left**. Right of way is theoretically on the right; but Indonesians drive fast, so the biggest vehicle or the person who honks loudest usually has priority! Locals seem to have no qualms about passing on a curve without the slightest visibility. In theory the **speed limit** is 50kph in towns and 90kph elsewhere.

Be careful, as roads are not lit up at night. Always pay attention because an obstacle may appear out of nowhere at any time. Many people walk on the side of the road – particularly hordes of little schoolchildren – sometimes with herds of animals, not to mention the stray dogs that suddenly bolt across your path. Do as the Indonesians do: honk unrestrainedly to warn pedestrians, cyclists and animals.

Fuel

Fuel is very cheap (less than 60 cents per gallon). Fill the tank before leaving and enquire about service station locations if you're going on a long trip (**Pertamina**, the national company, has a monopoly) as they are few and far between in some areas. Although it is a bit more expensive, fuel (*bensin*) sold at small shops on the side of the road is not good quality, but it will do in a fix.

Directions

Good **road maps**, as well as town maps, can be obtained on site. If you ask for directions, remember that Indonesians aren't used to reading maps. They may look at yours with curiosity, but their good intentions won't be of much help.

• Police

Police rackets are fairly common on certain roads in Indonesia, particularly in Bali. The policemen usually lie in wait around a curve, always find something to fine you for and thus supplement their income. It is often useless trying to prove your good faith. The same is true if you are the victim or cause of an accident (you will be held responsible in most cases and the policemen will be of no help to you). Don't be intimidated if you are arbitrarily arrested and ordered to pay an exorbitant sum of money. The golden rule is to keep your cool. Stay calm, defend yourself clearly and firmly, and be patient. Don't use this as a chance to practice your *Bahasa indonesia*, which might open the door to an "agreement" that could be unfavourable to you. The ideal solution is to get an Indonesian "friend", or the owner of your hotel or *losmen*, to intervene and negotiate for you. The fine usually drops considerably if an Indonesian is present.

An Indonesian-style family vehicle

• Chartering a vehicle

Groups of several people can hire a *bemo* or other vehicle for long trips, thus avoiding the loss of time and fatigue of bus travel. By sharing the cost with the other passengers, expenses will be less than if you rented a private car. Be tough when negotiating the price before leaving, specifying the planned itinerary and length of the trip. Drivers often have an unfortunate habit of wanting to take other passengers en route, so if you don't refuse firmly you'll soon feel like you're riding in a slow *bemo* that makes a halt at every stop.

• By motorcycle

This is a very pleasant – and thrilling! – way to visit the islands. But be careful, as riding a motorcycle can be trying and dangerous, especially on steep roads (in Bali and in several regions on other islands). So this means of transport requires extreme caution and is reserved for experienced motorcyclists.

Count on Rp40000-80000 per day for a **moped** (*bebek*) or motorbike (engine capacity never more than 150cc). They can be rented in most tourist areas, in particular at certain *losmen*. Although a **driver's licence** is in theory mandatory, you will rarely be asked to show it. Check the condition of the motorbike and the insurance contract carefully. Drive slowly and don't hug the edge of the road, which is often unstable and crowded with pedestrians and animals. Remember that **helmets** are mandatory, although many Indonesians (and tourists) neglect to wear them – risking their safety and incurring a fine.

• By bicycle

Bicycling is a pleasant and practical way to get around town (ideal in Yogyakarta, for instance) or to go short distances. Study the lie of the land before striking out (Indonesia is not a flat country!), check your tyres and brakes, and bring water if you're going off the beaten track. Rentals in tourist centres (especially in Java and Bali) go for about Rp25 000 per day.

• Hitch-hiking

Don't count on hitch-hiking across Indonesia. It isn't a local custom, and private cars are less common than buses and *bemos*. But you can always try. You may be asked for a small contribution.

• By taxi

Taxis are convenient for getting around towns, where there are usually plenty of them and they are cheap. Ask the driver to turn on the **meter**. If it isn't working, negotiate the price of the trip before starting out (enquire about normal rates with the hotel staff or other locals). In large cities, try to locate where you are on a map in order to avoid being "taken for a ride".

• By bemo

The countless *bemos* – also called *oplet*, *mikrolet*, *colt* and other names in different regions – are **minibuses** that run short and medium distances around town and in the environs. They have numbers or colours, depending on the place, and their destination is often written on the windscreen; but it's wiser to ask the driver if he's heading where you want to go. *Bemos* leave from terminals as soon as they're full, usually jam-packed, or drive around town honking to solicit travellers. Passengers hail them with a wave of the hand from the edge of the road. If you want to **get off**, clap your hands or yell "kiri!" (left!) – although the word varies from one region to another – or ask a local to tell you when you get to your destination. You may be asked to pay extra if you have luggage. It might be faster and more practical to charter a *bemo* (*see above*).

• By becak

Becaks (three-wheel cycle rickshaws) are everywhere in most cities in the archipelago and remain a well-used means of transport for short distances. But they are forbidden in congested metropolises (such as Jakarta and Surabaya) and are often restricted to secondary roads in other cities. Negotiate the fare before setting off in order to avoid any unpleasant surprises upon arrival, and make sure the driver has understood where you want to go.

• In a horse-drawn cart

Dokar, **andong**, **bendi**, whatever their local name (*benhur* in Sumbawa!), horse-drawn carts are still widely used in small towns and rural areas. They are two- or four-wheel carts painted in bright colours and often adorned with little bells that jingle along the way – a picturesque means of transport for short distances or for taking a leisurely ride.

A becak

R. Marca

• Organised tours and excursions

Travel agencies in tourist areas (Bali and Yogyakarta, as well as Lombok, Bukittingi, Toba Lake, the Toraja region etc) organise tailor-made excursions in private cars with guide and driver, as well as various group tours in buses. You can also enquire at your hotel or *losmen*.

BED AND BOARD

• Various categories

Tourist areas offer a wide range of accommodation, from a small room in a rudimentary guesthouse to a spacious and refined suite in a luxury hotel. But be prepared for a very basic standard of comfort if you go off the beaten track. Ask to see several rooms (they tend to only show you the fancier ones), check the condition of the **bathroom** and air conditioning, and make sure that the windows (if there are any!) don't overlook a busy street, a morning market, a mosque (the first prayer is at 5am!), a bus terminal or a port. In most cases you can **bargain** over the price of a room, especially in tourist areas (mention more competitive rates), during the off-season (up to 50% off), if you're planning on staying several nights or if you're alone. Parents can share a room with one or two of their children under the age of 12 at most hotels.

Hotels

This category covers a broad range of establishments, from the most run-down to the most luxurious. Every hotel has several types of rooms, and the rates can triple depending on the standard of comfort (fan or air conditioning, with or without hot water, private or shared bathroom, television, telephone, mini-bar and other facilities) and the room's location (on the beach or set back from it, with or without a view, etc). An 11% government **tax** and a 10% service charge are tacked on at the most expensive hotels, where rates are usually quoted in US dollars. In addition, they raise their rates an average of 25% during the busy season (July-August and December-January).

Losmen, pondok, wisma, and penginapan

These names all refer to inexpensive guesthouses and small hotels. They are usually family-run establishments with no employees or a small staff, and a limited number of rooms. Meals are sometimes served and breakfast is usually included in the price of the room (tea or coffee most often served with toast, pancakes or eggs, and fruit salad in some cases). What such places lack in creature comforts (mattresses, lighting and bathrooms sometimes leave a lot to be desired!) they make up for in conviviality, as you'll meet both Indonesians and other travellers from many countries. In most cases, **bathrooms** have a vat filled with clean, cold water **(bak mandi)** instead of a shower. Rather than sitting in it like a bathtub, splash water on yourself with the plastic bucket *(gayung)* placed next to it! This system is also used for cleaning toilets (often Turkish-style without a flush) and for rinsing oneself off, according to local custom (but you're free to buy toilet paper if you like).

Price range

The addresses given in the "Where to stay" section of the "Making the most of..." pages for each place are listed according to off-season price ranges (only luxury hotels raise their rates considerably during the busy season), on the basis of a double room (including breakfast and taxes) in a middle-range category (when there are several categories in the same hotel). Given the economic crisis and galloping inflation in Indonesia, we cannot quote specific rates. We have therefore chosen to use 5 categories defined according to the following balanced quality-price ratio:

modest   less than US$5 (minimum to basic comfort)
average   from US$5-12 (comfortable with a touch of charm)
high end   from US$12-50 (stylish or high-end hotel)
luxury   from US$50-100 (refinement and top-notch service)
super deluxe   over US$100

There are also some very nice establishments with amazingly low rates.

• Eating out

Types of restaurants are as varied as accommodation. There are places to eat everywhere you go (but not open at all hours); and they often prepare delicious meals, always at ridiculously low prices.

"Warung", markets and pushcarts

Whether in town, in a remote village or by the roadside, there is always a street vendor (**kaki lima**, literally "five feet": two belonging to the vendor and the other three to his cart!) peddling *bakso* (noodle soup), *sate* (kebabs), *nasi goreng* (fried rice), *mie goreng* (fried noodles), or *martabak* (pancakes with eggs or peanuts), as well as sweets (with bananas, coconut, sticky rice, peanuts and palm sugar). Check out the night markets, **pasar malam** (most open around 5 or 6pm and close at various times during the night depending on business), and **warung** – a few tables with benches or stools protected by plastic coverings – where a limited selection of local dishes is served.

The country also abounds in **rumah makan**, cheap restaurants with no pretensions but where the food is often good and tasty, and the atmosphere is always fun. In theory one eats with the right hand after washing in the small bowl of water provided; but cutlery will probably be offered. There are also many **rumah makan Padang**, which specialise in spicy dishes from Sumatra. You choose an assortment of them in the window or directly at the table and pay only for what you have eaten. Contrary to common belief, there is less chance of food poisoning in these modest but very popular places, where there is a high turnover, than in certain better-looking restaurants.

In restaurants

The word **restoran** covers a variety of establishments, from the simplest to the most elegant. There is an abundance of choice in tourist areas from among the multitude of average-priced restaurants with basically identical menus. The competition has become so stiff that there is a trend towards standardisation, so the choice will be more about the setting than the menu. In some places restaurants try to outdo each other with happy hours, dance **performances** and film screenings, as well as charming hostesses hired to attract customers with their biggest smiles to stop them sitting down at a table at a neighbouring restaurant. With varying degrees of success, in an attempt at international cuisine, Indonesian, Chinese, Indian, Italian, French, Tex-Mex, Japanese, Thai and seafood dishes fight for the place of honour. As a rule, the best food to be had is in restaurants specialising in one type of cuisine; and since you're in Indonesia, why not stick with local fare! However, **fast-food restaurants** with American-style air conditioning are becoming increasingly popular in big cities.

In hotels

The big hotels all have one or more (sometimes air-conditioned) restaurants serving various kinds of cuisine. The quite common **open buffet** system allows food-lovers to taste a wide variety of dishes. Prices, often listed in dollars, are exorbitant for the country's standard of living. With rare exceptions, the food isn't as good as in other places; and since the turnover isn't as high as in more modest establishments, you will not necessarily be less subject to intestinal woes!

Beverages

Sodas (*Coca-Cola, Sprite, Fanta*), beer (*Bintang, Angker, San Miguel*), tea and coffee, mineral water (*Aqua*) or boiled water (*air putih*) can be found almost everywhere. In cities and tourist areas, drinks are served cold or with ice (made with boiled water). It's amazing how many places claim to sell the coldest beer in town! Elsewhere, you'll have to get used to drinks that are warm or have ice cubes. Restaurants serve delicious **fresh fruit juices**. Only establishments of a certain standing offer wine – both local (Bali produces a rosé called *Hatten*), Australian, and more rarely French. And why not try some Indonesian **spirits**: *arak* (distilled palm wine to be drunk in moderation!), *tuak* (made from fermented palm sap) or *brem* (fermented rice wine).

Price range
The restaurants mentioned in the "Eating out" section in the "Making the most of..." pages for each place have been grouped according to prices on the basis of an average meal not including beverages. Although eating out is incredibly cheap in Indonesia, you can still choose from the following three price ranges:

basic for markets, *warung* and other open-air restaurants where you can eat for less than US$2;

moderate for restaurants where the bill ranges from US$2 to US$5;

more select for establishments that are more refined and have more elaborate food that will cost you over US$6.

SPORTS AND PASTIMES

• Cross country
Walking
Whether you prefer athletic or leisurely hikes, Indonesia is the place for you. You can go up a volcano (Bromo and Merapi in Java, Batur in Bali, Rinjani in Lombok, etc), on an expedition to a national park or to the jungle (Gunung Leuser in Sumatra, Ujung Kulon in Java, Lore Lindu in Sulawesi) or on a simple walk through rice fields. Most hikes can be done alone; but some require the services of a **guide**. Make sure that he speaks English and, above all, that he is from the area and knows the hike well. It's better to hire officially certified guides, who must have a registration card. Whenever possible, enquire beforehand about the weather forecast (sudden torrential rains occur during all seasons) and volcanic conditions (several volcanoes are still active). Bring a good pair of hiking shoes that are lightweight, waterproof and have good treads, as well as some provisions and above all enough **water** in case you're going far away from inhabited areas (you get quite dehydrated on volcanoes due to the sulphur fumes, and also in muggy jungles). Take something to protect you from the rain and **cold** (in the mountains), the sun (sunblock, glasses and hat) and mosquitoes (in forests), and don't wear shorts.

Mountain biking
Most roads on the Indonesian islands are very steep, but experienced cyclists will be rewarded for their efforts by the warm welcome they'll receive from the locals. *See also the "By bicycle" section, p 95.*

Rafting
In addition to a multitude of waterways, the landscape and precipitation combine to create some turbulent rapids that are ideal for rafting. Travel agencies are increasingly exploiting this potential, particularly in Bali (on the Ayung), in Sulawesi (on the Sa'dan in the Toraja region), in Sumatra (the Wampu) and in West Java (the Citarik in Gunung Halimun Park).

• The Sea

Exploring the seabed

The most spectacular seabeds are in Sumatra (Pulau We), Bali (Pulau Menjangan, Tulamben, Nusa Lembongan and Penida), Sulawesi (the Togian and Bunaken islands), Lombok (the Gili islands) and Flores (Maumere and Labuhanbajo). Hotels, *losmen* and diving clubs rent masks (not always watertight!), snorkels and sometimes flippers, but you might regret not having brought your own equipment. You might be able to buy some in Jakarta, Yogyakarta, Ujung Pandang, Manado or Bali.

Scuba diving clubs at all the seaside resorts – especially in big hotels – organise excursions to the most beautiful coral reefs in the area. There's something for everyone, from first dives for beginners to daytime or night-time diving for more experienced divers (remember to bring your certificate). Bali has the most reliable outfits. However, you should check the condition of the equipment (sometimes old and not well maintained) and the instructors' experience. During the rainy season, from approximately October to April, the sea can get rough and visibility may be reduced. The less daring can admire coral and fish from a **glass-bottomed boat** (at big tourist beaches such as Sanur in Bali).

Riding the waves

Indonesia has some of the best surfing spots in the world. Shops and agencies specialising in surfing are concentrated in **Kuta** (Bali), a Mecca for surfers. From there you can embark on a memorable cruise to some of the numerous deserted spots on neighbouring or more distant islands (especially around Sumbawa). The island of **Nias** (Sumatra) and the beach at Kuta **(Lombok)** also attract many surfing buffs. For those in search of big thrills: beware before taking on the wild waves! This sport requires total mastery. June and July are the best season, but the best "tubes" are taken by storm then. For more information about particular conditions at each site, buy a copy of *Tripsurf* or *Surf Session* magazines. They can be found in Kuta (Bali) at the **Tubes bar and restaurant** (Poppies Gang II), THE hangout for surfers from around the world. Other venues in Kuta where you can find equipment and expertise include Ulu's Surf Shop, Bali Barrel, and The Surf Shop.

Chartering boats

Several companies organise cruises through the archipelago – mostly luxury ones that are expensive.

Take your pick: pleasure cruising, or enjoying the best surfing and scuba diving spots. For more details contact one of the local travel agencies, mostly concentrated in southern Bali (Sanur, Kuta, Nusa Dua and Benoa).

Other sports

Only a few beaches such as Sanur, Nusa Dua and Benoa (Bali) rent jet skis, windsurfing boards, inner tubes, pedal-boats etc.

Just to get you started, here are a few of the many places that will take care of your water sports needs (*see p 110 for books on Diving & Surfing*):

Bali Marine Sports, Denpasar, ☏ 62 361 289 308, Fax 62 361 287 872, bmsdive@indosat.net.id

ENA Dive Center, Denpasar, ☏/Fax 62 361 287 948, enadive@denpasar.wasantara.net.id

Pro-Dive Bali, Kuta, ☏ 62 361 753 951

Dream Divers, Lombok, ☏ 62 370 634 547

Wanasari Wisata Surfing Tours, Kuta, ☏ 62 361 755 588, Fax 62 361 755 690, bobby@denpasar.wasantara.net.id

Sports and pastimes

Ruling the roost

R. Merca

• Night life
Bars and nightclubs
Always up for a party, young Indonesians are fond of going to bars and nightclubs in big cities and tourist areas (especially in Kuta in Bali, where Western women are frequently approached).

Cinema
Young Indonesians enjoy films and crowd into cinemas in large and middle-sized cities as soon as night falls. Competing genres include big Western productions, sentimental Indian musical comedies (from "Bollywood") and *kung-fu* films. More and more bars and restaurants are showing films in the evening in tourist areas (mainly in Java and Bali).

Concerts and live shows
Your exploration of Indonesian life wouldn't be complete without a theatre, puppet, dance or music performance. There is always something to see in Yogyakarta (Java) with its lively nightlife, and naturally in Bali too (especially in Ubud). *See p 295 and 416.*

SHOPPING

Indonesia is full of tempting things to buy! The widest range of items – from all of the islands in the archipelago – and the most competitive prices are without a doubt to be found in Bali (especially in Kuta and in the area of Ubud) and Java (particularly in Yogyakarta and its environs). But finding an *ikat* in the depths of Flores or a basket in a remote little village in Lombok will lend a special charm to your purchase. *See also the chapter on "Crafts", p 64.*

• What's on offer
Fabrics
A speciality of Central Java (Yogyakarta and Solo), **batik making** has also won fame on the northern coast of Java (Cirebon and Pekalongan) and to a lesser degree in southern Sumatra (Lampung). Each region has its own style with different colours and patterns *(see p 64)*.

Batik sarongs (handmade or printed) can be purchased in most markets in the archipelago, but the most beautiful ones are sold in shops in tourist towns in Java in particular, as well as in Bali.

Ikats *(see p 66)* can be found everywhere in Flores, Sumba and Timor; and there are also variants in Bali, Lombok, Sumatra and Sulawesi. There are different levels of quality (in dyeing – natural or chemical – and weaving), and prices are often higher on site because competition isn't as stiff as elsewhere.

Shopping

101

Clothes

This is your chance to renew your summer wardrobe at absolutely unbeatable prices (in Bali and Java). If you don't like the ready-to-wear items in the shops (the trend is towards "one size fits all" and, increasingly, synthetics), buy the fabric of your dreams and have your clothes made by a **tailor**. It's better to provide an example of what you want in order to avoid the unpleasant surprise of something "tailor-made" that is not quite up to the mark.

Jewellery

Indonesia has diamond mines and produces cultured pearls; but most jewellery is made of silver or gold and can be bought at low prices, although the quality varies a great deal. Found especially in Bali and Central Java (Kota Gede, near Yogyakarta.)

Painting

Different painting styles thrive in Bali, particularly in the Ubud area, as well as in Yogyakarta, where batik and silk painting techniques predominate.

Sculpture

Sculpture production is concentrated in Bali, but the quality of work has gone down because it's so commercial. Much more beautiful and original pieces are to be found in Java, in particular near Borobudur and in Trowulan (East Java). Elsewhere you may discover more primitive works, such as in the Batak region (Sumatra).

Puppets and masks

Leather or wooden puppets (*wayang kulit* or *wayang golek*) – so decorative and easy to slip into a suitcase – are not made exclusively in Java or Bali; but that's where you'll see the most beautiful ones. Or you may decide on a wooden mask, often painted in bright colours (Lombok, Bali and Java).

Basketwork

Baskets, mats and hats designed for everyday use in all shapes and sizes also make pretty decorative souvenirs. Shops in Bali (such as the ones in Ubud) also sell handsome *Dayak* bags from Kalimantan and various creations from all over the archipelago.

Antiques

You'll probably see more fake antiques (such as Majapahit terracotta ware and Hindu bronzes, not to mention all the "real Borobudur statues"!) than genuine old pieces (over 20 years old). If you know enough to tell the difference, ask around to find the best shops, which are usually concentrated in large cities. In any case, it is **forbidden** to export objects over 50 years old. Besides relics from the Dutch colonial period and some Chinese (ceramic) pieces, you may find some lovely local crafts made of wood or metal. Since old **kris** daggers have become extremely rare, most of the ones you'll be shown will only be copies. That doesn't mean you shouldn't buy one, as long as you aren't made to pay the price of a genuine antique!

Coffee and spices

To brighten up your kitchen with exotic colours, smells and tastes, buy a small assortment of spices and coffee (the best come from the Toraja region) at the local market.

Music

Cassettes and **CDs** of local and Western music can be found in tourist areas and big cities at unbeatable prices (ask to listen to them in order to check their condition before buying).

• Where to shop

Local markets

You'll find all sorts of aromatic spices, sarongs and magnificent everyday objects here (basketwork, boxes, kitchen utensils, toys etc), and sometimes items designed more specifically for tourists (mobiles, kites and other colourful knick-knacks). Bargaining is a must!

Shops

The innumerable and varied shops contain either local items at fixed prices or tourist products that you can bargain over, with a smile.

Supermarkets

Large cities have numerous supermarkets and malls where you can find everything you need (fixed prices).

• Bartering

See the "A to Z" section, p 105.

• Mailing things home

See the paragraph on "Mail", p 89.

HEALTH AND SAFETY

• Vaccinations

See p 84.

• Precautions

The sun

The tropical sun you travelled so far to get to can also be a formidable enemy! And it is intense even when skies are cloudy. Using sun block with a high protection factor, wearing a hat and sunglasses, and exposing yourself to the sun gradually over the first few days will reduce the risk of **sunburn** and sunstroke that could ruin your holidays. Be particularly careful when exploring the sea bed with your mask and snorkel. A T-shirt and trousers will save you from the worst burns, but bring along a tube of *benzocaine* burn cream. Avoid **dehydration** by drinking lots of water and taking a bottle of it with you when out and about, especially on hikes in the jungle and up volcanoes. And beware of sudden changes in temperature due to **air conditioning**.

Mosquitoes

Malaria – transmitted by anopheles mosquitoes that bite between sunset and sunrise – is rampant on most islands in the archipelago, with the exception of Bali and Java. Outside of those islands some precautions are necessary. At nightfall wear long clothing, put on an anti-mosquito lotion containing DEET (*Off!*; or *Autan*, the most effective one found in Indonesia) on uncovered parts of your body and possibly on your clothes, and sleep under a mosquito net (the ones that can be bought there, in large cities and at some markets, are of mediocre quality). Coils for burning and insecticide plugs are also effective and can be bought throughout the country. In certain areas with high malaria rates it is recommended to follow a prophylactic anti-malaria treatment (*Proguanil + Chloroquine*, or *Mefloquine*) during your stay and for four weeks after you return home. Enquire at a tropical medicine centre before leaving (*see the "Vaccinations" section, p 84*). Be careful, as scuba diving can be dangerous when taking *Mefloquine*. In case of an attack (high fever, shivers, sweating, intense headaches, delirium etc) take along some curative medicines (*Halofantine*, or *Mefloquine* if you aren't taking any as a preventive). You should also bring along some antihistamine cream to soothe itches! *Tiger Balm*, sold on site, is quite effective.

Dengue, another ailment transmitted by certain mosquitoes, is a viral disease. Its symptoms are a high fever, intense headaches, and articular and muscular pains, sometimes followed by a skin rash, which keep you bed-ridden for several days without calling for any specific treatment. However, one should contact a doctor immediately because in Southeast Asia the disease can have serious effects (haemorrhaging) necessitating hospitalisation.

Food
Stomach upsets (sometimes known as "Bali belly") due to varying degrees of intestinal problems are familiar to all tourists. They may be caused simply by the change in climate and food or, more seriously, from a lack of hygiene or food that isn't fresh. Bring along some *Imodium* (for diarrhoea) and *Tilbroquineol* or *Nifuroxazide* (to treat the bacterial infection that may have caused the diarrhoea). If it's a serious case, drink lots of water (not too cold!) to prevent dehydration, eat white rice, vegetable broth, salt and bananas.

Tap water must be boiled (20min, longer at high altitudes) or purified with tablets (such as *Micropur*) before drinking it. However, such disinfectants do not kill all parasites, in particular amoebas. You can drink the water served at a *warung* or in someone's home, as it is always boiled beforehand (ask if you are in doubt about it). In theory, the same goes for the ice cubes used to cool drinks. Otherwise, bottled mineral water *(aqua)* can be found everywhere. Avoid eating fruits and vegetables if you're not sure about the water that was used to prepare them. Wherever possible, check the freshness of the meat, fish and shellfish that you are served, and above all make sure they are well cooked.

AIDS
The virus has been as devastating in Indonesia as in other parts of the world. So remember to protect yourself.

● **Medical kit**
Soap, shampoo, toothpaste and toilet paper can be obtained everywhere (women will have a harder time finding tampons). In addition to the supplies already mentioned against sun, malaria and stomach upsets, it is advisable to bring along some antiseptic cream *(Betadine)*, band aids, aspirin or paracetamol, broad-spectrum antibiotics in case of infection, as well as an anti-fungal cream, antihistamines (for allergies due to plants or insect bites), and some eye drops. Take along a sterile syringe in case you need to have an emergency injection or give a blood sample (with a prescription). Ask your doctor for advice before leaving.

International travel insurers, based in Singapore:
International SOS Assistance, Singapore, ☎ (65) 221 3981, Fax (65) 226 3937, Telex: 24422 SOSAFE
AEA (Asia Emergency Assistance International), Singapore, ☎ (65) 338 2311, (65) 338 7611. Offer insurance packages for travellers including medical evacuation to Singapore.
In Bali: **Bali Tourist International Assist:** ☎ 228996 (emergency number: 227271/ 231443; Fax 231442).

(See p 85 for travel/health insurance)

● **Health**
The quality of medical care depends a great deal on where you are. When in need, call the nearest embassy or consulate first, or else one of the big hotels. They usually have a medical service where you can at least get first aid; and they can recommend a doctor or hospital.

Hospitals

All cities have a hospital (*rumah sakit*) and most villages have dispensaries (*puskesmas*) that aren't very inviting, but you can go there when in need. Jakarta and other major cities have good hospitals where some of the doctors speak English. In an emergency, take the first plane for Singapore, which has the best medical infrastructure in the region.

Traditional doctors

Traditional doctors who use plant remedies are often the most experienced and capable people for treating certain tropical diseases. Ask Indonesians for their advice to help you find the best person.

Chemists/Pharmacies

There is at least one relatively well-stocked pharmacy (*apotik*) in every city where you will have no problem finding basic over-the-counter medicines. More specialised treatment is less easy to come by. Since the names of medicines vary from one country to another, it's better to know the generic names of the ones you might need. Always check the expiry date of the medicine. Sun block and tampons can only be found in certain supermarkets, in cities and in the most tourist-oriented areas.

Dentists

The same rules apply for dentists as for hospitals (*see above*). In case of a serious dental problem, Bangkok is known for its high-quality dentists (*dokter gigi*). Singapore is closer, but more expensive.

• Emergencies

Police ☎ 110 – **Fire Brigade** ☎ 113 – **Ambulance** ☎ 118

FROM A TO Z

• Antiques

It is forbidden to export objects over 50 years old from Indonesia (*see "Shopping" section, p 101*).

• Bartering

Bargaining is a must in many circumstances. In any case, enquire in advance (asking several disinterested parties) about the usual prices. That way, you'll be sure not to offend the seller by belittling his work or services by suggesting too low a price, and you won't be "swindled" either. But remember that, whatever your standard of living, you'll always seem immensely wealthy to an Indonesian. Naturally you'll pay more than the local customers; but that's only fair! Rather than being offended, try to see it as a kind of "tax on wealth" that is really quite minimal.

You can almost always negotiate the price of a ride in a **taxi** (with no meter) or **becak**. But don't forget that *becak* drivers are among the most underprivileged people in the country and that, for them, every hundred rupiah counts. **Bemo** rates are fixed, but drivers tend to raise prices for Westerners (watch how much an Indonesian pays to get an idea of regular rates). The same holds for car, motorcycle and bicycle **rentals**. Don't be shy about negotiating the price of your **room** in tourist areas (Bali, Yogyakarta and Lake Toba), especially during the off-season or if you're staying for several nights. You can also bargain over **purchases** at markets and in shops (except if they have a price tag). If you can't get a decent discount and the price is obviously excessive, pretend to leave. In most cases – if your price is reasonable – the seller will call you back and offer a better price. It's not easy to assess an item's value, especially since some people double or triple prices in tourist areas. You can expect a 20-50% price-cut on average in such places. It would be considered extremely rude not to make the purchase if the seller accepts your price. By shopping in the morning you might get the "good omen" price that some salespeople traditionally grant their first customer of the day.

● Drinking water
Tap water is not drinkable, but bottled water can be found nearly everywhere. Indonesians themselves drink boiled water, so there's not much to worry about if you are offered a glass of water (ask just to be on the safe side). Ice cubes are also made with boiled water (*see the "Health" section above*).

● Electricity
Most places have converted to 220 volts, but some still use 110 volts (buy an adaptor if you're planning to go off the beaten track). Plugs are of the rounded two-pronged variety almost everywhere. Power shortages are common outside of large cities, so a flashlight often comes in handy.

● Laundry
All hotels – even the most humble *losmen* – will do your laundry for a modest sum. But avoid giving them your more delicate or favourite clothes.

● Narcotics
Possessing or using narcotics in Indonesia is punishable by 20 years in prison.

● Newspapers
Local newspapers are in Indonesian with the exception of the **Jakarta Post** – an English-language daily sold on the streets, in bookshops and supermarkets in major cities and in the main tourist areas – and the *Indonesian Observer,* which is harder to find. You can also find certain American, Australian and English-language Asian newspapers and magazines.

● Radio
Radio Republik Indonesia (RRI), the national radio, is broadcast throughout the archipelago. Certain foreign stations such as the **BBC World Service**, **Voice of America** and **Radio France Internationale (RFI)** can be picked up in addition to the private local ones.

● Smoking
Indonesians (the men almost exclusively) are among the biggest smokers in the world. So there are hardly any non-smoking areas, and the smell of tobacco doesn't seem to be considered a pollutant. But you may be surprised by the smell of the local clove cigarettes (*kretek*), which has been known to please even the most adamant anti-smokers! Very cheap American cigarettes (made locally) can be found in all tourist areas; elsewhere, they may be harder to get.

● Taking photographs
Film can be bought and developed in all tourist areas. Prices are much lower than in Europe, but the choice of film isn't as great (especially for slides and black-and-white) and the quality of the **development** and prints is often mediocre (make sure

it is clear when you want slides). Check expiry dates carefully for film and make sure it hasn't been exposed to the sun for months in a shop window. **Cassettes** for video cameras can be bought in big cities and at major tourist sites.

On the whole Indonesians don't mind being photographed and even enjoy posing. They often give you their address so you can send them a snap. But in the country or in remote areas, women – and sometimes children – are often more reticent. Be sensitive as to what situations and subjects may be appropriate, ask for permission before snapping away, and thank them with a smile. Keep a proper distance and don't break the silence of a prayer with your clicks and flashes. Out of respect, never photograph a person who is bathing (at a public bath, on the side of a road or river). Lastly, it is **forbidden** to photograph or film airports, train stations, military bases or any other strategic sites.

• Television

Television is broadcast via satellite without interruption in *warung* and in suitably equipped homes, attracting friends and neighbours. You'll be surprised by the number of satellite dishes set up in front of houses, even in the poorest and most remote areas. Besides the government channel, **Televisi Republik Indonesia (TVRI)**, there are several private channels broadcasting with varying degrees of freedom of expression. Hotels usually pick up international channels (CNN, BBC etc). Local programmes alternate between long news broadcasts focusing on Javanese news and trendy, violent or soppy TV films.

• Thefts

Indonesians aren't known for stealing, but don't forget that you are far richer than they are and that the country is going through a deep economic crisis. Consequently, there has been a noticeable increase in petty larceny in tourist areas. So don't tempt fate! Avoid showing off your wealth, and lock the doors and shut the windows in your **room** and bathroom when you go out at night. Don't leave your camera or your wallet on the **beach** while you go in for a swim, leave nothing in your **car**, and keep an eye on valuable objects when riding on a bus or *bemo* (often jam-packed) and during stopovers at bus stations. Keep them in a safe place (in a belt under your clothes or in a small bag always within reach) if you sleep on a **train**. Bags are often piled on top of buses, so lock yours with a little padlock. Such precautions can also spare you from having things stolen from your hotel room. Safes for depositing money, papers and other valuable goods are often available for clients. You might also entrust your things to the owner of your *losmen*. Listen to warnings from other travellers but don't become paranoid. Be particularly careful in **Kuta** (Bali), on the **Gili** Islands (Lombok), on the **Yogyakarta-Jakarta** (Java) train and on the island of **Nias** (Sumatra), favourite sites for thieves.

• Tipping/Gratuities

You will never be asked for a tip. Tipping is not a very widespread custom except in big hotels (doormen, porters) and in taxis and car parks in large cities. That doesn't mean it isn't appreciated. The 11% government tax often added onto the bill at tourist hotels and restaurants doesn't go to the staff, who usually earn miserable salaries. So some places increase the bill by another 10% for service. Leave an equivalent tip if this hasn't been added. As a rule, try to calculate the right sum so as not to leave a disproportionate tip.

• Units of Measurement

Indonesia has adopted the metric system and distances in this guide are given in kilometres. As a rule of thumb, one kilometre is five-eighths of a mile: 5 miles is therefore about 8 kilometres, 10 miles is about 16 kilometres and 20 miles is about 32 kilometres.

Consult the table below for other useful metric equivalents:

Degrees Celsius	35°	30°	25°	20°	15°	10°	5°	0°	-5°	-10°
Degrees Fahrenheit	95°	86°	77°	68°	59°	50°	41°	32°	23°	15°

1 centimetre (cm) = 0.4 inch
1 metre (m) = 3.3 feet
1 metre (m) = 1.09 yards
1 litre = 1.06 quart
1 litre = 0.22 gallon
1 kilogram (kg) = 2.2 pounds

• Weather forecasts

Weather bulletins are broadcast daily on television and given in local newspapers. You don't need to understand Indonesian: those little sun and cloud symbols covering the map of the islands speak for themselves.

LOOK AND LEARN

• General

BEHR Edward, *Indonesia: A Voyage through the Archipelago*, Archipelago Press, Singapore. Photographs by 45 of the world's best photographers.

BYFIELD Graham (paintings) & DARLING Diana (text), *Bali Sketchbook*, Archipelago Press, Singapore. Watercolours that capture the spirit of the island with accompanying text.

DALTON Bill & MULLER Kal (photographer), *Indonesia: The World's Largest Archipelago*, Passport Books, 1992.

MERRILLEES Scott, *Batavia in 19-Century Photographs*, Archipelago Press, Singapore. Jakarta seen through 19C photographs.

PICARD Michel, *Bali: Cultural Tourism and Touristic Culture*, Archipelago Press, Singapore.

VATIKIOTIS Michael (text), GERSTER G, HELMI R, LUERAS L, ROSSI G A (photography), *Over Indonesia*, Archipelago Press, Singapore. Aerial photographs with commentary.

• Indonesian Literature

BROWN I, DAVIS J (editors), *Di Serambi: On the verandah*. A bilingual anthology of modern Indonesian poetry, Cambridge University Press, 1995.

KARTINI Raden Ajeng, *Letters of a Javanese Princess*, University Press of America, 1985.

LUBIS Mochtar, *Twilight in Djakarta,* Oxford University Press, 1986.

PRAEMOEDYA Ananta Toer, *This Earth of Mankind; House of Glass; The Mute's Soliloquy: A Memoir*, Penguin.

LINGARD Jeanette (translator), *Diverse Lives: Contemporary Stories from Indonesia*, Oxford in Asia Paperbacks, 1996.

• Foreign Literature

BARLEY Nigel, **Not a Hazardous Sport**, Viking/Penguin. An entertaining book by anthropologist Barley.

BAUM Vicky, **A Tale from Bali**, Oxford in Asia. The "puputan" of 1906 and the Dutch take-over of Bali provide the backdrop for this portrayal of everyday life on the "island of the gods" in the early 20C.

CONRAD Joseph, **Lord Jim**, Bantam Classic, 1995. Conrad's adventure novel that takes place in the remote corners of Kalimantan; and **Almayer's Folly: A Story of an Eastern River** (The Cambridge edition of Conrad's first novel), 1994.

CORN Charles, **Distant Islands**, Viking 1991. Travels through Indonesia.

COVARRUBIAS Miguel, **Island of Bali**, Knopf, 1937. A classic with excellent insights into Balinese life and culture.

MULTATULI, **Max Havelaar, or the Coffee Auctions of the Dutch Trading Company**, Penguin, 1995. A chronicle of Dutch colonial exploitation in the 19C that created a considerable stir when it came out.

NAIPAUL VS, **Among the Believers**, Knopf, 1981.

O'HANLON Redmond, **In the Heart of Borneo**, Penguin, 1985.

• Nature

JEPSON Paul, **Birding Indonesia: A Birdwatcher's Guide to the World's largest Archipelago**, Periplus, 1997.

SMITH Holly S, **Adventuring in Indonesia: Exploring the Natural Areas of the Pacific's Ring of Fire**, Sierra Club Adventure Travel Guide, 1997.

STONE David (text), COMPOST Alain, AW Michael, SEVERNS Mike (Photography), **Biodiversity of Indonesia**, Archipelago Press, Singapore.

WARREN William (text), TETTONI LI (photography), **Tropical Flowers Of Indonesia**, Periplus, 1996.

WHITTEN Tony, SOERIAATMADJA, RE & AFIFF, SA, **The Ecology of Java and Bali**, Periplus, 1996.

• History, religion, society

EISEMAN Fred B, SUKARTHA IN (illustrator), **Bali: Sekala and Niskala: Essays on Religion, Ritual and Art**, Periplus, 1989.

FOX James J (editor) & ADAMS Marie Jeanne, **The Flow of Life: Essays on Eastern Indonesia**, (Harvard Studies in Cultural Anthropology, 2), 1980.

FOX James J, **Religion and Rituals**, Archipelago Press, Singapore.

GEERTZ Clifford, **Religion of Java**, University of Chicago Press, 1976. **The Interpretation of Culture**, Princeton University Press, 1980.

MIKSIC John, **Ancient History**, Archipelago Press, Singapore.

REID Anthony, **Early Modern History**, Archipelago Press, Singapore.

SCHWARZ Adam, **A Nation in Waiting: Indonesia in the 1990s**, Westview Press, 1994. **Inside Indonesian Society: Cultural Change in Java**, The Pepin Press, 1996.

• Architecture, arts and crafts

ACHJADI Judi (editor), **Batik: Spirit of Indonesia**, Archipelago Press.

CARPENTER Bruce, **Emilio Ambron: An Italian in Bali**, Archipelago Press.

DAVISON Julian, GRANQUIST Bruce, **Balinese Architecture**, Periplus, 2000.

DAWSON Barry, GILLOW J, **The Traditional Architecture of Indonesia**, Thames & Hudson, London, 1994.

FISCHER Joseph, **The Folk Art of Java**, Oxford University Press, 1994.

GITTINGER Mattiebelle, **Splendid Symbols: Textiles and Tradition in Indonesia**, Oxford University Press, 1979.

JESSUP Helen I, **Court Arts of Indonesia**, Abrams, 1990.

SOSROWARDOYO Tara, **Java Style**, Archipelago Press.

WIGGERS Frank, CARPENTER Bruce (eds.), **Mentawai Art**, Archipelago Press.

WIJAYA Made with DARLING Diana, **The Architecture of Bali**, Archipelago Press.

WIJAYA Made, **Tropical Garden Design,** Archipelago Press.

Pusaka: Art of Indonesia, Archipelago Press.

The Crafts of Malaysia, Archipelago Press.

Treasures of the National Museum, Jakarta, Archipelago Press.

● Cooking

OWEN Sri, **Indonesian Food and Cookery.**

VON HOLZEN Heinz, ARSANA Lother, **The Food of Bali**, Periplus, Singapore. A complete guide to Balinese cooking with beautiful illustrations. Von Holzen also conducts cooking classes at his Bumbu Bali restaurant (☎ 62/361 774 502; Fax 62/361 701 577; www.balifood.com).

VON HOLZEN Heinz, ARSANA Lother, **The Food of Indonesia**, Periplus, 1995. Mouth-watering recipes featuring the many flavours of the Spice Islands.

● Language

BARKER John, **Speaking Indonesian**, Apa, 1989. A language manual sold in bookstores on site.

McGlynn John, **Languages and Literature**, Archipelago Press, Singapore.

● Performing Arts

FOLEY Kathy (editor), **Essays on Southeast Asian Performing Arts: Local manifestations and Cross-Cultural Implications**, Paperback, 1993.

RAFFERTY Ellen, **Putu Wijaya in Performance: A Script and Study of Indonesian Theatre**, University of Wisconsin Madison, 1989.

SEDYAWATI Edi, **Performing Arts**, Archipelago Press, Singapore.

TENZER Michael, **Balinese Music**, Periplus, Singapore. An excellent introduction to Balinese music.

● Adventure, Sports

LUERAS Leonard, **Surfing Indonesia**, Periplus Action Guides.

MULLER Kal, **Underwater Indonesia: A Guide to the World's Greatest Diving**, Periplus Action Guides, 1993.

ROCK Tim, **Diving and Snorkeling Guide to Bali and the Komodo Region**, Paperback, 1996.

● Films and documentaries

NUGRUHO Garin, **Leaf on a Pillow (Daun di atas bantal)**, 1998. A touching film on poverty and street children in Yogyakarta.

The Year of Living Dangerously The film adaptation of a novel by CJ Koch dealing with the 1965 attempted coup in Java.

Art of Indonesia: Tales from the Shadow World, Public Media Inc, 1990.

The Search for Indonesia's most Secret Animals: A Video Safari, United American Video Inc, 1998.

Indonesia (Travel Preview Series), Education 2000, 1992.

Indonesia: Jeweled Archipelago, IVN Entertainment, 1996.

• Music

Java, Javanese Court Gamelan of Pura Pau Alaman, Yogyakarta, Elektra Nonesuch, Explorer Series. A wonderful CD for those who have been bewitched by the sounds of the gamelan (with chorus).

Music of Indonesia, 1-20, Smithsonian Folkways Series.

Music for the Gods: The Fahnestock South Sea Expedition, Indonesia, Rykodisc. A classic of ethnomusicology recorded in the 1940s.

Nonesuch, Ocora Radio France, Playa Sound and **Auvidis Unesco** have also produced a number of CDs.

• Maps

Several companies publish maps of the islands and major Indonesian cities, the most accurate being those put out by **Periplus** and **Nelles Verlag**. They can be found in travel bookstores in the West, but they can be bought much more cheaply in cities and tourist areas on site.

USEFUL WORDS AND EXPRESSIONS

All of the Indonesian words used in the text and on the maps can be found with their English translation on the inside cover at the back of the book. See also "Body language", p 74.

Although English is spoken in most tourist areas, knowing a few basic Indonesian words will greatly facilitate your negotiations, bargaining, travelling and, above all, your contact with the local population. Dictionaries and pocket language primers can be bought on site *(see "Language" section above). Bahasa Indonesia* is a gratifying language for beginners because it is quite easy to pronounce, and has no conjugations or major grammatical difficulties – at least when learning its basic elements. For more in-depth studies, you can take classes on the spot, particularly in Yogyakarta and Bali *(see "Making the most of…" sections for those destinations).*

One curious aspect of the language is its **plural** form created by doubling words (child: *anak*; children: *anak-anak*). Indonesians put a "2" after a singular word *(anak-2,* pronounced *"anak-dua")* for the sake of brevity. Although this written form has been officially abolished in favour of the doubled noun, it is commonly used in both written and spoken language.

Pronunciation

Indonesian uses the Latin alphabet and most of its letters are pronounced like English. Spelling is phonetic as a rule, but with the following tips you will find it easier to make yourself understood. As the system of spelling has changed four times over the past hundred years, it is common to see the same word spelled several different ways, especially on some signs and maps; but pronunciation has remain virtually unchanged.

ai   is pronounced like a long "i" + a long "e" when followed by a consonant, and like a long "i" when it comes at the end of a word

au   is pronounced "ow" as in "owl"

c   "ch" (as in "church")

e	depending on where it comes in the word: like the "é" in "touché"; like "the" (schwa); and like a short "e" (bet)
g	hard (as in "guard")
h	usually soft in the middle of a word; hard between two like vowels ("mahal", expensive); almost silent at the beginning or end of a word
j	as in "judge"
k	unvoiced stop at the end of a word, otherwise like "kite"
kh	like "kite" but harder
ng	soft (as in "sing")
ngg	always hard (as in "mango")
p	pronounced almost like an "f"
r	rolled, as in Spanish or Italian
u	long as in "clue"

Numbers

zero	kosong	fourteen	empat belas
(one/and a half)	setengah	twenty	dua puluh
one	satu	twenty-one	dua puluh satu
two	dua	thirty	tiga puluh
three	tiga	fourty	empat puluh
four	empat	one hundred	seratus
five	lima	two hundred	dua ratus
six	enam	three hundred	tiga ratus
seven	tujuh	one thousand	seribu
eight	delapan	two thousand	dua ribu
nine	sembilan	ten thousand	sepuluh ribu
ten	sepuluh	one hundred thousand	seratus ribu
eleven	sebelas	one million	satu juta/sejuta
twelve	dua belas	ten million	sepuluh juta
thirteen	tiga belas		

Common expressions

hello (mornings until about 11am)	selamat pagi
hello (11am to 3pm)	selamat siang
hello (3pm to nightfall)	selamat sore
good evening (when it's dark)	selamat malam
good night	selamat tidur
welcome	selamat datang
good bye, bon voyage (to someone leaving)	selamat jalan
good bye, bon voyage (when you are leaving)	selamat tinggal
see you soon	sampai jumpa lagi
how's it's going (what's new?)	apa kabar?
fine/well!	kabar baik! baik baik!
please (asking for something politely)	tolong
thank you (very much)	terima kasih (banyak)
you're welcome/don't mention it	sama-sama/kembali
please (have a seat)!	silakan (duduk)!
excuse me! (making a request)	permisi!
sorry! (excusing yourself)	ma'af!

Basic conversation

yes	ya
no, not (after a verb or adjective)	tidak
there is/is there?/there isn't	ada/ada?/tidak ada
no problem!	tidak apa-apa/tidak ada masalah/bukan masalah!
Do you speak Indonesian?	bisa bahasa indonesia?
Yes, a bit	ya, bisa sedikit
I don't understand	(saya) tidak mengerti

112

You speak Indonesian quite well	sudah pintar/lancar bahasa indonesia		
What is your name?	namanya siapa?/siapa nama anda?		
My name is	nama saya...		
Where are you going?	mau ke mana?		
I'm taking a walk	jalan-jalan saja		
I'm going to Bali	(saya) mau ke Bali		
I'm getting some fresh air	makan angin		
Where are you from?/	dari mana? /		
what country (origin, nationality)	asal(nya) dari mana?		
from Australia/I'm Australian	dari Australi/saya orang Australi		
from Canada/I'm Canadian	dari Kanada/saya orang Kanada		
from the UK/I'm British	dari Inggeris/saya orang Inggeris		
from the US/I'm American	dari Amerika/saya orang Amerika		
I'm from the Toraja region	dari tana Toraja		
Where are you staying? (what hotel)	dimana tinggal/menginap?		
How old are you?	umur(nya) berapa?		
Are you married?	sudah kawin/nikah?		
Do you have children?	sudah punya anak?		
Mrs/mother, mum	ibu, bu, ibu		
Mr/father, dad	bapak, pak, bapak		
Husband	suami		
Wife	isteri		
Boy/girlfriend/fiancé(e)	pacar		
Friend	teman		
Child	anak		
person, human being	orang		
(are you) all alone?	sendiri/sendirian?		
What is your religion?	anda agama apa?		

Questions

what?	apa?	how much?	berapa?
who?	siapa?	where?	(di) mana?
why?	kenapa?	when?	kapan?
how?	bagaimana?		

Key words

but	tapi, tetapi	only	cuma, saja
or	atau	again	lagi
and	dan	more	lebih (banyak)
because	karena	very	sekali
this	ini	much	banyak
that	itu	too much	terlalu
with	dengan, sama, pakai	a (little) bit	sedikit
without	tanpa	less, not enough	kurang
for	untuk	all	semua
also, likewise	juga	perhaps	mungkin

Useful verbs

come in	masuk	stay, live	tinggal
go out	keluar	ask	tanya/minta
		(for information/the bill)	
understand	mengerti	lose	hilang
know	tahu	see, look at	lihat
can/be able	bisa	look for	cari
may, have permission	boleh	try	coba
have, possess/	punya	wash, bathe	mandi
belong to		work	kerja
want	mau	study	belajar
pay	bayar	like (to be willing/	suka/cinta
wait for	tunggu	love)	

Common adjectives

good, fine,	bagus, baik	slow	pelan, lambat
good-looking (thing)		finished, gone	habis
good-looking (man)	gantang, gagah	same, equal/with	sama
beautiful (woman)	cantik	mixed	campur
ugly, bad	jelek	normal, common	biasa
expensive	mahal	full	penuh
inexpensive	murah	empty, vacant	kosong
new/just now	baru	occupied	sibuk
old (thing)	lama	lively, noisy	ramai
old (person)	tua	calm, quiet	sepi
young	muda	forbidden	dilarang
big	besar	difficult, complicated	susah, sulit,
small	kecil		sukar
simple, easy	mudah,		gampang
hot	panas	tired	capek
cold	dingin	starving (hungry)	lapar
fast, quick	cepat	thirsty	haus

Time

flexible time	jam karet	evening, night	malam
now	sekarang	(from nightfall)	
in a minute	sebentar	late	terlambat
first, before (once)	dulu	today	hari ini
already	sudah	tomorrow	besok
not yet	belum	the day after tomorrow	lusa
how long	berapa lama	yesterday	kemarin
long , a long time	lama	day	hari
minute	menit	week	minggu
hour	jam	month	bulan
what time is it?	jam berapa sekarang?	year	tahun
It's 3 o'clock	jam tiga	date	tanggal
morning (5-7am)	pagi-pagi	what day (of the week)	ini hari apa?
morning (7-11am)	pagi	is it?	
noon (11am-3pm)	siang	what is the date?	hari ini
afternoon (3-7pm)	sore		tanggal
			berapa?

Days of the week

Monday	(hari) senin	Friday	(hari) jumat
Tuesday	(hari) selasa	Saturday	(hari) sabtu
Wednesday	(hari) rabu	Sunday	(hari) minggu
Thursday	(hari) kamis	Holiday	hari raya

Weather

sun	matahari	star	bintang
rain	hujan	moon	bulan
wind	angin		

Directions

at, on, in	di	outside	di luar
to (direction)	ke	right	kanan
here	(di) sini	left	kiri
over there	(di) sana, (di) situ	in front of	di depan
on (top of), over	di atas	behind	di belakang
under, down	di bawah	straight, continue	terus
next to	di sebelah	north	utara
near	dekat	south	selatan
far	jauh	east	timur
inside	di dalam	west	barat

Public Transport

(by) bus (at night)	(naik) bis (malam)
(by) ferry	(naik) kapal
(by) boat	(naik) perahu
(by) plane	(naik) pesawat terbang
(by) train	(naik) kereta api
(by) car	(naik) mobil
(on a) motorcycle/ moped	(naik) sepeda motor/ bebek
(on a) bicycle	(naik) sepeda
rent	sewa
with driver	pakai sopir
taxi	taksi
seat	tempat duduk

leave, go	pergi
come back, return	kembali
go up	naik
go down	turun
from ... to ...	dari... ke...
until/arrive	sampai
direct	langsung
bus station	terminal (bis)
port	(pe)labuhan
airport	lapangan terbang
train station	setasiun (kereta api)
ticket	karcis
fuel	bensin

Visiting

go for a walk	jalan-jalan
go on foot	jalan kaki
city (centre)	(pusat) kota
village	desa/kampung
street, (main) road	jalan (raya)
alley	gang
house	rumah
school	sekolah
beach	pantai
sea	laut
lake	danau
island	pulau
river	sungai
cave	gua
mountain/volcano	gunung/gunung api
forest, jungle	hutan
tourist office	dinas/kantor pariwisata
tourist site	obyek wisata
museum	museum
ceremony	upacara

temple	pura (in Bali)/ candi (in Java)
mosque	mesjid
church	gereja
palace	kraton (in Java)/ puri (in Bali)
park	taman
garden (botanical/ zoological)	kebun (raya/binatang)
nature reserve	cagar alam
waterfall	air terjun
hot springs	air panas
entrance	masuk
exit	keluar
open	buka
closed	tutup
ticket	karcis
cinema	bioskop
dance	tarian

Hotel

room	kamar
passport	paspor
key	kunci
bathroom	kamar mandi
shower, bath, have a wash	mandi
hot/cold water	air panas/dingin
toilet	kamar kecil, WC
toilet paper	kertas WC
ladies'/men's toilet	wanita/pria
woman/man	perumpuan/laki-laki
sleep	tidur
bed	tempat tidur

sheet	seprei
blanket	selimut
soap	sabun
bath towel	handuk
door	pintu
window	jendela
fan	fan/kipas angin
air conditioning	AC
lamp	lampu
mosquito	nyamuk
breakfast	sarapan (pagi)
pool	kolam renang
wash, clean	cuci, bersihkan

Restaurant

eat, may we eat?	makan, bisa makan?
drink	minum
waiter!/miss!	Mas!/Mbak!
there's none left	(sudah) habis
enough	cukup
full	kenyang

seafood	makanan laut
prawns	udang
lobster/crayfish	lobster
squid, cuttlefish	cumi-cumi
crab	kepiting
eggs	telur

good, pleasant/ delicious, tasty	enak/sedap	soup	sop, soto, kuah
bill	minta bon	small kebabs	sate
glass	gelas	noodle soup with meatballs	mie bakso
plate	piring		
knife	pisau	grilled	bakar
fork	garpu	fried, sautéed	goreng
spoon	sendok	boiled	rebus
food	makanan	ice-cream	es krim
menu	daftar makan	cake	kue
bread	roti	spicy	pedas
rice	nasi	soy sauce	kecap
noodles	mee/mie	(savoury/sweet)	(asin/manis)
potato	kentang	chilli	lombok, cabe
vegetables	sayur	chilli sauce	sambal
fruit	buah	sweet	manis
banana	pisang	salt	garam
pineapple	nanas	butter	mentega
papaya	papaya	sugar	gula
jackfruit	nangka	sweets	gula-gula
mango	mangga	drinks	minuman
orange	jeruk manis	water (bottled)	air
lemon	jeruk nipis		(botol/Aqua)
peanuts	kacang	black coffee with sugar	kopi
coconut (young)	kelapa (muda)	(bitter/with milk)	(pahit/susu)
tofu (soybean curd)	tahu	meat	daging
soy seed cake	tempe	without sugar	tanpa gula
chicken	ayam	tea	teh
pork	babi	milk	susu
beef	sapi	milk chocolate	susu coklat
goat, mutton	kambing	orange juice	es jeruk
duck	bebek	beer	bir
fish	ikan	wine (red/white)	anggur (merah/putih)

Shopping

shop, boutique	toko	change (small notes)	uang kecil
market	pasar	silver	perak
how much does this cost?	berapa harganya?	gold	mas
		wood	kayu
price (normal, usual)	harga (biasa)	leather	kulit
it's too expensive	terlalu mahal	fabric	kain
buy	beli	clothes	baju, pakaian
bargain	tawar	shoes	sepatu
I'm just looking	lihat-lihat saja	mask	topeng
for a quick look	cuci mata	sculpture	ukiran
can you bring the price down a bit?	bisa kurang sedikit?	painting	lukisan
		cigarettes	rokok
I'm losing out	saya rugi	roll of film	film

Colours

black	hitam	green	hijau
white	putih	blue	biru
red	merah	yellow	kuning

Post Office

post office	kantor pos	parcel	paket
stamp	perangko	pen	pen
envelope	amplop	address	alamat
post card	kartu pos	send	kirim
letter	surat	telegram	telgram

Telephone

telephone office	kantor telpon, Wartel, Telkom	phone that takes cards	telpon kartu
local/inter-city/	lokal/interlokal/	telephone card	kartu telpon
international	luar negeri	telephone number	nomor telpon

Banking

bank	bank	change	tukar
money	uang	exchange rate	kurs

Health

hospital	rumah sakit	head	kepala
doctor	dokter	stomach	perut
dentist	dokter gigi	feet, legs	kaki
ill/unwell	sakit	arms	lengan
emergency	darurat	eye	mata
ambulance	ambulans	skin	kulit
pharmacy	apotik	teeth	gigi
medicine	obat	hair	rambut

Police

police	polisi	thief	pencuri

Tadi Oary.
Terima Kasi

Exploring Indonesia

Sumatra,
Lake Maninjau

On the shores of Lake Toba

SUMATRA

What name can equal that of Sumatra to evoke a land of distant otherness, harbours at the end of the world and shadowy jungles that are home to unknown peoples? Other days, other ways, but modern Sumatra can still raise its distinctive shiver. It is a wild land, where nature enthusiasts can feel truly at home. With its area of 473 606sqkm, this enormous island (the fifth largest in the world) has an infinite variety of landscapes dominated by the line of a gigantic dorsal ridge, the **Barisan Mountains** that form a vertiginous rocky cliff running along most of the west coast. Smoking **volcanoes** stand out along its spine, some of them reaching heights of over 3 000m (Gunung Leuser and Gunung Kerinci). **Mountain lakes** lie hidden in their folds like stately mirrors that reflect the sky, while fertile valleys ripple with the green shelves of the **rice fields**. The mountain slopes are clad in exuberant **forests** that are steadily diminishing under the axe and the chainsaw. The forests are still home to the great apes and the Sumatra tiger, tapirs and elephants, hornbills and flying lizards. To the east, the slopes of the Barisan mountains plunge without any transitional stage onto a broad plain with **plantations** of hevea trees, coffee and tobacco stretching out as far as the sea. Closer to the Straits of Malacca, the rivers that irrigate the plain spread out into **marshy deltas** lying over a subsoil that is rich in oil. On the west, a narrow strip of alluvial soil separates the flanks of the Barisans from the Indian Ocean. It is from here that, disregarding the turbulent waters, boats set out for the **Mentawai Archipelago**, a natural barrier that stretches out along about a hundred kilometres of the coastline. As well as their **corals**, these islands with their harsh beauty – covering the area from the warlike Nias to the "primitive" Siberut have an aura of mystery. The adventure of Sumatra is also the discovery of its peoples: more than ten ethnic groups live together on the island, in a constellation of distinct and unique cultures. Yet they have one point in common: the wealth of their ancestral tradition, which will leave you with memories as substantial as the jungle.

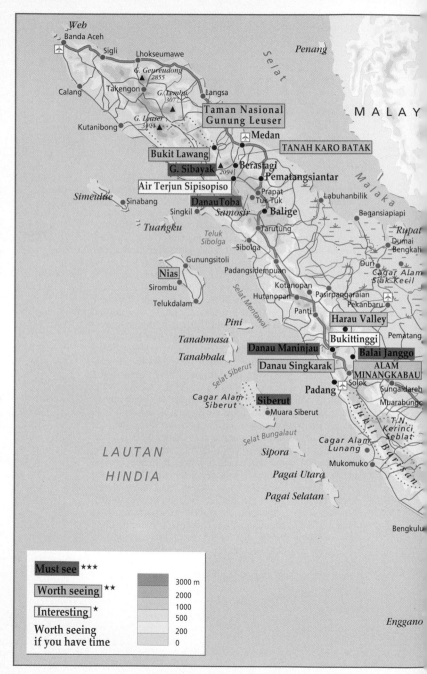

Web
Banda Aceh
Sigli
Lhokseumawe
Penang
G. Geureudong 2855
Takengon
Calang
G. Lembu 3072
Langsa
G. Leuser 3404
Kutanibong
Taman Nasional Gunung Leuser
MALAY
Medan
Bukit Lawang
TANAH KARO BATAK
G. Sibayak
Berastagi 2094
Pematangsiantar
Simeulue
Sinabang
Air Terjun Sipisopiso
Prapat
Labuhanbilik
Tuk Tuk
DanauToba
Samosir
Bagansiapiapi
Singkil
Balige
Rupat
Tarutung
Dumai
Teluk Sibolga
Bengkali
Tuangku
Sibolga
Duri
Cagar Alam Siak Kecil
Gunungsitoli
Padangsidempuan
Nias
Kotanopan
Sirombu
Hutanopan
Pasirpangaraian
Pekanbaru
Telukdalam
Panti
Pini
Harau Valley
Tanahmasa
Bukittinggi
Pematang
Tanahbala
Danau Maninjau
Balai Janggo
Danau Singkarak
ALAM MINANGKABAU
Cagar Alam Siberut
Siberut
Padang
Solok
Sungaidareh
Muara Siberut
Muarabungo
LAUTAN
HINDIA
Selat Siberut
T.N. Kerinci Seblat
Selat Bungalaut
Cagar Alam Lunang
Sipora
Lunang
Mukomuko
Pagai Utara
Pagai Selatan
Bengkulu
Enggano

Selat Malaka
Selat Mentawai

Must see ***
Worth seeing **
Interesting *
Worth seeing if you have time

3000 m
2000
1000
500
200
0

Record humidity levels

Sumatra's climate is just as full of contrasts as its other features: stifling heat on the coast (generally around 30°C) and welcome coolness in the mountains, with nights that are genuinely cold near the lakes. However, crossed as it is by the equator, Sumatra makes no distinction between dry and wet seasons. In simple terms, it rains more or less all the year round! The average rainfall is close to the record in the west of the island, with between 4 000 and 6 000mm of rain each year. During the driest months (June to August), the heavy clouds hold off in the morning but the heavens open at the end of the day.

At the crossroads of history

Few traces of Sumatra's ancient history have survived the damp climate. Only the bronze drums that have been discovered in the south reveal the presence of the **Dongson** civilisation that developed in southeast continental Asia around the 5C BC (*see p 31*). In a single leap, history moves on to the first millennium of the modern era, with Indian influences and the appearance of the first kingdoms. The traces that have survived the centuries show reigns that were as dazzling as they were short.

The first kings of "the golden isle"

Beginning in the 7C, the Buddhist **Srivijaya** kingdom flourished in the area of the modern Palembang. The name of "the golden island" was known at this time from the Indian Ocean to the Pacific. Taking advantage of its strategic location, the kingdom effectively based its power on trade in textiles, spices and rhinoceros horn. It retained the monopoly in these goods until the year 1000, when it was brutally crushed and eliminated by an Indian fleet. Its collapse left the field open to the expansion of the modern province of Jambi, where the state of **Malayu** prospered in the 12 and 13C. This success was not welcomed by the Javanese kingdom of Singosari: war broke out in 1278, to be settled with the abduction of a Malayu princess who married the Javanese king and gave him a son **Adityavarman**. As an adult the latter returned to the land of his mother's birth and settled in a region that was particularly rich in gold, the modern Minangkabau, where he sought to set up a royal model based on that in Java.

Islam and trade

In the 13C, however, traders from Persia and India began to spread their religion, which first took hold on the northeast coast of the island. Sumatra then became the springboard for Islam, enabling it to expand towards Malaya and the northern coasts of Java. In the 16C all Sumatra's large ports – one of which, **Samudra**, in the Pasai estuary, was to give the island its name – followed Muslim customs, as did the mountainous regions of the Minangkabau. The young coastal states built their fortunes on a spice, **pepper**, which was grown in the interior of their lands and sold at enormous prices. Sumatra became recognised as the leading supplier of pepper to distant China (around 1500).

The pepper war

In the early 16C the **Straits of Malacca** became a maritime crossroads of world significance, and were highly coveted, particularly by the Portuguese who seized them in 1511. As Catholics, the Portuguese intended to take over the Muslim **Aceh**, the most powerful port of the area, at the northern end of Sumatra. A vain hope: the sultanate increased its influence and was soon supplying half the pepper in Europe.

This became a golden age, marked by the reign of the "New Alexander", Sultan **Iskandar Muda** (1607-36), whose ostentatious court ceremonies brought him renown in the Western world. His territory extended from Padang to the future Singapore. Late in his life, however, madness overtook him, and the **decline** of Aceh accelerated with the **Dutch** capture of Malacca in 1641. Batavia (Jakarta) became the new centre of the spice route, and Aceh's trade passed into European hands.

The colonial era

In 1663 the Dutch captured Padang, but it was not until 1824 that they brought Sumatra fully under their control, taking it from the English and giving them Malaya in exchange. This also meant that the government in Batavia inherited the struggle with the **Padri**, radical Muslims who were waging a holy war in the Minang lands.

Nonetheless, in the late 19C, the Dutch tobacco **plantations** were flourishing, as were new products – which are still grown in the plain of Medan – such as rubber (introduced in 1877) and palm oil (after 1910).

It was also in the second half of the 19C that Lutheran **missions** – Dutch and above all German – had their earliest successes, among the Batak of northern Sumatra and then on the neighbouring island of Nias, which was conquered in 1890.

The Padri
Led by Imam Bonjol and his generals, "the eight tigers", the Padri put Minang to fire and the sword in the 19C. On their return from Mecca (taking their name from the port of their arrival, Padri in North Sumatra), these radical Muslims undertook to impose the orthodox practice of Islam on the population. The Dutch took a hand in matters, however, taking advantage of the situation to seize military control of the region. The war, which broke out in 1803, ended with the capture of the Imam in 1837, in his stronghold of Bonjol (West Sumatra). Since then Bonjol has become a national hero, symbol of the struggle, against colonialism, for independence.

Aceh, the enduring stronghold

From the time of the Dutch arrival, Aceh sought its **independence**: the old commercial power rejected commercial contracts imposed by the masters in Batavia. The consequence was a series of wars between 1873 and 1903. Aceh was defeated but did not surrender. Its determination to achieve independence was copied and inspired other resistance movements on the island, including that of the sultan of Jambi, on the east coast (1906) and of the Batak priest-king **Sisingamangaraja**, in the north (1907). These rebellions were crushed, however, and the Dutch forces gradually seized all parts of Sumatra, bringing the island under **unified rule** in 1910.

Spearheading national identity

The first Indonesian nationalist movements burst onto the scene a few years later. As in Java, the **Sarekat Islam**, the Muslim Union founded in 1912, stirred up mass revolts across the island. Benefiting from recent access to Dutch advanced education, students set up their first societies: **The Sumatra League of Youth** in 1917, and **The Organisation of Batak Students** in the 1920s. They sought independence for the archipelago and supported the Minangkabau **Mohammed Hatta**, Sumatra's most famous intellectual, who travelled to the Netherlands to plead the cause of Indonesia and later became vice-president at Sukarno's side. Lastly, the island's main language, **Malay**, was adopted as part of the project for a national language (Bahasa Indonesia), in 1939.

At the crossroads of history

Sumatra in revolt

When the **Japanese forces** invaded Sumatra in 1942 they found support among the nationalist factions, which were ready to fight against the colonial allies. On the departure of the Japanese, after Hiroshima, these armed groups embarked on what was sometimes a bloody struggle for power with the Muslim traditionalists. In 1945, however, with the proclamation of **independence**, a common cause united the population: insurrection against Jakarta and its centralising socialism. In 1958 Toba Batak and Minangkabau combined to form a rival government, the **PRRI** (Revolutionary Government of the Republic of Indonesia). Bukittinggi claimed the status of revolutionary capital but was silenced with bombing from Java. In the north Aceh rejected its attachment to the province of North Sumatra, populated by Christian Bataks. The peace of 1959 granted it a degree of independence by promoting it to the status of a special autonomous district, **Banda Aceh**.

Discontent in regional Sumatra did not diminish until the time of Suharto's presidency, beginning in 1966, and his government, which favoured economic liberalism. Pacification of the island next enabled progress in education, health and also communications that included the **Trans Sumatra** – a 2 500km road linking all the island provinces from north to south.

Treasure island

Sumatra has been generously endowed with **fertile soil** by its volcanoes. This resource attracted European planters in 1860. **Tobacco** was rapidly followed by hevea trees **(rubber)**, **sisal** (its leaves are used in textiles), **tea**, **pepper** and **oil palms**. By the turn of the century more than a million hectares had been cleared and cultivated along the *Oostkust* ("the east coast", corresponding to the present-day plain of Medan). These plantations enjoyed a second expansion after a serious crisis that was created by a wave of nationalisations between 1958 and 1965. **Rice** naturally completes the range of food crops. It is grown throughout the year, feeds the whole population and even generates income through export trade.

The subsoil also has its treasures: **oil**, **coal**, **tin** and **natural gas** have formed the basis of industry since the 1950s. The future of Sumatra, however, is expressed nowadays in ecological terms. Despite the creation of large nature reserves, the forests of Sumatra, so tempting for industry, are as threatened as those in Amazonia.

Rafflesia, the giant flower

The forests of Sumatra are home to the largest flower in the world: rafflesia ("Rafflesia Arnoldii"). A parasite flower, it has no stem, leaves nor roots, only a network of filaments, which it deploys inside the climbing liana that it colonises. It produces a series of buds that unfold once a year into giant purple flowers, a metre in diameter. This flower is as magnificent as it is astonishing – its petals are as hard as wood. It gives off a revolting smell, which has earned it the local name of "carrion flower" ("bunga bangkai"), and attracts pollinating insects.

The endangered forest

According to the World Wildlife Fund, 5 million hectares of equatorial forest vanished in Sumatra in 1997 alone. The origins of these ravages lie in forest fires, the timber industry and its derivatives (resins transformed into incense), and also the expansion of the plantations. Since the 1980s the government has been trying to preserve what remains of this biological treasure through the creation of national parks. The forest is home to an outstanding range of flora (insectivorous pitcher plants, **rafflesia**, etc) and an equally unique range of fauna: nearly 200 species of mammal, including endemic primates (**orang-utan**, **gibbon**, the **joja** of Siberut), as well as tapir, wild pigs, russet bats, 600 species of birds, snakes and rare butterflies. The island's two natural parks, Gunung Leuser in the north and Kerinci-Seblat in the south, provide shelter for species that are threatened with extinction, such as the Sumatra **rhinoceros** (the smallest of the animal's five species), tiger and elephant. The latter are being pushed back into an ever-diminishing area, forcing them to invade agricultural land. Since 1985 the Way Elephant Kambas Reserve (in the province of Lampung) has opened a centre to renew the tradition of training, the only way of channelling the elephants' aggressions while using its working strength. And at Bukit Lawang (northern Sumatra), a rehabilitation centre for orang-utans is reintroducing the apes, which have lived in captivity, to their natural environment. However, there is silence from Siberut and forest clearing continues.

A full range of faces

The thousand faces of Sumatra are a physical expression of all the influences that have landed on its shores, beginning with **Islam**. Introduced in the 16C, the faith of the Persian traders has never left the island. Since then Sumatra has become one of Indonesia's most Muslim regions. Three of the four main ethnic groups that make up its population of **42 million** refer to the Koran as their religious authority. This applies to the **Malays** (a quarter of the population), who crossed the Straits of Malacca with the expansion of trade and now live mainly in eastern Sumatra. The second largest group, the 6 million **Minangkabau**, lives in the wealthy province of West Sumatra. The Minangkabau are also Muslim, but their belief is blended with an ancestral **matrilineal** tradition. In the far north the 4 million **Acehnese** also display a strong individual identity, combining Islam with claims of autonomy which regularly result in violent confrontations with the army. Lastly, Sumatra's fourth major ethnic group is that of the **Batak**, who probably arrived from Borneo in the 1C BC. They settled in the highlands of North Sumatra, around the centre of their adopted homeland, Lake Toba. Most embraced the Christian religion of the Protestant and Catholic missionaries in the late 19C, and today form the **leading Christian community** in Indonesia. The two exceptions to this are the Batak Mandailing and the Angkola (in the south of the region), two sub-groups that converted to the Islam of the neighbouring Minangkabau in the 19C.

A profusion of minorities complement these major cultural groups. The **Buddhist Chinese,** who provided the labour for the 19C mines and plantations, take part in the business life concentrated in Medan and Padang, major urban centres whose frantic activity has also attracted **Javanese** immigrants. The **Indians** of the Tamil Nadu have moved from the elevated rank of *shahbandar* – managers of the commercial trading centres of the 17C – to that of general workmen in the urban world (*becak* drivers, street vendors, etc). Sumatra is also the home of very ancient peoples whose customs have remained virtually unchanged since the earliest days of mankind. This is the case with the inhabitants of the island of **Nias**, where neither church nor mosque has managed to oust **ancestor worship**. The animist **Mentawai** of Siberut continue with their **Shamanism**. The strange **Kubu**, agricultural **nomads** in the province of Jambi, avoid all contact with the modern world. Few kilometres separate these groups but their language, domestic housing and style of dress have nothing in common, which adds to the pleasure and interest of the visitor.

A full range of faces

Making the most of Sumatra

Making the most of Sumatra

COMING AND GOING

By air – If your visit is limited to the island of Sumatra, remember that Singapore and Malaysia are much closer than any other city in the archipelago. Medan is the main point of arrival (daily flights with Malaysia Airlines, Garuda and Silk Air to and from Penang, Kuala Lumpur and Singapore, regular flights from Bangkok). Padang, the capital of West Sumatra, is linked to Kuala Lumpur by daily flights (with Pelangi and Sempati) and to Singapore three times a week (Silk Air). Both cities have daily flights to Jakarta and the provincial capitals of Sumatra. Pekanbaru has two flights weekly to Singapore (Merpati) and Malacca (Pelangi).

By sea – Hydrofoils from Penang (Malaysia) take 5 hours to cross the Straits of Malacca to Belawan, the port for Medan, (daily except Sundays). In the opposite direction, there are daily departures except Mondays. From Java two **PELNI** boats make the crossing between Tanjung Priok (the port for Jakarta) and Medan (departures Mondays, 1pm, crossing time: 50hr). The **PELNI** steamer "Kerinci" does the Jakarta-Padang-Sibolga route, along the west coast, departing alternative Fridays at 1pm; in the Sibolba-Padang-Jakarta direction, departure is on alternative Saturdays (travelling time, 2 days). Economy class costs about Rp300 000 fully inclusive of meals, drinks and comfortable cabin). Ferries between Merak (West Java, access by coach from Jakarta) and Bakauheni (in the south of the province of Lampung, departure point for the Trans Sumatra road). From here, coaches depart all day for the major cities in Sumatra.

By coach – The **ANS** company ("Aman-Nyaman-Sejuk", which promises "Safety-comfort-coolness") offers coach + ferry tickets between Sumatra and Java. It links Jakarta with Padang in 30 hours.

GETTING AROUND SUMATRA

By air – From Medan: flights to the capitals of all the provinces in Sumatra. With **Merpati** and **Sempati**: Banda Aceh, Bengkulu, Jambi, Padang, Palembang and Pekanbaru. With **Bouraq**: Palembang. With **Garuda**: Bandar Lampung, Bengkulu, Jambi, Padang, Palembang and Pekanbaru. With **SMAC**: daily flights between Medan and Gunung Sitoli (Nias).

By coach – Several companies offer a daily service on the Trans-Sumatra road. The best, from the point of view of comfort and air-conditioning, is **ANS**. Coaches generally leave on time, but the duration of the journey is variable. For these journeys on the Trans Sumatra tickets should be bought at the departure coach-station no later than the previous day. (In Medan some travel agents may make a charge for booking your ticket.) The main stopping points along the Trans-Sumatra are Bakauheni (Sumatra-Java ferry port), Bandar Lampung, Muaraenim (South Sumatra), Tebingtinggi, Bangko, Muarabungo (Jambi), Padangpanjang, Bukittinggi (West Sumatra), Prapat, Pematangsiantar, Medan (North Sumatra) and Aceh (Banda Aceh).

By minibus – Colt or bemo. Varying in standards of comfort (with or without air-conditioning), they go everywhere. Hail them, bargain with them, and ask them to drop you off where you wish. The most practical solution is to charter one as a group (average capacity, 7 places) and organise your own route. You will usually have to pay the set price, plus fuel and the driver. If you are not planning a round trip, remember that you will have to pay for the empty return trip to the departure point.

By car – Renting a car is the most expensive option, but the most interesting for excursions or day trips. You will only be able to hire a car with a driver, which – in view of the driving conditions – is the best choice.

C. Bourzat

The village of Ambarita in the Toba Batak region

MEDAN
Capital of North Sumatra Province – Map p 131
Pop 2 000 000 (11 000 000 including outer areas) – Hot climate

Not to be missed
Try the local drink, "bandrek",
a spice-flavoured spirit with a powerful cheering effect.
And remember...
Avoid exploring on foot in the middle of the day
when the heat and pollution reach maximum levels.

The Medan metropolis, Indonesia's second largest port and the gateway to North Sumatra, lives up to its name, "battlefield". The name takes on its full meaning when, at the end of the day, the city centre resounds with the echoes of car horns and ailing engines. At first sight the galloping modernism of the centre seems to have entirely overwhelmed it, with towers springing up everywhere – offices, banks and commercial centres. Fortunately the city is still a blend of different eras, revealing here and there – for those who take the time to seek them out – picturesque images of the Medan of older times. A *sate* seller, for instance, peacefully pushing his old cart along the tarmac among the four-wheel drive cars, the ultimate sign of achievement for businessmen.

Yet while some quarters display true chic with their tree-lined avenues of old colonial houses, for the modern traveller Medan is more a departure point than a destination in itself. A few hours will be enough for the history enthusiast to cover the past of **Deli**, the old name of the city under which the whole region developed in the shadow of Aceh. "Deli" comes from Delhi, showing how its monarchs wished to incorporate all the power of the sultans of 12C Muslim India.

The "Battlefield"
The name Medan sustains the memory of the strong rivalry that set the sultanate of Deli against the kingdom of Aceh in the 16C. The heart of the struggle was the prized **pepper trade**. Yet the inhabitants of Medan set aside these economic considerations in favour of a legend: the story of the **"green princess"**, a young Medan girl whose outstanding beauty impressed the Sultan of Aceh. Under cover of a serenade, he despatched his troops against the city and abducted the princess. Sadly, an invincible dragon seized her in turn and made her disappear for good. From one dragon to another! In the 19C Medan was once again the scene of a "battlefield", this time for the Dutch investors who came to develop **tobacco plantations**. The work that they created together with the later discovery of **oil**, have made Medan modern Sumatra's most heavily populated area: a conurbation of 11 million people, a vast ethnic melting pot made up of Bataks, Malays and Javanese, as well as Chinese and Indians. So many faces and characters that become unconsciously engraved on the visitor's memory.

Tour of the city
Allow a full half-day. Start southeast of the city centre.

Historic walk
Cool and calm, the **Maimoun Palace**＊ (Istana Maimoun) (D4) is a good departure point for understanding Medan. This self-important house with its eclectic architectural style, part Malay, and part Victorian, was built in 1888 by Sultan Mohammet El

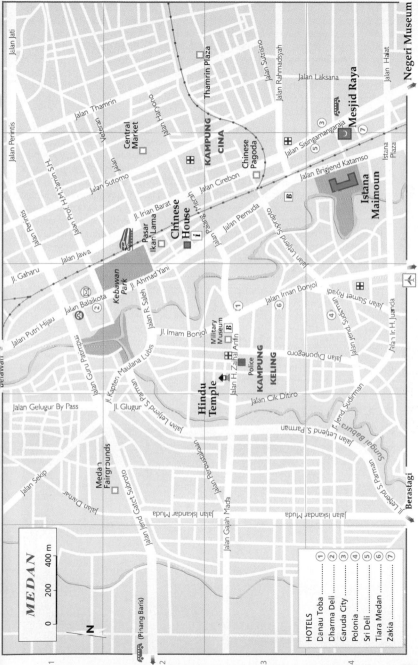

MEDAN

0 200 400 m

N

(Pinang Baris)

Jalan Jati
Jalan Perintis
Jalan Perintis
Jl. Gaharu
Jalari Putri Hijau
Belawan
Jalan Guru Patimpus
Jalan Jend Gatot Subroto
Jalan Sekip
Jalan Danar
Jl. Kapter Maulana Lubis
Jalan Gelugur By Pass
Jl. Glugur
Jalan Perpustakaan
Jalan Gajah Mada
Jalan Iskandar Muda
Jalan Iskandar Muda
Jalan Thamrin
Jalan Prof. H.M. Yamin S.H.
Jalan Sutomo
Jalan Jawa
Jalan Balaikota
Jalan R. Saleh
Jalan Ahmad Yani
Jl. Imam Bonjol
Jl. Irian Barat
Jalan Harjono
Veteran
Jalan Paang Merah
Jalan Cirebon
Jalan Brigjend Katamso
Jalan Pemuda
Jalan Letjend Suprapto
Jalan Letjend S. Parman
Jalan Letjend S. Parman
Sungai Babura
Jalan Cik Ditiro
Jalan Diponegoro
Jalan Irnan Bonjol
Jalan Slamet Riyadi
Jalan Jend. Sudirman
Jalan Ir. H. Juanda
Jl. Letjend S. Parman
Jalan Sutrisno
Jalan Rahmadsyah
Jalan Laksana
Jalan Halat
Jalan Sisingamangaraja
Jalan H. Zainul Arifin

Thamrin Plaza
Central Market
KAMPUNG CINA
Chinese Pagoda
Mesjid Raya
Chinese House i
Pasar Ikan Lama
Kebawan Park
Istana Maimoun
Istana Plaza
Military Museum B
Police
KAMPUNG KELING
Hindu Temple
Medan Fairgrounds
Negeri Museum
Berastagi
B

(1)
(2)
(3)
(5)
(7)
(6)
(4)

HOTELS
(1) Danau Toba ....
(2) Dharma Deli ....
(3) Garuda City ....
(4) Polonia ....
(5) Sri Deli ....
(6) Tiara Medan ....
(7) Zakia ....

Rasjid Perkasa Alam, who had recently made his fortune from tobacco plantations. Handsome gardens surround the palace where local children play football every evening. The Sultan and his family still live in the right wing of the building.

Behind its pale yellow walls, however, Maimoun is no more than a ghost palace. Only the **Audience hall**★ still comes to life, particularly to celebrate the end of Ramadan *(entrance free)*. People can approach the sultan here as he sits beneath his yellow canopy at the end of the hall, which is decorated in green, the Islamic colour. The marble floor comes from Italy and the chandeliers – the height of kitsch! – from Paris, *via* the Netherlands.

The wealthy Muhammad was also responsible for the **Great Mosque**★★ (Mesjid Raya) (D4) which stands opposite *(on the other side of the railway line and Jl Brigjen Katamso)*. Built in 1906, it displays the riches accumulated by the sultans when they gave the territory to the planters – which did not all belong to them. Indonesia's second largest mosque, it is regarded as one of the most beautiful in the archipelago and indeed, with its five imposing **black domes** and its walls lined with blue ceramics, the Mesjid Raya is the pride of the city. It is also a consolation for the citizens of Medan who cannot afford to undertake the pilgrimage to Mecca and thereby become "hadji". It is the focus for incessant activity: children fly their kites on the lawns while men gossip on the steps next to street vendors selling *peci* and brochettes. Women have their own entrance: they can be seen, shrouded in white, sitting in the coolness of the arcades.

If you can spare the time, continue a little further south to visit the **Museum of the Province of North Sumatra**★ (Negeri Museum) (from E4) *(Jl H. M. Joni 51, 8.30am-12noon/1-5pm; closed Monday. Post Office at the museum entrance. Small guide, free, but in Indonesian, at the ticket office)*. The museum provides an excellent introduction to the history and culture of the region's peoples. In the very varied halls on the ground floor you can see, among other items, some fine **Karo Batak jewellery**★ made of copper and silver (note the enormous double spiral earring), and the **models** of various kinds of housing in North Sumatra.

The Great Mosque, Medan

G. Gerster/Rapho

The most interesting section, on the first floor, is on daily life: cooking and crockery, hunting and fishing, and farming and harvesting. Rituals surrounding death are also evoked by the model of a **Karo coffin tower** and by two **Toba Batak sarcophagi** that have been carved out of hollow tree-trunks and finely worked. Another section shows **traditional musical instruments**, while the last room illustrates the role of Sumatra in the war of independence *(see p 126)*.

The city centre (D2)

Continue your walk further to the north, round Jalan Ahmad Yani. Stronghold of the wealthy 19C planters, the city centre still has some beautiful Dutch **colonial houses*** built in the "tropical neo-Classical" style. In particular, do not miss the **Chinese House****, the former residence of the head of the Chinese community, whose district, **Kampung Cina**, extends to the east. With its great wooden doors flanked by two dragons, it is a striking building *(still inhabited. You may enter as you would open the door to a friend's house, without payment but at a reasonable time)*. Inside the porch lies a well-cared-for **garden**. Behind the enormous red and gold **mother-of-pearl screen***, which stands in the great entrance hall of the house, is a series of salons furnished with rattan armchairs waiting for unlikely visitors. Despite the dim light, yellowing photographs can be seen on the walls showing wealthy Chinese – in Western dress, cigar in hand – portraits of the representatives of the Chinese diaspora in Sumatra until the early 20C. In the silence, the candle-lit **altar** standing at the end of the second courtyard contributes to the air of mystery.

Vampires for sale

Three black creatures with damp skins hang down from a bamboo pole, swinging by their feet. The trader, of Chinese origin, has chosen one of the most polluted avenues in central Medan, Jl Zaihal Arifin, to display his treasures: live bats. The forests of Sumatra are home to the largest species in the world. Unfortunately for the "Pteropus Vampyrus" – its scientific name – its entrails possess unparalleled virtues according to traditional Chinese medicine, especially when fresh. This has led to a lively trade in the animals, and for a few thousand rupiah, the trader will eviscerate the creature at the roadside.

Kampung Keling, the Indian quarter* (C3)

Go west along Jl Palang Merah, which becomes Jl Zaihal Arifin. The Indian district, one of the most lively quarters in Medan, grew up around the **Hindu temple*** (Parisada hindu dharma), a large building whose gaudy colours and countless statues of gods recall the extravagance of India. Facing it, a shop run by a young Medanese of Tamil origin offers all kinds of articles from the subcontinent, such as *kum-kum*, the red powder used to make the sacred round red mark on the forehead of the faithful. The home of southern Indians with dark skins, the surrounding streets are full of stalls – **sari merchants** from Bombay, and **Indian grocer's** full to the ceiling with aromatic jars. Here you have the opportunity to enjoy a curry *(in Jl Teuku Cik Ditiro, see "Making the most of Medan")*, while handcarts pass to and fro, overflowing with merchandise.

The plain of Medan

The road that leaves Medan for the Batak region heads across the plain, a green chessboard of vast plantations of tea and tobacco, and also great forests of **hevea trees**, with a characteristic bitter smell of latex. Every morning grooves are cut into the pitted trunks to encourage the flow of sap, which is gathered in large basins.

Medan

Apart from hevea, the dominant plantations here are **cacao trees** and **oil palms** (*Elaeis guinensis*), which provide oil from their fruit for making glycerine and margarine.

If you are interested in plant life, make time for a visit to the **Sibolangit arboretum** *(42km from Medan on the Brastagi road)*. Its splendid collection of native plants will help you to recognise and appreciate the full range of Sumatra's flora. One of the most common plants is the **sugar palm** *(Arenga saccharifiera)*, one of Indonesia's most heavily exploited products. Its sap is used in making molasses and also *tuak*, palm alcohol, its fruit makes a delicious jam and its black fibre is used for thatching. You will also be able to identify the **betel liana** and the **areca palm**, with its long straight trunk. The leaves of the former and the nuts from the latter are both used in preparing the very popular betel for chewing, *siri*. Don't miss the **clove tree**, a shrub with gleaming leaves touched with red, forming a round bush, or **cinnamon**, with its highly flavoured bark that looks like beech.

Medan, going to school with bicycle and veil

Making the most of Medan

COMING AND GOING

By air – The gateway to North Sumatra, **Polonia airport** lies 3km south of the Great Mosque. If you decide to take a *becak* rather than a taxi, remember that they cannot wait inside the airport, but you will find them waiting 500m from the exit.

Domestic lines: **Merpati**, Jl Brigjen Katamso 41, ☎ (061) 51 44 02 (D4). **Sempati**, Polonia airport, **SMAC**, Jl Imam Bonjol 59, ☎ (061) 51 69 34 (C3). **Mandala**, Jl Brigjen Katamso 37E, ☎ (061) 51 33 09 (D4)

International lines: **Garuda**, Jl Cut Mutia, ☎ (061) 51 68 71 (C3). **Singapore Airlines**, Jl Jend Sudirman 24, ☎ (061) 32 53 00 (C4). **Malaysian Airlines**, junction of Jl Imam Bonjol and Jl Palang Merah, ☎ (061) 51 43 00/ 51 93 33 (C3).

By sea – **Belawan**, Medan harbour (26km north of the city) links Sumatra with Java, Malaysia and Singapore. Shuttle services provide transport from the port to the city centre and Penang Baris coach station. Shipping lines: **PELNI**, Jl Kol Sugiono Cakrawati 5-7, ☎ (061) 51 89 80.

By coach – Two coach stations provide links with North Sumatra (20min by taxi from the city centre): **Amplas** for towns on the Trans-Sumatra highway and inter-island journeys, and **Penang Baris** for other towns in North Sumatra. Regular lines use the Trans-Sumatra to Medan, Pematangsiantar, Prapat, Sibolga and Padangsidempuan. Most of the country's interesting sites are also accessible by road, by coach or car.

By car – If you intend to explore the Batak region, travelling around the villages, a car (with driver) is the ideal form of transport, and can be rented from the travel agents listed below.

Travel agents – For ferry tickets: **Tropitours**, Jl Katamso, ☎ (061) 50 48 88 (D4) and **Sukma**, Jl Sisingamangaraja 92A, ☎ (061) 72 09 54 (E4). For coach travel on the Trans-Sumatra: **ANS**, Jl Amaliun 2A, near the Great Mosque, ☎ (061) 220 14 (D4).

GETTING AROUND

By minibus – Cheap and frequent, minibuses follow set routes. Yellow vehicles run along the main thoroughfares and stop at the city's main centres of interest. They can be picked up in front of the Maimoun Palace.

By taxi – Also numerous, some have a meter fitted. The main taxi rank is in Jl Teladan.

By car – The dense and unpredictable traffic in the city will soon convince you not to drive.

By becak/by bemo – If you are not in a hurry. A little more expensive than taxis, but practical, they cover the whole city and are easily found near hotels. Agree on the fare before you set out.

ADDRESS BOOK

Tourist information – In the colonial quarter, in Jl A Yani, ☎ (061) 51 11 01 (D2). The staff speak English and are friendly. Town plan and good advice.

Bank/Currency exchange – For travellers who enter Indonesia through Medan it is difficult to change large sums at the airport. However, the city has plenty of banks, and exchange rates for dollars are good. **Luppo**, Jl A Yani (D3), offers one of the best rates. You will easily be able to change currencies other than US dollars in the following banks.
– **BDSU** (Development Bank of North Sumatra), near the Tiara hotel (C3);
– **Kesawan**, Jl Zaihal Arifin (C3);
– **Duta**, Jl Pemuda (D3). Currency withdrawals with Visa card. Also at **Standard & Chartered**, at the junction of Jl Zaihal Arifin and Jl Imam Bonjol (C3), for a small fee.
Automatic cash machines are rare. **BCA** (Bank Central of Asia) has a dispenser in Jl Zaihal Arifin (C3) close to Maimoun, in Jl Brigjen Katambo 56 (D4).

Post office/Telephone – **Main post office**, at the junction of Jl Putri Hijau and Jl Prof H M Muhammad Yamin (C1).

Internet – **Indo-net**, Jl Brigjen Katamso, beyond the Daihatsu garage (D3). The best rate in the city but, as is the case elsewhere, the logging on time is very slow. Fee charged per hour.

Medical service – Medan has plenty of well-equipped hospitals, including the **St Elizabeth**, Jl Imam Bonjol, ☎ (061) 51 24 55, near the airport.

Consulates – British Consulate, Jl Brig Jend A Yani 2, ☎ (061) 51 86 99.

WHERE TO STAY

As the commercial and business centre, Medan has the best hotels in North Sumatra – but there is no point in searching for traditional places to stay; accommodation, like the city, is functional and anonymous. Most establishments, regardless of category, are clustered together in Jl Sisingamangaraja (E4-D4).

Modest

Zakia, Jl Sipisopiso 10, ☎ (061) 72 24 13 – 32rm and a dormitory. ☞ ✈ ✗ Family atmosphere and humming with activity. A haunt for long-distance travellers. Rooms are basic but very clean and, above all, enjoy a dream setting, facing the Great Mosque. The view by night is superb from the roof and the peacefulness is striking – except for the call to prayer, which begins very early in the morning and continues until very late at night.

Average

🐌 **Sri Deli**, Jl Sisingamangaraja 30, ☎ (061) 71 35 71 – 55rm. ☞ 🍽 cc Public telephone (card payment). The best value for money for small budgets, provided you ask for one of the rooms on the mosque side – "sound effects" at set times – and not on the street side – with permanent sound effects! Friendly and very well maintained.

Garuda City (do not confuse this with the Garuda Plaza, similar to the Natour Dharma Deli), Jl Sisingamangaraja 27-39, ☎ (061) 71 77 33, Fax (061) 71 44 11 – 70rm. cc Go for a room in the new wing if possible, rather than the older part, which leaves something to be desired.

High end – Luxury

Danau, Jl Imam Bonjol 17, ☎ (061) 55 70 00, Fax (061) 53 05 53 – 258rm. ☞ ✗ ⬙ cc The rooms are slightly less comfortable than in the Tiara (see below), but the luxury style of the hotel is less impersonal. Its Javanese restaurant and magnificent swimming pool make it worth a visit.

Dharma Deli, Jl Balai Kota 2, ☎ (061) 32 79 99 – 178rm. ✗ cc A stylish place that has retained part of its colonial origins. Apart from this the style is fairly kitsch "international Chinese", with minibar, armchairs and Thermos flasks. On the whole the hotel is well maintained, with friendly service. Chinese and Indonesian cuisine.

Polonia, Jl Jend Sudirman 14, ☎ (061) 54 22 22, Fax (061) 51 95 53 – 144rm. cc A good establishment for its category. The 44 rooms in the old building are slightly cheaper than those in the new one (100 rooms). Silk Air has its head office in the hotel.

Super deluxe

Tiara Medan, Jl Cut Mutiah, ☎ (061) 57 40 00, Fax (061) 51 01 76 – 72rm. cc International luxury in North Sumatra's best hotel, used by the President, ministers, and Garuda staff. The hotel also houses the offices of Garuda, Cathay Pacific and Sempati, together with Import-Export Bank.

EATING OUT

Medan has a wide selection of places where you can enjoy Malaysian and Padang cooking (the latter is very highly spiced). You should also try the local drink, "bandrek". Its euphoric effects are not the result of alcohol but of the quantity of spices that are macerated in it. Look out as well for street vendors selling "lontong", a Medan speciality, which can be enjoyed for breakfast. This is a rice sausage poached in a banana leaf and accompanied by sauce, beans, coconut milk, prawns, fried pimentos and grated and grilled coconut. A treat!

The large park opposite the Mesjid Raya (D4) is a good place for eating out in the evening. You can eat in the open air beside a little artificial lake, in one of the numerous inexpensive restaurants that offer delicious dishes of "sate" or "tempe". Lively and relaxed, this is where the young people of Medan like to meet. Check the bill.

• **Indonesian flavours**

Basic

Bakso Amat, Jl Juanda, near the harbour, 500m from the airport (C4). Only one dish is served here: bakso soup (meatballs). A treat for less than US$0.50, which brings smart Medan running.

Moderate

Garuda, Jl Gaja Mada 8 (C2). This is the best place in Medan to try out hot Padang cuisine. If it is full, try the **Centaner**, Jl Pemuda (D3), which offers the same type of experience.

Famili, Jl Sisingamangaraja, in the Ibunda hotel (E4). A well-named restaurant, which is very popular at weekends. The service is sophisticated and the menu offers a great choice of specialities from all over Indonesia, from fish grilled with red peppers to tofu prepared in many different ways.

More select

@ **Tip Top**, Jl Ahmat Yani (D2). You will want to try everything on the extensive menu, which offers the widest possible range of specialities from Indonesia, China and even the West. If you cannot make up your mind, head for the appetising buffet: stuffed vegetables, grilled fish – the choice is yours. The restaurant has elegant decor with woodwork and plants. Avoid the terrace, which opens on to the street (noisy).

● **Seafood**

Restaurants are concentrated in Jl Selat Panjang, behind the City Shopping Centre (E2). Try the excellent **Nelayan**, Jl Thamrin, in Thamrin Plaza.

● **Indian flavours**

Moderate

Cahaya Baru, Jl Teuku Cik Ditiro 106, Kampung Keling (the Indian quarter) (B3). A small restaurant, but where large parties from the Indian community meet round chicken biryanis or spicy curries with steaming and slightly sweet chapatis. **Maharaja**, 50m away, at number 82, ☎ (061) 55 48 21 (B3). Similar style but more sophisticated decor. The menu, which offers curries, chapatis, lassi and lentil dhal is up to par.

OTHER THINGS TO DO

Excursions and stays – A selection of tourist agencies: **Saint Christophe**

Voyages, Jl Halat 73 C, ☎ (061) 71 09 93, Fax (061) 71 09 93. The director, Christophe Marbun, is a Toba Batak. He is a former guide, like his competitor Suyanto who has set up the **Archipelago** agency, Jl Katamso (near Istana Plaza), ☎ (061) 51 29 87 (D4).

Also: **Pacto**, Jl Katamso, ☎ (061) 51 00 81 (D4) and **Seiba**, Jl Bukit Barisan, near the Post Office ☎ (061) 51 18 50 (C1). **Edelweiss**, Jl Irian Barat 47, ☎ (061) 51 72 97 (D4), organises adventure tours (jungle walks and river rafting).

A new agency: **Sumaterra**, Taman Setia Budi Indah (Tasbi), Jl Cycas 11, Block DD12, ☎ (061) 820 13 02, Fax (061) 821 66 81, sumatra@indosat.net.id Also specialised in individual adventure tours (rafting, canyoning, camping and Jeep excursions), at reasonable prices. The director, Yader Rostello, is a young Swiss who has lived in Sumatra for 10 years and is devoted to the Kerinci National Park (West Sumatra). A mine of information for nature-lovers!

SHOPPING GUIDE

Fabrics – The large **Pasar Ikan Lama** market, Jl A Yani (D2) is a fascinating maze that recalls oriental souks. Tiny stalls crowd the length of covered alleys, offering a vast selection of sarongs and songkets embroidered with golden thread.

The centre for textile manufacturing is at **Tebing Tinggi**, 76km south of Medan on the Prapat road via Pematang Siantar. Here you will find sumptuous Batubara songkets (silk brocade in traditional Malayu style) woven in attractive Malaysian houses (Jl Badak).

If you want antiques, keep your money until you reach the Batak region, although most antique items disappeared a long time ago. Bargain knowledgeably and select items for the quality of the workmanship, not for the amount of dust on them.

Making the most of Medan

BUKIT LAWANG ★★
GUNUNG LEUSER NATIONAL PARK
North Sumatra Province – Map p 122-123
85km northwest of Medan
For access to the park, see "Making the most of Bukit Lawang"

Not to be missed
A night out listening to jungle sounds until dawn.
A visit to the Orang-utan Rehabilitation Centre to see the animals at feeding time.
And remember...
Avoid approaching orang-utans that are roaming free,
as their time in captivity has not endeared them to humans.

With its 75 000sqkm, Mount Leuser National Park **(Taman Nasional Gunung Leuser)** – one of the first of its kind in Indonesia – is the largest in Southeast Asia. It is an immense jungle that the State has decided to preserve in order to protect all that remains of an extraordinary natural inheritance that is in increasing danger. The only human settlement near this wild terrain is the peaceful village of Bukit Lawang. Nestling in a valley at the southern edge of the park, it stretches along the **Bohorok**, a turbulent little river with rapids that marks the frontier between the world of humans and that of monkeys. On the other bank lies nothing but jungle. Dense, overpowering and dark, it is alive with myriad rustlings. At nightfall the concert of sounds redoubles in the starlight.

The gateway to freedom

In 1973, a **centre for the rehabilitation of orang-utans** was opened with the support of the WWF (World Wide Fund for Nature) and Frankfurt Zoo. What started as a simple wooden hut has now become one of the largest of the few orang-utan refuges in the world, receiving animals that have been kept in illegal captivity. On arrival the new resident is isolated in a cage for observation. This 3-4 month period of quarantine enables the detection and treatment of illnesses that often develop in captivity, for example, tuberculosis, hepatitis and malaria, and which must not be exposed to orang-utans that have been returned to the jungle. Once the health check is over, the orang-utan begins a period of re-acclimatisation. This is deemed successful when the animal no longer returns to the platform set up near the centre, where food is put out every day. On average, the centre rehabilitates around ten apes each year, but some may need more than two years before they recover total independence.

The last "men of the jungle"
Orang-utans (literally "men of the jungle" in Bahasa Indonesia) are now only found in the wild in Sumatra and Borneo (Kalimantan) and are listed as an endangered species. Larger and thinner than its cousin, the Sumatra orang-utan is ginger in colour and has a longer face. Its arms are 50% longer than its legs, enabling it to move from branch to branch with wonderful dexterity. But because of decades of uncontrolled deforestation, poaching has become easier, an activity encouraged by the fact that huge sums of money can be made from the sale of wild animals to wealthy individuals in Singapore or Malaysia. Indonesian law now forbids their captivity, and the species appears to be recovering gradually. In total, its numbers are estimated to be 2 000 in Sumatra and 3 000 in Borneo.

M Shah/Fotogram-Stone

The "man of the jungle"

Forest spirits and "Mosquito party"

Bukit Lawang village is the ideal setting for a prolonged stay. River bathing is possible, a chance to get a glimpse of the monkeys that live on the far bank. A visit to the centre with its famous platform, on the edge of the jungle, provides a closer look at these distant cousins. Seeing them in their natural surroundings, on the road to freedom, is a moving experience.

It is also an opportunity to learn, during walks organised by the rangers and local guides, about the charms (and dangers) of the equatorial jungle. There is likely to be a warm welcome, for the residents of Bukit Lawang are thrilled to meet foreigners who, like them, respect and love nature. The extremely peaceful site has tempted many travellers to prolong their visit, and it is easy to meet people there. Young Indonesians, with their long hair floating free, will undoubtedly invite you to one of their "Mosquito parties". These are pleasant evenings in which they play a few Western songs on their guitars before recounting some legends of the jungle and the spirits that haunt it.

The man who became an "orang-utan"

The Indonesians call him La-Lou. Here, everyone knows the quiet Frenchman who goes about barefoot. Local residents like him for two reasons. Firstly, for several months now he has been a volunteer at the Orang-utan Rehabilitation Centre. "After giving them their food, their cages are taken out into the jungle and they are observed as they come out gradually and gain in confidence", this wildlife enthusiast tells the visitor. "After two hours, we call them and they return. This goes on until the call of the jungle is stronger than that of the human voice". The second reason for his popularity makes the local people laugh: during a walk in the park on his own, the young Westerner got lost and spent a night in the jungle. Since then the joke has gone round the village: in Bukit Lawang, La-Lou the volunteer has actually become an "orang-utan", a "man of the woods".

Visiting "The Platform" ★★★

The Orang-utan Rehabilitation Centre is a 30min walk from the edge of the village, along a footpath beside the river (which you cross in a canoe). The Platform is open to the public twice a day, at 8am and 3pm, the orang-utans' feeding times. Access is via a steep path, which is slippery after rain.

Complete quiet. Suddenly, the trees in the distance seem to be stirred into waves. Then the nearest greenery begins to shake in turn, branches crack, something is approaching. Behind the wooden fence, cameras are held ready – here it is the humans who are penned in. The foliage continues to wave around, until finally a strange russet shape bursts out of the vegetation, into human sight. Two or three teetering balancing movements in the air and the acrobat lands on the right spot, a few metres above the Platform set up on piles. The many onlookers hold their breath, gazing at this remarkable expert of the high wire. There is a little pause. Then the orang-utan casually pretends to look elsewhere, before lazily stretching out his hand towards the rangers. A fresh rustling attracts attention. Soon there are two, three, then four orang-utans that appear, attracted by the sound of the feeding bowls being tapped on wood. The different faces turn placidly towards the impressed spectators. On the menu: bananas! Twice a day the staff from the centre bring them whole bunches, together with milk. This frugal menu is designed to encourage the apes to seek their own nourishment. In the meantime, rangers and orang-utans embark on a game, part complicity, part intimidation, an amusing spectacle that does not exclude the tourists. But as soon as the meal is over the great primates are firmly despatched back to their natural setting.

The Bats Cave ★

This is 2km south of Bukit Lawang (35min on foot). Take a good torch and stout shoes. Set out in the morning to benefit from the relative coolness and take a guide from the village to show you the way. There is a (modest) entrance fee.

Before embarking on the jungle adventure *(see below)*, it is worth a trip to see this cave near the village. First walk in the shade through a **plantation of hevea trees**, a neat alignment of light-coloured trunks with half coconut shells fixed onto them to catch the latex that oozes out. Across a small water-course is a wooden hut, the "entrance kiosk" where the warden, delighted to have a visit, will undoubtedly offer refreshment of some sort (usually hot!) and start up a conversation. Access to the cave, up a ladder with widely spaced and very slippery rungs, requires full attention! Similarly, crossing a mossy tree-trunk and climbing the second ladder, equally rudimentary, also demands care. Finally, you reach the cave entrance, a gaping dark mouth covered in lianas as thick as a man's arm. The interior is home to hundreds of bats that spend the day asleep. The only sign of their presence is their pervasive bitter smell, and a few uncertain flights. There are **three halls** to explore, if you are not afraid of threading your way along a narrow **passageway**. A strange green light illuminating the rocks and stalactites comes from chimneys carved out of the rocks by water. Open to the sky, the halls are partly blocked by creepers, mosses and foliage, waterfalls of greenery. The whole place is of course laden with legends and magical powers. The depths of the cave are said to house the spirits of ancestors. Among the rumours that are unconfirmed, is the secret passage which leads directly to the very popular **Acoustic Cave** *(see "Making the most of Bukit Lawang")*.

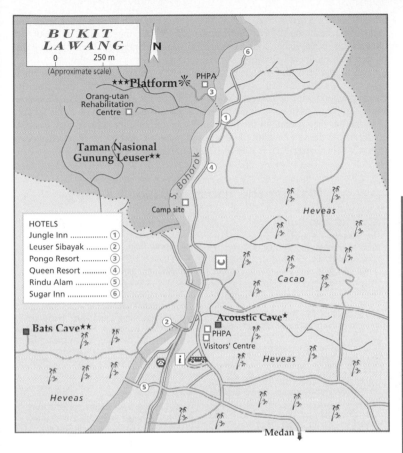

Adventure in the jungle★★

Trekking in the jungle. See "Making the most of Bukit Lawang".

A few minutes' walk from Bukit Lawang is enough to get away from the tourist bustle. The route leads through giant trees such as the **santiria**, of the dipterocarpaceae family, which often reach a height of more than 40m. The visitor feels dwarfed among their enormous roots, an impression reinforced by the surrounding chaos of plant life. There are tangles of creepers, stems and enormous leaves, all brilliant green and gleaming with rainwater. Flowers grow on the trunks, visited by **butterflies** of every colour, zigzagging between the branches.

Lying almost astride the equator, Leuser Park enjoys a remarkable amount of rainfall: an average of 4m of water each year! The result is a dense flora that is constantly renewed and extremely rich: no fewer than 3 500 plant species have been recorded, including the very rare **rafflesia** *(see p 126)*.

This is a paradise for monkeys, birds, reptiles and other creatures with fur, feathers or scales. Each layer of the forest (five in all) has its own residents. The different monkey species generally keep their distance, each one with its own living level. The orang-utans have established their empire 20m above the ground. In about ten minutes they put together a kind of platform made of branches. Their presence can be identified more easily by their signals: echoing kisses

But it is at night that the concert reaches full pitch, peaking at dawn. This is when their cries are mingled with those of all the other local residents, including the **siamang** gibbon with its powerful vocal chords, or the agile **Thomas leaf monkey** and the 285 species of birds (including the **argus pheasant**) that hide in the foliage. Then there is the croaking of the frogs and other amphibians (35 recorded species), not forgetting the various cries of 90 types of mammal, and over a hundred species of reptile. The Leuser Park is sure to be an unforgettable experience.

Making the most of Bukit Lawang

COMING AND GOING

By coach – Allow 3hr from Medan. Choose between the "Tourist bus" service and local buses. The former, ten times more expensive, will pick you up at your hotel. Departures are usually at 11.30am and 3pm. The latter leave every 20min from Penang Baris station. They take longer because they stop along the way to pick up more passengers. The advantage is that when you arrive, the hotel touts will not be waiting to solicit your custom. Both services go to the same spot in Bukit Lawang, a small square surrounded by cheap eating places, the tourist office, PHPA office and various shops. Return trips on the same basis, with departures throughout the day.

ADDRESS BOOK

PHPA – *Forest Protection and Environment Conservation Office*, near the coach station. Open daily until 3pm. Written permission is required to visit the Platform, available from the PHPA, where you show your passport and pay a fee. The permission is valid for both visits of the day (8am and 3pm). The PHPA is also a good place to make contact with local guides (licensed by the Indonesian Guide Association). Ask for Nasib.

Arrangements to work as a volunteer taking part in the daily tasks, are also made here. No special qualifications are needed. The only conditions are that candidates undertake to stay for a minimum of two weeks, and the number of volunteers must not exceed 6 people at any one time.

Tourist information – A white building behind the parking area for buses. The staff speak English, can book bus tickets and organise trekking parties.

Bank/Currency exchange – Take care to change money in Medan: there are no practical opportunities in the village.

Post office/Telephone – No post office, postage stamps and letter boxes are available in the shops. For **Telkom**, follow the canal, heading left opposite the Wisma Leuser Sibayak bridge. The **Wartel** is indicated by a sign on the right, after 50m.

WHERE TO STAY

Bukit Lawang is an ideal stop for nature lovers. The hotels and guesthouses listed below look onto the Bohorok River.

Modest

Sugar Inn – 6rm. ⌂ ✗ The haunt of most of the volunteers at the Rehabilitation Centre. For those who are not afraid of the steep path up to it (allow 10-15min on foot from the jetty up the hill, dangerous at night), nor of the basic accommodation (a bungalow without electricity). Advantages: total isolation in a clearing in the middle of the jungle, and a warm welcome.

Queen Resort – 12rm. ⌂ ✗ On the way to the Orang-utan Rehabilitation Centre. Basic, but friendly and lively, thanks to the bar-restaurant with its low tables. Perfect for lovers of rock music and billiards.

Jungle Inn – 11rm. ⌂ ✗ Just before the boarding point for canoes to the centre. Deserves its name on account of the decor: the main hut has an upper floor set on tree-trunks, with vegetation on the inside as well as the outside. Even the monkeys are confused by it! The music, jazz or reggae, brings in people in the evenings. Good food. The 4 bungalows on the river, which are more expensive, are the most attractive with their rattan furnishings. The Tarzan-style "Honeymoon room" is worth seeing.

Average

Leuser Sibayak – 60rm. ☎ and Fax (061) 55 05 76 – 🛏 ⚊ [TV] ✕ The first of the hotels after the coach station. Facilities vary according to the room (avoid the upstairs rooms). The bungalows (with a small private terrace), set round an enormous garden with banana palms and avocado trees are very good value for their price. From the terrace restaurant there is a fine view over the bustling village.

High end

🏯**Pongo Resort**, ☎ (061) 54 25 74, Fax (061) 55 42 84 – 14rm. 🛏 ▤ / ⚊ 🅿 [TV] ✕ The price includes the visit permit. A perfectly maintained thatched hotel, located on the other side of the river (crossed by ferry), beside the entrance to the Orang-utan Rehabilitation Centre. The bungalows, furnished with taste in colonial style, are full of charm. Then there is the amazing setting, in a valley far away from everything. Impeccable service. Good restaurant overlooking the water, with soft lighting.

Luxury

Rindu Alam, ☎ (061) 57 53 70, Fax (061) 54 50 15 – 55rm. 🛏 ⚊ [TV] ✕ This is the most expensive place to stay. It is pleasant, but lacks charm. The rooms are spacious but impersonal.

EATING OUT

As Bukit Lawang is essentially devoted to tourism, there are virtually no restaurants in the village except in the hotels. Among them, the restaurant at the **Pongo Resort** offers the most pleasing setting, and has a good and varied menu. The exception is the delicious family establishment, full of caged songbirds, which faces the Acoustic Cave (see below). Look out for a white wooden house as the place has no name.

HAVING A DRINK

Acoustic Cave, 200m on the right beyond the PHPA office, just before the bridge. Stone Age atmosphere! Laid out in a natural cave (the entrance is through a tunnel carved out of the rock), the bar is lit by candles and furnished with bamboo. The charming owner is a young Batak, a talented sculptor when he is off duty. One of the rocks in the cave is used as a stage for local musicians, who come most days (around 9pm) to play jazz, rock or Indonesian pop, depending on the evening. Cross the cave to find a botanical garden tucked between the rocks. Footpaths lead up onto the heights, from where there are splendid views over the surrounding jungle. The place is the headquarters for a group of friends who are passionate about climbing and who will suggest outings. Enquire at the bar.

OTHER THINGS TO DO

Trekking – The experience of trekking in the jungle is rarely disappointing provided you take a good guide. Information from the PHPA or the tourist office. All the hotels also offer excursions, lasting between 3hr and 3 days, with nights out in the open. In 3 days you can visit Berastagi, going through jungle and spectacular valleys. While you walk, your luggage can be transported by road in a car.

Some excursions include **rafting** on the Wampu and **tubing** (going down the river in inner tubes). This is great fun, but there are no safety measures.

Climbing – Information at the Acoustic Cave, see above.

Films – A good quality film on the process of releasing orang-utans, shot with the researchers at the Rehabilitation Centre, is shown at the **Visitors' Centre** at 8pm, three times a week: Sunday, Tuesday and Thursday.

SHOPPING GUIDE

The many local artists illustrate the theme of the orang-utan from every angle. You will find their paintings, batiks or sculptures more or less everywhere in souvenir shops, which line the path beside the river, and even in the Telkom office!

Making the most of Bukit Lawang

THE KARO BATAK REGION★★

BERASTAGI

North Sumatra Province – 65km south of Medan – Map p 122-123
Alt 1 400m – Temperature 16-18°C

Not to be missed
A dip in the hot springs at Dubuk-Dubuk.

And remember...
When you set off to visit Karo villages, take packets of cigarettes with you,
they are an excellent way of making contact with the locals.
In the Karo region, "Hello" is "Mejuah juah".

From the Muslim city of Medan the road leaves the plain for the heights, winding up through the hevea plantations to another world, the home of the Batak Karo. This region is the source of one of Sumatra's oldest cultures, full of standing stones and above all the famous "long houses" with enormous uptilted roofs, like ships with narrow prows, piercing the sky.

Although today the Karo are Christians – the legacy of Dutch missionaries – the mark of their traditions remains steadfast. It is easy to see this as you explore the region, discovering the most impressive villages and the stones that kings ordered to be set up, permanent emblems of their power and nobility.

Berastagi, a small hill station, is a haven of coolness in the heart of the country, drowning in orchards of *marquisa* (passion fruit) and rambutans. Use it as a base camp for exploring the surrounding volcanoes, all equally magical. It is not difficult to climb them, but the excursion is bound to be quite an experience.

The Karo, "the first-comers"

The fertile soil of the vast plateau which borders the plain of Medan made the earliest colonials – *"Karo"* in the Batak language – the most prosperous of the whole region. Their villages and houses reflect this wealth, and are the largest of all the Batak groups.

Sadly, with the development of communication methods and the exodus of the rural population, many of the Karo Batak villages are now semi-abandoned. Some of the houses are still inhabited, but their occupants are often no more than tenants, and their way of life no longer follows the traditional clan system. Tourism continues, and it is to be hoped that its growth may at least help to preserve these great wooden vessels.

Excursions around Berastagi

Tour of 2 days minimum.

As preparation for your exploration of the **Tanah Karo Batak** (the Karo Batak region), you should preferably visit the **Bukit Barisan National Park** (*49km south of Medan,*

A house between land and sky
According to Batak cosmogony, the Karo house is built according to a vertical plan that forms a link between the worlds of heaven and earth. The central level is the living space, which is linked by its piles to the territory of devils, while the roof rears up towards the gods. Not a single nail is used in building the house: only wooden pegs, skilfully used according to the traditional "paku" system, a technique that is sadly tending to disappear. The interior space, very large among the Karos, is divided into four homes, each one occupied by two families (thus eight families in all!) without dividing walls. A single passageway runs the length of the house, linking the two outside doors that open at the gable ends.

A Karo Batak house and rice store

R. Marca

15km from Berastagi). You will find life-size examples (half wood, half concrete) of the traditional houses of North Sumatra, from Nias to Mandailing, via the Malaysian house and those of the six great Batak groups.

The first stop on your tour is the hamlet of **Peceren** *(on the way out of Berastagi on the Medan road, just before the Megaview Hotel)*, although the setting offers little invitation to linger. The few traditional houses that survive stand close to "modern" houses with satellite dishes.

Head instead for **Gurusinga**★★ *(southwest of Berastagi)*, a superb village that is little visited even

The "long house" of the Karo Batak

Standing on piles between 3 and 6m tall, which protect it from animals, the communal house of the Karo has a generous roof with a slightly hourglass shape, covered in fibres from the sugar palm. It is crowned with stylised buffalo heads, considered to ward off ill fortune. The lizard is a symbol of prosperity and honesty, and patterns of its footprints in plaited cord decorate the planks of the side walls. A ladder leads up to the bamboo verandah. The number of its rungs indicates the social standing of the household: an uneven number for an aristocratic clan, and an even number for a family of more humble status. The house is divided into three floors, with three corresponding colours: white for the roof (home of the gods), red for the living space, and black for the piles and the ground, home of death and bad spirits. The Toba Batak and the Minangkabau also use the same symbolism.

though it is accessible by bus. Daily life has not changed here for decades: the farmers continue to go out to the fields with their age-old ox-ploughs, and coffee still dries on the doorsteps. A beautiful **traditional house**★ stands here in reasonably good condition and is still alive with the daily activity of its eight resident families. For a small donation a wrinkled little grandmother will happily invite you in to see the interior.

The much more heavily visited village of **Lingga**★ *(15km from Berastagi, 6km from Kabanjahe)* is full of the commercial spirit that tourism has generated, and the Karo tradition of welcome has to some extent been changed by it. Yet the village is worth a look: a dozen **houses★** are still inhabited, and you can see an impressive **griten★**, a mausoleum on the upper storey containing ancestral relics, decorated with Karo motifs and a buffalo skull. The funeral ceremony for putting the relics in the griten is one of the major moments in Karo life. It must be said that the family may wait for between five and ten years before providing the dead person with his or her final resting place (until then the body receives a temporary burial). It is important to have favourable omens and to have gathered together enough money to celebrate the placing in the tomb with all the inhabitants. Note also the enormous **banyan tree★★** on the edge of the village, said to have been planted here during the construction of the first house, three hundred years ago.

More remote (and therefore less visited), **Barusjahe** *(accessible only by bemo, 40km to the east of Kabanjahe, via Tigapartah)* is mainly worthwhile for the superb **road★★** that leads there. It is lined with orchards, bougainvillaea and hibiscus, and occasionally looks over delightful valleys clad in terraced rice fields. The sign that indicates the village, to the right at the last fork, is written in the Karo alphabet. At the entrance to Barusjahe, on the left, don't miss the surprising **church★** crowned with a layered Karo roof and capped with buffalo horns.

On the road to Lake Toba, **Dokan** *(approximately 30km south of Berastagi, near the Sipisopiso waterfall; a bus leaves from Kabanjahe)* is the haunt for groups who visit Samosir. You should, however, take the time to see the **lesung** built at the foot of a small hill. This is an enormous community house where rice is stored. Around it, the few houses of the village are sadly dilapidated.

The best is kept to the end: further south you reach **Cingkes★★★** *(35km south of Kabanjahe, from where a bus leaves early in the morning; return, early afternoon. Or you can hire a car in Berastagi)*, a village with a population of 500, lying in the heart of a beautiful **forest of bamboos**. Cingkes is without doubt the most interesting village in the region, on account of the number of its **houses★★**, which are also well preserved. Their pediments bear the carved word "Mediofah": "Welcome" in Karo. The bus arrives in the square, under the inquisitive look of the village men talking in the shade of a magnificent bougainvillaea. As you go along the well-tended paths of beaten earth with children running round, you will find a **rice store** here, a **griten** there, and further on a lovingly maintained **pigeon-house**. The inhabitants are very proud of their village, which is still prosperous, and take pride in letting their land to outside tenants.

AROUND BERASTAGI
0   8 km
(Approximate scale)

The volcano route★★★

Allow a full day to climb a volcano. Take stout shoes, something to eat and rainproof clothing: showers are frequent in the early afternoon.

From Berastagi it is very tempting to set off up the smoking summits that stand out against the horizon to the north. Although Sinabung is the highest and the most mysterious, Sibayak is perfect for an adventurous but less demanding expedition. Make your choice – or indeed go for both.

Sinabung★★

In Berastagi, take a bus to Lake Kawar. You will be able to find guides on arrival. You need a good ten hours' walk to reach the crater, at an altitude of 2 451m. The climb is generally undertaken at night, in order to make the most of the **view★★**, which in the dawn light is very impressive and covers the whole of the Karo area. The walk starts in dense jungle on the steep sides of the volcano, then comes out on the crater ridge, a gaping mouth wreathed in the myriad clouds of vapour from its **fumaroles**. In the centre there is a **lake** which smells strongly of sulphur *(do not linger here as these vapours may be dangerous)*.

Sibayak★★★

Two possible tracks lead up to the summit (2 172m). More gradual and therefore less demanding, the **west route★★** ends in a paved road with a magnificent **panorama★★** *(from Berastagi, take the Gundaling hill road, go through the connecting village of Jalang Nouda and then continue straight ahead; allow 3hr for the walk)*.

Finer still, the **east route★★★** leads directly to the foot of the volcano, carpeted with thick, rustling jungle *(take a bus for Medan and stop at the "Panorama Waterfall" beyond the junction with the road for Doulu village, approximately 5km beyond Berastagi)*. Before starting the climb, take a little detour to see the **Sikulicap falls★**, a chance to enjoy a pleasant ten-minute walk through the forest. This place is as romantic as you could wish, and is a draw for many young people.

Back on the main road, go down for another 500m. The path leading to the top of the volcano heads off opposite the panorama.

The climb begins abruptly in the heart of the jungle, in the middle of wild bay bushes and **pitcher plants**, the strange insectivorous flowers that look like tubular water-jugs, fearsome coloured traps. Five hours later, having crossed a slippery riverbed and various tunnels of vegetation, you reach the crater. A lunar landscape appears through clouds of smoke. This is a chaotic mass of stones of phosphorescent green, smoking hot, formed by the sulphur concretions that crop up here and there from the **sulphur springs**, in the middle of evil-smelling curls of smoke.

A narrow path takes you right round the **caldera★★★**, with your ears full of the whistling of the wind and the creaks and groans from the centre of the volcano. On all sides clouds form and dissolve, surrounding you suddenly in cotton wool and then a few seconds later revealing fragments of landscape. In the foreground you see red and grey heather, and the blue-black stones of the flanks of the volcano.

When you leave you go down the southern slope, following very steep stone steps. It is a somewhat tricky descent, particularly if you look up to admire the view.

The **bamboo forest** announces your return to terra firma. You will have thoroughly earned a dip in the **Dubuk-Dubuk hot springs★★**. These sulphurous waters feed several pools, of varying degrees of heat (very well maintained). Here you can sip a cool drink, doing what everyone else does, letting the soothing properties of the water work on your weary muscles until the place closes and the bus arrives to take you back to Berastagi.

The Karo Batak region

Making the most of Berastagi

COMING AND GOING
From Medan, most of the Batak Karo region's centres of interest are accessible by road, by car or bus.

By bus – To reach Berastagi, leave from the **Penang Baris terminal** (Medan), in the direction of Kabanjahe. Frequent buses, throughout the day until 5pm.
In Berastagi, the **Tugu bus station** is next to the southern market, beside the cinema. This is where you go to take a bus for Kabanjahe. For Medan or Prapat, the bus leaves from beside the memorial.

By bemo – To explore surrounding villages, the simplest way is to hire a *bemo* with a driver, through your hotel or the tourist office. It is also possible to hire the services of a *bemo* in Kanbanjahe.

GETTING AROUND
For short distances, the "sado" is perfect (a horse-drawn vehicle for two in which passengers and coachman sit back-to-back). Agree on the fare before getting in.

FINDING YOUR WAY
The town consists of one long street, Jl Veteran. The daily fruit market is north of the town, near the memorial. South of the town is a strange sculpture of a cabbage. This is a well-earned honour: cabbages from the Karo region feed the whole of Indonesia and are exported further afield to Japan and Australia.

ADDRESS BOOK
Tourist information – Rafflesia Tourist Information Office, Jl Veteran (facing the post office, near the fruit market), ☎ (0628) 915 58. Plenty of practical information on the region, and an English-speaking guide can be provided for your excursions, as well as vehicles with drivers.
Post office/Telephone – Telkom and post office opposite the tourist office.

WHERE TO STAY
No need for air conditioning or fans in the hotel bedrooms: the nights are cool in Berastagi. Those who are travelling on a small budget can find accommodation near the fruit market and anywhere along Jl Veteran. The best hotels are a little further out, but it is easy to hail one of the many minibuses that ply the streets.

Modest
Wisma Ikut, Jl Gundaling 24, ☎ (0628) 911 71 – 15rm. ⚏ ✕ Five minutes from the fruit market, perched on a little hillside with grazing horses, between a church, a Buddhist monastery and a mosque! This former Dutch house with its slightly flaking paintwork has retained all its charm, with its high ceilings and large rustic dining room. Attentive welcomes, and simply furnished but clean rooms. Numbers 11 and 12 have their own private verandah at the rear, overlooking the garden, from where you hear the call to prayer at the mosque.
El Shaddai, Jl Veteran 65, ☎ (0628) 910 23, Fax (0628) 915 13 – ⚏ ✕ Formerly the Crispo Inn. The rooms are plain but very clean. The owners are friendly and can provide useful information on the region.
Sibayak Guesthouse, Jl Veteran 119, ☎ (0628) 910 95, Fax (0628) 911 22 – 22rm. ⚏ ✕ cc The front is not appealing, but a second building behind it has 3 lovely rooms on the roof. They are very large, lined with bamboo, and very inexpensive. All open onto the terrace, where you can eat and have a drink, peacefully taking in the bustle of the town and the surrounding district. Ramli, the owner, provides useful information and organises excursions on foot.
Do not confuse this with the **Wisma Sibayak**, Jl Udara, which is friendly but very basic.

Average
Bukit Kubu, Jl Sempurna 2, ☎ (0628) 915 24, Fax (0628) 915 13 – 40rm. ⚏ TV ✕ ✨ 🐎 Attractive setting in the middle of the golf course, with all the charm of a colonial villa. Well equipped bedrooms. This lively hotel has an Indonesian clientele, including numerous families on holiday. Pleasant restaurant and bar looking onto greenery.
Berastagi Cottages, Jl Gundaling, ☎ (0628) 913 45 – 74rm. ⚏ 🍴 TV ✕ ✨ cc Disco, billiards. A notch above the

previous hotel, with extremely well maintained Karo-style roofed bungalows dotted about on a magnificent lawn. Regrettably, the rooms are uninteresting and the bathrooms mediocre (although the water is hot).

High end to luxury

Sibayak International, Jl Merdeka, ☎ (0628) 913 01, Fax (0628) 913 07 – 113rm. A large complex that nevertheless manages to retain a welcoming atmosphere. The bungalows round the swimming pool are decorated with batiks. Beautiful garden with jogging track and 24-hour restaurant, all with a fine view of the plumes of smoke from Sibayak.

Megaview Hotel, 3km before reaching Berastagi, Jl Raya Medan, near the Karo village of Peceren, ☎ (0628) 916 50, Fax (0628) 916 52 – 140rm. The hotel fully deserves its name. The restaurant has one of the best views possible of Sinabung volcano. The hotel opened in 1993 and offers its clientele of wealthy Asian families every luxury: rooms facing the swimming pool, piano, and karaoke.

EATING OUT

Apart from eating at the hotels indicated above, you could try the very popular **Ginsata**, Jl Veteran, facing the memorial. It serves all kinds of simple, spicy family dishes. Very good vegetable curry. The delicious "gado-gado" overflows with peanut sauce. Open relatively late. "Nasi Goreng" to take away (in a banana leaf) when you set off on an excursion.

OTHER THINGS TO DO

Trekking – All the hotels and agencies offer tours to traditional villages and to the volcanoes. You will find good guides at the **Ginsata** (Manto, or Junior). The friendly Ismael can be found in the **El Shaddai** hotel. The **Raimond Coffee House** also offers excursions of all kinds: don't hesitate to bargain. The tourist office can also recommend guides. Here too, take the time to discuss and negotiate.

Excursions on horseback – Enquire at the **Sibayak International** or **Bukit Kubu** hotels. This is a good way to explore the area if you have already done a little riding.

Swimming – Berastagi is one of the few towns in Sumatra to have a public swimming pool, **Kolam Renang**, a few minutes from the centre (800m from the fuel station on the road to Sibayak, then 200m on the right beyond the Wisma Ikut). Open daily until 5pm, very crowded at weekends.

Making the most of Berastagi

NIAS ISLAND★★★

North Sumatra Province
Mentawai Islands – 125km off the coast of Sibolga
130km long (north-south) – 45km wide (east-west)

Not to be missed
The spectacular traditional "batu hombo" leaps,
in the southern villages.

And remember...
Never leave anything of value on the beach or in an unlocked bungalow:
theft and police corruption have been growing steadily in recent years.
When you visit villages, take a reliable guide to ensure that the customary
"donation" does not turn into extortion.
Plan to spend your last night in Gunung Sitoli, ready to take the return flight next day.

With its deserted beaches ringed with coconut palms, Nias has all the features of an island paradise. Lost in the turquoise waters of the Indian Ocean, it is part of the long chain of islands which, from the Gulf of Bengal (the Andaman and Nicobar islands), extend as far as the western coast of Sumatra (Mentawai Islands). A green island, Nias has wonderful landscapes that alternate between dense forest and plantations of hevea trees or coffee bushes. Hidden in thick jungle, villages from the depths of time still survive, linked by an extraordinary network of stone-paved tracks.

The treasures of the island, strange megaliths, can be seen standing at the foot of spectacular houses. They are effigies of ancient kings or reminders of their battles, fascinating for ethnologists and for collectors of primitive art.

Mysterious origins

The origin of the native people of Nias remains a mystery. Some believe that the Niasans are descended from the Nagas of Assam, in India (head-hunters, like the inhabitants of Nias not so long ago!). Others think that they are related to the Bataks, or other peoples of the Mentawai Islands.

An exiled queen
Legend locates the cradle of the Niasans on the banks of the Gomo, in the middle of the island. It was here that an exiled queen took refuge at the end of a long sea crossing, bearing the child of an adulterous love affair. Her only companion on board her frail craft was a dog that her husband had put on board to protect her (which would explain why the Niasans do not eat dog meat). Months passed and the young woman gave birth to a son. She took him later as her mate, and together they created the native people of Nias.

There are also navigators' accounts. The oldest references – Arab and Persian – date back to 851, and then 1154. The first people to land on the island were, however, probably Chinese and Indian traders, with the influence on the island of the latter in evidence from as early as the 1C of the modern era.

Whatever the truth may be, the name of "Nias" did not appear on European maritime charts until the 16C. Today, in the local language, the island is called Tano Niha, "The Island of the People", whose inhabitants are the *Ono Niha*, the "Children of the People", who greet you with an enthusiastic *"Ya'ahowu"* (pronounced "Yahou").

From slavery to Christianity

In the 17C Nias sustained regular links with Aceh and the other sultanates in Sumatra. At the heart of this relationship was a sinister slave trade, from which the Nias chiefs derived enormous profits, in the form of gold. At the end of the century the Dutch established a post on the island in exchange for commercial agreements, and developed the trade in humans, who were despatched to Dutch and French colonies. The trade only ended with the arrival of Christianity, in the

Blood-stained gold

When it came to gold, the Niasan chiefs had only one rule: more, more and more! The many ceremonies — marriages, banquets designed to add to the prestige of the nobility — were a pretext for creating new jewellery and finery. But, once the creation was finished, custom demanded the tribute of a human life — the object in effect had its own magical power, which was dangerous to whoever was the first to wear it. It was therefore first put on to a slave, who then had to give up his life, and with it, the jewels.

19C. Officially, 85% of Niasans are now Christian (mostly Protestant) although in remote areas the beliefs are blended with a vast ancestral pantheon of animist gods. The coastal towns have immigrant traders among their population: 10% are Muslims from Sumatra, 3% Chinese Buddhists and 2% Hindu Indians.

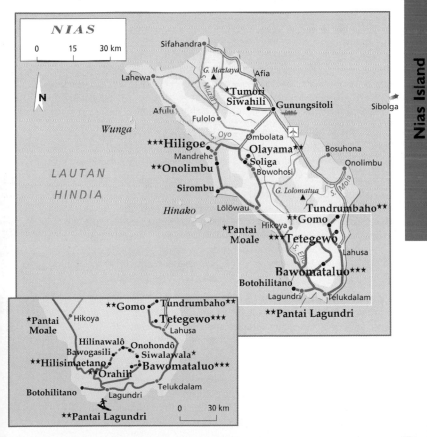

151

Sumatra

The island of megaliths

Hidden in the depths of the jungle or set up in front of a village house (thus providing an ideal drying rack for washing!), the **adu** stones are still highly venerated by the Niasans, despite Christianity and the looting by private or public collectors. The *adu zatua*, protective statues of ancestors, are decorated with traditional jewellery: for men, a single ring in the right ear and the *nifatali*, the warriors' necklace, symbol of the passage from childhood to adulthood. Next to these figurative statues are taller standing stones, menhirs or *osa-osa* with animal features. All the great ceremonies were focused round these ceremonial offerings, particularly the *owasa*, the feast of merit, accompanied by its indispensable attributes: pigs, jewels and decapitated heads.

Two islands in one

Although for a long time the island was divided into tiny kingdoms, consisting of a village or a group of villages, they all respected the same social system. The king ruled over a population of nobles (*si'ulu* in the south, and *salawa* in the centre and the north), served by the common people (*sato* or *sihönö*) and slaves (*sawuyu* or *harakana*). The king was seen as the direct descendant of the founding ancestors, with the same warrior prestige predominating throughout the island.

At some unknown date, between one branch and another of an equally undefined line, a split arose between the two regions, revealing two cultures that were distinct in both language and housing. What was the origin of this "divorce"? We only have a legend to throw light on it: formerly, the sovereigns were polygamous; one of them had two wives who quarrelled over everything. Irritated, the king decided to have separate houses built for each of them, one oval (the northern type), and the other one in the shape of a ship (southern style).

The north, the land of oval houses★

*Allow a full day. Preferably, keep your time for the south,
where there are countless, richer sites, and accommodation standards
are generally better.*

■ **Gunungsitoli** – The island capital, a town dominated by corrugated iron and concrete, has little of interest apart from the **Pusaka Nias Museum★**, the museum of the History of Nias, (*800m before the harbour, Monday-Saturday, 9am-5pm, Sunday 2-4pm; fee*). Opened by a German pastor who was anxious to protect the island treasures from looting, the museum houses some unique **megaliths★**. You can also see an interesting video on the history and civilisation of Nias.

■ **Tumori Siwahili★** – *15km to the northwest.* This is a tiny village hidden behind a line of hills (hence the name *Siwahili*: "the nine hills"). The road climbs the steep slopes in a series of switchback bends. Like flying saucers that have come to earth in the jungle, the century-old **oval houses★★** stand on their framework of massive piles. The **roof★**, made of sago palm leaves, is set with skylights which the residents close when they depart for the fields. Inside, a single large room is home to between one and three families. The bodies of their ancestors lie in family tombs close to the house.

The south, the land of ship-houses★★★

There are two roads to Lagundri, a centre for hotels and guesthouses, 14km from Telukdalam: the faster inland road (128km, 4hr), or the coast road which affords beautiful glimpses of the ocean towards the end of the route. If you use public transport, you will have no choice. If you hire a vehicle and guide, take advantage of them to visit sites along the way (Olayama to the west or Gomo in the east), as different trips around the island can be fairly tiring. Allow 4 days.

In Telukdalam there are plenty of motorbikes or covered trucks to take you to Lagundri. A paradise for the Australian surfers who have colonised it since the 1980s, **Lagundri beach★★** (Pantai Lagundri) hosts the famous World Qualifying Series in June-July. It must be said that, according to local experts, its rollers guarantee you "the seven best seconds of your life". Nonetheless, if you want to live a little longer, turn your attention to the reefs and their colourful fish, armed with mask and snorkel. You can also go to the nearby fishing village of **Botohilitano**, *(20min on foot, along the road leaving Lagundri to the west)*. **Megaliths** with symbolic motifs stand at several points along the main street.

Southern Nias: "ship-houses"

R. Marca

Nias Island

From village to village★★★

A one-day walking visit (allow 6hr including visits). Take a guide with you, make sure you have shoes that will cope with stone-paved tracks, and take a picnic. Do not forget to register your visit with the chief of each village, who will take a fee for the right to pass through. The villages of Bawomataluo and Hilisimaetano are also accessible by road. In this case it is advisable to organise transport, through your hotel, so you can be dropped off in the first village (12km from Lagundri) and collected from the last.

The villages that are dotted around the southern tip of the island are perched on hilltops to have a better view of approaching enemies. They barely emerge from the jungle, which is still home to wild pigs, and, like fortified towns are reached by inter-minable flights of steps. Each village once represented a small state, complete with chief and council (the term *banua*, which means "village", also designates a larger entity, encompassing the sky, the world, and the land of one's birth). The council met together in an open-sided hall, the *bale*, to discuss the sharing of collective tasks and matters of customary justice. In front of it now stands the assembly court bristling with the village's finest **megaliths**, while each house displays its **oli batu** ("wall of stones") that commemorates major family events. Horizontal stones are for funerals, and standing stones for other ceremonies.

■ The 250 year-old village of **Bawomataluo★★★** is recognised as one of the most typ-ical of the region (naturally heavily visited). Wooden houses stand shoulder to shoul-der along both sides of a wide paved street.

But what makes Bawomataluo famous is the impressive outline of the **omo sebu★★★**, the chief's house standing 20m high. In its great inner hall a series of **bas-reliefs★** embellishes the wooden walls, in which the royal emblems are recognisable: a pair of horns crowned with two stars, together with a necklace and an earring. And don't miss the Dutch ship under attack by fish, an illustration of the king's invincibility. As in Hilisimaetano, you can watch the **war dance★** of the head-hunters, performed for tourists on request. This is also the opportunity to see the impressive leaps over the **batu hombo★★**, the "jumping stone". Warriors used to practise leaping over the stone in a single bound, so as to be ready to scale the ramparts of enemy kingdoms. The performances of the young villagers are still enough to take your breath away.

■ A pretty village lying 600m below Bawomataluo, **Orahili★★** fully deserves its name: "the hillside steps". In fact, access is via a winding track of 480 stone steps, plung-ing down from the road *(be warned, this is a cul-de-sac: you will have to climb up again and then up the Bawomataluo steps, to continue the excursion).*

■ At an hour's walk from Bawomataluo, **Siwalawala★** also occupies an enchanting site. To reach it, cross the **Bawomataluo baths**: two loops of the river have been made into baths, one for men and the other for women. You should take the path through the area that corresponds to your sex!

■ A village-street with 3 000 inhabitants, **Onohondo** *(20min walk above Siwalawala)* still retains some beautiful **painted façades** and its **royal house**. According to local legend, the king had his carpenters thrown from the top of the roof to avoid any pos-sible copy being built of his "palace".

■ Continuing to the north *(45min walk)*, you will come to the main street of **Hilinawalo**, a little village whose **church** illustrates a rare case of successful compro-mise with traditional building styles.

Nias: the traditional leap over the "batu hombo" (Onohondo)

C Bourzat

■ *A narrow unpaved path takes you back westwards to the tarmac road.* It goes through **Bawogasili** *(1hr from Hilinawalo)*, which still maintains a very fine **megalith**★ with carved decoration.

■ After a 45min walk, the path joins the road to the village of **Hilisimaetano**★★, which is interesting for its **assembly court**, still furnished with stone seats.

From here you are not very far from Lagundri (10km along the road) and a well-deserved bath.

Gomo★★

62km northeast of Lagundri. Forking off from the main thoroughfare in Lahusa, the road leaves the coast to wind through banana plantations, palm trees and rice fields. Standing on the banks of the river with the same name, Gomo was probably the cradle of the Niasans: here you can see the island's most famous megaliths. They actually stand 5km away from Gomo, in the village of **Tundrumbaho**★★. Here, under a leaden sky, you will find the **osa-osa**★★, royal thrones carved with three-headed dragons, abandoned to the enveloping vegetation. Here you will also see a phallic **behu**, stretching skywards to transmit the pleas of mortals to heavenly beings.

On your way back take a little detour to **Tetegewo**★★★ *(20min walk, going through Gomo again)*, which also has some fine black stones, lost in the midst of acacias and bamboos. Moss has covered their dragons with soft green velvet, spreading right into the depths of their gaping mouths. **Stone tables** stand all around, serving as symbols of women.

Back in Gomo, you can stop for refreshments.

The wild west★★★
2-day tour from Telukdalam (long distances by car). Plan to spend a night in Onolimbu.

This itinerary off the tourist trail will certainly leave you with powerful impressions. The very bumpy road is strewn with fallen rocks and earth, and the six bridges along the way have all been destroyed. They have now been replaced by simple tree trunks passable only by a motorbike pushed by its passengers on foot! The inhabitants of the regions are naturally very isolated, and are therefore all the more charming.

On the way the road passes alongside **Moale beach**★ (Pantai Moale) *(approximately 40km from Telukdalam)*, a superb and completely empty ribbon of white sand. Sadly this is not a good place for swimming: the spectacular rollers dissuade even the most experienced Australian surfers.

■ **Olayama**★★ – *A few kilometres north of Moale.* This village contains an astonishing group of **adu figures**★★. At the top of three granite steps stands a row of statues from the time of King **Halawa**, a traitor who killed his father to bring forward the day of his enthronement. He is the central figure, shown on his knees on his throne, dominating all the other statues. His father stands on his left, without a seat. A group of commoners stands to the left of the royal group: there is no crown, the finery is different, and an erect penis is much smaller in size than that of the royal characters. Needless to say, such genital representations have very rarely survived the activism of the Christian missionaries.

Facing the statues a small wooden hut houses a **patchouli distillation laboratory**. You can buy a little bottle of the unrefined oil here.

About 1km away, along a narrow track below, you will come face to face with four more enormous **statues**, unique in that they have been carved out of pink stone, and bear virtually no relief *(local children will guide you through the thick forest)*.

■ **Hiligoe**★★★ – *90min by road from here; 3km from Mandrehe.* Once across a river you reach a long steep stone track, where you will meet women with kilos of fresh latex on their heads. Finally, the delightful **Malaysian houses** of the village appear, painted green and blue. Statues protect them, which the older people continue to venerate. The most accessible, hidden in a cabin on the edge of the village, has always been known to the inhabitants as **techembowo**★. Although it is very eroded, it remains formidable and is regarded as having powers of speech. History relates that it suffered from the shots of Dutch soldiers, for whom this lack of tact proved fatal: eleven of them are supposed to be buried behind the statue. The figure is consulted on marriages and dowries, and interprets the omens read in the entrails of chickens sacrificed on the altar.

Two more sites★★ that are even more spectacular await you outside the village. To find them, buried in the jungle, you have to cut your way through with a machete (5min walk). Then, emerging from the greenery you will see a group of megaliths: four statues of varying sizes, some holding in their hands the sacred **betel cup**. The third site consists only of a single **statue**★ – but what a statue! Set up in the middle of a clearing in a forest of banana trees, it stands like a gigantic matchstick, measuring almost twice the height of a human. Now it leans over to one side, like a tower of Pisa with a human head. No one knows why – perhaps the work of spirits or a landslide.

■ **Onolimbu**★★ – *On the way back, 30min from Hiligoe along a very rough road. The village chief is happy to accommodate visitors in his large house.*
On the way into the village, on the right, the **Catholic Church**★ catches the eye with its vivid colours. The interior is even more remarkable, with its naive **frescoes** that you could gaze at for hours. Onolimbu – literally "child of the spring" – was founded a dozen generations ago and legend has it that the water surrounding the village has prevented the inhabitants from leaving it. Recently, however, the outside world has come to meet them, in the form of a television set acquired by the village chief. There is public viewing every evening. Apart from this attraction, Onolimbu is unique in the region on account of its **megaliths**★★, which are innumerable. The long central pathway, lined with both ship-houses and oval houses, has a succession of *adu* without faces, but whose shapes and decoration give each one a genuine personality.

Continue southwards (a challenging 2-3hr walk). After crossing the six tree-trunk bridges, you reach Sirombu.

■ **Sirombu** – A charming fishing village far from the rest of the world, with light boats constantly putting out to sea, Sirombu stretches out along an enormous beach. This has been so hardened by the tides that locals ride their bicycles on it. Lastly, beyond the fork for the village of **Lolowau**, you will see the beach of Moale stretching out, as empty as ever.

Nias Island

Making the most of Nias Island

COMING AND GOING

By air – Flights twice a day (8-11am) Medan-Gunungsitoli with the charter company SMAC (50min-1hr10min). Booking offices at Medan and Gunungsitoli. At the airport SMAC organises transfers for Gunungsitoli (the airport is 19km south of the town).

By sea – Daily service (except Sundays) by overnight boat from Sibolga, on the west coast of Sumatra (9-11hr). A PELNI ferry crosses three times a week between Sibolga and Gunungsitoli (Wednesdays, Fridays and Sundays; return on Tuesdays, Thursdays and Saturdays). On Saturdays the boat continues to Padang and Jakarta. In the Sibolga-Nias direction you can buy your ticket directly at the port, by applying to the Customs Office and paying a "commission". It is better to go through a travel agent. Be warned: with its combination of night-time heat, racketeering and thefts, the boat journey can be an unpleasant experience. Go by air instead.

SIBOLGA ADDRESS BOOK

Bank/Currency exchange – **BNI**, Jl Katamso.

Post Office/Telephone – The **main post office**, Jl Sutomo, has a long-distance telephone and Internet service.

Travel agency – The **Tourist Information Center**, Jl Bridg Katamso 51, facing the Wisata Indah Hotel, ☎ (0631) 228 87, is a private tour operator run by Mr Bandung, an efficient and friendly Toba Batak who is now famous in the town. Bookings for ferry and plane tickets (agent for SMAC, Garuda and Sempati) and for bus tickets.

GETTING AROUND

Regular bus services connect Gunnungsitoli with Lagundri. There are also public minibus and mini-van services (the latter officially equipped for six passengers). For short distances: *becak* (cycle rickshaws), "babybuses" (theoretically designed for 35 people) and motorbikes that can be hired in *losmen* in Lagundri.

EATING OUT

Except in Lagundri, there are few restaurants on Nias. Most meals are served in the hotels and *losmen*.

Making the most of Gunungsitoli

ADDRESS BOOK

Tourist information – Jl Soekarno 6. Its opening hours are extremely unpredictable and its resources minimal.

Bank/Currency exchange – **BNI**, Jl Pattimura, **BPDSU**, Jl Hatta.

Post office/Telephone – **Main post office** and **Telkom** together at the intersection of Jl Hatta and Jl Gomo.

Travel agents – **Nias Holidays**, Miga Beach Hotel, ☎ (0639) 214 60. The only such establishment available on the island, the hotel is an agent for SMAC. English-speaking guides. In the town centre there is a small **PELNI** office, Jl Lagundri (left fork beyond the Buddhist temple).

WHERE TO STAY

Modest

Miga Beach, Jl Diponegoro 507, ☎ (0639) 214 60, Fax (0639) 211 88 – 12rm. ☏ 🗎 ☷ ✗ Cold water. Room 10 is the only one with air conditioning. Located between Gunungsitoli and the airport. The little wooden bungalows with sago-palm roofs are set round a garden. Quiet, but the service is fairly blasé.

Gomo Hotel, Jl Gomo 148, ☎ (0639) 219 26 – 30rm. ☏ 🗎 ☷ ✗ A favourite hotel with surfers. The same Spartan standards: the concrete of the hotel reverberates day and night with the sound of the capital's traffic.

Making the most of Lagundri

ADDRESS BOOK

You will find various services at **Teluk-dalam**, 14km east of Lagundri.

Bank/Currency exchange – BPDSU, Jl A Yani 46, weekdays 8am-3pm, Saturdays until 12noon. Changes travellers' cheques, dollars and the major European currencies.

Post office/Telephone – On the same side of the street, 500m further on.

WHERE TO STAY

The selection is restricted to two hotels (a third one is opening soon). Those on a small budget will easily find numerous Spartan *losmen*, bamboo bungalows with a communal concrete bathroom block.

Seabreeze has a good reputation. It is ideally placed for surfers and for international competitions – hence its distinctive clientele, permanently carrying boards.

Modest
Lagundri Holiday Cottage, ☎ (0630) 210 50 – 16rm. 📶 ☲ Its bungalows on the waterfront would provide an ideal spot but there is no competition in the range: service is indifferent and the rooms depressing (no sheets, and flickering neon lights from outside).

Luxury
Sorake Beach Resort, Pantai Lagundri, ☎ (0630) 211 95, Fax (0630) 211 97 –

80rm. 📶 ☲ 🖋 📺 ✕ ⚒ ☂ 🆑 Open since the summer of 1994, this is representative of the invasion of great luxury in Nias, with hot water (non-existent everywhere else) and mini-bars. Tastefully designed wooden bungalows dotted about in a vast garden.

EATING OUT

Zita, Jl Sorake 12 A, Lagundri. A Chinese restaurant on Sorake beach. They serve the inevitable steaks done to Western taste. Also excellent fish.

HAVING A DRINK

Toho, 100m beyond **Seabreeze**. A bar that is popular with surfers and residents alike. The palm leaf roof lets in the sea air. People come here for a cool beer, with Indonesian pop music in the background. The alternative is the bar at the **Sorake Beach Resort**, which is far more chic and romantic.

OTHER THINGS TO DO

Surfing and snorkelling – For the professional as well as the beginner, **Seabreeze** rents out surf-boards or "body boards", as well as masks and snorkels for observing the fish and the enormous turtles that abound in Lagundri Bay.

Making the most of Lagundri

LAKE TOBA★★★
THE ISLAND OF SAMOSIR
North Sumatra Province
Prapat: 176km from Medan – Map p 161
Alt 900m – Cool climate

Not to be missed
The Lake Toba Festival, in June.
A swim in the lake.
The road from Prapat to Bukittinggi, one of the most beautiful
stretches along the Trans-Sumatra.

And remember...
Say "Hello" in the local language, with a cheerful "Horas!"
Buy one of the superb songkets (embroidered silk) in Tebing Tinggi.
At Pematang Siantar, take a ride in a "becak siantar", a unique form of transport
in Indonesia.

The history of the region is a tale of giants: the story of a volcano which, 75 000 years ago, blew up in a colossal explosion. Its crater collapsed in on itself, opening up a large cauldron that filled with water. This was the birth of Lake Toba, an inland sea with blue-mauve water, 100km long and 31km wide. But that was not the end of the story: 45 000 years later, fresh upheavals convulsed the original volcano. The base of the caldera split and broke apart, and whole slabs of the volcano's sides came away and plunged into the water. Two enormous pieces of rock are visible above the surface: one on the northeast side of the lake, forming the Prapat peninsula, and the other in the middle, creating Samosir, "the Isle of the Dead". And all around are the shining waters, with their 450m depths unexplored.

Such a majestic and fertile site could not but attract settlers. Around the 6C AD Batak colonisers set up there to develop one of the most prosperous communities of their ethnic group, the Toba. The local nobility displayed the wealth in their tombs, impressive megaliths on which they spent fortunes. Modern times have transformed the stone memorials into cement mausoleums, but the ostentations of Toba funerary art still provoke jeers (or jealousy?) among other Batak groups.

Arriving from the Karo region
For those who arrive from Berastagi without using the Trans-Sumatra highway.

Beyond Kabanjahe the road soon meets the shores of Lake Toba. After **Merek**, a little village a few kilometres to the south, it runs along the northeast shore in an asphalt ribbon winding along the green ridge of the former caldera. Before taking this road, make a small detour along the road that drops down from Merek to the edge of the lake, towards **Tongging**. Just before the town, at the mouth of a cave, the **Sipisopiso waterfall**★ ("like a knife-blade") bursts out above a wall of green and plunges noisily down in a torrent, a spectacular dive of 120m.

Return to Merek, then turn right along the road to Prapat.

Pematang Purba★★
32km east of Merek. A veritable museum-village, Pematang Purba recreates the full warlike atmosphere of the **Batak simalungun** strongholds. Founded in the 17C, the village still has its access tunnel, a narrow and easily defended passage. It opens out

onto an esplanade in the middle of eight **long houses*** on piles, noble ships with soaring roofs that were once protected by stone walls or bamboo and earth palisades. While they display the high standing of the chiefs of the Purba clan, the local dynasty, they also illustrate the lack of comfort and hygiene that made 19C European missionaries and travellers shudder.

The **royal residence***, more than two hundred years old, is open to visitors. In the dim light of the first room, on the right, is the alcove of the **royal bedroom**. This was where the companion chosen for the night was brought in by a eunuch. But it is the **women's room** that occupies the largest space, a long dark smoky room that accommodated around ten wives (the royal offspring – 88 children according to the record established by the thirteenth sovereign! – slept in a separate pavilion). Items preserved here include crockery, goblets and bottles hollowed out of bamboo tubes, and a **royal sarcophagus** bearing a decorative bird in relief, a Batak version of the Garuda. A succession of 14 kings in all ruled from this dwelling, their genealogy recorded in a series of buffalo horns set on the house's inner pile, which is painted in the three Batak colours – white, red and black. All are remembered for an iniquitous power under which the ruler treated his serfs like a herd of animals, to be chastised with death according to the *adat* (customary law) or the ruler's whim. During the social upheavals of 1947, however, the fourteenth king was assassinated, an event that marked the abandonment of the village.

Beyond Pematang Purba take the road to **Simarjarunjung**** which offers magnificent views over the lake. In particular, take time to stop at the **panoramic restaurant** at the Simarjarunjung crossroads. Here you can enjoy one of the most beautiful **views**** while you sip a *bandreh*, a drink full of the flavours of the Medan region, mixing ginger, pepper, cardamom, cinnamon, cloves, aniseed, citronella and sugar cane.

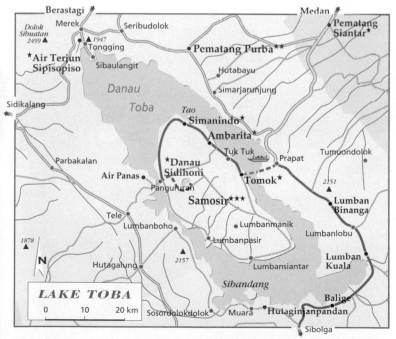

On the Trans-Sumatra

For travellers who come direct from Medan.

If you reach the Toba region along the Trans-Sumatra, take advantage of it to make a brief stop in the village of **Tebing Tinggi** *(76km from Medan, 96km from Prapat)*. Here the family of Zaleha Hasyim continues the Malayu tradition of **songket batubara★★**, sumptuous silk brocades. On the threshold of his Malay house *(in the residential quarter, Jl Badak 30)* full of songbirds, you can watch the complex weaving of these fabrics.

Those who are travelling in their own vehicle can also stop for a moment at **Pematang Siantar★** *(48km before Prapat)*. For at least three reasons: the surprising **becak**, unique in Indonesia – Nortons or BSAs dating from the Second World War! – the peanut snacks sold in the Chinese stalls in the town centre, and the **Simalungun Museum★** *(Jl Sudirman, Monday-Thursday and Saturday, 8am-2pm, Friday, 8-11am; closed on Sundays and public holidays)*. As its name indicates, the museum is devoted to Batak Simalungun culture (books of magic written on tree-bark, stone sculptures of protective gods, etc).

As you approach **Prapat** the road descends in hairpin bends, bathed in a sweet scent of flowers and damp earth, with superb **views★★** of Lake Toba all the way. The peninsula itself, however, offers very little of interest, apart from its **fish market** *(daily, on the ferry pier)*. A spa resort since the early 20C, Prapat village is above all the point of entry for the island of Samosir. Here you will find every holiday facility: post office, bus station, hotels, restaurants and so on.

The island of Samosir★★★

One-day tour on motorbikes (can be hired at your hotel).
Distances are given from Tuk Tuk.

Samosir, the cradle of Batak culture, is naturally a very popular place. But it is worth knowing that away from Tuk Tuk and the coast facing Prapat, constantly busy with boats disgorging hordes of tourists, the interior of the island and its western shores remain extremely peaceful.

■ **Tomok★** – *4km south of Tuk Tuk.*
Apart from a fine **traditional Toba house** that contains a dusty museum *(fee)*, Tomok has a **royal necropolis★**, the domain of a large number of tombs bearing their *singa*, or guardian demon. A group of stone statues stands on a platform *(follow the alley of shops to find the site)*, sacred figures seated on chairs. They appear to have taken root in the rock while talking together. Created in the early 20C, these figures are of the first king of Tomok, **Seributu**, and his wife (17C), surrounded by dignitaries.

Tomok, a royal sarcophagus

M Lemerie

Cannibal practices

In terms of cruelty, mankind has never lacked imagination. The Toba proved no exception with their own style of capital punishment. Tied to a rock, the condemned man had two deep cuts slashed in his chest, which the executioner sprinkled with aromatic lemon and salt. Then the executioner put the victim's head on a large stone before slowly cutting his throat, like a pig. Next, the watching crowd drank the man's blood and shared his heart and liver, raw, but purified by the "makrut" juice. The last executions of this kind took place in the late 19C.

Standing nearby are **royal tombs****, weighty stone sarcophagi (*500m below, towards the lake*). The most imposing is that of the king's grandson. Like a figurehead, the carved head with its long hair juts out from the tomb. A woman squats astride the tombstone, bearing on her head a bowl for *makrut* (aromatic lemon of the bergamot family, used in many Batak rituals), the symbol of young unmarried girls. As the unhappy fiancée of the sovereign, who preferred war, she fell in love with another man and the king, furious, used his magic powers to make her go mad. The surrounding tombs include the final resting-place of the last descendant of the line (1929-74) who died in Jakarta, while an enormous banyan tree shades the more modest burial places of the faithful soldiers of Seributu, who died in battle.

■ **Ambarita*** – *6km north of Tuk Tuk. From the quay, a continuous line of souvenir stalls leads directly to the site (a donation is requested)*. The village itself offers little of interest apart from the well-preserved **houses of the king and his family**. The open-air "law court" stands in front of the royal residence, shaded by a traditional banyan tree, where several **stone seats** have been assembled from various villages around Samosir. A **jail** has been installed between the piles of the house, with a fabric model representing a prisoner, its feet held in a frame.

In the adjoining square another **group of stones** illustrates the rituals of capital punishment that were carried out here, a cruel custom that gave the Toba Batak a sinister reputation. Expect to see the local guides hugely enjoying giving a "historic reconstruction", delighting in the most bloodthirsty details.

■ **Simanindo** – *On the northern tip of the island (19km from Tuk Tuk). Daily performances of traditional dance (two in the morning, one on Sundays, fee)*. The large number of fish breeding grounds that can be seen from the boat indicates that a village is near. At the entrance to the village a beautiful traditional house has a small **Museum of Batak traditions*** (*notices in Batak and Bahasa Indonesia, a few in English*). Here you will find everything that relates to Toba magic and beliefs, including the formidable *tunggal panaluan*, the sacred staff used by the datu (sorcerer-priest) to visit sickness or death on a hostile clan, or simply call up rain. Delicate **statues of gods** illustrate the skill of the Bataks in woodwork. A cremation urn, from which the ashes were taken and used as fertiliser stands next to a *makrut* press and books on divination. There are also objects from everyday life: looms for weaving *ulos* – traditional Batak fabrics – dried pumpkins used for storing *tuak*, spoons made of coconut, communal dishes, etc.

On the right on the way into the village is a row of **royal family mausoleums**, the final resting-place of the Sidauruk clan (the last burial dates from 1991). Near it is the **sacrifice pavilion** (animal and human), preceded by its **altar for offerings**. Inside the village walls is a very handsome group of five **houses with grain stores***, standing in two rows facing each other. On the right, the side with the grain stores – which were also used as sleeping space for bachelors – a pavilion houses the communal *lesung*, the pestle used for husking the rice.

Lake Toba

Sigalegale, the puppet of the dead
To mark the end of the performance at Simanindo, a Sigalegale puppet makes its appearance. In the past this life-size wooden puppet would be made when an important man died without a male heir, to prevent his soul returning to haunt the surviving members of the clan. The officiating priests would treat it with due respect during the funeral ceremony before reducing it to shreds and chasing its maker out of the village, who would take with him the appeased spirit of the dead man.

On the left is the **royal house★**, identifiable by its handsome **singa masks★**. The interior still has the **royal bed**, a large piece of furniture in the shape of a boat with a chest concealed beneath it (the king thus slept over his treasure). As you leave you can watch a dance performance in front of the building. Although these are designed for tourists, they are nonetheless impressive.

Follow the road running along the western coast of the island, before forking left to Pangururan (16km from Simanindo). The final stretch involves a very uneven and difficult road, requiring the experience of a local driver.

■ **Danau Sidihoni★** – Few tourists visit the heart of Samosir – the road is not encouraging. Yet the journey is undoubtedly worth the trip. Isolated on a high plateau, a lake measuring one square kilometre lies like a little emerald in its landlocked casket above the blue waters of Lake Toba. An odd sight, a lake within a lake; its changeable colours have given rise to more than one legend. One version relates that when the Dutch arrived the waters of the lake turned blood red. Still

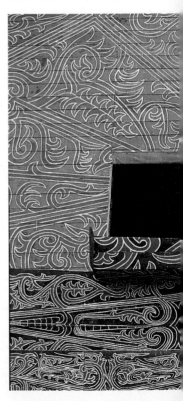

today the local inhabitants, fishermen and peasants, consider that its changing colours reflect their worries and struggles. Cut off from the rest of the island, this small dark-skinned population has developed a distinct way of life, with an oral tradition that perpetuates numerous legends.

Along the way you will come across peasants armed with machetes, going barefoot to the fields, or women carrying wood on their shoulders.

On the return journey the steep road affords breathtaking **panoramas★★** of the western banks of Lake Toba. Rich vegetation cloaks the mountains with soft brown-green velvet. Next comes **Pangururan**, from where you can visit the **hot springs** *(4km to the west, turn right at Pangururan bridge)*. This is your opportunity for a relaxing bathe, even if the surrounding concrete spoils the setting.

Around the lake★

After visiting Samosir, leave Prapat to take the Trans-Sumatra highway that runs beside Lake Toba. The Prapat-Padang Sidempuan section is one of the most spectacular on this long stretch of road: from Prapat, the road first runs along the eastern and southern shores of the lake, carving its way across the pastoral landscape of **Uluan★** ("the springs").

Up as far as **Porsea** you go through a series of beautiful villages – simple, peaceful places that are ignored by tourists. One such is **Lumban Binanga II** (*30km from Prapat*), the centre of the Manurung clan, whose houses still have their thatched roofs (disregarding the intrusive Malay house nearby with its satellite dish).

Further on, **Lumban Kuala** (*14km away*) marks the entrance to the Asahan valley. Here you can see a handsome **royal tomb***** made of stone.

Another place for a stop is **Balige** (*65km from Prapat, 3hr by bus*) where you can explore an enormous **market*****, capped by a series of traditional Batak roofs. Fish, meat, fruit and spice smells mingle for better or for worse. The market is a combination of an ants' nest and Ali Baba's cave, containing superb **ulos******. These are made up and sold on the spot by charming old ladies who come in from the surrounding villages. The fabrics are piled up in their hundreds, with every colour and style, and go for unbeatable prices since there is no middleman (*to find them, turn left at the entrance*). Nearby, working in the soft light, a group of women untangle freshly dyed woollen strands while they gossip and chat together.

Beyond Balige, head for **Muara**, by taking a fork on the right that leads (*15km from the Trans-Sumatra*) to **Hutaginjanpandan**, the site of a superb **viewpoint***** overlooking the lake, Samosir and the peninsula of Pardomuansigaol (*this itinerary can also be done as an excursion from Prapat*).

Then return to the Trans-Sumatra.

The vast royal house at Simanindo (detail)

Lake Toba

R Zeboulon/DIAF

The road to the West⋆

The Trans-Sumatra road leaves the Lake Toba region at **Siborongborong** (*approximately 20km from Balige*) and winds through the heights of the two parallel chains of the **Bukit Barisan**. Beyond the last Toba villages it affords the finest **panorama⋆⋆⋆** imaginable over the lake.

Next it reaches **Tarutung** (*26km from Siborongborong*), a little town that lives off the trade in incense harvested in the benjamin-tree plantations on the surrounding hillsides. No fewer than 1 200 bends punctuate the 66km of road that separate Tarutung from Sibolga, the port for the ferries to the island of Nias (*see p 158*), all of it through the forests of giant heather in the **Silindung valley**.

Beyond Sibolga the road climbs up again to the higher lands of the Batak Pak Pak, to reach **Padang Sidempuan** (*approximately 90km from Sibolga*), the gateway to the Mandailing region. The town has no intrinsic charm but is a necessary stopping point on the road to Bukittinggi (*you should allow 15hr to cover the 500km of surfaced road*).

In the Mandailing region

Like their Pak Pak neighbours, the Mandailing live an enormous contradiction: they are simultaneously Batak (they still use their language)

The ship-houses of Lake Toba

With their roofs curved like a ship's hull, the houses of Lake Toba and the island of Samosir are somewhat similar to those of the Toraja on Sulawesi, almost at the other end of the archipelago. Lined up along a village street each one faces its own rice store or "sopo", an outward sign of wealth. As with the Karo, the entrance is at the gable end through a trap door set into the floor. Elaborate carved motifs decorate the façade, coloured red, black and white. Against the geometric compositions of spirals and stars the protective mask of the "singa" can often be seen. This half-lion and half-buffalo with gaping mouth and a double pair of breasts is a symbol of fertility.

A Toba Batak house

R Marca

and Muslim, since the Padri *(see p 125)* converted them by force (1815-37). A puritanical form of Islam took root in the region, particularly at **Purbabaru**, a village to the south of Panyabungan *(about 100km from Padang Sidempuan)*, which can pride itself on having the largest **pesantren** (Koranic school) in Indonesia, founded by one of the Mandailing in 1912. There are students (5 000 boys and 3 000 girls) from all over Indonesia as well as from Malaysia, Singapore and Brunei.

The **Hutanopan region** *(35km from Panyabungan)* still has several types of traditional Mandailing housing. **Usortolang** village on the banks of the Gadis retains wooden houses with high Batak gables, carved with decorative features borrowed from their Minangkabau neighbours.

Making the most of Lake Toba

COMING AND GOING

By bus – From Medan (the east road): several departures daily from the Amplas bus station. If you are travelling on the Trans-Sumatra, via Pematang Siantar, the terminal is Parluasan. With regular coach services, the Trans-Sumatra is the most direct route (allow 5hr).

If you are coming from Berastagi, take the road along the eastern shore of Lake Toba, via Merek (Berastagi-Prapat: 169km). In this case there is no regular bus service; you will have to go to Kabanjahe, take a bus for Pematang Siantar, and change again at the Parluasan terminal for the Prapat road. The alternative is to take one of the tourist minibuses that leave every day. More expensive, but comfortable and direct, they make a stop at the Sipisopiso falls and at the museum village of Pematang Purba.

By car – The simplest and most convenient form of transport. Rent a car or a minibus from a hotel or the tourist office in Berastagi (in the fruit market). The recommended route runs along the east bank of Lake Toba, an opportunity to see a good many places of interest.

For **Padang Sidempuan** (West Sumatra): by car or tourist bus. Daily departures at 6am, pick-up points at some of the hotels in Prapat (enquire at your hotel). You can also book seats from Samosir.

By boat to Samosir – Double-decker boats provide a shuttle service between Prapat and Tuk Tuk or Tomok. Last departures at 6.30pm. You can also charter a small motorboat at the **Danau Toba** hotel jetty at Prapat.

GETTING AROUND

The island of Samosir has no public transport services. The best solution is therefore to hire bicycles from **Pepy's**, or small motorbikes from your hotel.

ADDRESS BOOK

Prapat Tourist Office – On Jl Pulau Samosir. Not very helpful.

Bank/Currency exchange – Better to err on the side of caution and exchange currency in Medan where the rates are better. In Prapat, the **BNI** has an automatic cash-dispenser for MasterCard. The **Singgalang** restaurant, Jl Sisingamangaraja 52, ☎ (0625) 412 60, and **Charlie's Guesthouse**, near the market (on the ferry pier) change money (dollars) at a reasonable rate, with a small commission charge. The same applies to the **Dolok Silau** travel agency.

Post office/Telephone – Small post office in Ambarita. In Prapat, **Wartel** in Jl Harranggaol.
In Samosir, **Telkom** next to Anju Cottage, at the northern end of the Tuk Tuk peninsula. Reverse-charge calls possible in most hotels. **Internet** in the restaurant at **Tabo Cottages**, in Tuk Tuk.

Medical service – The best-equipped establishment is the **Specialist Center**, Pemantang Siantar, 1hr by bus from Prapat. In Tuk Tuk, there is a small **Health Center** on the roadside, 800m beyond the Carolina Hotel.

Travel agencies – In Prapat, **Dolok Silau**, near the market (on the ferry pier), has a good reputation. **Pesiar Indah Tour and Travel**, Jl Harranggaol 75, ☎ (0625) 416 83, makes bus and domestic airline reservations. In Tuk Tuk, **Pepy's**, next to the Carolina Hotel, lays on tours and operates as a modest travel agency.

WHERE TO STAY

● Prapat

Modest

On the Haranggaol road you will find plenty of *losmen*-tourist offices for modest budgets, with basic facilities. They organise excursions in the surrounding area and transport to Bukittinggi. The main ones are **Riris Inn**, **Pago Pago Inn**, **Penginapan Melati**, **Andilo Nancy Travel** and **Tobali**.

Average

Danau Toba International Cottages, Jl Nelson Purba, ☎ (0625) 411 72/416 41 – 91rm. 🛏 🥢 TV ✗ 🏊 ♨ CC Its bungalows with spacious bedrooms are spread up the slopes of a hill facing one of the lakeside beaches. You can do various water sports here.

Natour Prapat, Jl Marihat 1, ☎ (0625) 410 12, Fax (0625) 410 19 – 100rm. 🛏 🥢 TV CC This is the oldest hotel in Prapat. Comfortable rooms in a large three-storey building facing the lake (avoid the rooms on the street side of the building, which overlook Prapat's main crossroads). The food here is not recommended, but in the evenings the "pub" atmosphere is pleasant.

Luxury

Niagara, Jl Pembangunan 1, ☎ (0625) 410 28, Fax (0625) 412 33 – 145rm. 🛏 🥢 TV ✗ 🏊 CC A sophisticated establishment perched up on a hillside. Not near the lake beaches, but it has its own enormous swimming pool.

● Samosir

Modest

In the curve of the eastern bay on Tuk Tuk peninsula you will find a string of small places such as the **Yogi**, the **Sony** and **Nina's**. The price per night is derisory, with facilities to match: the interior furnishing of the large traditional Batak houses is just a plain mattress on the floor. There is a "kamar mandi" outside. Bring your own sleeping bag and mosquito net.

Average

Bagus Bay, Tuk Tuk, ☎ (0625) 41481 – 17rm. 🛏 ✗ A favourite with travellers, no doubt on account of its semi-Western menu and its American films. The hotel

has lovely rooms, which are very clean, including some in two wooden Batak houses. Magnificent garden with an unrestricted view of Tuk Tuk bay.

Anju Cottage, Tuk Tuk, ☎ (0625) 413 48 – 10rm. 🛏 ("mandi") Simple rooms with cupboards that lock, hot water, and a **Telkom** office near by (24hr a day). The staff will book bus tickets for Bukittinggi, Medan and Berastagi.

Samosir Cottages, Tuk Tuk, next door, ☎ (0625) 410 50, Fax (0625) 45 11 70 – 30rm. 🛏 ✗ The hotel shares with the Anju Cottage (above) the most beautiful natural swimming pool in the lake. It has the same type of rooms, reasonable but without great charm.

Pulau Tao Cottages, on Pulau Tao, an islet facing Simanindo – 20 cottages (no telephone). 🛏 ✗ Access by boat. The cottages are small and clean. The Olympian calm of the setting is only disturbed by the comings and goings of the fishermen.

High end

🏨**Liberta**, Tuk Tuk, ☎ (0625) 45 10 35 – 8rm. 🛏 ✗ Run by Helga who has very tastefully appointed the attractive Batak houses set in a magnificent garden. Apartments rather than rooms, at unbeatable value for money. Family atmosphere, and fresh bread!

🏨**Tabo Cottages**, Tuk Tuk, ☎ (0625) 416 14, tabores@indo.net.id – 6rm. 🛏 ✈ ✗ Similar to the above in atmosphere, but with higher rates. Batiks and panelling embellish the rooms with their very personal touch, harmoniously blending tradition and modernism. In the evening, settle down on purple cushions in the restaurant overlooking the garden to enjoy vegetarian food in one of the best places to eat in Tuk Tuk.

Toledo Inn, Tuk Tuk, between Ambarita and Tomok, ☎ (0625) 411 81, Fax (0625) 411 74 – 65rm. Booking in Medan: ☎ (061) 52 75 50 – 🛏 Hot water at certain times. The bungalows, some of which are built in the traditional style, form a somewhat old-fashioned ensemble. The roofs are made of corrugated iron so you may feel the heat. Currency exchange, shops, postal service.

Carolina, Tuk Tuk, ☎ (0625) 415 20, Fax (0625) 415 21 – 50 rm. 🛏 ✗ Its large bungalows in Toba Batak style have plain but comfortable rooms. From the recently redecorated restaurant you can watch the sun set over the lake. Very pleasant.

Silingtong, Tuk Tuk, ☎ (0625) 413 45 – 51rm. ⚓ ✗ The pretty garden lends it charm. The rooms are not very original, but pleasant. It is a pity that the enormous dining room seems to be more suitable for groups than for individual travellers. Not very convivial.

● **Padang Sidempuan**

Average

Danau Marsabut, Jl Sisingamangaraja, ☎ (0634) 218 72 – 50rm. ⚓ ✗ ⚓ A simple, pleasant hotel, popular with Indonesian groups. A pity that it is so far out.

Natama, Jl Sisingamangaraja 100, ☎ (0634) 223 05, Fax (0634) 210 35 – 60rm. ⚓ 🖳 ✗ The best, most comfortable hotel in town. The restaurant stays open late and, unlike the entry above, the staff here speak English.

EATING OUT

● **Prapat**

Basic

Most of the "rumah makhan" are concentrated on Jl Haranggaol. One of the best places is **Islam Murni**, ☎ (0625) 410 43. Excellent Padang cuisine.

At **Marina**, at number 18, you choose from the dishes displayed behind the window. You can try everything in small quantities, from spicy prawns to chicken flavoured with green chilli – simple, delicious – and highly seasoned.

● **Samosir**

Moderate

On the coast road from Tuk Tuk to Tomok, behind the Toledo Inn hotel there are several restaurants and small cafes, including **Leo's Bar**, in a curious "Swiss chalet" style.

Tarian, next door. The restaurant is in a breathtaking position overlooking the lake. It serves very good vegetarian food in competition with the excellent **Tabo**, in the hotel of the same name.

GOING OUT, HAVING A DRINK

Bar – Brando's Blues Bar, where young Indonesians and tourists meet for billiards or beers.

Batak dance performances – At the **Bagus Bay**, every Wednesday and Saturday; entrance free. The hotel will take the audience back after the show.

OTHER THINGS TO DO

Festivals – Every year, in June, Prapat holds the **Lake Toba Festival**, 6 days when streamlined boats fight it out in regattas. Concerts of traditional music by day, rock and disco music by night.

Excursions – The hotels provide guides and hire out bicycles and motorbikes for the many excursions possible on Samosir. **Pepy's**, next to the Carolina Hotel, will give you an idea of the cost and the different tours.

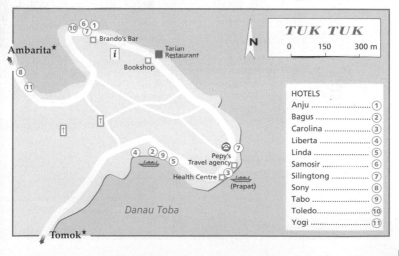

Making the most of Lake Toba

TUK TUK

0   150   300 m

Ambarita★

Brando's Bar

i

Tarian Restaurant

Bookshop

Pepy's Travel agency

Health Centre

(Prapat)

Danau Toba

Tomok★

HOTELS

Anju .... ①
Bagus .... ②
Carolina .... ③
Liberta .... ④
Linda .... ⑤
Samosir .... ⑥
Silingtong .... ⑦
Sony .... ⑧
Tabo .... ⑨
Toledo....................... ⑩
Yogi .... ⑪

The Minang region★★
Bukittinggi
West Sumatra Province – Map p 122-123
108km from Padang
Alt average 930m – Cool dry climate

Not to be missed
Bukittinggi market, the largest in Sumatra.
A buffalo fight at Kota Baru.
A swim in Lake Maninjau.

And remember...
Try the local form of transport, the "bendi" (horse-drawn carriage) at Bukittinggi
Avoid skimpy clothing, which may shock the Minang who,
although not fundamentalist, are devout Muslims.

The heart of the Minang region, a farming area, stretches out at the foot of **Merapi** volcano (2 891m). On its fertile slopes, carved into terraces of rice fields, there are fantastic canyons bursting with waterfalls, all drowned by jungle. At dawn, when the mist still clings to the delicate foliage of the cinnamon trees, the landscape recalls the pastoral beauties of Bali.

As for the inhabitants, they are unlike any other people. In town the veiled women govern the commercial world, transforming the markets into animated beehives. In the countryside they reign over the amazing traditional houses with horned roofs,

In the land of the "all powerful buffalo" (village of Padang Magek)

A Boutteville

where their brothers discuss the *adat*, the set of customs that regulates everyday life. Thus the Minangkabau perpetuate the paradox of a society that is both matrilineal and Muslim. A fascinating duality, to which can be added their unfailing warmth towards foreigners.

One people, three valleys

According to legend, the Minangkabau are directly descended from Alexander the Great, who had three sons with an Indian princess. One settled in the lands of the East, another in the West, while the third, **Maharaja Diraja** ("great king of kings"), set up between the two. His ship hit a rock the size of an egg – the summit of Mount Merapi – where he waited until the waters receded. He then founded his kingdom in the surrounding area on the site of modern-day **Pariangan**. His wife – a young local girl – gave him a son, Sutan Paduka Basa. From a second marriage she then had another child, Jantang Sutan Balun.

Buffalo against buffalo calf
The people of West Sumatra take their name from a mythical joust, which set them against Javanese forces in the 14C. The powerful Majapahit kingdom had despatched Prince Adityavarman to make Sumatra its vassal. He seized the mountains of the Minangkabau, where he was forced to submit to a trial of strength: a buffalo contest. Facing the enormous male brought by the Javanese, which had been trained to fight, the Minangkabau only came up with a ridiculous buffalo calf. Game lost even before it had begun? Hidden between its sprouting horns the young animal wore two sharpened blades. As it tried to suckle its adversary, it ripped the other open. The public acclaimed the calf "Menang Kerabau" – "buffalo victor" – which thereafter designated the Minang people and their region.

When the time came to divide their inheritance, the elder son wished to reign over the country's three valleys – **Tanah Datar** (*see p 180*), **Agam** and **Limapuluh Kota** – but the two half-brothers clashed. The younger set a challenge, near Lima Kaum: victory would go to the one who managed to plunge his kris dagger into a stone. The two blades sliced into the stone – to equal depths – with the result that each brother separately set up his own political system. As a descendant of a noble lineage, the elder son established a strongly hierarchical aristocracy, the *koto-piliang*; the younger chose a collegiate and egalitarian administration, the *bodi-caniago*. The Agam valley belonged to the first, the Tanah Datar to the second, and the valley of Limapuluh Kota combined the two systems.

Women's rule
These distant times are said to be the original setting for the *adat*, the customary law that created the famous matrilineal system of the Minang. According to this "ancient legacy that the rainfall does not rot and the sun does not wither", only the women have the right to own property and to pass it on. The whole

The Minang region

171

Minang house

family is subservient to the senior grandmother and although the administration of the village falls to her eldest brother the final decision remains with the women. In the face of this female power the young men set out on *marantau*, exile in another region where they seek experience and wealth before returning home to take a wife. In this way society has developed its own logic: mothers are guardians of the nourishing earth but it is the sons' responsibility to make the produce from it bear fruit. The legend of Malin Kundang, a prodigal son, illustrates the power of this tradition. On returning home the prodigal son refused to recognise his mother, now a poverty-stricken widow. Shocked by his attitude, the old woman cursed him and when Malin Kundang returned to sea a storm blew up. He died out of lack of respect for the *adat*.

The marriage of the adat and Islam

According to a Minang proverb, "the adat came down from the mountains, religion came up from the coast". In this unexpected encounter – matrilineal tradition and Islam – the Koran took the first step. The riches of the Minang region, in the form of gold deposits and then pepper, attracted Islamised traders from Aceh and, in the late 16C a Muslim, **Sutan Alif**, took the throne of **Pagaruyung**, the capital of Tanah Datar. Two regents ruled at his side: the *raja adat*, representing customary law, and the *raja ibadat*, who was responsible for religious questions.

The horned houses of the Minangkabau
The large house ("rumah gadang") of the Minangkabau has a long façade. Some think that the curve of the roof was adopted to avoid collapse of the ridge beam; but for the Minangkabau, it represents the horns of a buffalo, their symbolic animal. The wooden façade is covered with a profusion of carved and coloured motifs, an ornamental language that repeats the patterns on the Minangkabau brocades, the "songket". The interior space consists of a single long hall, which is used as a reception room; each end has a dais, the "anjung", for important guests. The back wall, consisting of a panel of plaited bamboo to allow air to pass through, is set with a series of alcoves: the sleeping rooms for the women of the family.

In the 19C, however, this balance was upset by the arrival of the **Padri** (see p 125). Led by **Imam Bonjol**, these armed believers embarked on a holy war, which turned into an instrument of nationalism against the Dutch. The *adat* now became seen as contrary to orthodox Muslim principles, particularly since the Minangkabau royal families maintained economic links – too close for their taste – with the colonial power. Abandoned by Batavia, the king of Pagaruyung and his family were then decimated by the Padri in the 1820s, before the Dutch finally crushed and eliminated the jihad. Islam was the loser at the end of this episode, but for a long time it continued to represent nationalism and the hope for independence. For this reason the people of West Sumatra have remained some of the most fervently devout in Indonesia. The choice between the old customary law and the Koranic law now remains within the family, and the village Council looks to one or the other, depending on the circumstances, to resolve a problem. Another development is that while property owners are still mainly women, the current trend is increasingly encouraging the sharing of inheritance between brothers and sisters.

The land of the "long houses"

Despite the changes in society, the Minangkabau have kept a powerful identity. The members of the *marantau* diaspora remain deeply attached to their land, and still send their mothers part of their income. This is how, in the ancestral lands, the traditional **rumah gadang** – the great wooden houses – are still being preserved and built (even though corrugated iron has begun to appear). As the house is the domain of the women, husbands are "invited" there as night falls. The immense roof, curved like buffalo horns with brilliant jewels set into the tips, recalls the totem animal of their origins. Naturally the houses appear somewhat empty with all the young people away seeking their fortune. But when there is a wedding – one of the most spectacular ceremonies in the archipelago – they become a magnificent decor shimmering with silk and gold.

On the road to Bukittinggi★

After crossing the Batak Mandailing region (North Sumatra), you reach the town of Rau, the gateway to West Sumatra Province. Beyond this point, the road is lined with a variety of places of interest.

Overhung by ridges of rock covered with clinging heather, the road runs alongside the **Rimba Panti Reserve★**, a luxuriant enclave of 3 120ha containing several rare species – tigers, bears, and birds of paradise *(the first point of access lies 100km north of Bukittinggi)*. Next to the road you can see boiling springs that spit out black sulphur at temperatures of 90-100°C. The reserve is also a sanctuary for the **rafflesia★**, a giant plant that only flowers once a year *(see s access near the south gate of the reserve, via the village of Batang Palupuh, 16km north of Bukittinggi; information at the tourist office in Bukittinggi)*.

Further south, you can make a detour through the small town of **Bonjol** *(60km north of Bukittinggi)*, known throughout Indonesia for its imam (Imam Bonjol), leader of the Padri war, and for its hunting dogs, which hunt wild pig! Interestingly, this is also where you can cross the **equator**. A monument and a small adjoining museum (rather dull) indicate the line of demarcation.

Bukittinggi★

The small town of Bukittinggi is the departure point for exploring the Minang region and has several advantages: the weather is good, the food is good, and you can go about on foot. At 5am the calls from all the mosques blend together in a piercing polyphony. The faithful hurry along through the misty darkness while the peasants, already at work, lead their cattle through the empty streets. By day these streets ring with the sound of iron-shod hoofs: the hundred **bendi** of Bukittinggi, horse-drawn carriages decorated with red pompoms, are the subject of cheerful popular songs. But make no mistake: beneath its peaceful atmosphere the little town represents the cultural focus of the Minangkabau, and it was used as the country's temporary capital during the war of independence *(see p 126)*.

Tour of the town

Its many points of interest will easily fill 2 days. In the very centre of the town, the **Jam Gadang** (B3), or "great clock" is impossible to miss. This Dutch clock tower capped with a Minang roof, was built in 1827. It is believed to have been used by the Dutch army to spy on the movements of Imam Bonjol. At its feet lies the traditional **upper market**★★ (Pasar Atas) (C2), which looks over the **lower market** (Pasar Bawah), used for imported goods. Both have extremely lively **warung** eateries and gather together all the riches of the Minang region: fruit, handicrafts, not to mention the mountains of **krupuk** chips with their varied colours and flavours. On Saturdays the entire town centre turns into a vast stall, justifying Bukittinggi's reputation as the largest market in Sumatra. Resign yourself to getting lost, thrown off course by the innumerable flights of steps and the flood of customers. In the middle are the **oldest alleyways**★★ in the town, lined with small low houses in faded colours that date from colonial times. Under their shady arcades, men with their *peci* on their heads play boisterous games of dominoes, indicating with a tap of the fist that they are passing their turn.

To escape the frenzy of the market, take the steps to Jl A Yani, then climb up the steps to the *benteng* quarter, the "citadel". Better known as **Fort de Kock** (B1), it was built by the Dutch during the Padri uprising. Only the cannon survive, but it is just the right place, at sunrise and sunset, to enjoy a **panoramic view**★ of the town.

From here take the metal footbridge over Jl A Yani.

The hill with the fort faces another hill, where the **zoo** (C1) *(9am-6pm, modest fee)* contains tigers, tapirs, Komodo dragons and pelicans kept in less than perfect conditions. The park is also home to the museum of Minangkabau culture, the **Bundo Kandung Museum**★ *(8am-5pm, Friday 8-11am/2-5pm. Every evening at 8.30pm there are dance performances in the open-air auditorium).* The museum building is a beautiful traditional house. The interior has a medley of ethnographic documents (marriage is abundantly illustrated), models of regional architecture and stuffed animals. Precious **songkets**★, superb local silk brocades, show attractive Chinese, Indian and Arab influences, which contribute to the richness of the Minang art of weaving.

End your tour of the town with an escape to the impressive **Panorama Park**★ (A3) *(Jl Panorama)*, a garden laid out on the corniche of a rocky canyon to the southwest of the town. Here you will find the **Japanese caves**★ *(8am-6pm, small fee. Tours, 1hr; guides on site)*, 1 400m of galleries carved out by the occupying Japanese forces in 1942 to store their weapons out of reach of the Allies.

One of the exits opens out in the **Sianok Canyon**★★, an impressive fault which is visible from the top of the belvedere in the park. Its sequence of cliffs with their changing colours directs the gaze to the imposing **Gunung Singgalang** (2 877m). You can then walk down to the bottom of the canyon, through jungle carved out by water-courses, to **Koto Gadang**★, a little village nestling in the greenery where skilful craftsmen make silver jewellery. *(45min walk. Several paths. The easiest is to follow Jl Tengku Umar, near the belvedere. Below the road, turn left, cross the river by the bridge then climb the steps leading up to the village, indicated by a sign.)*

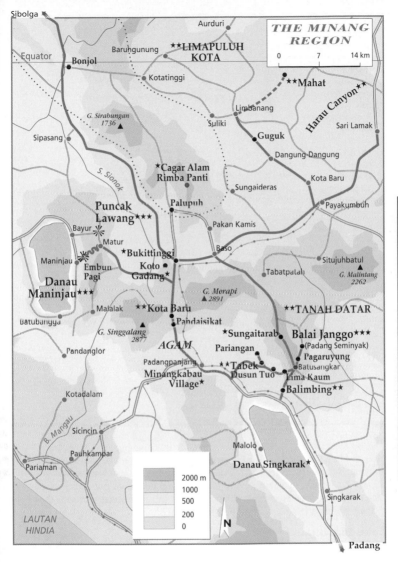

Around Bukittinggi

Kota Baru★★

13km south of Bukittinggi, on the road to Padangpanjang (do not confuse it with the other village of the same name, further to the east). Buffalo fights are usually staged on Saturdays and Tuesdays at 5pm. Enquire at the tourist office, your hotel or the coffee shops.

This village owes its fame to its spectacular **buffalo fights**, which take place in the large clearing on the edge of the village. On the days of the fights, hundreds of men

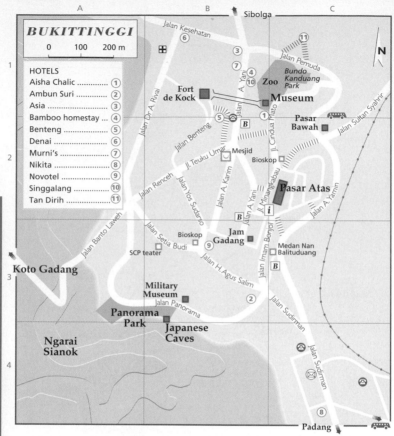

meet to place their bets. The event is full of symbolic meaning. In a sea of mud the two massive adversaries lock horns violently until one of them breaks away and runs off. However, it is said that victory is not played out there but rather among the ranks of the owners: away from the crowd they murmur secret words as they hold in their fingers a few hairs from their beast's tail.

Lake Maninjau★★★

36km west of Bukittinggi (but allow 2hr for the journey). Several walks are possible round the lake, and you can swim in it. Boats provide a ferry service between the villages on the opposite banks. Accommodation available (see "Making the most of Bukittinggi").

After a long descent of 44 hairpin bends *(numbered!)*, the road finally reaches the shores of Danau Maninjau, a superb crater lake. Although at 17km long it does not match the size of Lake Toba, it is a close rival in terms of majesty. You can test this at leisure from the **panoramic views at Embun Pagi or Puncak Lawang★★★** *(north of Bayur, on the main road)*. The atmosphere of the site is so romantic that local legend tells of desperate lovers who drowned here. When their respective families refused to see them marry, they threw themselves off the top of a high cliff together, near the village of Bayur. Water then sprang out from the spot, welling up day after day to form Lake Maninjau (literally, "that you see from afar"). Today the fishermen glide along close to the banks in their pirogues. Watching them as they gather in their nets, slender outlines reflected in the purple waters at sunset, gives a wonderful feeling of timelessness.

Kota Limapuluh, the valley of standing stones**

Access to the various sites in the valley is from Payakumbuh, 33km east of Bukittinggi.
The many **megaliths** (*"batu" in Minang*) that stud the valley are evidence that the earliest ancestors of the Minangkabau settled around **Payakumbuh**. The tradition still continues in the villages that when a chief dies his successor should set up two menhirs in his memory. At **Guguk** (*13km northwest of Payakumbuh*), seventeen **decorated batu*** spring up from the ground.

It is, however, the **Mahat cirque**, surprisingly very little visited, that will leave you with the strongest memories (*access from Limbanang, 7km east of Guguk; take the bad track from the bar; allow 4hr on foot or hire a four-wheel drive vehicle*). Several hundred **stones**** with strange curves lie here, a whole forest of megaliths adding a magical atmosphere to this natural bowl that lies bathed in silence.

Close to this is the opening to the spectacular **Harau canyon**** (*15km northeast of Payakumbuh; excursions possible, enquire at the Harau Cliff Cafe in Bukittinggi or at the entrance to the reserve, indicated on the road beyond the village of Lamaksari*). The equatorial forest, alive with birdsong, has invaded this fault with its 100m high sides transformed in places, by waterfalls, into shimmering curtains. Above, the 270ha plateau was declared a **nature reserve** in 1933 in order to preserve the rare species that live here: bears and tigers, porcupines and macaques, as well as bamboos, heather and hundred-year old lianas.

Making the most of Bukittinggi

COMING AND GOING

By bus – To get to Bukittinggi, the hotels in **Prapat** organise daily departures on regular bus services (departure at 6am, enquire at your hotel). Take care, however: this system does not allow you to make a stop along the way. You can also make a reservation for the journey through the hotels in **Samosir**. From **Sibolga**, a night bus leaves around 8pm, arriving in the very early morning (information at the Tourist Information Centre). From the bus terminal in Bukittinggi (15min east of the centre) several departures throughout the day for Padangpanjang, Maninjau, Payakumbuh and Padang.

GETTING AROUND

In Bukittinggi itself you can easily get around on foot, or try the carriages ("bendi").

By bemo – The red and yellow ones will take you to the bus station. They inter- connect at the junction of Jl Permuda and Jl A Yani, and at the lower market (Pasar Bawah).

ADDRESS BOOK

Tourist information – In the clock square (B2), near the market. Fairly basic documentation, but you can find guides here and good information about excursions.

Bank/Currency exchange – The **BNI** (C3) has an enormous branch at the foot of the clock hill, below Jl Sudirman (closed on Sunday and Saturday afternoon), where you can change travellers' cheques, also at the **Bank Rayat** (B2), on the clock square. Automatic Visa dispenser in the office of the **BII** (B2), at the top of Jl A Yani. Plenty of opportunities to change currency in coffee shops and travel agencies, but at an unfavourable rate.

Sumatra

Post office/Telephone – *Main post office* (C4), Jl Sudirman (8am-4pm, Friday until 11am, Saturday until 3pm, Sunday until 10am). **Telkom**, opposite the post office. **Wartel**, Jl A Yani (B1), under the metal footbridge. Open late at night. **Internet**, access in almost all coffee shops and at the post office.

Medical service – *General hospital*, Jl A Rivai, reception open 24hr a day.

Travel agencies – There is no shortage on Jl A Yani (B1). At n° 85, the staff at **Jogja Wisata Travel**, ☎ (0752) 335 07, are efficient. Acts as agent for the main domestic airlines, and also supplies good guides for a one-day tour of Harau canyon or a visit to Minagkabau villages.
Shaan Holidays (C1), Jl Permuda 9, ☎ (0752) 325 30, Fax (0752) 321 30, shaan@bukittinggi.wasatara.net.id, is full of information on the region.

WHERE TO STAY

● **Bukittinggi**

Modest

In Jl A Yani (B1) there is a series of modest *losmen* where you can also find information, such as the **Murni**, the **Singgalang** or the **Bamboo Home Stay**, set in an area of noisy coffee shops.
⌂**Aisha Chalic**, Jl Cindua Mato 101, ☎ (0752) 352 60 – 8rm. ✗ Shared bathroom. For the same price as the above you can sleep in a thatched inn, fitted out in an old Dutch house with enormous rooms, with everything made of wood and polished by time.

Average

Benteng, Jl. Benteng 1, ☎ (0752) 211 15, Fax (0752) 225 96 – 40rm. ⌐ ⌖ ✗ ☰ In the quarter round the fort. Used by Indonesian families. A peaceful hotel (its main advantage).
Nikita Hotel, Jl Jend. Sudirman 55, ☎ (0752) 316 29, Fax (0752) 311 77 – 17rm. ⌐ ⌖ / ☰ ✗ ☑ The rooms, with every facility, are welcoming, and some have lovely views over the rooftops, the mosques and the mountains.
Asia Hotel, Jl Kesehatan 38, ☎ (0752) 625 277, Fax (0752) 625 278 – 32rm. ⌐ ☑ ✗ This large modern building opened in 1999. White tiling predominates, and there are very large rooms maintained by irreproachable staff. However, avoid rooms facing the street, because of the traffic.

Ambun Suri, Jl Panorama 2, ☎ (0752) 344 06, Fax (0752) 314 27 – 28rm. ⌐ ⌖ ☑ ✗ ☰ You will sleep in beautiful rooms decorated with an international style with light-coloured wood. The hotel, which is new, is perfectly placed opposite the splendid Sianok Canyon.
⌂**Tan Dirih Hotel**, Jl Pemuda 12, ☎ (0752) 232 07, Fax (0752) 232 07 – 15rm. ⌐ ☑ ✗ Excellent value for the price. All the rooms are at ground level with a small private terrace, and some have bathrooms with a bath. You are guaranteed peace and quiet, as well as a friendly greeting from the manager.
Cindua Mato, Jl Cindua Mato 96, ☎ (0752) 213 46, Fax (0752) 228 08 – 9rm. ⌐ ✗ Very well located on the edge of the upper market, this large house with its traditional Minang roof dominates the whole town. Unfortunately the rooms do not have the benefit of the view.

High end

Denai, Jl A Rivai 26, ☎ (0752) 329 20, Fax (0752) 334 90 – 35rm and bungalows. ⌐ ☰ ⌖ ☑ ✗ ☰ Located near the canyon, it has luxurious rooms with soft light and white curtains. Rooms facing the garden offer peace and quiet.

Luxury

Pusako, Jl Sukarno Hatta 7, ☎ (0752) 221 11, Fax (0752) 326 67 –191rm. ⌐ ☰ ⌖ ☑ ✗ ⌂ ☰ Standing on a hillside, with swimming pool and casino, the hotel belonging to Garuda is the most luxurious in Bukittinggi.
Novotel, Jl Laras Datuk Bandaro, ☎ (0752) 350 00, Fax (0752) 238 00, novotel-bkt@mail.com – 100rm. ⌐ ☰ ⌖ ☑ ✗ ⌂ ☰ This enormous hotel, with slightly overdone Moorish architecture, has competed with the Pusako (above) since 1995. Its great advantage is its central location, a superb swimming pool and a smart bar. Small rooms.

● **Maninjau**

Modest

⌂**Rizal Home Stay**, Bayur/Maninjau, ☎ (0752) 614 04 – 6 bungalows. ✗ All the bus drivers know this popular establishment. They will drop you off at the roadside and all you have to do is cross a rice field from where you will see the main hut, set on piles in the lake. The bungalows, very plain, stand on the edge of the beach. The food is good, the view unequalled, and the welcome friendly.

Average
Tan Dirih Hotel, 1km Desa Air Panas, ☎ (0752) 612 63 – 15rm. ⌖ TV ✗ A little smarter than the place with the same name in Bukittinggi. The rooms are charming and the view from the upstairs restaurant is magical.

High end
Maninjau Indah, Jl Raya Pasir Panjang, Desa Gasang, ☎ (0752) 610 18 – 25rm. ⌖ ▤ ✗ This is a welcoming hotel, designed to blend in with its surroundings. Most prestigious of the lake hotels.

EATING OUT

You are in the capital of delicious, finger-licking Padang cuisine. You will need to lick your fingers, since custom requires you to eat without cutlery. You can however ask for a spoon – and less chilli pepper.

◉**Pondok Bakso**, Jl Cindua Mato 94H, in the alleyway that runs behind the Gloria cinema (C2). This little tavern clinging to the hillside enjoys a fascinating view of the market directly below. It is always full, the result of the reputation of its soup with meatballs and crisp onions.
Gon Raya (C2), Jl Sukarno Hatta 90, ☎ (0752) 223 96. Wonderful grilled chicken, and very attentive staff.
Simpang Raya (C2), Jl Minangkabau, ☎ (0752) 235 93. Several restaurants, including one near the market and the tourist office. The quality is consistent and the service very fast.
Family (B1), Benteng Indah, ☎ (0752) 211 02. Reliable, popular with large families on their way down to the benteng (the fort). Enjoy the pleasant, shaded terrace on the hillside.
◉**Mona Lisa** (B2), Jl A Yani 18. The salad of jungle fruits and the Chinese ravioli draw in a crowd of locals and tourists, in a bamboo-decorated dining room.

GOING OUT, HAVING A DRINK

Jl A Yani (B1) has friendly bars that stay open late (you can also find food, if you have had enough of Padang cuisine).

Cafes, discos – Jazz and Blues Cafe, Jl A Yani 95/105, ☎ (0752) 227 23 Jazz and good town guides.
Harau Cliff Cafe, Jl A Yani 134, ☎ (0752) 318 50. Dodi, head of a team of climbing enthusiasts, has created a very attractive atmosphere with soft lighting and comfortable seating.

Central, Jl A Yani, next to the Star Cafe. Noisy, techno-lovers' haunt.
Gangga Hotel, at the top of Jl A Yani, has an equally popular disco in its basement, with decor imitating a cave. Here you can dance to the traditional rousing rhythms of "dangdut" music.

Live shows – At **Medan Nan Bali-tuduang** (C3), in a large hall with tiered red velvet seating. A fascinating performance of traditional Minang dance on Saturday and Sunday evenings.

OTHER THINGS TO DO

Excursions – Hiring a minibus is the most practical way of exploring the region. Ask your hotel about hiring one, for several people and for the day.
Batours Agung, Jl A Yani 105, ☎ (0752) 223 06, Fax (0752) 223 79, can organise excursions into valleys in the Minang region (rates for half-days and longer, hire of vehicles with driver, walking tours, etc).
At the **Jazz and Blues Cafe** (see above), you may meet Hengky, who will talk passionately about Siberut Island (see p 100). The many groups that set off trekking round the island are put together here, or through the **Rendez Vous Cafe**, at the bottom of Jl A Yani, or also at the **Star Cafe**, opposite. Among the guides, who will all claim to speak fluent Mentawai and to have explored the island thoroughly for 10 years (which is rarely the case), Eddy and Julianus, native Mentawai, are recommended.

Climbing – The team from the **Harau Cliff Cafe** is always keen to go, and has good equipment for climbing in Harau Canyon.

SHOPPING GUIDE

Handicrafts – The great craft speciality of the Minangkabau is still silk brocade, or "songket". The most beautiful are on sale at **Pandaisikat**, in the Agam region (see p 182).

Music – The Minang are great music-lovers and have invented their own genre, "Minang Techno", which narrates the sadness of young girls waiting for their fiancés who have set off on "marantau". The music has a powerful rhythmic beat. **Toko Cassette Maju Jaya** in the Pasar Atas market, Jl Minangkabau 10.

Making the most of Bukittinggi

TANAH DATAR VALLEY★★
West Sumatra Province – Map p 122-123 and p 175
Round trip from Bukittinggi, via Batusangkar – (approximately 120km)

Not to be missed
Balai Janggo Palace, a royal example of Minang architecture.
And remember...
Buy one of the superb "songket" embroidered silks from Pandaisikat.

Tanah Datar is bathed in legend. The soil is rich, fertilised by the surrounding volcanoes, Merapi and Singgalang, whose brooding outlines rise against a lowering sky, the origin of nourishing rains and light. Tanah Datar is marked by the turbulent history of its rulers. It is traditionally held that the land was conquered by the youngest son of Alexander the Great, the mythical **Maharaja Diraja** (see p 171). Indeed, who else would have been able to set up the great megaliths that stud the region, ghosts of stone hidden in a mosaic of forests and rice fields? You should also follow the traces of the Pagaruyung, the noble family who made the country so prosperous and whose spirit still haunts the villages. The journey will take you to the heart of Minang memory.

The Pagaruyung kingdom
In the late 16C the royal family of Pagaruyung dominated not only the valley of Tanah Datar – its early preserve – but also most of the Minang area, stamping its influence on the whole region. But the Padri movement in the middle of the 19C (see p 125) was to mark the brutal end of the dynasty, with the massacre of its members. The only proof of its splendour is the Balai Janggo Palace in Padang Seminyak, undoubtedly the finest example of the region's traditional architecture. Sadly, ravaged by a fire in 1976, all the original palace pavilions were reduced to ashes. Undeterred, Minang craftsmen set about bringing it to life again: from 1976 to 1987, the most skilful wood-carvers exercised all their talents, and the result is on a par with the original. The only change is in the site, moved from that of the original palace in Pagaruyung to a neighbouring village, Padang Seminyak (see below).

The Valley of the Kings★★

The historic sites of Tanah Datar are concentrated round Batusangkar (39km to the southeast of Bukittinggi). Minibuses run between Bukittinggi and Batusangkar. You will also find bemos and bendis to explore the nearest sites, within a radius of 10km.

At **Baso** (10km east of Bukittinggi), a small **road**★★ heads off to the south along the flanks of Mount Merapi affording several very "Balinese" **views**★★ of terraced rice fields. The road then skirts round the north/northeast of the volcano before dropping down to the valley, threading its way through village after village. The area is bathed in a gentle pastoral atmosphere, ideal for walks.

The same can be said of **Sungaitarab**★ (approximately 30km southeast of Baso), where you should stop to admire the particularly pretty **houses with horns**. The village has a delicious smell of coffee, which is still ground in mills worked by the waters of the Selo. In the surrounding forest you can see men leading monkeys, trained to pick mangoes from the treetops.

Beyond Sungaitarab, almost without transition you come to the modern town of **Batusangkar**, the administrative centre of the valley. There is no point in lingering here: even **Fort van der Capellen**, built by the Dutch during the struggle against the Padri (1821) is invisible now, all its walls having been enveloped by recent public buildings. The only sight of interest is the **Council Chamber** (1967) in the main square, built in the local traditional style.

Northeast of Batusangkar, take the little road that runs beside the river (in the direction of Sungayang).

■ **Pagaruyung** – *1.5km from Batusangkar.* The former fiefdom of the Minang royalty is now no more than a modest single-street village. At the centre, by the roadside, you will see a small **cemetery***, in the shade of an enormous banyan tree. This is the resting-place of the rulers of Pagaruyung, an entertaining mixture of megaliths and Muslim tombs, some of them topped with a stele whose shape is reminiscent of Minang roofs (some have been moved to a shelter).

At the foot of the banyan lies the **batu kasur**, a flat stone used for a strange trial by ordeal. When a prince wished to set out on his *marantau (see p 171)*, custom required him to stretch out on this stone, to which a Minang version of itching powder had previously been applied! If the young man felt nothing, he was allowed to depart, but if his back itched he had to stay. This practice would still be used today, although the Pagaruyung dynasty now only consists of a single member. This prince has had a miniature **palace** built *(a few hundred metres from here, on the same side of the road)*, which he rarely occupies. For this reason the very helpful warden will allow you to visit it, in return for a generous tip.

■ **Padang Seminyak** – *5km from Batusangkar.* The village is the site that was chosen for the construction of an exact copy of the **Balai Janggo*****, the magnificent palace of the Pagaruyung *(daily, 8am-7pm; note that unfortunately the main façade is against the light in the morning).* Surrounded by lawns, the various pavilions provide a fascinating opportunity to explore life in the Minang region. In the middle of the complex, the **palace***** proper, with three storeys, rears its enormous roof with its curves and five pairs of giant horns pointing up to the sky.

At ground level a series of alcoves frames the throne dais: these are the rooms of the royal wives, all ornamented with *songket*, the shimmering Minang brocades. The alcove of the latest wife, known as the "hot chamber" *(in the southeast corner)*, opens close to the king's room *(on the same side)*, while the upper floor houses the princesses. The king's meditation chamber, a magnificent and entirely panelled space *(open to visitors for a small supplement)* occupies the whole of the top floor, panelled in wood carved with foliage enhanced by colour.

Apart from the king, no man was allowed into the palace. Pubescent boys and married men lived in another building behind, the **surau** (men's house), where they were initiated into the teachings of the Koran and martial arts. They did not leave the building to join their wives until after nightfall.

In another pavilion, joined to the palace by a gallery, the **kitchens** still have their crockery together with large glazed storage jars. Lastly, on the main esplanade, there is the elegant decorated tower of the **rice store*** together with the two **drum pavilions** where the times for prayer were sounded and new laws proclaimed.

From here, make a small detour southwest of Batusangkar: shortly before Lima Kaum, leave the main road and head left towards Balimbing-Singkarak.

Tanah Datar valley

■ **Balimbing**★★ – *Approximately 13km from Batusangkar.* Although it is true that corrugated iron has replaced *ijuk*, the fibre which used to cover roofs, time does not appear to hold any sway over this rural village hidden away in the forest. Balimbing, which means "starfruit" in Bahasa Indonesia, has some very **old houses**★★, some of them probably over 300 years old. The oldest among them, with its wooden walls blackened and hardened by smoke until they look like stone, has seven sleeping chambers, tiny alcoves lined along the side wall.

■ **Lake Singkarak**★ – *Approximately 3km from Balimbing.* Beyond Balimbing, the road winds through sparkling **rice fields**★ where ducks paddle, before it suddenly comes out above the largest crater lake in West Sumatra. A vast stretch of clear water surrounded by mountains, the scene is almost as spectacular as that of Lake Maninjau. Less peaceful, however, as the Trans-Sumatra highway runs all the way along its east shore.

Return along the same road to Batusangkar, then head for Bukittinggi (39km from Batusangkar).

Crossing the Agam★★

To the west of Batusangkar the road crosses the Agam. A region rich in megaliths, much like its neighbour the Limapuluh Kota valley *(see p 177)*, to which are attached all the founding myths of the Minang royal family.

■ **Lima Kaum** – *5km from Batusangkar.* According to legend, the three standing stones in the middle of the village are the royal "triumvirate" that Sutan Alif set in place in the late 16C – unless they are simply an open-air location for deliberation, like those that you can see in Nias or among the Toba Batak.

■ **Dusun Tuo** – *2km from Lima Kaum.* Here too, history gives way to legend. The two sons of Indo Jelito, the wife of the mythical Maharaja Diraja, are said to have pierced the village stone **Batu batikam** with their kris, to prove their valour *(see p 171)*.

■ **Tabek** – *4km from Dusun Tuo.* An enormous ship-house with its horned roof soaring over the village, the **Balairung sari**★★ (meeting place and council chamber) is one of the oldest examples of traditional Minang architecture. If you stop briefly you will also be able to enjoy the unique **panoramas**★★ over the valley with its slopes clothed in lush terraced rice fields.

From Tabek, a footpath climbs up to **Pariangan** *(1km)*, a modest village where Maharaja Diraja established the first Minang kingdom. Here the **surau** (men's house) still retains its functions.

Beyond Tabek the road from Tanah Datar joins the Trans-Sumatra highway.

■ **Padangpanjang** – *17km south of Bukittinggi.* Don't miss a visit to the Minang Region Information and Documentation Centre, or **Minangkabau Village**★, which has opened recently, laid out in a magnificent traditional house. You can look at rare books devoted to the Minang culture and admire a moving collection of old photographs.

■ **Pandaisikat** – *6km north of Padangpanjang.* Before returning to Bukittinggi, make a final detour through the village of the **songket**. Around a thousand looms are still active here and weaving is still the main activity. But you will also find a number of woodcarving workshops, producing items that can be found in every house in the region.

A Bouttevielle

A Minang wedding at Padang Pajang

PADANG
Capital of West Sumatra Province
91km from Bukittinggi – Map p 122-123
Pop 700 000 – Hot climate throughout the year

Not to be missed
The spicy flavours of Padang cuisine.
A nostalgic walk through the Chinese quarter.

And remember...
Avoid the beach at night, it is not safe and is badly lit.
The city is stifling, so book a room with air conditioning.

As the connecting point for air and sea transport along the west coast, Padang is not particularly inviting for a prolonged stay. Its vast polluted avenues do not encourage walks and the narrow beach next to the city dispels any thoughts of bathing. But before you depart for more agreeable climates or the nearby island of Siberut, spend an hour or two strolling through the Chinese quarter, which brings the 19C back to life. Then try the "hot" flavours, to say the least, of Padang cuisine: after all, you are in its hometown.

"Rumah makan Padang", a culinary diaspora

Every town in the archipelago has restaurants that aim to reproduce those in the capital of West Sumatra. The secret of their success is to provide a spicy feast and to display it in a unique way. There is no menu. Rather, waiters rush to your table with a dozen dishes balanced down their arms from shoulder to hand. You choose whatever tempts you from the rainbow of flavours and colours. Only the dishes that you eat appear on the bill. Apart from pork, everything is available, from cows' udders to chicken gizzards, simmered for hours in the famous *rendang* sauce, a blend of spices thickened with coconut milk. It is the burning *rendang* that makes – or breaks – the reputation of a restaurant.

A tour of the city★
Allow a day.

Before disappearing into the narrow lanes of the Chinese quarter, head off to the south of the city, well away from the frenzy, to visit the **Museum of West Sumatra Province** (Negeri Adityavarman Museum) (B3) *(Jl Pangeran Diponegoro 10; 8.30am-12noon /1-5pm; closed on Mondays; fee; allow 1hr)*. The museum was built in a style reminiscent of Minang palaces, and contains various objects illustrating Mentawai culture. Its attraction lies also in its large park, which is shady and very pleasant.

The Chinese quarter★★★ (Kampung Cina) (B4)
As you leave the museum, turn left and continue along Jl Bundo Kandung. At the end on the right go down Jl Pondok to the next junction, where you should take Jl HOS Cokroaminoto to the left. Then, after 300m, turn right into Jl Niaga, the heart of the quarter.
The Chinese arrived in Padang in the late 19C to work in the mines and the docks. The atmosphere of this period is fully alive in **Jalan Niaga★★** with its rows of little coloured houses built of stone by the Dutch in the 1920s. Incense burns on each doorstep, while elderly Chinese enjoy a little respite from the heat in cool tearooms with tiled walls. Do not miss the **Chinese Temple★★★** *(on the right)*, a magnificent building all in red and gold, a sight mentioned by travellers in 1880. Two dragons

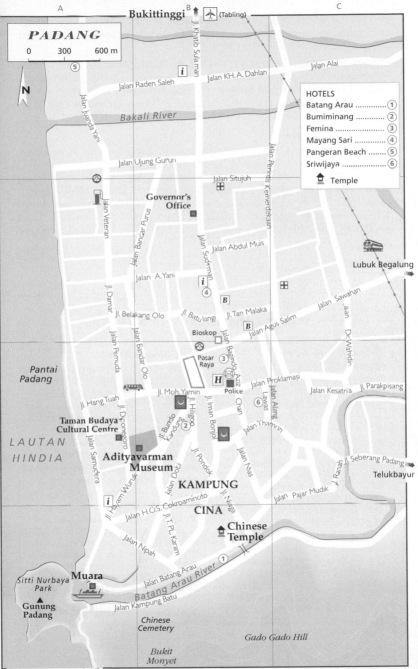

SUMATRA

Bukittinggi ✈ (Tabling)

PADANG

0   300   600 m

Ⓝ

HOTELS
Batang Arau .... ①
Bumiminang .... ②
Femina .... ③
Mayang Sari .... ④
Pangeran Beach .... ⑤
Sriwijaya .... ⑥
🏛 Temple

Jalan Khatib Sulaman
Jalan KH. A. Dahlan
Jalan Alai
Jalan Raden Saleh
Bakali River
Jalan Juanda Yani
Jalan Ujung Gurun
Jalan Situjuh
Jalan Veteran
Governor's Office
Jalan Bandar Purus
Jalan Sudirman
Jalan Abdul Muis
Jalan Permis Kemerdekaan
Jalan A.Yani
Jl. Damar
Jl. Belakang Olo
Jl. Batu langi
Jl. Tan Malaka
Jalan Agus Salim
Jalan Sawahan
Dr. Wahidin
Lubuk Begalung
Bioskop
Jalan Pemuda
Jalan Bandar Olo
Pasar Raya
Jalan Bagindo Aziz Chan
Jalan Proklamasi
Jalan Kesatria
Jl. Parakpisang
Pantai Padang
Jl. Hang Tuah
Jl. Moh.Yamin
Jl. Hiligoo
H Police
Layas
Jalan Alang
Taman Budaya Cultural Centre
Jl. Diponegoro
Jl. Bundo Kandung
Jl. Iman Bonjol
Jalan Thamrin
LAUTAN HINDIA
Adityavarman Museum
Jalan Samudera
Jl. Pondok
Jl. Nas
Jl. Ranah
Jl. Seberang Padang
Telukbayur
Jl. Hazam Wuruk
KAMPUNG
Jalan Doti
Jalan Pajar Mudik
Jalan H.O.S. Cokroaminoto
CINA
Jalan Nipah
Jl. T.PL.Karam
Jl. Niaga
🏛 **Chinese Temple**
Sitti Nurbaya Park
Muara
Jalan Batang Arau
Batang Arau River ①
Jl.
Gunung Padang
Jalan Kampung Batu
Chinese Cemetery
Gado Gado Hill
Bukit Monyet
Pantai Air Manis

185

with protruding eyes flank the imposing **mother of pearl panels*** on the entrance door. Inside, in the play of light and shade, scented scrolls hang above the altars, hiding an antique iron bell from China.

Opposite the temple, the peaceful banks of the **Batang Arau** are home to **stone warehouses*** where pepper, timber and coffee were once stored. Further on you reach the estuary and the **old harbour**** (Muara) *(500m on the right)* where a **tavern** *(next to the Harbour-master's Office)* with lazy fans harks back to the days when sailors arrived from distant lands.

Air Manis beach*

5km from the old harbour, 1hr on foot. Return by public minibus. From the Chinese quarter, take the footbridge over the Batang Arau and follow the estuary to the sea.

Like a lighthouse standing at the entrance to the harbour, the luxuriant **Padang hillside*** (Gunung Padang) rises up, with a large number of ceramic **Chinese tombs*** on its slopes. But the walk here is especially rewarding for the superb **panorama**** from the edge of the plateau, overlooking the blue waters of the sea with the beach and the bay outlined below. At low tide you can walk out to the little islet opposite.

Making the most of Padang

COMING AND GOING

By air – Padang airport, **Tabing**, is 6km north of the city, on the Bukittinggi road, ☎ (0751) 234 71. It has links with Medan and Jakarta (flights to Merpati and Mandala), and also with Singapore (Garuda flights, 3 times a week) and Kuala Lumpur (Sempati flights). Domestic lines: **Merpati**, Jl Jend Sudirman 2 (B2), ☎ (0751) 320 10; **Sempati**, ground floor of the Pangeran Beach hotel (A1), ☎ (0751) 316 24; **Mandala**, Jl Pemuda 29A (A3), ☎ (0751) 219 79. International lines: **Garuda**, Jl Jend. Sudirman 2 (B2), ☎ (0751) 320 11.

By sea – Padang port, **Teluk Bayur**, 7km south of the city, ☎(0751) 221 09. The PELNI line ferry "KM Kerinci" serves the port of Jakarta on alternate Sundays. There is another link with Sibolga, in North Sumatra. Shipping lines: **PELNI**, Jl Tanjung Priok 32 (B2), ☎ (0751) 221 09.

By bus – From the **central terminus** (A3), Jl Pemuda, departures twice daily (in theory) for most towns in Sumatra, including Bukittinggi.

GETTING AROUND

By car – Driving is definitely not advised in the city, where the traffic is frantic.

By bemo – These are blue and always overflowing. They cover the whole city from the central terminus, Jl Pemuda, and interconnect at the major junctions.

By taxi – Yellow or white. Take care, they all object to setting the meter.

By bendi – Horse-drawn carriages stand all along the beach in the late evening.

ADDRESS BOOK

Tourist information – Jl Khatrib Suleiman, on the road between Padang and the airport (B1), ☎ (0751) 221 18. You will get the same information as in Bukittinggi. For Siberut: **Siberut National Park Padang Representative**, Jl Raden Saleh 8C (B1), ☎/Fax (0751) 554 61.

Bank/Currency exchange – The **BII** (B2), Jl Sudirman, opposite no 9, offers reasonable rates of exchange and has an automatic Visa and MasterCard dispenser. **BCA**, Jl Agus Salim (B2).

Post Office/Telephone – The **main post office**, Jl Aziz Chan 7 (B3), has an **Internet** service. Closed on Friday and Saturday afternoon. **Wartel** open 24hu a day, Jl Pekas 2, and numerous **Telkom** in the centre, including one in Jl Pasar Baru, near the cinema.

Medical service – **Yos Sudarso Hospital**, Jl Situjuh (B2).

WHERE TO STAY

Modest

Hotel Sriwijaya, Jl Alang Lawas, ☎ (0751) 235 77 – 18rm. This unpretentious *losmen* is tucked away in a small quiet street near the centre. Apply here to contact Julianus, an excellent guide for Siberut and a native of the island.

Average

Femina, Jl Bagindo Aziz Chan 15, ☎ (0751) 343 09 – 14rm. Good value for money and conveniently placed, but without charm. Avoid the restaurant.

Wisma Mayang Sari, Jl Jend Sudiman 19, ☎ (0751) 226 47 – 14rm. Unbeatable value for the price, with charm on top. A large Dutch house has been converted into a guesthouse with period furniture and small decorative items that make it very attractive. Friendly family atmosphere and bright rooms. What more could you want?

High end

Pangeran Beach, Jl Juanda 79 ☎ (0751) 513 33, Fax (0751) 316 13 – 139rm. Located north of the city on the road to the airport. Its restaurant serves good Western cuisine.

Luxury

Hotel Batang Arau, Jl Batang Arau 33, ☎ (0751) 274 00 – 7rm. Established in a former Dutch bank dating from 1908, in the heart of the Chinese quarter. The hotel combines luxury and charm. Large parties are given here, but it is also possible just to have a drink by the waterside.

Hotel Bumiminang, Jl Bundo Kandung, ☎ (0751) 375 55, Fax (0751) 375 67, hbminang@indosat.net.id – 164rm. This enormous hotel with its international-style luxury has everything that you would expect: marble and a fountain, a magnificent swimming pool and spacious rooms. The view from the first floor over the city and the sea is breathtaking.

EATING OUT

Basic

Simpang Raya, Jl Aziz Cham 24. (B3) The specialist for "Es Teller", an ice-cream made with fresh fruit. Shady terrace where you can enjoy some of the best Padang cuisine.

Pagi/Sore, Jl Pondok 143. (B3) Similar quality but larger choice, notably for vegetarians.

Select

Nelayan, Jl HOS Cockroaminoto 44 A, (B3) ☎ (0751) 322 38. Padang's middle classes justifiably appreciate the marine decor, air-conditioned dining room and succulent specialities: fresh fish on a smoking cast-iron dish, or tasty crabmeat.

OTHER THINGS TO DO

Excursions – For Siberut, see p 191.

Other – A small train has recently been restored and links Padang with Solok. It crosses the superb landscape of the Anai valley and goes round the edge of Lake Singkarak. The round trip is done in a day. Information at the tourist office.

Making the most of Padang

SIBERUT ISLAND★★★

155km west of Padang – 4 500sqkm – Map p 122-123
Pop 25 000 – Equatorial climate, hot and wet

Not to be missed

Watching arrows being smeared with the redoubtable "poisoneros" before a monkey hunt.
Going fishing with local residents using hoop nets.

And remember...

Bring a supply of cigarettes: the Mentawai often ask for them.
Try not to flaunt jewellery or precious personal items.
Leave your money and papers in a safe until you return,
to protect them from the damp.

The largest of the four inhabited islands of the **Mentawai Archipelago** also has more tourists and traders than the others. This is only relative, as the island, with its coasts lined with mangrove swamps, its exuberant jungle and the virtual absence of roads, is difficult to explore.

The Mentawai move about in canoes on the red rivers, or on foot thanks to an extraordinary network of tree-trunks set across streams and marshes. They are a friendly people to meet, and exposure to their culture, which is imbued with shamanism, is a real adventure. But these encounters also contribute to a change in the culture, and there are noticeable shifts in attitude and thinking. For some these changes are proof of the evils of a tourism that claims to be "ethnological", while for others they are the mark of inexorable development.

From the Bronze Age to the year 2000

The earliest inhabitants of Siberut may have shared their origins with the Batak of northern Sumatra, but there is little that can shed light on their arrival. The island was declared a Dutch territory – a purely theoretical one only – from the moment of colonisation. But it did not really come into contact with the outside world until the middle of the 20C, with the arrival of Italian Catholic missionaries, and traders who cast greedy eyes at the rich profits to be gained from exploiting the forest. After independence, the government embarked on a plan to convert the population to Islam. Mosques were built, as were prefabricated villages into which families were moved to be nearer the schools provided to teach children the national language. In a similar project to achieve acculturation, animist rites, tattooing and loincloths were forbidden. Since the 1990s, however, the tendency has been put into reverse, for a pragmatic reason. Tourists are passionately interested in this ancient culture which, in a single generation, is moving out of the Bronze Age into the 21C.

Dances and trances

The man is perspiring in a blanket. He watches the ceremony unfold – with himself at the centre – on the sheltered platform of the "uma". No fewer than seven Shamans ("Sikerei") have come in from surrounding villages to call upon the soul to return into the body of the sick man, who is himself a Shaman. The Shamans are decorated with flowers and palm-leaves, and on their foreheads they wear a "luat", a band of pearls that indicates their function, which is passed down from father to son. For seven days and seven nights, they take it in turns to sing and dance, imitating eagles and monkeys, and stamping on the ground until they reach a state of trance. Around them, dozens of members of the community join in, laughing continuously as if their sides would split. For despite the weariness and the shadow of death, this is how it has to be. The soul will not return unless the house is happy.

Sumatra

Flower-men, a life of harmony

The men set off hunting with red hibiscus flowers in their hair. Thus adorned, the Mentawai ask the forest and its spirits – those of the stones, the trees, in fact everything in the jungle – to grant them good luck. In the heart of the forest man lives in harmony with nature and with himself. As a reflection of this personal equilibrium, the body has to be beautiful, so as to continually attract the soul which, otherwise, would depart. Jewellery, and teeth filed to a point contribute to the appearance, but nothing matches the value of **tattoos**, a truly symbolic language. Thus, arrows heading down the arms evoke strength, and the monkeys that men draw on their thighs recall their successful hunting expeditions. The pain that is part of the tattooing process is just as sharp as the pride the Mentawai take in their skin. But when they go to Muara Siberut, the town on the east coast, the flower-men cover themselves with a T-shirt – as if attracting the spirits of the town were less significant.

The taste of sago

Since the dawn of time, the Mentawai have extracted an extremely nutritious powder from the crumbly heart of the sago palm (metroxylon), a variety of palm that sinks its great roots into marshes. Grated on a platform overhanging the river, the sago is gathered in a pirogue placed underneath, before being sieved and washed. Once grilled, it is preserved in palm leaves, and provides the basis for all meals. It has little taste.

"Uma", the village-house

Isolated in the jungle near a watercourse, the *uma* used to house beneath its vast palm roof a community of between five and ten families, all linked through the paternal line. Every event in social life took place here, including meals, weddings, and Shamanism. The living area up on its piles was reached by a notched wooden tree-trunk. Before the evening meal men and women, in two separate groups, would talk and smoke under the great *jaraik*, a painting set up above the entrance, depicting the symbolism of the monkey, a totemic animal. As night fell, the men would take an oil lamp and settle in the first room, decorated with monkey skulls and pigs' jaws, evocations of benevolent spirits, while the women and children would stretch out under a mosquito net near the still-warm hearth in the kitchen.

Siberut, the island of "flower-men" (three Shamans)

P. de Vallombreuse/Rapho

Siberut Island

Meeting the Mentawai

This expedition – worthy of an Indiana Jones! – requires good physical condition, and time (at least 10 days). It is better to do the long hours of walking between villages in the morning, since the afternoon generally brings rain. To organise a trip, see "Making the most of Siberut".

Muara Siberut★

The water is too shallow for ferries to approach but canoes with engines provide a shuttle service to take visitors to land. With its port, its **mosque** and its shops run by Minang or Javanese, the little town with a population of 1 000 is the last outpost of modernity before the jungle. Already the **seafront★** has an end-of-the-world atmosphere, particularly when the sky turns crimson, and the call of the muezzin rings out over the ocean. To the south, there is an attractive tropical-style **church** and an Italian mission, before which stands a large cube of concrete, the school that takes in all the children from the forest as boarders.

The jungle villages★★★

In general, a motorised pirogue drops visitors off at Rogdog, a government village (15km to the west, 45min travelling time). This is the starting point for the tracks into the depths of the jungle. The first tree trunks thrown into the mud indicate the way. The path plunges into the heart of intertwined palms, coconut and banana trees, invaded by lianas and red lichen. You come across a succession of mangrove marshes, rattan and thick bamboos, while the melodious song of the *bilou* monkeys and the cries of flocks of macaques ring out, stopping suddenly at the approach of intruders. Progress, made difficult by the mud underfoot, presents no problem at all for the Mentawai, who are used to walking barefoot. With their springy step they greet you with a cheerful *"Alohita!"* before disappearing once more into the forest.

A recently established village, **Madobag** *(7km northwest of Rogdog, 4hr walking)* suddenly emerges in the middle of a plain. The inhabitants of the surrounding *uma* come here for their supplies of tobacco, bringing out of their loincloths the money that they have recently begun to use. As you leave, note the **laleps** on piles, small-scale models of the *uma* used as annexes in the banana plantations.

Further on you come to **Ugai★★** *(3km northwest, 1hr on foot)* with the imposing buildings of two of the oldest *Sikerei* – authorities on moral matters – at each end of the main street of beaten earth.

The surrounding jungle contains numerous isolated **uma**, perched above the Butui, which is full of fish. Here the clan's traditional way of life has been preserved. If you are tactful and patient, members of the family will let you share in their daily tasks, such as **fishing**. Armed with hoop nets, the women invoke the spirit of the waters as they move in silence through the mud, waist deep in sludge, to dislodge the fish and prawns hiding in the mangroves. **Hunting** involves the head of the family patiently spreading the formidable *poisoneros* onto arrowheads *(Silogoui)*. This deadly substance, extracted from the roots of the *dagi*, kills a monkey or a wild pig within a minute. The evening gathering takes place to the soothing song of the Mentawai, while *pepen* (fireflies) dart about in the air – the only lights in this age-old night.

Making the most of Siberut

COMING AND GOING

By boat – The ferries leave Padang three times a week at 8pm to arrive the next day at 6am. Check up on the days of departure (usually Monday, Wednesday and Thursday) and return, which vary according to the state of the boat, the arrival of goods or climatic conditions. For cabins, book several days in advance. Tickets can be bought in Padang, at **PT Rusko Lines Padang**, Jl Batang Arau 31, ☎ (0751) 219 41, opposite the entrance to the port. They cost the equivalent of a night in a cheap hotel. On board, a variety of groceries (fruit, instant soups and biscuits) for the island are on sale in the hold, almost like a supermarket.

PREPARATION FOR SIBERUT

Equipment – Make sure you have walking shoes, a good raincoat, and plastic bags to protect your possessions from the rain, all in a small rucksack. You may also want to take a light camping mattress.

In groups – This is the easiest way to travel. Take care all the same to find a congenial guide and fellow visitors (6 people seems to be the maximum). The most experienced guides can be found in Bukittinggi (see p 178) and – fewer – in Padang.

Alone – Organisation will take more time and money but, on the other hand, you will have freedom and individual contact with the local people. The permit ("surat jalan") is available at the Padang police station, in Jl M Yamin. Once at Muara Siberut, you can find an English-speaking guide who is a native of the island at the **Visitor's Center** (Maileppet beach, *2km from the town, 30min on foot to the north along the main road*), which also houses the office of the **Siberut National Park**. This body manages the western part of the island that has been protected since 1993. The State guides will take you there, to explore the caves, waterfalls and marshes, but will also agree to an itinerary to the south where there are more traditional "uma". Your main expenses will include pirogue journeys into the interior, and equipment. You should prepare for your own needs by taking (in addition to the items mentioned above) a mosquito net, insecticide, medicines (anti-malarial treatment, antibiotics, anti-diarrhoea treatment, water purifiers, disinfectant for the many scratches that heal with difficulty, and vitamins), a torch and food (instant soups, pasta, rice, tea, sugar, etc).

GETTING AROUND

On the island, people go about on foot or by canoe (some have paddles, others engines).

ADDRESS BOOK

Tourist information – Siberut National Park Padang Representative, Jl Raden Saleh 8C, in Padang, ☎/Fax (0751) 554 61. This is an official body that depends on the national park and is responsible for promoting the nature reserve in the west of the island and providing licenced guides who offer flexible itineraries.

On the island, the Siberut National Park office, Maileppet, Muara Siberut, ☎ (0759) 210 57, provides a small booklet and guides. The **Visitors' Center**, which has a collection of Mentawai objects with explanatory notes, is in the same complex

Post office/Telephone – Wartel and small **post office** in the south of the town, opposite the football ground, on the main road.

Bank/Currency exchange – There are no banks on the island. Make your arrangements in Padang.

Medical service – Basic **Health Center**, north of the town, on the main road.

WHERE TO STAY

In the villages you will sleep in the inhabitants' homes, on the floor.
Muara Siberut has two modest losmen, which are friendly and cheap:
Siberut National Park Guest House, Maillepet, next to the Visitors' Center, ☎ (0759) 210 57 – 6rm. ⌐⌐
Syahruddin Hotel, no telephone – 10rm. ⌐⌐

EATING OUT

You will find some satisfactory *warung* round the mosque in Muara Siberut.

Merdeka Square, Jakarta

JAVA

Awesome smoking volcanoes, steeply tilted rice fields with glimmering palm trees, impenetrable primary forests and long ribbons of wave-battered sand. Java, the jewel of the Sunda Islands, fires the Western imagination with its exotic tropical landscapes. Whatever geographers' views on Java, to visitors crossing the island it seems more like an immense overpopulated village in which a gentle way of life and rural traditions endure intact. For its inhabitants, however, Java is much more than a village or an island. It is a whole universe, the very centre of the world, in keeping with the mandala at Borobudur. With its great mix of religions, peoples and cultures, Java has been nourished for a long time by unsolicited outside influences; however, the island's true nature has never really disappeared from view.

Java is an exuberant, luxuriant land where the senses are awakened at every turn. Visitors are immediately hit by the heady smell of *kretek* cigarettes, the forest scents of flowers and humus, the bitter mixtures of perspiration, the fried foods concocted on the pavements in the middle of exhaust fumes, the sulphur emanations from volcanoes and the fragrance of a thousand spices. Java is certainly not a sterile environment. Silence is rare, with constant calls from street vendors, children laughing, and the chattering in unknown languages occasionally interrupted in answer to a call to prayer. Then there is the noise of chaotic traffic, the metallic notes of gamelan music and, sometimes, the rumbling of volcanoes. The senses may find some respite in the quiet contemplation of colourful batiks in the chiaroscuro of the markets, or the peace of a rice field.

Rice and fire

With its abundant vegetation and explosive volcanoes Java has an unsuspected diversity. What, indeed, is there in common between the high green valleys in the west, the rice plains in the centre, and the Baluran savannah in the east? Three types of landscape form the island ribbon that is 1 000km long and between 60 and 200km wide. The **north coast** along the Java Sea gives onto a vast alluvial plain with the major cities of Jakarta, Cirebon, Semarang and Surabaya. Dismal expanses of flooded rice fields stretch uninterrupted. The **mountain chain** in the centre has the highest concentration of active volcanoes in the world (Gede 2 958m, Slamet 3 432m, Sumbing 3 371m, Merapi 2 911m, Lawu 3 265m, Arjuna 3 331m, Semeru 3 676m, and Raung 3 332m). Lastly, the Indian Ocean coast consists of a succession of **karst hills**, where water has carved out the limestone, and **alluvial plains**.

Lying 1 000km south of the equator, the island has a **tropical monsoon climate** with alternating wet and dry seasons. The very heavy precipitation (with humidity of over 75 %), culminates in the rainy season from January to March. The exceptions are the high areas where the temperature drops to 4°C, and the Baluran savannah, which has a rainfall of less than 1 500mm a year. The El Niño warm ocean surge sometimes disturbs the crop cycle, spelling disaster for farmers.

Rich volcanic deposits contribute to the extraordinary fertility of the soil. Almost two-thirds of the land is cultivated, with fields (mostly **rice**) that are sometimes irrigated, or plantations (cloves, tea, sugar cane and teak). But the greater part of the island is under constant threat from natural disaster, whether it be volcanic eruption, landslide or flood.

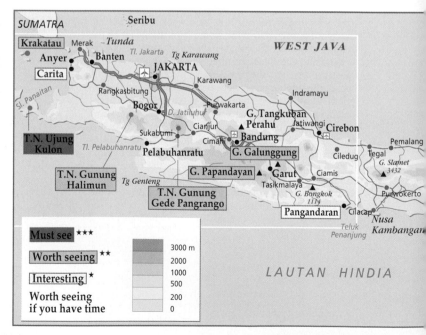

Shaped by its volcanoes and eroded by the rain, Java has several different regions that succeed one another from west to east. In **West Java**, the superb Priangan massif contrasts markedly with the Jakarta plain. The region, with some of the highest rainfall on the island, has a large network of watercourses and some of the world's last remaining virgin forests. Long dominated by the cultivation of crops in dry fields (*tegalan*), farmers turned to growing rice on irrigated land (*sawah*) in the 19C at a time when the Dutch were developing plantations of coffee, tea and hevea trees. Paradoxically, West Java is also the most industrialised region in Indonesia, with activity around the hubs of Jakarta, Serang and Bandung.

In **Central Java**, the fertile plains can grow two or three rice crops a year, but some non-volcanic areas have very poor soil (Pekalongan and Gunung Kidul). Semarang on the north coast has most of the industrial activity, while its neighbour Jepara specialises in arts and crafts (furniture and textiles) on a large scale.

Wilder and less populated **East Java** has no less than six large volcanoes, including Tengger. The fertile soil in the valleys grows two crops a year (rice and sometimes maize), while the plantations (sugar cane, coffee, tobacco and vegetables) bring in substantial revenue. By contrast, the poor soil on the coastal plain only grows one crop of rice a year. Lastly, northeast of Java is the satellite island of **Madura**, which has no volcanic relief and is strikingly arid.

Bountiful Java

In spite of its overpopulation, Java has outstanding **flora**, but the legendary jungles that once fascinated Western travellers have almost disappeared. On the plain, there are barely any **tropical rain forests** apart from those of Ujung Kulon, Nusa

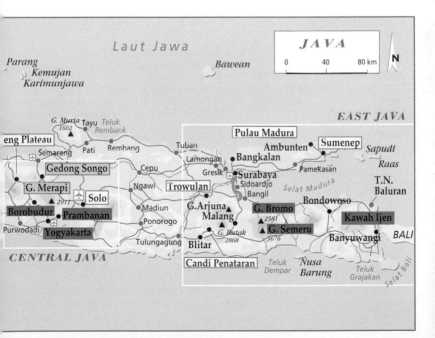

Mangroves – salt water forests

The low, dense swamps that flourish in the tidal waters form one of the most fascinating ecological environments in the tropics. Segara Anakan, Java's largest mangrove swamp, lies at the mouth of a river and stretches over an area of 13 500ha. Submerged right up to their foliage at high tide, the mangroves bare their tangled network of adventitious roots at low tide. Apart from serving to anchor the plants in the mud, the roots also provide them with oxygen, which is very rare in this habitat. The amazing resistance of these halophytic plants to their hostile environment can be explained by the fact that their cells are enriched with sodium chloride, which enables them to draw the water they need from the sea. The leaves have the ability to store salt water and to limit vapour emissions, all the while maintaining the salt content at an acceptable level. Some plants even have special glands for eliminating salt.

Kambangan, Mount Wayan, Lebakharjo and Alas Purwo. As for wet or dry **tropical deciduous forests**, the only remaining ones are in Baluran and Madura. **Mountain forests**, on the other hand, are better preserved, particularly in the west (on the Priangan massif), and in the east (on the Tengger, Argopuro and Raung massifs) where the teak flourishes. A veritable tropical Eden, Java abounds with palm trees, breadfruit trees, bamboos (about thirty species), teak trees, rattan palms, sundaris, tree ferns, flamboyants, frangipanis, banyan trees, umbrella trees, pandanus, ficus and kapok trees.

Apart from its 217 types of **orchids**, Java has some unusual species, like the **rafflesia** (see p 16 and sidebar p 126), the world's largest flower, which gives off a putrid smell. **Edelweiss**, of which the Javanese are very fond, only grows on high ground, on recent volcanic soil. Lastly, the very rare *wijaya kusuma*, which is related to the bougainvillaea, is only found in a few rocky sites on the south coast.

Most of the more common **exogenous plants** – flamboyants, cinchona, cassava, sweet potato, maize, peppers, tobacco, etc – come from America, and the others from Asia (taro, soya) or Africa (oil-palm, coffee). One of them, however, is endemic to Java: *Saccharum officinarum*, the most widespread species of **sugar cane** in the world.

The last kings of the jungle

Java's **fauna** can be compared with that of the Asian continent, to which it was attached until the Ice Age. Of the 137 species of mammals (around thirty are endemic), the most common are the Java pig, wild boar, water buffalo, rats and bats. Tigers have had a less happy fate and probably dis-

A fast-shrinking tropical forest

The forest in fact began to shrink during the time of the early Indianised kingdoms, because of the increased use of teak as well as the development of irrigated rice fields. In 1800 the jungle still covered 75% of the island. It was the beginning of the Kultuurstelsel (1830) or forced agricultural system that brought about its inexorable decline on the plains and hills. Millions of hectares were cleared to exploit the valuable timber, create plantations, or supply the combustibles required for producing sugar and indigo. Rapid population growth accentuated the phenomenon, and problems of erosion began to appear. Between 1898 and 1937, 22 000sqkm were cleared, and since the late 1930s the surface area of virgin forest has shrunk from 23% to 7%.

appeared in the 1980s. Similarly threatened in the short term are the famous **Java rhinoceros**, of which only around fifty survive (in Ujung Kulon), crocodiles (also in Ujung Kulon), the Java panther (several hundred in the forests in the centre and the west) and the wild dog. The **Java gibbon**, prince of the forests in the west, with its black face and grey fur, is the only primate to live in a couple (apart from humans of course), keeping the same mate for life. However, the species is diminishing alarmingly fast through hunting and the decline of its habitat. Less affected by proximity to man are the *lutung* and the **long-tailed macaque**, which abound.

The **banteng**, an enormous ox that can measure up to 1.8m at the neck and weigh 900kg, lives in the forests and remote grasslands in the east and west. The **Bawean deer**, the world's rarest, can only be found in Bawean, an island off Surabaya. Far more widespread, the **Java muntjac** (*kijang*) lives in the Baluran savannah, and a third smaller species of deer may be found in the Pangandaran area.

The sultan's flower

While it has no special appeal and no scent, the "wijaya kusuma" was once reserved for the sultan of Solo alone, and anyone else caught with it was liable to face the death sentence. Its picking involved an expedition of about sixty people led by a priest. Once picked, with great difficulty, it was shut in a gold box lined with silk, which itself was placed in an ornamented box and then transported to the "kraton" or royal residence on a palanquin protected by a golden parasol. Once it had been given to the sultan it was placed among the most precious attributes of the sovereignty. Legend has it that expectant sultanas who ate a "wijaya kusuma" were sure to have a male heir, hence its name "flower of victory".

The puny-looking *cicak* is a matchless insect hunter, and can be seen scurrying about on every wall in Java. Its comrade the *tocke*, a large kind of green **gecko** with red spots, is more difficult to see. It hides in gardens and thatched roofs, and as soon as night falls, begins to call (seven times is a sign of luck!). While not the most popular of creatures, **snakes** nonetheless play a vital role in the biosphere, and only some are dangerous (including triangular-headed vipers, royal cobras, and reticulate pythons). Lastly, the south coast is a refuge for five kinds of **sea turtle**, unfortunately endangered by the trade in their eggs.

The island has around 300 species of **birds**, of which about twenty are endemic, living in the swamps and forests in the east and west. The Java lapwing has disappeared and the same fate awaits the Java eagle-hawk, the national emblem, of which only fifty or so couples remain, and the magnificent Java sparrow, victim of its beauty. Other species include the black-winged starling and the Java kingfisher. Among the more widespread birds are egrets, herons and ibises. **Hornbills** have suffered from deforestation on the plains, but in the mountains in the west there are still blue Sunda robins, black eagles, thrushes, red-tailed flycatchers and Java partridges. As for the charming *ayam kampung* (common cockerel) with the irrepressible suicidal urge to hurl itself under car wheels, it is none other than the cousin of the proud *ayam hutan*, which still lives in the forests.

An island in the heart of History

Java has been inhabited for 500 000 to 1 million years, and was subject to migrations at an early stage in its history. But little is known about the **Australoid** hunter-gatherers, ancestors of the Aboriginal peoples of Australia and the Melanesians. Much later, in 3000 BC, the arrival of the **Austronesians**, who came from the north via Borneo, marked the advent of the Neolithic Age and paved the way for settled societies making a living from farming. The area opened up to trade during the Bronze Age and the **Dongson** civilisation, which originated in northern Vietnam, expanded in the last centuries BC. From then on Java found itself at the crossroads of two influential civilisations: those of India and China. *See also "A Fragmented History", p 29.*

Between India and China

Known to the Indians in the 3C BC, Java appears in a version of the *Ramayana* under the name Yavadvipa. It is likely that Indonesian merchants went to the subcontinent at the time to sell camphor, sandalwood and spices. Furthermore, Indian pottery dating from the first two centuries AD has been found in Sundanese territory. The famous **carved stone in Bogor**, Java's oldest written trace (450 AD), mentions **Purnarvarman**, king of **Tarumanegara**. From then on West Java found itself within the Indian cultural sphere of influence and adopted Hinduism. But it was three centuries later, in the middle of the island, that the great concentric kingdoms emerged. The name of the Hindu king **Sanjaya**, who held sway over the Kedu plain, appears for the first time in an inscription in 732 found near Borobudur. During the two following centuries two dynasties were to dominate the kingdom, which took the name **Mataram** and united Central and East Java. There was an upheaval in 778 with the emergence of the Buddhist **Sailendras** ("kings of the mountain"). However, their domination did not last long and in 832 a Sailendra queen married a Sanjaya prince who took control of the kingdom.

Chinese designs

The first relations between a foreigner and Java are found in a text by Faxian, a Chinese Buddhist monk who stopped there in 413, on his way to Sri Lanka. In 449 the Chinese emperor sent a messenger to the rulers of the island, notably to a certain He-Luo-Dan (possibly Tarumanegara), whom we know sent missions to China. From then on, Javanese kingdoms are mentioned increasingly in Chinese chronicles. Dan-Dan, a Hindu Javanese kingdom sent missions to China beginning in 530, and then, from 640 to 818, China struck up relations with the Buddhist kingdom of He-Ling in Central Java. These were perhaps respectively the kingdoms of Sailendra and Sanjaya.

The temples at **Dieng**, **Prambanan** and **Borobudur** bear witness to the magnificence of Mataram, which was able to mobilise great numbers of farm workers for building purposes. In this way the kingdom put in place a highly centralised power system modelled on the concentric states in India. Hinduism was adopted to a greater extent than Buddhism, judging by the number of Brahmin sanctuaries, but the two managed to live smoothly side by side. Indeed it would seem that the conversion of sovereigns to Indian religions did not have deep repercussions on society, which kept some forms of ancestor worship. On the other hand, little is known about the customs of the time, apart from the fact that women benefited from a relatively egalitarian status and that the Indian caste system was never introduced. Furthermore, there was a clear dividing line between the north coast and the interior of the kingdom, which foreigners were not allowed to enter.

After 919, however, all trace is lost of the kingdom of Mataram, victim perhaps of an eruption of Merapi, an epidemic or an invasion by Sriwijaya.

The eastern kingdoms

East Java became the centre of power for more than five centuries. In 929 King **Sindok** had a palace built on the north bank of the Brantas (southwest of Surabaya). Through an alliance his successors were able to take control of Bali and launched an attack against Sumatra in the late 10C. But the kingdom was weakened by division and its capital was destroyed in 1016. The young **Airlangga**, the son of a Balinese king, took refuge into a retreat. On his return four years later he built a *kraton* near Surabaya and in barely ten years had managed to reconstruct the domains of his ancestors. On his death in 1049 the kingdom was divided into **Janggala** (near Malang) and **Kediri** (west of Surabaya) and, in 1150, the latter ended up by annexing its rival. The splendour of the Kediri court, where the nobles (*panji*) developed a refined culture, is borne out by the temples and the prolific literature of the time.

A new page in history began when the usurper Angrok, the founder of the **Singosari** dynasty, acceded to the throne in 1222. The history of this agrarian kingdom, which late in life became a great sea trading power, is a mixture of grandeur and bloody events. At its height in the late 13C it controlled the most heavily populated areas of Java, as well as Sumatra and the Straits of Malacca. The last Singosari ruler, Kertanegara (1286-92), died on the eve of a short-lived Sino-Mongol invasion.

Majapahit, or the apogee of the agrarian kingdoms

Once Kublai Khan's armada had departed in 1293, **Raden Wijaya** cleared the Terik forest with the help of the Madurese and set up his capital there. The Majapahit Empire was born. The golden age of the agrarian kingdoms reached its peak in the 14C during the reign of **Hayam Wuruk** (1350-89) and his prime minister **Gajah Mada**. Following the example of Singosari, the Majapahit Empire was based on developing a combination of agriculture and maritime trade. An immense trading network radiated out to most of the islands that make up modern Indonesia, right up to the Malayan Peninsula. For the first time ever, Java affirmed its predominance over the archipelago.

Its slow decline in the 15C coincided with the expansion of Islam, but to the Javanese the Majapahit Empire remains the symbol of the splendour of the great concentric kingdoms that were founded on rice-growing.

The beginnings of Islam

While the earliest conversions to Islam date back to the 11C, the religion took several centuries to spread over Java. Indian and Chinese traders brought it to the towns on the north coast (Pasisir), and it was known at the Majapahit court in the 14C. Of all the small city states that emerged, the **Sultanate of Demak** was destined to have the greatest success. In the first half of the 16C, its influence spread over East Java all the way to Kalimantan, and it tried to take Malacca twice. It was even said to have dealt the final blow to the Majapahit Empire in 1527.

The great Islamised kingdoms

To establish its domination in Sundanese territory in the west, Islam took advantage of the fact that the Indianised states lacked a central structure. In 1527 the sultan of **Cirebon** took **Banten**, the main port of the **Pajajaran kingdom**, and set up a sultanate that was to become one of the greatest powers on the island until the following century.

In the 17C, in the rest of Java, power passed from the hands of the coastal sultanates to those of the **Mataram kingdom** (the second kingdom to

An island in the heart of History

R Marca

A mosque with a three-tiered roof in Demak

The Wali Songo, pioneers of Javanese Islam

Golden legend has it that the "nine holy men" were responsible for the great spread of Islam throughout the archipelago in the 15C. Endowed with miraculous powers, they are believed to have built the Demak mosque in a single night. Sunan Giri changed a feather into a kris dagger to put the unbelievers to flight, and he shared with Sunan Botang the ability to walk on water. As for Sunan Kali Jaga, he converted sand into gold to convince a ruler of his faith. The legend attaches former traditions to the Wali Songo, and so Sunan Gunung Jati, founder of the Sultanate of Cirebon, is believed to have made use of "wayang kulit" in his preachings. Sunan Kali Jaga is said to have been entrusted with a text – a profession of faith for Muslims – by Yudistira, a hero of the "Mahabharata". The Wali Songo also took up the Hindu concept of the cosmic mountain. Some of them are buried on hilltops (Gunung Jati and Muria), and these sites have become places of pilgrimage. However, while the Javanese have no doubt whatsoever about the feats of the Wali Songo, few admit that – as historians have established – some of them were actually Chinese.

hold the name), founded by Senopati at Kota Gede (1575). Unlike what happened in the Sundanese areas, however, here the Indo-Javanese tradition held firm beside Islam. The royal palaces (*kratons*) developed an original model combining animist rituals, Islamic practices, and European-style pomp and ceremony.

The early stages of the Batavian era

The arrival of the Dutch in the 16C drastically changed the political scene. In the race by the great European powers to control the spice route the Portuguese were pipped at the post. After an initial foray in 1596, the Dutch set up the **Dutch East India Company (VOC)** in 1602. This was to provide a basic structure for their colonisation. In 1619 governor-general Coen flattened Jayakarta and founded Batavia, modelling it on Amsterdam.

But the Dutch bases remained fragile in the face of the Sultanate of Banten and the rising power of Mataram. Master of Central and East Java, **Sultan Agung** (1613-46) secured control of the trading towns on the north coast, and attacked Batavia twice (in 1628 and 1629). But in vain: taking advantage of the rivalry between the Javanese kingdoms, the VOC gradually spread its influence.

A cycle of war

In 1671 to oppose a rebellion by the Madurese prince **Trunajaya**, the heir to the Mataram kingdom, Mangkurat II, called upon the Dutch, and once he was reinstalled on the throne moved his capital to Kartasura, near Solo. From then on, however, the Dutch constantly interfered in the internal affairs of the kingdom.

While the VOC had definitively conquered Banten in the west in 1684, it took it several decades to subdue the small principality in Pasuruan in the east founded by the Balinese slave **Surapati**. Mataram was shaken by a war of succession in 1704, but it was the massacre of the Chinese in Batavia by the Dutch in 1740 that precipitated the decline of the kingdom. The revolt spread like wildfire, obliging the Dutch to intervene. Victorious without encountering any opposition, they forced Pakubuwono II to cede possession of the north coast and the east of the island to them, and to accept a tax levy. The **War of Succession** that followed (1740-55) sealed the fate of Mataram. After Kartasura was sacked (1742), Pakubuwono II moved his capital to **Surakarta** (Solo), but two members of his family refused to capitulate. In 1755 Prince Mangkubumi brought about the partition of Mataram by moving to **Yogyakarta**. Pakubuwono's troubles were still not over. In 1757 a small independent principality was set up in Solo itself, with the name **Mangkunegaran**. A second dynasty also emerged in Yogyakarta, in 1813. The long military campaign (1767-77) led by the Dutch against **Blambangan**, the last Hindu Javanese kingdom, then secured them total control of the island.

A profitable colony

In spite of its conquests the VOC found itself on the verge of bankruptcy and, in 1800, the archipelago was taken over by the Dutch crown. But the commotion of the wars in Europe soon reached Java's shores. As Napoleon had put his brother Louis on the throne in the Netherlands, it was a pro-French governor, **Daendels**, who was posted to Batavia in 1808. An energetic man, he planned the first trans-Java road, which opened up the interior of the island but cost the lives of many workmen. In 1811 Daendels was removed from office by the English, who installed **Thomas Stamford Raffles** as the new governor. Raffles opposed the local nobility (priyayi) and the sultans. An outstanding administrator, he carried out the first census of the population, inaugurated a tax system and fought against slavery. But Raffles had no time to reap the fruits of this enhancement as the colony reverted to the Dutch crown in 1815.

All these reforms considerably weakened the sultan of Yogyakarta, who was now dispossessed of some of his goods and land. A revolt led by Prince **Diponegoro** broke out in 1825. A devout Muslim, though steeped in the Javanese tradition, he benefited from wide popular support and led guerrilla action on the island for five years. The **Java War** ended with his arrest and exile in 1830.

With the island bled dry the Dutch decided to have the land worked for their own profit. To do this, the **Kultuurstelsel**, or system of forced agriculture, was established by Van den Bosch, transforming the island into a vast plantation to the detriment of traditional farming. On several occasions the population was decimated by starvation. To organise forced labour, the Dutch relied on the priyayi, who formed a kind of bureaucracy to serve the colonial power, while the Javanese courts confined themselves to the role of preserving art and tradition.

The nationalist awakening

In the late 19C the colonial system became more flexible, notably thanks to the furore in the Netherlands created by the book Max Havelaar, which denounced its excesses. The education system developed, and with it the teaching of Dutch. But the farmers remained in poverty, which was further accentuated by the growing population.

Paradoxically, the westernisation of the local elite, which was meant to put a brake on the Islamic awakening, favoured the emergence of nationalism. It was in Java in 1908 that the **Budi Utomo** organisation was born, seeking to spread modern ideas within the class of the priyayi. At the same time, the **Sarekat Islam** mass movement, founded in 1909 by Javanese traders, spread its influence throughout the archipelago and recruited members among the farmers. It was also in Java that the **Indonesian Communist Party (PKI)** was formed. Founder of the **Partai Nasional Indonesia** (1927), with Hatta and Sjahrir, Sukarno tried to bring the diverse movements together. But the economic and social crisis worsened and repression struck the nationalist leaders, who were imprisoned.

However, the **Japanese invasion** (March 1942) was to deal a fatal blow to the colonial power and its image of invincibility. Three years of terrible occupation followed, during which the idea of emancipation progressed rapidly.

After the Dutch left (1949), the history of Java, which had been the driving force in the war for independence, merged with that of the Republic of Indonesia, and from then on the island was divided into five provinces (DKI Jakarta, West Java, Central Java, DKI Yogyakarta and East Java). However, the Javanese are increasingly being accused of monopolising the wheels of power and appropriating the country's resources for their own profit.

An island in the heart of History

An over-populated island

With almost 120 million inhabitants (including Madura) 60% of the Indonesian population is concentrated on Java, on less than 7% of the country's land. Comparable to that of Bangladesh, the density (900 inhabitants/sqkm) is one of the highest in the world. In some areas in the centre (Klaten), it verges on 2 000 inhabitants / sqkm and in Jakarta it even goes up to 14 000 inhabitants/sqkm! The rare areas with a low density are the highland plateaux, the forested massifs on the western and eastern ends of the island as well as the south coast of West Java.

And yet Java's over-population is a recent phenomenon, as there were only 28 million people at the beginning of the 20C. The exceptional fertility of the soil means that the population can feed itself, although this self-sufficiency seems to be under permanent threat. While the population growth has slowed thanks to family planning, it was still 1.5% in the 1990s. On the other hand, the policy of *transmigrasi*, which aims to move people to less densely populated areas in the archipelago, has had a limited impact and the economic dynamism of Java continues to attract workers from all over Indonesia. However, the most immediate problem is the rural exodus: almost 36% of the population lives in towns, compared with only 20% in 1970. Apart from Jakarta – the eighth largest metropolis in the world with almost 10 million inhabitants – three towns have over a million inhabitants: Surabaya (4 million), Bandung (1.7 million) and Semarang (1 million).

The peoples of Java

There are several ethnic groups (*suku*) on the island, which are distinguishable through language, history and culture, although they share the same basic social unit, the village (or *desa*). Furthermore, the differences between them are becoming blurred with the effect of globalisation and Islamisation.

The **Javanese** – almost two thirds of the island's population – live on the central plain, and along the north and east coasts, in the former areas occupied by the Mataram kingdom. Yogyakarta and Solo form the heart of the *kejawen* culture, while **Pasisir**, stretching from Cirebon to Surabaya bears the stamp of the sultanates. Proud of its arts, the former remains characterised by the predominance of the irrigated rice-growing that it inherited from the great Indianised kingdoms. A syncretic type of Islam is practiced here, unlike in Pasisir which follows a more orthodox line of faith and is attached to an urban, commercial tradition.

The **Osing** people in the east, who have been assimilated into the Javanese population, have barely kept the legacy of the ancient Hindu kingdom of Blambangan. Their cultural identity has been diluted through contact with the many Madurese in the region. Only a handful of implacable **Tengger** keep the Hindu flame alive in Java (see p 341).

Etiquette and respect for older people

A pillar of Javanese society, the respect for older people transcends all social classes to the extent that a nouveau riche at the wheel of his BMW will always show deference to the old beggar who asks him for money at the traffic lights. Society remains very unequal, as is borne out by the three levels of the Javanese language depending on who is speaking to whom. "Krama" is used for people of high social rank. "Madya", an intermediary form, is used by farmers and workers, or when "krama" seems inappropriate. "Ngoko" is simpler and less formal, and is used for close relationships or people in the same social class. Such subtleties require constant linguistic gymnastics, a kind of tightrope act when people cannot categorise the person they are speaking to. Children are taught good manners from a very young age: two-year-olds, for instance, are used to never giving or receiving anything with the left hand.

The contributions of Islam

The influence of Islam is evident in every domain, over and above that of religion. Linked to the trade boom in the Malay world, it is associated with the expansion of the economy as well as with the introduction of a new form of politics, the city-state, run by a sultan. Ironing out the differences in the social hierarchy has been accompanied by a reduced role in civil society for women, who are now put in an inferior position, which was not the case before. There is also the lunar calendar, which is adapted to urban activities, and the increase in the land areas given over to clearing and settlement. Concepts of the individual, linear time, morals and justice have also been brought in by Islam. Lastly, from an artistic point of view, Muslims have notably enriched the "wayang" repertoire.

The **Sundanese** in West Java, the second largest population (25 million), have a reputation for gentleness and tact. Their language is related to those in Sumatra and Malaysia, although it has borrowed the use of different registers from Javanese. In general, there has been strong cultural interpenetration with the neighbouring Javanese (borne out by gamelan music, shadow theatre and irrigated rice fields), except in religious matters where the Sundanese stick to an orthodox line. Furthermore, social hierarchy has always been less marked in this wild, mountainous land. The Kasepuhan villages on Mount Halimun and the Kampung Naga village-museum have perpetuated their ancient way of life, but without doubt it is the small animist community of the **Badui** (*see p 240*) that makes up Java's most traditional society.

Originally from the poor, overpopulated island of Madura, the **Madurese** (12 million) have emigrated throughout the archipelago, particularly to East Java. Devout Muslims, they are famous for their code of honour and are reputed to be hot-blooded, which has earned them the nickname of the "Sicilians" of Indonesia. Unlike the Javanese, the Madurese have a seafaring soul, and fish and exploit the salt marshes.

A becak in the streets of "Jogja"

C Goup/SCOPE

An over-populated island

In the heart of cosmopolitan Jakarta, where all the archipelago's ethnic groups mix, are the **Betawis**, who have developed their own culture and have their own language.

Lastly, the **Chinese** are an important minority in Java, and generally live in the towns. They have been on the island since the 3C, but in theory have no right to own property, which limits their scope in business, industry and finance.

"Javanism"

90% Muslim, Java has several Christian, Hindu and Buddhist minorities. Nearly all of them share a deep spirituality and have recourse to mysticism and magic. Healers, exorcists and masseurs all in one, the *dukun* are masters of occult sciences, which are often called upon, even if official Islam condemns such practices. The anthropologist Clifford Geertz has

Relative time

The highly complex Javanese calendar draws on Indo-Javanese and Muslim computations (the "Saka" era began in 78 AD, while the Hegira began in 622 AD). Alongside the official Gregorian calendar, some aspects of daily life continue to be governed by the old lunar "Saka" system. The "Pawukon" year (210 days) consists of five-day weeks ("pasaran"), following the old market cycle, and seven-day weeks ("wuku") used in divining rituals. The period obtained by combining the two weeks (35 days) serves to govern public events (ceremonies and "wayang" performances) as well as private events (and the combination of particular days, such as "selasa kliwon", is considered a good omen). In the 17C the Javanese calendar was Islamised and major palace ceremonies such as Sekaten were moved to correspond to holy days. The Muslim year consists of 354 days spread over months of 29 or 30 days. Lastly, to simplify matters further, don't forget that in Java a day begins at nightfall. So "sabtu malam" (Saturday evening) is in fact on Friday evening!

distinguished three types of Islamic practice in Java. Villagers (*abangan*) go in for a lighter form of popular faith tinged with animism. Heirs to the former aristocracy, the *priyayi*, who often hold high posts in administration, remain attached to Javanese tradition and have incorporated Islam into a Hindu-Buddhist belief system. Merchants (*santri*) for their part, practice a religion that is more faithful to the Koran. Appearing in the 19C, this tension between the upholders of orthodoxy and the defenders of Javanised Islam is still very much alive today. But tradition is showing signs of a decline, particularly among the urban middle classes who find an answer in the Koran to the spiritual crisis brought on by the onrush of modernity.

Miraculous "jamu"

Wrapped in a sarong, her back bent under an enormous basket of coloured bottles, the "jamu" seller paces the streets of Java in search of customers. Only she knows the composition of the concoctions that she has made herself with natural products. With a tamarind, eucalyptus or ginger base, they are generally seasoned with palm sugar or cinnamon to add to the flavour. For good measure, she sometimes adds ash, sulphur, eggs or even animal organs (testicles, skin, tail). The Javanese are very fond of these remedies, which conquer all: migraines, colds, cramps, skin problems, impotence, etc. Since the 1930s industrialists have entered the market and sell millions of sachets of the stuff every year.

The centre of the island forms the heart of the *kejawen* culture, a syncretism that is present at all levels of society. The sultans hold themselves to be defenders of the faith and send gifts to Mecca, but they also want to be the guardians of Javanese mysticism and have always opposed the emergence of an autonomous, powerful clergy. And so the **gunungan** (rice mountain) offered to the island's protective spirits during the *Garebeg Maulud* festival, the birthday of the Prophet Muhammad, is also an offering to Allah. Once a year the sultan revives the sacred and carnal ties that link him to **Loro Kidul**, the Goddess of the South Seas and guarantor of the fertility of the land. Numerous rites of passage also govern the life of the Javanese. Among them are the marriage rites (in fourteen stages!), the seventh month of pregnancy *(mitoni)*, the first lock of a child's hair or the first time a child touches the ground *(tedak siten)*, circumcision, crop seasons, and death. The most widespread ritual is *slametan*, the communion meal accompanied by prayers.

Art and architecture in Java

From "candis" to "kratons"

Little is known about the origin of the architecture of the early Indianised kingdoms from the 4-5C, as the wood buildings have not survived the ravages of time. Be that as it may, the early 8C andesite temples in **Dieng** *(see p 298)* show how the Hindu dynasty of the Sanjayas appropriated and reformulated the art of the Pallavas (southern India). The advent of the Sailendras, who saw the construction of Candi Kalasan (778), overshadowed the Sanjayas for half a century, in which time they built the sublime mandala in **Borobudur** *(see p 302)*. In 825 the Hindu revival was enriched by new Indian contributions, particularly in building techniques, thus enabling the Sanjayas to build their major work, **Candi Prambanan** *(see p 306)*. This was also a period in which temples flourished, borrowing from the two religions. The *candis* built in East Java by the Kediris and then the Singosaris (13C) preceded the advent of **Majapahit art**, which reached its peak in the 14C. A far cry from the monumental designs that governed the buildings in Central Java, this architecture was more intimate. The principle of symmetry was abandoned in favour of a plan with courtyards in rows rather than concentric shapes. And so the main sanctuary no longer opened onto the centre but at the end of the sacred perimeter (Penataran). The traditional structure of temples in East Java consists of a base on several levels on which stands a narrow *cella* which is reached by a staircase with a balustrade. On the top is a pyramidal superstructure soaring skywards, as at **Candi Jawi**, **Candi Kidal** and **Candi Singosari**. **Candi Jago** and the main temple at **Penataran** offer a variation on the theme, with high superposed terraces. These sacred mountain sanctuaries grad-

Detail of a bas-relief at Borobudur

B Brillion/Michelin

ually dominated the religious architectural style. The terrace-temples built at the end of the Majapahit era (15C) on Mount Penanggungan (west of Malang) and at **Candi Sukuh**, illustrate a mountain-temple cult that draws on the old Javanese belief system. Unlike the andesite temples, the examples of civil architecture unearthed at **Trowulan**, the old Majapahit capital, are more often built of red brick. The splendid split porchways, made up of two independent side structures, with no lintel nor any linking arch, bear some resemblance to Balinese architecture.

Muslim architecture

Although there are obvious borrowings from the Majapahit style, Muslim architecture has adopted different principles. This is borne out by the early mosques (*mesjid*) with their many roofs (Banten, Cirebon, Demak) based on the Hindu *meru* model. The high, massive square base recalls the ancient Javanese temples and the use of red brick (Kudus) evokes Majapahit architecture, as do the tiles adorning some of the outer walls. A small adjacent building was used as a prayer room for women, although this was later replaced by a simple partition separating the two spaces. **Contemporary mosques** are generally preceded by a covered colonnade that supports a central dome over the prayer area. The mosques contain the traditional features of Muslim architecture: mihrab (wall niche indicating the direction of Mecca), minbar (raised pulpit) and minaret for the call to prayer. Friday prayers, the most important of all, are celebrated in **mesjid agungs** (grand mosques), associated with the *kratons*.

An emblematic building, the **kraton** appeared in its present form in the 15C along with the early sultanates, but borrowed symbolic features from the Indo-Javanese tradition. A sacred place, it could never be profaned, and if an enemy seized it another *kraton* had to be built in its place. Built on the site of a 15C Hindu palace, the **Kesepuhan kraton at Cirebon** is the oldest one still standing (*see p 261*). It is surrounded by a red brick enclosure inlaid with Chinese and Dutch tiles, without any mortar. The shape of the *kraton* was to evolve later but the features and layout of those in Yogyakarta and Solo are already apparent. Built to a regular plan, between two vast square esplanades **(Alun-alun)**, the *kraton* forms a series of courtyards laid out along a north-south axis. The **pendopos**, a major feature of palace architecture, are open reception pavilions, topped by a roof supported by four pillars.

The private rooms in the palace follow an east-west axis and include the *Sesana Sewaka*, a vast ceremonial hall, flanked to the west by the *Dalem Prabayasa*, where the royal attributes are kept. This layout recalls that of traditional Javanese houses, with their characteristic sloped, truncated roofs.

Other influences

Two outside influences, the Chinese and the Dutch, have left their mark on Java. **Chinese architecture** has given the cities some superb buildings, recognisable by their gables, tiled roofs with upturned edges, and wide awnings preceding the entrances. Glodok (Jakarta) still has numerous house-shops with living quarters on the first floor, flanked by a balcony. These, however, suffer through not being recognised as valuable heritage, and from the modernisation of town centres. Lastly, the **kelentengs** (Chinese temples), some of which date back several centuries, are strikingly decorated with exuberant colours.

The elegant neo-Classical buildings with colonnades and pinnacles that sometimes adorn the old Dutch districts are a fine illustration of **Dutch architecture**, particularly in Jakarta **(Kota)** and Bogor **(Istana Bogor)**. The cities have often kept their old residential areas (such as Menteng in Jakarta). With its **art deco** edifices,

R Marca

A traditional house in northern Java

Bandung has escaped the anarchic, charmless modernisation that has most often affected the large towns. The pompous, grandiloquent style of the glass and marble towers that have sprung up in Jakarta has, however, produced some interesting curiosities.

Sacred arts and crafts

In the *kraton* courts as in the villages, the Javanese genius endeavours to magnify everyday objects, as if to reveal the little bit of sacredness that they all contain. Far from being a static art, these crafts with their rich outside influences continue to evolve along with the changing society.

There are two dominant styles of **batik** *(see p 64)*. The bright, shimmering **Pasisir batiks** (brown, indigo, red, ivory) have been highly affected by outside influences. These can be detected in the delicate floral motifs in Pekalongan (inspired by Dutch and Chinese ceramics), in the well-known, originally Chinese "rock and cloud" theme from Cirebon, and in the Arabic calligraphy in Demak and Kudus. In Central Java, on the other hand, Yogyakarta and Solo produce darker batiks (brown, white, indigo) whose patterns, which are always geometric, have precise symbolic meaning, often linked to the *kratons*.

Much more than a mere dagger, the **kris** is a sacred object believed to enclose the soul of its owner (a dignitary may have himself represented at a meeting by his kris). The double-edged dagger originating in Malaysia is endowed with a wavy blade with an odd number of curves (from 7 to 25). The finest have a chiselled metal or carved ivory handle, adorned with mythical animals. Metalworkers are traditionally believed to have mystical powers, and cleaning the blade, with water scattered with rose petals is a very precise ritual. **Kris holders**, superb pieces of carved wood, are usually painted or sculpted with the heroes of the *Ramayana* or *Mahabharata*.

Screen painting, a north coast speciality, depicts, in a naive style, subjects borrowed from Islam, Javanese myths, and even contemporary history. Mention should be made of **pottery** and wood **carvings**, particularly of the *loro budoyo* couple symbolising the goddess of fertility, Dewi Sri, and her spouse Sadono. Traditionally associated with major rites of passage, they sit enthroned beside the nuptial bed during weddings. However, imagination is also apparent in more ordinary items such as games, **masks**, musical instruments, ridge tiles, curtain rails, boxes for storing betel, kitchen utensils, instruments for cutting rice (*ani-ani*), the list is endless.

Ancient performing arts

While Yogyakarta and Solo are rightly thought of as centres of culture, many areas, particularly the Sundanese lands, have developed their own traditions. **Wayang kulit** shadow theatre (*see p 57*), the unrivalled master of the performing arts, fits in so well with the wit and mentality of the Javanese that it is hard to tell whether it is the puppet or puppeteer who is doing the manipulating. A variation of the art, *wayang katolik* uses a repertoire that draws on the Bible.

Semar, Java's star turn

Banned from heaven because of his compulsive eating and coarseness, Semar ended up in Java on Mount Tidar. To stop the island drifting away on the ocean, he decided to plant a nail to fix it in place. Semar soon became the protector of the island and the benefactor of the lower classes. When Islam arrived, he predicted that the Indian religions would return in 500 years, and took refuge on his mountain, which has since been considered to be the centre of Java. Some historians believe that Semar could be an ancestral divinity who has been reintegrated into Indo-Javanese mythology. Facetious but wise, he is plump with androgynous features, and moves about with a distinctive swaying walk. The most popular character in "wayang", his interventions invariably produce peals of laughter. Along with his three sons (Gareng the oldest with a club foot, Bagong the youngest with an enormous mouth, and crafty Petruk, tall and thin with a long nose), he makes up the group of "Punokawan" characters, buffoons who symbolise simple folk and are totally free with language.

Originating in Sundanese territory, **wayang golek** theatre uses puppets carved in the round controlled by slender wooden batons. Gamelan music accompanies the dialogues narrated by the *dalang*. Here again, the repertoire draws on the *Mahabharata* and *Ramayana*, but the most popular character is **Cepot**, a troublemaker with a red face.

The puppets in **wayang klitik** are also made of wood but are flat. Their repertoire is mainly based on the adventures of Damar Wulan, a hero of the Majapahit era.

There is evidence since the 15C of **Wayang beber**, a performance without actors but which takes place on an illustrated canvas which the *dalang* unrolls as he narrates. It has only survived in some villages in Central Java.

Lastly, some *kelentengs* on the north coast organise performances of **wayang potehi** with glove puppets, that draw on Chinese legends.

Body language

Imperceptible flickering of fingers and eyes, controlled angular arm movements, immobile chests, impassive faces. Javanese reserve and grace find perfect expression in dance. The body movements of the actors, who seem to proceed in a two-dimensional universe, draw largely on *wayang kulit*. Only the frequent and surprisingly lively combat scenes interrupt the peaceful unfolding of the action. Recognisable by their costume, voice and bearing, the innumerable characters are highly stereotyped. Little space is taken up by women, who have delicate movements, in the manner of **Sita**. The perfect example of a refined man, **Arjuna** has similar manners but stands firmly with his legs apart. Lastly, **Bima**, a symbol of male strength, moves about a lot and speaks in a deep voice. The repertoires of theatre and dance in Java draw not only on the *Mahabharata* and *Ramayana*, but also on the cycle of the adventures of *Panji*, and the Arab-style tales of Menak, as well as on royal Javanese chronicles (*babad*).

Originating within the walls of the *kratons* in Yogyakarta and Solo, **classical dance** bears the stamp of its aristocratic roots. The *kraton* culture spread into the countryside and today there are still schools of dance and drama.

In **Srimpi** performances four warrior-like women confront each other in a duel, played out in a graceful mirroring act. In the past the roles were played by the women of the palace. **Golek** on the other hand, was first performed in villages before being accepted by the *kratons*. In it a young woman mimes the discovery of femininity. Less dynamic than choreographies in Yogyakarta, those in Solo nearly always feature lovers. **Bedoyo Ketawang**, reserved for sultans in the past, is a sacred dance in which nine young women move in unison until they seem to merge together. The dance tells the story of the legendary union of the first king of Mataram with the Goddess of the South Seas. **Sendratari** has recently emerged in response to the desire to make dance more accessible, by stressing body movements rather than dialogue. The flamboyant performances of the *Ramayana* put on at Prambanan are derived from this.

Far more lively than *wayang kulit*, on which it draws, **wayang wong** (*wayang orang*) is a kind of **danced drama**, mainly based on the repertoires of the *Mahabharata* and *Ramayana* (*see p 58*). With its country roots, **ketoprak** is the most widespread form of popular drama. Dialogues are improvised and much is made of melodrama, like an eastern soap opera. Also well versed in romantic stories, **ludruk** (East Java) is a sung drama that appeared in the 20C, with women's roles being played by men.

Java, particularly the Sundanese region, has a great many **folk dances** that punctuate village festivals, such as the **reog ponoro** (tiger dance in Central Java), or the **gundrang** (East Java). In the Cirebon region, the **tari topeng** (mask dance) has as many variations as there are villages! Only the characters stay the same (Panji, Pamindo, Tumenggung, Kelana and Rumyang). Choreographies of **pencak silat**, a martial art, are also staged in West Java, while the most spectacular performance is the **kuda kepang** (or *kuda lumping*) dance in which the actors rush about frantically as though on horseback until they fall down in a trance!

Far from being static, the performing arts are changing and evolving, opening up to the avant-garde. In dance, Didik Nini Thowok skilfully and humorously blends the traditional repertoire with daring modernist inventions, while contemporary drama sometimes ventures into ruthless social criticism (*see p 62*).

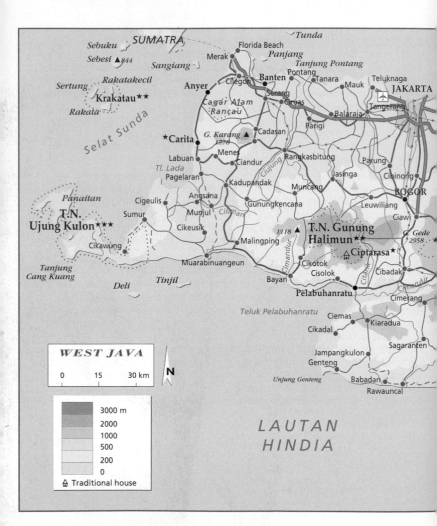

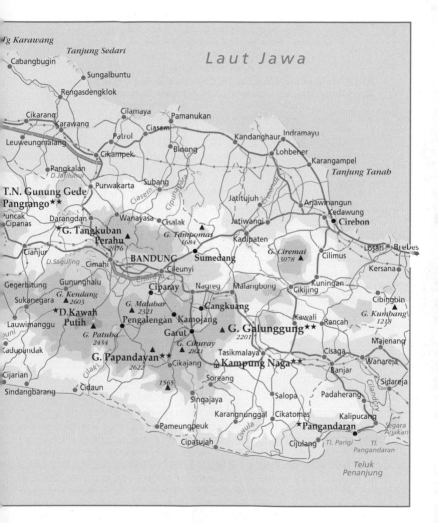

West Java

JAKARTA

DKI Jakarta Province
Capital of the Republic of Indonesia – Map p 210-211 and Plan p 216-217
Pop 10 000 000 – Hot, wet climate

Not to be missed
A wander along the quays in Sunda Kelapa.
A visit to the National Museum and Istiqlal Mosque.
Cultural shows and the night-life.

And remember...
Forget about getting around on foot and avoid driving during the rush hour.
Do your shopping for traditional items and major international brands here.
Watch out for pickpockets on public transport.
Allow 2 days to see the city's main sights.

Infernal traffic, outlandish distances, sticky heat and pollution all make Jakarta a hellish place for travellers. Its own inhabitants call it the "big durian" – after the foul-smelling fruit with the spiky skin which tastes as if it were in a high state of fermentation – which they love. A mirror for Indonesia's successes, the megalopolis also reflects all the nation's excesses. After the good years of growth Jakarta is now taking the full blast of the economic crisis that has prevailed in Indonesia since 1997. Traumatised by the riots in May 1998, it is trying to return to normal life; but it remains a kind of shadow theatre playing out the country's future, a symbolic image of a society undergoing massive changes. The capital can boast that it is the only truly Indonesian town in the archipelago, a cosmopolitan centre where Bataks, Bugis, Timorese, Moluccans, Sundanese and Javanese rub shoulders. This ever-growing population of immigrants adds to the indigenous people of Jakarta, the welcoming, smiling **Betawis**, so proud of their language and culture.

Once visitors get over the shock of their first impressions, they will find a fascinating, multifaceted city: the cluttered quays in Sunda Kelapa, the old colonial Kota district, the alleyways in the Chinese quarter, the *kampungs* (*see sidebar p 218*) and the flamboyant buildings of Kuningan. Visit the city's major museums and tour the countless shops and arcades where the arts and crafts of the whole archipelago are displayed. Then in the evening, discover the bright lights of a lively bar and experience the bustle of Jakarta by night.

Sunda Kelapa, a small harbour destined for great things

It was during the time of the Hindu kingdom of Pajajaran (12C) that the destiny of Sunda Kelapa began to emerge. Under the Pajarans it became one of the main ports in West Java. Its history took off in 1522 when the **Portuguese**, the new masters of Malacca, were given the right by the Pajajarans to build a fort near Sunda Kelapa, a prime stopping place on the spice route. The project was just what everybody needed: while the Portuguese wanted to set up a trading post there, the Sundanese found in them an ally against the Muslim Sultanate of **Demak**. The Portuguese returned five years later, with the intention of building their port. But the Muslims were in the final stages of conquering Pajajaran, and founded the Sultanate of Banten. On 22 June 1527, the Muslim prince Fatahillah took Sunda Kelapa, which he then renamed Jayakarta: "city of victory".

M Lewis/Fotogram-Stone

Another new era began in 1610 when the Dutchman **Jan Pieterszoon Coen**, governor-general of the East India Company (VOC), chose Jayakarta as the location of a trading post that would be independent of Banten. The sultanate fell victim to the VOC's monopoly over the spice trade and the situation quickly became critical. In 1618 the Prince of Jayakarta laid siege to the Dutch fort but Coen managed to escape to the Moluccas. He returned a year later with reinforcements and razed Jayakarta to the ground. A new city, **Batavia**, was built and remained the centre of Dutch colonisation in Indonesia until the 20C.

The "Queen of the East" – Batavia gradually asserted itself as the largest port in the archipelago. This rising economic power was against the interests of the ruler of Mataram, **Sultan Agung**, whose repeated attacks (1628 and 1629) resulted in heavy destruction. To rebuild the town, Coen's successor, **Specx**, followed the model for Dutch cities and criss-crossed Batavia with elegant **canals**. To revitalise the economy, he brought in Malays, Makassars, Balinese, and Chinese, who proved to be particularly dynamic. However, the Sundanese hinterland continued to be ignored: the town's rulers concentrated on maritime affairs and foreign trade and it was not until the second half of the 17C that the rest of the island was involved.

The 18C proved to be a period of decline for Batavia. Specx's canals were unsuitable for a tropical climate: the stagnant water attracted mosquitoes and served as an open sewer. Malaria and cholera soon became rife. The success of the Chinese community aroused jealousy and this led to a **massacre** in 1740. All these factors put a brake on the economy, and the VOC, which was already in debt on account of war, found itself on the verge of bankruptcy. In 1800, Batavia was handed over to the Dutch government.

When he arrived in 1808 the governor-general **Daendels** decided to restore Batavia's lustre. The canals were cleaned, the old fort was destroyed, and a new town centre – the embryo of modern Jakarta – was built 4km to the south. In 1811, an Englishman, **Thomas Stamford Raffles**, succeeded him and introduced numerous reforms. When the town reverted to Dutch rule five years later in 1816, a new golden age began. Jakarta became the flourishing capital of a colony in full expansion, earning the name **"Pearl of the Orient"** and the elegant Menteng and Cikini districts prospered. The resulting improvement in sanitary conditions led to an increase in the population of the town, which by the early 20C numbered 300 000. The era of splendour came to an abrupt halt on 5 March 1942 when the Japanese invaded. Jakarta was severely damaged in the violence that ensued.

Capital of the Republic of Indonesia – Following the Japanese surrender, Sukarno and Hatta proclaimed Indonesia's **independence** from the steps of a house in the Menteng district of Jakarta on 17 August 1945. The return of the Dutch forced them to transfer the capital of the Republican government to

Indonesia's Chinese: scapegoats

There were many Chinese in Sunda Kelapa in the 16C, and in the century that followed they proved to be highly dynamic in trade and arts and crafts, participating closely in the growth of the town. But this competition, together with the anxiety inflamed by rumours of a plot, led the VOC to ruthless repression: in 1740, 5 000 to 10 000 Chinese were killed by the Dutch (including 500 prisoners, on the governor's orders) and most of the old town was destroyed. Nonetheless, immigration soon picked up again and the Chinese, who had been moved to Glodok, regained their economic status. History, alas, repeated itself in 1965, when the Chinese Indonesians were once more victims of large-scale massacres. And during riots in 1998, their community was again targeted: there were dozens of victims and hundreds of Chinese shops were destroyed.

Yogyakarta but when the former colonial power left for good in 1949, Jakarta became the capital again. Monuments to the glory of the young nation were built and wide boulevards constructed.

This revival was short-lived, however, and ended with the *coup d'état* in 1965 (*see p 40*). Since then the capital has experienced **phenomenal population growth**, increasing from three to 10 million inhabitants between 1963 and 1998. High-rise buildings sprang up and a middle class emerged, both signs of the substantial economic success Indonesia was enjoying. But the economic crisis of 1997 has highlighted Jakarta as a centre of inequality and poverty. The **riots of May 1998** (1 200 deaths and 5 000 buildings destroyed or damaged) traumatised the city: such violence had not been seen in Jakarta for more than thirty years. The high point of the student protest was the occupation of Parliament, which was to lead to Suharto's resignation several days later.

"Jabotabek", the Javanese octopus

The megalopolis of Jakarta (see Plans I and II) stretches from north to south over more than 20km, engulfing the plain bordering the Java Sea. It forms a mosaic of urban centres linked by a network of wide thoroughfares. In the north, the old **Sunda Kelapa** harbour (Centre, A1-B1) and **Kota**, the colonial district (Centre, B1-B2) border on **Glodok** (Centre, B2), the Chinese quarter. Heading south, Jalan Gajah Mada opens onto **Merdeka Square** (Centre, B3-C3), on which are grouped the

Changing times

You can't miss the statues on all the main crossroads in the capital celebrating the national mood in the realistic-socialist style in vogue at the time of Sukarno. From "Welcome" (Plaza Indonesia), showing a couple with upraised arms, to the person with oversized hands in "Freedom breaking the chains" (near the Borobudur Intercontinental Hotel), which commemorates the liberation of Irian Jaya (now Papua), these lofty figures have been given highly irreverent names. Such is the case of "Dirgantara" (in Pancoran), and the statue of Hanuman (the monkey-hero of the "Ramayana"), renamed "Seven Up" because of the shape of its base. But the best one is "Semangat Pemuda" (Jl Jend Sudirman, Kebayoran), the proud symbol of the spirit of youth, now called "Pizza Man"!

Presidential Palace, Gambir train station and the National Museum. South of the square, Jalan Thamrin – Jakarta's "Champs-Elysées" – leaves the residential areas of **Menteng** and **Cikini** to the east (Centre, C4), while the working-class district of **Tanah Abang** (Centre, A3) opens up to the west. Jalan Thamrin extends into Jalan Jend Sudirman, which together with Jalan HR Rasuna Said outlines the "golden triangle" of **Kuningan** (Built-Up Area, C3-D3), bristling with skyscrapers. Lastly, beyond Jalan Gatot Subroto (the ring road), stretch **Kebayoran Baru** (Blok M) (Built-Up Area, C3) and **Kemang** (Built-Up Area, C3-C4), the expatriate district. And Jakarta is still expanding. While it has grown it has engulfed the surrounding towns to form a gigantic built-up area known as **Jabotabek**: Jakarta-Bogor-Tangerang-Besaki.

The old town

See the "Jakarta Centre" plan. Allow half a day, preferably the morning, for the historical districts.

Around the harbour★ (B1)

Moored tightly along the lively quays in **Sunda Kelapa**★★ (*fee*), a host of multicoloured **pinisis**★ seems to loom up from another era. These famous **Bugis boats**, which are recognisable by their heavy bulging hulls and upturned prows seem to

Jakarta

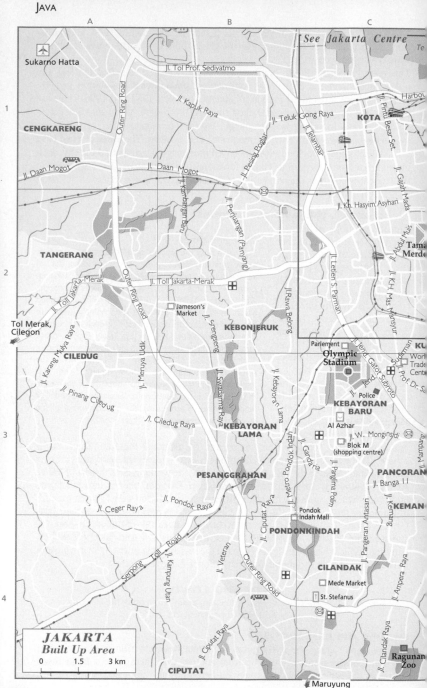

JAVA

have been designed without a plan. Nostalgic travellers go out in them for a few days on the Java Sea *(information at the Harbour-Master's Office)*, but you may also just go aboard one to have a look. Engines have replaced sails, which are now only used as a back-up. As soon as the *pinisis* draw alongside, an army of agile dockers goes aboard to unload the holds which are full to bursting with timber from Kalimantan or Sumatra. Like ants they come and go at top speed across narrow gangplanks, after which the boats head out to sea again full of rice or cement.

Sunda Kelapa (*kelapa* means "coconut palm") has been used as a moorage since the 12C, but it was under the Dutch that it had its hour of glory, when it became one of the main stopping places on the spice route. Jakarta's industrial port is to the east, in **Tanjungpriok**.

On reaching the end of the quay at Sunda Kelapa (*500m*), you can take a boat directly to the **fish market** (Pasar Ikan). Here a real olfactory adventure awaits you, especially between 9pm and 2am when the market is at its liveliest. Set in the middle of a picturesque **kampung**, Pasar Ikan is without doubt one of the best places to get an idea of the soul of Jakarta's ordinary people. But avoid wearing dainty shoes, as you will be bumped into by porters loaded with crates of fish as you make your way as best you can through the dimly-lit, muddy alleyways. The surrounding shops are entirely given over to marine activities, selling ropes, anchors, lamps, and shells.

Fitted out in a former 18C spice warehouse, the **Maritime Museum*** (Bahari Museum) *(Jl Pasar Ikan, outside the market, Tuesday-Thursday and Sunday 9am-3pm, Friday 9am-12.30pm, Saturday 9am-12.30pm. Fee. Allow 30min)* houses a fine collection of **proas** and **canoes**, as well as a range of countless types of boats that have crossed the waters of the archipelago through the centuries, including *pilnis*, schooners, freighters and warships. **Navigation instruments** and **old photographs** are displayed on the first floor.

"Kampungs", city villages

"Kampungs" ("villages") are working-class districts found in all of the Indonesian metropolises that reproduce the lifestyle and housing types found in the countryside. In Jakarta they are home to more than half the city's population. Some are shanty towns without running water or street lighting, crammed full of the casualties of the economic crisis. Others, however, consist of neat stone houses with tiled roofs, lived in by the middle classes who balk at living in apartments. Most of the time "kampungs" bring together people from the same ethnic group, who keep up a traditional system of helping one another.

An old **Customs Tower** (Menara Syahbandar) belonging to the Maritime Museum stands near the **Kali Besar** (Grand Canal). Built in 1839, it was successively a watchtower and a meteorological station. From the top there is an excellent **view** of Sunda Kelapa.

Jl Tongkol Cengkeh leads directly to Taman Fatahillah (1km), in the heart of Kota. Bike-taxis often offer their services.

The Kota district (B1-B2)

Taman Fatahillah is one of the rare places that gives an idea of what it was like under the Dutch, who were in Indonesia for 350 years. The vast paved square adorned with a **fountain** is surrounded by the main surviving buildings from the **colonial era**, most of which have been converted into museums. Before visiting them, have a look at the amazing **Portuguese cannon**, **Si Jagur**, which sits imposingly beside the Batavia restaurant *(see "Making the most of Jakarta")*. Taken from Malacca in 1641, its breech is decorated with highly suggestive imagery.

West Java

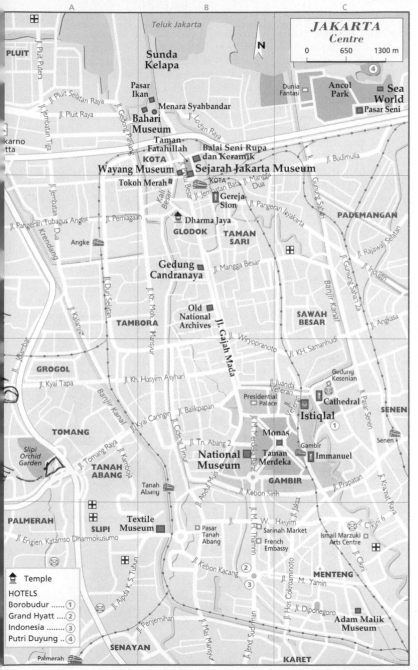

A   B   C

Teluk Jakarta

N

JAKARTA
Centre
0   650   1300 m

PLUIT

Jl. Pluit Putera

Jl. Pluit Selatan Raya

Jl. Jembatan Tiga

Jl. Pluit Raya

Jl. Gedong Panjang

Dunia
Fantasi

**Ancol
Park**

Sea
World

Pasar Seni

Karno
tta

Sunda
Kelapa

Pasar
Ikan

Menara Syahbandar

**Bahari
Museum**

Jl. Lodan Raya

Taman
Fatahillah

Balai Seni Rupa
dan Keramik

KOTA

Wayang Museum   **Sejarah Jakarta Museum**

Tokoh Merah

Jl. Pintu Besar

KOTA

Jl. Jembatan Batu   Jl. Mangga
Dua

Jl. Budimulia

Gunung Sahari

PADEMANGAN

Jl. Pangeran Tubagus Angke

Jl. Perniagaan

Kali Besar

Gereja
Sion

Jl. Pangeran Jayakarta

Jl. Jembatan Dua

Jl. Krendang

Angke

Dharma Jaya

GLODOK

**TAMAN
SARI**

Jl. Rajawali Selatan

Jl. Gunung Sahari 2a

Jl. Indusin

Jl. Duri Selatan

Jl. Kt. Moh. Mansyur

**Gedung
Candranaya**

Jl. Mangga Besar

Banjir Kanal

**SAWAH
BESAR**

Jl. Angkasa

Jl. Kalianyar

TAMBORA

Old
National
Archives

Jl. Wiryopranoto

Jl. KH. Samanhudi

GROGOL

Jl. Kyai Tapa

Jl. Jelambar

Banjir Kanal

Jl. Kh. Hasyim Asyhari

Jl. Gajah Mada

Gedung
Kesenian

SENEN

Jl. Pasar Senen

TOMANG

Jl. Kyai Caringin

Jl. Balikpapan

Jl. Cideng Timur

Jl. Kyai Caringin

Jl. Tomang Raya

Jl. Karboja

Presidential
Palace

Juanda
Veteran

Jl. Veteran

Cathedral

Istiqlal

①

Senen

*Slipi
Orchid
Garden*

**TANAH
ABANG**

Tanah
Abang

Jl. Tn. Abang 2

Monas

Gambir

**Taman
Merdeka**

Immanuel

**National
Museum**

Jl. Abdul Muis

Jl. Merdeka Barat

GAMBIR

Jl. Prapatan

Jl. Kramat Raya

Jl. Kebon Sirih

PALMERAH

Jl. Erigien, Katamso Dharmokusumo

SLIPI

**Textile
Museum**

Jl. Abdul K. S. Tubun

Pasar
Tanah
Abang

Jl.

Jl. M.H. Thamrin

Jl. Laksa

W. Hasyim
Sarinah Market

French
Embassy

Ismail Marzuki
Arts Centre

Cikini 6

Jl. Cikini

MENTENG

Jl. Kebon Kacang

②

③

Jl. M. Yamin

Jl. Hos Cokroaminoto

Jl. Penjernihan

Jl. Mas Mansyur

Jl. Jend Sudirman

Jl. Diponegoro

**Adam Malik
Museum**

SENAYAN

Palmerah

KARET

🏛 **Temple**

HOTELS
Borobudur ...... ①
Grand Hyatt .... ②
Indonesia .... ③
Putri Duyung .. ④

219

With its elegant neo-Classical façade topped by a steeple (1707), the **Jakarta History Museum*** (Sejarah Jakarta Museum) (B1) takes up the whole of the south side of the square *(Tuesday-Thursday and Sunday 9am-3pm, Friday 9am-2pm, Saturday 9am-1pm. Fee. Allow 20min)*. The symbol of colonial authority, the building housed the governor-general's offices and the town hall ("Stadhuis"), as well as a prison and a court, both of which had sinister reputations. The ground floor displays reproductions of **stone carvings** from the Pajajaran kingdom. But what mainly attracts the attention are the rooms themselves with their high ceilings and magnificent **period furniture****. At any moment you expect to see one of the governors burst in to chair a Cabinet meeting. A portrait of one of them hangs on the wall *(the others are being restored)*.

No need to be fascinated by puppets to enjoy the **Wayang Museum**** (B1-B2) *(Jl Pintu Besar Utara 27, Tuesday-Thursday and Sunday 9am-3pm, Friday 9am-2pm, Saturday 9am-1pm, Sunday show 10am-2pm. Fee. Allow 45min)*. Apart from the delightful

R. Marca

West Java

Memories of the colonial era: elegant buildings in Kota

shadow theatre **wayang kulit** leather puppets, the flat wooden **wayang kelitik** puppets and the wooden **wayang golek** puppets carved in the round, there are several unusual ones such as the **Christian wayang** puppets from Central Java featuring Adam and Eve, or the *wayang suluk* puppets used for anti-Dutch propaganda during the war of independence. The museum also has all sorts of puppets from Sumatra and Bali, Malaysia, Vietnam, Cambodia, India, Sri Lanka, China, Italy and France.

To the east of the square, the former law courts (19C) house the **Fine Arts and Ceramics Museum** (Balai Seni Rupa dan Keramik) (B1) *(Tuesday-Saturday 9am-3pm, Fee. Allow 45min)*, which is currently being renovated but remains open (heavy rain makes puddles on the parquet floor). **Chinese ceramics** are not as well represented as at the National Museum, but there are superb Song and Yuan pieces – notably a 14C series of **celadon** plates and dishes – as well as Thai, Vietnamese and European ceramics discovered on the archipelago. A section is reserved for the works of some of the great **Indonesian painters of the 19 and 20C** (including Affandi, Hendra, Raden Saleh, Sudjojono, and Basuki Abdullah).

Nearby stands the **Portuguese Church** (Gereja Sion) (B2) *(Jl Pangeran Jayakarta, east of Taman Fatahillah, behind Kota station)*, the oldest in the capital (1695). It was built for the *mardijker* ("freed slaves"), the descendants of Angolan and Indian slaves, or the descendants of mixed marriages between Asians and Portuguese. The church has a rectangular plan, and contains an original **pulpit** and **organ**.

To reach the Chinese quarter *(on foot or by taxi)*, go along the **Kali Besar** canal *(west of Taman Fatahillah)*, whose banks are lined with elegant 18C houses. Note the **Tokoh Merah** (Red Shop), the former home of a governor.

Glodok, the Chinese quarter (B2)

Unlike other "Chinatowns" in the world, the one in Jakarta barely makes a show of its identity, as ideograms are banned in Indonesia. There are, however, several superb *kelentengs* ("temples") and old houses. And you have to walk through the quarter to take in the atmosphere: a Westerner seen in the lively alleyways generally gives rise to amused curiosity. The many **warung** foodstalls provide ample opportunity for some good hot soup.

Following the canal southwards, you will see some pretty **Chinese houses** with gables and red-tile roofs. In Jalan Petak Sembilan, have a look inside the **Dharma Jaya Temple**, built in 1652. It is dedicated to the Buddhist goddess Kuan Yin, and is bathed in the fragrance of incense. Further on *(Jl Kemenangan III/47)*, the **Marla of Fatima Church** and the adjacent school are a reminder that many Chinese Indonesians are Catholics. There is another temple in the same street.

Avenue Gajah Mada is lined with countless electronics shops selling the latest wares (many were ransacked during the riots in May 1998). Drowned in the middle of this urban jungle are several old buildings that have resisted the concrete invasion, including **Gedung Candranaya**★ *(No 188)*, a superb 17C ensemble where the "Captain" of the Chinese once lived. The building is now squashed between two giant sacrilegious towers, whose building has been interrupted because of the economic crisis. Continuing southwards, you will see the **Old National Archives** (18C) on the right.

From Kota and Glodok, you can go back to the centre of town by taxi, or escape for a few hours to Ancol Park on the seafront.

Jakarta

West Java

G Guérard

Jakarta, a Chinese in Glodok

Ancol Park (C1)

Open 24 hours a day. Fee. The park is a vast island of greenery to the north of the capital, with all sorts of outdoor activities ranging from golf to sailing. There is a marina, a **swimming pool** (*see "Making the most of Jakarta"*) and several luxury hotels, as well as the **Dunia Fantasi Amusement Park** (*Monday-Saturday 2pm-9pm, Sunday10am-9am*). Over the weekend, the place is hugely popular with Jakarta families.

Seaworld* (*Monday-Saturday 9am-6pm, Sunday 9am-8pm. Fee. Commentaries in English*) is a remarkable achievement, with a fascinating variety of water species: crocodiles, piranhas, box-fish, moray eels, sharks, turtles, spotted rays, and giant spider crabs from Japan. The **main pool*** is crossed by a Plexiglas viewing tunnel and contains no less than 5 000 fish.

In **Pasar Seni** (Art Market) you can shop for works by Indonesian artists, or listen to one of the groups that play there every evening.

The town centre (Centre, B3-C3) ✓

Take a taxi to Taman Merdeka. From there it is best to go first to the National Museum and then walk to the Monas Monument (see below). Note the distances involved. Allow half a day.

A large square with trees and lawns in the heart of the capital, **Taman Merdeka** (Independence Square) is the scene for the parades and fairs that punctuate life in Jakarta. The rest of the time the place is almost deserted apart from the tourists going to Monas. Right in the middle of Taman Merdeka, the **Monas** Monument (*daily 8am-5pm. Fee. East side*), literally "National Monument", is an immense obelisk 137m tall, crowned by a flame of 35kg of fine gold. The Indonesians associate it with linga and yoni, the Hindu symbols of fertility, or sometimes with the virility of Sukarno, Indonesia's first president! From the top (*lift*), the **panorama*** of the town is exceptional.

At the foot of the obelisk, the **Freedom Museum** contains a series of **dioramas** illustrating the heroic deeds of the war for independence. For history enthusiasts only.

The National Museum*** (Centre, B3)

Jl Merdeka Barat, Tuesday-Thursday and Sunday 8.30am-2.30pm, Friday 8.30am-11.30am, Saturday 8.30am-1.30pm. Fee. Allow 90min. Guided tours daily except Sunday. Indonesia's oldest museum is indisputably its most interesting. The new wing being built is an identical reproduction of the noble neo-Classical façade of the original building (1860).

The **ethnographic section***** is a particularly rich illustration of the archipelago's cultural diversity, with masks, wickerwork, liturgical objects, jewellery, weapons, statues and also interesting **models of traditional houses**.

Bearing witness to the ancient ties between Indonesia and the Chinese Middle Kingdom, the collection of **Chinese ceramics***** covers the Han, Tang, Song, Yuan and Ming periods. It adjoins the room displaying **Majapahit terracotta objects** (14-15C), characteristic of East Java.

Hindu-Buddhist art*** is given pride of place in the courtyard, with sculptures – including a beautiful **Ganesha**** (an elephant-headed deity) – numerous Javanese bas-reliefs dating from the 8 and 9C, as well as rare statues from Kalimantan (9C). Beyond the **bronze section**, are some magnificent **Dongson drums***** (500 BC) discovered near Komodo. Other beautiful Hindu statues from a much later date (13 and 14C) are also displayed.

While the **textile collection**** is relatively small, the pieces on show are of great quality, notably the **original batiks**** from West Java, and the ikats.

But on no account should you miss the **treasure room***** upstairs, with its exceptional collection of jewellery, kris daggers and gold, silver and bronze dishes. The sumptuous **Hindu objects**** dating from the 9C were unearthed in 1990 near Prambanan in Central Java.

Further east

Making a perfect ecumenical image, the country's largest mosque and biggest cathedral stand side by side northeast of Taman Merdeka. The very sober, elegant **Istiqlal Mosque*** (Centre, C3) *(Jl Veteran. Donation at the entrance)* – designed in 1978 by a Christian architect – was once the largest in Southeast Asia. Remove your shoes before entering the mosque *(no shorts or bare shoulders)* and go along the marble walkways which look over the prayer hall, an immense space bathed in light that can hold 10 000 people. Twelve circular pillars covered in aluminium intensify the breathtaking impression of the ensemble soaring skywards.

As you leave, turn right into Jl Kathedral Banteng B (just behind the mosque).

With its two neo-Gothic spires, the **Cathedral** (1901) looks rather out of place. The neo-Classical architecture of the **Immanuel Church** (1835), which is in the same street heading towards Gambir station, is more restrained.

If you have time...

Near Tanah Abang station, the superb colonnaded home of a Huguenot family (18C) now houses the **Textile Museum** (Centre, B4) *(Jl K S Tubun 4, Tuesday-Thursday and Sunday 9am-3pm, Friday 9am-12.30pm, Saturday 9am-1.30pm. Fee. Allow 20min)*. This is a little disappointing and will mainly interest batik enthusiasts.

Far more remarkable, the eclectic **Adam Malik Museum*** (Centre, C4) *(Jl Diponegoro 29; Tuesday-Saturday 9.30am-3pm, Sunday 9.30am-4pm. Fee. Allow 20min)* houses the objects collected by the Minister for Foreign Affairs during his career at the time of Suharto. The place is a real Aladdin's cave with **Hindu statues** from Java (9C), **wooden sculptures from Kalimantan**, as well as cameras, kris daggers, ivory objects from Africa, Chinese ceramics, and even some **Russian icons**.

Jakarta

The southern outskirts
See the "Built-Up Area" plan. Allow half a day after visiting the town.

Taman Mini Park★ (Built-Up Area, E4)

Jl Toll Jagorawi, Cipayung, 45min by taxi from southeast of Jl Thamrin, or 90min by bus to the Kampung Rambutan terminus, then take the T55. Daily 8am-5pm. Fee. Allow half a day. "Mini", as in miniature, with the whole of Indonesia (or almost) in Lilliputian format! This amazing theme park covering 100ha intelligently combines relaxation, nature and culture, and is literally invaded over the weekend (*go during the week if you can*). Between sights, visit one of the outdoor restaurants or lounge beside the **man-made lake**. Its islands form a relief map of the archipelago.

The **Indonesia Museum** (*9.30am-4.30pm. Fee*), has a fine collection of textiles, sculptures, puppets and gamelan instruments. The "Indonesia Indah" film (*35min*), a vast fresco of all the beauties of Indonesia, is shown on a giant screen at the **Imax cinema**. But Taman Mini's main attraction is the group of 27 **traditional pavilions**★★ (one per province), intended to give a general picture of the incredible architectural diversity of the archipelago. Designed as small arts and craft museums, they each put on dance performances.

The park also features an immense **aviary**★ (Taman Burung), as well as an **aquarium** and numerous **gardens**.

Lastly, if you have the energy, continue on to the **Ragunan Zoo** (Built-Up Area, C4) by taxi or bus (*Daily 7am-6pm. Pasar Minggu, 15km south of Jl Thamrin, by taxi or bus 19. Fee. Allow 90min. Restaurants*). You will see diverse species from the archipelago – **dragons from Komodo, tigers from Sumatra, orang-utans from Kalimantan, cobras, macaques, crocodiles** – and from the rest of the world (**bears**, **giraffes** and **lions**). Unfortunately, due to a lack of funds, some of the animals are kept in awful conditions. The place nonetheless provides an opportunity for a pleasant walk in the woods.

The Seribu Islands (Pulau Seribu)

Boats leave from the Ancol Marina (outward crossings between 20min and 2hr depending on the island). Frequent departures. Day trips to the nearest islands are available if you don't want to sleep there. For the islands further north (Kotok, Pelangi, etc), you are likely to have to stay the night. As there are no links between the islands you have to return to Jakarta each time.

With its white sand beaches shaded by coconut palms, the Pulau Seribu ("Thousand Islands") archipelago is a privileged place of escape for Jakarta's wealthy inhabitants and foreign students who need some open air and quiet. It is classified as a national park, and has 340 islets. The resort that is both the nearest and the fastest to get to is on **Pulau Bidadari** (*30min by speedboat*), but it is not of great interest. From there, however, you can visit **Pulau Onrust**, which has the remains of a **Dutch fort**. **Pulau Ayer** is another day-trip possibility, for its beach.

As you go further away from Ancol, the water turns a soft turquoise, and you gradually forget the greyness of the capital. Take advantage of the **diving sites**★ in the area: **Pulau Kotok**★ is one of the best in Seribu. Further north, **Pulau Pelangi** and **Pulau Putri** have lovely white sand **beaches** fringed with pines and coconut palms. Lastly, neighbouring **Pulau Papa Theo** is renowned for its beautiful **seabed**★.

Making the most of Jakarta

COMING AND GOING

By air – Indonesia's capital has direct links with all the major towns in the country, as well as with major international cities. *Sukarno-Hatta International Airport* (Built-Up Area Plan, A1) has six terminals: A, B and C for domestic flights and Garuda flights; D, E and F for international flights. It is 10km west of Merdeka Square (between 45 and 90min by taxi). A minibus leaves directly from the airport for Gambir station, near Jl Jaksa (Centre Plan, C3).
Arrivals/departures information: ☎ 021) 550 53 07.
Have change ready for airport tax (international and local).

By train – *Gambir*, Jakarta's main station, takes up the east side of Merdeka Square (Centre Plan, C3). It serves all the large towns on Java. If you take a taxi, make sure that the meter is switched on. Reservations: ☎ (021) 386 23 63, for long distances only (7.30am-7pm).
Kota station (Centre, B2), in the north, serves Merak and Bandung, as well as Yogyakarta, Solo and Surabaya. *Tanah Abang* station serves West Java.
– For Bogor: numerous departures, between 6am and 9.30pm (1hr). Price: around Rp6 000.
– For Cirebon: departure at 10.10am from Kota, and at 4.55pm, from Gambir (3hr). Between Rp25 000 and Rp40 000
– For Bandung: 13 departures, between 5.30am and 8.30pm, (3hr). "Argogede", the fastest, has "Eksekutif" classes. Between RP30 000 and Rp50 000.
– For Surabaya: 8 departures between 7.50am and 9.30pm (9hr-14hr). The "Argobromo Anggrek" service has been running since 1997. It is the fastest (9hr) and the most luxurious ("Eksekutif" classes). The 9.30pm one is very practical, arriving at 6.30am. Rp60 000 to Rp185 000.
– For Yogyakarta: 3 departures, between 6.10am and 8.50pm (7hr-8hr30min). Rp50 000 to Rp76 000.
– For Solo: 3 departures, between 8am and 7pm (7-10hr). "Argolawu", the most luxurious service, (7hr30min), runs at

night, but "Dwipangga" is a little faster (7hr). Rp60 000 to Rp100 000.
There is also the "Bima" train (comfortable and fast), which leaves Jakarta for Surabaya at 6pm, via Yogyakarta and Solo (around Rp120 000).

By bus – Jakarta has four terminals, each about an hour from the centre. You can get to them by bus from Gambir, Sarinah (Jl Thamrin) or Blok M (Kebayoran Baru). Tickets are sold on the spot or from hotels and travel agencies.
Kalideres terminal (15km to the west) (Built-Up Area, A1) serves the west coast of Java, and Sumatra.
Kampung Rambutan (18km to the south) (Built-Up Area, E4) is a new, enormous bus station serving Bandung, Bogor, Tasikmalaya, Cirebon, Sumatra, Yogyakarta, and Surabaya.
The capital's main bus station, *Pulo Gadung* (12km to the east) (Built-Up Area, E2) has two terminals. One serves Sumatra and the other covers Java (Bandung, Cirebon, Yogyakarta, Solo, Surabaya, Malang) and Bali.
Lebak Bulus terminal (12km to the south) (Built-Up Area, B4) serves Yogyakarta, Surabaya, and Bali.
Main routes: Labuan (150km, 3hr30min), Bogor (60km, 30min), Bandung (150km, 4hr30min), Cirebon (260km, 5hr), Yogyakarta (560km, 12hr), Solo (580km, 12hr), Surabaya (780km, 18hr), Denpasar (1 260km, 24hr).

By minibus – *Arfina Margi Wisata*, Jl Kebon Sirih 39 (Centre, B3), ☎ (021) 315 59 08. Minibuses for Pangandaran.
Alpina, ☎ (021) 314 25 66. Other minibuses for Pangandaran.

By long distance taxi – *4848*, Jl Prapatan (Centre, C3), ☎ (021) 381 44 88 60. For Bandung.

By boat – Tanjung Priok harbour is 15km from the centre (Built-Up Area, D1-E1).
PELNI, Jl Angkasa 20, Kemayoran (C2), ☎ (021) 421 74 06, the national company, runs numerous routes throughout the archipelago.

GETTING AROUND

Generally speaking, the traffic in Jakarta is a nightmare. During rush hour (6.30am-9am and 4pm-8pm) it is forbidden to drive along the major thoroughfares (Jl Thamrin, Jl Jend Sudirman, Jl R Rasuna Said, etc) with fewer than three people per car. To get round the rule, some locals take passengers with them who get paid for the ride! Outside the main thoroughfares, it is difficult to find your way, and, in most cases, the numbers on the buildings seem to follow a logic all of their own. In addition, some streets are customarily known by their old names (Jl Pangeran Antasari is still called Jl Arteri, and Jl H Agus Salim is better known as Jl Sabang).

By bus – This is a very economic means of transport, but you have to be able to put up with the crush and the heat. You can get information on the various lines from the tourist office. The letter "P" on a bus means that it is express ("patas") – theoretically less packed – and PAC means there is air conditioning. From the Blok M (Kebayoran Baru) shopping centre, from near Sarinah (Jl Thamrin) and from Gambir, you can catch buses to most destinations.

By minibus – "Oplets" and "Mikrolets" travel along the main thoroughfares and the secondary streets that are not served by buses.

By train – A very practical line (elevated between Gambir and Kota) crosses the town from north to south. Often packed.

By taxi – Local taxi drivers have a bad press, but they work between 80 and 100hr a week for a pittance. So they are often reluctant to switch on the meter, and may give you a long drive round the town simply because they do not know the way or do not have a map. You should always look as though you are paying great attention to the route, but do note that sometimes traffic has to make detours to get somewhere quite close by. Round tips up to the nearest thousand. Jakarta has around thirty taxi companies, which generally have a minimum price if you call for a cab (from the airport to Taman Merdeka, for instance, count on around Rp35 000, plus Rp10 000 for tolls).

Bluebird (blue cabs), ☎ (021) 794 12 34 /798 10 01. A little more expensive than the others, but with faultless service. **Gamya**, **Cendrawhasi** and **Morante** are Bluebird subsidiaries.

Kosti Jaya, (blue cabs) ☎ (021) 781 77 71. The company belongs to Tutut, the daughter of Suharto, the former president.

Tiffany, ☎ (021) 585 45 45.

President (red and yellow cabs) is the company with the most taxis, but some are a real mess, and the drivers do not know their way round very well.

By bajaj – With no *becaks* around, as they are banned from Jakarta, these little orange motorised tricycles for two (pronounced "ba-jai") are convenient for short distances (but are not allowed on major thoroughfares). However, watch out for carbon dioxide fumes and decide on a price before you set out.

By bike-taxi – There are bike-taxis in some quarters, notably between Sunda Kelapa and Kota.

On foot – Heat, long distances, pollution and pavements full of potholes – walking is an adventure every step of the way.

By motorbike-taxi – "Ojeks" wait at some of the crossroads. If you are not afraid of zigzagging between cars, you can save considerable time.

By car – To hire a car from a local agent, enquire at hotels and travel agencies. The major companies are the most dependable but they are more expensive.

Avis, Jl Diponegoro 25 (Centre, C4), ☎ (021) 390 47 45.

Golden Bird Metro, ☎ (021) 798 90 00.

Hertz, Jl Jend Sudirman, Podium Plaza 7th floor (Centre, B4), ☎ (021) 570 36 83.

National Rent-a-Car, Jl Thamrin 10, Kartika Plaza Hotel, ☎ (021) 314 34 23.

ADDRESS BOOK

Most of the luxury hotels (see "Where to stay" below) in Jl Thamrin and Jl Jend Sudirman have all sorts of services on the premises: travel agencies, airline companies, bookshops, cake shops, and bars.

Tourist information – *Kantor Penerangan Wisata*, Jakarta Theatre, Jl Thamrin 9 (near Sarinah Market) (Centre, B4), ☎ (021) 33 20 67 (Monday-Saturday, 9am-4.30pm). Brochures in English, but unhelpful staff.

PHPA – *Forest Protection and Environment Conservation Office*, Jl Jend Gatot Subroto (Built-Up Area, C3), Mangala Wanabakti building, Blok 1, 8th floor, ☎ (021) 573 03 00. Issues permits for visiting national parks.

Bank/Currency exchange – The many banks in the main hotels and shopping centres, in Jl Thamrin (Centre, B4), Jl Jend Sudirman (Centre, B4) and Jl Rasuna Said (Built-Up Area, C3-D3) change foreign currency and are equipped with automated teller machines (ATMs). Jl Jaksa (Centre, C3-C4) has several currency exchanges. They are generally open Monday to Friday, 8.30am-2.30pm.

American Express, Jl Rasuna Said Bl X 1 (Built-Up Area, C3-D3). ☎ (021) 521 67 78.

Bank Central Asia, Jl Jend Sudirman Kav (Built-Up Area, C2).

Bank Indonesia, Jl Thamrin 2 (Centre, B4).

Bank Internasional Indonesia, Plaza Indonesia (Centre, B4). You can have money sent from abroad, with a big commission.

Bank Lippo, Jl Jend Gatot Subroto (Built-Up Area, C3).

Barclays Bank, Wisma Metropolitan 1.

Citibank, Jl Jend Sudirman 1, Landmark building (Centre, B4).

Standard Chartered Bank, Jl Jend Sudirman, Kav 33A (Centre, B4).

Main post office – Jl Pos Utara 2, Pasar Baru (poste restante, Monday-Friday 8am-4pm, Saturday 8am-1pm). Other post offices at Taman Fatahillah (Kota) (Centre, B1), Jl Sumenep 9 (Menteng), Jl Cikini Raya (Centre, C4).

Telephone – *Telkom*, Jakarta Theatre, Jl Thamrin 81 (Centre, B4). 24hr a day. There are numerous ***Wartels*** in Jl Jaksa (Centre, C3-C4).

Internet – *Internet Twilite Café*, Jl Kemang Raya 24A, Kemang (Built-Up Area, C3).

Duta Perdana Raya, Jl Jaksa 15 (Centre, C3). 8.30am-11.30pm. Fax, telephone, Internet, parcel post, and travel agencies.

Click!, Jl Jaksa 29 (Centre, C3). Monday-Friday 9am-10pm, Saturday 9am-8pm.

Embassies – *British Embassy*, Jl Thamrin 75 (Centre, B4), ☎ (021) 315 62 64.

British Consulate General, Deutsche Bank Building, 19th Floor, Jl Imam Bonjol 80, ☎ (021) 390 74 84.

American Embassy, Jl Merdeka Selatan 5 (Centre, B3-C3),☎ (021) 344 22 11.

Australian Embassy, Jl Rasuna Said Kav C 15-16 (Built-Up Area, C3-D3), ☎ (021) 522 71 11.

Canadian Embassy, Wisma Metropolitan I, 15th floor, Jl Jend Sudirman, Kav 29 (Centre, B4), ☎ (021) 525 07 09.

New Zealand Embassy, BRI II Building, 23rd Floor, Jl Jend Surdiman, Kav 44-46 (Centre, B4), ☎ (021) 570 94 60.

Airline companies – *Garuda*, Jl Merdeka Barat Selatan 13 (Centre, B3), ☎ (021) 231 18 01; Borobudur Intercontinental, ☎ (021) 231 03 39; Hotel Indonesia, ☎ (021) 320 05 68; Sukarno-Hatta Airport, ☎ (021) 550 13 70.

Merpati, Jl Angkasa 2 (Centre, C2), ☎ (021) 654 88 88.

Bouraq, Jl Angkasa 1-3 (Centre, C2), ☎ (021) 628 88 27.

Mandala, Jl Veteran I/34 (Centre, C3). ☎ (021) 424 61 00.

Air France, Jl Jend Sudirman Kav 61-62, Summitmas I, 9th floor (Centre, B4), ☎ (021) 520 22 62.

KLM, Jl Jend Sudirman, Kav 61-62, Summitmas II, 17th floor (Centre, B4), ☎ (021) 252 67 30.

British Airways, Jl Jend Sudirman Kav 29-31, World Trade Center, 10th floor (Built-Up Area, C3), ☎ (021) 521 15 00.

Lufthansa, Jl Jend Sudirman 1, Panin Center Building 2nd floor (Centre, B4), ☎ (021) 570 20 05.

Singapore Airlines, Jl Jend Sudirman Kav 21, Chase building (Centre, B4), ☎ (021) 520 68 81.

Silk Air, same address, ☎ (021) 520 68 99.

Travel agencies – *Pacto*, Borobudur Intercontinental (see below) (Centre, C3), ☎ (021) 797 58 74. One of the major Indonesian agencies.

Making the most of Jakarta

West Java

Patih Indo Tours & Travel, Jl Brawijaya XII/1, ☎ (021) 725 45 91, Fax (021) 726 52 11. Trips to West Java (Krakatau, Ujung Kulon, etc), Yogyakarta, Bali, Lombok and Papua.

Gray Line, Komplex Roxy Mas, Blok D2 /25, Jl Kh Hasyim Ashari (Centre, B3), ☎ (021) 350 21 55, Fax (021) 52 04 61. Day trips in and around the capital.

Wafa Jaya Tours & Travel, Jl Jaksa 7 (Centre, C3), ☎ (021) 32 30 23. Trips to West Java (Carita, Ujung Kulon, Pangandaran, Bandung, Pelabuhan Ratu), and car rental.

Mitra Semestra Raya, Marina building, Jl Lodan Timur 7, ☎ / Fax (021) 640 67 07. Specialises in the Seribu Islands.

Mitra Marsada Utama, Jl Kebon Sirih Barat Dalam I/56, ☎ (021) 314 25 66. Buses for Pangandaran, Yogyakarta, Mount Bromo and Bali. Car rental.

Medical services – Metropolitan Medical Centre, Jl Rasuna Said (Built-Up Area, C3-D3), Kav C21, Kuningan, ☎ (021) 520 34 35. Private hospital used by diplomats.

Rumah Sakit Pondok Indah, Jl Metro Duta Kav VE, Pondok Indah (Built-Up area, B3), ☎ (021) 750 01 57. A good hospital and a refuge for expatriates.

Guardian Pharmacy, Plaza Indonesia, Blok M (Built-Up Area, C3), and the Pondok Indah Mall (Built-Up Area, B3-B4).

WHERE TO STAY

As a business centre, Jakarta has a wide choice of accommodation, but prices are high compared to the rest of the country, and inexpensive guesthouses are of a poor standard. Most of the luxury hotels, which sprang up in the 1990s, are concentrated around Jl Thamrin and Jl Jend Sudirman. Even if you do not actually intend to stay in any of them you will no doubt have the opportunity to take advantage of their many services (travel agencies, airline companies, bookshops, cake shops and bars). Well placed in the city centre, a stone's throw from Gambir station, Jl Jaksa (Centre, C3-C4) is the hotel area for low to midrange budgets. The northern, outlying Ancol Park area is a haven of peace.

● City centre

Modest

Djody Hostel, Jl Jaksa 27 – 22rm. A small *losmen* with little in the way of comfort, and the service and cleanliness are nothing special. But given the price…

Bloem Steen Homestay, Jl Jaksa 173, ☎ (021) 32 30 02 – 18rm. 𝕩 Small but well-kept rooms. Very inexpensive (no breakfast).

Wisma Delima, Jl Jaksa 5, ☎ (021) 33 70 26 – 14rm. 𝕩 Shared bathrooms with debatable cleanliness, small Spartan rooms, and a rather cool reception.

Average

Nick's Corner Hostel, Jl Jaksa 16, ☎ (021) 314 19 88 – 9rm. Different types of accommodation, from dormitories without bathrooms to air-conditioned rooms with bathrooms and televisions.

Djody Hotel, Jl Jaksa 35, ☎ (021) 315 14 04 – 50rm. 𝕩 / 🍴 ✗ Some rooms have air conditioning and bathrooms, but on the whole they are small and poorly kept. Breakfast included.

Hotel Tator, Jl Jaksa 37, ☎ (021) 32 39 40 – 22rm. 🛏𝕩 / 🍴✗ Nothing outstanding about the rooms but they are well-kept and those with air conditioning are good value for money. Breakfast included.

Bumi Asih, Jl Solo 4, Menteng, ☎ (021) 315 52 35, Fax (021) 390 03 55 – 15rm. 🛏🍴 ✗ 💳 This quiet, central hotel run by Christians is an excellent option. The rooms could do with a little freshening up, but the place is good value for money and you are given a charming welcome.

High end

Hotel Le Margot, Jl Jaksa 15 ☎ (021) 391 38 30 – 34rm. 🛏🍴 📺 ✗ 💳 This recently-opened four storey hotel seems well used to Western tourists. The white-tiled rooms are rather small. Breakfast included. Car rentals with drivers.

Sabang Metropolitan Hotel, Jl H Agus Salim 11 ☎ (021) 385 76 21, Fax (021) 384 35 46 – 128rm. 🛏🍴 📺 🌊 💳 Centrally placed, with a standard of comfort that easily passes muster. But note that there's a huge difference between the prices quoted in dollars and those in rupiah.

Hotel Marco Polo, Jl Teuku Cik Ditiro 19, Cikini, ☎ (021) 230 17 77, Fax (021) 310 71 38 – 200rm. 🍴 🗐 ℰ 📺 ✗ ≋ 🆑 Fairly central and excellent value for money. The white corridors may look slightly clinical, but the rooms are clean and comfortable.

Hotel Indra Internasional, Jl K H Wahid Hasyim 63, ☎ (021) 315 28 58, Fax (021) 32 34 65 – 53rm. 🍴 🗐 ℰ 📺 ✗ 🆑 Recently renovated, with rather small impersonal rooms but an impeccable standard of comfort. The restaurant is in a pleasant inner courtyard.

Hotel Cipta, Jl K H Wahid Hasyim 53, ☎ (021) 390 47 01, Fax (021) 32 65 31 – 48rm. 🍴 🗐 ℰ 📺 ✗ 🆑 A four-storey hotel with very well-kept rooms. Among the best value for money of the hotels covered in this category.

🏨 **Hotel Karya**, Jl Jaksa 32-34, ☎ (021) 314 04 84, Fax (021) 314 27 81 – 73rm. 🍴 🗐 ℰ 📺 ✗ 🆑 The luxurious marble foyer, and the comfortable and impeccably kept rooms make this one of the best addresses in this category, for a very reasonable price.

Super deluxe

Ibis Tamarin, Jl Wahid Hasyim 77 ☎ (021) 391 23 23, Fax (021) 315 77 07 – 125rm. 🍴 🗐 ℰ 📺 ✗ ≋ 🆑 The least expensive in its range, this very comfortable, well-placed hotel, although devoid of any particular charm, offers a wide variety of services (sports centre, travel agency, bookshop). Off-season you can negotiate a small reduction.

Grand Hyatt, Jl Thamrin, Plaza Indonesia, ☎ (021) 390 12 34, Fax (021) 390 64 26 – 447rm. 🍴 🗐 ℰ 📺 ✗ ≋ 🆑 One of the capital's grand hotels, with a vast range of services. Exceptionally comfortable, with prices to match. Apparently the Sultan of Brunei is very fond of the presidential suite! Several bars and restaurants.

Mandarin, Jl Thamrin, in Plaza Indonesia, ☎ (021) 314 13 07, Fax (021) 314 86 80 – 438rm. 🍴 🗐 ℰ 📺 ✗ ≋ 🆑 This is another of Jakarta's luxury hotels and was used as temporary headquarters by the world's TV crews in May 1998. Its bars and restaurants feature among Jakarta's top night-spots. All manner of services (international bookshop, sports centre).

Borobudur Intercontinental, Jl Lapangan Banteng Selatan, east of Merdeka Square, ☎ (021) 380 55 55, Fax (021) 380 95 95 – 700rm. 🍴 🆑 This ocean liner-like hotel has long been the benchmark for luxury in Jakarta, and has just been renovated. Its refined decoration, excellent restaurants and cake shop, and vast gardens make it a haven of peace.

● **South**

Super deluxe

Dharmawangsa, Jl Brawijaya Raya 26, Kebayoran Baru, near Blok M, ☎ (021) 725 81 81, Fax (021) 725 83 83 – 100rm. 🍴 🗐 ℰ 📺 ✗ ≋ 🆑 The latest luxury hotel with very elegant stone architecture is also the most expensive. If you can't afford to stay there, try a cake in one of the superb salons. The presidential suite has a swimming pool on the terrace and overlooks the garden

● **North**

Luxury

Horison, Jl Pantai Indah, ☎ (021) 640 60 00, Fax (021) 640 60 06 – 444rm. 🍴 🗐 ℰ 📺 ✗ ≋ 🆑 A little less expensive than the other Ancol hotels. Comfortable rooms with superb views of the sea or Jakarta. The vast marble foyer has an air of old-fashioned luxury.

Putri Duyung, Jl Lodan Timur 7, ☎ (021) 260 16 80, Fax (021) 260 16 91 – 128rm. 🍴 🗐 ℰ 📺 ✗ ≋ 🏊 ♨ 🆑 The bungalows with terraces giving onto the sea provide an original alternative to a stay in the capital. Numerous outdoor pursuits, including boat trips and golf.

Super deluxe

Park Royal, Jl Lodan Timur 7, ☎ (021) 640 56 41, Fax (021) 640 56 45 – 301rm. 🍴 🗐 ℰ 📺 ≋ 🆑 This large hotel is ideal for a family stay far from the bustle of the city. The rooms are comfortable but expensive for the standard they offer. Negotiate a reduction if you're staying during the week.

● **Sukarno-Hatta Airport**

Super deluxe

Quality Hotel Aspac, Terminal 2/E, ☎ (021) 559 00 08, Fax (021) 559 00 18 – 82rm. 🍴 🗐 ℰ 📺 ✗ 🆑 A solution if you are in transit and do not want to go into the city. Rooms can be let for a few hours at a very low price.

Making the most of Jakarta

EATING OUT

The capital is the perfect place for trying out the specialities of the archipelago, and of other Asian countries. But if you have had enough of culinary experiences you can always fall back on the many Western restaurants. As for fast food, the choice is just as varied, from snacks on the hoof bought from a "kaki lima" (street vendor), to meals from *warung* with their tables on the pavement, not forgetting the inevitable McDonald's and Pizza Huts along Jl Thamrin.

Every evening a host of *warung* and small neon-lit Chinese restaurants open up in Jl Mangga Besar (in the north, near Glodok) (Centre, B2). The place is hardly a tourist attraction, but the soups are delicious. In the evening (until around 11pm), excellent seafood can be had in Jl Pecanongan (north of Taman Merdeka) (Centre, C3). For Indonesian cuisine, try Jl Kendal (Menteng) (Centre, C4), beside the railway that borders the residential district.

● Centre

Basic

Rumah Makan Jasa Bundo, Jl Jaksa 20A (Centre, C3), ☎ (021) 390 56 07. A small Padang restaurant, practical for a quick meal.

Angie's cafe, Jl Jaksa 15 (Centre, C3). A travellers' hangout with Western and Indonesian dishes ("nasi goreng", "cap cay"), and rock and funk music in the background. Copious breakfasts.

Rumah Makan Jaksa International, Jl Jaksa 18 (Centre, C3). A classic that all seasoned travellers know about. The food is good but not very original (meat, salads, fish, Indonesian dishes), and they also serve breakfast. There's a billiard room at the back.

Restoran Sederhana, Jl H Agus Salim 35 (Centre, B4). Some of the best Padang cuisine in the city, despite the loud techno music. However, there is also a quiet air-conditioned dining room.

Moderate

Tan Goei, Jl Besuki 14, Menteng (Centre, C4). This very pleasant Sundanese restaurant (fish, brochettes) has an air-conditioned dining room and another (covered) outside.

🍃**Raden Kuring**, Jl Raden Saleh Raya 62, Cikini (Centre, C4). Certainly some of the best Sundanese food in the capital, served in a bamboo setting around a small inner pool, with very relaxing traditional music in the background.

Kasara, Jl Wahid Hasyim 112, Menteng (Centre, C4). This fashionable Indian restaurant with Oriental decor serves excellent food, but it is not the place if you are looking for peace and quiet. The bar upstairs is ideal for a drink.

Kafe Pisa, Jl Gereja Theresia I (Centre, B4). A vast air-conditioned restaurant with a trendy clientele. The pizzas, a little more expensive than the average, are delicious. Live music on Saturday evenings.

Sate Khas Senayan, Jl Kebon Sirih 31A, on the corner of Jl Jaksa (Centre, C3). This large, recently refurbished restaurant attracts office workers at midday and tourists in the evening. Excellent brochettes, but a rather cold setting.

More select

Lanna Thai, Jl Kusuma Atmaja 85, Menteng (near Plaza Indonesia) (Centre, C4). A new Thai restaurant in an elegant setting decorated with antiques. The food is excellent, but it is a pity that the portions are small and the prices high. A bar should soon be opening upstairs.

🍃**Oasis**, Jl Raden Saleh Raya 47, Cikini (Centre, C4), ☎ (021) 315 06 46, Fax (021) 33 71 31 (closed Sunday lunchtime). The capital's most renowned restaurant is housed in a superb colonial home, its walls decorated with antiques. Impeccable service and refined cooking (Indonesian and Western). Try the "rijstaffel", an assortment of thirteen dishes served by as many waitresses (Sundays only).

● North

Basic

Phinisi Cafe, on the Sunda Kelapa quays (7am-7pm) (Centre, B1). A small restaurant shaped like a boat. Ideal for a drink or a bite after visiting the harbour.

Queen's Tandoor, Jl Veteran I/6 (near the Istiqlal Mosque) (Centre, C3). Just north of Merdeka Square, the restaurant is a canteen for the Indian community. Chicken tandoori makes a change from "nasi goreng".

Maharani, Jl Veteran I/17 (Centre, C3). Slightly more chic than the former. Food from both the north and south of India, as well as seafood and Chinese dishes.

More select

👁 **Batavia**, Taman Fatahillah, Kota (Centre, B1). This magnificent 19C Dutch home has two large dining rooms with a colonial atmosphere, where refined Western and Indonesian food is served.

● **South**

More select

Suan Thai, Jl Jend Sudirman Kav 11, Senayan (Centre, B4). Closes at 10pm. Hiding at the foot of an office block is one of the best Thai and seafood restaurants in Jakarta. With prices to match.

HAVING A DRINK

For evenings out, the English daily, "Jakarta Post", is a mine of information.

Bars, night life – In spite of a number of closures due to the economic crisis, the capital still lives up to its reputation as a city that never sleeps.

Jaya Pub, Jl Thamrin 12 (Centre, B4). One of Jakarta's classic night-spots, where you can have a drink and listen to local or Philippine groups playing standard rock numbers.

Batavia, see above under "Eating out". A chic venue, with jazz groups in a colonial setting (bar open 24hr a day).

Tanamur, Jl Tanah Abang Timur 14 (Centre, B3). The oldest (open since 1970) and liveliest of Indonesia's night-clubs has kept its wild reputation. Techno music until 3am during the week, 4am at the weekend.

Jamz, Lippo Surdiman, Grand Suite Hotel, Jl Garnsun Dalam 8, Karet Semangi. The capital's latest venue for listening to jazz.

JJ Duit, Jl Tanah Abang Timur 16 (Centre, B3). A tastefully decorated bar and restaurant just beside the Tanamur (whose reputation it shares), where you can have a drink, eat on the terrace or dance inside until the early hours.

Tavern, Hotel Aryaduta, Jl Prapatan 44-48, Senen (Centre, C3). You can have a meal or a drink as you listen to groups playing rock and disco hits. Very lively some evenings.

Harry's Bar, Hotel Mandarin, Plaza Indonesia (Centre, C4). A quiet, elegant bar where jazz groups perform from 9 to 11.30pm.

Latin Bar, Jl Veteran 32, (near the Istiqlal Mosque) (Centre, C3). This new Cuban bar is a welcome venue for salsa lovers. Excellent cigars.

Cafes, tea shops – A new kind of cafe has sprung up in Jakarta. Known as "tenda cafes" or *warung artis*, these places are opened by local cinema stars and singers who have been forced out of work by the slump. Food and drink from 6pm to midnight (sometimes 2am). The best known are in Jl Prapanca (near Blok M) (Built-Up Area, C3), Jl Casablanca (near the Ambassador Mall) (Built-Up Area, D3), Jl Asia Afrika (near the Senayan Plaza Mall) (Built-Up Area, C3) and in the Semanggi district. But remember that addresses often change.

Other places:

Sari Pan Pacific, Jl Thamrin 6 (Centre, B4). The hotel has a cake shop with a mouth-watering selection, and a cafe that serves excellent espresso.

Ragusa es Italia, Jl Veteran I/10 (near the Istiqlal Mosque) (Centre, C3). A charming little ice-cream parlour that has been open since 1932, with fans and wicker chairs.

Galeri TC, Jl Kemang Raya 24A, Kemang (Built-Up Area, C3). A venue for expatriates, who meet for a drink or a wander around the stores (books, furniture).

Arts and live shows – Taman Ismail Marzuki (TIM), Jl Cikini Raya (Centre, C4). This is the centre for contemporary drama. It also holds exhibitions and has a cinema and small open-air restaurants.

Gedung Kesenian, Jl Pos / Jl Gedung Kesenian 1 (behind the Istiqlal Mosque) (Centre, C3), ☎ (021) 380 82 83. The capital's most beautiful theatre, with its neo-Classical architecture (1821), puts on an excellent programme of Indonesian and Western performances (dance, drama, music).

Wayang Orang Bharata, Jl Pasar Senen 15, Senen (Centre, C3), ☎ (021) 421 49 37. A popular theatre that puts on an episode of the "Ramayana" or the "Mahabharata" almost every evening (8pm-midnight). The verve of the actors makes up for the frustration you may feel in not understanding the dialogues in Javanese. There are also "ketoprak" performances from a contemporary repertoire that draws on popular legends.

Making the most of Jakarta

Wayang Museum, see "The Kota district" above. Puppet performances on Sundays from 10am to 2pm (when there are five Sundays in the month, no performance is held on the first Sunday).

Taman Mini Park, see "The southern outskirts" above. Traditional dances on Sundays (9am-2pm).

Pasar Seni, Ancol (Centre, C1). Open-air concerts every evening (8-11pm).

French Cultural Centre (Pusat Kebudayan Perancis), Jl Salemba Raya 25, Cikini (Centre, C4), ☎ (021) 390 77 16. The centre has a library and a cafeteria frequented by Indonesian students. It organises exhibitions, performances and film shows on a regular basis.

Gœthe Institut, Jl Mataram Raya 23, ☎ (021) 850 91 32. The German cultural centre organises film festivals.

British Council, Widjojo Centre, 1st Floor, Jl Jend Sudirman 71, ☎ (021) 252 41 15. Cultural activities are organised; a library is also on offer.

Erasmus Huis, Jl Rasuna Said (Built-Up Area, D3), ☎ (021) 525 23 21. Dutch cultural centre.

OTHER THINGS TO DO

Swimming pools – The immense (and clean) **Ancol swimming-pool complex** (Gelanggang Renang) (Centre, C1) has about fifteen different pools, some with fountains, slides and artificial waves (Monday-Saturday 8am-8pm, Sunday 7am-8pm).

Some of the large hotels allow non-residents to use their pools (entrance fee). The **Hotel Indonesia** has a pleasant pool in a garden setting.

Feasts and festivals – Jakarta Fair, July. The capital celebrates the birth of the city with cultural events lasting several days.

National holiday, 17 August. Sports events, puppet shows and a carnival.

Films – TIM and most of the foreign cultural centres (see above) put on varied programmes.

SHOPPING GUIDE

Markets – A stroll through the capital's markets is guaranteed to give you a colourful taste of life in Jakarta.

Pasar Burung, Jl Pramuka, Jatinegara (Built-Up Area, D2). A lively animal market which will give you some idea of Indonesia's rich fauna.

Pasar Ikan, see "Through the old town" (Centre, B1), p 000.

Pasar Senen, east of Merdeka Square (Centre, C3). Handicrafts, batiks, fresh produce.

Pasar Tanah Abang, at the western end of Jl K H Wahid Hasyim (Centre, B4). The batiks are cheap, but bargaining is still *de rigueur*.

Shopping centres – Large shopping centres based on the American mall model sprang up like mushrooms in the nineties. There you will find major international brands (clothes, electronics, etc) at prohibitive prices for most Indonesians, but less expensive than in Europe. **Blok M**, Kebayoran Baru (in southwest Jakarta) (Built-Up Area, C3). Indonesia's largest concentration of shops, ranging from little stalls to gigantic malls such as **Mega Pasar Raya** (on 9 floors) and Pasar Senen (see above) (Centre, C3), which offers a vast choice of handicrafts. **Plaza Indonesia**, Jl Thamrin (at the foot of the Grand Hyatt) (Centre, B4). Includes a shop belonging to the Japanese Sogo chain.

Taman Anggrek, Jl Letjend S Parman, to the west (Built-Up Area, C2). The most recently built of the capital's malls is also the largest.

Jakarta also has concentrations of shops that specialise to varying degrees:

Pasar Baru, north of Merdeka Square (Centre, B3-C3). A host of inexpensive shops selling textiles, clothes and shoes.

Jalan Cokroaminoto, Menteng (Centre, C4). A small street in the city centre with numerous shops (including a supermarket, galleries and photography shops).

Glodok Plaza, Jl Gajah Mada (near Kota) (Centre, C1). In the heart of the Chinese quarter. The electronics centre was destroyed during the riots of May 1998.

Local arts and crafts, souvenirs – **Pasar Seni**, Ancol (Centre, C1). Around 200 stalls sell contemporary paintings and sculptures of varying degrees of quality.

Sarinah, Jl Thamrin 11; Jl Ir H Huanda 27 (Centre, B4). Handy for last minute buys (silverware, batiks, woodwork, books and sportswear).

Jalan Surabaya, Menteng (9am-5pm) (Centre, C4). Reproductions of Indonesian handicrafts, old records.

Batiks – Keris Galeri, Jl Cokroaminoto 87-89, Menteng (Centre, C4).

Batik Danar Hadi, Jl Raden Saleh 1A (Centre, C3).

Iwan Tirta, Jl Panarukan 25 Menteng (Centre, C4).

Sarinah, Jl Thamrin (Centre, B4). The most famous designer of batik clothes. Official supplier to Ronald Reagan, Margaret Thatcher, Hillary Clinton and Pope John Paul II!

Antiques – Along with Bali, Jakarta is the best place in Indonesia to hunt around for antiques, but prices are higher than in Yogyakarta. Shops in Jl Jaksa (Centre, C3-C4) and Jl Kebon Sirih Timur Dalam (Centre, B3-C4) have a good selection of handicrafts at reasonable prices:

Agam Art Curios, Jl Kebon Sirih Timur Dalam 161 (Centre, B3-C3), ☎ (021) 32 46 64. Masks, wooden statues, puppets and fabrics.

Jaya, Jl Kebon Sirih Timur Dalam 5B (Centre, B3-C3), ☎ (021) 32 50 21. Masks, puppets, arts and crafts from Sumatra (Batak).

Terracota, Kebon Sirih Timur Dalam 5 (Centre, B3-C3), ☎ (021) 391 42 01. Excellent choice of Javanese handicrafts (terracotta items, wood panels, puppets).

Further south, up-market antique dealers are concentrated along Jl Ciputat Raya.

Lampung Indah Art Shop, Jl Ciputat Raya, ☎ (021) 749 43 60. Wonderful selection of handicrafts from Sumatra (rattan objects, textiles, cupboards), and Chinese-Indonesian items (cupboards, porcelain).

Dharma Mulia Complex, Jl Ciputat Raya 50, ☎ (021) 749 28 50. This is a real museum of a place with outstanding fabrics, statues and ethnic artworks, unfortunately at prohibitive prices.

Gallery Fifty-Nine, Jl Ciputat Raya, ☎ (021) 749 43 60. Attractive shop selling Javanese and Chinese furniture.

Bookshops – You will find English newspapers in the main hotels.

In Plaza Indonesia (Centre, C4), the **Times** and **Books Kinokuniya** bookshops are considered to be the best stocked in the capital.

Kirama Bookshop, Hotel Indonesia, Plaza Indonesia (Centre, C4) Postcards, press and books in English (art, culture).

Gramedia, Jl Melawai IV/13, Blok M (Built-Up Area, C3).

Photography – The shops in Jl H Agus Salim and Pasar Baru (Centre, B4) have a good choice of equipment. Elsewhere, you will find stores in all the shopping centres.

Ekta Photo, Jl Cideng Barat (west of Taman Merdeka). Professional photo development.

Music – Near the French Embassy (Centre, B4), **Duta Suara** (Jl H Agus Salim 24F) and **Duta Disc** (Jl H Agus Salim 26F) sell Indonesian and Western CDs and cassettes, at good prices.

Making the most of Jakarta

THE WEST COAST★

West Java Province – Map p 210-211
A hot, wet climate

Not to be missed
Ujung Kulon National Park and Krakatau volcano.
The beaches.

And remember...
Avoid visiting Krakatau and Ujung Kulon during the rainy season (November-April).
Before going to Ujung Kulon, ensure you have anti-malarial treatment.

In spite of being so close to the capital, Java's west coast is still off the major tourist routes – a blessing for nature lovers and those in search of peace and quiet. From green Banten with its antiquated air, to mythical, smoking Krakatau, via the hot sand of the beaches along the coast, your days will be full of discoveries, some of them surprising.

Banten, a Dutch city

65km west of Jakarta, 10km north of Serang. Allow half a day.

It is difficult to believe that in the late 16C this small sleepy fishing port in the suburbs of **Serang** was Southeast Asia's largest city and a flourishing pepper trading port.

An eventful past
Founded in the 11 or 12C, Banten became the main port of the Sundanese kingdom of Pajajaran in the 14C. In the early 16C, to counter the threat posed by the Muslim Sultanate of Demak, the Sundanese – who were Hindus – sought an alliance with the Portuguese, who wanted to set up a trading post there, on the spice route. In vain: in 1527, Hasanuddin subjugated Banten, and set up a Muslim dynasty. This marked the beginning of a new golden age. Portuguese, Arab, Persian, Indian and Chinese merchants flocked to the city. Canals were dug and ramparts built. Coveting such prosperity, the Dutch settled in Sunda Kelapa in 1619 and imposed a commercial blockade. Weakened by disputes within the dynasty and by rivalry with the kingdom of Mataram, Sultan Ageng, Banten's last major sovereign, capitulated to the Dutch in 1682.

For people keen on old buildings, the city bears unique witness to a page of Indonesia's history that is often forgotten.

All that remains of the vast **Surosowan palace** (1680), destroyed by the Dutch in 1832, is the base of the **surrounding wall** that is now covered in weeds and borders the **Alun-alun**, the main square of ancient Banten. On the other hand, the **Mesjid Agung** (16C), which rises on the other side of the green square, is perfectly preserved and is typical of the architecture of early Javanese mosques with its three-tiered roof of red tiles.

Its imposing white **minaret**★ stands like a lighthouse, affording the best **view**★ of Banten, the surrounding palm grove and the salt marshes that fringe the seafront. If you have the time, take a look at the small **Historical and Archeological Museum** nearby (*Tuesday-Sunday, 9am-4pm*).

Fort Speelwijk, a small structure with lava walls, was built on the coast by the Dutch in 1682. It now stands a few hundred metres from the coast because of the silting which has occurred in the area. Not far away, the **Chinese Temple** (18C) and the **Chinese Mosque** (Pacinan Tinggi) with its remaining mihrab and white minaret on a square base, recall the city's cosmopolitan past.

West Java

Beaches, a volcano and rhinos

Head northwest from Serang to Cilegon, then fork left southwards along the coast. The road to the right leads to Merak (30km), the departure point for ferries to Sumatra.

The sand beaches in Anyer and Carita★

With their coconut palms and beautiful white sand, the beaches on the west coast are some of the Jakarta jet-set's favourite destinations. Hardly surprising then that so many luxury hotels are springing up. Furthermore – unusually for Java – there is no danger **swimming** here.

An important harbour during colonial times, **Anyer** *(19km from Cilegon)* has not forgotten the fatal tidal wave that followed the eruption of Krakatau in 1883. Two years after the catastrophe, Queen Wilhelmina of Holland had a **lighthouse** built for the village. It stands among the palm trees near the beach.

Off the coast of Anyer is **Sangiang Island** with its beautiful **coral reefs★**, perfect for an excursion *(90min crossing in a chartered boat)*.

Further south the road runs alongside a ribbon of white sand to **Karang Bolong** *(11km from Anyer)* before reaching **Carita★** *(21km from Anyer)*, one of the finest beaches on the coast.

Ujung Kulon National Park★★★

Expeditions depart from the evil-smelling waters of the small port of Labuan (9km from Carita) For access, see the "Excursions" section in "Making the most of the West Coast" below. Fee. Allow at least 3 days.

Sticking out from Java's southwestern point is a narrow peninsula fringed with remote, wild islets. The tropical forest covering the area (76 000ha) is on **UNESCO's World Heritage** list and has exceptionally rich flora and fauna. Apart from the invisible **Java rhinoceros**, one of the world's rarest mammals (with only about fifty left), there are **banteng** oxen, imposing animals that are endemic to the region, weighing

The elegant minaret
of the mosque in Banten

R. Marca

The West Coast

900kg and measuring 1.8m at the neck. Crocodiles, turtles, numerous species of monkeys, and a multitude of birds are also on view. For the adventurous at heart, various trails enable you to do a **tour of the peninsula** right into the wildest parts (*guides are indispensable*). There are also **beaches** and **coral reefs****, guaranteed to provide memorable opportunities for relaxation.

Lastly, with its fringe of golden beaches, **Pulau Peucang**** islet lies several hundred metres off the peninsula, and offers diving, walking and river canoeing.

Krakatau**

For access, see the "Excursions" section in "Making the most of the West Coast" below. Allow 1 day. Posted at the entrance to the Sunda Strait (Selat Sunda), an arm of the sea separating Java from Sumatra, Krakatau (or Krakatoa) can count itself amongst the most famous of the world's volcanoes.

To it we owe one of the most powerful natural cataclysms in the history of mankind (*see sidebar*). Of the original massif, which literally flew into pieces during the famous eruption, there remain three islands covered in vegetation, visible parts of the submerged caldera. Clockwise, they are **Lang**, **Rakata** and **Sertung**. In the middle stands **Anak Krakatau** (the child of Krakatau), an arid rock that rose up in 1928, and forms the chimney of the volcano. There have been signs of activity here since 1992, and it is forbidden to walk round the crater.

Krakatau's rumblings

The eruption of Krakatau, which had begun in May 1883, reached its height on 27 August. At 10.02am there was a fantastic explosion that pulverised the volcano and could even be heard in Alice Springs in Australia, 3 500km away. Soon a thick, 20 cubic kilometre column of ash rose into the atmosphere, 80km high, plunging the Sunda Strait into total darkness until the following day. This cloud continued to circle the globe for three years before dissipating! More importantly, the collapse of the volcano gave rise to an enormous tidal wave rising 30 to 40m high that devastated the coasts of Java and Sumatra, sweeping away 165 villages and killing more than 36 000 people. The wave reached the Arab peninsula within 12 hours, and could even be felt in the English Channel! Since then the volcano has erupted once, in 1979, and is a constant threat.

Making the most of the West Coast

COMING AND GOING

By bus and bemo – *Kalideres terminal* in Jakarta serves the west coast. Most of the main hotels in Anyer and Carita organise transport from Jakarta, if you book.
– For Banten: bus to Serang (90min), then *bemo* (10km).
– For Anyer: bus to Cilegon (2hr), then *bemo* (30min).
– For Carita: bus to Labuan (3hr30min), then *bemo* (15min).

By car – For car rental, see Jakarta p 226. Allow 3hr to reach Anyer on the toll motorway via Cilegon, but beware of traffic jams on weekends.

ADDRESS BOOK

Telephone – There are no post offices, even at Banten. You can usually phone from hotels, but its best to have nothing urgent to deal with.

WHERE TO STAY

The hotels in the region generally provide excellent service, but with prices to match. Places in Carita are cheaper than those in Anyer. The prices for the hotel categories below are based on weekend rates, mostly two or three times higher than during the week.

• Anyer

Luxury

Ancott, ☎ (0254) 60 15 56 – 24rm. 🏠
🍽 🅿 📺 ✕ 🛏 🏊 cc Very pleasant
bungalows with upper wooden terraces.
Some are equipped with kitchens. The
beach is one of the finest in the area.

Super deluxe

Mambruk Quality Resort, just after the
lighthouse, ☎ (0254) 60 16 02,
Fax (0254) 60 17 23 – 200rm. 🏠🍽✕
🏊 🛁 🏊 cc The best hotel on the coast.
Not much soul, but impeccable service.
You have a choice between rooms in the
main building or bungalows in the garden. An artificial beach has even been laid
out (watch out for the rocks at the bottom). Diving and deep-sea fishing can be
organised.

• Carita

Modest

Badak Hitam, ☎ (0253) 810 72 – 12rm.
This simple, friendly, very inexpensive
hotel (with no private bathrooms) has relatively comfortable rooms given the price.
The beach is just across the road. Breakfast is included.

Sunset View (beside the Badak Hitam),
☎ (0253) 810 75 – 10rm. 🏠 Another inexpensive hotel, but set back a little from
the beach. Clean rooms and friendly staff.
Numerous restaurants nearby.

Average

Hotel Wira Carita, ☎ (0253) 811 16 –
20rm. 🏠 🌂 / 🍽 🛏 🏊 cc This simple
but beautifully kept hotel has a wide
range of rooms, from basic to bungalows.
The beach is just across the road.

• Ujung Kulon

High end

Handeulum Island Guesthouse – The
bungalows run by the PHPA are of a rustic style. Not cheap, but affordable
nonetheless.

Ciputih Beach Resort Hotel, Sumur (at
the entrance to the park), ☎ (021) 828
10 93, Fax (021) 829 90 02 (reservations
in Jakarta) – 60rm. 🏠🍽✕🛏🛁 This is
a new hotel with impeccably comfortable
modern or traditional style bungalows.
Tours of the park, diving, water-skiing,
deep-sea fishing. Prices for full board,
with or without transport.

Peucang Island Flora Lodge – 16rm. 🏠
🍽 📺 ✕ Unexpected luxury in such a
remote place, but with prices to match.

Eating out

Most of the hotels in Carita and Anyer
have restaurants, but don't hesitate to try
the family-run *warung* which provide
cheaper, simple local cooking.

• Carita

Warung Kita, a friendly eating-house
serving standard but inexpensive Indonesian food.

Cafe de Paris, heading towards Anyer.
This is an air-conditioned meeting-place
for those who miss Western food

EXCURSIONS

• Ujung Kulon National Park

To do this expedition you need time (at
least 3 days) and money. Going through
a travel agent can save you a lot of hassle.
Kantor Taman Nasional Ujung Kulon,
Jl Perintis Kemerdekaan 51, Labuan,
☎ (021) 817 31. The Forestry Commission issues permits and helps people find
guides and porters.
PT Wanawisata Alamhayati, Mang-
gala Wanabhakti building, Blok IV,
Building A, 2nd floor, Jl Gatot Subroto,
Jakarta, ☎ (021) 571 03 92. The agency,
which also has an office in Labuan, takes
care of permits, transport and accommodation.
Even if you don't go through a travel
agent you must still have a guide. Get a
group together to share transport costs.
In Labuan you can hire a fishing boat
(crossing: 6hr), or a much more expensive speedboat for 15 passengers (crossing: 3hr). Bring food, water, mosquito
nets, torches, goggles and snorkels,
binoculars and anti-malarial treatment.

• Krakatau

Carita is an ideal departure point for
Krakatau. You may either go through a
travel agent or charter a private boat. Al-
low 8hr return for the crossing.
Be warned that weather conditions some-
times make the crossing impossible.
Black Rhino, Carita, ☎ (0253) 810 72.
Krakatau Ujung Kulon Tour & Travel,
Rakata Hotel, Carita, ☎ (0253) 811 24.

BOGOR
PUNCAK AND THE NATIONAL PARKS★★
West Java Province
60km from Jakarta – Map p 210-211
Alt 235m – Pop 700 000 – Mild, rainy climate

Not to be missed
The Botanical Gardens in Bogor.
Gunung Gede Pangrango and Halimun National Parks.
And remember...
Avoid the rainy season, from November to April.
Between April and August, reserve your hotel at Cibodas in advance.

Bogor, the first stopping place on a tour of the Sundanese region, stretches out at the foot of **Salak volcano** (2 211m), in beautiful undulating countryside. With barely any traces of the ancient Pajaran kingdom, the place mainly feels like a small colonial town with an uneventful past. The return trip from Jakarta to take in the famous Botanical Gardens and the local traditional arts and crafts can easily be done in one day. But if possible, you should venture further afield into the green heart of Java: beyond Bogor the **Priangan mountain chain** has an infinite variety of landscapes, some tame like those around Puncak hill station, others wild like the Halimun and Gunung Gede Pangrango National Parks.

Short tour of the town
Allow half a day.

Perched in the hills, Bogor has a cooler climate than the capital. It was this asset that won over the Dutch who built a manor here in the 18C and called it **Buitenzorg** ("free of worries"). This is the centre of the present-day town. However, with each tropical downpour, the Cisadane and Ciliwung rivers that flow through the town swell into impetuous torrents, and Bogor deserves its nickname *kota ujan* or "city of rain". But it is this rain that gives the Kebun Raya Botanical Gardens all their beauty, creating an oasis right in the heart of the town.

Before losing yourself there, go to the **Zoological Museum★** (B3-B4) (*Jl Otto Iskandardinata, near the main entrance to the Botanical Gardens, open daily 8am-4pm, allow 30min*), a taxidermist's dream! Apart from a **Java panther**, an orang-utan, a **pangolin** and birds of paradise, there are several curiosities, including a **banteng** (giant ox) and an enormous **rhino** (2 280kg) killed in the Tasikmalaya area in 1934.

West Java

Kebun Raya Botanical Gardens★★

Main entrance in Jl Otto Iskandardinata (B3). *8am-5pm, fee.* Whether or not you are passionately interested in plants, a visit to this large botanic park (110ha) is an enchanting experience as well as an ideal introduction to tropical flora. At the weekend, friendly crowds stroll along the pathways bordered by giant bamboos, tree ferns, palm trees, pandanus and teak trees, all bathed in the fragrance of bougainvillaeas, frangipanis and orchids.

Laid out in the 19C, the botanical gardens were instrumental in the introduction of new species into the archipelago (flamboyants, oil-palms, cassava, tobacco, maize, coffee and cinchona), and today the institution is dedicated to preserving endangered species and studying plants for medicinal and agricultural purposes.

In the northwest reaches of the park, near a pond, **Istana Bogor** (Bogor Palace) (B3) stands on the site of the former Buitenzorg manor. It was built in the 19C and became the official residence of Dutch governors from 1870 to 1942. At the time of Independence it was converted into a summer presidential palace and became a kind of gilded cage for the former president Sukarno from 1967 until his death in 1970. The palace is closed to the public *(the Tourist Office can organise group visits)* so you have to admire its elegant **neo-Classical façade**, topped by a steeple, from the outside.

Before leaving, stop by at the **Botanicus Café**, with its pleasant terrace overlooking the entire park.

Lastly, if you have time, take a look at the stone at **Batutulis** *(south of the town, Jl Batutulis; take colt no 02; open daily 8am-4pm; donation; you must remove your shoes)*. This was engraved in 1533 by King Surawisesa in honour of his father, Sri Baduga Maharaja. It is one of the rare remains of the **Pajajaran kingdom**, which nonetheless held sway over the region for centuries.

Bogor rooftops

G Guérard

Bogor

From jungles to volcanoes

Allow at least 3 days for excursions. Accommodation in Cibodas.

Mount Halimun National Park★★

About 50km southwest of Bogor. See "Making the most of Mount Halimun" for details on access. Allow 2 days for the excursion. The latest of Indonesia's national parks, Halimun (40 000ha) contains the largest area of **primary equatorial forest★★★** in Java. It is a sanctuary for the very rare **Java gibbon**, the long-tailed macaque and more than 130 species of birds. Bristling with peaks, including that of **Halimun** (1 929m), this immense forest area plays a vital role in West Java, affecting the climate and irrigation (no less than 4 to 6m of precipitation a year!).

The Badui, guardians of sacred places

One of Indonesia's most unusual communities lives several hours from Jakarta, near Rangkasbitung. Resolutely cut off from all modernity, the Badui live in bamboo houses and speak an archaic form of Sundanese. But when a delegation of them goes to the capital (on foot), they are welcomed by the highest authorities. The Badui are the descendants of a community of "mandalas", guardians of sacred places, and even the Muslims recognise them as being able to intercede with supernatural powers. Their religion mixes primitive Hinduism with ancestor worship, and they believe that Adam was the first man. Dressed in dark clothes, the 7 000 Badui Luar ("from the outside") serve as intermediaries between the Badui Dalam ("from the inside"), who are dressed in white and live in three villages totally cut off from the rest of the world.

Between the beautiful **Nirmala tea plantation** (Citalahab) and the **waterfalls** that spring up all over the jungle, the park offers all sorts of sporting activities, from **walking** to **rafting**. There is something for history buffs too: apart from the small **Cibedug Temple** (*a 2hr walk west of Citorek*), the **traditional Kasepuhan villages (local communities)** – mainly **Ciptarasa★** – are really worth a visit, with their attractive bamboo houses.

Puncak Pass★

Southeast of Bogor the road snakes through the **tea plantations★★** that cover Mount Gede, a thick dark green mantle that the surrounding trees splash with bright red as soon as the rainy season begins. Rich Jakartans in search of pure air and cool temperatures have made this superb setting into a holiday resort. Hotels and luxury mansions line the road from **Ciawi** (*10km from Bogor*) to **Cianjur** (*on the other side of the pass*) right up to the Puncak Pass, perched at an altitude of 1 500m.

Beyond Cisarua (*20km from Bogor*), a road to the right climbs towards **Taman Safari Park** (*2km from Cisarua; daily; fee*), a delight for animal lovers. Elephants, zebras, bison, deer, zebu oxen, hippos, bears and tigers roam freely through the vast reserve, which may be visited by minibus (*30min*). The site also has a swimming pool, a hotel, restaurants and an amusement park.

To learn more about tea picking, visit the very large **Gunung Mas Tea Plantation★** (*just before the pass*) and its **factory** (*which operates in the morning*).

Just beyond the pass, a road leads down to **Lake Telaga Warna** (*donation*), a limpid sheet of water stretching through the woods. According to legend, the variations in colour are due to a princess who drowned there with her jewels.

Several kilometres beyond Cipanas, a pretty road lined with flowers (*on the right*) leads to the **Cibodas Botanical Gardens★** (*45km from Bogor, daily 7am-4pm*). The site is run in conjunction with the Kebun Raya gardens in Bogor and is devoted to the

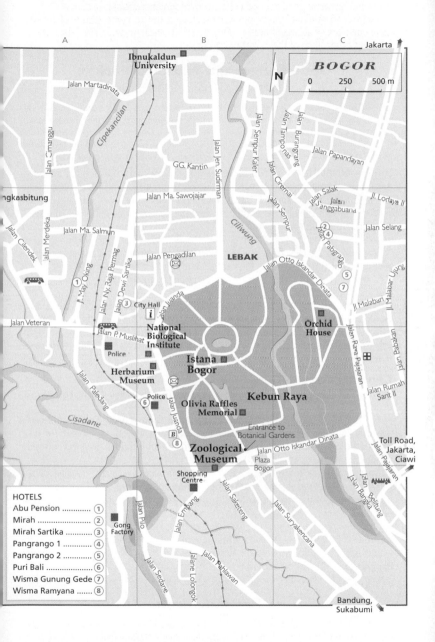

BOGOR

N

0   250   500 m

Jakarta

Ibnukaldun University

Jalan Martadinata

Cipekancilan

GG. Kantin

Jalan Jen. Sudirman

Jalan Jen. Tamponas

Jalan Sempur Kaler

Jalan Burangrang

Jalan Papandayan

Jalan Cimanggu

ngkasbitung

Jalan Merdeka

Jalan Ma. Sawojajar

Jalan Ciremai

Jalan Salak

Jalan Anggabuana

Jl. Lodaya II

Jalan Ma. Salmun

Jalan Ciliwung

Jalan Sempur

Jalan Pabrang

Jalan Selang

Jalan Cilendek

J. May Oking

Jalan Nj. Raja Permag

Jalan Dewi Sartika

Jalan Pengadilan

LEBAK

Jalan Otto Iskandar Dinata

Jl. Malabar

Jl. Malabar Ujung

Jl. Babakan Jalan

①

City Hall

i

Jalan Juanda

②
④

⑤
⑦

Jalan Veteran

Jalan P. Muslihat

National Biological Institute

Police

Orchid House

Jalan Raya Pajajaran

Herbarium Museum

Police

⑥

Istana Bogor

Kebun Raya

Jalan Rumah Sarit II

Jalan Paledang

Cisadane

Olivia Raffles Memorial

B

⑧

Entrance to Botanical Gardens

Zoological Museum

Plaza Bogor

Jalan Otto Iskandar Dinata

Toll Road, Jakarta, Ciawi

Jalan Pajajaran

Jalan Belitung

Jalan Bangka

Shopping Centre

Jalan Saketeng

Jalan Suryakencana

Jalan Pilo

Jalan Empang

Gong Factory

Jalan Plo

Jalan Sedare

Jalane Lolongok

Jalan Pahlawan

Bandung, Sukabumi

HOTELS

Abu Pension .... ①
Mirah .... ②
Mirah Sartika .... ③
Pangrango 1 .... ④
Pangrango 2 .... ⑤
Puri Bali .... ⑥
Wisma Gunung Gede ⑦
Wisma Ramyana .... ⑧

study and preservation of tropical plants from mountain areas. More than 200 species come from Mount Halimun National Park alone. Perched at an altitude of 1 400m, the garden covers 125ha of neatly ordered orchids, cacti and tree ferns that contrast with the exuberance of the surrounding forest.

Gede Pangrango National Park★★
(Taman Nasional Gunung Gede Pangrango)

Access near the Botanical Gardens (which stretch out before the entrance). There are two other gates to the park, one at Selabintana (to the south, via Sukabumi), and the other at Gunung Putri (to the north, near Cipanas). Allow a morning for a walk in the forest, and a full day if you continue to the top of Mount Gede (in which case it is best to spend the night before nearby in order to have an early start). Fee. See also "Making the most of Mount Gede".

Listed by **UNESCO** as a world nature reserve, the park's 15 000ha boast an exceptional natural heritage, with more than 300 species per hectare! It is a tropical garden of Eden, a maze of entangled lianas, tree ferns, and giant trees creating different shades of green that shimmer and glint when the flowers come out or when it rains. Apart from the oaks and chestnut trees, 15 varieties of ficus have been counted (used in medicine and batik dyes), 150 types of ferns, delicate rattans (growing up to 40m!) which die after a single flowering, strangler figs, pandanus, countless epiphytes, as well as **styrax** (*rasamala*) trees that can grow to a height of 60m and live for 300 to 500 years. There are also flowers in abundance: orange rhododendrons, green orchids, white jasmine, and purple passionflowers.

This inextricable tangle of plants hums with the song of 245 species of birds (**blue Sunda robins**, black eagles and thrushes), as well as the piercing cries of Java gibbons. While the rhinos and tigers disappeared in the 19C, there are still some leopards and Bengal cats. But you have more of a chance of seeing **long-tailed macaques**, polecats and squirrels.

Climbing Gunung Gede★★★
You can climb the mountain without a guide. Leave early in the morning and take waterproof clothes.

After a short walk in the jungle (*45min*), the **Blue Lake★** (Telaga Biru) soon appears between the trees, an excellent site for bird-watching. Its colour varies from deep blue to greeny-brown, depending on organic matter and mineral discharge from the volcano.

Further on, a fork leads to the beautiful **Cibeureum waterfalls★** (*90min*). Then, halfway along the walk, you reach a **hot spring★★** (air panas) (*3hr*) that spouts up from the sides of the volcano at a temperature of 75°C, covering the woods in an eerie mist.

Beyond the pass (2 400m), the path follows the ridge of the volcano up to the **summit★★★** (2 958m) (*6hr30min*), affording a magnificent **panoramic view★★★** of the whole region. While the volcano has been inactive for 50 years unlike its twin **Pangrango** (3 019m) on the other side of the pass, this does not mean that it is extinct, just dormant. But for how long?

Pelabuhanratu

90km from Bogor. Avoid weekends and public holidays when prices shoot up. Be careful when swimming in the sea, as currents can be dangerous at certain times of the year. Allow 1 or 2 days to enjoy the surrounding beaches.

Once a small fishing village, Pelabuhanratu has developed into a seaside resort which is taken over by Jakartans every weekend. The village is set in the curve of a large bay bordered with green vegetation. Attractive beaches of grey sand are dotted along the coast to the west of the village, between the wooded slopes of **Priangan** and the blue ocean rollers, a haven for surfers.

Queen's harbour

Pelabuhanratu ("Queen's harbour") takes its name from the mythical Queen of the South Seas. The town itself is of little interest, apart from the harbour, home to a host of iridescent prahu boats that wait, pennants to the wind, to put to sea. In the early morning when the fishermen return, the catch is sold at the nearby market which comes to life in a joyous hubbub.

The legend of the Queen of the South Seas

Prabu Siliwangi, the wise and powerful king of West Java, lived happily with his wife and daughter, who were both matchless beauties. Alas, this happiness aroused the jealousy of the concubines, who decided to use black magic to turn the two women into thoroughly repugnant creatures. Driven from the palace, the Queen soon died of sorrow, leaving her daughter to head south alone, through the forest. When the young woman reached the edge of the Karanghawu cliffs, she had a dream: by diving into the roaring water she would regain all her charm. So she jumped... and never reappeared. Since then, however, the "Queen of the South Seas", beautiful but extremely bitter, has haunted the whole of the Indian Ocean. She carries off anyone who dares swim in green, her special colour, which she loathes sharing.

From beach to beach

Before heading west on the trail of beautiful Ratu Kidul, make a short detour south to **Goa Lalay** cave *(4km from the village)*. Every day at sunset an enormous flock of **bats** flies out, whirling around in an impressive ballet in the sky.

Wilder and less frequented than the beaches at Pelabuhanratu, those to the west *(which may be reached by bemo)* are the major reason for a stay in the area. Stop first at **Citepus** *(4km)*, the most popular, where excellent fish is served in stalls set up on the sand.

Further along, there are pebbles at **Cimaja** *(8km)*, a popular spot for **surfing**. Be careful if you want to swim, the breakers can be dangerous.

Beyond rise the dark **cliffs of Karanghawu** *(15km)*, the petrified remains of a lava flow, and the place where Ratu made her legendary swallow dive. Then, just beyond Cisolok, you come to a pretty beach at **Cibangban***, a long ribbon of grey sand.

After a dip in the Indian Ocean waves, there's nothing like a hot shower in the **Cipanas hot springs**, which gush out of the ground in the middle of the woods *(2km from Cisolok, by motorbike-taxi or on foot. Not to be confused with the thermal spa of the same name, 60km from Bandung)*.

Lastly, continuing west towards **Malingping**, from the coast road you will see some magnificent **landscapes**** with rice fields and forests stretching right down to Java's western shore.

Bogor

Making the most of Bogor

COMING AND GOING

By train – From Jakarta (Gambir), departures every 20min (1hr).

By bus – From Jakarta, departures every 10min from Kampung Rambutan terminal (30min on the motorway).
Buses from Bandung avoid Puncak over the weekend and go via Sukabumi (4hr). In Bogor, the main terminal is in Jl Pajajaran.

By minibus – Several "Travel" minibuses (air conditioning and door-to-door service) go to and from Bandung. Travel agents: **Rini Travel**, ☎ (0251) 33 51 60, and **Erny**, ☎ (0251) 32 25 63.

GETTING AROUND

On foot – The mild climate and short distances tempt you to walk, but watch out for sudden showers!

By taxi – **Omega Motor**, Jl Pajajaran 217 (C3), ☎ (0251) 31 12 42.

By becak – Hosts of *becaks* wait for clients near the station. Convenient for short distances, but they are forbidden on main thoroughfares.

By minibus – "Colt" minibuses ply the streets throughout town.

Car rental – The most practical way to go about hiring a car is to enquire at hotels.

ADDRESS BOOK

Tourist information – At the town hall, Jl IRH Juanda (B2), Monday-Saturday, 7am-2pm.

Bank/Currency exchange – Currency exchange in Jl Siliwangi 62 (in the south). Open Sundays and public holidays. Banks also change money and are open until 2pm: **BNI**, Jl IRH Juanda 46 (B3) and **BCA**, Jl IRH Juanda 24 (B3).

Post office/Telephone – **Main post office**, Jl IRH Juanda 3 (B2). **Wartel**, Jl Pengadilan 8 (B2).

Internet – **Bogor Internet**, Jl Pajajaran (near the Olympic building) (C3).

PHPA – **Forest Protection and Environment Conservation Office**, Jl IRH Juanda 9 (B2). Information and entry permits for the various parks.

WHERE TO STAY

With its legacy from the Dutch period and particularly from the Asia-Pacific international conference held in 1994, Bogor has a wide choice of accommodation.

Modest

Puri Bali, Jl Paledang 50, ☎ (0251) 37 49 06 – 6rm. ⁂ A small family guesthouse with a cafeteria, in an old Dutch house. The rooms with their high ceilings are somewhat neglected but are good value for money (breakfast included). The lady owner, a mine of information on the region, offers tours.

Wisma Ramayana, Jl IRH Juanda 54, ☎ (0251) 32 03 64 – 25rm. ⌁ A quiet, pleasant hotel, somewhat Spartan but very inexpensive. Some rooms have private bathrooms.

Average

Abu Pension, Jl Mayor Oking 15, ☎ (0251) 32 28 93, Fax (0251) 33 56 34 – 43rm. ✕ Set beside the river, this is a popular place with travellers and has a wide range of rooms. Some have their own bathrooms and air conditioning. Friendly welcome and decent prices.

Mirah Sartika, Jl Dewi Sartika 6A, ☎ (0251) 31 23 43, Fax (0251) 34 03 87 – 34rm. ⁂ 🍽 ⌨ 📺 ✕ CC Between the station and the Botanical Gardens. A modern, functional hotel without much charm but extremely clean and comfortable.

High end

Hotel Mirah, Jl Pangrango 9A, ☎ (0251) 32 90 44, Fax (0251) 31 23 85 – 75rm. ⁂ 🍽 ⌨ 📺 ✕ ⌁ CC In a residential area full of Dutch houses. The hotel was enlarged to include a second building in 1997. Marble hall, comfortable carpeted rooms with satellite television (breakfast included).

Hotel Pangrango I, Jl Pangrango 23, ☎ (0251) 32 86 70, Fax (0251) 31 40 60 – 73rm. ⁂ 🍽 ⌨ 📺 ✕ ⌁ CC A little more expensive than the Mirah, and equally comfortable (breakfast included). Has a small bar. Satellite television.

Luxury

Hotel Pangrango 2, Jl Raya Pajajaran 32, ☎ (0251) 32 14 82, Fax (0251) 37 77 50 – 100rm. ⁂ 🍽 ⌨ 📺 ✕ ⌁ CC The most expensive hotel in town. Comfort to match. Satellite television.

EATING OUT

In the evening, try the *warung* along Jl Dewi Sartika (A2).

Basic to moderate

Jongko Ibu, Jl IRH Juanda 36 (B3). A small terrace restaurant where you can help yourself (to "ayam bakar" grilled chicken, brochettes, fruit juice).

☜Restoran Sri Kabayan, Jl Bina Marga I/2 (in the southeast). One of the best Sundanese restaurants in town, in a charming setting: tables dotted around a garden, bamboo decor.

Bogor Permai, Jl Jend Sudirman 23A (B2). 11am-9pm. Excellent Indonesian, Chinese and European dishes.

Cahaya Baru, Jl Pajajaran 7 (almost at the end of Jl Toll) (C4), ☎ (0251) 32 84 66. The best Chinese restaurant in town, where you can also try delicious seafood. A shame the dining room is a little chilly.

Trio Permai, Jl Raya Pajajaran 23 (C3). A large Padang (spicy) restaurant, where you can have a quick meal at any time.

Lembak Anai, Jl IRH Juanda 88 (B3), opposite the entrance to the Botanical Gardens (daily, 24 hours a day). A good Padang restaurant, where they serve exquisite fish head ("kepala ikan kakap") and lightly fried chicken ("ayam pok").

☜Salak Sunset Cafe, Jl Paledang 38 (A3). A small restaurant located behind the Alliance Française, with a wonderful view of Mount Salak. Try the very good "mie goreng" with cheese. Open until 11pm.

A street in Bogor

R. Marca

Making the most of **Bogor**

OTHER THINGS TO DO

Excursions – Most of the hotels organise tours. One of the travel agents: **Arcana Tours & Travel**, Jl Jend Sudirman 21 (B2), ☏ (0251) 32 86 29.

SHOPPING GUIDE

Jalan Suryakencana is the main shopping street. You can also wander through **Pasar Anyar**, Jl NY Raja Permag (near the station) (A2-A3), a popular market where you find anything and everything.

Local arts and crafts – **Gong Home Factory**, Jl Pancasan 17 (A4). The gongs made by Mr Pak Sukarna are renowned throughout West Java. Even if you don't want to buy any, the workshop with its traditional metal shaping methods is worth a visit.

DASE AS, Lebak, Kantin Rt 2/VI (B2). A small wayang golek workshop.

West Java

Making the most of Halimun National Park

COMING AND GOING

No buses go as far as the park gates. Whatever direction you approach from, you will either have to go by *bemo*, motorbike or on foot. So it is easier to hire a car in Bogor. It is possible to get an entry permit to the park at the gate.

By bus – From the north: bus to Cigudeg, near Leuwiliang (30min), then by minibus or motorbike to Cisarua and then on foot to Leuwijamang (a 1hr walk).

– From the east: bus to Parung Kuda (1hr), then by minibus to Kabandungan (1hr), and then by motorbike to Citalahab.

– From the south: bus to Pelabuhanratu (3hr), then by minibus or motorbike to Pangguyangan (1hr), and by motorbike to Ciptarasa (45min).

WHERE TO STAY, EATING OUT

The park has 3 camps, at **Leuwijamang**, **Citalahab** and **Pangguyangan**. Attractive wooden cabins that are basic but inexpensive are available to stay in.

OTHER THINGS TO DO

Walking – **Konsorsium Program Pengembangan Ekoturism Taman Nasional Gunung Halimun**, Jl Samiaji Raya 33, Bogor, ☏ (0251) 33 68 86. A friendly professional team organises tours and provides very detailed documentation in English.

Rafting – Unforgettable thrills going down the Citarik as far as Pelabuhanratu. The following travel agents take care of everything:
PT Lintas Jeram Nusantara, Jakarta, ☏ (021) 835 58 85.
BJ's, Jl Pondok Raya IV/23C, Jakarta, ☏ (021) 923 33 12.

Shows and festivals – "Wayang golek" and "jaipongan" (Sundanese dance) shows are organised for visitors. Among them is the **Seren Tahun** show, held in Ciptarasa in July. There is also the Harvest Festival, with traditional dancing, "wayang" shows and "angklung" (bamboo percussion) concerts.

Making the most of Mount Gede

COMING AND GOING

By bus and minibus – From Jakarta, buses leave from Kampung Rambutan terminal (90min).

From Bogor, take a bus or an "oplet" minibus heading for Cianjur, and tell the driver where you want to get off (45min). To go to Cibodas, take another oplet.

To go to Bandung, take a Jakarta-Bandung bus (2hr), or take a minibus to Cianjur, and then a bus.

GETTING AROUND PUNCAK

Car and minibus rentals – The hotels will help you with hiring a car or chartering a *bemo*.

ADDRESS BOOK

Telephone/Internet – **Wartel** in Cibodas, Jl Puncak Raya (9am-4pm), and in Cipanas (24hr a day). Internet access.

National Park Office – At the park entrance. Issues permits for climbing to the summit (Monday-Thursday: 7.30am-3.30pm, Friday: 7.30am-2.30pm and 7-9pm, Saturday-Sunday: 8am-2.30pm/7-9pm).

WHERE TO STAY

Puncak is full of luxury hotels and villas for rent. In Cibodas, however, there are cheaper places to stay.

• Cibodas

Modest

Cibodas Botanical Garden Guesthouse, ☎ (0263) 51 22 33 – 7rm. This colonial-style house offers a basic standard of comfort (shared bathrooms and no hot water). The setting, right in the middle of a garden, is unique. Essential to book (in the morning). Kitchen provided, but bring your own food.

Freddy's Homestay, Jl Kebun Raya (500m before the entrance to the gardens), ☎ (0263) 51 54 73 – 7rm. ✗ A small, friendly, well-kept guesthouse. Lots of information on Mount Gede, and the flora and fauna of the region.

Kliwon Homestay, Jl Kebun Raya 145, ☎ (0263) 51 15 12 – 9rm. ✗ Just as warm a welcome as at Freddy's, but the rooms are more comfortable and the prices higher.

• Puncak

Modest

Kopo Youth Hostelling, Jl Raya Puncak 557, Cisarua (near the service station), ☎ (0263) 25 42 96 – 18rm. ✗ A youth hostel with dormitories and some private rooms with bathrooms.

High end

Bukit Indah, Jl Raya Puncak (on the pass), ☎ (0263) 51 29 03, Fax (0263) 51 31 67 – 107rm. ✻ ℰ TV ✗ ⌣ ✗ CC This large building on the side of the hill is not as attractive as the Puncak Pass Hotel, but it is extremely comfortable. Choose the rooms with views even though they are a little more expensive. Groups of musicians play in the bar until 1am.

Luxury

Puncak Pass Hotel, Jl Raya Puncak (on the pass), ☎ (0263) 51 25 03, Fax (0263) 51 21 80 – 41rm. ✻ ℰ TV ✗ ⌣ ✗ CC The bungalows spread out on the hillside around a colonial building have a superb view of the valley. A very charming place, with every comfort and professional service.

EATING OUT

Rindu Alam I, Jl Raya Puncak. A real tourist factory (seats 500 people), with a splendid view, not to be missed. A variety of dishes (Sundanese, Chinese, Indonesian, and seafood).

Bandung Indah, Jl Raya Sindanglaya (heading east out of Cipanas). A small restaurant with a terrace and a garden, serving Indonesian and Sundanese food (excellent "gurame" grilled fish).

Making the most of Mount Gede

Making the most of Pelabuhanratu

COMING AND GOING

By bus – From Bogor, frequent departures until 6pm (3hr). No direct link from Jakarta.

FINDING YOUR WAY

Pelabuhanratu is crossed by two major streets which are perpendicular to one another: Jl Siliwangi, which serves the centre and the harbour, and Jl Kidang Kencana, which runs alongside the harbour and the coast to the west. The bus station is near the point at which they intersect.

GETTING AROUND

By minibus – The town's *bemos* travel the length of the coast all the way to Labuan.

By motorbike-taxi – The many "ojeks" on the road and near the bus terminal either charge per trip or per hour. Before clambering aboard, check the state of the bike (they are all ancient, but some are worse than others…).

Car rental – *Pertiwi Rent a car*, Jl Kidang Kencana, ☎ (0266) 43 10 76.

ADDRESS BOOK

No post office.

Bank/Currency exchange – *BCA*, Jl Siliwangi 109.

WHERE TO STAY

The categories below are based on weekend rates. Prices rise during the holiday period and on public holidays, but can be two or three times less during the week. Breakfast is not usually included.

• Pelabuhanratu

Modest

Seder Hana, Jl Kidang Kencana (opposite the Pondok Dewata), ☎ (0266) 43 17 46 – 11rm. ⚐ ⩩ A guesthouse with relatively clean monastic rooms, for hard-up travellers.

Average

Bukit Indah, Jl Raya Cisolok, ☎ (0268) 43 13 31, Fax (0268) 43 12 23 – 8rm. ⚐ 🗒 📺 ✕ The rooms have a fine view of the sea, but there is minimum comfort and upkeep.

High end

Bunga Ayu, Jl Raya Cisolok (heading west out of town), ☎ (0266) 43 11 11, Fax (0266) 43 19 53 – 18rm. ⚐ ⩩ / 🗒 🖋 ✕ A small hotel clinging to the cliff, with clean spacious rooms. Some have terraces with superb views of the sea. Good value for money.

Bayu Amrta, Jl Karang Pamulang 31 (beyond the Bunga Ayu), ☎ (0268) 43 10 31, Fax (0268) 43 13 44 – 20rm. ⚐ 🗒 🖋 📺 ✕ 🜄 🆑 Perched on a rocky promontory overlooking a small private beach, this very comfortable hotel also has an unrestricted panoramic view and a fine terrace restaurant. Deep-sea fishing trips are organised.

Luxury

Pondok Dewata, Jl Kidang Kencana 22, ☎ (0268) 43 10 22, Fax (0268) 43 15 32 – 39rm. ⚐ 🗒 🖋 📺 ✕ 🜄 🝮 🆑 A comfortable hotel with brick and bamboo rooms recalling those in Bali. A shame that the prices are excessive.

• West of Pelabuhanratu

Modest

Mirasa Losmen, Jl Raya Cimaja 12 (8km) – 5rm. ⩩ ✕ 🝮 🜄 A hangout for surfers who don't mind the lack of comfort. Run by a very welcoming Indonesian family.

Sari Raos, Jl Raya Cimaja 11 (8km) – 6rm. ⚐ ⩩ A cleaner guesthouse than the Mirasa, with similar prices, and a lady owner who is just as friendly. Located on the other side of the road.

Average

Daun Daun, Jl Raya Cisolok 39 (8km), ☎ (0266) 431 501 – 8rm. ⩩ / 🗒 ✕ This comfortable hotel opened in 1997, and made a commendable effort with the decoration (yellow roughcast walls). Room prices and comfort vary. Some rooms have private bathrooms and air conditioning. The clientele is mainly made up of surfers.

Augusta, Citepus (4km), ☎ (0268) 43 22 73, Fax (0268) 43 22 74 – 60rm. ⚐ ⩩ / 🗒 📺 ✕ 🝮 🆑 A large double-storey building with impeccably kept rooms at reasonable prices. The swimming pool is surrounded by a beautiful lawn. The sea is across the road.

West Java

Cleopatra, Jl Raya Citepus 14 (3km), ☎/ Fax (0268) 43 11 85 – 49rm. ⚓ ✈ / 🗐 TV ✗ ⌇ CC A little expensive for its standard of comfort, this motel-like hotel nonetheless has clean, functional rooms.

High end
Kumala Samudra Indah, Jl Cisolok (7km), ☎ (0266) 43 13 63, Fax (0266) 43 22 88 – 26rm. ⚓ 🗐 ℰ TV ✗ ⌇ ⚘ ✗ CC Breakfast included. This three-storey hotel opened in 1998 and if it weren't for its electric yellow and green livery, would be irreproachable. The rooms are comfortable and equipped with satellite television. Boat trips are organised, as is deep-sea fishing.

Luxury
🏖**Ocean Queen** (16km), ☎ (0266) 43 25 67 – 18rm. ⚓ ✈ ✗ ⌇ ⚘ ⚑ The bamboo bungalows spread out on lawns beside the beach in a very peaceful setting are planned for families and groups which unfortunately makes them too expensive for individual travellers or couples. Surfboards may be hired.

Super deluxe
🏖**Padi Padi**, Jl Citepus Raya (3km), ☎ (0268) 45 21 24, Fax (0268) 45 21 25 – 24rm. ⚓🗐 ℰ TV ✗ ⌇ ⚘ ⚑ CC With their tiled roofs and roughcast walls these charming bungalows make the hotel look

like a hacienda (it's a pity that the rooms are a little dark). The hotel offers numerous services and activities: rafting, surfing, deep-sea fishing, diving, jet skiing, bicycle and car rental, and a library. Its two restaurants serve seafood and Australian wine.

EATING OUT
Karang Sari, Jl Raya Cisolok (heading west out of Pelabuhanratu). Run by Christians, this very pleasant terrace restaurant specialises in seafood (frozen). **Nelayan**, Jl Raya Cisolok, Cimaja. On the side of the road near the Sami Raos *losmen*. Chinese and Indonesian dishes, as well as seafood (frozen).
Mutiara Sarik, Citepus, Kebon Kelapa. Open until midnight on Saturdays. A very pleasant place on the beach where you can have delicious seafood with rice and vegetables (there are other similar places nearby).

OTHER THINGS TO DO
Fishermen's festival – In April. The programme includes offerings to the sea, including flowers and a buffalo head, as well as festivities organised in honour of the Queen of the South Seas: boat races, "wayang golek" and "pencak silat" shows, and dances.

Making the most of Pelabuhanratu

BANDUNG

IN THE HEART OF SUNDANESE TERRITORY

Capital of West Java Province – 190km from Jakarta
Map p 210-211 and Plan p 255 – Pop 1 700 000 (not including the built-up area)
Alt 750m – Mild, rainy climate

Not to be missed
The art deco architecture in the town.
The Geology Museum.
Tangkuban Perahu volcano and Ciwidey valley.

And remember...
Visit the town and its surroundings during the week, to avoid weekend crowds.
Take in a dance or puppet show.

West Java

Nestling in the heart of the **Priangan massif**, the large town of Bandung stretches out over a vast basin left by a former lake. Benefiting from a very pleasant climate, the town has spread considerably to become a modern, active metropolis, often considered to be a showcase for Indonesia's science and technology industries. But the capital of West Java also likes to think of itself as being at the centre of a Sundanese territory immersed in Islam and at the heart of a culture that is remarkably eclectic and energetic. Whether this culture takes the form of dance (*jaipongan*), puppets (*wayang golek*), mystical rituals (*debus*), local martial arts (*pencak silat*), music of the traditional (*angklung*) or pop variety (*dangdut*), or epic **ram fights**, you will come into contact with it everywhere, and it is always original.

Although Bandung is one of the three jewels of tropical art deco architecture – the other two are Miami in Florida and Napier in New Zealand – in the end it is rather poor in terms of historical sites. It is difficult to resist the call of the nearby countryside which has been miraculously preserved. Apart from the famous Tangkuban Perahu, which lies dormant at the gates of the city, the region is dotted with other volcanoes, constantly smoking, as well as lakes and hot springs, all of them tempting excursions. And yet, without a doubt, the most characteristic features of the region are the magnificent tea plantations, spreading like a gentle veil over the tortured landscape.

"Paris of the Orient"

While the first mention of Bandung dates back to 1488, it was not until after the trans-Java Road had been built in 1811 that the town really began to develop. In the 19C the city benefited from the expansion of tea plantations built up by the Dutch. The latter very soon made Bandung their favourite retreat and set up their army headquarters. The town boomed in the 1920s, with fashion designers and elegant shops, and the streets filled with art deco buildings which earned Bandung the nickname "Paris of the Orient". After the war, which brought things to an abrupt halt, Bandung had its hour of international glory when in 1955 it hosted the first conference of the **movement of non-aligned nations** (*see p 39*), attended by Sukarno, Nehru, Zhou Enlai and Nasser.

Today, together with its built-up area, Bandung forms a vast megalopolis of 4 million inhabitants – the country's third largest city – and is a large industrial and university centre. It is notably the headquarters of IPTN, the Indonesian aeronautics company, set up in 1976 by the then Minister for Research, **Habibie**. Once renowned for its elegance, the town is paying a price for its success, suffering the torments of anarchical traffic and urbanisation. Fortunately there still remain quite a few green spaces, as well as a mild climate, which make visits to the town less trying.

Capital of Sundanese territory

Allow one day.

Several jewels of **art deco architecture** are concentrated in the town centre, and may be seen on foot. For instance, in Jalan Braga, the former colonial district and nightlife hot spot, rise the **Pembangunan Daerah Bank** and the **Bank of Indonesia**, both with fine, elegant façades with geometric lines. Not far away, in Jalan Asia Afrika, the main thoroughfare, don't miss the superb façade of the **Savoy Homann Hotel**, designed by AF Aalbers in 1938, nor that of the **Preanger Hotel**, designed by Wolf Schoemaker in 1928.

But the town's best known building is without doubt the **Gedung Merdeka** (B3) (Liberty Building), built in 1895, and renovated in 1926, again by Schoemaker *(Jl Asia Afrika, Monday-Friday 8am-12noon/1-6pm)*. It is famous not only for its architecture, but also for its history: it was here that the first conference of the movement of non-aligned nations was held in 1955. After the **exhibition of photos**, take a look at the **auditorium**, with its larger-than-life wax figures of the speakers.

From Jl Asia Afrika, take a taxi south to the Museum of West Java Province.

Although a little disappointing, the **Museum of West Java Province** (Negeri Propinsi Jawa Barat) (A4) *(Jl Lingkar Selatan Tunggal 2, daily 8am-3pm)* nonetheless has some fine examples of **Sundanese arts and crafts**: basketwork, musical instruments, and *wayang kulit*. The main piece in the museum is unquestionably the extraordinary **ceremonial chariot** of the Sultan of Cirebon (1608), which features a large red dragon, and looks like a bathtub on castors!

Return to the north of town by taxi, where most of the other sights are concentrated.

Bandung

Bandung art deco: the elegant Bumi Siliwangi

R. Marca

SILIWANGI

With its yellowing labels, dusty showcases and the swarms of schoolchildren in uniform rushing joyously through the galleries, the **Geology Museum** (Museum Geologi) (C1) (*Jl Diponegoro 57, Monday-Thursday, 9am-3pm; Saturday-Sunday, 9am-1pm*) has all the charm of the museums of yesteryear, despite the background music, which features Elvis Presley's *Only You* among other songs. There are superb **fossils**, skeletons of a stegadon (prehistoric elephant) and giant tortoises, as well as a reproduction of the skull of the famous "Java man".

Just as interesting are the **collections of minerals and meteorites** and the **vulcanological section** with displays of fine models of the main massifs in the archipelago.

On the other side of the street, attractively set in a park is another well-known Bandung building, the **Gedung Sate** (skewer building) (C2), which takes its name from its unusual shape. Its architecture combines different features in an original way: Javanese triple roof and Western arcs. The building was designed in the 1920s by the Dutch, at a time when they were considering moving the capital to Bandung, and now houses the administrative offices of the governor of the province.

The tour of the town continues in the northern districts, where the points of interest are more spread out.

In Jalan Ganeca, you will pass the **Bandung Technology Institute** (ITB) (B1), one of the most renowned establishments in Indonesia. Since the time when Sukarno was a student here, the building has remained a centre of political unrest. It was built in the 1920s and also combines diverse features of Javanese architecture – such as the *pendopo* – and art deco.

Continue up to the **Dago Tea House** (Dago Thee Huis) (north of B1) (*Jl Juanda*), perched on a hill in the heart of one of the chic parts of town. There is a superb **panoramic view** of Bandung and the surrounding area. From here, there is a pleasant walk to a pretty **waterfall** (*1km*).

Art deco enthusiasts may like to continue further north to near the Ledeng terminal, to see the **Bumi Siliwangi** (or **Villa Isola**) (*Jl Setiabudi, 6km from the centre, towards Lembang*), a masterpiece of the genre with its white façade of bold curves. The building is part of the IKIP complex, a teacher training college.

North of Bandung
Allow half a day for the trip.

Beyond Lembang the road passes through lovely orchards, affording delightful **panoramas** of the valley. Then it enters a pine forest before climbing to Tangkuban Perahu, which opens out into craters at an altitude of 2 076m.

Tangkuban Perahu
30km from Bandung. Fee. Dormant since its last eruption in 1969, Tangkuban Perahu ("upturned boat") attracts a great many visitors. This is unsurprising as it is the nearest volcano to Bandung, and is accessible by car. A victim of its own success, it has fallen prey to crowds of souvenir sellers, ready to leap on the first tourist who appears. Leaving these mercenary aspects aside, the site really is worth a visit.

Y Travert/DIAF

Tea picking

West Java

The road climbs first to **Kawah Ratu**★★ (Queen's Crater), a spectacular rocky basin. On a clear day you can see the **Ciater tea plantations**★★ and, beyond, the chain of volcanoes that overlooks Bandung plain. On the right, a path along the ridge leads to the second crater, **Kawah Upas**★★ (*avoid the path leading left, which is more slippery. 30min walk; you don't need a guide*), which is just as impressive.

If you have time, take the path which leads down from the car park to **Kawah Domas** (*30min*), an isolated crater riddled with bubbling mud pools, from which emanate sulphurous vapours which smell like bad eggs.

From Tangkuban Perahu, return to the main road and take a bemo (8km).

Ciater hot springs

Ciater is evidence of the Javanese people's passionate interest in hot springs which they view as privileged relaxation sites for families and lovers and which are believed to have healing virtues. Nestling amongst **tea plantations**★ is the extremely pleasant **Sari Ater Hot Spring Resort** with a hotel and several pools (*fee*).

Sumedang
60km northeast of Bandung. Allow half a day.

Off the tourist trail, Sumedang can be visited as a stop on the way to Cirebon, or as a trip out of Bandung. If you choose to do the latter and have access to a car, take the northern road via Ciater, a bucolic journey through a beautiful landscape of mountains and **terraced rice fields**★★.

The direct road from Bandung follows the route of the famous *Grot Postweg* ("Great Post Road"), which was built in the early 19C, costing the lives of thousands of workers. When you reach the mouth of a narrow valley, Sumedang suddenly appears, set right in the middle of a magnificent **mountain cirque**★ rising like a natural fortress.

Sumedang Museum★ (Prabu Gensan Ulun)

Daily, 8am-12noon, allow 45min. Sumedang was the last capital of the Hindu kingdom of Pajajaran in the late 16C. A witness to this prestigious past, the museum – one of the most interesting in the whole of Java – will enthral history buffs. It has been laid out in the pavilions of the former sultan's palace (1706), and houses numerous items inherited from the Hindu and Muslim kingdoms that succeeded one another in West Java from the 10 to the 19C.

Apart from the **ceremonial chariot** (19C), the collections of *wayang golek* and *wayang kulit*, of ancient weapons and gamelan instruments, the highlight of the museum is unquestionably the **treasure chamber**★★, containing the **crown**★★ set in gold leaf, which belonged to King Prabu Geusan Ulun (who reigned from 1578 to 1601), as well as superb 15C kris daggers and royal sabres. Lastly, in the highly elegant, sober **royal pavilion**★, the stuffed tigers and **Chinese ceramics** evoke the magnificence of the kings of Sumedang. Performances of Sundanese dancing are held here on Sundays (*9am-12noon*).

South of Bandung
Allow half a day for each excursion.

Cisangkuy valley★

Take the Banjaran road out of Bandung. At the foot of **Mount Malabar** (2 350m), **Situ Cileunca** artificial lake, a shimmering expanse of water, stretches out in the middle of **tea plantations**★★ that spread as far as the eye can see. On the way, stop

for lunch at **Pengalengan** (*35km, by bemo*), a small town famous for its caramels, before visiting the interesting **Malabar tea factory** between Pasir Malang and Pintu (*haphazard public transport*).

12km from Pengalegan (*turn left at Pintu*), freshen up in the water at the **Cibolang hot springs***. Far less frequented than those at Ciater, the springs benefit from a delightful setting among the greenery.

A road from Purwosari (*closed by railings in the late afternoon and in very poor condition*) leads to Gambung and Ciwidey. After several kilometres of market gardens it enters a luxuriant **forest**** of pines, tree ferns and eucalyptus that fill the air with heavenly scents.

Ciwidey valley**

Clinging to the steep sides of a superb gorge sculpted by **terraced rice fields**, **Ciwidey** (*25km*) is famous for its blacksmiths. Beyond the village, the road disappears again into the forest.

After 10km, a road to the left climbs up to **Kawah Putih**** and its summit 6km further on (*take a motorbike-taxi from Ciwidey as bemos do not come here; they go directly to Lake Situ Patengan*). Perched at a height of 2 350m, the wooded sides of the "white crater" encase a wonderful **turquoise lake****. When the mists rise off it to disappear over the ridge, you are left with an almost supernatural sight (and the temperature becomes unusually cool).

Returning to the main road, you soon come to **Cimanggu hot springs**. Further on, where a small undulating plateau covered in **tea plantations**** opens out, **Lake Situ Patengan** comes into view. Picnickers flock to its peaceful shores every weekend.

Making the most of Bandung

COMING AND GOING

By plane – The **Husein Sastranegara airport** is 4km east of the town centre, at the end of Jl Pajajaran. It serves Jakarta, Yogyakarta, Surabaya, Mataram, Ujung Pandang and Singapore.

By train – The station is east of the town centre and has two entrances: in Jl Kebon Kawung and Jl Suniaraja (A2-A3).
– For Jakarta: 16 trains a day, between 12.45am and 7pm (2hr30min to 3hr30min). The route is wonderful, with several suspension bridges.
– For Yogyakarta: 1 train a day, at 8.50am (9hr).
– For Surabaya: 3 trains a day, between 5.50am and 7pm (11hr30min-13hr30min).

By bus – **Cicaheum terminal**, Jl A. Yani (in the east), serves Sumedang (90min), Cirebon (3hr30min), Garut (2hr), Pangandaran (8hr) and Yogyakarta (12hr).
Leuwi Panjang terminal, south of the town, via Jl Kopo (south of A4), serves Jakarta (arriving at Kampung Rambutan terminal, 4hr) and Bogor (2hr30min).
By minibus – The **Ciroyom** (west), **Dago** (northeast) and **Ledeng** (in the north, for Lembang) terminals serve the towns round about. For Ciwidey and Pengalengan, leave from **Leuwi Panjang** terminal (south of A4) (1hr30min each). For Tangkuban Perahu and Ciater, leave from the terminal near the train station (A3) (1hr each).

GETTING AROUND
The traffic is fairly reasonable in Bandung, except over the weekend when it sometimes takes a good hour to get out of town.

By minibus – The 35 "angkot" lines, regular minibuses that run between the terminals, can be distinguished by their colour (their routes are shown on the windscreen). Prices vary according to distance. **Kebon Kelapa** (A4-B4) is the main angkot terminal in the town centre.

By taxi – Plenty of taxis near the train station (A2-A3).
4848, Jl Suniaraja Timur 14 (A3), ☎ (022) 23 48 48. They also have rates depending on time (2hr minimum).

Car rental – Ask in hotels for local agents.
Avis, Sheraton Inn Hotel, Jl IR H Juanda 390 (in the north), ☎ (022) 250 03 03.
Tara car rental, Jl Asia Afrika 81 (Preanger Hotel) (B3), ☎ (022) 43 16 31.

ADDRESS BOOK

Tourist information – As the office in Jl Asia Afrika (on the corner of the Alunalun) (B3), ☎ 420 66 44) is closed for the time being, try the branch at the train station (A2-A3).

Bank/Currency exchange – **BII**, Jl RE Martadinata 23, ☎ (022) 44 07 20. Accepts transfers from abroad, but for a large commission.
Money change at **Golden Megah Corp**, Jl Otto Iskandardinata 180 (A4). Monday-Friday 8.30am-4.30pm; Saturday 8.30am-2pm. The best rates in town.

Post office/Telephone – **Main post office**, corner of Jl Banceuy and Jl Asia Afrika (A3). Monday-Saturday, 8am-9pm.
Tolkom, Jl Lembong 64 (B3). Open 24hr a day. **Wartel**, in the station (A2-A3).

Internet – **EGA**, Jl Braga 111 (B3), ☎ (022) 420 62 91. Monday-Saturday, 8am-5pm.

Airline companies – **Garuda**, at the Preanger hotel, Jl Asia Afrika 81 (B3), ☎ (022) 420 94 67.
Merpati, Jl Asia Afrika 73 (B3), ☎ (022) 44 12 26.
Bouraq, Jl Cihampelas 27 (A2), ☎ (022) 43 78 93.

Travel agents – **Pacto**, Savoy Homann, Jl Asia Afrika 112 (B3), ☎ (022) 43 61 01, Fax (022) 43 44 15. Tours, car rental, ticket reservation.
Interlink, Jl Wastu Kencana 5, ☎ (022) 43 55 29.

French Cultural Centre – **CCF**, Jl Purnawarman 32 (B2), ☎ (022) 421 24 17. Library, cinema, shows and exhibitions.

WHERE TO STAY

● **Bandung**
There are plenty of cheap hotels near the train station.

Modest

New Le Yossie, Jl Belakang Pasar 1123, ☏ (022) 420 54 53 – 10rm. A small, quiet hotel in a renovated Dutch house. Numerous services: currency exchange, car rental, reservations, tours.

By Moritz, Jl Belakang Pasar, ☏ (022) 420 57 88 – 12rm. ✗ Popular with travellers. Small, austere, modest rooms with modest prices. The Austrian owner offers all sorts of services (reservations, tours, car rental). The restaurant is very lively some evenings.

Average

Surabaya, Jl Kebon Jati 71, ☏(022) 43 67 91 – 50rm. Some rooms have their own bathrooms. This vast Dutch house, with its terraces, corridors, nooks and crannies is a real maze. The tiles and period furniture easily make you forget the rather worn rooms. A shame about the cold welcome.

Hotel New Sartika, Jl Dewi Sartika 18, ☏ (022) 43 11 90, Fax (022) 421 98 90 – 30rm. ⚓ ✈ / ▤ ♪ TV CC A clean, comfortable hotel, without any special charm, but with a mostly Jakartan clientele. Good value for money.

Patradissa I, Jl H Moch I/8, ☏ (022) 420 66 80 – 33rm. ⚓ Another place without much charm, but clean and cheap, near the train station. Some of the rooms have television and air conditioning.

High end

Sukajadi Hotel, Jl Sukajadi 176, ☏ (022) 23 38 88, Fax (022) 23 40 20 – 80rm. ⚓ ▤ TV ♪ ▥ CC This pleasant hotel with a small swimming pool and a courtyard garden has rather characterless but comfortable rooms. Negotiate a discount.

Bumi Asih, Jl Cimaya 1, ☏ (022) 420 18 22, Fax (022) 43 32 08 – 40rm. ⚓ ▤ ♪ TV ✗ CC An elegant Dutch building near the Gedung Sate. The comfortable rooms surround a pretty courtyard garden. Very good value for money, and friendly staff to boot.

Luxury

Preanger, Jl Asia Afrika 81, ☏ (022) 43 16 31, Fax (022) 43 00 34 – 198rm. ⚓ ▤ ♪ TV ✗ ▥ CC A luxury hotel that is rather cold but very professional, with all kinds of services (satellite TV, travel agent, pharmacy, bars, currency exchange, car rental and Internet).

Savoy Homann, Jl Asia Afrika 112, ☏ (022) 43 22 44, Fax (022) 43 61 87 – 153rm. ⚓ ▤ ♪ TV ✗ ▥ CC In the same league as the former, but with more charm. The hotel has real soul in spite of an impression of past glory, and its art deco façade is a pure masterpiece. Charlie Chaplin once stayed here. Satellite TV, travel agents, pharmacy, car rental.

Super deluxe

Chedi, Jl Ranca Bentang, Ciumbuleuit, ☏ (022) 23 03 33, Fax (022) 23 06 33 – 53rm. ⚓ ♪ TV ✗ ▥ CC A little isolated in the green heights of Bandung, the hotel has a magnificent setting and elegant architecture, all marble and wood. It is a pity that the rooms are so small. Even if you cannot afford to stay here, you can come and try the excellent cakes beside the swimming pool.

● **Ciater**

Sari Ater, Jl Raya Ciater, ☏ (0260) 47 03 51, Fax (0260) 47 03 33 – 101rm. ⚓ ♪ TV ✗ ▥ ✼ CC Comfortable bungalows set in an enormous garden. The "standard deluxe" rooms are the best value for money. The hot water comes directly from the local springs. "Dangdut" concerts at the weekend. Big discounts available during the week.

EATING OUT

● **Bandung**

Allow yourself to be tempted by the *warung* in Jl Cikanpundung Barat (B3), near Ramayana shopping centre, and those in Jl Gardu Jati (A3), open until the morning, where you eat sitting on mats ("lesehan").

Daun Pisang, Jl Dr Setiabudhi 154 (in the north). An elegant, open place where they serve good Sundanese and Javanese fare. Unfortunately the portions are small.

Rangoon Prihangan, Jl Surapati 191-193 (in the east). A place to tide you over, frequented by the district's office workers. Convenient if you want a quick meal (the "ayam bakar" grilled chicken is excellent).

Toko You, Jl Hasanudin 12 (B1). A real museum furnished with Dutch tables and 1930s Javanese chairs, and decorated with an 18C Madurese pendopo. Original Chinese fare is served on a covered terrace (try the "mie" with prawns and vegetables). French wine.

Sindang Reret, Jl Naripan 9 (B3). A vast performance hall with neon lighting that puts on "wayang golek" shows, which alas are rather mediocre. The food, while nothing special, is nonetheless varied (fish, soup, brochettes, "mie goreng").
Warung Makan Sisijalan, Taman Sari 90. 11am-midnight, all night on Saturday. Restaurant serving Chinese dishes and seafood.

● **Pengalengan**
Rumah Makan Mandalawangi, Jl Raya Pengalengan (2km from the town). Small bamboo bungalows around an artificial lake, where you eat sitting on mats admiring the superb landscape. Sundanese dishes (fish and vegetables).

GOING OUT, HAVING A DRINK
CCF (see "Address Book" above), a very pleasant cafeteria (open until 10pm).
Canary, Jl Braga 16 (B3), a bakery selling excellent cakes.

Nightclubs – Caesars Palace, Jl Braga 129 (B3). 8pm-3am. Bandung's chic nightclub. Plays techno music and "dangdut".
Braga, Jl Braga 17-19 (B3). Nightclub specialising in techno open until 6am at the weekend.

OTHER THINGS TO DO
Shows – STSI, Jl Buah Batu 212 (in the southeast). The Fine Arts Institute in Bandung organises "angklung" performances.
Yayasan Pusat Kebudayaan, Jl Naripan 7-9 (B3), ☎ (022) 43 56 39. "Wayang golek", "jaipongan" and "pencak silat" shows.
Taman Budaya, Jl Buit Daga Selatan 53A (near the Dago Tea House) (north of B1), ☎ (022) 250 49 12. The complex puts on shows of contemporary art.
Rumentang Siang, Jl Baranang Siang 1 (C3), ☎ (022) 43 35 62. Popular drama on Fridays and "wayang golek" shows two Saturdays a month.

Kebun Binatang, Jl Taman Sari (B1), ☎ (022) 250 73 02. Shows of "ketut tilu" dancing, "pencak silat" and "wayang golek".
Motorbike races, Jl Bagusrangin (C2), west of the Gedung Sate. Every day in the late afternoon. Local youths come to compete in improvised races on motorbikes or motorised bicycles.

Ram fights – The "adu domba" is a colourful event that takes place on some Sunday mornings at Cilimus (take Jl Sersan Bajuridu from Ledeng terminal and walk 500m).

SHOPPING GUIDE
The main shopping streets are Jl A Yani (C3) and Jl Dalem Kaum (B3). In **"Jeans Street"** (Jl Cihampelas) (A1), shops sell jeans and printed T-shirts. Their façades fight to outdo one another in their sheer eccentricity.

Markets – Pasar Jatayu, Jl Arjuna (in the west). A flea market that opens every day.
Pasar Baru, Jl Otto Iskandardinata (Otista) (A3), in the Chinese district. A large central market, where you can find clothes, batiks, vegetables, etc.
Flower market, Jl Wastu Kencana (A2).

Shopping centres – Gramedia, Jl Merdeka 43 (B2). Open until 9pm. A large store with a bookshop, sports section, and stationery.
Plaza Bandung Indah, Jl Merdeka 56 (B2). The largest mall in town.

Local arts and crafts – Pak Ruhiyat, Jl Pangerang Bawah IV 78/17B (B3). "Wayang golek" workshop.
Saung Udjo, Jl Padasuka 118, ☎ (022) 77 17 14 (in the east). This "angklung" workshop (8am-4pm) organises shows for tourists.

Local delicacies – Try the "dodol susu" caramels from Pengalengan – absolutely delicious!

CIREBON★
West Java Province
248km east of Jakarta – Map p 210-211
Pop 250 000

Not to be missed
Kesepuhan kraton.
A stroll in the harbour.
A Tari Topeng show.

And remember...
Try the seafood sold in the warung in Jalan Bahagia and Kalibaru Selatan.

Cirebon opens onto the Java Sea, turning its back on the large monotonous plain that stretches along the coast all the way to Jakarta. With its calm atmosphere and pleasant architecture of low buildings, the hectic pace of the capital is soon forgotten. Relax in the **harbour★** with its coloured boats held in tight moorings, or visit the elegant *kratons* and the ancient Chinese temples that bear witness to a glorious past. Cirebon was once a flourishing port to which merchants flocked from all over the world. Like other towns on the north coast, it was one of the major gateways to Java for both Muslims and the Chinese. In fact the town's original name – *"Caruban"*, meaning "mixture" – confirms the cosmopolitan nature of this area of Sundanese-Javanese hinterland. This mixture of influences extends to the local **batiks**, whose shimmering patterns of flowers and animals carry the mark of China, the Arab world, and Europe.

The town's three sultans
It is thanks to saint **Sunan Gunung Jati** that Cirebon was made into a sultanate in the 16C. Its prosperity was not lost on its neighbours, and in the next century it became the prize in a conflict between the powerful kingdoms of Banten to the west, and Mataram to the east. As a result the city was carved up, and kept that way by the Dutch when they took Cirebon in 1677. However, several decades later (1705), the new masters decided to break up the courts of the three

Sunan Gunung Jati
Among the nine Muslim saints (the Wali Songo) who are traditionally held responsible for spreading Islam throughout the archipelago (see p 35), is Sunan Gunung Jati, who was originally from Sumatra. In 1552 he disembarked at Cirebon with a pilgrimage to Mecca under his belt, a very rare achievement at the time. Gunung Jati soon managed to spread the word of Allah throughout the region by skilfully making use of ancient local beliefs. He founded the line of Cirebon sultans, and became a highly revered person; he was even credited with having healed a woman with leprosy.

sultans installed there, which were deemed too restless. In the 19C the city's continued wealth attracted many Chinese who took part in the development of the prawn fishing industry. Today Cirebon is still known as "prawn town".

A tour of the town

Allow 1 day, by becak or on foot. Most of the places of interest are grouped together in the south of the town, only several hundred metres apart.

If you go to Cirebon during the month before **Maulud Nabi** (festival of the Prophet), don't be surprised at the number of beggars. An old tradition laid down by a raja requires the rich to show charity to the poor at this time. Hence the large gathering of the penniless.

Of Cirebon's three *kratons* – complexes of buildings that are more like villas than palaces – two are open to the public. Your first stop is **Kesepuhan kraton***, which opens onto the northern Alun-alun (*8am-4pm, Sunday 8am-5pm. Fee. Allow 45min. English-speaking guide*). The kraton was mainly built in 1677 on the foundations of a 15C Hindu palace. It is one of the rare examples of civil Indo-Javanese architecture still standing, and mixes Hinduism and Islam. The decoration, on the other hand, fully expresses the cosmopolitanism of the town, mixing Javanese, Chinese and European patterns and furniture.

Surrounded by a wall of red bricks inlaid with Dutch and Chinese earthenware, the **Siti Inggil*** (1529) courtyard encloses five small Hindu style *pendopos*. From there a split gate of the Balinese kind opens into another courtyard. There is yet another courtyard, containing the sultan's residence. The extraordinary **façade*** is carved in large rock and cloud patterns (*wadasan awan*), which draw on the Chinese decoration

Coloured prows in Cirebon harbour

Cirebon

Charliaz/Rapho

to be found on Cirebon batiks. The **interior★**, with its oriental baroque style, combines green panelling, carved friezes of iridescent flowers, as well as china, delftware (illustrated with scenes from the Bible) and European furniture.

Before leaving, take a look at the adjacent **museum★**, an interesting jumble of 14C Javanese gamelans, Egyptian mother-of-pearl chests, Javanese weapons, and 16C Portuguese coats of mail. Whatever you do, do not miss the separate room containing the **Kereta Singa Barong★★** (1549), an incredible royal red and gold coach in the shape of a winged dragon with an elephant's head. The mixture of influences combines Chinese, Hindu and Arab symbols.

A stone's throw from the kraton is the **Grand Mosque** (Mesjid Agung), one of the most sacred in Java. Its triple roof, typical of the early Javanese mosques (around 1500), features outstanding **timber-work★**.

From Kesepuhan kraton, it is best to take a becak to Kanoman kraton (about 500m north, in Jl Kanoman).

Before visiting the second kraton, why not mingle with the crowd in a Javanese atmosphere amongst the colours and fragrances of **Kanoman market**, which is very lively in the morning. Just behind it is **Kanoman kraton** (1588), hidden at the back of a quiet shaded courtyard *(haphazard opening times. Donation. Allow 20min)*. The present resident is Sultan Kanoman XI. Behind the high Balinese-style wall of red brick is an elegant sky-blue **pendopo** decorated with Dutch and Chinese earthenware, and furnished with European items. In the small **museum** nearby, you will see two amazing 16C **coaches★**, like the one in Kesepuhan kraton, as well as magnificent **carved wooden doors★**.

From the market, take Jl Kantor towards the harbour (east) and walk for 200m.

Lastly, on the way to the harbour, don't miss **Kelenteng Tiao Kak Si★** (or Dewi Welas Asih), one of the oldest Chinese temples in Indonesia (17C), dedicated to the Buddhist goddess of forgiveness. Note the superb **painted doors★** and the **frescoes**. The enormous **anchor** resting against the outside wall comes from a Chinese sampan that was lost off Java in the 18C.

Around Cirebon

The tomb of Sunan Gunung Jati
5km from Cirebon, on the coast. The tomb of the founding saint of the Cirebon dynasty *(see sidebar above)* is perched on the top of a hill *(gunung)* covered in teak trees *(jati)*. Some of the nine saints were named after the mountain on which they were buried, an example of how Indonesian society adapted Islam. The **princes' necropolis** is a highly important place marking the conversion to Islam, and still attracts many pilgrims from all over Java. It consists of several small cemeteries bristling with mausoleums, of which the oldest date back to the 15C. The sultans of Cirebon have been laid to rest here near a small mosque, beside Gunung Jati.

Gua Sunyaragi water palace
4km southwest of the town, by becak or minibus no 4, via boulevard Jend. Yani. 7am-6pm. Donation; allow 20min. Created in 1741 for the sultans of Cirebon to relax and meditate in, this strange "garden-palace" (unfortunately in a state of neglect) recalls the follies and artificial landscapes that European nobility had a liking for at around the same time. The decoration consists of artificial caves *(gua)*, pools (empty), and small hillocks made of rockwork and bricks pierced with recesses and winding galleries. According to legend the two recesses in the **Ruang Meja Perundingan** (one of the caves) are directly linked to Mecca and to China!

Making the most of Cirebon

COMING AND GOING

By train – The *station* is in Jl Tanda Barat (north of the town). Trains day and night for Jakarta (3hr) and Yogyakarta (5hr).

By bus – *Terminal*, Jl Jend. Yani (south). For Jakarta (5hr), Bandung (3hr30min) and Yogyakarta (9hr).

By minibus – *ACC Kopyor*, Jl Karanggetas 7, ☎ (0231) 20 43 43.

GETTING AROUND

By minibus – Ask your hotel about the different "angkutan" bus lines.

By taxi – *Taxi Central* ☎ (0231) 20 60 28. Note that drivers refuse to switch on their meters at night. So you have to bargain.

By becak – Plentiful and convenient (as they are lower than those in Yogyakarta, they are easier to hop aboard!).

ADDRESS BOOK

Tourist information – Jl Brijen Darsono 5, ☎ (0231) 20 88 56.

Bank/Currency exchange – There are several banks in Jl Karanggetas and Jl Siliwangi.

Post office/Telephone – *Wartel* at the train station and in the town centre. *Main post office*, south of the harbour, in Jl Yos Sudarso.

WHERE TO STAY

Modest
Asia Hotel, Jl Kali Baru Selatan 15 / 17, ☎ (0231) 29 21 83 – 31rm. In a good position, housed in a Dutch building dating from the 1940s. The best rooms have fans and their own bathrooms. Basic comfort and cleanliness.

Average
Cordova, Jl Siliwangi 87-89, opposite the station, ☎ (0231) 20 46 77 – 59rm. ☝ ✗ ᴄᴄ Marble hall, clean rooms, but without much soul. Nonetheless, good value for money.

Aurora Baru, Jl Siliwangi 62, near the station, ☎ (0231) 23 31 43 – 41rm. ☝ ✗ ᴄᴄ Some rooms have hot water, air conditioning, telephone and television. A comfortable hotel, but with rather worn carpeting. In short, less value for money than the Cordova.

Luxury
Puri Santika, Jl Dr Wahidin 32, west of the station, ☎ (0231) 20 05 70 – 87rm. ☝ 🍽 🖋 ᴛᴠ ✗ 🏊 ᴄᴄ The best in town. The staff speak English and can help you hire a car.

EATING OUT

In keeping with its reputation for delicious prawns, Cirebon has many excellent *warung* selling seafood, mainly in Jl Bahagia and Jl Kaltbaru Selatan. Those near the picturesque **Kanoman market** are also worth a try.

SHOPPING GUIDE

Batiks – In Cirebon: *Linas*, Jl Kanoman 54, in Kanoman market. Local silk or cotton batiks.

The batiks in Trusmi village, 5km from Cirebon, are amongst the most renowned in Java. Go to **Ibu Masina's** and **Ibu Ega Sugeng**, the two best workshops in the village.

Antiques – *Benny Santoro*, Jl Lemahwungkuk 67, ☎ (0231) 24 31 29. Screen paintings (a speciality of Java's north coast), and carved wood panels for hanging kris daggers.

OTHER THINGS TO DO

Tari Topeng – At *Kesepuhan kraton*, Sunday, 8-10am.

Festivals, ceremonies – *Sekatan Muludan* (June-July) commemorates the birth of the Prophet Muhammad. On the occasion, sacred items from the kratons are cleaned, and taken in procession to the Grand Mosque to be blessed. An enormous "gunugan" (mountain of rice and vegetables) is borne along with them.

Making the most of Cirebon

FROM BANDUNG TO PANGANDARAN★★

West Java Province
225km tour – Map p 210-211
Humid climate, cool in the heights

Not to be missed
The Papandayan, Kamojang and Galunggung volcanoes.
Kampung Naga traditional village.

And remember...
Stop over at Cipanas.
Hire a car to tour the area.
Bring a jersey for climbing the volcanoes.

Some of the most beautiful landscapes in Java are to be found to the east of Bandung. In this countryside of volcanoes, green forests and paddy fields, rare examples of a peaceful and rather wild Java are still to be found. The bustle of the town is soon forgotten in these last reaches of Sundanese territory, which will delight history and nature lovers as well as those in search of complete relaxation. Hindu temples set in rice fields, bamboo villages shaded by coconut palms, mountain paths leading through tropical forests, and hot springs perfect for some languid bathing offer a chance to recuperate before venturing into Central Java – another world altogether.

On the borders of Sundanese territory

Allow 2 days including a trip up a volcano.

Beyond **Cicalengka**, the road climbs a very steep slope which opens out onto a desolate plateau where several *warung* wait hopefully for customers.

In Nagreg, turn right heading south towards Garut.

■ **Candi Cangkuang** – *In Leles (50km from Bandung and about 9km from Nagreg), take a horse-drawn cart to the temple, which is 3km east of the village.* As if set on a plain, the small temple of Cangkuang rises up in the middle of a pool, isolated on a peninsula covered in pines *(access by boat).* The choice of the **site★** – a green sea criss-crossed by rice paddies surrounded by dark volcanoes – seems to have left nothing to chance, as the place gives off such a deep feeling of peace. However, compared to the temple in Prambanan, West Java's oldest Hindu temple cuts a modest figure with its height of 8.5m. Built in the 8C,

during the time of the Sundanese Galuh kingdom, Cangkuang nevertheless bears unique testimony to the history of the area, and was reconstructed stone by stone in the 1970s. Inside there is a fine **statue of Siva** on a buffalo.

■ **Cipanas** – *60km from Bandung, 2km from the main road.* Set at the foot of **Guntur volcano** (2 247m), this small thermal spa is an ideal stopping place to base yourself as you visit the area. The local hotels have a distinctive plus in that their swimming pools and baths are fed by the water from **hot springs**, making a stay there a deliciously relaxing experience.

In Tarogong, 2km beyond Cipanas, turn right and climb up to Samarang (8km). The road on the right leads to Mount Kamojang (14km) and that on the left to Papandayan (22km).

■ **Mount Papandayan**★★ – *In Cisurupan, a bumpy 9km road leads up to the summit. Leave Cipanas at about 4.30am to be at the volcano by sunrise.* On the climb, you will no doubt pass lorries overflowing with vetiver roots *(usar)*, which are used in the perfume industry. The gaping crater of Papandayan (2 622m) can be seen from far off, an enormous gash that has split the side of the volcano since the terrible eruption in 1772. From the car park *(several warung serve hot coffee)*, a path makes its way through a strange muddle of red and yellow stones, where sulphurous vapours steam out with a very strong smell. At the end of this almost lunar landscape *(30min walk)*, the **crater** basin paradoxically offers up a soothing sight with its sides carpeted in brushwood. From here, there is an exceptional **view**★★ of the volcanic cirque.

In the mouth of Papandayan

G Guérard

■ **Mount Kamojang**∗ – The road affords **panoramas**∗∗ that are no less spectacular. Without realising it, you soon enter Kamojang crater, a large wooded plateau punctuated by impressively powerful **steam geysers**∗. Don't miss the small smoking **mud pool**∗ lost in the middle of the woods, which has formed near the geothermal power plant *(follow the pipeline. The road once enabling you to reach Bandung directly, via Majalaya, is now impracticable).*

From here, you may return to Cipanas, or go on to Garut to continue the tour.

■ **Garut** – *65km from Bandung.* Garut, a neat, quiet provincial town is a pleasant place to stop for lunch. After which you may like to have a stroll round the **market** or visit one of the **handicraft workshops** for silks or caramels. Beyond Garut, the **road**∗∗ zigzags superbly through a steep-sided gorge with terraced rice fields.

■ **Kampung Naga**∗∗ – *23km from Garut, walk down along a path for 1km.* In the bright green rice fields a small clump of coconut palms suddenly stands out, shading the white houses of a delightful village. Made only of painted bamboo, the houses line up with their black thatched roofs facing the river in impeccably neat tight rows. Classified as a village-museum, Kampung Naga keeps up its **traditional way of life** – there is no electricity – for the sake of tourism. You will be asked to sign the visitors' book and to leave a donation with the village chief *(kepala desa),* who will be happy to put you in the picture, if he is not busy with his rice paddy.

■ **Mount Galunggung**∗∗ – *In Singaparna (about 15km from Kampung Naga), take a bumpy road left, then turn left at Cisayong.* Peaceful enough from the outside, Galunggung (2 168m) is in fact a quick-tempered volcano that from time to time likes to shake the sleepy surrounding countryside out of its torpor. While the eruption in 1982 was not as violent as that of 1822 (4 000 deaths), it nonetheless caused an exodus of almost 30 000 people. From the car park, a 45min walk *(easy)* brings you to the **crater**∗∗, a spectacular rocky cauldron enclosing a beautiful shimmering green **lake**∗.

The last stopping place before you change provinces, Tasikmalaya (60km from Garut) has little of interest. It is better to continue directly to Pangandaran (100km).

Making the most of the area: from Bandung to Pangandaran

COMING AND GOING

By bus – Plenty of buses from the **Cicaheum** and **Kebon Kelapa** terminals in Bandung go to Garut (2hr) and Pangandaran (the direct road via Ciawi is not so beautiful; 5hr).

By minibus – All you have to do between Bandung and Garut is hail a *bemo*.

By car – See Bandung for rentals.

ADDRESS BOOK

Tourist information – Dinas Pariwisata Daerah, Jl Pembangunan, Garut, ☎ (0262) 54 04 44.

Telephone – Wartel, Jl Siliwangi 31 and Jl Pramuka 7, Garut.

WHERE TO STAY

• **Cipanas**

Here you will find rustic *losmen* as well as luxury hotels. Breakfast is usually included. Prices rise during weekends and festivals. Most hotels have restaurants, but they close early.

Average

Antralina, Jl Cipanas 150, ☎ (0262) 23 27 78 – 13rm. 🍴 An economic choice, but rather Spartan. A place to go to tide you over.

Lembar Kuring, ☎ (0262) 23 94 71 – 20rm. 🍴 ✕ 🏊 Pleasantly set on the edge of a wood at the foot of a hill. A shame that the rooms are austere and poorly kept. Breakfast is not included.

Average to high end

🏨**Sumber Alam**, Jl Raya Cipanas 122, ☎ (0262) 23 80 00, Fax (0262) 23 25 69 – 28rm. 🍴 🅿 📺 ✕ 🏊 cc The cheapest rooms are small. The thatched pavilions overlooking a pond are charming; the suite with its own swimming pool and terrace a perfect love nest. The hotel has a large swimming pool supplied with water from hot springs. Be warned, prices double in the high season. Car rental.

Tirtagangga, Jl Raya Cipanas 130, ☎ (0262) 23 25 48, Fax (0262) 23 18 11 – 40rm. 🍴 🅿 🏊 cc Apart from the "economy rooms" (which are basic), most of the rooms are comfortable (private bathrooms and television) although quite characterless. Prices go up in the high season. Car rental.

EATING OUT

🏨**Sumber Rasa**, Jl Otista 89 (between Cipanas and Garut), ☎ (0262) 23 17 79. A pleasant restaurant where you eat sitting on mats in bungalows around a pond, to the strains of Sundanese music. Excellent fish.

SHOPPING GUIDE

Silks – Aman Sahuri, Jl Otto Iskandardinata 12/279, Garut. A silk factory where every stage, from cocoons to weaving, is on view. Items for sale.

Local delicacies – Picnic, Jl Pasundan 102, Garut. A confectioner's which makes "dodol" (crystallised fruit), "noga kacang" (caramel with peanuts), and "noga wijen" (caramel with sesame).

From Bandung to Pangandaran

PANGANDARAN★

West Java Province
185km from Bandung – 165km from Yogyakarta
Map p 210-211 – Pop 11 000

Not to be missed
A visit to the nature reserve.
A trip up Green Canyon.

And remember...
Avoid the weekend, especially in summer when hotels are full and prices rise.
Swim in the southern part of the west beach, the only safe spot on the coast.
To see the area, it is best to go on an organised tour or hire a car.

Pangandaran stands at the entrance to a peninsula covered in forest. This is a narrow tongue of land between two bays of black sand stretching as far as the eye can see, facing the blue waters of the Indian Ocean. An idyllic site, which has turned the modest fishing village into Java's main seaside resort. But while the hotels and restaurants have taken the place over, almost 60% of the local population still make a living from fishing, and in the surrounding villages life goes on peacefully as in the past, in the shade of the coconut trees.

The Sundanese hinterland – a green patchwork of rice paddies and thick clumps of forest crisscrossed by a hundred rivers, ideal for excursions – has held its own. Pangandaran and its region have been able to manage the change brought about by tourism, and you will be surprised by the warmth of the inhabitants.

Pangandaran and the surrounding area

Allow 2 days.

As well as being a small, well-placed seaside resort known for its beaches, with a good tourist infrastructure, Pangandaran is also an ideal departure point for exploring the region. Bordered by an ugly concrete quay and strewn with litter, the east beach, **Teluk Pangandaran** (C3), is hardly an inviting place to swim. But you never tire of seeing the *prahu* boats coming in and the clusters of fishermen hauling their bulging nets ashore.

The best place for a swim is the west beach, **Teluk Parigi**★ (A3), an immense crescent of black sand stretching all the way to Batu Karas. Be careful of the currents, though, as they are very strong everywhere, except in the easternmost area near the nature reserve.

Pananjung Nature Reserve★★

See the small map. Coming from Pangandaran, the entrance is at the end of Jl Kidang Pananjung. Fee. Bring a torch to explore the caves. The site of a magnificent secondary forest, the Pangandaran peninsula is a nature reserve that abounds in tropical flora and fauna. As you go further into the jungle, you soon feel like some kind of Indiana Jones looking for natural treasure, for instance the well-hidden **rafflesia patura**, a smaller relation of the Sumatran rafflesia, the largest flower in the world *(see p 126)*. There is, however, more chance of seeing deer *(kijang)*, **hornbills** or **macaques**.

After this, complete the tour by taking a boat trip round the peninsula *(45min)*, to see the **waterfall**★ plunging down from the cliffs, and the **white sand beach at Pasir Putih**.

Green Canyon**

See the small map. 35km west of Pangandaran. Fee for access and boat hire. Bring a swimming costume. The highlight of the area is Green Canyon, which owes its name to the little river that hollowed it out, a green stream full of volcanic alluvial deposits that turns brown after rain. The luxuriant vegetation on its banks is just as green, and the setting is enchanting. After 30min upriver by boat through the jungle, the river bed narrows, and the stream, now a torrent, surges into a spectacular **gorge★** carved out of the rock, while small, deliciously refreshing waterfalls run down the sides like curtains of rain.

For a pleasant end to the excursion, go to the small **Batu Karas beach** *(42km west of Pangandaran)*, wedged between two rocky promontories. The place is one of the best **surfing spots** along the coast *(surfboards for hire)*.

Heading for Yogyakarta

If you are going to Yogyakarta, rather than going the whole way by road, do part of the trip by sea, taking the ferry that goes from **Kalipucang** to **Cilacap**. This route, while it is a little longer *(4hr)*, will be more memorable. The ferry follows the channel that separates the coast from the **Pulau Nusakambangan** ornithological park. The island stretches all the way to Cilacap, protecting the entrance to **Segara Anakan bay**, home to the largest **mangrove swamp★** in Java. This strange tangle of roots with its fragile ecosystem is unfortunately in danger of drying up because of the

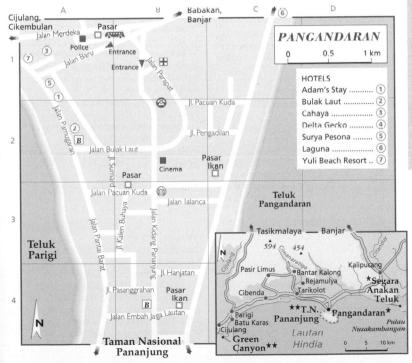

accumulation of alluvial deposits silting up the bay. The ferry crossing is punctuated by rare stopovers in villages that rise up out of nowhere, a fishing vessel passing by, or the sight of a heron or kingfisher. To the east of the island you will see a **prison** where some of the longest serving political prisoners in the world have been left to rot.

Making the most of Pangandaran

COMING AND GOING

You have to pay an entrance fee for the town, which forms part of the nature reserve.

By train – From Jakarta (7 to 10hr), Bandung (4hr) and Yogyakarta (5 to 7hr). The train goes as far as Banjar, then you have to take a bus to Pangandaran (90min).

By bus – Direct buses from Jakarta (Bekasi terminal (9hr) and Bandung (5hr). From Yogyakarta, you have to change at Banjar (7 to 8hr).

By bus and ferry – From Yogyakarta, take a bus to Cilacap (5hr), then the ferry to Kalipucang (4hr; departures at 8am and 1pm, same times in the other direction). In Kalipucang, take a minibus to Pangandaran (30min). The same route with *Agung minibuses* (see below) saves a lot of hassle.

By minibus – Private minibuses run a direct link from Pangandaran to Jakarta (10hr on the road) and Bandung (5hr). The *Agung* agency organises transport for Yogyakarta, including a minibus to Kalipucang, the ferry to Cilacap and another minibus to Yogyakarta (4hr30min).

GETTING AROUND

By becak – Very convenient for getting around the town.

By bike – Pangandaran is one of the rare places in Java where it is easy and pleasant to get around by bike. You will find people renting bikes everywhere.

By motorbike – Ideal for visiting the surrounding area, and prices are reasonable. Ask at your hotel or at a travel agency.

By car – Here again, there are many rental possibilities and prices are affordable. Usually the car comes with a driver.

ADDRESS BOOK

Guide Association – *Indonesian Guide Association*, Mangkubumi Hotel, Jl Jaga Lautan (B4). Don't hesitate to call upon their services to visit the reserve and the surrounding area.

PHPA – *Forest Protection and Environment Conservation Office*, Jl Kidang Pananjung 266 (in the south). Runs Pangandaran's nature reserve.

Bank/Currency exchange – There are no automated teller machines but moneychangers are plentiful.
Bank Rakyat Indonesia, Jl Kidang Pananjung 133 (B4). Be warned, the exchange rates are sometimes not as good as those at currency exchanges.

Post office/Telephone – *Main post office*, Jl Kidang Pananjung 111 (B3), Monday to Saturday (7am-2pm). ***Telkom***, Jl Kidang Pananjung (24hr a day). ***Wartel***, Adam's Homestay (A1). 7am-11pm.

WHERE TO STAY

Pangandaran is a very lively place, but you can always stay in the surrounding villages, in Cikembulan, Batu Karas (west) or Babakan (east). Hotels have been shooting up in Pangandaran, but it is sometimes hard to find a decent room in high season (weekends, summer, Christmas, and the end of Ramadan), when prices rocket.

• Pangandaran

Modest

Cahaya Hostel, in an alleyway leading into Jl Pamugaran, in the north, ☎ (0265) 63 04 83 – 6rm. ☜ A new, clean, comfortable *losmen*, not far from the beach. Very warm welcome. Breakfast included.

Average

Adam's Homestay, Jl Pamugaran, ☎/Fax (0265) 63 91 64 – 13rm. ✕ ⌕ ☼ A comfortable, elegant building with a pleasant courtyard garden. Pity that the rooms are small. Various services: wartel, library, ticket reservation.

Bulak Laut, Jl Pamugaran, ☎ (0265) 63 93 77 – 18rm. ☜ TV ☼ Courtyard garden. The clean, comfortable rooms are excellent value for money. Only one, the most luxurious, looks onto the sea, and consists of a suite with a sitting room, bedroom upstairs, and air conditioning.

Delta Gecko, Sindang Laut RT 07/02, Cikembulan (2km west of Pangandaran), ☎ (0265) 63 02 86 – 22rm. ☜ ✕ ☼ A charming hotel consisting of bamboo bungalows and a courtyard garden. Environmentally-minded atmosphere: no electricity and the food is vegetarian. Watch out for the mosquitoes.

Laguna, Jl Pengadilan Kebon Carik, Babakan (3km east of Pangandaran), ☎ (0265) 63 97 61 – 14rm. ☜ ⌕ ✕ ☼ The rooms are arranged around a pool. Those facing the sea have a terrace and a hammock. Warm welcome.

High end

Hotel Surya Pesona, Jl Pamugaran, ☎ (0265) 63 94 28, Fax (0265) 63 92 89 – 79rm. ☜ ▤ ✕ ⌕ ☼ CC The largest hotel in Pangandaran, with a marble hall. The "deluxe" rooms are impeccable, but with no character.

Yuli Beach Resort, Jl Pamugaran, ☎ (0265) 63 93 75 – 7rm. ☜ ✕ ⌕ ☼ The height of kitsch: marble tables in the shape of hearts, an eagle carved into the wall etc. Enthusiasts of the genre will be delighted. It is nevertheless a pleasant hotel with a lovely swimming pool and little courtyard garden.

• Batu Karas

Modest

Hotel Alana – 6rm. ✕ ☼ Bamboo bungalows scattered amongst the palm trees. Rustic but very inexpensive.

Average

Pondok Putri, ☎ (0265) 33 41 49 – 14rm. ☜ ⌕ ⌀ TV ⌕ ☼ A quiet hotel in a pleasant site. Irreproachable standard of comfort and cleanliness, but the staff are incredibly languid.

EATING OUT

• Pangandaran

Basic

Chez Mama Cilacap, Jl Kidang Pananjung 197 (B4), ☎ (0265) 63 90 98. Run by a French-Indonesian couple who serve a variety of dishes (including Indonesian, and seafood). As proof of its quality, the place is often packed.

Number One, Jl Bulak Laut 66 (A2), ☎ (0265) 63 03 83. One of the best places, and welcoming to boot. Try the "nasi liwet" (rice, garlic, tomato and vegetables with chicken or seafood) or the steamed chicken served in banana leaf.

Risma Fresh Sea Food, Jl Talanca 1, Pasar Ikan (B4). The restaurants in the fish market serve wonderfully fresh seafood.

Bunga Laut, Jl Bulak Laut (A2). The best Indonesian food in the village and a welcome that charms all travellers.

• Batu Karas

Moderate

Kang Ayi, seafood restaurant facing the beach.

GOING OUT, HAVING A DRINK

Bars, nightclubs – **Disko Meridian**, Jl Pamugaran (A2). Techno music.

Pub Matahari, Jl Baru (A1). A small bar with good music by local groups.

OTHER THINGS TO DO

Excursions – **Jock Tours Travel**, Jl Pamugaran (A2), ☎ (0265) 63 03 07, Fax (0265) 63 97 62.

Surfing – Surfboards can be hired locally.

Making the most of Pangandaran

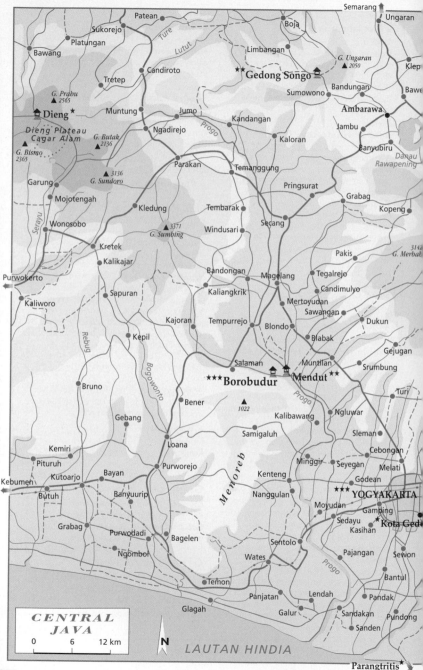

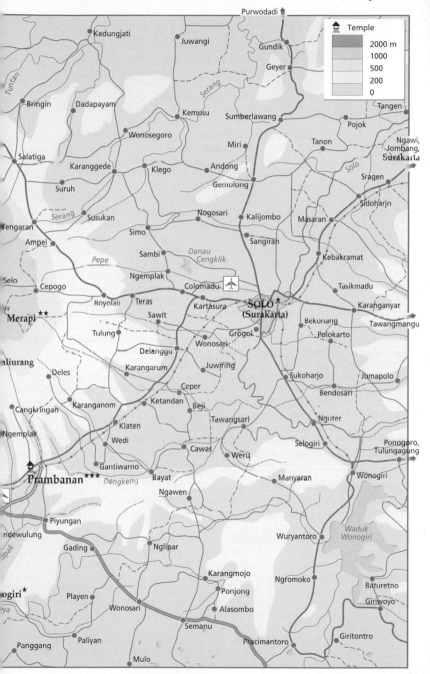

Purwodadi

Kedungjati

Juwangi

Gundik

Geyer

Temple
- 2000 m
- 1000
- 500
- 200
- 0

Tuntan

Bringin

Dadapayam

Kemusu

Sumberlawang

Tangen

Pojok

Serang

Wonosegoro

Miri

Tanon

Ngawi,
Jombang,
Surakarta

Salatiga

Karanggede

Klego

Andong

Solo

Sragen

Suruh

Gemolong

Sidoharjo

Serang

Susukan

Nogosari

Kalijombo

Masaran

Kebakramat

Tengaran

Simo

Sangiran

Ampel

Pepe

Sambi

Danau
Cengklik

Ngemplak

Selo

Cepogo

Colomadu

Tasikmadu

Boyolali

Teras

Kartasura

SOLO
(Surakarta)

Karanganyar

Merapi ★★

Sawit

Bekonang

Tawangmangu

Tulung

Grogol

Polokarto

Delanggu

Wonosari

liurang

Karangarum

Juwiring

Sukoharjo

Jumapolo

Deles

Ceper

Bendosari

Cangkringan

Karanganom

Ketandan

Beji

Ngemplak

Klaten

Tawangsari

Nguter

Wedi

Selogiri

Ponogoro,
Tulungagung

Cawas

Weru

Prambanan ★★★

Gantiwarno

Dengkeng

Bayat

Manyaran

Wonogiri

Ngawen

Piyungan

Waduk
Wonogiri

ndewulung

Gading

Nglipar

Wuryantoro

Upak

Karangmojo

Ngromoko

Baturetno

ogiri ★

Playen

Ponjong

Giriwoyo

Wonosari

Alasombo

Panggang

Paliyan

Semanu

Giritontro

Mulo

Pracimantoro

YOGYAKARTA ★★★
Capital of DKI Yogyakarta Province
60km from Solo – Map p 272-273 and Plan p 277
Pop 500 000 – Alt 90m – Hot and humid climate

Not to be missed
The kraton and the surrounding alleyways. Sono Budoyo Museum.
A stroll through Kota Gede.
The royal cemetery at Imogiri. A climb up Merapi volcano.

And remember...
See the sights in the morning and devote the afternoon to shopping.
Go to a Javanese dance or puppet show.

Yogyakarta stands in the heart of Java, between Mount Merapi and the shores of the Indian Ocean. An almost symbolic location for this hugely important city which is one of the most attractive places in Indonesia. Carefree and mystical, traditional and cosmopolitan, aristocratic and touristy, as well as being a place for students and workers – Yogyakarta (commonly known as "Yogya", pronounced "Jogja") blends its contrasts with consummate artistry. Neither the Paris nor the Venice of the Orient, simply "Jogja the gentle", the town has no real architectural jewel, but its narrow alleyways, low houses with tiled roofs, and colourful markets have indescribable charm. For the mystery of Yogyakarta lies above all in its atmosphere, in its peaceful, enchanting neighbourhoods, and its warm, welcoming inhabitants. The city is certainly changing, but although the air is thick with exhaust fumes, it is still a large country town, and the heart of all Javanese culture. As proof of the latter, the never-ending performances of *wayang kulit* draw a sociable crowd to the gates of the *kraton* every month, with people staying until the first light of dawn.

Most of the places of interest are south of the railway line, which cuts the city in two. At the end of Jalan Malioboro, the commercial nerve centre, the *kraton* district forms the historical and cultural heart of the town. However, to appreciate Yogyakarta to the full, and to mingle with its inhabitants, you should lose yourself in the alleyways and kampungs and wander through the markets. Outside the city, the rice paddies and hills provide ample opportunity for excursions to Mount Merapi, the royal tombs at Imogiri, or the beach at Parangtritis. Not forgetting the extremely famous sanctuaries at Borobudur and Prambanan *(see the following chapters)*.

Princely patrons of the arts
While Yogyakarta was founded relatively recently, its tradition is anchored in sources from Javanese epics: even its name comes from *Ayodya*, the mythical capital of Rama, the hero of the Ramayana.

The region has been occupied for at least two thousand years, but it was not until between the 8C and 10C, under the Sanjaya and Sailendra kings, that it experienced its first golden age, to which the Buddhist mandala at Borobudur and the Sivaite temples at Prambanan bear witness. In the 16C, after a very long period of eclipse, the area once again became the political epicentre of the island, at the time of the Muslim kingdom of Mataram. Indeed it was at Kota Gede, now a suburb of Yogyakarta, that Senopati chose to base his capital in 1575 (the town was to remain capital until 1614).

The birth of Yogyakarta dates back to 1755, after the Treaty of Giyanti, which established the partition of the kingdom, organised by the Dutch. Having obtained half the territory, Mangkubumi, the uncle of the ruler of Solo, chose a symbolic place for his new capital, halfway between Mount Merapi and the ocean. As **Hamengkubuwono I** ("He who holds the world in his lap"), he set up a robust and prosperous state.

But his successor had to face increasingly threatening designs by the Dutch. In 1810 Hamengkubuwono II was forced to abdicate in favour of his more docile son, but this did not prevent him from returning to power the year after. Fearing an alliance between Yogyakarta and Solo, **Raffles**, the new governor-general, deposed the ruler once again and reinstalled his son. In 1813, to weaken the throne, he favoured the installation of a second dynasty in Yogyakarta, that of the **Pakualamans.** There followed a period of troubles that did not end until after the bloody Java War (1825-30) *(see p 37 and 201).*

Dispossessed of its political power, the kraton then became a centre for the arts, overseen by the sultans. It is to them that we owe the classical aesthetic canons that are still in force today. The 19C saw the blossoming of literature and dance, while the repertoire of wayang kulit grew and inspired a new art form, wayang *orang* (drama with actors). At the same time, Yogyakarta's surrounding countryside saw an intense growth in population and underwent profound change.

A key role in politics

A new political wind began to blow in the early 20C with the emergence of nationalist movements. In the period following the Second World War Yogyakarta participated fully in the fight for independence, and for a while, in 1946, even became the capital of the Republic. The rebels benefited from the unfailing support of Hamengkubuwono IX, who founded the country's first university within the walls of the *kraton*. Yogyakarta was captured without a struggle by the Dutch in 1948, but freed the following year. For its role in the revolution the region was given the status of province ("Daerah Istimewa Yogyakarta") while the sultan exchanged his royal attributes for those of governor.

Today Yogyakarta is a lively city full of students from the whole of Indonesia and tourists from all over the world. Proud of its art and culture, it cultivates values that promote tradition and tolerance, in keeping with Sultan Hamengkubuwono X, who succeeded his father in 1989. While it was at the forefront during the student movement that led to President Suharto stepping down in May 1998, Yogyakarta did not experience the scenes of looting seen in Jakarta and Solo. But like the rest of the country it has taken the full blast of the economic crisis.

Heading towards the kraton

Allow a morning to visit the kraton district and the palace itself.

A stone's throw from the frenzied bustle on Jalan Malioboro, **Alun-alun Utara★** (or Alun-alun **Lor**) (Plan I, B3), a vast square of grass with two sacred banyan trees, is the setting for Yogyakarta's parades and major events. A month-long fair is held here once a year *(see "Making the most of Yogyakarta")* and outside this period the square is home to a multitude of *warung* which every evening serve *martabak* pancakes in the light of swaying oil lamps.

Sono Budoyo Museum★★ (Plan I, B3)

To the northeast of the square, Tuesday-Thursday, 8am-1.30pm, Friday 8-11am; Saturday-Sunday 8am-12noon. This is without doubt one of the most interesting museums in Java. Past the sumptuous **gamelan from Cirebon** that sits imposingly at the entrance, there is a **krobongan (ceremonial bed of the goddess Sri Dewi)** (1691) flanked by two wooden statues. Next come the **Dongson bronzes** from

Yogyakarta

eastern Indonesia, **megalithic statues** from Wonosari and magnificent **Hindu goddesses★★** made of bronze (10C-12C) from Gunung Kidul. Pottery and terra-cotta items illustrate Majapahit art from East Java, while among the objects from Java's north coast region known as Pasisir are old **Korans** and magnificent **panels of carved wood★**.

The **batik section** is rather disappointing, but the **puppet collection★★**, on the other hand, is fascinating. Through the various figures on display you will see that the *wayang* repertoire, far from limiting itself to Hindu epics, draws just as much on Muslim belief, the Old Testament, Chinese legends and heroic accounts of the war of independence.

Apart from the fine Topeng **masks**, the **kris daggers**, the **furniture** and **wooden statues**, don't miss the collection of **Hindu statues and gargoyles★★** stored outside, covering the classical (8C-10C) and Majapahit (13C-15C) periods.

Head towards the kraton from the museum, passing the Grand Mosque.

Built in 1773 under Hamengkubuwono I, the **Mesjid Agung★** (Grand Mosque) (B3) has kept all its original features *(visit outside of prayer times; remove your shoes; remember that shorts and bare shoulders are not allowed)*. The mosque is closely linked to the kraton and all its ceremonies and comes under the responsibility of the pangulu, a notable generally chosen from the **kauman**, the adjoining Muslim quarter. A wide portico bathed in light precedes the prayer room itself, which is paved in marble from Italy. The triple tiled **roof**, characteristic of Javanese architecture, rests on magnificent **timber-work★** supported by 36 teak pillars.

The kraton district★★★ (Plan I, A3-B3)
South of Alun-alun Utara. Tour on foot or by becak.

A city within a city, the *kraton* district forms a vast residential area crossed by alley-ways. It is protected by a white wall (1785), which is 3-6m high and pierced by four arched gateways. The sultan is not allowed to use the well-preserved south gate **Nirbaya**, until the day of his burial. The district's charms are obvious to everyone who enters. There are women selling *jamu* weighed down by their baskets of medic-inal concoctions, batik painters, and large families clinging together on their mopeds. Venerable old men wrapped in sarongs, young guides proposing improvised services to tourists, devout worshippers heading for the mosque, mothers going to market and school children in uniform, all make up a joyful crowd.

The low-built houses in the district were traditionally reserved for the palace ser-vants and workers as well as for members of the court and Yogyakarta's minor nobility. But the rule has eased a little over the last few years although theoretically foreigners are still not allowed to live here. In addition to the *kraton* itself, the batik workshops, the Bird Market and Taman Sari (hidden behind a second wall in the heart of the district) are just as inviting places to explore.

Ngayogyakarta Hadiningrat kraton★ (Plan I, B3)
Saturday-Thursday 8.30am-2pm; Friday 8.30am-1pm. Fee. The *kraton* is Yogyakarta's royal and spiritual centre as well as being the conservatory of Javanese arts (dance, music, drama and literature). The elegant pavilions carry with them a note of splen-dour, and an aura of Javanese mysticism fills the place. As a living incarnation of this, Sultan Hamengkubuwono X is both a guardian of traditions and a progres-sive figure, a shrewd businessman and a key politician – he is governor of the province. He has more than 500 people in his service (most of whom also have

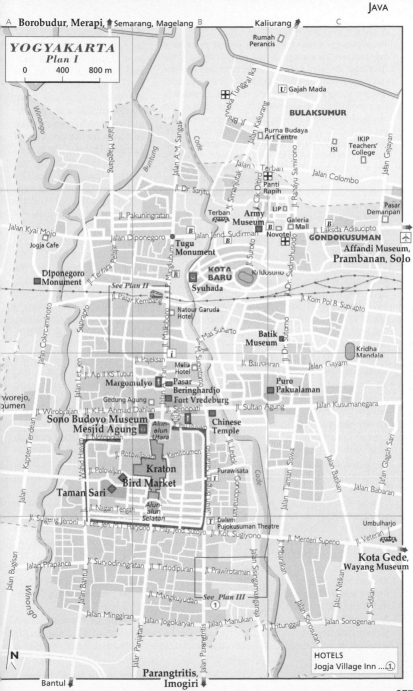

JAVA

A Borobudur, Merapi, Semarang, Magelang B Kaliurang C

YOGYAKARTA
Plan I
0   400   800 m

Rumah Perancis

U Gajah Mada

BULAKSUMUR

Purna Budaya
Art Centre

IKIP
Teachers'
College

ISI

Jalan Colombo

Jalan Magelang

Winongo

Jalan A.M. Sangaji

Jalan Bhineka Tunggal Ika

Jl. Bhu

Jalan Kaliurang

Jalan Simanjutak

Jalan Terban

Jl. Cik Ditiro

Jl. Dr. Sarjito

Jl. Pakuningratan

Jalan Kyai Mojo

Jalan Diponegoro

Jogja Cafe

Jalan Terfara/Pelajar

Bintung

Code

Terban

Panti
Rapih

LIP

Army
Museum

Galeria
Mall

Pasar
Demanpan

B

B

Jalan Jend. Sudirman

B

Novotel

GONDOKUSUMAN

Jl. Laksda Adisucipto

**Affandi Museum,
Prambanan, Solo**

**Diponegoro
Monument**

Tugu
Monument

Jl. Mangkubumi

**KOTA
BARU**

Kridosono

Jl. Suroto

Jl. Ranayu Samirono

Jl. Dr. Sudirohusodo

Jl. Kom Pol B. Suprapto

Jl. Dr. Sutomo

Jl. Cokroaminoto

Jl. Suprapto

Jl. Let. Jen.

See Plan II

Jl. Pasar Kembang

Syuhada

Natour Garuda
Hotel

Jl. Malioboro

Jl. Mas Suharto

Jl. Pajeksan

**Batik
Museum**

Kridha
Mandala

i

Jl. Sungotoro

Jl. Bausasran

Jalan Gayam

-worejo,
-umen

Jl. Aip II KS Tubun

Melia
Hotel

Margomulyo

Pasar
Beringhardjo

Puro
Pakualaman

Jl. Wirobrajan

Jl. K.H. Ahmad Dahlan

Gedung Agung

Fort Vredeburg

Jl. Sultan Agung

Jalan Kusumanegara

Jl. Kapten Tenderan

**Sono Budoyo Museum
Mesjid Agung**

Jl. Senopati

Jl. Ibu Ruswo

Chinese
Temple

Jl. Ledok

Jl. Notoprajan

**Kraton
Bird Market**

Alun-
alun
Utara

Jl. Rotowijayan

Jl. Kemitbumen

Jl. Polowijan

Purawisata

Jl. Taman Siswa

Jalan Batikan

Taman Sari

Jl. Nagan Tengah

Alun-
alun
Selatan

Jl. Bintaran

Jl. Katamso

Code

Condoman

Jalan Babaran

Jl. Sugeng Jeroni

Jl. Let. Jen. M.T. Haryono

Jl. May. Jend. Suroyo

Jl. Kol. Sugiyono

T Dalem
Pujokusuman Theatre

Umbulharjo

Jl. Veteran

**Kota Gede,
Wayang Museum**

Jalan Bugisan

Jalan Prapanca

Jl. Suryodiningratan

Jl. Tirtodipuran

Jl. Prawirotaman

Jl. Menteri Supeno

Jl. Mbarakan

Jl. Nitikan

Jl. Sidkan

Winongo

Jalan Bantul

Jl. Mangkuyudan

See Plan III
①

Jl. Sisongamangaraja

Jalan Sorosutan

Jl. Sorogenan

N

Jalan Minggiran

Jalan Jogokaryan

Jalan Manukan

Jl. Titunggal

Jalan Panjatan

Jalan Parangtritis

HOTELS
Jogja Village Inn ... ①

Bantul

**Parangtritis,
Imogiri**

Central Java

A palace and a symbol

The plan of the kraton follows very precise precepts of Indo-Javanese cosmology. In the main courtyard, the "pendopo" (an open audience chamber topped by a vast roof) represents the sacred mountain. From this point radiates a mosaic of courtyards that are carpeted in black sand (from the beaches of the Indian Ocean) and occupied by various buildings, respectively symbolising the sea and the islands of the archipelago. Each courtyard is protected by a wall pierced with gateways that mark the different levels of the cosmology: the northern entrance faces Merapi volcano, the home of the gods, while the southern one faces the sea, the domain of the goddess Nyai Loro Kidul. According to legend, the sovereign is in direct contact with her. The position of the palace's 64 banyan trees (the age of the Prophet on his death) has not been left to chance either: the two oldest ones, in the middle of the northern Alun-alun represent the union of the sovereign and his people.

separate occupations). Built in 1756 by Hamengkubuwono I, the *kraton* is organised in such a way that the buildings running in a north-south direction make up the official and ceremonial area, and those running east-west are for private and sacred purposes. The former link the Alun-alun in the north to that in the south by means of seven successive courtyards separated by monumental gates, while the latter stand around the Pelataran courtyard.

From Alun-alun Utara (*in the north*) a grille opens onto the **Pagelaran**, a *pendopo* where dignitaries would wait for an audience, and which is now used for traditional performances. It was from here that during the riots in May 1998 Hamengkubuwono X addressed his people massed in the square, making a formal appeal to them to keep calm, and calling for President Suharto to step down. Just beside the pendopo the raised terrace known as **Siti Inggil** (High Place) is where the sultans are crowned (*separate visit for this part of the kraton*).

Once through the **main entrance** (*on the west side in Jl Rotowijayan*) you come to the **Kemandungan** courtyard (*south of Siti Inggil*). The noise of the town dies away and the atmosphere becomes serene and dignified. Old palace servants stand guard wearing sarongs with a kris tucked into the back, and the inevitable *blangkon* (traditional headdress). Once past a sturdy wall (*where tickets can be bought*) you reach the **Srimenganti** courtyard with its two elegant **pendopos.**

Two silver **raksasa** (protective demons) flank the gateway that leads to the **Pelataran** courtyard, the *kraton's* nerve centre where the superb **Bangsal Kencana**** (Golden Pavilion) immediately draws the eye. This vast open *pendopo* symbolises Mount Meru, the centre of the universe. Its four **teak pillars**, delicately carved with Hindu, Buddhist and Muslim motifs, provide a perfect illustration of Javanese syncretism. This is where the major private events that mark the life of the palace (circumcisions, weddings, etc) are held.

Just beside this is the **Bangsal Manis** *pendopo*, the banqueting hall, while charming **kiosks** and bandstands rise here and there, like islets on the sea of black sand.

The most sacred part of the *kraton*, the **Dalem Prabayeksa** (*closed to the public*), lies east of the Bangsal Kencana. It serves as a tabernacle for royal attributes, and is where ancestors and the goddess Sri are venerated. It opens onto the **Keputren**, a sort of harem where the sultan had his apartments, and which now houses various departments including administrative offices and the kitchens.

At the end of the courtyard, on the left, the **Hamengkubuwono IX Museum** houses objects that belonged to the father of the present sultan, a man who was greatly admired by his people (1912-88). The hero of independence did not consider it

G. Guérard

Yogyakarta, the burial of a prince

beneath him to do the cooking (you can see his oven gloves!), and while he enjoyed appearing in traditional costume, Dutch uniform or dinner jacket, he also kept his scout uniform.

The **tea pavilion★** nearby, an attractive Dutch-style building with green and yellow panelling has an amazing water filter made of volcanic stone. It takes one month for the water to filter through.

On the east side a gateway leads to the **Kesatrian courtyard**, a pleasant space planted with trees where, in a *pendopo*, gamelan concerts are held twice a week. The former apartments of the sultans' sons have been converted into a **Museum of Paintings**, where you can see **family trees★** and a series of **portraits of the sultans★**.

South of the Pelataran courtyard the plan of the palace reflects the symmetry of the northern part. Beyond the first courtyard, which was used for military exercises, rises **Sasono Inggil**, a wide pavilion where *wayang kulit* shows are performed. You reach it via **Alun-alun Kidul★** *(at the end of Jl Ngadisuryan)*, a charming little square with two majestic banyan trees (the Javanese have a game in which you have to cross the esplanade blindfolded, passing between the trees). On the west side two **sacred elephants** enjoy a siesta, oblivious to the gaze of onlookers. Once a year, a **birdsinging contest** takes place, the square bristles with poles on which hang multicoloured cages, whose finest prisoners are then sold by auction for astronomical sums.

The palace visit may be completed by a tour of the **Kereta Kraton Museum** *(Jl Rotowijayan, near the entrance to the kraton, same times as the kraton)*. This houses royal carriages, most of which were made in Europe.

West of the kraton, in Jl Rotowijayan, turn southwards into Jl Ngasem.

Budgerigars, birds of paradise, golden orioles and turtledoves – the **Bird Market★** (Pasar Ngasem) (Plan I, B3) hums with the songs of all the feathered creatures of the archipelago. In backyards sellers wear themselves out convincing customers of the merits of their homing pigeons, while silent beasts like snakes and vampire bats wait for rare collectors.

You can go directly to the Taman Sari ruins from the market although the main entrance is to the south in Jl Taman.

Taman Sari★ (Plan I, A3)

Daily, 9am-3pm. Fee. Better known as the **Water Castle**, the palace the sultans once used (18C) for relaxation and meditation has greatly suffered from the ravages of time, wars and earthquakes. It takes a huge effort of the imagination to recreate the atmosphere that once reigned in the gardens now that the fountains have disappeared and the buildings are in ruins. Nevertheless Taman Sari was a mythical place to which the early sultans of Yogyakarta would come every year to renew the sacred marriage that joined them to Nyai Loro Kidul, the mother Goddess of the South Seas. According to legend, a secret passage led directly to her palace at Parangtritis on the ocean shore.

After going through a small octagonal courtyard you reach the best preserved part of the gardens, comprising three raised **pools** surrounded by faded walls. One of the pools was for the wives and children of the sultan, another was for his concubines and the third was for the sovereign himself. From the **tower** that stands between the pools the sultan could watch the women bathing undisturbed. Steps to the west lead down to another octagonal courtyard where there is a massive **portico** with carvings of birds. A narrow corridor to the south leads to the former **royal chambers**, which were designed with a Chinese influence. On the other side of the courtyard the site of the former artificial lake has now been invaded by houses. There is an unrestricted **view★** of Yogyakarta from the ruined **manor** (Gedung Kenongo) standing on a small

B. Brillion/Michelin

Yogyakarta, scouts on an outing to Taman Sari

hill. You can see, for instance, the towers dotted about that were used to light up and aerate the lake's **underground passages***, which are still negotiable.

Barely visible steps lead into a dark tunnel that goes to the most remarkable part of Taman Sari, the **Underground Mosque**** (Sumur Gumuling). This is now a large shaft with moss growing up the sides. Two superposed circular galleries lit by bays ring the shaft. In the middle, four small flights of steps make up a pyramid, on top of which four other flights of steps lead to the upper gallery. Several alcoves back up the theory that this is indeed an old mosque, but the only certainty is that the place was used for meditation.

The area surrounding Taman Sari is packed with **batik workshops** that form a co-operative. They are tourist orientated, and their output (with both primitive and modern patterns) is unfortunately rather mediocre.

Jalan Malioboro (Plan I-B2 or Plan II)

Yogyakarta's main thoroughfare is more than 1km long and passes through the centre of the town from north to south. The historic boulevard, which was laid out by Hamengkubuwono I along a line that goes from the *kraton* towards Mount Merapi extends north of the railway (Jl Mangkubumi) to **Tugu**, a small white obelisk that was erected when Yogyakarta was founded. No doubt the sultan would be greatly vexed to find the monument surrounded by today's infernal traffic and the many shops beneath the arcades in the side streets. The final insult is that the traffic flows in the opposite direction to that once taken by royal processions. A project is currently under examination to pedestrianise the street.

Some believe that the name Malioboro is a deformation of Marlborough, but it is more likely to derive from the Sanskrit *malya bhara*, which means "carrying a garland of flowers". As Jalan Malioboro is near the Sosrowijayan district, which is popular with travellers, anyone who comes to Yogyakarta is bound to cross it. However, the street itself is far from charming and visitors are often exasperated by the *becak* drivers and impromptu guides, or feel traumatised trying to get through the incessant flow of bebek (the local name for mopeds, which means "duck"). Nonetheless Jalan Malioboro is lively and colourful, the ideal place for shopping, having a bite to eat in the evening *(see "Making the most of Yogyakarta")* and generally feeling the pulse of the city.

Coming from the north, the first building you see *(set back on the left)* is the **Natour Garuda Hotel**, with the **Sosrowijayan** district on the right *(see Plan II, p 291)*. Further along on the left the **Gedung DPRD** houses the province's parliament. On the same side of the street a flashy mall, the ultimate concession to modernity, stands at the foot of the Ibis Hotel. Still on the same side, halfway along the street, near the Tourist Office, an imposing gateway marks the headquarters of the municipal administration, the **Kepatihan**.

For a fistful of rice

In Java as in Bali, daily life revolves around countless festivals and ceremonies. These are pure products of local syncretism. They happily mix Muslim, Hindu and Javanese rituals even if, to ensure they stand out, they are brought forward a day out of line with the Muslim calendar. On these intense occasions the sacred link that unites the sultan with his people is reaffirmed. The most important among them, "Garebeg Maulaud" ("Garebeg" means "noisy" in Javanese) is particularly colourful. Guards in freakish costumes, which were certainly never intended to frighten anybody, precede a "gunungan", an enormous pile of rice and vegetables that symbolises abundance. When the procession reaches the mosque, the crowd rushes forward in a terrific scramble to grab a few pieces, which are meant to bring luck.

The street changes name in the lower part, becoming Jl A Yani.

Pasar Beringhardjo (Plan I, B3), the large central market, has occupied a vast concrete building since the early 1990s. While the building lacks charm it is extremely lively. It is fun to walk among the stalls overflowing with batiks that line the aisles bathed in smells of all kinds, or along the neighbouring alleyways invaded by shops. The prices are unbeatable (bargaining is a must), but watch out for pickpockets!

Fort Vredeburg (Plan I, B3) *(Tuesday-Thursday 8.30am-1.30pm, Friday 8.30-11am, Saturday-Sunday 8.30am-12noon)* is the former headquarters of the Dutch garrison in Yogyakarta. The solid building, typical of colonial military architecture (18C) now houses the **Benteng Yogyakarta Museum**, which is devoted to the fight for independence. Its photos and dioramas will fascinate history buffs.

Just beyond the fort a **statue** commemorates the taking of Yogyakarta by the Indonesians on 1 March 1949. Opposite stands the state guest house, **Gedung Agung** (Plan I, B3) (1823, rebuilt in 1869), which is used for distinguished foreign visitors, such as Queen Elizabeth II. The street then opens into Jalan K H Ahmad Dahlan, a wide avenue lined with very white colonial buildings. On the left is the **Bank Negara Indonesia** (1923), and on the right the **main Post Office** (1910), behind which is the **Church of St Francis Xavier**. Lastly, on the other side of the crossroads an arch marks the entrance to the *kraton* district.

Central Java

The eastern part of the town

There are several places of interest scattered about the eastern part of Yogyakarta where you can learn more about Javanese culture.

Puro Pakualaman (Plan I, C3)

Jl Sultan Agung. Tuesday, Thursday, Sunday 9am-1.30pm. The palace was built in 1813 for Yogyakarta's second dynasty, that of the Pakualamans ("hub of the universe"), and faces south as a sign of deference to the Ngayogyakarta Hadiningrat *kraton*. Like the latter (but on a much smaller scale), it consists of a series of courtyards dotted with *pendopos*. In the south a small *Alun-alun* precedes the main courtyard *(the only one open to the public)*, in which stands the **Bangsal Sewotomo** with its typically Javanese architecture. There is a small European-style **pavilion*** next to it *(on the right)*, with a finely carved wooden façade. A modest **museum** to the right of the entrance houses weapons and old uniforms as well as old photos and some fine coaches that have been restored.

The palace has always been a centre for the arts and culture and continues to hold dance and gamelan performances. In September 1998 the funeral here of Pakualaman VIII brought together all the town's two-wheeled vehicles in an extraordinary mix, combining the newest models and the rustiest old wrecks!

The Batik Museum* (Plan I, C2)

Jl Sutomo 13, behind the Pakualaman palace (you can reach it on foot from Puro Pakualaman). Monday-Saturday, 9am-2pm; donation. Yogyakarta suffered acutely from not having a batik museum. The lack has been partly made up for by this modest but fascinating private collection, which survives as well as it can on donations from the dozen or so visitors it has every month. Only some of the 400 pieces it houses are on view (most come from **Pekalongan** on the northern coast), but you get an idea of the infinite variety of colours and patterns, whether abstract or drawn from nature. The ingenious **pagi sore sarongs** ("morning and evening" sarongs), are adorned with patterns and inverted according to the time of day. Don't miss the superb 19C **embroidery and Chinese costumes*** at the back of the museum.

The Affandi Museum (Plan I, from C2)

Jl Solo, airport road, as you leave the town, before the bridge (take a taxi or a "becak"). Daily 8.30am-3pm. The house of the famous Indonesian painter Affandi – a pioneer of avant-garde, who died in 1991 – has been converted into a museum which shows a wide range of his works. The first building was designed in a strange curved shape by Affandi himself in 1962. Large **canvasses** and works in **Indian ink** painted in Europe after the war are exhibited here alongside a customised Mitsubishi, also by the artist. The painter's **house** in the shape of a banana leaf overlooks a cafe and a **caravan** where his wife lived. Below there is a **swimming pool** paved with an attractive mosaic, again by Affandi. The **second gallery** contains other canvasses by the artist as well as works by his daughter Kartika. A new building currently under construction will be for exhibiting other paintings.

Kota Gede* (Plan I, from C4)

May be reached by bus from Umbulharjo terminal (no 11) or from Jl Prawirotaman (no 14). Today, the first capital of Mataram, founded in 1575 by Panembahan Senopati is no more than a peaceful suburb of Yogyakarta *(5km to the southeast).* However, from its golden age it has kept the thriving **silverware** tradition. The workshops are concentrated in the alleyways around Jalan Kemasan.

Yogyakarta

A visit to the small **central market*** *(intersection of Jl Kemasan and Jl Mondorakan)* installed in an old building is like going to a kind of shadow theatre drama with its effects of light and shade. Between the piles of rice bags, the stalls of flowers and the shelves of dried fish old women philosophise about the price of the produce. Highly venerated by the Javanese, the **tomb of Senopati**, hidden behind a small brick wall *(200m south of the market, Friday 1-3pm; Sunday, Monday, Wednesday 10am-1pm)*, is of little interest to the visitor apart from its pretty setting. Rather, why not take the time to stroll or bicycle along the shaded walks, or along Jalan Mondorakan, between the elegant early 20C **Javanese houses** with their attractive verandas.

The Wayang Museum

Southeast of Yogyakarta, may be reached by bus from Umbulharjo terminal (get off at Rejowirangun). Jl Raya Yogya-Wonosari km 7, Monday-Saturday 8am-3pm, fee. The sumptuous Javanese building hidden in a park houses a collection of **Javanese puppets** made of wood or leather. The display forms a vast panorama through the ages (with periods ranging from the Classical, the Majapahit, through to the War of Liberation) and the different styles (Muslim, Christian, and Hindu and other epics). Most of the puppets are reproductions, although there is also a wayang *golek* that is 250 years old.

South of Yogyakarta

Catch a bus in Jl Parangtritis, near Jl Prawirotaman. Allow a day.

Imogiri*

17km from Yogyakarta. Tour of the tombs, Monday 10am-1pm and Friday 1.30-4pm. Donation.

Perched on a low hill halfway between Yogyakarta and the Indian Ocean, the site of the cemetery of the sultans of Mataram owes nothing to chance. It is said that the first person to be buried here, the famous **Sultan Agung** (1613-1646) had chosen the place so as to be able to see his mistress Nyai Loro Kidul, the Queen of the South Seas. Imogiri holds a special place in Javanese culture and is a perfect illustration of Javanese syncretism – so extraordinary to the Western mind – mixing ancestor worship, various mystical beliefs, and the Islamic faith.

A flight of 345 steps leads to the tombs of the 23 sovereigns of Yogyakarta *(on the left)* and Solo *(on the right)* who have been buried here since the 17C. Hamengkubuwono IX, the most recently buried sultan (d 1988), lies in the far eastern part of the cemetery.

As a sacred place Imogiri is to be visited barefoot and in traditional costume *(hired at the entrance)*. Once through the walled enclosure, you file one by one into the wooden **mausoleum** of Sultan Agung, to pay your respects in the incense filled room in front of the tomb covered in rose petals. An officiating elder recites a few words and then, with an imperceptible sign indicates that your prayer has been passed on and it is time to make way for the next person.

On the south coast**

Heading south through the green Javanese countryside, you come next to **Parangtritis*** *(28km)*, a favourite spot for Yogyakartans to relax in, and an important pilgrimage site. The **beach**, a long ribbon of grey sand stretching for 4km and dominated by superb white **cliffs** is invaded every weekend by Jakartans who fly kites, go for rides in horse-drawn carts or simply sunbathe (note, no bikinis). But the ocean still belongs to Nyai Loro Kidul, who, legend has it, drags anyone under who dares swim in green, her special colour. The currents are in fact really dangerous.

Stalls on the sand and hotel-restaurants set back from the beach serve frugal meals. There is a fine **panoramic view*** of the site from the **Queen of the South** hotel on the hill (see "Making the most of Yogyakarta").

According to legend, it was at **Parangkusumo** (1km to the west) that Senopati, the first king of Mataram, reappeared after spending three days at the bottom of the sea in the company of Nyai Loro Kidul, where he learnt the arts of love and power. Some of the major kraton ceremonies of Yogyakarta take place here. Pools have been laid out at the **Parangwedang hot springs** nearby.

Small fishing villages along the south coast off the tourist trail may be reached from Yogyakarta by bus (via Wonosari) or hired car.

Baron* village (60km from Yogya) nestling in the curve of a small steep-sided bay makes for a pleasant stop. There is a fine **beach** (unfortunately dangerous for swimming) facing which are some excellent seafood restaurants. Further on are less renowned beaches at **Kukup** (1km to the east) and **Krakal** (6km), where it is possible to stay the night.

Small Javanese mosque
(near Imogiri)

R. Marca

Yogyakarta

G Guérard

Central Java

Going for rides in Parangtritis

Mount Merapi★★
Allow half a day to climb to the top.
See also the "Other things to do" section in "Making the most of Yogyakarta".

Thirty kilometres north of Yogyakarta the perfect cone of Mount Merapi (2 911m) rises above the Javanese countryside. Majestic, but disturbing. Indeed, Gunung Merapi means "mountain of fire", a name that is particularly apt when you know that the volcano is one of the most active in the world. Scientists watch it closely and have set up numerous observation stations. In November 1994 62 people died in a cloud of hot lava near Kaliurang, and old people still remember the eruption in 1930, which caused 1 369 deaths. What now most worries vulcanologists is the enormous dome of solid lava, measuring 1 million cubic metres, which is still growing and threatens to collapse onto the villages to the south and west.

For the Javanese, Merapi is far more than a simple geological phenomenon. It forms the vertical part of the sacred trilogy that unites the *kraton* in Yogyakarta with the Indian Ocean and the mountain. While the sea, symbolising the womb and serving as the dwelling place of Loro Kidul represents the link between the sultan and his people, the volcano, home of the gods and image of the linga (phallic symbol of Siva) represents his relationship with the divine. If you happen to meet Mbah Marijan, a mischievous old sage, virtuoso *dalang* (puppet-master) when the fancy takes him, and keeper of the keys to Merapi *(juru kunci)*, ask him to tell you the legends of the volcano.

Kaliurang
25km, fee. Clinging to the southern slopes of Merapi, this small hill station (900m) provides the opportunity for a refreshing escape from Yogyakarta's muggy heat. Villas and chalets are spread out amongst the greenery on the edge of the woods. Kaliurang is a hangout for young lovers *(pacaran)*, and also the departure point for **walks** in the foothills of Merapi *(see the "Excursions" section in "Making the most of Yogyakarta")*.

The **Ullen Sentalu Museum** (*Tuesday-Saturday 10am-4pm, Sunday 10am-2pm; fee*) set in the middle of a very elegant **park** provides an excellent introduction to the symbolism of the court arts of Yogyakarta, and especially of Solo. It is devoted to women's Javanese traditional costume, and is the fruit of much museographical thought as it is not content just to exhibit **batiks**, but explains the exact meaning of sarong patterns. The collection of **photos and paintings** gives you an idea of what life was like in the *kratons*, and you may like to end the tour with a **traditional tea** served in a superb room, before paying a visit to the souvenir shop.

Climbing the volcano

The departure point is **Selo** (*it is no longer possible to climb from Kaliurang*), a small village nestled on the northern slopes of Merapi, on the pass that separates it from Mount Merbabu (3 150m). While there is no particular technical difficulty involved in this climb, it is nonetheless quite a tiring trek and you need to be in good physical condition (*allow 4hr for the climb up and almost 3hr for the descent, which is generally agreed to be interminable*). Avoid climbing in the rainy season, from November to April, as the path is slippery and the view restricted. Enquire at a travel agency to find out whether the volcano is showing signs of activity. When the level of alarm reaches 3 (out of 4), climbing is forbidden as the danger becomes real.

The first third of the walk is through **woods** and **tobacco fields**, then the path leads to a crest that opens onto a plateau. The last and most exhausting part of the climb is up through stones. At the end of this ordeal, you are rewarded at the **summit** with a spectacular **panorama***** that takes in the lunar landscape on Mount Merbabu (to the north), Mount Sumbing and Mount Sundoro (to the west), and the whole plain of Central Java.

Making the most of Yogyakarta

COMING AND GOING

By plane – The airport is 10km east of the town. By taking a taxi at the rank (fixed rates) you will avoid complications. You may also catch a bus or minibus on the main road, outside the airport.
Yogyakarta has links with Jakarta and Denpasar (several flights a day), as well as with Bandung, Surabaya and Mataram.

By train – Theft by pickpockets is unfortunately a common occurrence especially in economy class: keep your valuables on you and guard them closely.
Tugu, the main station is in the town centre, at the northern end of Jl Malioboro (Plan I-B2 or Plan II). There is an information office ("Kepala stasion") on the platform. If you don't have much luggage, you can reach Malioboro and Sosrowijayan on foot (on the other side of the railway line).
– Jakarta: 9 trains a day. The most comfortable, with air conditioning, are

"Dwipangga" (leaves at 9.48pm, arrives at 5am), "Argo Lawu" (leaves at 8.46am, arrives at 3.30pm) and "Bima" (leaves at 10.48pm, arrives at 6.26am). Less comfortable but more colourful: "Fenjar Utama" and "Senjar Utama" (8hr30min-10hr; some trains have air conditioning).
– Bandung: 3 departures in the evening. "Turangga" is the most expensive and the fastest (travelling time: 7hr).
– Solo: Plenty of trains (1hr).
– Surabaya: 5 trains, in the afternoon and the evening (4hr30min-5hr). The most comfortable is "Bima"; the least expensive is "Mutiara Selatan".

By bus – **Umbulharjo**, the main terminal (Jl Veteran) (Plan I, C4) is near Kota Gede (bus no 4 or direct *bemo* for Malioboro). Prices are a little higher if you go through a travel agent but you will avoid hassle, and can be collected at your hotel. Some agents offer bus transport all the way to Bali, via Bromo volcano.

Terban terminal, Jl Simanjutak (Plan I, B2), near the Novotel, serves Bandung.
Major routes: Borobudur (90min), Parangtritis (1hr), Kaliurang (1hr), Imogiri (40min), Solo (2hr), Cilacap (5hr), Jakarta (12hr), Bandung (10hr), Surabaya (8hr), Probolinggo near Bromo volcano (9hr), Denpasar (16hr).

By minibus – At **Terban terminal** (Plan I, B2) there are *bemos* for Prambanan and Kaliurang.
Minibuses known as Travel minibuses will collect you and drop you off at your hotel when you arrive at your destination. If you go directly through a minibus company you will not have to pay a large commission to a travel agent.
Agung Star, Jl Parangtritis 42 (Plan I, B4), ☎ (0274) 37 18 11. The only ones serving Pangandaran (departure at 7am).
SAA, Jl Diponegoro 9A (Plan I, B2), ☎ (0274) 58 49 76.
Rahayu, Jl Diponegoro 15 (Plan I, B2), ☎ (0274) 56 13 22.
Rama Sakti, Jl Diponegoro 85 (Plan I, B2), ☎ (0274) 51 47 94.

GETTING AROUND

By bus – This is the least expensive form of transport, but not the simplest. Most lines, with variations, connect the UGM University (in the north) with Umbulharjo terminal. No 4 bus goes along Jl Malioboro.

By taxi – **Jas Taxi**, Jl Kapten Tendean 39 (Plan, A3), ☎ (0274) 37 37 37.
Pandawa Taxi, Jl Sosrokusuman 16 (Plan II), ☎ (0274) 56 31 11.
Armada, Pingit Kidul 12 (Plan I, A2), ☎ (0274) 51 27 87.

By becak – These little coloured cycle rickshaws for two have almost become a symbol of Yogyakarta, although you find them all over Java. They are an ideal means for visiting the town, particularly the area around the kraton (elsewhere you get drowned in traffic). There are so many in Jl Malioboro and Jl Prawirotaman that you may feel pestered, but you can always cut the conversation short with a polite "Alan jalan" ("I'm going for a walk").
Annoyingly "Tukang *becak*" drivers tend to take you to a shop or a hotel of their choice (not necessarily the best ones), where they get a commission even if you do not become a customer. Negotiate the trip before you set off, remembering at the same time that these drivers work hard and earn just enough to live on and to pay for the rent on their vehicles.

By horse-drawn carriage – Known as "andong", these have two or four seats and their drivers wear traditional costume. The carriages are an ordinary means of transport and not just a tourist attraction. You can, however, go on hourlong tours.

Bicycle rental – Enquire at hotels and travel agents.
Kartika, Jl Sosrowijayan 8 (Plan II), ☎ (0274) 51 34 24.

Motorbike rental – Very convenient for Yogyakarta and the surrounding area, but watch out for the unpredictable local driving habits. Negotiate the price if you are hiring for several days, and check the state of the bike carefully and how much the excess is in the insurance.
Indonesia Rental, Jl Pasar Kembang 64 (Plan II), ☎ (0274) 51 81 03.
Fortuna, Jl Jlagran 20-21 (Plan II) (near the Kota Hotel), ☎ (0274) 56 46 80. Motorbikes and cars.
Dewata, Jl Prawirotaman 27 (Plan III), ☎ (0274) 38 43 89. Motorbikes and cars.

Car rental – If you hire a driver find out whether or not you are expected to pay for his board and lodging if you are going away for more than a day. Enquire also at travel agents.
Bali Car Rental, in front of the airport, ☎ (0274) 51 20 54.
Star Car Rental, Jl Laksada Adisucipto 22 (Plan I, C2), ☎ (0274) 56 24 03.
Fortuna (see above).
Dewata (see above).

ADDRESS BOOK

Tourist information – **Dinas Pariwisata**, Jl Malioboro 16 (Plan I-B2 or Plan II), ☎ (0274) 56 60 00 (Monday-Thursday 7.30am-7.30pm, Friday-Saturday 7.30am-6pm). Maps, brochures, programmes for performances as well as an annual calendar of events (in English).

Central Java

Travel agencies – Yogyakarta has a wide range of Indonesian tour operators:
Media Tour, Jl Wahid Hasyim 258 (Plan I, A3), ☎ (0274) 56 37 72.
Pacto, Natour Garuda Hotel, Jl Malioboro 60 (Plan I, B2), ☎ 56 29 06.
Mekar Wisata, Jl Seturan Raya 5A (behind the Sahid Hotel), ☎ (0274) 52 36 53. Tours in Yogyakarta, Central Java and West Java. A reliable agency for climbing Mount Merapi.
– In Sosrowijayan and Prawirotaman:
Nitour, Jl KHA Dahlan 71 (Plan I, A3), ☎ (0274) 37 51 65.
Bu Yam Kartika, Jl Sosrowijayan 8 (Plan II), ☎ (0274) 51 34 24. Tours, bicycle rental, sending parcels abroad.
Kresna, Jl Prawirotaman 18 and 5 (Plan I-B4 or Plan III), ☎ (0274) 37 75 02. Tours in the Yogyakarta area and to Bromo; car rental with or without drivers.
Agung Tourist Service, Jl Prawirotaman 31 (Plan I-B4 or Plan III), ☎ (0274) 37 01 87. The only other local agency that sets up its own tours and offers every guarantee.
Sanuka, Jl Prawirotaman 12 (Plan I-B4 or Plan III), ☎ (0274) 37 71 57. A new agency whose services have not yet been tested by us, but whose staff speak several languages.
Azimuth Adventure Travel, Gang Seruni CTW-1, ☎ (0274) 54 28 12, Fax (0274) 58 28 47. A young outfit set up by a Frenchman, offering a walk in Borobudur, treks up volcanoes and 3-week tours (Java, Bali, Lombok, Sumatra and Sulawesi).

Bank/Currency exchange – Most of the major banks have their head office in Jl Jend Sudirman (Plan I, B2) and have branches throughout the town. Plenty of ATMs and currency exchanges.
BII, Jl Jend Sudirman 46, ☎ (0274) 56 14 16 (you may have money transferred from abroad, for a very high commission); Natour Garuda Hotel, Jl Malioboro 60 (Visa ATM).
Bank Central Asia, Jl Jend Sudirman 7 (near the Novotel); Jl Ahmad Dahlan 25; Jl Brigjen Katamso 141. Dollars, travellers' cheques and Visa ATM. Monday-Friday, 10am-12noon for travellers' cheques.
Bank Negara Indonesia, Jl Jend Sudirman 52; Jl Ahmad Dahlan 71; Jl Parangtritis. Monday-Friday, 7.30am-3pm. Dollars and travellers' cheques.

Lippo, Natour Garuda Hotel, Jl Malioboro 60 (Plan I, B2). Monday-Friday, 10.30am-2pm. Dollars, travellers' cheques and Visa ATM.
– In Sosrowijayan and Prawirotaman:
Intrahilex, Jl Senopati, main post office (Plan I, B3). Monday-Saturday, 8am-8pm; Sunday, 8am-7pm. Currency exchange.
PT Barumun Abadi, Natour Garuda Hotel, Jl Malioboro 60 (Plan I, B2). Monday-Saturday, 7am-4pm. Currency exchange with good rates.

Post office – **Main post office**, Jl Senopati (Plan I, B3). Monday-Saturday, 7am-9pm; Sunday, 8am-8pm.
Large parcel dispatch: **Poste Divisi Paket**, Jl Mayor Suryotomo 8 (Plan I, B3). The post office's parcel office. **Ritra Cargo**, Jl Parangtritis 132 (Plan I, B4), ☎ (0274) 37 04 05. Bulk mailing. **MSA Kargo**, Jl Parangtritis 132 (Plan I, B4), ☎ (0274) 37 10 80. Bulk mailing.

Telephone – Yogyakarta has plenty of Wartels, particularly in Sosrowijayan (Plan II) and Prawirotaman (Plan III).

Internet – **Warnet**, at the main post office (Plan I, B3). Monday-Saturday, 8am-9pm; Sunday, 9am-8pm.
Whizz Kidz, Sosrowijayan, Gang I (Plan II). Daily, 8.30am-10pm. Slow connection.
Protech 8, Jl Prawirotaman 24 (Plan III). Comfortable booths and fast connection (daily, 9am-midnight).

Airline companies – **Garuda**, Ambarrukmo Hotel, Jl Adisucipto (Plan I, C2) (airport road), ☎ (0274) 56 58 35 or 56 37 06 (airport).
Merpati, Jl Diponegoro 31 (Plan I, B2), ☎ (0274) 51 42 72.

Immigration – Jl Solo km 10 (before the airport), ☎ (0274) 58 61 30.

Medical service – **Panti Rapih Hospital** Jl Cik Di Tiro 30 (Plan I, B1-C1) (near the UGM university), ☎ (0274) 51 57 09. The hospital is run by Christians and is one of the best in town. Doctors (some of whom speak English) give surgery consultations.
Rumah Sakit Bethesda, Jl Jend Sudirman 70 (Plan I, B2), ☎ (0274) 56 22 46.
Kimia Farma 20, Jl Malioboro 179 & 123 (Plan I, B2 or Plan II). Two pharmacies or "apotik" that are open daily, 24hr a day.

Apotik Ratna, Jl Parangtritis 44 (Plan I, B4 or Plan III), to the right coming from Jl Prawirotaman (Monday-Saturday 7am-9pm).

WHERE TO STAY

Yogyakarta has more than 200 hotels. The Ambarrukmo, with its air of faded glory, was the only luxury hotel for a long time but several international chains have set up over the last few years (Novotel, Ibis, Hyatt, Holiday Inn and Radisson). For those travelling independently, two areas (Sosrowijayan and Prawirotaman) have a wide range of accommodation with easily accessible services (travel agents, restaurants and shops). Sosrowijayan is located near the station and the town centre and attracts a clientele of travellers, while Prawirotaman, south of the kraton, has a good deal of mid-range hotels. Breakfast is included in most cases.

● **Sosrowijayan and Malioboro** (Plan II)

Modest

Hotel Indonesia, Jl Sosrowijayan 9, ☎ (0274) 58 76 59 – 25rm. ⁅ ⤢ ✕ A friendly, very inexpensive hotel. Ask for rooms at the back, which are darker and cooler. Breakfast not included.

Aziatic, Jl Sosrowijayan 6 – 10rm. ✕ Housed in an old building dating from the time of the Dutch, the hotel is unfortunately rather noisy and the rooms are somewhat monastic. You will get a warm welcome from the mosquitoes.

Monica Hotel, Jl Sosrowijayan, Gang I/192, ☎ (0274) 58 05 98 – 15rm. Some of the rooms have private bathrooms. The small, extremely well-kept hotel opened in 1995. The rooms are set around a charming courtyard garden.

Hotel Selekta, Jl Sosrowijayan, Gang I/150 – 11rm. ⤢ Some of the rooms have their own bathroom. More spacious than the nearby Monica, this hotel has a courtyard garden, but the cleanliness and comfort are of a slightly lower standard. You are, however, given a friendly welcome.

Average

Bladok, Jl Sosrowijayan 76, ☎/Fax (0274) 56 04 52 – 24rm. ⁅⤢✕ ⤢ ㏄ Some of the best value for money in the district. Some rooms have a pleasant private terrace or balcony. Such a success

that it is often full in the high season. The good breakfast is not included in the price.

Oryza Hotel, Jl Sosrowijayan 49-51, ☎ (0274) 51 24 95, Fax (0274) 51 20 04 – 15rm. ⤢ ㏄ A neat, comfortable little hotel without any particular charm but good value for money. Most of the rooms have a bathroom with a mandi.

High end

Mendut, Jl Pasar Kembang 49, ☎ (0274) 56 34 35 – 58rm. ⁅ 🗏 ♪ ⓣⓥ ⤢ ㏄ A large hotel with clean but impersonal rooms at relatively high prices. Useful if you are in a fix. A bar with "dangdut" (local pop) singers has just opened. Breakfast not included.

*⌂***Kota**, Jl Jlagran 1, ☎ (0274) 51 58 44, Fax (0274) 51 35 86 – 17rm. ⁅ ⤢ ㏄ The warm welcome and lovely decor (magnificent ceramic tiles in warm colours, and period furniture) make this an extremely charming hotel. The only problem is that the rooms are tiny.

Luxury

Hotel Batik Yogyakarta II, Taman Yuwono Complex, Dagen, ☎ (0274) 56 18 28, Fax (0274) 56 18 23 – 22rm. ⁅ ⤢ / 🗏 ✕ ⤢ Slightly out of the centre of Sosrowijayan in a quiet neighbourhood. Large swimming pool and spacious rooms.

Super deluxe

Natour Garuda, Jl Malioboro 60, ☎ (0274) 56 63 22, Fax (0274) 56 30 74 – 233rm. ⁅⤢/🗏♪ⓣⓥ✕⤢✕㏄ This vast very well located Dutch building has unfortunately not kept much of its former style. The rooms are comfortable but lack character and are quite expensive. Numerous services on offer (currency exchange and travel agencies).

● **Prawirotaman** (Plan III)

Modest

Prayogo, Jl Prawirotaman I/26-34, ☎ (0274) 37 71 15, Fax (0274) 37 99 25 – 47rm. ⁅ ⤢ Now converted into a losmen, this batik factory dating from the 1930s has a pleasant hall, but the rooms are a little monastic. Convenient if you are in a fix.

Average

Sriwijaya, Jl Prawirotaman I/7, ☎ (0274) 37 18 70 – 30rm. ⁅⤢ / 🗏 ⤢ Another batik factory converted into a hotel. The place has kept a certain style, save for the rooms that are rustic but clean (some have hot water). The swimming pool is hidden at the back in a peaceful little garden.

� **Sumaryo**, Jl Prawirotaman 1/22, ☎ (0274) 37 75 52, Fax (0274) 37 35 07 – 40rm. In the same spirit as the former, an immense single-storey building with clean rooms and high ceilings.

Average

Airlangga, Jl Prawirotaman 1/6-8, ☎ (0274) 37 80 44, Fax (0274) 37 14 27 – 40rm. You cannot miss this huge multi-storeyed building that dominates the street. The rooms, which are clean but lack charm, are good value for money (ask for the ones upstairs that have more light).

Kirana, Jl Prawirotaman 1/30-38, ☎ (0274) 37 66 00, Fax (0274) 37 22 62 – 23rm. A quiet, charming ho-

tel with little sitting rooms here and there, and wonderful old tiling. The decoration in the rooms has a touch of kitsch. The second building, opposite, is more down-market.

Rose, Jl Prawirotaman 1/22, ☎ (0274) 37 79 91, Fax (0274) 38 00 11 – 42rm. A wide range of rooms generally offering good value for money. The rooms surround a courtyard garden that stretches out lengthwise according to traditional layout.

Mercury, Jl Prawirotaman II, ☎ (0274) 37 08 46, Fax (0274) 37 20 37 – 13rm. A superb early 20C residence that looks like a small kraton. The main room, preceded by a finely-worked awning, is a restaurant. It is a pity that the rooms are rather austere.

Prambanan, Jl Prawirotaman 1/47, ☎ (0274) 37 61 67 – 16rm. The rooms arranged around a patio

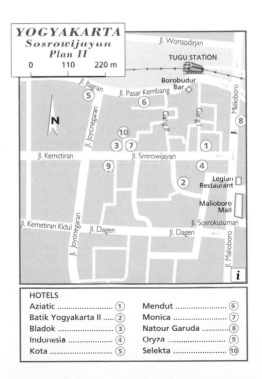

YOGYAKARTA
Sosrowijayun
Plan II
0   110   220 m

Jl. Wonsodiran

TUGU STATION

Jl. Jlagran

Jl. Pasar Kembang   Borobudur Bar

Jl. Joyonegaran

Gang II   Gang I

Jl. Malioboro

⑤

⑥

⑩

③ ⑦

①

Jl. Kemetiran

Jl. Sosrowijayan

⑨

④

②   Legian Restaurant

Malioboro Mall

Jl. Kemetiran Kidul

Jl. Joyonegaran

Jl. Dagen

Jl. Dagen

Jl. Sosrokusuman

Jl. Malioboro

i

HOTELS

Aziatic	①	Mendut	⑥
Batik Yogyakarta II	②	Monica	⑦
Bladok	③	Natour Garuda	⑧
Indonesia	④	Oryza	⑨
Kota	⑤	Selekta	⑩

with a little garden and swimming pool are comfortable and well-kept, but unfortunately on the small side.

Metro I, Jl Prawirotaman II/71, ☎ (0274) 37 23 64, Fax (0274) 37 20 04 – 66rm. 🍴 ✗ 🏊 Take a look at several rooms before choosing as size and comfort vary considerably. The hotel has one of the largest swimming pools in the area, as well as a bookshop and Internet access.

High end

Duta, Jl Prawirotaman 1/26, ☎/Fax (0274) 37 20 64 – 36rm. 🍴 ⛲ / 📺 ✗ 🏊 cc A maze of corridors with very comfortable rooms, although a little expensive. Those at the far end of the garden are particularly quiet.

Luxury

Jogja Village Inn, Jl Menukan 5 (300m south of Prawirotaman), ☎ (0274) 37 30 31, Fax (0274) 38 22 02 – 24rm. 🍴⛲/📺 🌿 ✗ 🏊 cc A charming hotel, one of the nicest in Yogyakarta. Rooms have wooden furniture and four-poster beds (the ones on the ground floor have magical open-air bathrooms). On top of all this, the service is irreproachable and it is difficult to resist a swim in the (salt-water) pool.

● **Parangtritis**

Modest

Agung Garden, in the main street that leads to the beach – 9rm. 🍴 ✗ Rather austere in terms of comfort and cleanliness (not much light and furniture reduced to a bed and a chair), as in most of the losmen in Parangtritis. Some of the rooms have air conditioning.

Widodo Losmen, just beyond the one above – 11rm. 🍴 ✗ The rooms are just as monastic as those in the Agung Garden, but lighter and more comfortable. Some have fans. The owner runs another hotel at the entrance to the village.

Luxury

Queen of the South, (3km beyond Parangtritis, in the hills), ☎ (0274) 36 71 96, Fax (0274) 36 71 97 – 40rm. 🍴 📺 🌿 📺 ✗ 🏊 🐾 cc In an unbeatable site on a cliff overlooking the sea (with steps leading down to the beach). Comfortable rooms, although they have no particular style. It is worth coming here just for the panoramic view from the

swimming pool. Diverse spiritual activities are on offer, including yoga and Javanese ceremonies. The hotel plans to expand.

● **Near Mount Merapi**

Modest

Pak Auto, Selo. The real name is Pak Darto. The hotel provides rustic but inexpensive accommodation. This is where you stay before climbing the volcano if you go through a travel agent in Yogyakarta.

Agung Merapi, Selo. A little more comfortable than Pak Auto, but more expensive. Some rooms have private bathrooms.

Vogels, Jl Astamulya 76, Kaliurang, ☎ (0274) 89 52 08 – ✗ Installed in a former home belonging to the nobility (the more recent building has less charm), this small family guesthouse has rooms that provide basic comfort but are quite satisfactory (some have private bathrooms). The very friendly owner is a mine of information on the volcano.

EATING OUT

Yogyakarta has a large amount of excellent restaurants, ranging from "rumah makan" (unpretentious restaurants) frequented by Indonesians, to *warung* and "kaki lima" (street vendors serving hot dishes). It's also worth going off the beaten track in Sosrowijayan and Prawirotaman.

Some *warung* specialise in **seafood** (in Jl Solo, near the Ambarrukmo Hotel, and in Jl Wahidin Sudhirohusodo, south of the Galeria mall) (Plan I, C2).

In the late afternoon along Jl Malioboro and Jl Solo delicious snacks such as "martabak" (thick pancakes, either sweet with chocolate and peanuts, or savoury with vegetables), "klepon" (rice balls stuffed with palm sugar and coated in coconut), "tempe" (soya biscuits) and "onde onde" (fried sesame balls) are on sale.

If you have had enough culinary adventures try the buffets in the large hotels, particularly the one in the **Novotel** (Jl Jend Sudirman 89) (Plan I, C2). You can always fall back on the **McDonald's** in Jl Malioboro and the **Pizza Hut** in Jl Diponegoro if you miss Western food.

Be warned that after 9.30pm you are not likely to be served in restaurants.

A good way of meeting young locals is to go to one of the "lesehan" eateries (where you sit on a mat on the floor) at the top of Jl Malioboro (Plan II). They open at 10pm and serve kebabs and grilled chicken.

• Sosrowijayan and the Kraton

Basic

Superman, Jl Sosrowijayan Wetan Gang I/71 (Plan II), ☎ (0274) 51 34 72. The vast restaurant with bamboo walls is a hangout for travellers, but the cuisine (Indonesian and Western) and the welcome you get are nothing special.

Bu Sis Kafe, Jl Sosrowijayan Gang I/89 (Plan II) (at the end of the alleyway). A small inexpensive restaurant serving excellent fish. The fried bananas are unforgettable.

Cirebon, Jl A Yani, at the end of Jl Malioboro (Plan I, B3), opposite the Beringhardjo market. The large well-ventilated room is pleasant after the bustle in Malioboro, but the service is sometimes very slow. They serve "nasi goreng", "mie goreng", yoghurt and milk-shakes.

Water Castle Cafe, Taman Sari KT I/231 (Plan I, A3). An ideal spot to take a rest and try "gado gado", "nasi goreng" or fruit juice, after visiting the Bird Market and the Water Castle (Taman Sari).

Moderate

Bladok, Jl Sosrowijayan 76 (Plan II), ☎ (0274) 56 04 52. A good place if you feel like meat (coq au vin, barbecued beef), salad or onion soup. The restaurant opens onto a small courtyard garden.

More select

Legian, Jl Perwakilan 9, opposite the Ibis Hotel (Plan II), ☎ (0274) 56 46 44. This has become an institution that now tends to rely on its reputation, but the "nasi gudeg" (chicken served with jackfruit) is excellent. Watch out for the mosquitoes.

• Prawirotaman (Plan III)

Moderate

Going Bananas, Jl Prawirotaman 48, ☎ (0274) 37 71 69. A small terrace restaurant, ideal for lunch snacks (salads, bruschetta and cakes). But the service is quite slow, even if you can fill in the wait by visiting the shop on the premises.

Via via, Jl Prawirotaman 24, ☎ (0274) 38 65 57. Friendly place serving excellent Indonesian and Western food. The very active Belgian owner is able to arrange bicycle tours, batik classes and even an introduction to traditional Javanese medicine.

Lotus Garden, Prawirotaman II, ☎ (0274) 37 76 49. A wide variety of dishes (Indonesian, Western and seafood), served in attractive bamboo decor, with a small tropical garden. Rather small portions, but the marinated chicken is excellent (quite spicy).

Mercury (see the hotel with the same name). Feel like trying cobra?

Making the most of Yogyakarta

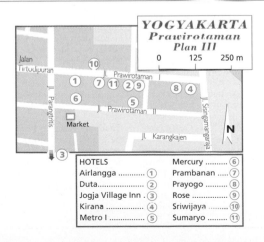

YOGYAKARTA
Prawirotaman
Plan III

0   125   250 m

Jalan Tirtodipuran

Jl. Prawirotaman I

Jl. Prawirotaman II

Market

Jl. Karangkajen

Parangtritis

Jl. Sisingamangaraja

N

HOTELS		Mercury	6
Airlangga	1	Prambanan	7
Duta	2	Prayogo	8
Jogja Village Inn	3	Rose	9
Kirana	4	Sriwijaya	10
Metro I	5	Sumaryo	11

More select

Kedai Kebun, Jl Tirtodipuran 3, ☎ (0274) 37 61 14. A friendly, elegant place with bamboo decor (yet another one!), where the food is of high quality: salads, prawns, chicken, fish ("gurame" sauce with a sweet-and-sour flavour or with peanuts). Exhibitions and performances are sometimes put on.

Jogja Village Inn (see the hotel with the same name). Refined Indonesian cuisine (chicken with spicy "rendang" sauce, or served in a coconut). Elegant setting.

● **North of the railway line**

More select

Gadjah Wong, Jl Gejayan (Plan I, C1) (near the bridge), ☎ (0274) 58 82 94. This new restaurant is already something of an institution. Its very pleasant setting consists of a garden with a small river running through it. The excellent fare shows originality: "ranapekel" (mutton in lemon sauce), "nasi kuning" (chicken in coconut sauce), ostrich and salmon.

Pring Sewu, Jl Magelang, (Plan I, A1), ☎ (0274) 56 49 93. At some distance from the centre, this vast restaurant with bamboo bungalows giving onto a garden is really worth the trip. The "gurame bakar" (grilled fresh-water fish) and the prawns in butter sauce are memorable.

Saung Kabayan, Jl Laksada Adisucipto, (Plan I, C2) (just beyond the Ambarrukmo Hotel). A long bamboo construction giving onto a pond, where very good West Java food is served. There is a karaoke bar just next door.

Chinese restaurants

Lie Djiong, Jl Brig Katamso 21 (Plan I, B3), ☎ (0274) 37 44 29. 11am-3pm and 6-9pm. Don't be put off by the "garage" atmosphere (walls covered in calendars, and the noise of the traffic) as this is the best Chinese restaurant in town. Try the prawns, the "mie goreng" and the shellfish. There are other Chinese restaurants in the same street further south.

Kobra, Jl Hayam Buruk 19 (Plan I, B2) (between the railway line and Puro Pakualaman), ☎ (0274) 51 67 71. A Chinese restaurant with rather cold decor (white tiles and neon lights), where you can try snake in every kind of way imaginable.

● **Parangtritis**

The *warung* beside the beach and the stalls set up on the sand serve frugal meals.

Widodo, adjoining the losmen with the same name. A good Indonesian restaurant that also serves seafood.

Queen of the South (see the hotel description). The main value of the place is in its setting, as the Indonesian and Western cuisine is nothing to write home about.

GOING OUT, HAVING A DRINK

Bars – Jogja café, Jl Kyai Mojo (Plan I, A2). Closes at 1am; entrance fee. An enormous place with bamboo decor and a dance floor. Every evening a local group plays international classics. The clientele is mainly Indonesian.

Borobudur bar, Jl Pasar Kembang (Plan II). Closes at 1am; entrance fee. Run on the same lines as the previous place, but with a more Western clientele and a wild atmosphere.

Dewata, Jl Gejayan, (Plan I, C1), near the Gadjah Wong restaurant (entrance fee). A more varied group repertoire, and the fact that there is a small garden below with a billiard table means you can take a break from the music.

Etnik Kafe, Purawisata, Jl Brigjen Katamso (Plan I, B3). A trendy little outside bar where you can have a drink after seeing a performance of the Ramayana.

Freetz, Jl Prawirotaman (Plan III). A restaurant-bar run by a friendly Frenchwoman who serves pastis.

Nightclubs – Yogyakarta is not as lively as Bali, but you will nonetheless find places to go out to in the evening.

Graha Parimitha, Jl Mayor Suryotomo (Plan I, B3), near the Melia Hotel (entrance fee). Better known by its old name "Papillon". An enormous, rather dark place that is very lively at the weekend with techno music.

Goedang Musik, Jl Pringgodari 22 (on the airport road; turn left as you leave town). Entrance fee. The brick and metal decoration is quite attractive, but the sound is too loud (techno music).

Cinema – Empire, Jl Urip Sumoharjo 104 (Plan I, C2) (above the Hero supermarket). 8 modern air-conditioned cinemas showing American films.

Central Java

LIVE SHOWS

The performing arts are very much alive in Yogyakarta, and the tradition is carried on in the schools – there's no trouble finding a show.

Indonesia Institute of Art (ISI), Jl Colombo (Plan I, C1). Dance rehearsals are open to the public (Monday-Saturday, 8am-2pm).

Bagong Kussudiarja, Jl Singosaren 9. The school of one of Indonesia's best choreographers.

Classical Javanese Dance, at the kraton (Plan I, B3). Thursday, Sunday, 10.30am-12noon.

Gamelan, at the kraton (Monday, Wednesday, 10.30am-12noon).

Ballet of the Ramayana – Purawisata, Jl Brigjen Katamso (Plan I, B3). Daily, 8 10pm. Quality performance but rather soulless.

Dalem Pujokusuman, Jl Brigjen Katamso 45 (Plan I, B4) Monday, Tuesday, Friday, 7-9pm.

In **Prambanan** (see "Making the most of Prambanan", p 311).

Wayang kulit – Sono Budoyo Museum (Plan I, B3). Daily, 8-10pm.

Alun-alun Selatan (Plan I, B3). Second Saturday of every month, 9pm-5am. You are guaranteed a local atmosphere.

Agastya Art Institute, Jl Gedongkiwo MD III/237 (Plan I, A4). Daily except Saturday, 3-5pm.

Ambarrukmo Hotel, Jl Laksda Adisucipto (Plan I, C2). Daily, 8-9.30pm.

Wayang golek – Kraton (Plan I, B3). Wednesday, 10am-12noon.

Agastya Art Institute (Plan I, A4). Saturday 3 5pm.

Nitour, Jl KH Ahmad Dahlan 71 (Plan I, A3). Monday-Saturday, 11am-1pm.

Other performances – Purawisata (Plan I, B3). "Dangdut" concerts (popular music with chants influenced by Arab song), performed by charming female singers.

French Cultural Centre (LIP), Jl Sagan 3 (Plan I, C2), ☎ (0274) 56 65 20, Fax (0274) 56 21 40. The centre puts on a very dynamic French-Indonesian programme (dance, drama, exhibitions and films). There is a library and a cafeteria.

Radio Republik Indonesia, Jl Gejayan (Plan I, C1). "Ketoprak" performances of popular Javanese drama (first Saturday of every month, 8pm).

FEASTS AND FESTIVALS

Pasar Malam, Alun-alun Utara (Plan I, B3). From May to July the square is transformed into a vast market that stays open until 11pm. The Javanese come with their families to buy toys for their children, and new clothes. They also consult healers, listen to "dangdut" and enjoy all the fun of the fair.

Yogyakarta Art Festival (Festival Kesenian Yogyakarta), June-July. Live shows, gamelan concerts, exhibitions and fairs are organised throughout the town for a month.

Birdsinging contest. In September there are bird auctions and birdsinging contests in Alun-alun Selatan (Plan I, B3).

Ceremonies – The Tourist Office will give you a very useful calendar. Linked with major Muslim festivals, the countless Javanese ceremonies ("upacara") and those at the kraton all have moveable dates.

Garebeg Syawal. At the end of Ramadan, at the kraton (Plan I, B3). In the northern Alun-alun a parade by the palace guard precedes the Gunungan procession that goes to the Grand Mosque.

Garebeg Besar. A ceremony at the kraton for Idul Adha (mutton feast) commemorates the sacrifice Abraham was asked to make of his son. The same festivities as for the preceding event. Children run through the streets with candles.

Javanese New Year. Parades and shows at Parangtritis.

Purification ceremony (month of Suro in the Javanese calendar). On this occasion kris daggers, spears and royal attributes are all cleaned with holy water afloat with flower petals (only the cleaning of the carriages takes place in public). Several days later it is the turn of the four sacred vases in Imogiri.

Sekaten and **Garebeg Maulud**. The Sekaten ceremony is linked to commemorations marking the birth of the Prophet Muhammad. It is an ancient harvest festival celebrated by the Javanese sultans and is believed to date back to the

Making the most of Yogyakarta

Majapahit era. The palace gamelans are taken in great pomp to the mosque, where sacred concerts are held. The week culminates with a "gunungan" procession. In the evening there is a performance of "wayang kulit" at the palace.

OTHER THINGS TO DO

Excursions – Travel agents offer tours to Imogiri, Parangtritis, Borobudur and Prambanan. To climb Merapi, go through an agent who will take care of paying the guides and especially organising the transport. If you are sure that you can walk sufficiently fast, insist on not leaving Selo before 1.30-2am, to avoid waiting in the cold at the summit for sunrise (at around 5.30am). At any rate, bring warm clothing as well as water and something to eat (and perhaps some binoculars). Guides are usually paid by the agent but to thank them some rupiah or clothing (shoes and T-shirts), are always appreciated.

The **Vogels Guesthouse**, in Kaliurang (see "Where to stay") organises night treks on the southern slopes of the volcano. With a bit of luck you will be able to see spectacular flows of glowing red lava.

Outdoor pursuits – Large hotels generally have swimming pools that non-residents pay to use. This is true of the **Radisson** (Jl Gejayan) (Plan I, C1), and the **Ambarrukmo** (airport road).

IKIP (Teachers' Training College), Jl Colombo (Plan I, C1): a lovely open Olympic pool, unfortunately not always very clean.

Rafting – Hotel Puri Asri, Jl Cempaka 9, Magelang (to the north of the town), ☎ (0293) 641 14. The hotel is set on the slopes of a hill on the banks of the Kali Progo. It organises tubing rides down the river (preferably in the rainy season). The view of Sumbing volcano and the rice fields is magnificent. You can sleep on site or leave Yogyakarta early in the morning (1hr journey).

Cycling – Some travel agents, and particularly **Via Via** restaurant (Plan III), organise tours around Yogyakarta.

Massages – Enquire at hotels.

Lotus moon, Jl Prawirotaman II (Plan III) (see the Lotus restaurant). Massages by old blind Javanese. Quite an experience!

Batik courses – Pak Hadjir, Taman Sari (Plan I, A3), ☎ (0274) 37 78 35.

Batik Research Center, Jl Kusumanegara 2 (Plan I, C3), ☎ (0274) 58 96 53. **Via Via** (see above).

Dance classes – Enquire at the **Dalem Pujokusuman** theatre (Plan I, B4).

Padepokan Puser Widya Nusantara Jawa, Suryodiningratan MJ II/837 (Plan I, A4), ☎ (0274) 37 23 63. Courses in traditional dance and puppets, as well as an introduction to Javanese culture (in English).

SHOPPING GUIDE

Markets – Beringhardjo, Jl Malioboro (Plan II). A large unattractive concrete building whose activity spills out into the adjoining streets (batiks, fruit and vegetables, etc).

Demanpan, Jl Gejayan (Plan I, C2), north of the intersection with Jl Laksda Adisucipto. A small popular market full of fragrances and colours (selling fruit, vegetables and various utensils), where you won't meet many tourists.

Batiks – You will find a wide range on offer in shops along Jl Malioboro and at Beringhardjo market (see above). You can watch demonstrations in workshops along Jl Tirtodipuran (Plan I, B4). Craftsmen around Taman Sari (Plan I, A3) try out modern patterns, with varying degrees of success. **Kenik**, Jl Cokrodipuran 18, ☎ (0274) 54 10 35. A cooperative of young artists from the Indonesia Institute of Art (ISI) who make batiks with modern and traditional patterns.

Mirota Batik, at the lower end of Malioboro, opposite Beringhardjo market (Plan II). Wide range of sarongs, tablecloths and hangings.

Batik Margaria, Jl A. Yani 69 (Plan I, B3) (continuation of Malioboro). Fine collection of silk batiks, but at exorbitant prices.

Winotosastro, Jl Tirtodipuran 54 (Plan I, B4). A building with several storeys where you can visit a workshop. Wide choice of sarongs and clothes at relatively high prices.

Central Java

Ikats – Borneo Gallery, Jl Tirtodipuran 49 (Plan I, B4). Magnificent ikats from Flores, Sumba and Timor and batiks from Java and Sumatra, at high prices. The very friendly owner, Rudi, will be happy to show you around.

Silverware – This is the speciality of Kota Gede, where you can even commission the work.

Nufa's Silver, Jl Kemasan 68, ☎ (0274) 37 55 89. Necklaces, rings and bracelets.

Ansor's Silver, Jl Tegalgendu 28 (near a bridge), ☎ (0274) 37 32 66. A workshop set up in an elegant building making jewellery and cutlery.

MD, Keboan, ☎ (0274) 37 50 63. Cutlery.

Salim Widardjo, Keboan KG 3/547, ☎ (0274) 37 66 01. Ethnic jewellery.

Furniture and antiques – The best place to hunt around is Jl Tirtodipuran, where the shops are full of old items as well as copies (furniture, masks, kris daggers, screen paintings, wooden sculptures, puppets, etc).

Kasumban, Jl Tirtodipuran 50 (Plan I, B4), ☎ (0274) 38 48 92. A smart, expensive shop selling furniture, chests, wooden panels and various kinds of handicrafts.

Java & Madura, Jl Sangaji (in the northern part of town, just before the Ring Road). A Madurese family owns several shops in the area. There is a wide choice of wooden chests, beds, benches and wardrobes.

Gallery 47, Jl Tirtodipuran 47 (Plan I, B4), ☎ (0274) 38 70 37. A fine choice of Javanese arts and crafts, as well as primitive art from the archipelago, terracotta items and ikats.

Hanoman & Delly, Jl Tirtodipuran 57 (Plan I, B4), ☎ (0274) 58 02 39. Handicrafts, primitive art and Indonesian and Chinese furniture.

Dieng Art Shop, Jl Tirtodipuran 50 (Plan I, B4). A good selection of Chinese and Javanese art and handicrafts (terracotta objects) at reasonable prices.

Local arts and crafts – Among Yogyakarta's specialities are puppets made of wood or leather, kris daggers, gamelan instruments and masks, although often these are produced in one of the many "antiques factories". There is an enormous choice in Jl Malioboro, but the quality is mediocre.

JV Novi, Jl A Yani 27 (Plan I, B3), ☎ (0274) 51 33 78. This is one of the few reliable antique shops in the street. Leather puppets and musical instruments.

Malls – Malioboro, Jl Malioboro (Plan II).

Galeria, on the intersection between Jl Sudirman and Jl Rahayu Samirono (Plan I, C2).

Bookshops, stationer's – Boomerang, Jl Sosrowijayan Gang I/67 (Plan II). A small well-stocked bookshop selling a variety of publications on Indonesia (nearly all in English). There is also a good stationery section.

Gramedia, Malioboro mall (Plan II) and Galeria mall (Plan II, C2). Wide range of books and other products.

Sari Ilmu, Jl Malioboro 117 (Plan II). English-language newspapers and guide books, as well as maps and postcards.

Djaja Widjaja, Jl Malioboro (Plan II) (near the Brahmana shop, at the lower end of the street). Makers of rubber stamps are legion in Yogyakarta. This shop has a wide choice of traditional and modern models, which you can have made on the spot.

Photography – The choice of equipment is quite limited but you can find film for prints and slides (100 and 200 ASA) in shops where they do speedy development, mainly in Jl Malioboro and in the malls.

Duta Foto, Jl Laksda Adisucipto 130 (Plan I, C2). This is the best place. You can also try shops nearby, notably Artha Foto. Duta Foto has another less interesting shop in Jl Parangtritis, near Jl Prawirotaman.

THE DIENG PLATEAU★

GEDONG SONGO★★

Central Java Province – Map p 272-273
370km tour – Allow 2 days
Cool climate

Not to be missed
Sunrise over the Dieng temples, or better still, those at Gedong Songo.
And remember...
Hire a car or go through a travel agent in Yogyakarta.
Visit the sites early in the morning.

Nestled in their majestic settings of volcanoes and rice fields, the temples in Dieng and Gedong Songo are fascinating samples of Indo-Javanese architecture. Take a trip back through time to the sources of Java's history. Each site can be seen in a day excursion from Yogyakarta. However, you can combine them with a trip to Borobudur and Prambanan, thereby tracing the history of Buddhism and Hinduism in Java. If you are not interested in old buildings, the journey off the tourist trail is perfect for a very pleasant drive through the mountains, across one of the most beautiful regions of the island.

Java's ancient temples

Take the main road from Yogyakarta, and when you reach Borobudur head west via Kepil.

The two-day visit from "Jogja" will take you through bucolic scenery. The undulating countryside is crossed by streams and there are **traditional houses** made of bamboo dotted about. Plantations of tapioca, maize and rice stretch as far as the eye can see, dominated by the imperial outline of **Sumbing volcano** (3 375m). Beyond Wonoboso, the road *(now rougher)* suddenly twists and turns steeply upwards, affording misty views of a superb landscape of **terraced market gardens★**, an immense mosaic of dark green steps tumbling down the vertiginous slopes.

■ **Dieng plateau★** – *160km from Yogyakarta, allow 3hr.* Perched at an altitude of more than 2 000m, this vast bare cirque is a refuge for Java's oldest Hindu temples, probably the remains of the Sanjaya kingdom (dating from around 750). The mountains surrounding the site are presumed to be the dwelling place of the gods, and so make the site sacred, an attribute that is enhanced by the presence of hot springs. "Dieng" derives from *di-hyang*, the "abode of the ancestors". This suggests that when the new Brahminical religion was introduced into Java, it chose to set up in places of worship already in existence, and traditionally devoted to ancestors. Archeologists doubt that the place ever had a large population because of the unfavourable climate, and believe rather that it was a monastic retreat. Be that as it may, the most recently discovered inscription (1210) proves that, even after the great kingdoms had disappeared from the centre of Java, the temples in Dieng continued to be known and revered.

On the Dieng plateau

Central Java

R. Marca

Many visitors who have seen Borobudur and Prambanan leave Dieng feeling a little disappointed. Indeed, the temples are a lot less spectacular, and a cold mist often covers the whole plateau. Nonetheless, a magical atmosphere emanates from the place – for the Javanese, Dieng is full of mysticism – and can be fully felt at dawn, when in the early light the mountain ridges stand out sharply against the sky. So, if you don't mind the modest local lodgings, it is best to spend the night on the spot.

Of the 200 original *candis* on the plateau – all dedicated to Siva – only eight have survived. There were once wooden constructions around them, but only their stone foundations remain. However, Dieng still has a multitude of buried remains that are waiting to be excavated.

Lost in the middle of the plateau, the five small *candis* in the central group are lined up along a path that disappears into the grass. Four of them follow after one another on the same side, facing west: **Candi Arjuna***, **Candi Srikandi**, **Candi Puntadewa** and **Candi Sembadra**, while **Candi Semar** in the row opposite, faces Candi Arjuna. The latter, the oldest of all, is equipped with an **evacuation system** for the holy water contained in the linga (can be seen inside). This is the only system of its kind in Indonesia, and enabled people to carry out the Sivaite ritual in accordance with the precepts of the temples in southern India.

The architecture of the Dieng temples bears out their Indian influence, which is characterised by the superposition of ever-decreasing cubes, enhanced by corner niches. The temples' stylistic originality is obvious, and they have inspired all the sanctuaries in Central Java, particularly by featuring both **makara** and **kala** protective demons on the outside walls (*see sidebar p 306*).

Candi Srikandi also has superb **bas-reliefs*** on the outside representing Vishnu (*north*), Siva (*east*) and Brahma (*south*). However, most of the sculptures found on the site are kept in the **Dieng Museum*** (*near Candi Gatotkaca, daily, theoretically 7am-4pm*). Although the museum is rather modest, it does have some unexpected treasures: Ganesha, Kali, linga, *raksasa* and Nandi (Shiva's sacred bull).

Apart from the central group, there are three other temples hidden in the hills on the edge of the cirque. Further to the west is **Candi Gatotkaca**, while to the north is the small **Candi Dvaravati**.

The most interesting is **Candi Bima**** (*a little further south*), the only one of its kind. It is well preserved and its architecture is characteristic of North India. A wide porch juts out over the building forming a pyramidal super-structure with horseshoe-shaped niches.

Near Candi Bima (*a few hundred metres on foot*) are the **hot springs** at **Kawah Sikidang**. With its sulphur emanations from the bowels of the earth, and pools of boiling mud, the site is in keeping with its mythical surroundings.

Return to Candi Bima and take the road that runs alongside the plateau heading southeast.

A strange atmosphere envelops Lake **Telaga Warna***, a peaceful sheet of green and turquoise water. The **caves** in the surrounding woods were once used for meditation.

The Dieng plateau

If you have your own car you can go directly from the Dieng plateau to Gedong Songo (110km) via Kreteg, Parakan, Temanggung and Kaloran.

The **road**★★ makes its way between **Mount Sundoro** (3 225m) and Mount Sumbing, then goes down into the Kali Progo valley before climbing a ridge that affords majestic **panoramic views**★★.

■ **The Gedong Songo temples**★★ – *Daily, 7am-5pm, donation, allow 2hr. You can also do the journey on horseback.* Built between 750 and 775 – except for the first one, which is thirty years younger – the Gedong Songo temples are just a little more recent than those at Dieng. Like their elders, they are dedicated to Siva and are of similar size and style. However, the atmosphere of the site is very different to that at Dieng. Here the temples are dotted about on the slopes of **Mount Ungaran**, at an altitude of 1 300m, where there is a magnificent, open **viewpoint**★★★. Mount Sumbing and Mount Sundoro rise to the southwest, Mount Merbabu to the south, and Mount Lawu to the east. Wherever you look volcanoes rise up out of the earth, each more spectacular than the last.

The name of the site is misleading. *"Gedong songo"* means "nine buildings" in Javanese, but in fact there are only six small groups of temples spread out on the edge of a forest *(you get to them along a paved path)*. The first three groups are gathered together to the east of a ravine hollowed out by hot springs.

Spend a little time at the main temple in the **third group**★★: it has some superb **statues**★★ and its bas-reliefs can still be seen clearly. **Ganesha**, Siva's elephant-headed son, appears on the back wall, while **Durga** features on the *north* wall, and the wise **Agastya** on the *south*. This layout foreshadows that of later Indo-Javanese temples. The fifth group of temples is mainly worthwhile for the **panorama**★★ it affords.

From Bandungan (7km) go to Ambarawa (6km) where you join the road that leads to Yogyakarta.

■ **Ambarawa** – This small town beside a lake at the foot of Mount Merbabu makes for a pleasant stop if you have the time. The **Kereta Api Museum** *(daily, theoretically 8am-5pm, donation)* installed in a vast **disused train station** has all the antiquated charm of old railway museums, right out of the 19C. Fifteen or so **steam locomotives** are exhibited in the open air. Excursions are organised in one of them, on a portion of the line that has been repaired *(see "Making the most of Dieng and Gedong Songo")*.

If you are in the town on the right date, don't miss the colourful **livestock market** that takes place every five days *(Pon, in the Javanese calendar)*. Deals are brisk, and prices for buffaloes, ducks, rams and other sheep are negotiated firmly. If you feel like buying a heifer, remember that they cost around 1.1 million rupiah a head. On the other hand, don't be taken in by the scorpion-based miracle cures extolled loudly by the *dukun* (healers) through their megaphones.

From Ambarawa you can take a direct road to Yogyakarta (100km), or take a slightly longer route via Prambanan, to finish off your temple tour.

Making the most of Dieng and Gedong Songo

COMING AND GOING

For Dieng – From Yogyakarta, take a bus to Magelang (90min), then another one to Wonosobo (90min) where you change again for Dieng (1hr). You cannot do the return trip in one day on public transport. **Rahayu**, Jl Diponegoro, Yogyakarta, ☎ (0274) 56 13 22. Minibuses without air conditioning, but direct to Wonosobo.

For Gedong Songo – From Yogyakarta there are plenty of direct buses to Ambarawa (3hr), then you take a minibus to Bandungan.

Tours and car rental – Numerous agents in Yogyakarta offer one-day tours to Dieng including a trip to Borobudur. If you have the time and the money, hire a car with a driver and visit Gedong Songo, and perhaps Prambanan as well (in which case allow 2 days).

WHERE TO STAY, EATING OUT

• Dieng

Several *losmen* offer very Spartan lodging and rather bland food.

Modest

Bu Djono, Jl Raya (just before reaching the plateau if you are coming from Wonosobo), ☎ (0286) 928 14 – 6rm. ✕ An inexpensive *losmen* that looks like a Swiss chalet, but with questionable comfort and cleanliness (shared showers). The restaurant serves soups and nasi goreng.

Average

Gunung Mas, Jl Raya 42 (on the plateau facing the temples), ☎ (0286) 924 17 – 14rm. ☝ The best *losmen* in Dieng, with

basic facilities. The most comfortable rooms are equipped with a television and have bathrooms with hot water (an appreciable luxury). Extension plans are under way. The mosque situated behind the *losmen* means that you are likely to be woken early in the morning.

• Bandungan

Bandung hill-station 7km from Gedong Songo has several good places to stay.

Modest

Dharma Nirmala, Jl Pandanaran (opposite the Rawa Pening), ☎ (0298) 911 40 – 8rm. ☝ This inexpensive little *losmen* in an old Dutch house has austere (low ceilings) but well-kept rooms. The larger rooms that give onto the street are unfortunately rather noisy.

High end

Rawa Pening, Jl Pandanaran 33, ☎ (0298) 71 14 45, Fax (0298) 71 15 42 – 11rm. ✕ ☝ ☝ ☝ A very pleasant hotel with a vast garden on a hillside. The rooms, in bungalows, are comfortable. Car rental.

OTHER THINGS TO DO

Tour in a steam engine – The **Train Museum in Ambarawa** organises trips ("Kereta Luarbiasa") along an old railway line from Ambarawa to Bedono. Return trip: 40km. Trips can be organised for groups on request. Booking is a must, on ☎ (0298) 910 35.

On the other hand, no bookings are necessary for the electric train ("lori wisata") that does a 5-10km tour.

BOROBUDUR★★★
Central Java Province
42km from Yogyakarta – Map p 272-273

Not to be missed
The bas-reliefs at Borobudur. Candi Mendut.
And remember...
Visit the temple early in the morning and avoid Sundays.

The **mandala** at Borobudur, a jewel of Buddhist art, moves the onlooker as much through the majesty of its architecture as the perfection of its bas-reliefs. This magnificent tropical stupa, older still than the city of Angkor, ranks amongst the finest of the world's architectural masterpieces (and amongst UNESCO's World Heritage sites). But to take in the full grandeur of Borobudur, you have to climb the surrounding hills. From there, lying surrounded by volcanoes stretching as far as the eye can see, in the middle of a plain of palm trees and rice fields, Borobudur appears as a nodal point, a centre of the world on which all energy converges. This enchantment dissipates somewhat as you enter the park, which is too regimented and has been taken over by a swarm of shoddy junk sellers. But the monument's image is restored once you begin looking at the kilometres of bas-reliefs that form an extraordinary stone book open to the elements.

The influence of Buddhism

In spite of the incomparable remains left by its golden age in Java (between 750 and 850), the history of Buddhism in Indonesia is still not well known. The oldest written evidence (414) is an account by a Chinese bonze (Buddhist priest) who made a stopover on Java on his return from a voyage to India. At the time, Buddhism was still in its early stages when compared with Brahmanism. But the situation changed in the 7C and 8C, and the Chinese monk I Ching, who lived in Sumatra between 686 and 691, was full of admiration for the high level of religious studies, although he noted some local peculiarities such as the veneration of serpent deities (*Naga*). In the early 8C the famous Indian guru Vajrabodhi came to Sumatra and Java, where he taught Amoghavajra. Later one of the latter's disciples, Huigo, was to found Shingon Buddhism, which is still practised in Japan and shares undeniable similarities with the Javanese Buddhism of the time.

The mandala kingdom ideal

All the Indo-Javanese kingdoms share a common reference to the Indian concept of the mandala, the fundamental circle representing the universe. On the religious plane – which in turn influenced architecture – mandalas designed on the ground were believed to create a space for prayer and meditation that was safe from evil spirits. The divinities were spread out symmetrically in concentric circles surrounded by a wall. On the political plane, the mandala symbolised the perfect kingdom that had been freed from evil forces. In the centre was the sovereign, who was given the supreme title of "Cakravartin" (He who turns the Wheel), surrounded by circles of officials, who were themselves in the centre of secondary circles. Lastly, on the social plane, the concept seems to have had a strong influence on the layout of villages, with the houses surrounding a central square.

The centre of the world

Although it draws on stupas from northeast India, Candi Borobudur nonetheless has unusual architecture, firstly due to its size, with its sides measuring 123m. The immense quadrilateral has no equivalent on earth.

Looking like a squashed pyramid, it consists of a base on which stand five square terraces, surmounted by three round terraces, which in turn are topped by a huge stupa. No fewer than 1 460 panels of narrative bas-reliefs and 1 222 panels of decorative motifs adorn the sides. These extraordinary stone masterpieces provide us with information on the beliefs and lifestyle of the Javanese of the time. 504 exquisitely beautiful statues of Buddha complete the whole. It is difficult for us to imagine what this would have looked like in its original state when it was all brightly coloured.

As far as its design is concerned, there is no other like Borobudur in the world. Strictly speaking it is not a temple but a **stupa**, as it has no cella containing the image of a god. Designed as a mandala, the monument is a concentric maze that the faithful walk through, following the ten **stages of initiation** along the path to enlightenment. The final stage is *shunyata*, or the experiential understanding of the emptiness of all things, the essence of Buddhist thought. Some historians believe that Borobudur could be the Bhumisambhara mentioned in a text dating from 842, to which was added the suffix *baudhara* ("mountain"), thus becoming "Mountain of the accumulation of Virtue in Stages". Others think that the name is a mixture of Sanskrit and Javanese meaning "Monastery on a Mountain", or a distortion of *Varabuddhapura*, "Sanctuary of the Great Buddha". Be that as it may, Borobudur's location, right in the middle of a volcanic cirque, has not been left to chance, and fulfils the precepts laid down by Indian texts. Indeed, Borobudur stands near Mount Tidar – a highly symbolic volcano – not far from the confluence of the Progo and the Elo, thus recalling the sacred confluence of the Ganges and the Yamuna in India. Furthermore, those who built Borobudur chose an artificial hill on which a terrace once stood, probably built by the ancient Javanese for ancestor worship.

The **building work**, which lasted about 70 years, took place in five stages under the **Sailendra** rulers, between 750 and 850. But the modifications undertaken as building progressed, notably during the emergence of Vajrayana theories, make the symbolism difficult to interpret. For instance, the enormous stupa that once topped the four square terraces was abandoned in favour of the three circular terraces topped by a smaller stupa that can be seen today.

Borobudur, a giant mandala

P Bourseiller/Altitude

Borobudur

In the footsteps of the initiated

Daily, tickets sold 6am-5pm. Site closes at 5.30pm. Allow 2hr.

Before beginning your initiatory journey, have a look at the **base**, which is half hidden by the edifice, and on which stands a large open terrace. It is adorned with 160 **panels of bas-reliefs★** that were unearthed during restoration (a portion is visible in the south-east corner). The frieze illustrates human features and symbolises the law of "Cause and Effect", which determines the reward for the thoughts and actions of humankind in the present life and in those to come. Some historians maintain that the frieze was hidden when the edifice was being modified, as it no longer fulfilled the building's purpose. Others believe that the base was added simply to consolidate the structure. On the four **galleries** above, there are a total of 2.5km of **bas-reliefs★★★** representing the world of forms (*Rupadhatu*), which you can see as you walk round the edifice clockwise. During this initiatory phase, the stupa on the very top is never visible, as the galleries are lined with high balustrades surmounted by little stupas. There are also niches set at regular intervals containing a statue of Buddha in one of his four representations (*Jina*).

The inner wall of the **first gallery** has two superposed series of 120 panels each. The upper one depicts events from the life of Buddha, from his birth to his teachings in Benares (*Lalitavistara*), while the lower one illustrates his earlier lives (*Jataka*). The same theme appears on the balustrade, except in the northeast corner where the former lives of Bodhisattvas are illustrated.

You reach the **second gallery** by means of the eastern steps (reserved for the journey up), where you can see 128 other panels, describing the *Gandawyuha*, one of the most important Buddhist texts, which tells the story of Sudhana and his path to enlightenment. The series ends in the **third gallery**.

The **fourth gallery** has 72 panels describing the *Bhadratjari*, the end of Sudhana's life, when he vows to follow in the footsteps of Bodhisattva Samantabhadra. A host of panels illustrate scenes of daily life depicting the people and the court at the time of the Sailendras.

On the fifth level with its balustrade you come out onto a **plateau** with a **panoramic view★** of the valley, contrasting sharply with the lower galleries. Indeed, at this stage, the faithful have learned enough about the world to be able to contemplate it. Moreover, this is the main occupation of the 72 meditating stone **Buddhas★★** in their little openwork stupas that stud the three **circular terraces**. The large **central stupa** crowning the mandala is empty, probably to lighten the structure.

As you leave the mandala, take a look at the **Borobudur Museum** (at its foot), which houses a collection of photos showing how the site was renovated. The site was first described by Sir Thomas Stamford Raffles in 1817. The vegetation covering it was first cleared, and then, in the early 20C, the Dutchman Theo Van Erp began to restore it. But the mandala still threatened to collapse on account of all the water that had seeped in, and so, from 1975 to 1984, UNESCO headed an extremely ambitious project, which has enabled the site to regain its former splendour. More than 1 million blocks were moved one by one, and then the mandala was reinforced by invisible concrete foundations and given a new drainage system.

Around Borobodur

As you approach Borobudur coming from Yogyakarta, there are two small temples near the site (*1km to the east*). **Candi Pawon**, which may have served as an antechamber for pilgrims, has a square base topped by a pyramidal roof providing support for tiers of stupas. Inside there are some fine **bas-reliefs** of female figures and *kalpataru*, trees dripping with jewels and surrounded by pots of silver, where people would make a wish.

Candi Mendut** was built by King Indra in 800, and is shaped like a cube (its roof, which no doubt would have been a stupa, was never finished). The balustrades on the steps and the outer walls are decorated with bas-reliefs and Bodhisattvas. But Candi Mendut's main interest lies in its three **statues***** (3m high) that sit impressively inside, no doubt the most beautiful that can be seen *in situ* on Java. Sitting with his legs in front of him, Buddha is flanked on his right by Bodhisattva Avalokitesvara, and on his left by the repentant demon Vajrapani. The feet of the statues have been rubbed smooth by the hands of the devout.

Making the most of Borobudur

COMING AND GOING

By bus and minibus – The **new terminus** north of Yogyakarta (beyond the intersection of Jl Magelang and the Ring Road) serves Borobudur terminus, 15min from the site (frequent departures between 5am and 5pm, 90min).

From **Umbulharjo terminus** in Yogyakarta, either take a bus direct, or one for Magelang and change at Muntilan.

Travel agencies – The simplest way of visiting Borobudur is to go through an agent (see "Making the most of Yogyakarta" p 287).

Taxi – A worthwhile solution is to hire a taxi for the trip with 3 or 4 people (see "Making the most of Yogyakarta" p 287).

Bicycle and car rental – (see "Making the most of Yogyakarta" p 287).

GETTING AROUND

Becak – This is convenient but not absolutely necessary for getting to the temple terminus or for visiting Candi Pawon and Candi Mendut.

Bicycle rental – Enquire at the *losmen*.

ADDRESS BOOK

Post office/Telephone – **Main post office**, Jl Pramudyawardani 10. **Wartel**, Jl Pramudyawardani.

WHERE TO STAY, EATING OUT

● **Borobudur**
Modest
Homestay Rajasa, Jl Badrawati 2, ☎ (0293) 882 76 – A small, simple comfortable and very friendly *losmen*.
Lotus Guesthouse, Jl Medang Kamulan 2, ☎ (0293) 882 81 (1km north of the entrance) – ☏ Same category as the above. Hires out bikes.
Saraswati, Jl Balaputradewa 10 (7am-7pm). Located east of the site, this restau-

rant-*losmen* with a terrace is the ideal place for a rest after the tour. It is run by Ibu Sri, who has seen generations of archeologists and tourists passing through. Simple, decent Indonesian cooking.
Super deluxe
Amanjiwo, Majaksingi, in the hills 3km from the temple, ☎ (0293) 883 33, Fax (0293) 883 55 – 35rm ☏ 📧 📠 ✕ ☒ 📺 It is worth making a trip to this new, extremely luxurious hotel just for the splendid panoramic view of Borobudur lying below. The suites, which are arranged in a semicircle around the central building shaped like a stupa, decorated with precious wood and some even have private swimming pools! The service is impeccable, but the prices, even for a simple coffee, are exorbitant.

● **Magelang**
Luxury
Hotel Puri Asri, Jl Cempaka 9, ☎ (0293) 641 14, Fax (0293) 644 00 – 100rm. ☏ 📠 📺 ✕ ☒ 📺 The hotel is comfortable but lacks charm (some rooms have air conditioning), although it stands in a pleasant setting on a hillside with a superb view of Sumbing volcano.

OTHER THINGS TO DO

Festivals – **Waicak** (May), a festival celebrating the birth and death of Buddha. A procession of bonzes goes from Candi Mendut to Candi Borobudur.
Borobudur festival (May). 5 days of parades, local arts and crafts, music and wayang kulit.
Outdoor pursuits – The Puri Asri hotel organises **rafting** trips (see "Making the most of Yogyakarta" p 287).
Local arts and crafts – On the main road between Muntilan and Yogyakarta craftsmen offer to make reproductions of the statues at Borobudur.

Making the most of Borobudur

PRAMBANAN★★★

Central Java and DKI Yogyakarta Provinces
17km from Yogyakarta – Map p 272-273

Not to be missed
The following candis: Loro Jonggrang, Sewu, Plaosan, Kalasan and Sari.
An evening performance of the Ramayana.

And remember...
Take a torch to see the inside of the temples.
Tour the sites in the morning.

Prambanan, a small village in the fertile Javanese countryside, has given its name to the largest concentration of Hindu-Buddhist temples in Indonesia. The tall outlines of Candi Prambanan, jewels of Indo-Javanese art, are a hymn to the gods of India, and figure among the masterpieces on UNESCO's World Heritage list. However, while these temples are the most famous, they form only a small part of a gigantic complex of 218 sanctuaries. Archeologists dream of making more discoveries like the one made by the peasant who inadvertently struck the roof of a temple buried beneath the ashes of Merapi with his pickaxe, or again the one by road workers who, in 1990, 5km from Prambanan, unearthed a fabulous treasure weighing 36kg, full of jewels and ritual objects made of gold and silver.

The "candi", mountain-temple

Born of the fertile rivalry (and later cohabitation) between the two great Javanese kingdoms of the classical period (8C-10C) – the Hindu **Sanjayas** and the Buddhist **Sailendras** – the Prambanan temples illustrate Indo-Javanese art at its peak. The *candi* were often built to the glory of a deceased monarch and are closely connected with death although they are not burial places. They are the earthly manifestation of a female divinity with whom the king was believed to merge in the afterlife, while in the cella, a statue indicated the presence of the monarch to pilgrims.

Even before the introduction of Indian religions, very ancient Javanese inscriptions refer to mountain-temples, which are right at the heart of the Hindu-Buddhist mythology. Mount **Meru**, the cosmic mountain in the centre of the universe, indicates the axis along which the world lies. Its base reaches right down to the bowels of the earth and its summit touches the highest heavens. It is with this symbolism in mind that the Prambanan temples should be observed.

Symbolic architecture

The temple base, bhurloka, the level of mortals, is covered in floral and geometric motifs. The atmosphere changes on the second level, bhuvarloka, the seat of purified beings where the faithful come into contact with the divinity, thanks to incantations by priests. Diverse bas-reliefs adorn the walls, including kala-makara, a combination of monstrous figures. "Kala", a legendary demon with protruding eyes and generally shown without a lower jaw (which is meant to be underground), stands atop doors and niches, while "makara", a chimaera with an elephant's trunk, a lion's mane, a parrot's beak and the tail of a fish, forms the handrail of the stairs leading to the cella. Lastly, the pyramidal roof features the world of the gods (svarloka). It is decorated with gandharva and vidyadhara, celestial creatures floating amongst "naga" (serpents) and lotus leaves. A small chamber beneath the cella still houses the peripih, a receptacle for the symbols of the material world, such as gold, silver, bronze and seeds.

Candi Prambanan★★★
(Loro Jonggrang)
The complex rises in the middle of a large well-kept park. Daily, 6am-5.15pm; fee.
Allow at least 2hr.

The complex, which can be seen from the road, is without doubt the finest and largest Hindu sanctuary ever built in Indonesia. Candi Prambanan was completed in 856, marking the Sailendras' return to glory with the reign of Rakai Pikata. Largely destroyed by an earthquake in the 16C, the complex has been patiently restored, work that began at the time of the Dutch.

The different temples stand on a vast quadrilateral divided into three concentric courtyards. Surrounded by a wall, the first is in fact a kind of no man's land without any buildings, while the second has a host of **small Perwara shrines** (a total of 224), standing in a chaotic mass of ruins out of which emerge here and there the odd restored miniature structure. Lastly, standing in the centre is the most sacred courtyard with the main temples dedicated to the Trimurti trinity. On either side of Candi Siva, the tallest and the holiest, are Candi Brahma (*south*) and Candi Vishnu (*north*). Each has a secondary temple opposite, a **vehicle temple**, which contains the *vahana*, the steed of the god.

There are also two annexe temples or **Candi Apits** on the site, whose function is not known. The enclosure wall itself is punctuated by little guardian temples: four **Kelir** temples stand at the gates and there are four **Sudut** temples in the corners.

Candi Siva★★★

The mountain-temple of Siva, a real technical feat, consists of stone blocks weighing 600kg, the highest of which are perched 20m from the ground. The building is 47m high, and forms a quadrilateral with sides measuring 30m. It is topped by a pyramidal roof on six levels, bristling with a host of little ribbed **stupas**.

Each façade is flanked by a **portico staircase** with a ramp featuring *makara* (*see sidebar on previous page*). This leads to a separate cella, a small chapel guarded at the entrance by a *kala* (only the east cella serves as a vestibule by communicating with the central cella, which is hidden in the heart of the building).

Each chapel contains a **statue★★★**, all of them masterpieces of Indo-Javanese art. In the central cella a majestic Siva stands meditating, gazing towards the east. The north cella features the goddess Durga, who is also known as Loro Jonggrang ("frail virgin"), a

The princess with a heart of stone
Bandung Bondowoso, King Boko's son, loved Princess Loro Jonggrang, who did not in the least return his feelings. But as luck would have it, the fact that King Boko conquered her father meant that the young woman was forced to agree to the marriage. However, she agreed on the condition that Bandung build a thousand temples in her honour in a single night. The prince called upon all the genii that the world could muster, and they set to work energetically. But while they were tackling the last structure, the princess – a bad loser – woke all her servants and ordered them to sow grains of rice everywhere. Delighted with the prospect of breakfast so early, the cocks broke into a crowing session, and the genii, no doubt a little hazy with fatigue, thought that dawn had come and so downed tools without having finished their work. Sorely grieved that he had been duped, Bandung nonetheless showed the young woman that he too could play little tricks and turned her into a statue. Since then, Loro Jonggrang has been brooding over her fate in a cella in Siva's temple, fixed forever with Durga's face.

young beauty after whom the site is named. The west cella contains elephant-headed Ganesh, while the wise man, Agastya occupies the south cella. Although the figures belong to the Indian pantheon, the way they are presented here is unique to Java.

Apart from admiring the statues, take the time to look at the detail in the **outside decoration***. Walk round the open gallery that runs round the temple. Its parapet is punctuated by 24 panels of **bas-reliefs*** that tell the story of the *Ramayana* epic (begin in the east and continue clockwise). The energy of the scenes and the delicacy of the features have filled generations

of archeologists and visitors with admiration. There are other superb bas-reliefs on the walls, depicting the god Dewa Lokapala, the guardian of the cardinal points.

Note also on the base of the edifice, the lions in medallions surrounded by *kalpatura* (celestial trees) and the *kinara* (a creature that is half man half singing bird), all motifs characteristic of what is known as the Prambanan style. Above, **gargoyles**, **ribbed stupas** and bas-reliefs illustrating Siva's dance complete the picture in a magnificent profusion of detail.

Candi Brahma and Candi Vishnu**

The interrupted story of the *Ramayana* – when Rama arrives in Lengka to do battle with Rawana – continues on the **bas-reliefs*** of Candi Brahma (*south*). The temple is smaller than Candi Siva, consisting only of a single cella with a **statue of Brahma**** with four heads, which is unfortunately damaged. The extent of the worship of the god is a Javanese peculiarity when compared with what happens in India, where there are few temples dedicated to Brahma.

The temple's twin brother, Candi Vishnu (*north*) also only consists of a single cella, with a **statue of Vishnu*** with four arms. Splendid **bas-reliefs*** telling the story of *Kresnayana* (the incarnation of Vishnu as Krishna) run along the outside walls.

Of the three vehicle temples (*vahana*), only **Candi Nandi** (*opposite Candi Siva*) has kept its statue, a magnificent **sacred bull***. The sacred goose of **Candi Angsa** (*opposite Candi Brahma*) and the mythical bird of **Candi Garuda** (*opposite Candi Vishnu*) have, alas, disappeared.

The Buddhist temples in the North Group**

1km on foot from Loro Jonggrang (Prambanan). Allow 2hr, fee.

■ **Candi Sewu**** – Known in ancient times as Manjusirirgrha, Candi Sewu ("a thousand temples") was built between 778 and 810 under the aegis of the Sailendras. The complex has recently been renovated, and is Indonesia's second largest Buddhist sanctuary after Borobudur.

B Wassman/Rapho

Prambanan, among the ruins of Candi Sewu

Four rows of 60 **minor shrines** (240 in all) topped by stupas cluster round the main temple, a building 30m high that is accompanied by eight annexe temples or **Candi Apits**. Crowned by a large central stupa, the main building follows the strict conventions of Vedic ritual (the foundations rest on a stone mandala), but its design shows a certain amount of stylistic freedom – due to the Sailendras – when compared with the Indian archetype. Its original square shape was modified in the 790s in favour of a cruciform plan with four side chapels to comply with the increasing influence of the Jina cult, the Buddha of the cardinal points. Four powerful **raksasas** armed with clubs guard the gates of the temple from evil spirits, while leading off from a partially covered inner gallery are five cellas (the one in the east opens onto the central cella).

Continue on foot through the rice fields and sugar cane plantations to Candi Plaosan, the site's easternmost temple, 2km from Candi Prambanan.

■ **Candi Plaosan**** – Building probably began in 835. This superb complex (*restored*) celebrated the marriage of a Buddhist Sailendra princess with a Hindu Sanjaya king, a union that was to herald a fascinating mixture of architectural features borrowed from the two religions.

Of the original complex comprising three large temples, there remains a **twin temple****, composed of two massive rectangular buildings separated by a low wall. No fewer than 116 **stupas** and 58 **shrines** (partly renovated) cluster round the twins in their sacred setting. All that remains of the third temple, made of wood, which stood to the north, is a stone base, while its matching temple to the south has completely disappeared.

Within their thick stone walls the temples each had three cells, dimly lit by small openings. The monks lived on the upper storey where the wooden floor has not survived. Each cella contains two **Bodhisattvas***, before which pilgrims would gather. When the pilgrims sat on the ground their eyes were level with the feet of the statues, the only divine figures accessible to man. A bronze Buddha (since disappeared) once

Prambanan

accompanied the two sculptures, and was slightly removed from human gaze, sitting on a raised platform. In the half-light it is quite difficult to see the **bas-reliefs★** that cover the walls, depicting the faithful at prayer. You will have more luck with the decoration on the outer walls, where there are finely-executed female **dancers★★** as well as terrifying **raksasas** responsible for chasing away evil spirits. The **kala** here are shown with a lower jaw, which is very rare.

Ratu Boko, a mysterious city★
(The South Group)

2km from Candi Prambanan. A flight of steps leads to the car park and to the entrance.
Open daily, 6.30am-5.30pm, fee.
Allow 1hr for Ratu Boko itself.

From Prambanan, walk to the hill that rises on the other side of the road, the site of some little-visited remains. The place nonetheless preserves a rare example of civil architecture dating from the classical period (8C and 9C). The city of Ratu Boko, built on a succession of small terraces on the hillside at an altitude of 200m, stretches over 16ha, enjoying a superb **panoramic view★★** of Prambanan and Merapi volcano. But is the place really a city? Strangely, this palatine group still remains much of a mystery. While some archeologists think it is the ancient capital of the Sanjayas (the position was easy to defend), others believe it was a monastery or a place for relaxation.

Once through the **Gapura**, a double ceremonial entrance comprising a **triple portico** followed by a **quintuple portico** made of stone, you come onto a vast raised platform dotted with stones. On the left you see the **incinerating temple**, a double square terrace with sides measuring 26m long and 3m high. A **well**, final resting-place for departed souls, once opened up in the middle. At the other end of the platform once stood the **paseban**, the former reception hall *(currently being restored)*, where you can still see a stone base and some ruins.

Beyond, near a hamlet of bamboo houses, are some of Ratu Boko's most interesting remains. They recall the *kraton* buildings that the sultans of Yogyakarta were to build almost a thousand years later. Holes in the paving of a **pendopo★** (20m by 20m), a pavilion that served as an audience chamber, have been left by the pillars that once supported a wooden roof. The pendopo extends onto the terrace of a **pringgitan**, which is not as wide. A wall *(renovated)* surrounds the two terraces, and is lined with a host of **miniature stupas.** Just southeast of the enclosure are three **miniature temples**.

Below, the **pools★** carved out of the rock may have been used for the princes' ablutions. There is also a large **Keputren** pool ("women's quarters"), at the eastern end of the site.

If you have the time and a vehicle, other temples are worth a trip:

Other small temples of the area

Nestled at the foot of the hill *(1.5km south of Ratu Boko)* is **Candi Banyunibo★** (9C), a small elegant Buddhist temple that has just been restored. It stands on a square base topped by a **stupa**, in beautiful natural surroundings. The many small openings that pierce the walls provide the inside with an unusual amount of light. Unfortunately, the **bas-reliefs** there have been heavily damaged.

In the hills south of Ratu Boko you can also see **Candi Barong**, a shrine comprising two charming little temples preceded by a terrace, currently being restored.

Lastly, further south, lost in the middle of stones and scrub, is **Candi Ijo**. This has very few visitors, apart from archeologists *(excavations under way)*, but is worth going to just for the **view★★** of the plain.

The West Group

Allow 90min.

■ **Candi Kalasan★** – A string of temples stretches out between Yogyakarta and Prambanan and remains little visited by tourists. On the main road, near Kalasan village is one of the oldest Buddhist temples in Indonesia (dating from 778, although what you see today is believed to date from the 10C). It is dedicated to Tara, a female stellar divinity in Tantric Buddhism. The temple has been partly restored and has a square plan with four additional porches giving it a cruciform appearance. Its high walls are surmounted by a complex roof, the whole ensemble bristling with **stupas**. Niches piercing the façades are surrounded by double *kala-makara* figures. But Candi Kalasan's stylistic originality lies mainly in the **kala★★** over the main doorway, surrounded by floral motifs with lions and *gandharvas* (celestial musicians).

Continue on foot to the next temple (200m to the north), standing in tropical vegetation.

■ **Candi Sari★★** – Although it is a contemporary of Candi Kalasan, this temple is radically different in style. It is a fine building in three parts, raised on a high base and topped by **stupas**, recalling Candi Plaosan. Like the latter, it was built on two levels but the wooden floor has since disappeared. On the façade pierced with openings stand superb **Buddhist divinities★★**. They are unusual on account of their height (2m), elongated limbs, and especially the graceful sway of their hips that is typically Indian. Unfortunately, nothing remains of the main doorway or of the statues inside.

12.5km along the main road, turn northwards and continue for 2km.

■ **Candi Sambisari★** – In 1966 a peasant discovered Candi Sambisari lying under a carpet of volcanic ash 6m thick, but it was not unearthed until 1996. It is probably one of the last Sivaite shrines built by the Sanjayas (10C). The pillars on the terrace are thought to have supported a wide wooden roof. The temple is remarkably well preserved and still has its **linga★** as well as elegant **statues★** of Durga, Ganesh and Angsa, which adorn the niches in the upper gallery.

Making the most of Prambanan

COMING AND GOING

By bus – From Yogyakarta there are frequent departures from the **Umbulharjo** terminus (30min).

By minibus – Bemos can be caught at the **Terban terminus** in Yogyakarta.

Travel agencies – All Yogyakarta's travel agencies organise trips to Prambanan, with or without guides.

Car, motorbike and bicycle rental – If you have your own means of transport you can visit the more isolated temples (see p 287 "Making the most of Yogyakarta").

OTHER THINGS TO DO

Live show – Prambanan puts on one of the finest *Ramayana* performances to be seen, the **Sendratari**. The show takes place in a vast open-air amphitheatre laid out on the site, recalling the architecture of the temples. There are choirs, two enormous gamelan orchestras, and Candi Prambanan in the background. Not to mention the atmosphere, with the Indonesians, who, while they know the story by heart, always form a large part of the audience and approve or disapprove every new development in the plot! From May to October, 7.30-9.30pm. Book through a travel agent. The rest of the year the performance takes place in the adjoining Trimurti Theatre.

Ceremonies – *Tawur Agung* (March, in Prambanan). The major Hindu purification ceremony held on the eve of Hary Raya Nyepi is marked by recitals of the sacred Veda texts and a gamelan concert.

SOLO★
(SURAKARTA)
Central Java Province
65km from Yogyakarta – Map p 272-273
Pop 600 000 – Alt 80m – Hot climate

Not to be missed
Buying batiks in Pasar Klewer.
Visiting the Sukuh and Ceto temples on Mount Lawu.
And remember...
Plan to visit the kratons and the museum in the morning (closed in the afternoon).
Hire a bicycle to get around the town and its environs.

Solo is surrounded by no fewer than three volcanoes whose threatening outlines can be seen through the distant mist. Merapi and Merbabu stand to the west, while Lawu rises to the east reaching a height of 3 265m. The town has a peaceful atmosphere which contrasts sharply with the agitation of its neighbour, Yogyakarta. While it is the cradle of Javanese artistic tradition, which it perpetuates through its **batiks**, and its performances of dance, *wayang orang* and *wayang kulit*, Solo also has a commercial calling that is evident in the market and along the very busy Jalan Gatot Subroto. From Solo you can escape by bike *(enquire at hotels)* into the serene countryside with its rice fields. Further away, on the slopes of Lawu, you can make a trip to see Sukuh and Ceto temples, impressive testimonies to late Javanese Hinduism, or head for **Sangiran** *(15km north of Solo)* to follow in the footsteps of **"Java Man"**, one of the oldest hominids in Asia *(see sidebar, p 29)*.

A city with two princes
The kings of Mataram – the last great Javanese kingdom – had built their capital in Kartasura but when the town was sacked by the Dutch in 1742, Pakubunowo II decided to move his court to a nearby village, Solo, which he renamed Surakarta. However, eight years later his successor had to deal with two dissident uncles. This power struggle, which suited the Dutch, lead to the partition of the Mataram kingdom in 1755. Half went to one of the uncles, Mangkubumi, who founded Yogyakarta, while the other half was divided between the *Sunan* (prince) and his vassal Mangkunegara, who both stayed in Solo. A period of prosperity then opened up for the town, whose population grew dramatically, but this was brutally interrupted in 1825 by the Java War *(see p 37 and 201)*. The early 20C saw the founding in Solo of Indonesia's first nationalist organisations. But during independence the *Sunan* was accused of having collaborated with the Dutch, stripped of all official function and no longer played any role at all in the new republic.

Tour of the town
Allow a morning to visit the two palaces and the museum, which close at 1pm.

Jalan Slamet Riyadi, a wide avenue beside which runs a railway line, crosses the town from east to west, separating the two *kratons* with a stream of shops, restaurants and hotels. A great many buildings were damaged (almost 250!) or destroyed during the riots in May 1998, and the district has not yet recovered its usual bustle. On Saturday evenings, however, youths once again converge on Jalan Dahlan to show off their gleaming scooters with their fake leopard skin adornments.

Central Java

Head south from Jalan Slamet Riyadi to **Alun-alun Lor** (C3), a vast quadrilateral full of weeds on which stand two majestic banyan trees planted by the sultan in 1745. The north side of the square is full of stamp collectors and people selling glasses, while the central strip of ground is used for festivities or spontaneous football matches. On the west side is the **Grand Mosque** (Mesjid Ageng) (C3), which belongs to the *kraton* and is recognisable by its **three-tiered roof** (1750) *(non-Muslims are not allowed in)*. A little further along you will see a large two-storey concrete building, the **Pasar Klewer★** (C3), Solo's textile market *(9am-5pm)*. This is the place to buy clothes and batiks. Take your time as you wander through the maze of stalls. The saleswomen, who constantly shout out to one another and have their meals served on the spot so as not to miss any customers, are sure to call you over to show you the most beautiful Solo batiks, with their predominant browns and yellows.

Surakarta Hadiningrat Kraton★ (Kasunanan) (C3)
Note that only a small part may be visited as many of the buildings are being renovated.

The *kraton*, a city within a city, is a quarter in its own right, protected by high white walls. Several thousand people live here, attached to the royal family. The complex was inaugurated in 1745 when Solo was founded, and like all *kratons* was designed

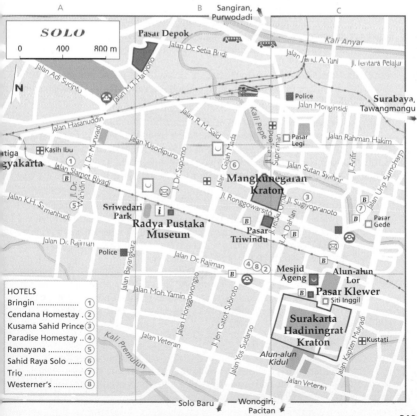

HOTELS
Bringin .... ①
Cendana Homestay . ②
Kusama Sahid Prince ③
Paradise Homestay .. ④
Ramayana .... ⑤
Sahid Raya Solo ...... ⑥
Trio .... ⑦
Westerner's .... ⑧

according to the precepts of Javanese cosmology *(see p 278)*. Legend also has it that the site was chosen by Loro Kidul, the Queen of the South Seas and protectress of the sovereign. The inhabitants of Solo are convinced that the fire that devastated the place in 1985 was punishment for a breach of the rules by *Sunan* Pakubuwono XII, who was more interested in business than in tradition. The *Sunan* has been in power (on an honorary basis) since 1945, and still lives in the private part of the palace.

The north part of the *kraton* is occupied by the **Pagelaran**, a pavilion formerly used for public audience, and the **Siti Inggil**, the coronation room *(both being renovated)*. To the south is the palace itself (700m x 500m), home to the *Sunan* and his 600 servants (access through the museum on the east side).

You enter the *kraton* through the **East Gate** *(south of Alun-alun Lor, head left following the balustrades)*. This opens onto a courtyard and the **Swaka Budaya Museum** *(8am-2pm; closed Friday. Fee. Allow 45min)*. Although they are somewhat dusty the collections are nonetheless full of interest. Apart from puppets, gongs, and *wayang* masks, you can see sculptures and gargoyles from the temples at Prambanan and Dieng, a collection of old photos dating from the time of Dutch colonisation, and some remarkable **royal carriages***.

On leaving the museum you come to the main courtyard in the complex, a sea of black sand planted with tall trees, from which emanates a deep feeling of peace. In the middle stands an imposing **pendopo** paved with marble, restored after the fire in 1985 to its original state following the design by Pakubuwono X. Standing beside it like a lighthouse is a tall **tower*** (Panggung Songgo Buwono) (1782). Every year the *Sunan* shuts himself off on its top floor to have a private meeting with the Queen of the South Seas.

The **Dalem**, the sultan's private quarters, are closed to the public but you can walk round the enclosure to admire the superb **finely carved gateway*** that closes off Alun-alun Kidul, the square to the south of the *kraton*.

Mangkunegaran Kraton* (B2-C2)

8.30am-2pm, 1pm on Sunday. Fee. Allow 30min. Solo's second palace is in fact a baronial hall *(pura)* and not a *kraton*. It was built in 1757 after the Mataram kingdom was partitioned, and is now the home of Prince Mangkunegara IX and his family. Apart from the collections, the tranquil atmosphere that pervades the place makes it a very pleasant visit.

In the middle of the courtyard – a vast square of lawn surrounded by a gallery lined with white pillars – stands an immense **pendopo*** (3 270sqm) that was for many years the largest in Java. Four gamelans are housed here, of which the oldest *(on the left)* was made in Demak in the 16C. Just behind is the **Pringgitan**, the official reception hall, decorated with portraits of the various *Sunans*.

You then enter the first room of the **Dalem**, which contains the **princes' collections****. Among the displays are jewellery, chastity belts for men and women, crockery, ivory globes, sabres, kris daggers and water glasses. The alcove at the back contains a bed on which rice is placed twice a week as an offering to Dewi Sri, the goddess of rice.

Around Mangkunegaran

Just beside *Pura Mangkunegaran*, as you head back towards Jalan Slamet Riyadi, there is a very small flea market, **Pasar Triwindu** (B2) *(Jl Diponegoro; 9am-4pm)*, which is worth a look. Among the odds and ends are statues, puppets, bronzes, old batiks, masks, porcelain, jewellery, etc (but watch out for copies).

Further west in an elegant colonial house with white walls and wooden ceilings, the **Radya Pustaka Museum*** (B2) *(8am-1pm, 11am Friday and Saturday; closed Monday. Fee. Allow 30min)* has an outstanding collection of **objets d'art and craft items from Central Java**. There are puppets, masks, kris daggers inlaid with ivory and precious stones, porcelain, crockery, weapons, gamelans, head-dresses, monstrous prows of royal ships, as well as beautiful **Hindu statues**.

On leaving the museum and turning left, you come to the **Sriwedari Amusement Park** (B2), a favourite spot for Solo's citizens in the evenings.

Bat stew

The Chinese are very fond of the creatures' flesh and the supposed aphrodisiac and therapeutic virtues of their organs. The flying mammals are caught in the forests of Sulawesi, where huge numbers of them live. Hunting them at nightfall is the privilege of the children. They trap them with kites armed with hooks on which the creatures get caught. Once captured, the bats are put live into large wickerwork baskets and sent to the markets in large towns where the Chinese (from Indonesia and China) come to choose them, unfolding their dark wings in broad daylight like fans. It is a lucrative market, as bats are expensive commodities. But if the trade grows it will place the bat population under increased threat, and the creatures are essential to maintain the ecological balance of the forest.

The bird market in Solo

R Marc

Solo

Apart from the inevitable bumper cars, there are souvenir shops, a *wayang* theatre and a cinema, as well as *lesehan* eateries open 24hr a day, where local groups perform (*see "Making the most of Solo"*).

If you have the time, take a *becak* to the **Bird Market** (Pasar Depok) (B1) (*at the end of Jl R M Said*), in the northwest of the town. This makes for a pleasant stroll and will give you the opportunity to understand the passion that Indonesians have for birds, from the fighting cocks that are sold secretly, to budgerigars and superb cockatoos. Keep an eye out also for bats, for sale!

On the slopes of Mount Lawu★★
30km east of Solo. A day's excursion.

Lawu volcano rises east of Solo, its dark green velvet slopes layered into tea plantations, rice fields and clumps of forest. Two little-known Hindu temples, hidden in this wild landscape, form romantic sites that are infused with a serenity and spirituality that are quite entrancing.

If you are travelling by car or motorbike, head east from Solo towards Wonogir. After 30km, in Karangpandan, turn left and continue for another 8km. Allow 1hr travelling time in all, as the last kilometres are on very steep terrain. If you are travelling by bus, take one for Tawangmangu. Get off at Karangpandan and then take a minibus (irregular service).

Magnificent **Candi Sukuh**★★ (around 1416-59), perched at an altitude of 900m, consists of three superposed terraces dominated by a **pyramid** that was once topped by a linga. From here, the **panoramic view**★★ of the forest and tea plantations is superb. The shrine was Central Java's last Hindu bastion in the face of the spread of Islam. It was devoted to the cult of a mysterious hero, thus making a break with Sivaite orthodoxy. This has been expressed through original images and symbols, including phallic figures and large tables in the shape of turtles, which may indicate the existence of initiatory or orgiastic rituals. There are also **bas-reliefs** on the outside of Bima and Sadewa, heroes of the Indian Mahabharata, set in purely Javanese episodes. A little further up at a height of 1 200m, **Candi Ceto**★★ appears like a mirage in the middle of the plants and the mist (*7km north of Sukuh, via Ngargoyoso*). It is a contemporary of Candi Sukuh (around 1468-75), and is dedicated to the same cult. On the other hand, its **seven terraces** recall the organisation of Balinese temples. The faithful still gather here, and while it was being restored wooden pavilions were added on the initiative of Suharto, who, it is said, liked to come here.

From the Sukuh temple you can go to **Tawangmangu waterfall**★, which rises in the middle of a forest reserve. It measures 40m, and feeds several **pools**, which make for a delightful swim. You can get here by car – the road through the rice fields is very pretty – but it is best to walk to drink in the atmosphere and the beautiful scenery (*2hr30min for the outward journey. Take a guide, as it is not easy to find your way*).

Central Java

Making the most of Solo

COMING AND GOING

By plane – Adi Sumarmo interna-tional airport is 10km northwest of the town. To get there, taxi is the easiest means of transport as there are no direct buses. Links with all the major towns on Java, Sumatra and Bali. **Silk Air** serves Singapore.

By train – Balapan station is in the north of the town (Jl Monginsidi) (B1). Frequent departures for Yogyakarta on the "Prambanan Express", which is convenient and fast (1hr). Several trains a day for Jakarta. "Argolawu" is the most comfortable and the fastest (7hr); "Senja Utama" (10hr) has air conditioning in "eksekutif" class. "Bima" and "Jayabaya" go from Surabaya to Jakarta via Solo. Lastly, "Argopuro" links Solo to Surabaya in 9hr.

By bus – Tirtonadi terminus is north of the station (Jl Jend A Yani) (B1). Most companies have their agencies in Jl Sutan Syahrir or Jl Urip Sumoharjo. Price depends on comfort (air conditioning, toilets, video) and speed. For night buses it is best to book. Approximate travelling times: Jakarta 12hr; Semarang 2hr30min; Yogyakarta 2hr; Surabaya 6hr.

By bemo – The terminus is just east of the bus station in Jl Jend A Yani (B1-C1). Bemos are convenient and comfortable for average distances.

GETTING AROUND

As distances between the different places of interest are fairly short, it is best to get around by becak, bicycle, or even on foot

By bike – Rental in the losmen.

By becak – More of them (but they have less decoration) than in Yogyakarta. Negotiate prices.

By cart – This is an ordinary form of transport and not a tourist attraction. Try it!

By taxi – The main rank is in Jl B J Slamet Riyadi, near the station in the town centre. Be warned, drivers are sometimes reluctant to switch on their meters.

By motorbike – Another pleasant and unusual way of visiting Solo and its environs (but be very careful on the main roads). Enquire at the losmen.

By car – You can hire a taxi with driver for the day from large hotels, travel agents or **PT Solo Central Taxi**, Jl Adisucipto 78 (A1), ☎ (0271) 71 94 10 and 71 56 78.

ADDRESS BOOK

Tourist information – Jl B J Slamet Riyadi 275 (B2), ☎ (0271) 71 14 35, Monday-Saturday, 8am-5pm.

Bank/Currency exchange – Plenty of banks (8am-2pm) and **ATMs** in Jl B J Slamet Riyadi (A2-B2-C2).
Bank Danamon, Jl Gatot Subroto 91F (B2-B3). Accepts travellers' cheques in US dollars.
Bank Central Asia, Jl B J Slamet Riyadi 3 (C2). Travellers' cheques accepted.

Post office/Telephone – Main post office, Jl Jend Sudirman 7 (C2). Monday-Friday 8am-4pm, Saturday 8am-1pm. **Telkom**, Jl Mayor Kusmanto (C2), 24hr a day, near the main post office. **Wartel** can be found everywhere, particularly in Jl B J Slamet Riyadi.

Internet – Solo Net, Jl Arifin 129 (C2), ☎ (0271) 478 78. **C 21**, Puja Sari (B2), an "Internet warung" near the Sriwedari Park(B2).

Airline companies – Bouraq, Jl Gajah Mada 86 (B2), ☎ (0271) 63 43 76.
Garuda and **Merpati**, Lippo Bank, Jl B J Slamet Riyadi 328 (B2), ☎ (0271) 449 55.
Silk Air, Bank Central Asia, 3rd floor, Jl B J Slamet Riyadi (C2), ☎ and Fax (0271) 413 69.

WHERE TO STAY

Solo has a vast choice of hotels ranging from the smartest (Sahid, Sheraton and Novotel) to family-run losmen. You will find cheap hotels in Jl Gatot Subroto and Jl Yos Sudarso. Average and high end places are concentrated around Jl B J Slamet Riyadi.

Modest
Westerner's, Kemlayan Kidul 11, an alleyway opposite the Matahari in Jl Gatot Subroto, ☎ (0271) 63 31 06 – 12rm. ⌧ Rustic but cheap, with the advantage of being central. Pak Mawardi has seen generations of travellers passing through. He

offers bike tours in the country with his guide Santoso. You can make bus and tour reservations here. **Paradise Homestay & Guesthouse**, Gang Kidul I/3, beside the one above, ☎(0271) 529 60 – 32rm. ✈ A former colonial dwelling with old-fashioned charm. The service is average, but the rooms are clean and comfortable. Hire of bikes and motorbikes, and reservation of tours. The rooms in the guesthouse have private bathrooms and air conditioning.

Cendana Homestay, Gang Empu Panuluh III/4, a stone's throw from the entry above, ☎ (0271) 578 21 – 14rm. ✈ Family welcome, and many services offered. Some rooms have their own shower.

Average to high end

Trio, Jl Urip Sumoharjo 25, ☎ (0271) 63 28 47 – 40rm. ✎ ✈ North of Pasar Gede, in a Dutch house with an elegant façade dating from 1932. Local clientele. Basic but very clean. The "presidential" rooms have double beds, television and hot water.

Ramayana, Jl Dr Wahidin 22, ☎ (0271) 71 28 14 – 10rm. ✎ ✈ A villa with very attractive architecture and a little garden full of superb birds. The place is quiet, and the decoration sober and elegant. Let's hope that the extensions planned will not spoil it.

Bringin, Jl B J Slamet Riyadi 392, ☎ (0271) 72 62 32, Fax (0271) 71 53 43 – 28rm. ✎ 🖹 🖉 TV CC A comfortable motel with an inner courtyard. Opened in 1997. Travel agencies.

Luxury

Kusuma Sahid Prince, Jl Sugiyopranoto 20, ☎ (0271) 463 56, Fax (0271 447 88 – 120rm. ✎ 🖹 🖉 TV ✗ ⟲ CC Laid out in a former stately home (1897) that has kept some of its original decor including a superb hall. Souvenir shops, bar, travel agent. Ask for the rooms looking onto the swimming pool. Excellent reception and perfect comfort. You are treated like a prince.

Hotel Sahid Raya Solo, Jl Gajah Mada 82, ☎ (0271) 441 44, Fax (0271) 441 33 – 138rm. ✎ 🖹 🖉 TV ✗ ⟲ CC Spacious carpeted rooms, and marble in the bathrooms. Indonesian and international cuisine. Sports centre, souvenir shops and car rental.

EATING OUT

The *warung* in Jl Teuku Umar (C2) (night market) close late, and the ones in Puja Sari (B2) near the tourist office are open 24hr a day. Try the delicious local specialities, such as "nasi liwet" (rice with chicken cooked in coconut milk), "kue putu" (small coconut cake steamed in bamboo) and "srabi" (banana rice cake with coconut or chocolate).

● **Around Jalan Ahmad Dahlan** (C2)

Moderate to more select

Cafe Gamelan, Jl Ahmad Dahlan 28, ☎ (0271) 416 40. Set in pleasant wickerwork decor with a straw matting ceiling and subdued lighting. Indonesian and Western dishes.

Warung Baru, Jl Ahmad Dahlan 23, ☎ (0271) 563 69. Travellers are all familiar with its bamboo decor. Western and Indonesian dishes (don't miss the tasty "nasi liwet"). Bicycle rental, bike tours, lending library, and batik classes.

Monggo Pinarak Cafe, Jl Ahmad Dahlan. Excellent Indian cuisine prepared by a Bengali cook. Indonesian and European dishes and breakfasts.

Ramayana, Jl Imam Bonjol 49, ☎ (0271) 466 43. Same category as the one above, and slightly fresher. Indonesian and Chinese dishes, and seafood.

● **In the main avenue**

Moderate

Kusama Sari, Jl B J Slamet Riyadi 111 (C2), on the junction with Jl Yos Sudarso, ☎ (0271) 569 55 – 🖹 Very popular with Solo's inhabitants who crowd in here from 8pm onwards. The owner runs three restaurants, as well as the Café Solo. Indonesian cooking and ice-cream.

Lumba Lumba, Jl Slamet Riyadi, Pujasari A04 (B2), ☎ (0271) 73 77 48 – This small trendy restaurant has recently been opened by two young Solonese. It serves eclectic dishes, including club sandwiches and nasi liwet, and you can also have cobra, which is prepared by the adjoining Warung Sehat! Open until midnight.

More select

Tio Ciu 99, Jl B J Slamet Riyadi 244 (B2), ☎ (0271) 443 61. Chinese dishes. A smart place serving good seafood.

• Elsewhere

More select

Pringgon Dani, Jl Sutan Syahrir 79 (C2), beside Mangkunegaran Kraton, ☎ (0271) 439 36. Bamboo decor and a warm welcome. Excellent Solonese specialities.

Café Solo, Jl Dr Rajiman 261 (A2), ☎ (0271) 63 29 35. Daily (Friday and Sunday until midnight). 📧 📶 Installed in a beautiful colonial home, this is without doubt the smartest restaurant in town. It's a pity that they only serve Western food (salads, steaks, spaghetti, and soups). Art gallery and Internet connection.

GOING OUT, HAVING A DRINK

Cafes, bars, nightclubs – Nirwana, Jl Urip Sumoharjo, in Pasar Gede (C2). "Dangdut" and techno music.

Kantin Bahagia, Jl Gatot Subroto 97 (B2), in front of the Matahari. A little terrace ideal for a drink.

Sriwedari Park (B2), frequented by a friendly male crowd. A mixture of light music and traditional Indonesian music (Wednesday 8pm, Thursday 10pm, Sunday 8pm).

Live shows – These are a tradition in Solo, where there are several performing arts schools.
– "Wayang orang" (drama with actors) at the **Sriwedari Park**, daily except Sunday, 8-10pm, and at the **RRI**, Jl Abdul Rahman Saleh 51 (B1), on the second Tuesday of the month, 8pm midnight.
– "Wayang kulit" (shadow theatre). Performances generally last from 9pm to dawn. **Anom Suroto**, Jl Gambir Anom 100, the best "dalang" in Solo (every fifth Tuesday). You may also go to the **RRI** (third Saturday of the month), and to **Taman Budaya Surakarta**, Jl Ir Sutami 57 (northeast), every fifth Friday, or to the **Surakarta Kraton**, Alun-alun Lor (C3) (Friday and Sunday, 7-9pm).
– "Ketoprak" (popular drama) at the **RRI** (B1), fourth Tuesday of the month, 8pm-midnight.
– Dance performances at the **Surakarta Kraton** (Sunday, 9am-3pm), at the **Mangkunegaran Kraton** (Wednesday, 10am-12noon), at the **SMKI** (College of Art and Dance), Jl Kepatihan Wetan (C2) (8am-12noon; closed Sunday), and at the **STSI** (Academy of Performing Arts), Kentingan Kampus (northeast), Jebres (every morning at 7.30am; closed Sunday).

OTHER THINGS TO DO

Excursions – Enquire at the hotels and restaurants (see above).

Niki Tour, Jl Yos Sudarso 17 (B3), ☎ (0271) 532 78. Tours and bus reservations.

Mandira, Jl Gajah Mada 77 (B1-B2), ☎ (0271) 71 85 58. Welcoming and efficient staff, offering tours, ticket reservations and bookings for performances.

GPS Tour and Travel, Jl Achmad Dahlan (C2). To be avoided as they have prohibitive prices.

Feasts and festivals – Kirab Pusaka Kraton, Javanese New Year is celebrated in the two palaces.
There is a craft fair, **Maleman Sriwedari**, in Sriwedari Park (B2) during the last two weeks of Ramadan.
Sekaten, a week of festivities preceding the birthday of Muhammad.

Other – Cinema: **Solo 21**, the best complex, Sriwedari Park (B2).
Batik courses at the **Warung Baru** restaurant (see above).

SHOPPING GUIDE

Most shops close at 4-5pm, except those in Jl Gatot Subroto (B3), open to 9pm.

Markets – Pasar Gede, Jl Urip Sumoharjo (C2) 9am-5pm, the central market (vegetables, fruit, fish and meat).

Pasar Legi, Jl L J Supraman (C1), a huge, extremely busy market. At 3am farmers set up their stalls, and at 4.30am *warung* chefs come to get supplies.

Handicrafts, antiques – Good copies of antiques at **Pasar Triwindu** (B2), the flea market, and at **Sriwedari Park**. Wide choice of kris in the **Alun-alun Lor** (C3), notably at **Balai Agung**. "Wayang beber" (painted canvas scrolls used by the narrator to tell the stories), "wayang kulit" puppets and kris. **Bali Art Shop**, Kios Pujasari, Sriwedari Park (B2), antiques, masks, ethnographic items.

Batiks – Pasar Klewer (C3) is the temple of batiks, whether industrial or hand made. The main batik makers are **Batik Keris**, Jl Yos Sudarso 62 (B3) (workshop in Lawiyan, 8km to the east), **Batik Danarhadi**, Jl Dr Rajiman 164, and **Batik Semar**, Jl R M Said 148.

Books –Toko Sekawan, Jl Kartini (B2), several books in English.

Photography – Plenty of shops in Jl B J Slamet Riyadi (B2).

Making the most of Solo

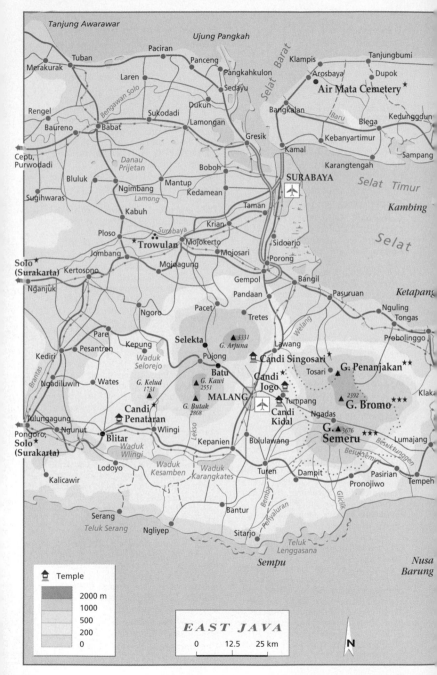

EAST JAVA

0   12.5   25 km

N

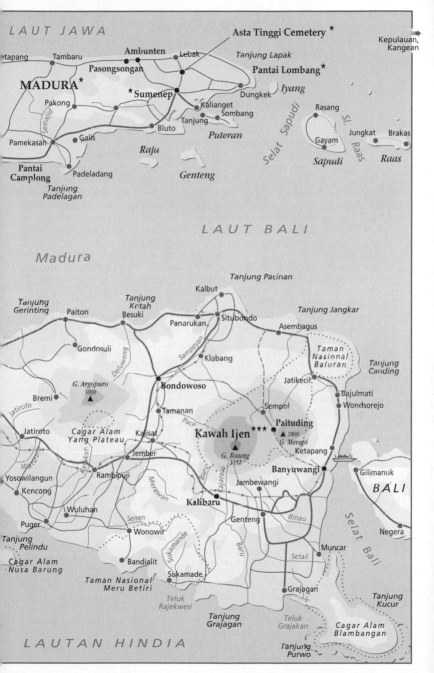

LAUT JAWA

Kepulauan, Kangean

Tambaru
etapang
Ambunten
Lebak
Asta Tinggi Cemetery ★
Tanjung Lapak
Pasongsongan
Pantai Lombang ★
MADURA ★
★ Sumenep
Dungkek
Iyang
Pakong
Kalianget
Sombang
Rasang
Sl. Raas
Bluto
Tanjung
Jungkat
Brakas
Galis
Puteran
Gayam
Pamekasah
Raju
Sapudi
Raas
Pantai
Camplong
Padeladang
Genteng
Tanjung
Padelagan

LAUT BALI

Madura

Tanjung Pacinan
Kalbut
Tanjung
Gerinting
Paiton
Tanjung
Ketah
Besuki
Tanjung Jangkar
Panarukan
Situbondo
Asembagus
Gondosuli
Klabang
Taman
Nasional
Baluran
Tanjung
Canding
G. Argopuro
3000
Bondowoso
Jatikecil
Bajulmati
Wondsorejo
Bremi
Tamanan
Sempol
Paltuding ★★★
Jatiroto
Cagar Alam
Yang Plateau
Kalisat
Kawah Ijen ★★★
▲ 2800
G. Merapi
Jember
Ketapang
Rambipuji
G. Raung
3332
Banyuwangi
Gilimanuk
Yosowilangun
BALI
Kencong
Jambewangi
Wuluhan
Kalibaru
Puger
Senen
Genteng
Binau
Negera
Tanjung
Pelindu
Wonowir
Setail
Muncar
Cagar Alam
Nusa Barung
Bandialit
Sukamade
Tanjung
Kucur
Taman Nasional
Meru Betiri
Grajagan
Teluk
Rajekwesi
Tanjung
Grajagan
Teluk
Grajakan
Cagar Alam
Blambangan

LAUTAN HINDIA
Tanjung
Purwo

East Java

SURABAYA
Capital of East Java Province
780km from Jakarta – Map p 320-321 and Plan p 325
Pop 4 million – Hot climate

Not to be missed
The Chinese and Arab quarters. Tanjung Perak harbour.
The Majapahit ruins at Trowulan.

And remember...
Avoid taking a taxi during rush hour.
Visit the Arab quarter during the day, when it is livelier.

Surabaya, the second largest city in Indonesia, is a large port town that seems to have grown too fast. With its glass and concrete buildings, and streets crowded with traffic sweltering in the extreme heat, it first strikes you as a place to pass through quickly. And yet it is one of the rare examples in Indonesia of an urban, cosmopolitan culture. Indeed, Surabaya is part of **Pasisir**, the northern fringe of Java that has long looked to the sea and outside influences, be they Madurese, Chinese or Arab. Its vocation for trade dates back several centuries, and testimonies to this can be seen in the quays in Tanjung Perak harbour, in the Buddhist temples or in the alleyways in the Arab quarter. By visiting the very exotic Pabean market, the museum and the zoo you will discover that Surabaya is more than a mere stopover on the way to Madura or Mount Bromo.

For history enthusiasts, the town is also the departure point for an excursion to Trowulan *(near Mojokerto)*, the former capital of the Majapahit Empire *(see p 34)*.

A cosmopolitan city
Surabaya was founded in the late 13C, and was long coveted by the princes of Madura and Central Java. However, in 1525, when it was turning to Islam, it was Surabaya itself that imposed its hegemony on neighbouring kingdoms. It even dared cross swords with the powerful Mataram kingdom, entering into a war that was to last almost a century. Yet the town ended up by capitulating to Sultan Agung (1625), before passing into the hands of the Dutch a century later. The 19C marked the beginning of a period of rapid expansion that reached its height with the building of the railway that linked the town with the capital, Batavia (Jakarta). The following century, in the 1930s, the town could boast of being the country's leading industrial centre. However, after the Japanese occupation (1942-45), the population had a hard time when the former colonisers returned. Surabaya was then the scene of one of the bloodiest battles in the War of Independence. Such was the resistance by the rebels that the young Republic of Indonesia set Surabaya up as the "city of heroes", the name by which the town is known.

Tour of the town
Allow 1 day, on foot and by taxi.

Surabaya developed from the port southwards, following the course of the canal (Kali Mas). Today, the heart of the modern city lies along Tunjungan (A3-B3), Basuki Rahmat (B4) and Pemuda (B3-C4), large crowded avenues lined with luxury hotels, banks and shopping centres. In Tunjungan, take a look at the **Majapahit Hotel**, a typically art deco jewel dating from the 1930s. Then head for the harbour where you will see reminders of the town as it used to be, in the times when merchants arrived from all over the world.

The old quarters

Take a taxi from the town centre to Jembatan Merah Bridge, halfway to the harbour (20min).

East of **Jembatan Merah Bridge** (Red Bridge) lies the **Chinese quarter** (B1), a maze of little shop-houses where pedestrians, *becaks*, cars and trucks fight for space. With its **Chinese Puppet Theatre** (Fu-Kien), the **Hok Tek Hian Buddhist Temple** (*Jl Dukuh*) is an extraordinary cultural mix. The repertoire is Chinese, while the puppets are Javanese.

The atmosphere changes at the **Pasar Pabean** (B1) (*Jl Panggung, 200m away*), a vast market crammed with fish, meat, spices, vegetables and all kinds of utensils. With their groceries balanced on their heads, women in colourful sarongs jostle each other as they bustle along the muddy alleyways, making their way through the general hubbub bathed in a thousand and one fragrances.

Since the 15C Surabaya has had an **Arab quarter** (B1), separated from the Chinese quarter by Jalan Mas Mansur. In the alleyway leading to the **Sunan Ampel Mosque** (*non-Muslims may not enter*) merchants compete fiercely, selling their fabrics, carpets and Korans, while Arab music can be heard everywhere. You are in another world. The cemetery adjoining the mosque is the burial place of Sunan Ampel, one of the most highly venerated **Wali Songos** in the country (*see p 35*).

The visit to the old town ends with **Kali Mas harbour** (beyond A1) (*2.5km to the north, by taxi*). This is home to the *pinisi*, the heavy wooden Bugis **sailing ships★** with colourful prows that are waiting to be loaded to the gunnels before setting off for eastern Indonesia. On the quays great carpets of silvery fish dry in the sun giving off a terrible smell, enough to put off even the most ravenous cats in the district!

In the south

For a little historic interlude, go to the **MPU Tantular Museum** (beyond B4), which is devoted to the art and prehistory of East Java (*Jl Taman Mayangkera 6; 8am-12.30/2.30pm, closed Monday. Take a bus from Jl Panglima Sudirman. Allow 45min*). Don't miss the outstanding **Dongson bronzes**, or the impressive series of 69 **bronze Hindu statuettes★** (10C-11C), unearthed in Ponorogo in 1992. You can also see some delicate **wayang puppets**, **Majapahit terracotta items** and elegant **Chinese ceramics**.

From there you can cool off with a stroll around the **zoo** (Kebun Binatang) (beyond B4) (*Jl Diponegoro, 7am-6pm*), the largest in Indonesia. Some of the archipelago's endemic species may be seen, including hornbills, **Komodo dragons** (spectacular at feeding time!), boa constrictors and **Java tigers**. The Surabayans come here in couples or family groups, and the rare Westerners visiting the zoo arouse just as much interest as the animals.

Surabaya, in the Ampel Mosque quarter

G Guérard

Surabaya

Trowulan★

60km west of Surabaya and 6km from Mojokerto. Site and museum: 7am-4pm. Allow a morning. As the edifices are spread out, it is better to have a car.

All that remains of the prestigious **capital of the Majapahit Empire** is just a stretch of countryside dotted with ruins. Unlike the stone temples in Central Java (which are nonetheless a lot older) Majapahit was built of wood and brick and has therefore not withstood the passing of time. However, some of the edifices, such as the odd isolated shrine or gateway dating mainly from the 14C when the empire was at its height, are well worth the trip.

Before beginning your excursion, visit the **Trowulan Museum★** *(1km south of the main road, closed Monday)*, an excellent introduction to Majapahit art and civilisation. Statues, pottery, ridge tiles and vases, all made of **terracotta** are given a prominent place. There are even **piggy banks** on display. Note especially the remarkable **linga and Hindu statues★**, as well as the many **Chinese ceramics** that bear witness to trade between the Majapahit Empire and the Middle Kingdom.

Opposite the museum is a vast **pool** (Kolam Segaran) measuring 375m by 175m, which is thought to have been the setting for Majapahit court festivities. Today it is a favourite spot for anglers.

The splendid **Gapura Bajang Ratu★** *(2km to the east)* (14C), is a narrow pyramidal gateway with cut-off corners, the last remains of what once was a wall. It is decorated with elegant **bas-reliefs** that draw on the *Ramayana*.

Continue to **Candi Tikus** *(1km to the east)*, a large royal pool made of red brick that was unearthed in 1914. The structure rising from the middle is a reproduction of **Mahameru**, the holy Hindu mountain. Note the superb stone **gargoyles★** featuring *makara*, the guardian of the water.

7km to the west, on the other side of the main road, you come to **Candi Brahu**, Trowulan's largest temple, but not its most elegant. It is shaped like a tower, and some historians believe that the ashes of the early Majahapit kings were kept here after cremation.

On the main road as you come from Mojokerto, you will see on the right, in the middle of nowhere, a majestic gateway with cut-off corners, standing more than 15m high. It is **Gapura Wringin Lawang**, which, according to local belief, is the entrance to the former palace of Gajah Mada, the great Majapahit statesman.

You may end the excursion at the **Troloyo** cemetery *(2km to the south)* that contains the oldest **Muslim tombs** on Java (1368 to 1475). Historians see them as proof of an Islamic presence at the court of the Majapahit kings.

Kali Mas

A B C

SURABAYA

0 250 500 m

N

Jalan Pesapen Kali

Jalan Kasuari

Jl. KH Mas Mansur

Jl. Nyamplungan

Sunan Ampel

Jalan Pegiran

SIMOKERTO

Jl. Sidodadi Baru

Jalan Simojawang

Jalan Rajawali

Jl. Sasak

Jalan Dukuh

Jalan Sidodadi

Jl. Smolawang Baru

Jl. Sidotopo Lor

Pasar Pabean

Hok Tek Hian

Jalan Panggung

Jalan Kembang Jepun

Jalan Songoyudan

Jl. Slompretan

Jalan Teparapuan

Jalan Burguan

Jalan Gembong

Jalan Kapasan

Chinese Temple (1)

Kanjeran Beach

Jembatan Merah

Chinese Temple

Karet

Jalan Waspada

Jalan Setasiun Kota

Jl. Kebon Rojo

Jalan Semut Kali

KOTA

Jalan Pengampon

Jalan Pecindilan

Jalan Kapasan

Jalan Indrapura

Kali Mas

Jalan Veteran

Jalan Jl. Semul Baru

Jl. Gembong Tebasan

Jalan Semut Baru

Jalan Dupak

Jalan Pasar Turi

Jalan Johar

Jalan Sulung

GENTENG

Jalan Temudan Pasar Besar

Jalan Jagalan

Jalan Ngaglik

Jalan Semarang

Mardi Sentoso

Jalan Raden Saleh

Jalan B. Jbutan

Jalan Pahlawan

Jalan Kramat Gantirg

Jalan Peneleh

Jalan Grogol Kalimir

Jalan Undaan Kulon

Jalan Kalianyar

Adi Husada

Jalan Undaan Wetan

Jalan Kusuma Bangsa

Taman Remaja

Gelora 10 November

Peneleh Cemetery

Jalan Baliwerti

Jalan Semblorgan

Jalan Akhmad Jais

Jalan Ambengan

Jalan Arjuno

Jalan Kranggan

Jalan Praban

Jalan Genteng Kali

Jalan Bubutan

Jalan Tidar

Jalan Anjasmoro

Jalan Embong Malang

Jalan Tunjungan

Jl. Genteng Desar

Taman Budaya

Jalan Ngemplak

Jalan Raya Jaksa

City Hall

Jalan Anggrek

(3)

(2)

Jl. Indrakila

Tunjungan Plaza

General Soerjo Statue

Jalan Ketabang Kali

Jalan Walikota Mustajab

General Sudirman Statue

Jalan Sudarso

Jl. Yos Sudarso

Jalan Kedung Doro

Grahadi

Dr. Gani

TEGALSARI

Joko Dolog Statue

Jl. Embong Wungu

Jl. Embong Kenongo

Delta Plaza

Kapal Selam Monument

Jalan Pemuda

Jalan Gubeng Pojok

GUBENG

Jl. Gubeng Klingsingan

Jalan Kedungsari

Jalan Tegalsari

Jalan Jenderal Basuki Rahmat

Jalan Panglima Sudirman

(4)

Jalan Kayun

Kali Mas

Jalan Wonorejo II

Jalan Kombes

Brata Husada

Jalan Sunatera

Jalan Raya Gubeng

Jalan Nias

Jalan Kampung Malang

Jl. Urip Sumoharjo

Jl. Keputran

Budi Mulia

Malang, Mojokerto
Zoo, MPU Tantular Museum

Temple

HOTELS

Ganefo .... (1)

Majapahit ..... (2)

Paviljoen .... (3)

Remaja .... (4)

Making the most of Surabaya

COMING AND GOING

By plane – Juanda airport is 15km south of the town. Buses and taxis provide a shuttle service (tickets for fixed-price taxis are on sale at the counter). Surabaya is linked to all the major towns in Indonesia.

By train – Gubeng station is near the town centre (C4). Travelling times: Jakarta 8hr30min-14hr, Yogyakarta 5hr30min-7hr, Solo 4hr30min-6hr, Malang 2hr, and Banyuwangi 7hr.

By boat – The **Pelni** boats going to Kalimantan, Sulawesi and eastern Indonesia all stop at Surabaya.

By bus – Bungurasih terminus is 10km to the south (accessible by bus). Travelling times: Pandaan 1hr, Malang 2hr, Blitar 4hr, Banyuwangi 6hr, Solo 6hr30min, Yogyakarta 8hr, and Jakarta 12-15hr.

By minibus – Surya Jaya, Jl Basuki Rahmat 72 (B4), ☎ (031) 534 24 63. **Panther**, Jl Suropati 47, ☎ (031) 531 03 41.

GETTING AROUND

On foot – When you cross a street you have to do so with a cool head and great care. Indicate firmly to drivers that they must stop, otherwise they won't!

By bus – The convenient P1 bus leaves from Bungurasih terminus and serves the zoo, Jl Basuki Rachmat, Jl Embong Malang, Pasar Turi station and the harbour.

By bemo – Most of the *bemo* lines run east-west.

By taxi – Srikandi Taxi, ☎ (031) 752 23 33. **Metro Executive**, ☎ (031) 870 85 85.

Car rental – Toyota Rent a Car, Jl Raya Achmad Yani 210, south of the town, ☎(031) 828 20 00. **Avis Rent a Car**, Jl Raya Darmo Indah Timur II Blok 632, to the east, ☎ (031) 734 41 33.

ADDRESS BOOK

Tourist information – Surabaya Tourist Office, Jl Pemuda 118 (C4) (temporary address), ☎ (031) 532 44 99 (Monday to Saturday, 9am-7pm).

Bank/Currency exchange – Banks in Jl Pemuda and Jl Tunjungan (B3-C4) accept foreign currency and travellers' cheques, and are equipped with ATMs. **BII**, Jl Pemuda 150, ☎ (031) 52 65 44. Money can be sent from abroad, for a very high commission. **Fath Surya**, Jl Panglima Sudirman 72I (B4), ☎ (031) 534 49 96. Daily. **Pacto** travel agent (see below).

Post office/Telephone – Main post office, Jl Kebon Rojo 10 (B2) (7am-10pm, Saturday 9am-12noon), Poste Restante. **Wartel Darmo**, Jl Raya Diponegoro/Jl Kapuas 51, in the south of the town. 24hr a day.

British Consulate – Hong Kong Bank, Hyatt Bumi Modern Skyline Building, 3rd floor, Jl Basuki Rachmat 106-128 (B4), ☎ (031) 532 63 81.

American Consulate General – Jl Raya Dr Sutomo 33, ☎ (031) 567 68 80.

Airline companies – Garuda, Jl Tunjungan 29 (B3), ☎ (031) 534 58 86 **Merpati**, Jl Raya Darmo 111 (east of the town), ☎ (031) 568 81 11. **Bouraq**, Jl Panglima Sudirman 70 (B4), ☎ (031) 52 16 21. **Mandala**, Jl Raya Diponegoro 73, ☎ (031) 57 89 73.

Shipping line – Pelni, Jl Pahlawan 112 (A2), ☎ (031) 57 19 65.

Travel agents – Pacto, Jl Tunjungan 65 (B3), ☎ (031) 433 51. **Aneka Kartika**, Jl Manyar Ketarojo 55 (southeast), ☎ (031) 592 90 00.

WHERE TO STAY

Surabaya has plenty of luxury hotels for businessmen but few mid-range places.

Modest to average

Hotel Ganefo, Jl Kapasan 168-171, ☎ (031) 371 11 69 – 52rm. The former "harbour master's office" for the Chinese has kept its decoration with mouldings, and its lady manager who does her accounts with an abacus! Some of the rooms have their own shower and air conditioning. The clientele is mostly local.

Hotel Paviljoen, Jl Genteng Besar 94, ☎ (031) 534 34 49 – 20rm. ☝ This is a pleasant colonial house with a courtyard garden set in a quiet central street. The rooms are clean and good value for money. Some of them have hot water and air conditioning.

Hotel Remaja, Jl Embong Kenongo 12, ☎ (031) 534 13 59 – 20rm. ☝✕🍽 Another quiet place in a good position. The rooms are comfortable but only tolerably clean.

Luxury

Majapahit, Jl Tunjungan 65, ☎ (031) 545 43 33, Fax (031) 545 41 11 – 150rm. ☝✈/🍽 🎵 📺 ✕ ⚓ cc A superb example of art deco architecture (1910), with an elegant façade overlooking a garden, all with unparalleled charm. People on small budgets may be content with trying the excellent cakes.

EATING OUT

The places in the malls selling fast food are convenient but for more exotic fare try the *warung* along Jl Genteng Besar (B3) or Jl Tidar (A3) (Chinese, Javanese and seafood dishes). Open late in the evening.

More select

Ria Restaurant, Jl Kombes Pol 7 (A4), ☎ (031) 534 31 30 (open until 11pm). This is Surabaya's smart restaurant (air-conditioned dining room). Service is professional and the food is good. Try the "gurame bakar" (grilled carp).

Cafe Venezia, Jl Ambengan 16 (B3), ☎ (031) 545 77 77 (open until 11pm). A vast choice of local and Western (barbe-cue) dishes served in a garden or an air-conditioned dining room. It's a pity that the welcome is so impersonal.

GOING OUT, HAVING A DRINK

Ice-cream parlour – Zangradi Ice Cream, Jl Yos Sudarso 15 (B3). 9am-9.30pm; closed Tuesday. A pleasant place, very popular with the local middle classes.

Nightclubs, bars – Flamingo, Jl Genteng Kali (B3). Funk and techno music.

Tavern, Hyatt Hotel, Jl Jend Basuki Rachmat (B4). Ideal for a drink, as you sit comfortably listening to local groups.

Lldo, Jl Magjen Sungkono, near the Shangri La Hotel (southeast of the town). Not as smart but friendlier than the place above. A bar where local groups play.

Live shows – Taman Budaya, Jl Genteng Kali (B3), near the river. Performances of traditional dance, drama and Javanese wayang are sometimes organised here (even the rehearsals are worth a look). There are also exhibitions

British Council – Jl Cokroaminoto 12, 3rd floor, ☎ (031) 568 99 58.

SHOPPING GUIDE

Shopping centres – At the **Plaza Surabaya** (Jl Pemuda) (C4) and the **Tunjungan Plaza** (Jl Tunjungan) (B3) you will find major international luxury brands.

Antiques – Anisah Art Shop, Jl Urip Sumoharjo 4 (B4). Basketwork, batiks, antiques, and items made of wood.

Yakop, Jl Keputran Kejambon I/49D (B4). Terracotta articles, bronzes and boxes from Madura.

MADURA ISLAND★

East Java Province – Pop 3 million
160km long, 35km wide – 4 250sqkm
Map of the island p 320-321 – Hot, dry climate

Not to be missed
The ox races at the end of summer.
The beautiful beaches in the east.

And remember...
Stay in Sumenep, the most pleasant town on the island.
As Islam on Madura is quite strict,
be careful not to shock by wearing or doing anything provocative.

The small island of Madura lies several hundred metres from the frenzy of Surabaya and the green coasts of Java. With its remarkable aridity it shows a very different side to Indonesia. Here there are no volcanoes with fertile ash, and barely a hill, apart from the low ones lining the north coast. Madura is an island of sun-scorched plains that makes a living mainly from fishing, salt and cattle rearing. The land is poor and harsh, and no doubt plays a part in the proverbial severity of the Madurese. They are said to be *kasar*, or hard and direct, even *panas* (irascible), with a temperament that contrasts with the civilised manners of their neighbours. Be that as it may, you will undoubtedly receive a kind, shy welcome. Likewise, while the island remains very attached to its language, traditions and to Islam, you should be wary of clichés. In the towns, on market day, the streets belong to the women, and their veils are the most sparkling imaginable.

Far from having any complexes, Madura flaunts its differences. Hence the profound exoticism that you will find in the little fishing ports crowded with colourful boats, on the deserted beaches lined with coconut palms, and especially when you attend one of the famous and extremely thrilling *Kerapan Sapi,* or **ox races**.

Kerapan Sapi

Every year at harvest time life on Madura revolves around the popular Kerapan Sapi and their accompanying festivities. The principle of the race, in which two yokes of young oxen compete, couldn't be simpler. The first yoke whose hindquarters pass the finishing line is declared winner by the jury. There are no holds barred, even doping is allowed (beer, eggs, even chillies on the animals' organs in order to increase their heartbeat)! In the early morning jubilant crowds mass along the track in the overpowering heat, while the owners finish adorning and beautifying their animals. Perched on a shaft that trails behind on the ground, each competitor lines up behind the starting line. The tension is extreme. A whip cracks, the drivers grab hold of their oxen's tails, and then everything happens very quickly. Balanced precariously, each driver tries somehow or other to direct his animals as they bolt ahead at full speed. It is not rare to see a team charging into the crowd amid shouts, and the most perilous part of the race is pulling up the team at the end of the track. All in all, highly dramatic!

A restless neighbour

It is to the great local family of the **Cakraningrats** that Madura owes the most illustrious pages of its history, from the 16C to the 18C. The year 1528, when one of its members, the prince of Arosbaya, converted to Islam, was a decisive turning point. The island then took itself to be one of the most ardent centres of Islam, and this has remained an essential element in the political and social life of the Madurese. Up until the 18C the Cakraningrats made life difficult for the rulers of Java.

While in 1624 the island fell into the hands of **Sultan Agung**, the king of Mataram, several decades later (1672) the legendary Madurese prince **Raden Trunojoyo** drove back the occupying forces and managed to push into the heart of Java, where he reduced the capital to ashes.

To quell the revolt the Javanese called upon the Dutch, who, alas, took advantage of the occasion to interfere with the internal affairs of the kingdom and in 1705 took control of the west of Madura. However, even under Dutch hegemony the local princes always managed to preserve a certain amount of autonomy, in exchange for back-up troops for the Dutch in the wars with Java and Sumatra.

In the 19C the exploitation of salt begun by the Dutch made Madura a prosperous island. It entered a golden age economically speaking, but this was brutally ruined by the Japanese occupation during the Second World War. Since then much of the island population has left, with people emigrating to Java and the rest of the archipelago. Administratively speaking, Madura is joined to East Java Province and is divided into four districts (*kabupaten*), Bangkalan, Sampang, Pamekasan and Sumenep.

Tour of the island
Allow 2 days.

From Kamal, where the ferries draw alongside, the main road heads towards **Bangkalan** (*16km north*), a small town without much of interest to see. Only history buffs may like to pay a visit to its modest **museum** devoted to the Cakraningrat kings (*8am-2pm, closed Sunday*).

Arosbaya

It's probably best to continue northwards to Arosbaya (*16km from Bangkalan, 30min by bemo*), a quiet town with nothing to suggest that it was the political centre of Madura in the 15C and 16C – apart from the **Royal Cemetery of Air Mata*** ("tears") that dominates it, perched on a little hill (*donation*). This is one of the three royal (Muslim) necropolises on the island, places that are always the subject of great devotion. Inside the two chambers adorned with stucco are the tombs of the Cakraningrat family, lined up in chronological order. At the top of the hill a finely worked **stele** marks the site of the oldest grave, which belongs to the highly venerated queen mother **Ratu Ibu**.

Return to Bangkalan to take the road south that leads to Sumenep in the east of the island. After crossing hills it drops to the sea at Sampang (61km from Bangkalan).

The south coast

Beyond **Sampang**, you may like to stop a while at **Camplong beach** (*9km to the east. Be warned, it is very crowded on weekends*). The coconut palms shading the sand, the little multicoloured **sailing boats** and the fishermen's bamboo platforms (*bagan*) bobbing on the water add a poetic touch. It is a pity that the tanks of the *Pertamina* oil company mar the landscape.

The road follows the coast to **Pamekasan** (*29km*), a small town that comes to life once a year with the *Kerapan Sapi* races, which are among the most colourful on the island. Just before you reach Sumenep, note the **pools** dotted along the road. They are covered in a host of little hoop nets for catching fish, and are lit by lamps that create a halo of magical light.

Madura Island

Sumenep*

64km from Pamekasan. Sumenep was the capital of the ancient kingdom of the Cakraningrat family, and has remained Madura's main town. It is a pleasant, quiet, neat town with a grid pattern of wide avenues crisscrossed by *bemos* and *becaks*. It is the ideal place for a stay on the island, whether you want to watch ox races or enjoy the warm sand on the surrounding beaches.

The **kraton** *(Jl Sutomo 5, daily 7am-4pm)* with its pretty pleasure garden is more like a large mansion than a princely palace. Built in 1750 it now houses the administrative headquarters of the *bupati* (prefecture), as well as a small **Regional Museum** (Museum Daerah) with a disorganised but interesting collection. There are carriages, Dutch and Chinese furniture, photographs of the sultan, ceremonial jewellery, copper betel caskets, masks, kris daggers, puppets, a 13C Hindu statue, and ceramics.

The **Jamic Mosque** *(300m from the Kraton, Jl Trunojoyo, donation)* dating from the same time as the palace, is thought to be the work of a Chinese architect. You enter through a massive portal painted white and yellow in an unexpectedly baroque style. Inside, nine wide pillars support the roof of the **prayer hall**, which is very bright. Perched on a little hill 2km northwest of Sumenep is the 18C **Asta Tinggi Royal Cemetery***, which dominates the town and its environs, affording a very fine **view***. You enter through a large white and yellow **portico** like the one at the Jamik Mosque. In the middle of the enclosure is the domed **mausoleum** of the last prince of Madura. The atmosphere of the place is tinged with mysticism, and the Madurese like to gather here with their families. You walk barefoot along the lanes lined with simple brick stelae, and visit the funerary buildings in silence.

After this cultural immersion it is difficult to resist a swim in the sea. So head for **Lombang beach*** *(30km east of Sumenep, near Legung; accessible by bemo; allow at least 1hr)*. This is one of the most beautiful beaches on the island – a long stretch of white sand lined with pine trees – and what is more, few people come here.

The northeast coast

The most interesting part of the north coast, between Slopeng and Tamberu, can be seen in a day's outing from Sumenep. The road goes through charming fishing villages, such as **Ambuten** and **Pasongsongan**, set amongst the palm trees beside little estuaries crowded with boats. Wherever you go you will see **Madurese sailing boats*** being built. These magnificent vessels have triangular rigging, finely carved wood and bright colours. They are mainly intended for fishing but also transport goods to far-away islands. Traffic is invariably interrupted at the entrance to each village by people requesting donations for a new mosque, while in the country white carpets of *cambodia* give you forewarning of a Muslim cemetery.

To end with, there's nothing better than relaxing on **Slopeng beach*** *(20km north of Sumenep, near Ambunten, access by bemo)*. It is an earthly paradise with its white sand dunes fringed with coconut palms, where the only people you are likely to see are fishermen from the neighbouring village.

Bugis boats in the harbour

Making the most of Madura

COMING AND GOING

By ferry – Ferries leave from Surabaya every 30min for Kamal on the southwest tip of Madura (30min crossing). Departures in the other direction are also every 30min.

GETTING AROUND

By bemo – This is the main means of transport. You just wave at the driver for him to stop. Allow 2hr30min from Kamal to reach Pamekasan and 4hr to reach Sumenep.

By becak – Convenient for getting around Sumenep.

Car rental – Enquire at Surabaya, or at hotels on the island if you would like to hire a *bemo* for the day (check the condition of the vehicle, and preferably hire a driver who has had experience of driving tourists around).

ADDRESS BOOK

Bank/Currency exchange – It is advisable to change money in Surabaya, where rates are better. There are several banks and cash dispensers on the island. *BCA*, Jl Jokotole, near the Alun-alun, Pamekasan. Travellers' cheques are accepted (8am-1pm, closes at 11am on Saturday).

BCA, Jl Trunojoyo, Sumenep. Accepts dollars and travellers' cheques. You can withdraw cash with a credit card at the counter (8am-3pm, closes at 12noon on Saturday).

Post office/Telephone – *Main post office* in Pamekasan, near the Alun-alun (8am-3pm), and in Sumenep, on the Kalianget road. *Telkom* in Sumenep, beyond the Chinese temple east of the town. *Wartel*, Jl Sudirman, Sumenep.

WHERE TO STAY

Be warned that Madura is under-equipped as far as its hotel infrastructure is concerned, and the few comfortable places are sometimes full during the Kerapan Sapi races. It is best to make your bookings in Surabaya.

• Bangkalan
Average
Hotel Ningrat, Jl K H MO Kholil 113, ☎ (031) 309 53 88 – 29rm. The only comfortable hotel in the town is in a renovated mansion. The most comfortable rooms are in the old building and come with air conditioning and a private bathroom, but they are a little noisy.

• Sampang
Average
Pondok Wisata Pantai Camplong, Camplong, near Sampang, ☎ (0323) 32 15 86 – 22rm. ⌘ 🏊 ✗ ⛱ 🐾 One of the best hotels on the island, just opposite the beach. The suites have air conditioning. Breakfast included.

• Sumenep
Modest
Wisma Penda, Jl Trunojoyo 53, ☎ (0328) 66 25 02 – 14rm. A quiet, inexpensive hotel. The air-conditioned rooms with their own bathrooms are good value for money.
Hotel Wijaya I, Jl Trunojoyo 45-47, ☎ (0328) 624 33 – 63rm. ✗ In spite of looking like a roadside motel, the place is more comfortable than its twin, Wijaya II. Some of the rooms have air conditioning and television, while the cheaper ones have shared bathrooms.

EATING OUT
Moderate
• Bangkalan
Depot Mirasa, Jl Trunojoyo 75. Indonesian and Chinese dishes.

• Pamekasan
Rumah Makan Telomoyo, Jl Trunojoyo 19. This is in a building dating from 1908, which is recognisable by the heavy pillars on its façade. Chinese and Indonesian ("nasi rawon") food.

• Sumenep
You can find something to eat night and day in the market near the mosque.
Rumah Makan 17 Augustus, Jl Sudirman 34. Chinese and Indonesian food.
Depot Anugerah, Jl Jend Sudirman 32. Family atmosphere and Indonesian food.

Rumah Makan Kartini, Jl Diponegoro 83. A small, very simple Indonesian restaurant run by charming Indonesian "Mamas" ("Ibu").

OTHER THINGS TO DO

Kerapan Sapi – The ox races on Madura take place once a year throughout the island (the most important are in Bangkalan, Sumenep, Sampang and Pamekasan). Heats begin on 17 August (the date of the national holiday), and continue on Saturdays and Sundays throughout September. The final is held either in Sumenep or in Pamekasan at the end of September.

SHOPPING GUIDE

Market – Anom Bar, Jl Trunojoyo, Sumenep. Fabrics, clothes, fruit and vegetables.

Batiks – Madurese batiks are particularly colourful, and are made by hand in the coastal villages. Hence their high prices. Have a look in Sumenep market, which has a wide range.

Batik Madura, Jl Diponegoro 96, Pamekasan. A workshop with items for sale.

Patimura, Tanjungbumi, on the north coast. Vast choice of locally made batiks.

Antiques – Madura is mainly known for its wooden handicrafts (panels, beds, chests and benches) – very beautiful work that can also be found in shops on Java and Bali.

Madura Art Shop Amak Baabud, Jl Jend Sudirman, Gang I/56B, Sumenep, ☎ (0328) 664 52.

Fiesta Madura, Jl Kabupaten 71, Pamekasan, ☎ (0324) 235 94.

Making the most of Madura

R. Marca

Madura, the royal cemetery at Asta Tinggi

THE TEMPLE ROAD ★
MALANG
East Java Province
Malang: 85km from Surabaya – Map p 320-321
Pop 650 000 – Alt 450m – Mild climate

Not to be missed
The Penataran and Singosari temples.
And remember...
Avoid Batu and Selekta at weekends.

The mild climate of the Malang region brings a welcome coolness after the sweltering heat and frenzy of Surabaya. The area provides the opportunity for a pleasant trip through a land where nature mixes harmoniously with history. Enigmatic Hindu shrines emerging from the rice fields, holy volcanoes surrounded by forest, isolated hill stations lying amongst coffee plantations and market gardens – the delightful scenery has an almost magical quality.

This is also the opportunity to discover a more intimate side to the Indo-Javanese civilisation, by hunting down little temples belonging to the ancient **Singosari** kingdom, which preceded the Majapahit Empire *(see p 34)*. For those not interested in history, there is the chance to have a relaxing bathe in the hot springs at Batu or cool off in its waterfall.

Malang
Allow half a day (on foot or by becak). From Tugu square,
you can easily reach the town centre on the other side of the river.

In the late 18C the Dutch settled in the Malang region to grow coffee. This was the beginning of an extraordinary boom for the little town judiciously positioned on the banks of the Brantas. Since then Malang has continued to prosper, diversifying into market gardens and tobacco. It is here, notably, that the famous cigarette manufacturer **Bantoel** has its head office, and a factory currently employing nearly 20 000 people. With its elegant **colonial houses** inherited from the Dutch era, and its lively streets, Malang is a charming place to stroll through.

The rebel stronghold
After Java's third War of Succession (1746-57) the Malang region, known for its difficult access, became a refuge for the last supporters of Prince Surapati, a descendant of a former Balinese slave who had founded a principality in Pasuruan in the late 17C. Fearing the arrival of Balinese reinforcements in the area – which was in constant revolt – the Dutch actively encouraged Muslims, whom they believed to be more reliable to settle there. But it was not until 1771 that they managed to capture the last of the line of rebel princes. Figures of courage and tenacity, the Surapatis have become legendary characters in Javanese drama.

From Tugu square, head for the cool, fragrant **Flower Market** (Pasar Bunga) *(take Jl Kahuripan, then Jl Brawijaya to the left)*. From there, as you go down towards the river, you come to a **Bird Market** (Pasar Burung) *(8am-4pm)*, which is just as colourful and will give you an idea of Indonesia's extraordinary fauna. There are not only falcons and parrots but also wild cats, all living side by side in a jumble of baskets and bamboo cages.

From here, you can either cross the Brantas and walk to Jl Jend Basuki Rahmat, or take a taxi to the colonial quarter.

The elegant **Jalan Ijen** *(2km to the northeast of the town)*, a wide boulevard planted with tall palm trees, marks the heart of Malang's chic quarter. Beside the venerable **Dutch houses** stand luxurious modern villas with rather flashy façades.

Lastly, to the south, the **Klenteng Eng Ang Kiong Chinese Temple** *(Jl Zainul Zakse, 300m east of Pasar Besar)* has strikingly exuberant bas-reliefs. Fish with staring eyes, monsters and birds all make up a decor typical of the Tri Dharma cult that mixes Buddhism, Confucianism and Taoism.

Looking for Singosari

A day's tour, beginning north of Malang. As the temples are spread out, it is best to hire a car and a guide. We have, however, also included details on public transport.

Nothing remains of the prestigious capital of the Singosaris that was founded in 1222. It has long been buried beneath the walls of the modern Malang. The only testimonies to its beauty are the funerary temples built in the surrounding area, which have been protected by their isolation.

■ **Candi Singosari**★ – *10km north of Malang. Take a minibus from Arjosari terminal. Donation, allow 15min.* The layout of Candi Singosari, a small Sivaite shrine dedicated to king **Kertanegara** (1268-92), draws on that of Java's classical edifices, positioned according to the cardinal points (the pyramidal roof has unfortunately disappeared). Magnificent red, white and grey stone **statues**★ stand at the entrance, while niches have been carved in the base of the building (and not on the upper part as is traditionally the case). Mysteriously, the **heads of the kala** figures that crown the doorways on the lower level remain unfinished.

200m to the west note the two **dwarapalas** that were meant to guard the entrance to the royal palace, now destroyed. The terrifying faces of these stone monsters were thought to discourage evil spirits.

■ **Candi Sumberawan** – *5km northwest of Singosari. Take a minibus from the market. A path leads through the rice fields for 500m to the temple, but it is difficult to find without a guide.* The 14C Buddhist **stupa** belongs to a different age and a different cult. It is a large stone bell-shaped shrine lost in the greenery, one of the rare stupas to be seen in East Java.

To reach the temples east of Malang, take a minibus from Arjosari terminal, 5km north of Malang.

■ **Candi Jago**★ – *18km east of Malang. Donation, allow 30min.* The melancholy ruins of Candi Jago, probably the funerary monument of the Singosari king **Wisnuwardhana** (d 1268), stand right in the middle of **Tumpang** village. The shrine, dedicated to Tantric Buddhism, consists of three superposed terraces, shaped like a mountain and topped by a little temple. Standing at the entrance is a magnificent headless **statue**★ of the sovereign, shown as the god Amoghapasa, recognisable by his eight arms. Like *wayang kulit* puppets made of stone, the sumptuous **bas-reliefs**★★ on the walls mix Buddhist *(Kunjakarna)*, Hindu *(Mahabharata)* and Javanese *(Angling Dharma)* themes.

■ **Candi Kidal** – *7km south of Candi Jago, minibus from Tumpang.* Barely earlier than the previous temple (1250), this one, however, has a completely different structure, narrow and tapering (the upper part of the building has disappeared). It stands in a pleasant country setting and has some outstanding **reliefs of Garuda**★ *(on three of its sides)*, the mythical bird that serves as Krishna's chariot. The temple is thought to be dedicated to the Singosari king **Anusapati**, who died in 1248.

The temple road

On the slopes of Mount Arjuna★

Excursions from Batu, a small town 20km west of Malang. Access by bemo.
While there are plenty of hotels, you need only spend a day there.

The mild climate and enchanting countryside on the slopes of Mount Arjuna (3 331m) have made the village of **Batu** a very popular holiday resort since the time of the Dutch. For tourists, Batu is mainly an excellent departure point for visiting the beautiful natural sites in the surrounding area.

One of these is the romantic **Caban Rondo waterfall** *(10km west of Batu, by taxi. Fee)*, which springs out of a small valley covered in pine trees. The spot is a favourite place for young lovers.

On the flanks of Mount Arjuna, above the little **Selekta** resort *(10km north of Batu)*, the road crosses through superb **countryside**★★ alternating between forest and terraced market gardens, often enveloped in mist in the late morning.

Beyond a pass (1 600m), you reach the **Cangar hot springs** (Air Panas Cangar) *(18km by bemo or taxi)* in the middle of a clearing. Given the cool temperature of the surroundings, this is one of the rare places in Java where you may appreciate a really hot bath.

Lastly, from Cangar you can either return to Malang or continue to Pacet *(13km)*, then Trowulan *(34km, or Surabaya, p 322)*. The road crosses a spectacular torrent before disappearing into thick **virgin forest**★★ that echoes with the cries of monkeys and the hum of birdsong.

Around Blitar

An excursion lasting half a day.
From Malang, you can visit the Blitar region in a day.

A peaceful, pleasant little town, Blitar's only claim to fame is that it is the birthplace of the very charismatic first president of the Republic of Indonesia, and his burial place. Erected in 1978, **Sukarno's tomb** (Makam Bung Karno) *(2km north, towards Panataran. Free entrance)* has little architectural interest, but nowhere else will you understand better the torments of present-day Indonesia *(see p 44)*. "Bung Karno", as Sukarno was affectionately known by the Indonesians, wanted to be buried in Bogor, near Jakarta. But on his death (1970), his successor Suharto, fearing that his tomb might become a gathering place for opponents, preferred to have him buried far away from the capital. In vain: the mausoleum of the ousted president has become an extremely popular place of pilgrimage.

Candi Penataran★

In Nglegok, 12km north of Blitar. Minibus or motorbike-taxi, 7am-5pm, donation, allow 1hr.
Rather than lingering in Blitar, take the road to the largest temple complex in East Java. Indeed, the Penataran site bears unique witness to the Singosari and Majapahit civilisations, as it was built over a period of 250 years (from 1200 to the middle of the 15C, with most of it dating from the 14C when the Majapahit kingdom was at its height). Perched at an altitude of 450m on the southern slopes of Kelud volcano, in the middle of coconut palms, the complex consists of three courtyards surrounded by a wall, a design that served as a prelude to that of Balinese temples.

In the first courtyard you will see *(on the left)* a wide stone **terrace**, where assemblies were held, as well as the base of a former **pendopo** (1375) that was used for offerings. Reliefs decorate the walls, recalling characters from *wayang kulit* narratives. But the most interesting feature in the courtyard is the little **Candi Ganesha**★ that contains a **statue** of the Indian elephant-god. A **head of Kala**, the terrifying lord of the forest in the *Ramayana*, crowns the entrance.

The second courtyard contains the **Naga temple★**, which owes its name to the enormous mythical snake that winds around the four sides of the building, supported by nine hieratic **regalian figures★**. A wooden roof like those of the *pura* in Bali would have covered the temple.

Nearer the mountain – the home of the gods – is the holiest of the three courtyards, where the **mother-temple★** stands imposingly. The edifice consists of a square base measuring 30m on the sides, on which are three tiered terraces. **Bas-reliefs★★** – among the most beautiful in East Java – run round the bases of the first two podiums, illustrating episodes from the *Ramayana* and the *Krisnayana* (Krishna's youth). Simple steps lead to the last terrace, which is adorned with winged serpents and lions. To the left of the temple is a little shrine that has been restored, and would originally have crowned the summit.

Lastly, behind the complex, do not miss the charming **pool★** (1415). This is decorated with bas-reliefs illustrating Indian fables from the *Panca Tantra*.

Making the most of Malang

COMING AND GOING

By plane – Merpati has a flight a day for Jakarta, which leaves from Malang military airport.

By train – Malang's main train station is at **Kota Baru**, 300m east of Tugu square. There are plenty of trains for Surabaya (8 departures a day, 2hr) and for Blitar (5 departures a day, 2hr). However, there is only one train a day for Yogyakarta (at 4pm, 7hr). The train for Banyuwangi leaves at 12.55pm and arrives at 7pm.

By bus – Malang has 3 bus terminals:
– **Arjosari terminal** (5km to the north) serves Surabaya (2hr), Probolinggo (2hr30min), Banyuwangi (via Jember, 6hr) and Denpasar (10hr).
– **Gadang terminal** (5km to the south) serves Blitar, (2hr).
– **Landungsari terminal** (5km to the northwest). A night bus leaves for Yogyakarta (7hr).
For long distances go through a travel agent, or through **Tugu Transport**, Jl Kertanegara, ☎ (0341) 36 83 63.

By minibus – Arjosari terminal for Singosari and Tumpang. **Landungsari terminal** for Batu. **Travel** minibuses are convenient for long distances.

Travel Surya, Jl Suropati, near the station, ☎ (0341) 35 41 17.
Putra Jaya, Jl Bromo 33, ☎ (0341) 223 33.

FINDING YOUR WAY

From Tugu square (between the Flower Market and the station), you can easily reach the centre of town, on the other side of the Brantas River. In Jl Jend Basuki Rahmat you will find plenty of restaurants, banks, shops and travel agents. The street extends south into Pasar Besar, the shopping district.

GETTING AROUND

By minibus – The "AG" "mikrolet" goes from Arjosari terminal to that of Gadang via the town centre. The "GL" provides a shuttle service between Gadang and Landungsari.

By taxi – Argo, ☎ (0341) 49 04 44.
Bima, ☎ (0341) 71 71 71.

By becak – Convenient for getting around the town centre. As usual, negotiate the fare.

Car rental – Enquire at hotels and travel agents. Favourable rates.

ADDRESS BOOK

Tourist information – Bapparda, Jl Tugu 1 (Monday to Saturday, 7.30am-1.30pm).

Bank/Currency exchange – Exchange rates are not very good in Malang.

BCA, Jl Jend Basuki Rahmat 70-74. The main foreign currencies are accepted. Visa cash dispenser.

Bank Bali, Jl Bromo 2. Visa cash dispenser.

BNI, Jl Jend Basuki Rahmat. Visa cash dispenser.

Post office/Telephone – Main post office, Jl Merdeka Selatan 5 (8am-8pm). Poste Restante (8am-2pm) and Internet (8am-12 midnight). **Telkom**, Jl Jend Basuki Rahmat 7-9 (open 24hr a day). **Wartel**, Jl Agus Salim, near the Santosa Hotel.

Cafe Internet, Jl Bromo 40, near the Bali Bank.

Pharmacy – Apotik Kabupaten, Jl Jend Basuki Rahmat 11 (8am-9.30pm).

Travel agents – Passopati, Jl Jend Basuki Rahmat 11E, ☎ (0341) 202 70.

Oen Tourism, Toko Oen restaurant, Jl Jend Basuki Rahmat 5, ☎ (0341) 36 40 52. An obliging, efficient team that offers a variety of tours and provides detailed information.

Mujur Surya, Jl Bromo 33, ☎ (0341) 223 33. Bus transport, car rental and tours.

WHERE TO STAY

There is a wide choice of hotels in and around Tugu square.

Modest

Hotel Helios, Jl Pattimura 37, ☎ (0341) 36 27 41 – 24rm. The best place for small budgets. The friendly staff are a mine of information on the region and can do your train and bus bookings. Take no heed of the taxi drivers who will tell you the hotel is full.

Average to high end

Splendid Inn, Jl Majapahit 4, near Tugu square, ☎ (0341) 36 68 60, Fax (0341) 36 36 18 – 27rm. ⌖ 廾 ✕ ⤳ The hotel laid out in a Dutch house provides excellent value for money. Obliging staff, and clean, comfortable rooms (some with air conditioning and hot water). It is a pity that the swimming pool is poorly maintained.

Hotel Kartika Kusuma, Jl Kahuripan 12 (near Tugu square), ☎ (0341) 35 22 66 – 31rm. ⌖ 廾 ✓ TV ✕ CC A place to tide you over if the Splendid is full. The rooms are comfortable (some with air conditioning), but have no special charm.

Hotel Pelangi, Jl Merdeka Selatan 3, ☎ (0341) 36 51 56, Fax (0341) 36 54 66 – 80rm. 廾 ✕ CC A vast hotel in a Dutch house in the town centre. Various categories of rooms ranging from modest to luxurious (some with air conditioning, hot water and bathtubs), but not always scrupulously clean.

Luxury

Tugu Park Hotel, Jl Tugu 3, ☎ (0341) 36 38 91, Fax (0341) 36 27 47 – 43rm. ⌖ ▤ ✓ TV ✕ ⤳ CC The hotel opened in 1990 and is already a legend with its antique furniture, refined decoration and pleasant garden swimming pool. Have a look at the antiques shop. The food in the restaurant and the cakes are delicious. Breakfast is not included. Negotiate a reduction.

EATING OUT

The *warung* in Jl Kawi serve excellent "bakmie" (Chinese noodles with condiments). Also try the "nasi rawon" (beef in a sauce with bean sprouts), the local delicacy.

Rumah Makan Agung, near the Alunalun. A simple, inexpensive restaurant serving succulent "martabak" (pancakes with a meat stuffing) and chicken Biryani.

Toko Oen, Jl Jend Basuki Rahmat 5. The uniformed waiters and the pianist are right out of the 1930s. Chinese and Western dishes, seafood and sandwiches, but we mainly recommend the ice-creams and cakes.

Melati Pavilion, Tugu Park Hotel. The setting, beside a swimming pool, is very pleasant, with cooking to match. Try the aubergine with breadcrumbs, the "nasi rawon" and the desserts. You can drink French wine here, but all pleasure has its price!

Cahyaningrat, Jl Soekarno-Hatta 18, to the north on the Ring Road, ☎ (0341) 47 14 72. A vast airy restaurant with a garden and a fountain, where you can eat sitting on mats ("lesehan"). Excellent Javanese cuisine.

East Java

Nikmat Lesat, Jl Gatot Subroto 94-96, near the Chinese temple. The best Chinese restaurant in town.

GOING OUT, HAVING A DRINK

Bars, tea rooms – Tugu Park, bar and excellent cakes.
Toko Oen, see above. Local ice-cream and cakes.

OTHER THINGS TO DO

Feasts and festivals – In July Malang's tourist week is the occasion for performances, exhibitions and birdsinging contests.

SHOPPING GUIDE

Markets – Pasar Besar, the big market in the south district in the street of the same name, has antiques, clothes, jewellery, electronic equipment and old books.
Pasar Bunga and **Pasar Burung**, the flower and bird markets (see description of "Malang" above).
In Blitar, **Pasar Legi** in the town centre is a charming popular market where you can find local handicrafts including basketry, bronzes, terracotta items and plaited paper hats that look like wastepaper baskets.

Shopping centres – Sarinah, Jl Jend Basuki Rahmat, Malang.

Antiques – Hendra Wira, Jl Ronggowarsito 19, near the station, ☎ (0341) 32 59 63. Thousands of old porcelain items and kitsch objects, as well as a little basketry at very reasonable prices.

Bookshop – Gramedia, Jl Jend Basuki Rahmat 3 (9am-9pm). You will find road maps and post cards, the "Jakarta Post" of the day, as well as English books and a sports section.

Photography – Fuji Image Plaza, Jl Jend Basuki Rahmat 15, Malang. Wide choice of film, and quick photo development.

Tobacconist's – Taman Tembakau, Jl Jend Basuki Rahmat 37, Malang. An old tobacco shop bathed in the fragrance of Javanese cigars, and run by the same couple for 50 years.

Making the most of Malang

MOUNT BROMO★★★

East Java Province – approximately 100km from Surabaya – Map p 320-321
A half-day excursion (with a 30min walk to the rim)
Alt 2 329m – Cool nights

Not to be missed
Sunrise over the Tengger caldera.

And remember...
Bring warm clothes and a torch, as well as water and
biscuits (hotels do not serve breakfast at 4am!)
Cover your camera carefully as the fine ash gets everywhere.

Perched at an altitude of 2 000m the **Tengger caldera** forms a gigantic sea of sand (8km by 6km) bristling with volcanic cones. In the background rises the threatening outline of **Mount Semeru**, Java's highest point (3 676m), which is regularly covered in thick dark cloud. The impressive landscape is like an image of the dawn of time. Daybreak is the best time to see the site, when the warm light of the first rays of the sun set the sky on fire, gradually outlining the steep crest of the cirque. As the sun rises the thick layer of mist wisps away, revealing three volcanoes standing close together in the middle of the caldera: **Kursi** (2 581m) with its green slopes, Bromo with its grey, smoking crater, and **Batok★★★** (2 440m), a perfect dark green cone, grooved with such regular ravines that they seem to have been dug out by a giant fork.

Mist and fire in the Tengger caldera (with Mount Semeru in the background)

East Java

G. Guérard

340

Sacred fire

Such a magical site inevitably has its myths and legends. The **Tengger**, a Hindu people who sought refuge here when Islam was spreading through Java are convinced that Mount Bromo, the last of the cirque's active volcanoes, is the dwelling place of Joko Seger, the holiest of their protective spirits.

As for **Mount Semeru***, it embodies Mahameru (or **Meru**), the holy mountain in Hindu cosmology. According to legend, when the gods were looking for a new abode they carried the mountain on their shoulders from the Himalayas to Java. The site, however, does not seem to please them as it is constantly shaken by explosions and

Mysterious Tengger

The 40 000 or so Tengger who live on the Tengger slopes are the last representatives of the Hindu kingdom of Blambangan, which disappeared in the 18C. Refusing to convert to Islam, the people retired to the mountains to form small religious communities, becoming the guardians of holy sites ("mandalas"). While they have renewed contact with the Hindus on Bali since the 1960s, the Tengger keep a strong hold on their own customs. They are deeply egalitarian, for instance, and only use one level of language no matter whom they are addressing. For lack of having developed a refined art form they have kept up a rich popular tradition, the highlight of which is the Kasada ceremony, a mixture of Hinduism and local beliefs. The festival commemorates the sacrifice of Roro Anteng and Joko Seger, who were forced to throw their 25th child into Bromo crater to keep their promise to the god Hyang Widi Wasa.

its latest deadly eruption dates back to 1994. Nonetheless, the energetic and the bold climb it, apparently an unforgettable experience *(see "Making the most of Mount Bromo")*.

Walking into the dawn

On the eve of the expedition, which begins in the middle of the night, most visitors sleep at Ngadisari or Cemara Lawang, small villages north of the caldera.

We should warn you that you will not be the only visitor. Apart from Tengger pilgrims, the site attracts hundreds of tourists a day (200 to 300 people, sometimes even 800 in summer).

The temperature here drops to 3°C, a rare event in Indonesia. The guides and locals look like Indians from the Andes, as they sit on their ponies in their ponchos and woollen hats *(on the way to Penanjakan, you will easily find hot coffee, gloves and a woolly hat)*.

The best place to see the sunrise is on **Gunung Penanjakan***, the highest volcano on the site (2 770m), which closes off the caldera to the west *(departure by jeep at 4am, 1hr)*. After a short (but bumpy!) crossing of the sea of sand, which is totally hidden by the darkness and the mist, the road snakes up the sides of the cliff to the top. Once there, it is just a question of waiting for the **spectacle*** of the dawn. First blue-grey, then pink, orange and scarlet, the whole caldera gradually appears in a blaze of different colours until the sun has fully risen.

Mount Bromo

Once the inevitable photo session is over, let the troops of jeeps depart before going down into the caldera to climb Mount Bromo.

The last active volcano in the cirque, **Bromo***** is the most famous although it is the smallest (2 329m). A tough flight of steps leads to the rim of the **crater*****. You are immediately seized by the sight of the hell-like opening below, out of which noisily escapes a thick white cloud smelling strongly of sulphur. This is where the Tengger throw their offerings of flowers, rice and even cockerels during the **Kasada** festival. Every year the ceremony attracts almost 200 000 pilgrims who come to the foot of the volcano and then climb to its rim.

Take the time to walk round the rim *(allow about 1hr; the path is easy)* to take in the extraordinary **panoramic view***** of the caldera and the other volcanoes. At the foot of Bromo and Batok, you suddenly see a **Hindu temple***, which was built by the Tengger, a forgotten shrine hidden in the mist.

Making the most of Mount Bromo

COMING AND GOING

In Yogyakarta some travel agents organise a tour that goes as far as Bali, via Mount Bromo, but the second half of the trip is in uncomfortable buses. In Surabaya and Malang you will find plenty of agents for Bromo. There are several tours possible.

• Via Probolinggo (northeast)

This is the most traditional route. Probolinggo has good bus services from Surabaya (2hr), Malang (2hr30min), Yogyakarta (8hr), Banyuwangi (5hr) and Denpasar (9hr). You can also take a train from Surabaya (2hr) or Banyuwangi (5hr). The bus station is 5km from Probolinggo (by *bemo*), on the volcano road. Take a minibus to Cemara Lawang (avoid going through touts to buy your ticket), situated on the edge of the cirque (45km, 90min). Once in **Cemara Lawang**, the simplest solution is to charter a jeep that will take you to Gunung Penanjakan (departure at 4am, 1hr for the drive up), then to Mount Bromo. When you come down from Penanjakan, you may choose to cross the sea of sand to Bromo on horseback or on foot, but the jeep traffic appreciably mars the charm of the trip.

Lastly, some people walk to Mount Bromo at night armed with a torch to see the dawn from its crater (which means getting up at 2.30am). While crossing the sea of sand is quite magical (in spite of the jeeps that catch up with you), daybreak is still much more beautiful from the top of Penanjakan. Up to you to choose.

• Via Wonokitri (north)

From Surabaya take a bus to Pasuruan (90min) then go to Warung Dowo (3km) where you can take a minibus to Tosari (40km, 90min), via Puspo. Then possibly a motorbike-taxi to Wonokitri (3km). In Tosari you will have no trouble finding a jeep for Gunung Penanjakan and Bromo. From Malang take a bus or minibus for Pasuruan and get off at Warung Dowo, then take a minibus to Tosari. Another possibility would be to take a bus to Purwodadi (30km, 30min), then a minibus to Wonokitri via Nongkojajar (37km, 90min). But you may have to finish the trip by motorbike-taxi.

To make things easier you can always charter a *bemo* or a taxi in Malang or Surabaya.

• Via Ngadas (southwest)

This is also the departure point for climbing **Mount Semeru**, and is an alternative route for the descent from Bromo and heading across the sea of sand towards Malang. The trip is tiring but superb.

From Malang take a minibus to Tumpang (20km, 30min) where you will be able to charter a jeep for Jemplang (29km, 90min), on the edge of the caldera. Mount Bromo is at the other end of the sea of sand (6km, 30min).

ADDRESS BOOK

PHPA – Forest Protection and Environment Conservation Office, Jl Raden Intan 6, Malang, ☎ (0341) 49 18 28.

WHERE TO STAY, EATING OUT

Hotels have rooms in all price ranges. The most luxurious have hot water (which is welcome, as the temperature is cool). Breakfast is not always included.

● Sukapura

Luxury

Hotel Raya Bromo, Sukapura, 18km from Cemara Lawang, ☎ (0335) 58 11 03, Fax (0335) 58 11 42 – 180rm. ⌐ ✆ TV ✗ ⌐ CC Hot water. The hotel is laid out on the mountainside and has a superb panoramic view. The swimming pool is huge, but the bungalows could do with a little renovation. You can hire a jeep here for Mount Bromo. The restaurant serves Western, Indonesian and Chinese food.

● Ngadisari

Average

Yoschi, 2km before you reach Ngadisari and 5km from the caldera, ☎ (0335) 233 87 – 22rm. ✗ A charming hotel, with lovely rooms decorated with wood and matting, and a pleasant garden. In the cheaper accommodation the bathrooms are shared. You can arrange transport by jeep with the staff.

● Cemara Lawang

Modest

Cafe Lava Hostel, ☎ (0335) 234 58 – 29rm. ✗ CC A good place for travellers. Friendly welcome. The rooms are well kept and some have their own bathrooms. The restaurant, which serves good Western and Indonesian food, has surprising decor, suggestive of a western film.

Average

Hotel Bromo Permai I, ☎ (0335) 54 10 21 – 52rm. A wide choice of clean, comfortable rooms, ranging from the cheapest (without private bathrooms), to the "VIPs", with television, private bathrooms and breakfast included.

Lava View Lodge, ☎ (0335) 54 10 09 – 16rm. ⌐ ✗ CC Located a little away from the others, near the terminal. The pavilions on the edge of the crater have an exceptionally fine view of Mount Bromo. Some of the rooms have hot water.

High end

Cemara Indah Hotel, ☎ (0335) 54 10 19 – 40rm. ✗ The reception is blasé, the standard of comfort and cleanliness is doubtful, and the restaurant serves mediocre food. All in all, a place to avoid. But there is a view of the crater.

● Tosari and Wonokitri

Modest

Penginapan Kartika Sari, Wonokitri, ☎ (0343) 57 10 58 – 8rm. You stay with the family, in simple, inexpensive accommodation. The bathrooms are shared, and breakfast is extra, but you are given a friendly welcome.

High end

Hotel Bromo Tosari, Tosari, ☎ (0343) 57 12 22, Fax (0343) 57 13 33 – 90rm. ⌐ ✗ CC A huge hotel with comfortable pavilions laid out on the mountainside, with a magnificent view of the outer slopes of the caldera. The hot water at all times is a very welcome luxury.

OTHER THINGS TO DO

Climbing Mount Semeru – Approximately 20km south of Bromo. To be able to climb, you must be in good physical condition (allow about 3 days). Get hold of a stout pair of walking boots and camping equipment, and an experienced guide. You must also obtain a permit from the **PHPA** in Malang, Jl Raden Intan 6, ☎(0341) 651 00. The best period to climb is in the dry season, from May to October. The trip begins in Ranu Pani, where you will find a guide. Be warned, the volcanic ejections (stones) at the summit can pose a real danger.

Kasada ceremony – The Kasada ceremony takes place on the 14th day of the month in the Hindu Tengger calendar (November). Apart from the procession to Bromo (see sidebar), there is a dance performance in Ngadisari village.

KAWAH IJEN★★★

BANYUWANGI

East Java Province – Map p 320-321
Approximately 150km from Malang – A half-day excursion on the site
Alt 2 500m – Cool nights

Not to be missed
The sulphur lake.

And remember...
Go up the volcano in the dry season, from May to October.
Bring warm clothing and basic supplies of food.

The eastern end of Java with its active volcanoes, huge primary forests and deserted beaches is a large area of unspoilt nature. But the jewel of the region is unquestionably Kawah Ijen, an impressive volcanic crater *("kawah")*. It is the setting for a turquoise lake upon which dance thick wreathes of sulphurous vapours. The volcano and its neighbours, **Mount Merapi** (2 800m) and **Mount Raung** (3 332m) to the south, have given their names to an immense nature reserve that spreads out at their feet covering a forested plateau of 130 000ha. This is a paradise of greenery inhabited by countless birds that sing out from every shrub and tree. At the northern tip of the area the adjoining **Baluran** national park also promises unforgettable walks. You may see deer and **banteng**, the enormous oxen endemic to Java. So, on with your boots and away you go!

On the sides of Kawah Ijen: sulphur miners

D Clarisse

Java's eastern peninsula

The road to Kawah Ijen crosses a fertile region where huge patches of forest alternate with coffee, cocoa and pepper plantations. **Bondowoso**, the last town before you disappear into the heart of the Ijen-Maelang-Raung reserve, owes its fame to its colourful **buffalo fights**. Apparently, a very long time ago, a landowner who was desperately trying to dry out and level his swampy land, thought of organising a buffalo fight and inviting all the villagers. The result, after several hours of tramping about, was better than anything he had ever hoped for.

The sulphur miners
Every day about a hundred porters climb up to the Ijen crater to collect sulphur. In the midst of suffocating fumes they dig out the precious yellow mineral with pickaxes, then load it into baskets hung onto poles, which they carry down to Paltuding 4km below. Before the Paltuding road was built (1995), they used to have to walk 30km. By doing one or two trips a day, with average loads of 70kg (worth Rp150 per kg), each porter earns between Rp10 000 and Rp20 000 a day. The strongest men manage to carry loads of up to 100kg!

Ijen-Maelang-Raung Nature Reserve★★

Between Sempol and Paltuding it is better to have your own vehicle, rather than waiting for a bemo that may or may not happen to come along. Lost in the middle of coffee plantations, **Sempol** village (*about 40km from Bondowoso*) is an ideal place to spend the night before climbing Kawah Ijen. In the morning you go to the forest station at **Paltuding** (*10km east of Sempol*), where a good track leads off through the forest to the crater (*1hr walk*). You pass **sulphur miners** who go back and forth to the crater by way of the **weighing station** (*slightly below the crater, on the edge of the forest*). These imperturbable men seem to do the trip without the slightest effort, even on the way back, when, laden like mules they tear down the volcano at top speed. Offering a cigarette is a polite gesture that is always welcome (*bring a stock with you*), especially if you want to take photos.

The high sides of the **crater**★★★ are completely bare, and from them you have a breathtaking view. The **lake**★★★, a still stretch of milky-green water, lies at the bottom of the rock cauldron, while on the shore you can see the yellow stain of an open **sulphur mine**★★ out of which rises a thick cloud of smoke.

You can go down to the lake along a rocky path (*30min*). Watch out, however, for the sulphur fumes. While they are only dangerous in repeated doses, they get into your clothes and leave an unpleasant smell of bad eggs. To avoid this you can go round the crater up to the summit, where you have a superb **view**★★. Lastly, from here you can continue to a small **dam** that closes off the lake at the other end.

From here you can go directly to Banyuwangi (*about 20km*) along a rough track that goes through a magnificent **tropical forest**★★ of tall trees full of monkeys.

Banyuwangi

In spite of its proximity to Bali, whose coast stretches out opposite, Java's easternmost town sees few tourists as most of them head directly for the jetty at **Ketapang**, 8km to the north. And yet this large town, where there are no tall buildings, is quite charming. Its **central market**, for instance, is a good goal for a walk, even if you have not planned to buy anything.

You should also take the time to visit the **Blambangan Regional Museum** (Museum Daerah Blambangan) (*Jl Sritanjung, 7am-12noon; closed Sunday, donation*), which is small but full of surprising objects. There are very old Hindu items, **kris** daggers that are just as old, as well as an enigmatic animist **bronze statue**★ that has never been properly researched.

Kawah Ijen

If you are thinking of going to Malang along the south road via Jember, the little town of **Kalibaru** *(80km west of Banyuwangi)* makes for a very pleasant stop in the middle of coffee and cocoa plantations. Along the way you will have some extraordinary **views***** of Mount Raung, Mount Argopuro and especially **Mount Semeru** *(see p 340)*.

Making the most of Kawah Ijen

East Java

COMING AND GOING

There are two access routes to Kawah Ijen: via Bondowoso, to the west of the reserve, or via Banyuwangi, to the east. As there is little in the way of public transport, it is best to have your own car.

By bus – You can go to Bondowoso by bus from Surabaya (200km) and Probolinggo (100km, 2hr). From Bondowoso, a minibus climbs twice a day to Sempol (60km). **Pos Paltuding**, the departure point for the walk, is 15km away.
– To reach Pos Paltuding from Banyuwangi (30km to the west), take a minibus from Blambangan terminal to Sasak Perot, then another one to Jambu (18km). But be careful, beyond that the track (12km) is only practicable by truck, jeep (enquire at your hotel) or on foot!

WHERE TO STAY

• **Sempol**
Average
Catimor Homestay, in Blawan, 2km beyond Sempol, then a track for 3km, ☎ (0331) 868 61 – 16rm. 📶 ✕ The guesthouse in the middle of a coffee plantation is a little difficult to reach, but the main Dutch-style building has character (on the other hand, the rooms in the outbuildings are rather ordinary). There is an impressive waterfall nearby, with a heavy flow.
Arabica Homestay, Kebun Kalisat, ☎ (031) 352 48 93 (reservations in Surabaya) – 18rm. 📶 The guesthouse is pleasantly located in the green surroundings of the Wisata Agro coffee plantation

and has huge, comfortable rooms. Be warned, it is sometimes full. Reserve for meals and breakfast.

• **Kalibaru**
High end
📶**Margo Utomo Homestay**, Jl Lapangan 10, ☎ (0333) 684 67 – 53rm. 📶 ✕ 📺 ✕ The spacious, comfortable rooms have a little terrace giving onto a luxuriant garden. If the hotel is full, try the other "Margo Utomo" a few kilometres away. Tours are organised in the plantations, to Kawah Ijen and to Meru Betiri national park.

EATING OUT

• **Sempol**
Warung Pak Hurdin, the only restaurant in the village serves reasonable but rather unimaginative food.

OTHER THINGS TO DO

Excursions – **Baluran national park** can be reached by bus from Banyuwangi (35km) but, once there, it is better to have a vehicle. You can stay at the **PHPA** (bring your own food), which organises jeep trips.
Meru Betiri and Alas Purwo (Blambangan) national parks are much more difficult to reach.

Feasts and festivals – **Aduan Sapi**, the traditional buffalo fights in Bondowoso, take place over the weekend from February to July and from October to December.

Making the most of Banyuwangi

COMING AND GOING

By bus – *Seri Tanjung Terminal*, north of Ketapang (8km north of Banyuwangi): buses for Probolinggo (3hr), Surabaya (5hr) and Malang.

The **main station**, near the Ketapang jetty serves Probolinggo (5hr), Surabaya (7hr), Malang (6hr) and Yogyakarta (15hr).

Brawijaya Terminal (or Karang Ente), 4km south of the town, serves Jember.

Going to Bali – *Ketapang jetty* has ferries every half-hour, 24hr a day, for Bali (crossing, 30min). From there, you can either take a tourist bus direct to Ubud (departure at 3pm) or, when you arrive at Gilimanuk, take a public bus to Denpasar.

GETTING AROUND

Becaks are ideal for short distances in town. **Blambangan**, the *bemo* terminal, is in Jl Basuki Rahmat.

ADDRESS BOOK

Tourist information – Jl Diponegoro 2.

PHPA – *Forest Protection and Environment Conservation Office*, Jl A Yani 108, ☎ (0333) 241 19. Information on the Baluran, Meru Betiri and Alas Purwo national parks.

Bank/Currency exchange – *BCA*, Jl Sudirman. *BNI*, Jl Banterang. Visa cash dispenser.

Post office/Telephone – *Telkom*, Jl Diponegoro 3. *Main post office*, Jl Diponegoro 1.

WHERE TO STAY

Modest

Hotel Baru, Jl MT Hariyono 82-84 (near the old station), ☎ (0333) 42 13 69 – 48rm. ✕ The rooms are austere but cheap (some have air conditioning and television). Ask for a room in the building opposite the restaurant.

Hotel Slamet, Jl Wahid Hasyim 96 (a stone's throw from the Baru), ☎ (0333) 42 46 75 – 37rm. ✕ Really Spartan facilities with minimal cleanliness but the reception is friendly and the prices good.

Average

Hotel Pinang Sari, Jl Basuki Rahmat 116/122, near the Blambangan terminal, ☎ (0333) 232 66 – 37rm. ⌂ ✕ In a good position, and full of charm. The best place in town. A wide range of rooms, with the most pleasant accommodation in bamboo bungalows giving onto the garden. Some rooms have air conditioning.

Hotel Ikhtiar Surya, Jl Gajah Mada 9, ☎ (0333) 42 10 63 – 39rm. ⌂ ✕ The hotel is a little way out of the centre. A huge choice of rooms, ranging from cheaper ones to more comfortable with air conditioning, hot water and television. The furniture and carpets seem to date from the 1970s, but the courtyard garden is quite pleasant.

Luxury

Hotel Ketapang Indah, Jl Gatot Subroto, 6km north of Banyuwangi, before Ketapang, ☎ (0333) 222 80, Fax (0333) 235 97 – 53rm. ⌂ 🗐 ✆ 📺 ✕ 🏊 ☲ ⌀ 💳 Laid out beside a rather dreary beach, this place is nonetheless the best hotel in the region. The most expensive rooms are not necessarily the best, and, whatever room you take, you should not hesitate to negotiate a reduction. Scuba diving and deep-sea fishing can be arranged.

EATING OUT

The little stalls along Jl Pattimura stay open late in the evening and serve specialities such as "dadak jagung" (small pies with eggs and corn).

Moderate

Rumah Makan Sariwangi, Jl Basuki Rahmat 130 (7am-11pm). A small, pleasant seafood restaurant not far from the Pinang Sari Hotel.

OTHER THINGS TO DO

Festivals – *Petik Laut*, the sea festival in Banyuwangi, takes place on Muncar beach in July. There are dances, and goat sacrifices in the sea.

The Mother Temple of Besakih on Gunung Agung's misty slopes

BALI

With its beaches fringed by coral reefs, terraced rice fields glinting emerald in the sun, narrow valleys overgrown with forests, and majestic, destructive volcanoes, it is by no means surprising that the Balinese consider their island to be the work of the gods.

Yet despite its modest size – not quite 140km from east to west by 80km north to south, ie 5 620sqkm – Bali is an island full of contrasts. The volcanic mountain chain stretching from east to west still comprises a few active craters, the highest being **Gunung Agung** at 3 014m. Their successive eruptions have fertilised the island soils while their summits of around 2 000m attract the rainfall that feeds lakes and rivers.

For water flows abundantly on Bali. Sitting 8° south of the equator, the island enjoys a pleasant **tropical climate** with a high level of humidity (80% on average). The year is divided into two seasons, dry from April and then damp and hotter from October, although rain does fall all year round, in short sharp bursts, and temperatures, which vary between 24°C and 31°C, depend more on relief than season.

This endless water, cleverly utilised thanks to a complex irrigation system, ensures two generous harvests a year. In the south, the island's rice granary, a multitude of lakes and rivers floods the rice fields terracing the gently sloping hills. On the drier narrow coastal plain in the north, the main activities are coffee and copra growing and livestock farming, all mainly for export. The higher regions, which are very humid and cooler, produce fruit and vegetables, flowers, coffee, cloves, tobacco, vanilla, cacao, etc. West Bali, covered by the vast forests of the national park, is poorer and less populated, as is the northeast, devastated by Gunung Agung's angry outbursts, and especially the limestone plateau of the **Bukit** peninsula and the arid islands of **Nusa Penida** and **Lembongan**.

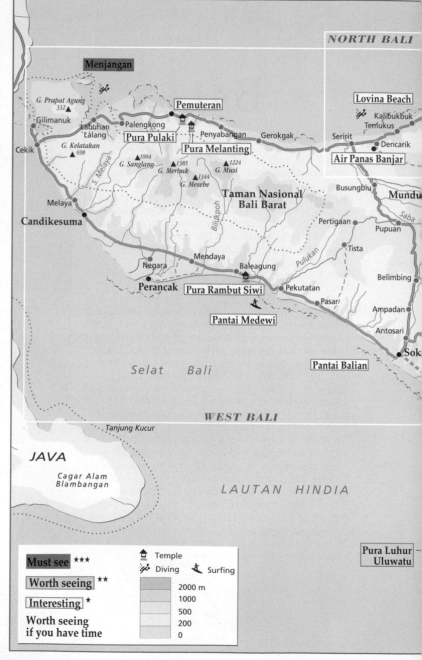

NORTH BALI

Menjangan

G. Prapat Agung
332

Gilimanuk

Pemuteran

Lovina Beach

Kalibukbuk
Temukus

Labuhan
Lalang

Palengkong

Penyabangan

Gerokgak

Seririt

Dencarik

Pura Pulaki

Cekik

G. Kelatakan
698

Pura Melanting

Air Panas Banjar

G. Sanglang 1004

G. Merbuk 1385

G. Musi 1224

Busungbiu

Mundu

G. Mesehe 1344

Saba

Melaya

Taman Nasional
Bali Barat

Pertigaan

Pupuan

Candikesuma

Bilukpoh

Tista

Belimbing

Negara

Mendaya

Baleagung

Pulukan

Perancak

Pura Rambut Siwi

Pekutatan

Ampadan

Antosari

Pantai Medewi

Pasar

Sok

Selat   Bali

Pantai Balian

WEST BALI

Tanjung Kucur

JAVA

Cagar Alam
Blambangan

LAUTAN   HINDIA

Pura Luhur
Uluwatu

Must see ★★★

Temple

Worth seeing ★★

Diving

Surfing

Interesting ★

2000 m

Worth seeing
if you have time

1000
500
200
0

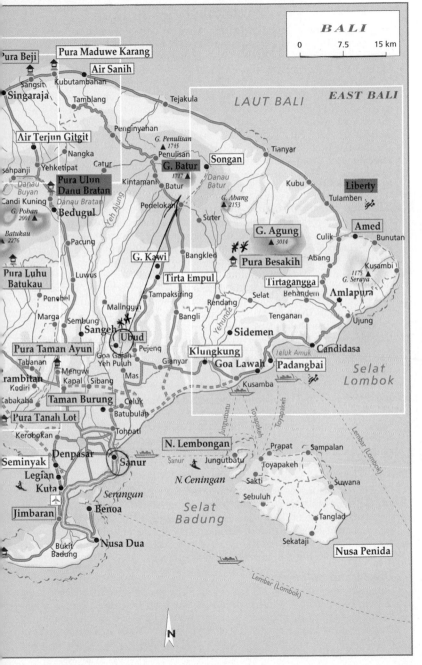

BALI

0   7.5   15 km

Pura Beji

Pura Maduwe Karang

Air Sanih

Sangsit   Kubutambahan
Singaraja
Tamblang

Tejakula   LAUT BALI   EAST BALI

Penginyahan

Air Terjun Gitgit

Nangka   G. Penulisan
Catur   ▲ 1745
Sahpanji   Yehketipat   Penulisan   Tianyar
Danau   G. Batur   Songan
Buyan   Pura Ulun   Kintamani   1717 ▲   Danau
Candi Kuning   Danu Bratan   Batur   Batur   Kubu   Liberty
G. Poban   Danau Bratan   Penelokan   G. Abang   Tulamben
2001 ▲   Bedugul   ▲ 2153   Amed
Batukau   Suter   G. Agung   Culik   Bunutan
▲ 2276   Pacung   ▲ 3014   Abang   Kusambi
G. Kawi   Bangkled   Pura Besakih   1175 ▲
Pura Luhu   Luwus   Tirta Empul   Tirtagangga   G. Seraya
Batukau   Selat   Behandem   Amlapura
Penebel   Tampaksiring   Rendang   Tenganan   Ujung
Marga   Mallngguh   Bangli   Tenganan
Sembung   Sangeh   Sidemen
Pura Taman Ayun   Ubud   Pejeng
Tabanan   Goa Gajah   Klungkung   Candidasa
Mengwi   Yeh Puluh   Gianyar   Goa Lawah   Teluk Amuk
Trambitan   Kapal   Sibang   Mas   Padangbai   Selat
Kodiri   Kusamba   Lombok
Kabakaba   Taman Burung   Celuk
Batubulan
Pura Tanah Lot   Tohpati
Kerobokan   N. Lembongan
Seminyak   Denpasar   Prapat   Sampalan
Legian   Sanur   Jungutbatu   Toyapakeh
Kuta   N. Ceningan   Sakti   Suwana
Serangan   Sebuluh
Jimbaran   Benoa   Selat   Tanglad
Badung
Bukit   Sekataji   Nusa Penida
Badung   Nusa Dua   Lembar (Lombok)

N

Bali

Uncertain origins

Archeological remains found in Bali – pottery and stone tools around 3 000 years old – prove that the island was inhabited as early as the **Neolithic Age**. Other artefacts, including the famous Moon of Pejeng (*see p 407*), date back to the **Bronze Age** (about 5000-1200 BC). According to the earliest written records so far discovered – 9C stone inscriptions – its inhabitants were already cultivating rice using a complex irrigation system and respecting some of the religious and cultural traditions that have continued up to the present day. The first inhabitants were **animists** who worshipped the spirits they believed lived everywhere and in everything; **ancestor worship** likewise dates back to very ancient times. The exact dating of Bali's Indianisation is not known, but clay tablets have been found bearing a religious 8C **Buddhist** text. Other documents dating from the 10C indicate that India's **Hindu civilisation** had already been present on the island for several centuries and show the growing influence of Java over Bali.

The last bastion of Indo-Javanese civilisation

In the first half of the 11C, the reign of the great Javanese ruler **Airlangga**, son of a Javanese princess and the Balinese king Udayana (*see p 34*), brought the two islands together under the same crown. Strong bonds developed between the two territories, to the benefit of Java whose culture flourished in Bali. On Airlangga's death, however, the island regained a certain level of independence, interrupted by brief spells of Javanese domination, particularly from 1284 to 1292 under **Kertanegara**. In 1343 it was firmly reconquered by the very powerful **Majapahit** dynasty (1294-1527) (*see p 34*). **Gajah Mada**, grand vizier of the Javanese realm, subjugated the great Balinese king **Dalem Bedaulu** and placed a Javanese priest on the throne who took the hereditary title of *Dewa Agung* (great god).

From the golden age to the war of the rajas

In the 15C, while Islam was being imposed in Java, Hinduism found refuge in Bali. On the fall of the Majapahit kingdom, the Javanese elite – priests and nobles as well as artists, dancers and musicians – emigrated to Bali in large numbers. Indo-Javanese influence spread rapidly, affecting every aspect of Balinese life: politics, the royal court, religion, the caste system, the arts and architecture, language and literature, etc. The rajas' palaces in **Gelgel**, the kingdom's new capital, developed into prestigious cultural centres where new artistic trends combining Javanese and Balinese elements flourished, reaching their heyday in the 16C.

But a sombre series of princely quarrels put an end to the *Dewa Agung*'s dynasty in the 17C. Several vassals aspiring to independence broke their allegiance to Gelgel and the island broke up into small independent territories. The descendants of the dynasty finally established their capital in **Klungkung** in 1710. There followed a long period of instability during which the island's political life was governed by rivalries between rajas, as well as wars and alliances, new States and fallen kingdoms. It was not until the 19C that the situation began to stabilise.

Divide and colonise

During the first half of the 19C Bali combined prosperity – thanks to its fertile soil and lucrative trading – with independence, two assets which were seen as a hindrance by the Dutch, who were seeking to build up a vast colonial empire by expanding their hegemony over the entire archipelago. Their military conquest of Bali began in 1846 with the launching of several expeditions. The north of the island was taken in 1849 and from 1882 a colonial government sat in **Singaraja**.

However, conflicts quickly broke out between almost all the Balinese kingdoms, a situation that the Dutch were to turn to their advantage. In 1894 their support for the **Sasak** rebellion *(see p 470)* helped to bring down the Balinese kings of **Lombok**. Some kingdoms, such as **Karangasem** (1895) and **Glanyar** (1900), agreed to recognise the coloniser's sovereignty in order to safeguard a semblance of power, but the rebel kingdoms of Tabanan, Badung and Klungkung, which remained obstinately opposed, were one by one conquered by force. Using the looting of a wrecked ship as a pretext, the Dutch landed on the Sanur coast in 1906 and marched on Denpasar. With only their kris to fight the cannon, the rulers of Badung preferred to take their own lives in a tragic **puputan** ("fight to the death") *(see sidebar p 366)*. Two years later the Klungkung *puputan* signed the death warrant of the last Balinese kingdom, and the island then came under the control of the Dutch crown.

The Balinisation of Bali

Was it guilt or genuine interest? In the years following their conquest, the Dutch attempted to blot out the Balinese bloodshed by presenting a flattering image of their colonial policy. They gave a predominant role to the local aristocracy, founded on respect for tradition and indigenous culture, and also strove to promote what they saw as a "living museum", the last bastion of Indo-Javanese civilisation, through tourism. In the 1920s and 1930s, wealthy aesthetes and intellectuals flocked from all over the world to sample the unique refinements of this exotic paradise.

For or against independence

In March 1942 the **Japanese Invasion** revived nationalist hopes long smothered by the colonial government. On 17 August 1945 the declaration of the **Republic of Indonesia** divided the Balinese. Many of them, mostly peasants, showed support for **Sukarno**, the new nation's President, and mobilised to oppose the return of the Dutch. However, the higher castes belonging to the more influential minority had established a compromise with the colonial power that safeguarded their privileges. The struggle between the two sides rapidly began to look like civil war, which culminated in the **Battle of Marga** on 20 November 1946, in which the last pocket of pro-independence fighters led by **Ngurah Rai** met a heroic end.

The Republic's bloody beginnings

After Indonesia proclaimed its independence in 1949, most of Bali remained faithful to **Sukarno**, the new nation's President, who was fond of the island and made it a special case, giving it the status of province in 1958 and working to develop tourism there. But the 1960s were particularly black years, with political and economic chaos, a devastating eruption of Mount Agung that claimed many lives (1963), followed by an attempted *coup d'état* (1965). The latter initiated bloody **anti-Communist repression** that was particularly severe in Bali, where almost 100 000 people were massacred. Their crime was to have advocated agrarian reform and the abolition of the caste system, both traditional foundations of Balinese society.

Paradise for all

When General **Suharto** became president in 1967 and instigated his New Order, the era of mass tourism opened in Bali. Aware of the island's potential due to its Garden of Eden image, the government chose to turn it into a **showcase for Indonesia**, the focus of its tourist development. Although the island was still a relatively unknown paradise, all that began to change from the early 1970s on. With the massive development of infrastructure (roads, water and electricity, telecommunications and, of course, hotels), everything was now in place to welcome visitors.

From less than 30 000 a year in the late 1960s, the number of visitors shot up to over a million a year in the early 1990s. Over the same period hotel capacity grew from under 500 rooms to over 25 000. A great frenzy took hold of investors (mostly non-Balinese), often to the detriment of the environment.

Cultural tourism or tourist culture?

So what does this tourist invasion mean for Bali today and for those specific cultural traits that have forged the island's reputation? The debate is a stormy one. Detractors lament nostalgically that there is really nothing authentic left on Bali. For them, tourism has turned a page that can never be turned back, and the lure of profits has corrupted all the traditions, henceforth focused on tourist tastes. Mercantile relations control creativity, and even religious ceremonies have been perverted so as to fulfil visitors' expectations!

The island's most fervent fans are more optimistic, conserving the romantic vision of the early Westerners. They maintain that the Balinese have succeeded in making the best of the upheavals caused by foreign intrusion and in turning them to their advantage, but without losing their souls.

Whatever the case, it seems that the **cultural tourism** (parawisata budaya) encouraged by the authorities has fulfilled its promises. Its aim was to develop the island's cultural resources in order to attract visitors, while at the same time utilising tourist revenue to preserve and promote its culture. At all events, it has to be admitted that this policy has at least had the positive effect of reviving the Balinese's interest in their own traditions and strengthening their attachment to their cultural identity. Whether people are sceptical or convinced, one thing is clear: the island has two faces, an authentic one that remains sheltered from foreign eyes, and another fashioned for the tourists and available for consumption.

Hindus and minorities

Ninety-five percent of the island's population of 3 million are **Balinese Hindus**. A tiny Hindu enclave in an immense Muslim country, this religious minority is descended from the Indo-Javanese civilisation, from which it inherited its **caste system**. Peasants and craftsmen form the largest sector and belong to the lowest caste, the Sudra. The local aristocracy is divided between Brahman (scholars and priests), Satria (the ruler caste) and Wesia, the caste traditionally composed of the kingdom's warriors and administrators. Although its role is now noticeably reduced, this hierarchy continues to govern certain religious rituals as well as the use of different levels of language.

Only the **Bali Aga** minority (see p 437, "Trunyan", and p 426, "Tenganan"), the island's original inhabitants, have resisted the caste system. During the Majapahit invasion in the 15C these indigenous Balinese fled into the secluded regions of the island and refused to adopt the Indo-Javanese culture, thus preserving their ancient Hindu traditions.

Family and social rank

How confusing when you meet the fifth Wayan of the day, or are introduced to yet another Nyoman! The explanation is that the Balinese name their children according to the order in which they were born, so that all first-born children, male or female, are named Wayan, the second-born Made, the third Nyoman and the fourth Ketut. A fifth baby coming into the family presents no problem: they just start again at Wayan, and so on. Variations nevertheless do exist (Gede, Putu, Kadek, etc) and there is no lack of nicknames. In addition, the titles such as Cokorda, Dewa or Gusti that precede some names indicate social position.

Alongside these, increasing numbers of **Indonesians**, from Java and Lombok as well as from islands further away are flocking to Bali, attracted by the tourist trade. Lastly, small groups of **Chinese** and **Indian** traders, plus, of course, the closed circle of **Western** expatriates, complete the island's ethnic portrait.

Society and cosmic order

For the Balinese, the social order reflects an unchanging cosmic order that governs all aspects of daily life. Their universe makes a distinction between the positive domain of the **celestial powers** – associated with ancestors, sky and mountains – that of **humans** and rites – linked to the earth – and that of the harmful **chthonic forces** corresponding to the sea and the underworld. This hierarchy is incorporated at every level in the form of microcosms that dictate everything from the layout of the houses, villages and temples to the very structure of the human body.

Community life

All Balinese obey a strict network of social, religious and economic institutions that define each individual's place in society, role and daily duties, as well as the community's rituals. A person exists first of all as a member of one group or another before existing as an individual. He belongs to his *desa* (village), to his *banjar* and to his *subak* (*see below*), but often to other associations as well (of gamelan musicians, for example).

Space and cosmic cycles

Villages, temples, houses, fields, religious rituals – in Bali everything is governed by the cardinal points dictated by the cosmic order. The mountains (particularly Mount Agung), considered from the very beginning to be where gods and ancestors dwell, represent the "kaja" direction, the purest and most sacred. This is where water comes from, source of the island's fertility and purification. Opposite this is the sea that receives wastewater and human ashes. It is the downstream, "kelod", direction representing the impure and the profane. Corresponding to the "kaja-kelod" cycle of water and souls is the solar cycle starting in the east ("kangin"), the positive focus, and terminating in the west ("kauh"), its negative counterpart. The same pattern applies to the human body, with the head housing the soul and corresponding to "kaja", the feet to "kelod", and right being superior to left.

The **villages** form the administrative units, and each constitutes the social and religious unit to which every Balinese remains linked. Even city-dwellers continue to participate in the life of their native village and to follow the customs (*adat*) passed on by the elders. A similar plan dictates the organisation of each village. Where the two main streets intersect there is generally a **square** (*alun-alun*) with the most important buildings: the **market**, the former ruler's **palace** (*puri*), sometimes accompanied by a tower housing the **kulkul** (a signal drum beaten to sound the alarm or to gather the villagers together), and a **banyan**, the sacred tree of the Hindus. The village's three main temples (*kahyangan tiga*) are laid out in accordance with the Balinese cardinal points (*see sidebar above*), each one being in addition associated with a god of the Hindu trinity. In the *kaja-kangin* part the **pura puseh** (temple of origins, dedicated to the village's founding ancestors) is associated with Brahma, in the centre the **pura desa** (devoted to the village's protective spirits) honours Vishnu, while the **pura dalem** (temple of the depths, the dead) on the *kelod-kauh* side near the cemetery and the cremation site, is devoted to Siva.

Houses are spread out in several districts or **banjar**, formed of rows of family compounds, which also form neighbourhood associations or sub-communities within the village. They serve both civil and religious purposes and are governed by their own customary law (*banjar adat*) and a system of mutual assistance. Each *banjar* has

Society and cosmic order

its temple, its *kulkul* and above all its **bale banjar**, a pavilion where the council formed of the married men from the *banjar* meets, and where people socialise, play cards or sometimes watch television.

All **sawah** (rice field) owners have to belong to an irrigation association, or **subak**. Membership, which is not connected to any other village institution, depends on the watercourse irrigating the fields. The *subak*'s role is to regulate and control the building and maintenance of the hydraulic system (channels, tunnels, aqueducts, dikes and dams) and the distribution of the water it supplies. It also co-ordinates the calendar for planting and transplanting, and organises offerings and ceremonies in honour of **Dewi Sri**, the goddess of rice. Like the *banjar*, each *subak* has its temple, *kulkul* and assembly.

The **house**, or rather family compound (*pekarangan*), is a private area enclosed by a wall and sheltering an extended family. It comprises several buildings whose locations and functions are strictly defined by the cosmic order (*see sidebar p 355*). In addition, a system of magic measurements ensures harmony within this microcosm. A small **protective wall** (*aling aling*) set slightly back from the entrance porch serves to keep out the evil spirits that might attempt to enter the compound. In the *kaja-kangin* corner – the purest – stands the **family temple** (*sanggah*) where each family honours its deified ancestors. Various **pavilions** (*bale*) open onto the courtyard, several of which house a nuclear family; when sons marry they settle in the family compound, while daughters have to move into the family compounds of their husbands' families. The **east pavilion** (*bale kangin*) serves for rites of passage and is also where guests are received. The functional areas such as kitchen and bathroom (*mandi*) are to be found on the *kelod* side.

Bale are to be seen everywhere, in family compounds, temples and *banjar* as well as, more recently, in hotels and restaurants. A place for meeting and relaxing, for shows and rituals, they vary according to their importance and function in social, ritual and religious life. These rectangular pavilions open on all sides provide delightful natural ventilation that is perfectly suited to the climate. The roof of thatch or palm leaves supported by pillars sometimes comprises several tiered layers.

Daily life

The household tasks are the responsibility of the **women**. After rising at dawn they cook the rice that forms the family's three daily meals, sweep the courtyard and house energetically, then distribute little offerings in specific places. Every three days (fixed by the calendar) they go to market. The rest of their day is mainly spent with the children and neighbours and looking after a shop or guesthouse (*losmen*); the ruling activity remains the untiring and painstaking making of offerings.

The **men** often work in the rice fields. In addition they have to take part in the meetings of the various councils (village, *subak*, *banjar*) to which they belong. But as soon as they have any free time they devote it to their fighting cocks, of which every Balinese possesses at least one or two, to the great displeasure of light-sleeping tourists! These cocks are cleaned, fed, taken out into the sun and, of course, trained to fight (*see p 359*).

Temples by the thousand

They are everywhere: in the villages, along the coast, beside lakes, lost on the slopes of volcanoes, in the middle of forests – Bali is covered with literally thousands of temples! These holy places where gods and humans come together often appear deserted and almost abandoned, but a ceremony is all that is needed to suddenly give them a whole new dimension.

All Balinese are connected to several temples depending on the various social or territorial groups (family, *banjar*, village, *subak*, profession, etc) to which they belong, and they take part in the rituals associated with each of them. Only the most important temples are frequented by the entire population whatever their community connections. These are the nine **directional temples**, the best known of which are Besakih, Batur, Uluwatu, Batukau and Bratan, and the six **Great Sanctuaries**, the list of which remains controversial and coincides in part with the former. Some of these are also **State temples**, in former times attached to the royal courts. Each kingdom thus had its main temple (such as Pura Taman Ayun in Mengwi and Pura Kehen in Bangli), its mountain temple (Batukau and Besakih) and its sea temple (Uluwatu and Rambut Siwi).

From split gates to multiple roofs

Just like the family compounds, Balinese temples are protected by **walls** built around the holy area. Within this enclosure, which often contains several slightly tiered **courtyards**, the buildings are laid out according to the spatial concept of the Balinese (*see sidebar p 355*). Access is generally on the *kelod-kauh* side through a **candi bentar**, the split gate symbolising the base of the sacred *Mahameru* (Mount Meru). The first courtyard comprises several **bale** (*see p 355*) used for preparing offerings, for gamelan orchestras or even for cockfights (*wantilan*). There is also a **kulkul** tower. A **kori agung**, or "great gate" depicting the outline of Mount Meru, leads into the inner courtyard. Guarded by monsters supposed to ward off evil spirits, this is opened only during ceremonies; visitors therefore use a small side entrance. The most sacred courtyard, which faces upstream, houses a row of secondary

Fragile architecture

The use of natural materials that wear rapidly – wood, bamboo, palm, brick and "paras" (very soft, greyish volcanic tuff) – tends to make all constructions short-lived and gives them an aged look even when recent. In addition to this the vagaries of history and the ravages of the island's volcanoes explain the lack of ancient remains. The temples and palaces that can be seen today are the result of faithful reconstructions and regular restorations (although the dull grey cement that has made a massive appearance over the last few years has none of the charm of the "paras").

altars on the *kangin* side whereas the most important ones are lined up on the *kaja* side; these serve as thrones for the gods when they "come down" to take part in rituals. The **meru**, elegant shrines with multiple roofs of dark thatch, stand at the far *kaja* end of the courtyard. The number of roofs (from 3 to 11) is always uneven and varies depending on the local status of the god being venerated. Symbols of the sacrosanct Mount Meru, these often honour natural powers – gods of volcanoes and goddesses of lakes – but can also glorify a deified ancestor or priest. In the *kaja-kangin* corner, which is the purest, a **padmasana** (lotus throne) is often found. This is a stone construction that in theory stands on the cosmic world-turtle and two *naga* serpents, the seats of the creation of the universe. It is devoted to the sun god Surya, the principal manifestation of the supreme god **Sanghyang Widi Wasa** (*see following page*).

Balinese Hinduism

The **"religion of divine Hindu law"** (*Agama Hindu Dharma*), the foundation of Balinese culture, is a system of beliefs that governs all the activities of daily life. The Balinese religion is the result of a surprising syncretism. It has assimilated the indigenous **ancestor worship** and **animist beliefs** passed down from very ancient times, while from India it has incorporated elements of the Hindu cosmogony and pantheon, as

Balinese Hinduism

well as certain esoteric aspects of Tantrism. The Balinese pantheon is dominated by the **Hindu trinity** of the gods Brahma, Vishnu and Siva, but it also comprises a galaxy of local divinities associated with natural forces and the spirits of ancestors. As the official Muslim **monotheism** imposed by the *Pancasila (see p 41)* would seem to be incompatible with such a religion, to have it recognised the Balinese were therefore obliged to affirm their belief in a supreme god, **Sanghyang Widi Wasa** (the godhead), of which all the other divinities are simply manifestations.

The art of offerings

A daily sacrificial ritual, offerings are an integral part of man's primordial duty of maintaining order in the universe by ensuring equilibrium between all the antagonistic forces composing it. These veritable works of art made up and presented according to complex, strictly codified rules are intended to placate the spirits that inhabit each entity – natural or supernatural, positive or negative – that is likely to contribute to cosmic harmony. They are mainly the prerogative of the women, who pass their knowledge down from mother to daughter. Whether vertiginous pyramids of fruits and cakes, little banana-leaf baskets filled with rice and coloured petals, palm-leaf panels

Cock-a-doodle-doo!

Dozens of motorbikes parked in an alleyway. Cock crows mingling with a confused hubbub. It is well worth watching a cockfight as the atmosphere is unforgettable. Only the men take part, with the few women present remaining in the background selling drinks and delicacies. The crowd jostles around the makeshift arena. Everybody talks, eats, drinks, smokes a lot and laughs all the time. Gradually the tension mounts. Each cock owner searches out a suitable opponent. Bank notes pass from hand to hand and cries ring out. It all appears totally anarchic but in fact it is not so at all. The owners massage their birds, excite them and then carefully fix a sharp pointed blade to the spur. Finally the birds are released, whereupon they either eye each other up or launch into savage attacks, egged on by the spectators, some of whom may well have placed heavy bets. It sometimes happens that one of the fighters makes its escape but more often the confrontation ends in a brief flurry of feathers and a few red stains on the ground.

Fighting cocks

P Bénet

with symbolic motifs woven in, or long intricately decorated bamboo stems lining the streets of villages during celebrations, these offerings come in every form. They may be laid on the ground in front of the house, placed in a small niche or on a makeshift shrine, stood at a dangerous crossroads or bend, or put in a rice field or on a beach. Those placed above ground level are intended for the celestial powers (which simply taste their essence) and are then consumed by the faithful, while those intended to pacify the chthonic forces are placed on the ground, where they are much appreciated by chickens and stray dogs!

Cockfighting

A real island passion, cockfights have officially been forbidden since 1981 because of the ruinous gambling they engender but are nevertheless still authorised as part of rituals. Their religious vocation, which the recreational side tends to obscure, is that of a sacrifice to the **chthonic spirits**, the bloodthirsty evil forces, to prevent them from doing harm. During important ceremonies such as cremations or the building of a temple, a purifying cockfight is organised in the courtyard for **wantilan** (*see p 357*). In daily life the passion for these fights is such that there is always one taking place somewhere, concealed from indiscreet eyes in semi-official secrecy, for the gamblers know just how to twist the authorities around their little fingers!

Sumptuous ceremonies

Not a day goes by without some ceremony or other filling the island of the gods with its sounds, colours and fragrances. Whether honouring coconut palms, musical instruments, prosperity or domestic animals, and following a cycle of five days, two weeks, six months or ten years, these always give rise to magnificent celebrations. Be they sacrificial or purifying, they all honour a divinity, an ancestor or some spirit that contributes to the harmonious unity of the world.

When wandering around visitors are certain to come across splendid **processions**. Advancing to the heady rhythms of the gamelan, the Balinese may accompany a divinity to the seashore or river bank for a purifying bath, carry the funeral tower of a family member, go to collect holy water from a spring for a ritual, or present baskets of offerings in some holy place.

During an important **temple ceremony** the area around the sanctuary looks like a village fête. From the little *warung* hastily erected for the occasion escape appetising smells of *sate* and *babi guling*. Other stalls display clothing, toys or household utensils, providing the opportunity for a bit of shopping. Further on, the gambling is in full swing. Bets are laid, bank notes flutter, money piles up – and is then shared out again. Luck changes and men get feverishly excited. In this relaxed, joyful, lively atmosphere the Balinese meet up over a coffee dressed in their best clothes, gossip over the latest news, or stroll around taking their time. The festivities last well into the night.

It is easy to forget the presence of the gods, who are the guests of honour at the party, seated on the thrones of their hallowed altars. An intoxicating fragrance fills the air from the burning incense that symbolically bears the offerings to the gods. From the loudspeakers the resonating percussion instruments of the gamelan answer the tinkling of the little bell calling the divinities. While the **priest** slowly performs his *mudra* (gestures full of magic powers), the faithful kneeling on the ground listen to the insistent recitation of the *mantras* (sacred invocations) with the deepest devotion. Their hands are clasped in front of their foreheads, holding flowers in the tips of their fingers. When the prayer is finished they take three small gulps of lustral water from the palm of the hand, then stick a few grains of rice onto forehead and temples. Ritual dances, sacrificial cockfights and performances of *topeng* (*see p 365*) or *wayang kulit* complete the celebrations.

Balinese Hinduism

Some major festivals

Odalan – Every 210 days each temple receives its gods by celebrating its *odalan*, the anniversary of its consecration, for three days.

Other festivals celebrated throughout the island:

Eka Dasa Rudra – The most important celebration, which ensures the general purification of the island, is held every 100 years at the temple of **Besakih** *(see sidebar, p 419)*.

M. Lemerle

Ganesh in festive garb

Nyepi – The Balinese **New Year** is marked by "emptiness". The previous day, the last day of the *saka* year *(see sidebar below)*, the universe is purified. Abundant offerings are presented to pacify the powers of evil, and all night long the streets are crowded with people who in a joyous cacophony make enormous demonic effigies dance in the **exorcising carnival**. But as soon as the first day of the new year dawns, the entire population remains cloistered at home, in darkness, so as to make the evil spirits believe that the island is deserted. The smallest sign of human life might compromise this ploy and incite them to stay and stir up trouble. Visitors should be careful, as no-one takes this belief lightly and anyone not respecting it is taking risks. It is particularly recommended to avoid arriving on this day *(check when it is, as the date changes every year)*. There is no transport, no lighting and it is forbidden to go out. Tourists obliged to camp out at the airport for the duration are a sorry sight.

Galungan – Every 210 days the Balinese celebrate their legendary victory over **Maya Danawa**, the demon-king who forbade them to practise their forms of worship. Symbolically it is a celebration of the "religion of divine Hindu law". Ceremonies take place in temples all over the island and everyone returns to their village to honour the procession of divinities and ancestral spirits that come for the occasion. The entire island goes into slow motion, with shops and government offices closed and hotels and restaurants deserted. The festivities draw to a close on the tenth day, named **Kuningan**, when the last offerings precede the return of the gods to their celestial residences.

Rites of passage

It is not possible to give a full description of all the ritual stages that mark Balinese existence, from conception and birth through to death and after-life. A newborn baby is seen as the reincarnation of an ancestor and considered to be divine. The first rite of passage comes at three months old when, at the end of a highly symbolic celebration, the baby bedecked in protective jewels touches the ground, considered impure, for the first time.

Two calendars
For some festivals, particularly agricultural rites, the "saka" calendar of Indian origin, based on the moon's cycles, is used. The days of the new, and especially full, moons are marked by important ceremonies. Other events follow the "wuku" calendar of 210 days, a Hindu-Javanese legacy. The interpretation of complex conjunctions is used to determine auspicious days, with divinatory consultation of the calendar still a prelude to every act of daily life. Shown graphically, each square represents a week of the year, illustrated by an auspicious fact associated with the period.

After being presented to the ancestral divinities, it is henceforth allowed into temples and officially becomes a member of the community. At puberty the ceremony of **tooth filing** marks entry into the adult world. The ritual's function is to level off six incisors that correspond to six human ills of bestial and demonic origin.

Most Balinese celebrate their **marriage** before they are thirty. Instead of the classic *mepadik*, a family courtesy visit after which the suitor asks for the hand of his beloved, young people often prefer the more romantic and extravagant scenario of the *ngerorod*, in which the young man simulates elopement with his (consenting) bride-to be, whose parents then pretend to seek her everywhere in vain. After their secret "honeymoon" the happy couple finally reappears and a big ceremony makes the joyful event official.

The final stage in life and the supreme goal of existence, the soul *(moksa)* is liberated for its reincarnation by **cremation**. Delivered by the flames, it can then leave its human body in order to be reborn in another form determined by its *karma* (the total sum of its acts in its past life). The deceased is generally buried temporarily in the cemetery, with cremation only taking place at a later, favourable, date, sometimes several years after. If the family cannot muster the necessary funds, it waits for a **collective cremation** in order to share the costs.

In the meantime the *banjar* members get busy building the **tower** to carry the coffin, a wood and bamboo structure richly decorated with coloured fabrics, flowers and mirrors, which symbolises the cosmos. The sarcophagus in the shape of an animal – cow, bull, winged lion or other mythical animal – is placed in the middle, between heaven and earth, under a tower with many roofs, the number of which depends on the deceased's caste. After a festive meal provided by the family, the **procession** suddenly gets under way to the sound of the gamelan. The bearers advance, retreat, turn this way and that, shaking the strange palanquin with a great commotion intended to trick malevolent spirits and prevent the deceased's soul from returning to haunt his home. Once the final rituals have been completed the tower is set alight. The resulting ashes are gathered in a coconut shell and thrown into the sea or a river from where they drift to the Ganges. As for the soul, now purified, it takes its place in the central altar in the family temple, the domain of deified ancestors, until it is reincarnated.

Balinese etiquette

Friendly, discreet, gentle and serene, the Balinese generally welcome visitors with pleasure. They attach the greatest importance to politeness, which is inherent in their art of living, and expect strangers to respect their customs *(adat)* by behaving suitably on all occasions. They are extremely tolerant, and while they will not make discourteous remarks about tactless mistakes, they are likely to observe the people who make them with a certain amount of condescension!

In temples

Visitors can attend ceremonies alone but it is preferable to be accompanied by a Balinese. If this is not possible, permission should be asked to enter the temple. A few **elementary rules** will help you avoid making a blunder. For discretion's sake always remain behind the worshippers, which also means you can watch what they do. It is essential to avoid standing in passageways, jostling or stepping over anyone, talking out loud, sitting down anywhere without having been invited, or walking around or standing up during rituals. Most important of all, visitors must never place themselves higher than a priest, or any other Balinese, even if it is the only chance

Balinese etiquette

Entry forbidden

Before entering a temple visitors should, like the Balinese themselves, read the notice outside carefully. Depending on the place, this notice specifies if entry is forbidden to women when they are menstruating, to pregnant women, to mothers of children who have not yet cut their first tooth, to children who have not yet lost their first tooth, to those in mourning (considered impure), to madmen and, finally, to those who are improperly dressed.

of seeing something. According to the "cosmic" conception of the human body *(see sidebar, p 355)* it is a sacrilege for the feet (which are impure) to be higher than the head of another person, which is sacred. It is therefore very important not to raise or point the feet, or even to draw attention to them in any way.

At home

The rites of passage (marriage, tooth filing, cremation, etc) take place within the family circle, extended to include neighbours and friends. Visitors are only welcome if they have been specifically invited, but a few rudiments of *Bahasa Indonesia* plus a skilful dosage of tact, audacity, politeness, serenity and patience gives a good chance of being invited to the festivities. It is important to **take a gift** for the hosts and to remember it is not a slight if they do not open it immediately. Lastly, visitors should remember to take their shoes off before entering a house and that the **right hand** alone should be used for giving, taking or eating, as the left is reserved for impure purposes.

Dress for the occasion

Dress forms an integral part of all religious ceremonies and is strictly regulated. Visitors should not be afraid of feeling "dressed-up" and ridiculous, as on the contrary this inspires the greatest of respect and facilitates contacts. If you have made the acquaintance of some Balinese, they will happily lend you a ceremonial outfit and help you to wear it elegantly. If an Indonesian suggests a visitor take a bath *(mandi)*, this is not a pointed allusion; being clean and tidy to celebrate the gods is a question of self-respect.

The **men** wear a *saput* over their sarong, two pieces of fabric held at the waist by a cloth sash, a sober jacket and a turban tied around the head. The **women** wear a long sarong and a *kebaya*, a fine long-sleeved tunic with a *sash* (sash) pulling it in at the waist. They take great care in dressing their hair, sometimes fixing in a hairpiece, and adorn themselves in their finest jewellery.

NB: It is unseemly to put on a sarong in public, nor is it done to keep trousers on under a sarong or a T-shirt under a *kebaya*. In principle, the colour **black** is reserved for cremations. Lastly, when dressed in ceremonial garb motorbike riders are not obliged to wear a helmet.

Photography

Whether using a video camera or taking photos, photographers should keep a reasonable distance. The silence of prayer time should not be broken by shutter clicks or flashes. Sometimes (rarely) a subject will make a gesture of refusal, particularly in the case of old women. Modesty dictates that photos should never be taken of anyone bathing (in public baths or by a road or river). *See also p 106.*

Art in the service of the gods

On the island of the gods all artistic expression is stamped with a spiritual dimension and is participated in out of religious feeling, and a feeling for universal harmony and cosmic equilibrium. The major aim of its recreational or aesthetic function is to honour the gods. Considered an integral part of community duties, it long remained a collective activity; no individual would have dreamed of being proud of his talent or of identifying his authorship of an artwork by signing it. The Balinese language does not in fact possess a word meaning "art" or "artist".

In the course of the 20C, however, due to Western influence, artists gradually came to assert themselves as such and their creations, now personal expressions, have taken on a commercial value. With the boom in tourism, the arts are thus tending to be aimed towards mass production, to the detriment of quality. Countless galleries and shops have sprung up all over the island, along with performances organised every day to entertain visitors.

Yet while Balinese arts may have lost part of their religious foundation, they nevertheless conserve a sense of aesthetics and a tremendous refinement that permeate the smallest aspects of daily life. These qualities can be felt in a whole range of objects from ritual ones (offerings, ceremonial dress, *wayang kulit*) to more utilitarian ones (palm leaf basketwork, coconut-shell household implements, bamboo furniture) and even to decoration on restaurant tables and in hotel gardens. They are present also in the notes of the gamelan and the movements of *legong*. Whether divine inspiration or innate talent, the charm still works.

An inexhaustible repertoire

Strongly inspired by the great Hindu epics, the **Mahabharata** and the **Ramayana** *(see p 58)*, on which all Balinese are brought up from birth, both the performing arts and plastic arts make ample use of mythical creatures and the heroes of **local folklore**. The **wayang kulit** puppets *(see p 57)* dominate the entire range, with performances often taking place in an exuberantly exotic natural setting. Whether classical or modern, all artistic manifestations remain a harmonious reflection of cosmic order. Hindu and animist references coexist, and realism and fantasy intermingle in a profusion of minute detail, an expressive ballet that characterises Balinese aesthetics as a whole.

Sculpture

Whether in soft stone *(paras)* or hard wood (teak or ebony), in narrative bas-reliefs or monumental statues, the carving found everywhere in Bali is devoted above all to ornamenting temples, palaces and public baths.

Every depiction, be it a protective divinity or terrifying demon, mythical *naga* serpent or *Garuda* bird with supernatural powers, occupies a specific site determined by its symbolic function. The general development of the arts in a commercial direction has turned the iconography towards a more profane repertoire, but sculpture still offers proof of perfect technical mastery and tremendous expressiveness. Since the 1930s various schools have sprung up but tourism has brought a trend for mass producing stereotyped subjects, which is impoverishing pure creation. *See also p 409, "The craft villages".*

Painting

Previously done on textile or plant panels (wood, bark or palm leaves), traditional painting adorned the temples and palaces, its creations characterised by a classical iconography, a narrative composition and conventional means of representation, plus a colour palette reduced to five natural pigments. The most common paintings, in the **wayang style**, are still perpetuated in the village of Kamasan *(see p 425)*. The European artists who settled on the island in the 1930s, mainly in the **region of Ubud**, gave a new lease of life to Balinese painting with regard to both themes and techniques *(see p 398, "Ubud")*. Interrupted by the war in 1942 then by the political

Art in the service of the gods

troubles of the 1950s and 1960s, pictorial development continued under the leadership of Dutch artist **Arie Smit**, the instigator of the **Young Artists movement** *(see p 401)*. Today the creative force is feeling its way forward, with varying degrees of inspiration and success.

The performing arts

Music, singing, dance and theatre are inseparable disciplines occupying a special place in the life of all Balinese. The gamelan's percussive polyphonic chords, the supple movements or rigid quivering of a dancer, the rasping voice or rolling, staring eyes of an actor instantly plunge the spectator into a singularly evocative universe. There is a poignant identification of performer with role. From a very early age, non-professional dancers and actors untiringly rehearse the studied gestures taught by their masters. Each very stylised movement metaphorically evokes a precise action or feeling, with the expressiveness of wrists and fingers being of the greatest importance. Costumes, masks and make-up, all just as codified, help to identify the characters; sudden changes in the volume and rhythm of the gamelan guide the choreography. Novice audiences should forget the impenetrable symbolism of the plot and simply let themselves be carried away by the beauty and musical virtuosity, all perfectly co-ordinated. The atmosphere is also helped along by the Balinese, who come in families and contribute with laughter and enthusiasm.

Diverted from their original vocation as entertainment for the village community and, in former days, for the princes' courts but above all as an offering to the gods during ritual celebrations, performances are now put on every evening for tourists, especially in the Ubud region.

Originally from Java, the Balinese gamelan – also called **gong** – differs from its Javanese counterpart in that it has a less formal style of playing. The name designates a set of instruments, mainly in bronze and bamboo and mostly percussion: gongs, drums, timpani, cymbals, xylophones, etc. But the island has over twenty different types of orchestra! Each one forms an indivisible entity, all the elements of which were designed simultaneously and tuned to be played interdependently, in the purest of harmonies. Every *banjar* (district) possesses at least one gamelan. After their day's work the musicians rehearse under the *bale gong*, without scores, playing from memory the chords they have been hearing since birth.

Drama and dance call on a rich repertoire of fifty or so genres, but with plots that are familiar to everyone as they always involve confrontations between the standard figures of good and evil, goodies and baddies. They show incredible virtuosity, with the most aesthetic emphasising the perfect resonance between music and choreography.

Legong was in former times performed in the courts of the rajas to which the young dancers belonged. The fascination of the extremely abstract *legong* lies in the delicate and refined gracefulness of its movements. Three young girls play all the roles; the *condong*, or attendant, opens the performance alone, then the two small *legong* appear. Aged around 8 to 12, radiant in their tight-fitting gold brocade costumes, their hair dressed with frangipani flowers and each holding a fan, they dance in perfect synchronisation, often creating a mirroring effect. They mime the story of the king of Lasem who, refusing to free the young Rangkesari whom he has taken captive, does battle with her brother. Ignoring the bird of ill omen (played by the *condong*) that he encounters on the way, the king is killed in the battle.

The **baris**, a ritual war dance, glorifies Balinese warriors. The dance is as demanding as the *legong* and is often performed by young boys. The battle theme provides the framework for the changing emotions and mood swings that animate the characters through a subtle and complex play of movement and facial expression, all highly emphatic and performed in response to the gamelan.

In the **kecak**, a group of men sitting in a circle lit by a flame and each wearing a *kain poleng* loincloth (a black-and-white check cloth symbolising balance between antagonistic forces) imitate the percussion sounds of the gamelan in an onomatopoeic chorus of "chak-ka-chak-ka-chak". Adapted from the vocal element in the ritual *Sanghyang* trance dance *(see below)*, the modern *kecak* accompanies choreography taken from the **Ramayana**. Often called the **monkey dance**, it recounts the victorious battle fought by Prince Rama, assisted by an army of monkeys led by Hanuman, to rescue his wife Sita, abducted by the demon-king Rawana.

Other performances come closer to theatre drama, putting more emphasis on the story that is told and playing on alternations in register ranging from intensely tragic through moving melodrama to outright buffoonery. In the **topeng** (mask dance) the actors interpret a succession of varied character archetypes (king, buffoon, flirt, deaf man, etc) while wearing corresponding masks. The **Ramayana ballet** incorporates comic improvisations into epic scenes by using animal roles. As for the **arja**, it narrates an interminable love story punctuated by heart-rending episodes and incredible plots.

Some dances remain an integral part of religious rituals and are only performed during ceremonies, such as the **pendet** that accompanies the presentation of offerings.

The **sanghyang** are fascinating dances performed by young worshippers in trances, their bodies taken over by celestial nymphs who communicate the demands of the gods. The original objective of these dances was to protect the village by exorcising malevolent spirits.

Lastly, the **Barong and Rangda** dance takes the form of a duel between the forces of good and evil. The *Barong*, a sacred mythical creature played by two men covered in a fleece and wearing a big mask with terrifying fangs, personifies the guardian spirit of every village, which it protects by chasing away evil forces. Its greatest enemy is the witch *Rangda*. In an exorcising ballet the confrontation culminates in the **kris dance** in which *Rangda* incites the *Barong*'s followers, bewitched by her demonic influence, to turn their weapons on themselves. By using its magic powers the *Barong* awakens them from their trance and makes good triumph over evil.

P. Bénet

Art in the service of the gods

A Balinese dancer full of island grace

DENPASAR
Capital of the province of Bali – Capital of Badung district
Map p 350-351
Pop 315 000 – Warm humid climate

Not to be missed
Taking a walk around the market district.
Exploring the alleyways.

And remember...
The town centre is best visited on foot.
Weekends are best avoided as many shops are closed.

Suffocating, polluted and noisy, Denpasar with its never-ending traffic is not exactly an enticing place to spend any length of time. With all the motorbikes, *bemo* minibuses, cars, lorries, bicycles and *dokar*, every crossroads poses the same puzzling question as to how the pulsating tide succeeds in advancing at all! For the last 20-odd years the city has been experiencing unlimited and somewhat anarchic expansion, which means it offers a side of Bali that is very unlike what you will see on the rest of the island.

The capital of the kingdom of Badung

Denpasar (literally, "north of the market") still bears the traces of its former vocation as a trading post. Its cosmopolitan population comprises large numbers of long-standing immigrants, mainly Bugis, Chinese, Arabs and Indians. In 1906 the town was one of the last bastions on the island still to hold out against the Dutch, but on 20 September 1906 it was the scene of a tragic **puputan**, a ritual collective suicide that was to sign the death-warrant of the kingdom of Badung (*see sidebar*). Denpasar, now a symbol of the Dutch hold over Bali, then became the new seat of colonial administration, replacing Singaraja in the north. After Indonesia became independent the town conserved its role by setting itself up as capital of the province of Bali (1960).

Liberty or death
The terrifying "puputan" of 1906 (adapted from Vicki Baum's account in "A Tale from Bali"): Men dressed in white and adorned with flowers advanced very slowly, as if unaware of the Dutch facing them with cannon and guns. Suddenly the prince brandished his weapon in his raised fist. An inhuman cry went up from the group, all the men took their kris in their hands and rushed forward. Shells and volleys of firing greeted the Balinese, who threw themselves headlong against the Dutch troops. Fresh waves of men surged through the gate, all armed with kris, all bearing the same expression of madness and mortal fury, all adorned and crowned with gold and flowers. The Balinese intended to die and nothing in the world could stop their death charge. Hundreds of them were cut down by bullets, hundreds more brandished their kris and plunged them into their own breasts, right to the heart, in accordance with ancient and holy custom. Behind the men came the women and children.

As the island's centre of administration, trade, industry and education, it attracted civil servants, merchants, workers and peasants in search of work from all over the archipelago.

A tour of the town
Allow half a day.

The main places worth visiting can be found on either side of Jl Gajah Mada, the major thoroughfare running east-west through the city centre. Street names – when they exist – are shown in white on a green background, and are placed perpendicular to the street.

The **statue of Catur Mukha**, the god of the four cardinal points,

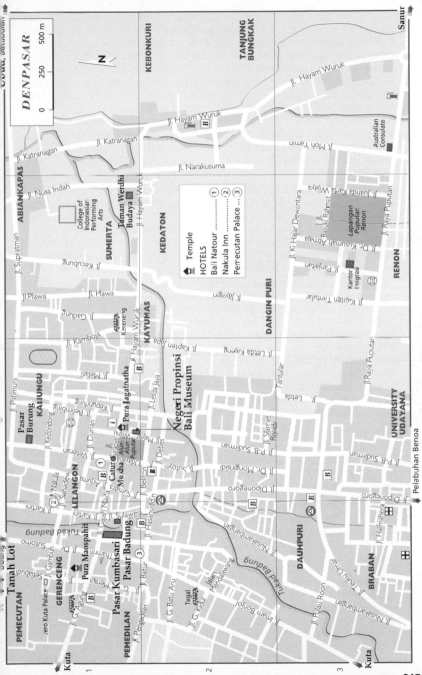

DENPASAR

0   250   500 m

N

Temple

HOTELS
Bali Natour .... ①
Nakula Inn .... ②
Perrecutan Palace ... ③

Negeri Propinsi
Bali Museum

Bali

watches over the junction where the Gajah Mada, Veteran, Surapati and Udayana streets meet, providing a useful landmark. The vast esplanade stretching alongside, **Puputan Square** (Alun-Alun Puputan) (B1), commemorates the collective suicide of the rulers of Badung and their courts during the decisive offensive by Dutch troops. A **statue** portraying a couple with their two children brandishing kris and spears stands as an allegory of the heroic act. The jewels the woman holds in her hand are a reminder of the Balinese women who threw their most precious belongings in the face of their assailants before stabbing themselves in the heart.

Today the inhabitants of Denpasar come here to lunch on the lawns, play ball or stroll around in the late afternoon. The square also regularly hosts impressive gatherings of civil servants, who can some days be seen standing to attention, in uniform, quietly listening to official harangues!

Cross Jl Mayor Wisnu, which runs along the east side of the square.

Behind railings stands **Pura Jagatnatha** (B1) (*usually closed to the public*), a recently built temple dedicated to the supreme god, **Sanghyang Widi Wasa**, the official affirmation of Balinese monotheism (*see p 358*). It houses an imposing **padmasana**, the lotus throne representing the creation of the world. Made entirely of white coral, it stands on the world-turtle and two mythological *naga* serpents. At every full and new moon important ceremonies are held here, with prayers and sometimes performances of *wayang kulit*. Visitors may be allowed to enter if wearing a sarong and sash.

Just next door is the **Bali Museum*** (Negeri Propinsi Bali Museum) (B1) (*8am-3.45pm; Fridays 8am-2.45pm; closed Mondays and public holidays. Fee. Allow 20min*). Its pavilions, built in 1932 under the Dutch, illustrate the various styles of traditional architecture on the island with some of the displays taken from temples and palaces of the ancient kingdoms of Bali. They house miscellaneous ethnographic collections of prehistoric tools and jewellery, primitive works of art, ceremonial costumes and accessories for specific rituals (marriage, tooth filing, ancestor worship, etc), traditional fabrics, *Barong* masks, *wayang kulit* puppets, kris, musical instruments and all sorts of everyday objects (cages for fighting cocks, kitchen implements, fishing tackle, etc). The way things are displayed is far from exciting but the architectural setting and some particularly interesting exhibits make it worth a short visit.

Cross or skirt Puputan Square to the statue of Catur Mukha.

A 500m detour via Jalan Veteran leads to the **Bird Market** (Pasar Burung) (B1). Here visitors can stroll around among the bamboo cages and brightly coloured birds, set in a pleasant turmoil of excitement and an almost melodious cacophony!

Return to Jl Gajah Mada and head towards the market.

Rather than taking the crowded major thoroughfares (*Jl Veteran, Jl Sumatra and Jl Gajah Mada*), it is more pleasant to walk through the **side streets** (*Jl Nakula, Jl Sahadewa, etc*), which are quieter and more picturesque. They also show you other aspects of city life that can be feverish when it is cool but more laid back in the heat of the day. Numerous tailors have their workshops here and the regular clicking of their sewing machines gives a pleasant rhythm to your walk! In the early morning school children in uniform hurry by, eyes half closed and perched on too-high bicycles, so as not to be late for class. You will see men watering plants while on several doorsteps fighting cocks take the morning air in their bamboo cages as they wait for their masters to discuss their merits and train them to fight. Once back from market, the women set to making offerings for the next ceremony. Later in the afternoon, as the day wanes, fragrant odours start to fill the neighbourhood; this is when the vendors of *bakso* and *sate* stride along the streets, pushing their carts along to the honking of old horns.

M. Lemerle

In the market

Standing back slightly from Jalan Gajah Mada, on the banks of the miserable Badung, are two vast covered markets (*daily 8am-5pm approximately*). On the east side the hustle and bustle of **Pasar Badung**★ (A1) overflows into the car park, where men and women from the countryside start selling their produce as soon they start unloading. Inside, the central stairway provides a fine bird's-eye view of the colourful stalls. The ground floor houses perishable goods, the first floor is devoted to **spices**, and clothing and **sarongs** share the top storey with kitchen utensils and religious material of all kinds. And everywhere, in the middle of all the goods, the women prepare offerings while gossiping about village life.

It is worth taking time to hunt around in **Pasar Kumbasari**★ (A1) opposite, a bazaar intended mainly for tourists but which offers samples of all the island's **handicrafts**. Many craftsmen can be seen at work and will try to persuade visitors – although not too insistently – to buy their jewellery, fabrics, basketwork, sculptures and paintings of very variable quality.

From here, continue down **Jalan Sulawesi** (*the street along the east side of the market*), which is home to traders of Arab and Indian origin. Gold merchants and goldsmiths, who form the majority, rub shoulders with fabric wholesalers whose rolls of material are sometimes stacked up right on the pavement. Gold, which is sold by the gram, is meticulously weighed on small manual scales before being worked to clients' tastes. Business is brisk and always good-humoured.

Leave the market and turn left down Jl Gajah Mada. After the junction with Jl Dr Sutomo, take the 2nd street on the right (towards Tanah Lot), then the first pedestrian alley (gang) on the right.

This picturesque working class alleyway leads peacefully to **Pura Maospahit** (A1), the oldest temple of the kingdom of Badung. It was restored after the 1917 earthquake and contains a few vestiges dating from the 14C Majapahit kingdom. Some old women look after the place as they go about their daily business. With great delicacy they will ask you to fill in the visitors' book and will lend out sarongs and sashes if required.

Denpasar

You need some form of transport to get to the **Cultural Centre** (Taman Werdhi Budaya) (C1), which is a little out of the centre of town (*Jl Nusa Indah; 8am-4pm. Kecak performance daily at 6.30pm; lasts 1hr. Fee*). The purpose of the centre, set amongst the greenery, is to promote the island's traditional arts. It really comes into its own during the **annual festival of Balinese arts** (*generally in June or July*). But throughout the year it holds exhibitions, concerts, and drama and dance performances (as well as rehearsals). Every evening it also puts on a **kecak performance**, for the tourists, but of good quality.

Making the most of Denpasar

COMING AND GOING

By bemo – The town has several bus stations. Bemo minibuses shuttle between **Kereneng** (C1) station and the main **Batubulan** station, from which buses and bemos serve eastern and northern Bali. **Ubung** station (beyond A1) serves the north and west of the island and **Tegal** station (A2) the south.

By bus – Shuttle buses do not serve Denpasar but daily buses leave from **Ubung** station for the main towns in Java.

GETTING AROUND

By car – Heavy traffic, parking problems and the large number of one-way streets make getting around by car difficult.

On foot – This is the best way of getting around if you stay in the centre. NB, as traffic lights are very scarce, crossing the road is sometimes a perilous undertaking. Wait for an Indonesian to get ready to cross and follow determinedly on his heels!

By dolkar – These romantic horse-drawn carriages act as taxis and offer a picturesque means of exploring the town, although they do not run along all the main thoroughfares.

By bemo – Very cheap but it is hard to identify the various routes they follow so they are not easy for strangers to use.

By taxi – Although numerous in the market district they become rarer as you move out of the centre. Can be called on ☎ (0361) 28 90 90/28 91 91.

ADDRESS BOOK

Tourist information – Jl Surapati 7 (B1), ☎ (0361) 23 45 69, 7am-2pm; Friday 7-11am; Saturday 7am-1.30pm. Only has a mediocre map of the town and the calendar of island events.

Alliance Française – Jl Pathi Jelantik (beyond A3), ☎ (0361) 22 41 23. Small French library.

Consulate/Embassy – *Australian Consulate*, Jl Prof Moh Yamin 4, Renon (D3), ☎ (0361) 23 50 92/93, emergency ☎ (0361) 23 41 39 ext 3311, Fax (0361) 23 19 90, ausconbali@denpasar. Wasantara.net.id Also deals with other Commonwealth citizens.

American Consulate, Jl Hayam Wuruk 188, Renon (D3), ☎ (0361) 23 36 05, emergency ☎ (0361) 23 41 39 ext 3575, Fax (0361) 22 24 26.

Bank/Currency exchange – Most of the banks that change foreign currency are on Jl Gajah Mada (A1-B1), Jl Diponegoro and Jl Thamrin (A1). At several of them you can withdraw cash with Visa or MasterCard. *BCA*, Jl Hasanudin 58 (A2); *Bank Duta*, Jl Hayam Wuruk 165 (B1).

Post office – *Main post office (Pos dan Giro)*, Jl Raya Puputan, Renon (C3), 8am-2pm; Friday 8am-12noon; Saturday 8am-1pm; closed Sunday. Poste restante, Internet. There are other post offices in Jl Kamboja (B1-C1), Jl Gunung Agung (A1), Jl Teuku Umar (A3) etc.

Bali

Telephone – There are numerous coin and card telephone boxes. **Telkom**, Jl Teuku Umar 6 (near Jl Diponegoro) (A3). There are **Wartel** offices on Jl Thamrin (A1), Jl Sudirman (B2-B3), Jl Gajah Mada 102 and Jl Diponegoro (A3).

Immigration office – Kantor Imigrasi, Jl Panjaitan 4, Renon (C3), ☎ (0361) 22 78 28. Monday-Thursday 8am-2pm; Friday 8am-11am; Saturday 8am-12noon. Dress very properly; you will quite simply be refused entry if you are wearing flip-flops, shorts or a skimpy dress!

Medical service – Rumah Sakit Umum Propinsi (RSUP), Sanglah (A3), ☎ (0361) 22 79 11. Probably the best general hospital in Bali.
SOS Gatotkaca Klinik, Jl Gatotkaca 21, ☎ (0361) 22 35 55. Private clinic.
Dr H Kusuman, Jl Raya Sesetan 190, ☎ (0361) 22 96 46. An excellent English-speaking dentist.

WHERE TO STAY

Denpasar has numerous hotels and *losmen* (guesthouses), mostly not very inviting and frequented mainly by visiting Indonesians. These addresses may nevertheless prove useful if you are stuck.

Modest
Nakula Inn, Jl Nakula 4, ☎ (0361) 22 64 46 – 8rm. A family guesthouse located in a pleasantly lively working-class quarter. Very basic little rooms with private terraces. The upstairs ones have better ventilation. The plants, hanging bird cages and shrine for offerings give the place a certain amount of charm.

Average
Pemecutan Palace Hotel, Jl Thamrin 2, ☎ (0361) 42 34 91 – 3/rm. The temple and palace that greet you at the entrance are illusory. Although the lovely garden with its many birds still forms a much-appreciated haven of peace in the centre of Denpasar, the place suffers from a serious lack of maintenance. Rooms without charm and dilapidated bathroom facilities.

Luxury
Bali Natour Hotel, Jl Veteran 3, ☎ (0361) 22 56 81, Fax (0361) 23 53 47 – 71rm. Hot water. International category hotel with no character but comfortable and clean. Rooms with private terraces lined up facing a garden or the swimming pool. Big, impersonal, air-conditioned restaurant.

EATING OUT

There is no lack of *warung* eateries and cheap restaurants. There are also several good, pleasant night markets (*pasar malam*) that come alive from 6pm, such as the one in **Pekambingan**, Jl Diponegoro (B2), or near the **Kereneng** bemo terminus (C1).
The following places are very close to Kumbasari market (A1).

Basic to moderate
Hawai restoran, on the 1st floor of the market. Practical for lunch or cooling off between bargaining sessions. Uninteresting decor but the food is reasonable. Salads, snacks and basic Indonesian dishes.

Moderate
Atoom Baru restaurant, Jl Gajah Mada 106-108, ☎ (0361) 43 47 77/ 42 67 09/ 42 26 23. Daily 8am-11pm. Large, rather cold dining room. Mainly Chinese food. Wide choice of dishes comprising rice, noodles, seafood, etc.

Moderate to more select
Hong Kong restaurant, Jl Gajah Mada 99, ☎ (0361) 43 48 45. Daily, 10am-2am. Air-conditioned dining room but with no charm. Large variety of Chinese specialities that you share sitting at a round table. All the dishes can be served in small, medium or large portions, as you wish. A little more expensive but somewhat better than the one above.

SHOPPING GUIDE

Apart from the markets described above there are also several shopping centres, in particular in Jl Sudirman and Jl Diponegoro.

Making the most of Denpasar

THE CONURBATION OF KUTA
LEGIAN AND SEMINYAK
Badung district
About 10km southwest of Denpasar – Map p 350-351
Hot humid climate

Not to be missed
Sunset on Kuta beach.
And remember...
Always shut the doors and windows of your room before going out.
Beware of pickpockets and bag snatchers (never leave anything of
value unattended when you go swimming).
Do not walk along the beach alone at night.

Paradise for some, purgatory for others, Bali's largest seaside resort stretching along an immense 8km beach is a subject of controversy. Its waves attract crowds of budding surfers, its bars and night-clubs delight the night-owls, while its innumerable cheap shops are heaven for shoppers. But its dizzying rhythm and commercial atmosphere also put many to flight. Extremely Westernised and excessively and anarchically urbanised, Kuta bears no resemblance today to the fishing village fringed with coconut palms that charmed the hippies in the 1970s.

Business...
Kuta is not the place to give you an idea of the authentic Bali. Nor, despite its overriding feeling of relaxation, are visitors likely to make many interesting contacts. The lightning development and inexhaustible manna of the tourist industry have turned it into a veritable Eldorado for Indonesians, who come here from all over the archipelago looking to make profits. So great is the phenomenon that it has attracted its share of crime and the atmosphere is tending to become somewhat unhealthy.

Congestion in Kuta has inevitably led to the development of **Legian**, the neighbouring township that is now barely distinguishable from Kuta.
Only **Seminyak***, although close by and now merging with Legian, has conserved a little of its country charm. It is more peaceful, playing the role of smart residential suburb where luxury hotels and expatriate villas sit side by side in a natural setting. Here you can still get lost in the maze of alleyways, far from traffic jams and perpetual harassment by vendors. But for how long? All the buildings going up are not a good omen.

...and hot sand
The only bright spot in this rather sombre picture is the **beach***, a wide ribbon of pale sand stretching away from Tuban to Seminyak. It is little frequented in the south because of its proximity to the airport, its nerve centre being located on a level with Kuta along a very busy avenue. Here, after a row of small beach bars, beach lovers have to brave the serried ranks of parasol and lounger hirers, masseuses and sellers of cheap sarongs, fake Rolex watches and cold drinks, to reach the area theoretically forbidden to vendors. If this prospect seems too daunting right from the start, it is worth knowing that the beach is considerably more pleasant up by Legian where the seafront road comes to an end, and even more peaceful at Seminyak.

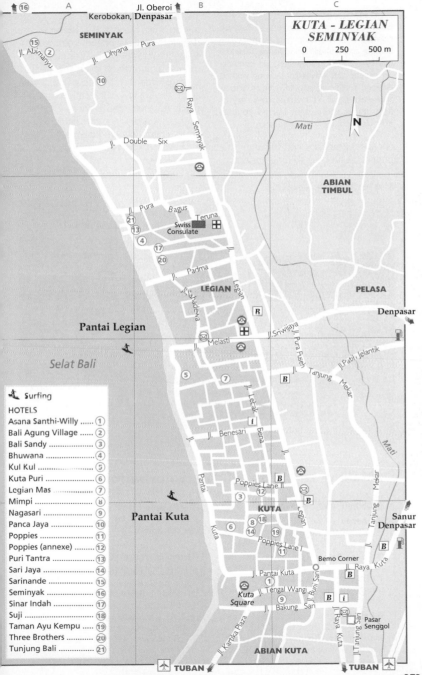

KUTA – LEGIAN
SEMINYAK

0   250   500 m

N

SEMINYAK

Jl. Oberoi
Kerobokan, Denpasar

Jl. Abimanyu

Jl. Dhyana Pura

Jl. Raya Seminyak

Jl. Double Six

Mati

ABIAN TIMBUL

Jl. Pura Bagus
Teruna
Swiss Consulate

Jl. Padma

LEGIAN

Jl. Sahadeva

Jl. Legian

Jl. Pura Puseh

PELASA

Denpasar

Pantai Legian

Selat Bali

Jl. Melasti

Jl. Sriwijaya

Jl. Tanjung Mekar

Jl. Patih Jelantik

R

B

Jl. Letak

Jl. Bena

Mati

Jl. Benesari

Pantai Kuta

Jl. Pantai

Poppies Lane II

KUTA

Jl. Legian

Jl. Kuta

Poppies Lane I

Bemo Corner

Jl. Raya Kuta

Sanur
Denpasar

B

B

Jl. Bumi Sari

Jl. Pantai Kuta

Kuta Square

Jl. Tengal Wangi

Jl. Bakung Sari

Jl. Raya Kuta

Jl. Gunung Lili

B

i

Pasar Senggol

Jl. Kartika Plaza

ABIAN KUTA

TUBAN   TUBAN

🏄 Surfing

HOTELS

Asana Santhi-Willy ...... ①
Bali Agung Village ...... ②
Bali Sandy .... ③
Bhuwana .... ④
Kul Kul .... ⑤
Kuta Puri .... ⑥
Legian Mas .... ⑦
Mimpi .... ⑧
Nagasari .... ⑨
Panca Jaya .... ⑩
Poppies .... ⑪
Poppies (annexe) .... ⑫
Puri Tantra .... ⑬
Sari Jaya .... ⑭
Sarinande .... ⑮
Seminyak .... ⑯
Sinar Indah .... ⑰
Suji .... ⑱
Taman Ayu Kempu ..... ⑲
Three Brothers .... ⑳
Tunjung Bali .... ㉑

373

Hati Hati!

Both swimmers and surfers should be careful. It is important to respect the bathing areas under surveillance (marked out by red and yellow flags), as currents are strong and waves sometimes violent. Anyone in difficulty should raise an arm as a distress signal. You should never try to fight against the current but let yourself drift to get out of the turbulence.

The obligatory climax after a day lounging on Kuta beach is the **sunset****, the daily gathering of a brightly coloured cosmopolitan crowd. During this moment of intense communion even the pedlars seem to forget their business. Lovers walk along the water's edge, children hastily patch up their sand castles as the tide washes them away, a grandfather enjoys an ice-cream in a deckchair, and everyone takes a ringside seat to watch the ballet of exalted surfers moving like shadow puppets against the flaming horizon.

Kuta beach: sun, sea and surf

P Bénet

Bali

Making the most of the conurbation of Kuta

COMING AND GOING

By bemo – One route serves Denpasar (Tegal station), Kuta and Legian and goes round Kuta via Jl Pantai Kuta, Jl Melasti and Jl Legian. Another goes from Denpasar (Tegal) to Kuta (Bemo Corner) then Tuban (very near the airport). Bemos do not go to the north of Legian or to Seminyak.

By shuttle bus – Several daily connections to Kuta from the island's main tourist centres (Sanur, Ubud, Lovina, Candidasa, Padangbai, Kintamani, etc).

The **Perama** company's office is in Kuta, Jl Legian 39 (C4) but all the tourist agencies sell tickets.

FINDING YOUR WAY

Jl Legian, a major thoroughfare permanently blocked by traffic, runs parallel to the beach through the entire conurbation from Kuta to Seminyak. In Kuta, Jl Pantai Kuta goes from Bemo Corner crossroads along the seafront to Jl Melasti, which then joins Jl Legian. Around Poppies Lane I and II numerous alleyways –

where motorbikes slalom dangerously around shops and tourists – criss-cross between Jl Legian and the beach.

GETTING AROUND

On foot – The best means of getting around the small crowded alleyways in the centre of Kuta. If you want some peace and quiet, walk along the beach at the water's edge; pedlars are forbidden there and you avoid the pollution and noise of Jl Pantai Kuta.

By bike/By motorbike – Some hotels, family guesthouses and shops rent them out. NB, the traffic is dense and somewhat anarchic.

By taxi – There are plenty along Jl Pantai Kuta and Jl Legian.

By car – To be avoided. Traffic jams are a virtually permanent fixture, diversions are frequent and the one-way streets change regularly!

By bemo – See above, "Coming and Going".

ADDRESS BOOK

Tourist Information – Kuta has two tourist offices where you can obtain a map of Bali and the annual calendar of island events, as well as a variety of advertising brochures.

Bali Tourist Information (B3), Century Plaza, Jl Benesari 7, Legian, ☎ (0361) 75 40 90/75 41 46. Daily 8am-8pm; closed Sunday.

Badung Government Tourism Office (C4), corner of Jl Raya Kuta/Jl Bakung Sari, ☎ (0361) 75 61 76. Daily 8am-6pm; closed Sunday.

Bank/Currency exchange – Most of the **banks** are in Jl Legian. At some of them you can withdraw cash with Visa (Danamon, Bali, Panin, BCA, Duta banks) or MasterCard (Bali, Lippo banks).

There are countless **moneychangers** who enable you to change cash or travellers' cheques at better rates than in the banks, but be careful since rates can double depending on the place, and visitors often get swindled. Some real professionals operate sleight-of-hand tricks that enable them to rob even the most vigilant tourists. Calculate the amount you should receive yourself (their calculating ma-

chines are sometimes rigged!), count your money several times over, do not let it out of your sight for a second and be extra vigilant if you are given small denomination notes. If you realise there is money missing you will of course demand the full sum. But do not be too smug about having avoided being swindled! The changer will apologise, give you what is missing and then recount the lot. And it is often at this point that he acts, by asking you, for instance, if he can keep a small note as a tip, thus distracting your attention from the wad he has just recounted before your eyes and pocketing some of it before handing it over and thanking you. It is usually pointless to go back and demand the rest.

Post office/Telephone – There are numerous **Wartel** agencies for making international calls and sending and receiving faxes.

Main post office, Jl Raya Kuta, Gang Slamet (C4).

Kuta post office, Jl Legian (C3). Poste restante and Internet.

Legian post offices, Jl Melasti (B3); Century Plaza, Jl Benesari 7 (B3).

Seminyak post office, Jl Raya Seminyak (B1).

Mailing parcels – The many air and sea freight companies are found mainly in Jl Legian.

Internet – Wartel Kambodianan, Kuta Square, Block C 18 (B4), Kuta. Expensive. **Hot Chilli Café**, Jl Benesari (B3), Legian. A real cybercafé for those who like to sip a drink while surfing the Web. **Bali Cyber Café**, Jl Pura Bagus Teruna, Legian. **Legian Cyber-Café** (B2), Jl Sahadewa 21 (B2), Legian. **Goa 2001 Cyber-Café**, Jl Raya Seminyak 501 (B1), Seminyak.

Tourist agencies – These are legion and all offer similar excursions.

Car rental – Numerous local agencies rent out cars, with or without drivers, as well as motorbikes. Compare prices, insurance policies and the state of the vehicles.

Medical service – Kuta Clinic, Jl Raya Kuta, ☎ (0361) 75 32 68. See also p 104.

WHERE TO STAY

Both the best and the worst are available: rooms for all tastes and all budgets, with quality and price not always going hand in hand. The luxury hotels are to be found mainly in Tuban and Seminyak, while Kuta and Legian have a large number of inexpensive places.

● **Kuta**

Modest

Bungalows Taman Ayu Kempu, Poppies Lane I, ☎ (0361) 75 18 55 – 10rm. ⌂ ☂ A family-run place set in a court-yard with trees. Simple but irreproach-ably clean rooms with woven bamboo decor, each with a small private terrace. Avoid room 1, which is right on the street.

Average

Bali Sandy Cottages, Poppies Lane II, ☎ (0361) 75 33 44 – 12rm. ⌂ ☂ Pretty bamboo-furnished rooms in a 2-storey building set in a spacious garden that is well ventilated if not luxuriant. The hotel gives excellent value for money and is quiet as it is off the street.

Nagasari Beach Inn, Jl Bakung Sari (re-named Singosari) 60, ☎ (0361 75 19 60/ 75 18 89, Fax (0361) 75 62 78 – 11rm. ⌂ ☂ ✕ Private 2-storey bungalows with woven bamboo decor and thatched roofs. The rather dilapidated bathroom facilities are on the ground floor. The bedrooms with balconies are upstairs, with pretty carved and coloured wooden doors. A good hotel for the category. The music in the restaurant is sometimes a little loud.

🐚**Mimpi Bungalows**, Poppies Lane I, ☎/Fax (0361) 75 18 48 – 9rm. ⌂ ☂ ⚱ Hot water in some rooms. Set in a little garden full of charm and decorated with Balinese parasols and statuettes, with birds singing in cages. The thatched-roof bungalows are furnished in bamboo with ikats or batiks. Avoid rooms 1 and 2, which are near the reception and the street. The place is nevertheless quiet for Kuta. Impeccably clean with a friendly welcome and a pleasant small swimming pool.

High end

Suji Bungalow, Poppies Lane I, ☎ (0361) 75 24 83, Fax (0361) 75 24 83 – 45rm. ⌂ ☰ / ☂ ✕ ⚱ cc Hot water in some rooms. Small 1- or 2-storey pavil-ions, clean and simple, in white brick with tiled roofs. The setting is not fantas-tic but the bungalows are nicely spaced out and well maintained.

Sari Jaya Cottages, Poppies Lane I, ☎ (0361) 75 69 09, Fax (0361) 75 29 48 – 25rm. ⌂ ☰ / ☂ ⚱ cc Hot water. Sober rooms with white brick on 2 floors set around the swimming pool. A clean, well-cared for setting but which lacks space and greenery.

High end to luxury

Kuta Puri Bungalows, Poppies Lane I, ☎ (0361) 75 19 03, Fax (0361) 75 25 85 – 22rm. ⌂ ☰ / ☂ ⚱ Hot water in some rooms. The nicely spaced out bungalows sit in the middle of a garden around a swimming pool. The cheaper rooms are ordinary but acceptable. Those in the higher category are prettier and more spacious and have a little living room area and an open bathroom with bath tub. The whole place is clean and pleasant.

Poppies (annex), Poppies Lane II, ☎ (0361) 75 10 59, Fax (0361) 75 23 64 – 4rm. ⌂ ☂ cc The annex to the hotel in Poppies Lane I. A pleasant place even if it is not as luxurious as the hotel itself (see below).

Asana Santhi - Willy, Jl Clung Wanara 17, ☎ (0361) 75 12 81/75 22 73, Fax (0361) 75 26 41, asanasw@ indo.net.id – 12rm. ⌂ ☰ ⚱ cc Hot water. A charm-ing little hotel although slightly cramped. Its advantage is to be away from the crowded shopping streets, but it is a little far from the beach and rather noisy. The rooms are furnished with refinement, and pretty screens divide the terraces.

Luxury to super deluxe

🐚**Poppies**, Poppies Lane I, ☎ (0361) 75 10 59, Fax (0361) 75 23 64, info@bali.poppies.net; www.poppies.net – 20rm. ⌂ ☰ ☂ ✎ ✕ ⚱ cc Hot wa-ter and fridges. Small private bungalows with white walls and thatched roofs, ele-gantly decorated with fabrics and craft-work and set in a harmonious garden criss-crossed by flower-lined paths. The open-air bathrooms are decorated with plants and have marble bath tubs set in the ground. Each terrace is discreetly hid-den by shrubs. Avoid room 28, which is noisier. A pretty swimming pool edged with rocks and shaded by bougainvillaea. The much-esteemed restaurant is 20m away (see "Eating out").

• Legian

Modest

The Legian Mas Beach Inn, Jl Melasti, Gang Iabak Bena, ☎ (0361) 75 53 34 – 12rm. A good little family-run place set back from the street in a friendly, peaceful neighbourhood. The rooms, which are clean although rather basic and a bit dilapidated, are set around a little garden and an offerings pavilion.

Average

Bhuwana Beach Cottages, Jl Padma Utara, Gang ABDI 2, ☎ (0361) 75 22 34 – 10rm. In a peaceful alleyway. Small private houses with 2 storeys separated from the central alley by a little wall. On the ground floor an open room serves as living room and kitchen, with the bedroom upstairs. There are also classic rooms, which are smaller and less intimate.

Sinar Indah Beach Cottages, Jl Padma Utara, ☎ (0361) 75 59 05 – 28rm. Clean, sparsely furnished rooms. An ordinary place whose main asset is its peace and quiet.

High end

Three Brothers Bungalows, ☎ (0361) 75 15 66, Fax (0361) 75 60 82 – 85rm. / Carved brick and stone decor. Large, sober and impeccable rooms. The nicest ones have 2 storeys under a thatched roof with bamboo blinds instead of windows, which means they have pleasant natural ventilation. Lovely swimming pool. Pleasant restaurant although a little noisy.

High end to luxury

Puri Tantra Beach Bungalows, Jl Padma Utara 50 X, ☎/Fax (0361) 75 31 95 – 6rm. Hot water. Small private white brick bungalows with thatched roofs reached by a central alleyway that leads through the garden to the beach. Balinese parasols on the terraces, pretty furniture made of bamboo or carved wood plus ikat curtains and bedspreads. Superb open-air bathrooms with tubs. Perfectly peaceful and charming.

Luxury

Tunjung Bali Resort, Jl Padma Utara, ☎ (0361) 75 60 13, Fax (0361) 75 68 89 – 8rm. / TV CC Hot water. Rooms and villas (for 2 to 5 people) with modern standard of comfort but no great charm. A friendly welcome.

Super deluxe

Resor Kul Kul, Jl Pantai Kuta, ☎ (0361) 75 25 20, Fax (0361) 75 25 19, kulkul@indosat.net.id – 76rm. TV CC A relatively quiet hotel standing back from the street. Prettily decorated rooms with balconies upstairs or terraces giving onto the garden. The more expensive bungalows have private entrances and terrace living rooms. Beautiful items of local craftwork brighten up the corridors: fabrics, statuettes and "kulkul" (wooden cowbells).

• Seminyak

Average

Panca Jaya Bungalows, Jl Dhyana Pura, ☎/Fax (0361) 73 04 58 – 12rm. Good value for money, simple, quiet and quite close to the beach. Some rooms open through Balinese doors onto big terraces, set around a rather small garden. There is also accommodation in woven bamboo bungalows with thatched roofs surrounded by fences. The bungalows are 2-storey, with living room, kitchenette and open-air bathroom (the latter a bit dilapidated).

High end

Annex to the Bali Agung Village (see below) CC Hot water. The bungalows are located just behind the main building in a slightly neglected garden and enable you to use the hotel's swimming pool and restaurant at a much lower price. The rooms are spacious although without charm and have an open-air bathroom with a goldfish pond.

Sarinande Beach Inn, Jl Sarinande 15 (Jl Dyana Pura), ☎ (0361) 73 03 83 – 26rm. / TV CC A small hotel with no particular character but clean, quiet and close to the beach. The rooms are on 2 floors set around the swimming pool. Pleasant staff.

Super deluxe

Bali Agung Village, Jl Abimanyu, ☎ (0361) 73 03 67, Fax (0361) 73 04 69 – 51rm. TV CC Hot water and 5min from the beach. The rooms are neither very big nor very beautiful but the lovely garden and peaceful surrounding countryside compensate considerably. Some of the rooms give onto rice fields. Twice as expensive are the individual villas separated by a little wall, which have more charm and offer total privacy.

Making the most of Kuta

Bali

Resor Seminyak (ex-Pesona Bali), Jl Lasmana, ☎ (0361) 73 08 14, Fax (0361) 73 08 15, pesonahtl@indosat.net.id – 69rm. 🛏️ 📺 🍴 ♨️ 🏊 CC Hot water and several categories of rooms. The cheapest are small and a bit drab. The others are roomier and have living room areas, plus a big jacuzzi bathtub in the most luxurious. They look onto either a magnificent garden, the sea or rice fields.

EATING OUT

So many restaurants open up, close down or change management with such rapidity that it is difficult to make a reliable selection. They generally serve local cuisine adapted to tourist tastes as well as Western cuisine that is often mediocre. We therefore list only the tried-and-tested places, plus others where the setting seems particularly pleasant.

● **Kuta**

Basic

Pasar Senggol, Jl Tanjung Sari, in the night market (C4), open from late afternoon. The Indonesians forget business while they eat a quick sate, nasi goreng or bakso. Be careful of pickpockets, this is one of their favourite spots.

Moderate

Tree House Restaurant, Poppies Lane I (B4), ☎ (0361) 75 13 21. A small, unpretentious place serving a wide choice of dishes from different countries. The upstairs terrace is quieter. Informal service.

Moderate to more select

Ryoshi, Jl Melasti 42 A (B3), ☎ (0361) 76 18 52. An inside dining room with gentle air conditioning where you eat Japanese-style sitting on cushions on the floor. A few ordinary tables as well. They serve sushi, sashimi, tempura, soba-udon and other Japanese delights. The fish is deliciously fresh, tender and tasty. Come early, the place is popular!

Made's Warung, Br Pande Mas (C4), ☎ (0361) 75 52 97. This café and restaurant opening onto the street not far from Bemo Corner is full from morning to night. In an old-fashioned decor with old black and white photos, long-standing regulars and recently arrived tourists come to eat on the terrace or the less noisy mezzanine floor. The menu offers a large choice of dishes served in generous helpings.

More select

🍲**Poppies Restaurant**, Poppies Lane I (C4), ☎(0361) 75 10 59 (it is advisable to book for evenings), daily 8am-11pm. A tropical oasis and haven of peace, the elegant restaurant seems to have been dumped here by mistake like an enclave in the heart of pulsating Kuta. Good local and Western cuisine in a hushed atmosphere.

● **Legian**

Moderate

Swassdee Kha Thai Restaurant, Jl Werkudara 523 (B2), Legian, ☎ (0361) 75 73 73. A small, charming, peaceful place for those getting tired of Indonesian food. Intimate, hushed setting livened up by a little fountain. Diners eat sitting on cushions around low tables. There is also a pleasant, more classical, terrace upstairs. Flavourful Thai cuisine plus good cakes and pastries for those with a sweet tooth.

Topi Koki, Jl Werdukara (B2), ☎ (0361) 75 63 30. A big, open dining room set a little back from the street. Good Indonesian and Western cuisine in an attractive setting.

Galih, Jl Melasti, Gang Camplung Mas (B3), Legian Kelod, ☎ (0361) 75 38 21. A very simple little restaurant but very pleasant too, with a large Balinese thatch roof. A friendly welcome and well-prepared local dishes.

More select

Poco Loco, Jl Padma Utara (B2), ☎ (0361) 75 60 79. 6pm-12midnight. The colourful setting, an original, cheerful place on several floors set back from the street, sets the tone for this Mexican restaurant. They serve nachos, quesadillas, tortillas, burritos, enchiladas, tacos, etc with music playing and all washed down with a good margarita.

● **Seminyak**

Basic

Café Moka, Jl Raya Seminyak (B1). A French cake shop that will make croissant fans more than happy.

Moderate to more select

Ryoshi, Jl Raya Seminyak 17 (B1), ☎ (0361) 73 11 52. See the description of the restaurant in Kuta.

More select

La Lucciola, Jl Oberoi, Kayu Aya Beach (beyond A1), ☎ (0361) 73 08 38. CC Essential to book for dinner. A sophisticated restaurant much appreciated for its setting. Ideal for a lazy day on the beach, an aperitif while watching the sunset or a romantic dinner. You eat either in an elegant thatched-roof pavilion that is pleasantly ventilated, or right on the beach between a massage and a quick dip. Good Italian-inspired cuisine and tasty desserts. Discreet, attentive service. Somewhat expensive but worth it.

Kafe Warisan, Jl Raya Kerobokan, Br Taman (beyond B1), ☎ (0361) 73 11 75. Dinner only. Outside terrace with a bistro ambience or little rooms with old-fashioned charm for more intimate dinners. Delicate, inventive cuisine prepared by a French chef. Among the specialities are duck terrine with pistachios, marinated fish salad, snails, fish stew, pasta with mustard, and salmon with coriander. And if you still have room it is well worth trying the crème brûlée or the glacé soufflé with cinnamon in an orange sauce.

HAVING A DRINK

The night-life is at its most frenzied along Jl Legian. Neon lighting, traffic jams and horns are the order of every evening.

Gado-Gado, Jl Dhyana Pura (A1), Legian. A big nightclub, ideally located right on the beach, where you can dance the night away. It also has a rather expensive restaurant.

Double Six, Jl Double Six (A1), Legian, ☎ (0361) 73 04 66. Italian restaurant open all day plus a night-club from midnight to dawn in an immense room opening onto the beach. A swimming pool as well for midnight swims.

Warung Tapas, Jl Raya Basangkasa (beyond B1), Seminyak, ☎ (0361) 73 00 29. Small night-club and bar. Concerts on Tuesday and Friday. Friendly.

OTHER THINGS TO DO

Surfing – The main rental shops are in Poppies Lane II (B3) in Kuta. Particularly well known is the **Tubes** bar and restaurant, a hangout for surfers from all over the world. But there are also surfboards for rent on the beach itself.

Massage – There are numerous masseuses working on the beach or beside the hotel swimming pools, when the management allows them in. You should agree on the price and duration before starting, and expect the masseuse to "forget" the time and/or double the massage up with a manicure. It is rarely disagreeable but never free! There are also many massage parlours if you prefer more privacy.

SHOPPING GUIDE

Kuta is THE shopping capital. There are hundreds of shops along Jl Legian and in the side streets, all selling much the same articles: sarongs, bags, clothing and jewellery, as well as furniture, carvings and other craftwork. Many shops sell cassettes and CDs too, at low prices. There are also several photographers.

Making the most of Kuta

BUKIT PENINSULA★
(BUKIT BADUNG)
Badung district – Map p 350-351
Half-day excursion (about 50km)
Arid climate

Not to be missed
Uluwatu temple (preferably at the end of the day).
Eating grilled fish on Jimbaran beach.
The sight of the surfers riding the most impressive waves on the island.

And remember...
Do this excursion in the afternoon so as to then enjoy the sunset.
Be careful of the very light-fingered monkeys at Uluwatu temple.

The Bukit peninsula, a small, isolated finger of land on the tip of southern Bali, has a very different physiognomy to the rest of the island. Here there are neither rice fields nor steep gorges, just a few small valleys cutting through a limestone plateau (*bukit* means "hill") covered in sparse, arid vegetation. Probably separated from Bali at some point in the far-distant past, Bukit is today joined to the island by a low, narrow isthmus. With the tourist boom it has become the setting for a few top luxury seaside resorts, but it also provides the opportunity for a pleasant excursion of a few hours.

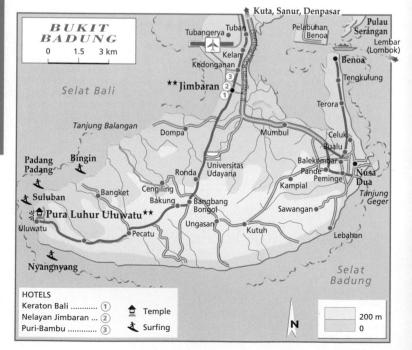

■ **Jimbaran**★★ — *From the airport, turn right into Jl I GST Ngurah Rai, then do a U-turn down the road to Uluwatu.* This peaceful fishing village on the way to the peninsula is composed of modest houses scattered along the roadside. The alleyways crossing the main road lead down to the **beach**★, a wide, curving swathe of pale sand washed by a calm sea, and virtually deserted. A few hotels have sprung up here but nothing seems to bother the fishermen who continue patching up their nets in the middle of the gaily-coloured *jukung*. Further north a flotilla of bright boats sits bobbing on the waves, waiting for nightfall to weigh anchor. This is the children's favourite time for playing pirates, climbing on board or diving off the highest prows, completely indifferent to the aeroplanes above their heads. In the morning a **market** is held where the fishermen's wives sell the day's catch.

On going south out of the village the road climbs up towards Uluwatu (signposted).

■ **Pura Luhur Uluwatu**★★ — *About 15km from Jimbaran (a 20min journey). Temple car park on the left. 8am-5pm. Fee (hire of sarongs and sashes). Allow 30min.* Standing in isolation on the southwestern tip of Bali, the temple rises up at the end of an abrupt rocky promontory (*uluwatu* means "at the top of the rocks") and looks down over the wild ocean more than 200m below. As it is dedicated to the sea divinities and is also one of the nine directional temples and one of the six great sanctuaries on Bali (*see p 357*), it is therefore one of the most venerated temples on the island.

But the most impressive thing about the place is the grandiose **panorama**★★★ over the cliffs and wild coast, where the breakers come crashing in violently. A picture that is even more magical at sunset when the sea catches fire.

But beautiful as the sight may be, visitors should still remain vigilant as the monkeys that inhabit the sanctuary are dreadful little thieves who have got into the bad habit of pinching cameras, wallets and sunglasses in the twinkling of an eye. Those who fall victim to them should lose no time in buying peanuts or bananas (there is no lack of vendors) to try to coax them into giving back their prizes.

Nirvana at Uluwatu

Legend has it that Uluwatu temple was built in the 11C by the Javanese priest Mpu Kuturan, then rebuilt in the 16C by Danghyang Nirartha (see p 461). The latter, a fellow priest, played a prime role in the Hinduist revival on Bali, and is said to have attained nirvana here (the supreme state of non-existence and purity of soul that enables the soul to merge with the cosmos), thus achieving moksa, the final deliverance of the soul, which puts an end to the cycle of rebirth (samsara).

On leaving the temple, turn left a few hundred metres beyond the car park and follow the road for about 2km.

■ **The surfing spots**★★★ — Uluwatu is also renowned for its waves, which attract the best surfers from all over the world (*Note: only very experienced surfers should venture out on the breakers. They are exhilarating but dangerous!*). From the road (*2km from the temple*) a stairway leads down to **Suluban beach**, where you can sip a cold drink in a *warung* while admiring the surfers. It is a fascinating **sight**★★★ to see their outlines dancing in the waves, flouting the unbridled elements. Other surfing spots such as **Padang Padang**, **Bingin** and **Nyangnyang**, which are difficult to find, can be located by asking local people.

■ **Nusa Dua** — This seaside resort built in the 1970s and 1980s was designed by the government as a top-class holiday centre, isolated but easy to get to and intended for the elite. Since security guards are responsible for getting rid of pedlars and other undesirable Indonesians, visitors are unlikely to meet any other natives than hotel

Bukit peninsula

staff and limousine chauffeurs, and there are more dollars in circulation than rupiah. The hotel complexes, some of which are so spread out that guests move around in electric vehicles, largely monopolise access to the sea. All in all, this does not really feel like Bali in the least.

■ **Tanjung Benoa** – Located along the narrow tongue of land stretching north of Nusa Dua, the village and holiday resort of Benoa have a somewhat simpler atmosphere. Here too hotels have sprung up all along the seafront but visitors feel less cut off from local life. It is here that most of the island's (expensive) **water sports** take place: parasailing, jet-skiing, windsurfing and water-skiing. The **beach** is fairly pleasant but the constant buzz of motorboats plus the narrow and rather shallow bathing area, marked out by floats for safety's sake, deprive it of all exoticism!

Just opposite the peninsula stands **Benoa harbour** (Pelabuhan Benoa), one of the most important in Bali. In its marina there are sometimes sumptuous **yachts** and it is from here that luxury cruises leave for the other islands (see p 396).

■ **Pulau Serangan** (Turtle Island) – *At low tide you can walk across but when the tide is in it is necessary to hire the services of a jukung from Sanur or Tanjung Benoa.* Sitting off the Suwung mangrove swamp and barely 500m from the shore, the little island of Serangan is home to a **sea turtle** farm. Although it is supposed to protect the species, which is in danger of extinction, the farm does in fact feed the market for turtle meat, which is much prized particularly for festive meals. Visiting the island is of no interest unless there is a ceremony taking place in one of the temples. On Kuningan day (see p 360) the *odalan* ceremony begins, celebrating the anniversary of the founding of **Sakenan temple**.

Bali

Making the most of Jimbaran

ADDRESS BOOK

Currency exchange – The exchange office on Jl Uluwatu accepts all major foreign currencies.

Post office/Telephone – The post office and *Wartel* office are in Jl Uluwatu, in the centre of the village.

Transport – To hire a motorbike or car or to go out in a boat, ask on the beach or in the hotels.

WHERE TO STAY

Average to high end

Nelayan Jimbaran, Jl Pantai Jimbaran 3, ☎/Fax (0361) 70 22 53 – 20rm. 🔺 🖥 / 🎾 ✕ ⚘ Impeccably clean rooms, quite pleasant all in all despite the lack of a real garden. Nevertheless, avoid the ones at the front. Only the more expensive rooms at the back have a terrace worthy of the name and a bit of greenery. Rooftop restaurant. The prices are a little high

Super deluxe

Hotel Puri-Bambu, Jl Pengeracikan, Kenonganan, ☎ (0361) 70 13 77/ 70 14 68/69, Fax (0361) 70 14 40 – 38rm. 🔺 🖥 🖋 📺 ✕ ⚘ 🆑 Hot water. The modern, comfortable but rather impersonal rooms are set around a swimming pool. A lovely garden with bamboo and frangipani. Rather high prices.

Keraton Bali, Jl Mrajapati, ☎ (0361) 70 19 61, Fax (0361) 70 19 91, german@denpasar.wasantara.net.id – 99rm. 🔺 🖥 🖋 📺 ✕ ⚘ 🎾 🍴 🆑 Hot water. Twice as expensive as the above hotel. The rooms are in several brick buildings with roofs reminiscent of Chinese pagodas. Only the size of the rooms and the view differentiate one category from another. The place is generally pleasant and set in a lovely garden.

EATING OUT

Select

🦐 Lined up on the beach in front of the hotels are several *warung* that prepare excellent fish and seafood, freshly caught. Customers choose their meal themselves from the ice tanks and it is then grilled over coconut shells. The series of *warung* nearest the airport is less touristy and the setting even more pleasant.

SANUR
Badung district
7km southeast of Denpasar – Maps p 350-351 and Plan p 386
Hot damp climate

Not to be missed
Taking a stroll along the seafront at sunrise.
Eating dinner in the Sinduh night market.

And remember...
Watch where you walk as the pavements are full of holes!
Be careful of sea urchins when bathing in the lagoon.

Sanur stretches along the eastern coast, seemingly turning its back on Kuta, of which it is indeed in many respects the opposite. Although resolutely dedicated to tourism over the last few decades, Sanur has succeeded in avoiding some of the excesses of its neighbour on the west coast. This fishing village, which was very fashionable among European artists in the 1930s, saw its first big hotel go up in 1966, financed by the war reparations paid by the Japanese. Since then the imposing **Bali Beach Hotel** has sat on the northern end of the beach – an eyesore blotting the coastal scenery. Most fortunately this architectural heresy has not had followers, since a later law forbade any building to be taller than the coconut palms. Today Sanur's moderate development and the sophistication of its hotel infrastructure place it in the category of up-market, family-orientated seaside resorts. Classier than Kuta although without the exclusiveness of Nusa Dua's luxury tourist enclave (see p 381), it charms all those seeking comfort and peace and quiet.

Street or beach

Sanur stretches along the coast for almost 4km on either side of its main street, Jl Danau Tamblingan. Numerous side streets lead down to the beach, whereas a big two-lane road, Jl Ngurah Rai (Bypass), skirts round the outside of the town.

Jalan Danau Tamblingan, an uninterrupted line-up of shops, hotels and restaurants, is the realm of shopkeepers and pedlars. It is impossible to stroll along it without being approached, but courtesy remains the order of the day. Anyone wishing for a glimpse of the more authentic side of Sanur should head into the alleyways going west, the only ones to have escaped the tourist invasion.

On the seafront★ bordered by the sumptuous tropical gardens of the luxury hotels, a pleasant promenade has been laid out that is closed to motor vehicles but not to vendors. All day long they try to sell sarongs, watches, caps, etc to visitors, while in the shade mattresses await clients for massages or manicures.

Early in the morning, when the sun sets the waves alight, the place belongs to the Balinese. Young people take advantage of the coolness to do a few gym exercises, others meditate in silence, while women walk down to the sea's edge to lay down offerings to the sea gods.

The long ribbon of pale sand edged with coconut palms forming the beach★ stretches to infinity facing the calm, clear waters of the lagoon. Out to sea, a few hundred metres from the shore, the waves roar and break over the coral reef, creating a thin strip of foam. The lagoon, which is very shallow, is of less interest for swimming than for exploring the seabed with mask and snorkel. At low tide swimming even becomes impossible. This is when the fishermen appear armed with lines and nets.

D Ball/DIAF

Sanur, or the delights of doing nothing

At weekends the inhabitants of Denpasar like to come and spend a few hours picnicking, playing ball or enjoying a lazy siesta.

Between sunbathing sessions it is pleasant to go round **Le Mayeur Museum*** (B1), formerly the home of the Belgian painter and his wife *(entry is from the seafront. 8am-2pm; Friday 8am-11am; Saturday 8am-12.30pm; closed Monday and public holidays. Fee. Allow 10mtn).*

A historic beach

In 1904 a Chinese boat hit the reef and ran aground on the Sanur shore. The crew survived but the precious cargo disappeared. The Dutch demanded compensation from the looters but the Raja of Badung obstinately refused. This resistance to colonial authority provided a pretext for armed intervention and, on 14 September 1906, troops landed on Sanur's sheltered beach, from where they launched a decisive offensive that was to subjugate the rebel province. On 20 September they marched on the palace in Badung, where the rajas, their families and retinues killed themselves before the adversary's cannon in a bloody "puputan".

Born in Brussels in 1880, Le Mayeur fell in love with Bali, where he settled in 1932 and married the beautiful Balinese dancer **Ni Polok**. After her husband's death in 1958, Ni Polok lived in the house until the end of her days, in 1985. The government has turned the place into a modest museum, which is not particularly well maintained. The paintings on show, unfortunately very badly preserved, bear witness to the artist's passion for the island, with scenes from everyday life and Balinese women providing inspiration for most of them.

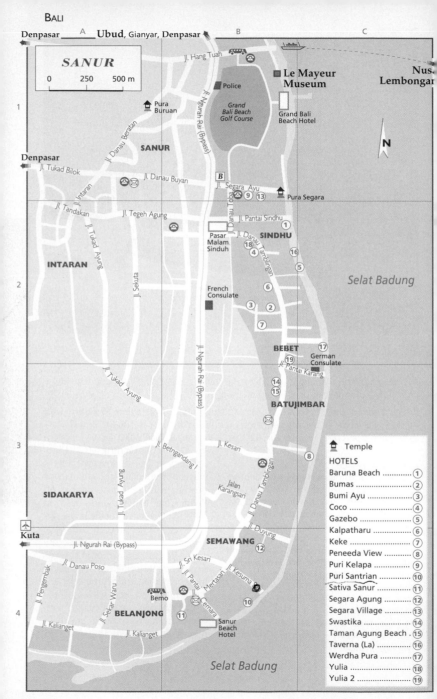

BALI

SANUR

0   250   500 m

Denpasar — Ubud, Gianyar, Denpasar

Jl. Hang Tuah

Le Mayeur Museum

Nus. Lembongar

Police

Pura Buruan

Grand Bali Beach Golf Course

Grand Bali Beach Hotel

N

SANUR

Denpasar

Jl. Tukad Bilok

Jl. Danau Beratan

Jl. Ngurah Rai (Bypass)

Jl. Danau Buyan

Jl. Intaran

B

Jl. Segara Ayu

⑨ ⑬

Pura Segara

Jl. Tandakan

Jl. Tegeh Agung

Jl. Tukad Ayung

Jl. Pantai Sindhu

①

Pasar Malam Sinduh

⑱ ④

SINDHU

⑯

INTARAN

Jl. Seluta

Jl. Danau Tamblingan

⑤

Selat Badung

French Consulate

⑥

③ ②

⑦

BEBET

⑰

⑲

German Consulate

Jl. Ngurah Rai (Bypass)

Jl. Pantai Karang

⑭ ⑮

BATUJIMBAR

Jl. Tukad Ayung

Jl. Kesari

⑧

Jl. Betngandang I

Jl. Danau Tamblingan

SIDAKARYA

Jalan Karangsari

Jl. Duyung

Jl. Tukad Ayung

Kuta

Jl. Ngurah Rai (Bypass)

SEMAWANG

⑫

Jl. Danau Poso

Jl. Sri Kesari

Jl. Selat Waru

Bemo

Jl. Pengembak

Jl. Pantai Mertasari

Jl. Kesuma

BELANJONG

⑩

⑪

Sanur Beach Hotel

Jl. Kalianget

Jl. Kalianget

Selat Badung

▲ Temple

HOTELS

Baruna Beach	①
Bumas	②
Bumi Ayu	③
Coco	④
Gazebo	⑤
Kalpatharu	⑥
Keke	⑦
Peneeda View	⑧
Puri Kelapa	⑨
Puri Santrian	⑩
Sativa Sanur	⑪
Segara Agung	⑫
Segara Village	⑬
Swastika	⑭
Taman Agung Beach .	⑮
Taverna (La)	⑯
Werdha Pura	⑰
Yulia	⑱
Yulia 2	⑲

Making the most of Sanur

COMING AND GOING

By shuttle bus – Several daily services between Sanur and the island's main tourist destinations (Kuta, Ubud, Lovina, Candidasa, Kintamani, etc) The **Perama** company's offices (B1) are opposite the entrance to the Grand Bali Beach Hotel, but many tourist agencies sell tickets.

By bemo – The northern terminal is in front of the Grand Bali Beach Hotel (B1); and the southern one is in Jl Mertasari (near the Semawang Beach Inn hotel) (B4). But you just need to wait along Jl Danau Tamblingan or Jl Bypass to hail a minibus. Bemos all go to Denpasar, the blue ones going to Tegal station and the green ones to Kereneng station.

GETTING AROUND

On foot – This is the best bet for short journeys and for the beach and main street. Be very careful of the potholes all over the pavements!

By taxi – They drive along Jl Danau Tamblingan and tout for custom by tooting their horns.

By bemo – See above, "Coming and Going".

ADDRESS BOOK

Tourist information – There is no tourist office in Sanur but all information required can be obtained from the hotels.

Bank/Currency exchange – There are dozens of exchange offices, mainly along Jl Danau Tamblingan. Compare their rates as they can vary enormously from one place to another.

Bank Lippo, Jl Bypass (beyond B1). Cash can be withdrawn with a Visa card.

American Express, in the grounds of the Grand Bali Beach Hotel (B1), ☎ (0361) 28 84 49/28 85 11. Monday-Friday 8am-4pm; Saturday 8am-12noon. They also agree to your having travellers' cheques sent.

Post office/Telephone – The main post office is in Jl Danau Buyan (A1) but it is more practical to go to the smaller post offices in Jl Danau Tamblingan (B3) or Jl Mertasari (B4), or to a big hotel.

There are several **Wartel** telephone agencies in the main street (B3), Jl Mertasari (B4) and on the corner of Jl Segara Ayu and Jl D Toba (B1).

Internet – An exchange office in Jl D Toba (B1-B2) provides this service. Average price. **Hotel Santai**, Jl Danau Tamblingan (B3) (in the hotel lobby). The most professional and the cheapest. **Grand Bali Beach Hotel** (B1), Lobby (1st floor), 8am-11pm. Expensive.

Mailing parcels – There are several air and sea freight companies in Jl Danau Tamblingan.

Tourist agencies – There are plenty in Jl Danau Tamblingan and Jl Bypass.

Car rental – Many local agencies rent out cars, with or without drivers, as well as motorbikes. Compare prices, insurance contracts and the state of the vehicles. Some hotels, guesthouses and shops also hire out bicycles.

Airline companies – The main companies have their offices at the **Grand Bali Beach Hotel** (B1), ☎ (0361) 28 85 11, or at the **Sanur Beach** (B4), ☎ (0361) 28 80 11. They are also represented by travel agencies.

Medical service – **Chemist**, Jl Danau Buyan 74. You may consult the doctor at the **Grand Bali Beach Hotel**, ☎ (0361) 28 85 11, or at the **Bali Hyatt**, ☎ (0361) 28 82 71.

WHERE TO STAY

Modest to average

Coco Home Stay, Jl Danau Tamblingan 42, ☎ (0361) 28 73 91 – 8rm. ⁴⁄ ⚒ A family guesthouse located behind a souvenir and arts and crafts shop. Small rooms with terraces on 2 floors. The place is simple, a bit cramped but clean and cheap. A friendly welcome.

Yulia Home Stay, Jl Danau Tamblingan 38, ☎ (0361) 28 80 89 – 8rm. ⁴⁄ ⚒ A charming family guesthouse set in a garden behind the owner's shop. Clean and peaceful. The most pleasant place in this category. The 2 rooms upstairs offer more peace and privacy.

Keke Home Stay, Gang Keke 3, Jl Danau Tamblingan 96, ☎ (0361) 28 72 82 – 7rm. ⚎ ✕ Clean, basic little rooms laid out around a quiet courtyard, at the end of an alley leading off the main street. Appreciable above all for the family's kindness and the warm welcome they give their guests.

Yulia 2 Homestay, Jl Danau Tamblingan 57, ☎ (0361) 28 74 95 – 6rm. ⚎ ✕ ✕ A small, simple family guesthouse that is impeccably clean. The 2 rooms upstairs are preferable, as they are lighter and more recent and have balconies looking over the roofs. Those on the ground floor have a shared terrace and therefore less privacy.

Average

Werdha Pura (Wisma Wisata Pantai), Jl Danau Tamblingan 49, ☎ (0361) 28 81 71/ 28 67 11 – 13rm. ⚎ 🖉 ▤ 🏊 Hot water. A series of brick bungalows with thatched roofs scattered around a vast, airy garden. Breakfast is served in a big straw hut facing the beach. This prototype of a 1960s' tourist hotel, a little dilapidated and austere, is just asking to be renovated. It is nevertheless the only cheap place on Sanur beach.

High end

Kalpatharu Hotel, Jl Danau Tamblingan 80, ☎/Fax (0361) 28 84 57 – 6rm. ⚎ ▤ 🖉 ✕ 🏊 CC A small hotel that is friendly and very clean, set back from the road. Minute swimming pool, more for cooling off than swimming. At the end of the garden are the family home and temple. Communal sitting room with television. Restaurant and bar opening onto the street, with concerts some evenings.

🏠**Hotel Segara Agung**, Jl Duyung 43, Semawang, ☎ (0361) 28 84 46/ 28 68 04, Fax (0361) 28 61 13 – 12rm. ⚎ ▤ / ✕ ✕ 🏊 CC At the end of a little dirt track. Various categories of rooms, depending on whether they have air conditioning and hot water or not. The cheapest one is to be avoided as it needs freshening up. Ikats or Balinese paintings decorate the walls. Small swimming pool, deckchairs and straw-roofed restaurant in the middle of a pretty garden. The place is well ventilated and peaceful and offers value for money for Sanur.

High end to luxury

Hotel Taman Agung Beach Inn, Jl Danau Tamblingan 146, ☎ (0361 28 85 49, ☎/Fax (0361) 28 91 61 – 33rm. ⚎ ▤ 🖉 TV ✕ 🏊 CC Hot water. Rooms in small 2-storey buildings. Little swimming pool in the garden. Although the place is well looked after it lacks space.

Luxury

🏠**Baruna Beach Inn**, Jl Pantai Sindhu, ☎ (0361) 28 85 46, Fax (0361) 28 96 29 – 9rm. ⚎ ▤ 🏊 CC A small, friendly place full of charm, more original and personal than the big hotels. The rooms give right onto a garden that opens onto the seafront. Walls made of woven rattan, and doors and furniture mostly made of carved wood. A few bits of formica as well! A lovely family house sits behind the bungalows. Warm welcome.

Swastika Bungalows, Jl Danau Tamblingan 128, ☎ (0361) 28 64 87/ 28 86 93, Fax (0361) 28 75 26 – 81rm. ⚎ ▤ / ✕ ✕ 🏊 CC Hot water. Magnificent luxuriant garden crisscrossed by little winding paths and with 2 lovely swimming pools. Several categories of rooms. The most pleasant ones are upstairs and have private terraces looking onto the garden from under a pretty roof. Some of the ground floor rooms have an open-air bathroom where you can sunbathe. It is nevertheless a good idea to inspect the bathroom facilities before choosing a room.

🏠**Bumi Ayu Bungalows**, Jl Bumi Ayu, ☎ (0361) 28 91 01/28 60 51, Fax (0361) 28 75 17 – 58rm. ⚎ ▤ 🖉 ✕ 🏊 CC Hot water. Far from the main street (and from the beach as well) in a quiet, friendly neighbourhood, this good quality hotel offers excellent value for money. Large, prettily furnished rooms scattered around a superb garden. Little alleyways lead to terraces that are rendered private thanks to the plants. Pleasant restaurant and vast swimming pool. Irreproachable service.

Gazebo Cottages Beach Hotel, Jl Danau Tamblingan 35, ☎ (0361) 28 82 12/28 92 56, Fax (0361) 28 83 00 – 75rm. ⚎ ▤ 🖉 TV ✕ 🏊 🏊 CC Hot water. Lovely Balinese bungalows with thatched roofs and carved wooden doors. The standard rooms, lined up on 2 floors, are spacious but rather ordinary. The magnificent garden is crisscrossed by pebble paths punctuated by little bridges and fountains. Musicians sometimes play in the gamelan stand near the swimming pool.

Peneeda View Hotel, Jl Danau Tamblingan 89, ☎ (0361) 28 84 25/ 28 90 45, Fax (0361) 28 62 24/28 83 00 – 44rm. ⌾ 🗐 𝄢 ✕ ⚒ 𝒫 cc Hot water. Little thatched pavilions set beside a long lane going from the hotel entrance to the beach. Well-maintained rooms decorated with Balinese paintings. Some of the terraces are separated by aquariums. Two small swimming pools and a billiard table. Charming welcome. Further from the beach there are also large 2-storey bungalows with 2 bedrooms each.

Super deluxe

Puri Kelapa Garden Cottages, Jl Segara Ayu 1, ☎ (0361) 28 61 35, Fax (0361) 28 74 17 – 47rm. ⌾ 🗐 𝄢 tv ✕ ⚒ cc Hot water. Pretty rooms spread around a splendid tropical garden with hibiscus, coconut palms and bamboo. Lovely architecture comprising white brick and Balinese carved wood doors. There is rattan furniture, and kites and batiks on the walls. The bungalows are more private but some of the bathroom facilities could do with being renovated. The restaurant unfortunately gives onto a busy street.

Bumas Hotel, Jl Bumi Ayu 4, ☎ (0361) 28 63 06/28 63 07, Fax (0361) 28 83 41 – 34rm. ⌾ 🗐 𝄢 tv ✕ ⚒ cc Hot water. Away from the main street in a quiet alleyway. Most of the spacious rooms have a pretty open-air bathroom decorated with pebbles and plants. They are on 2 floors around a lovely swimming pool and a vast garden with hibiscus, coconut trees and frangipani. Small straw huts provide shade for guests having a drink.

Sativa Sanur Cottages, Jl Danau Tamblingan 145, ☎/Fax (0361) 28 78 81 – 50rm. ⌾ 🗐 𝄢 tv ✕ ⚒ cc The luxurious but impersonal rooms are in several small 2-storey buildings giving onto either the garden or the swimming pool from which islets of coconut palms emerge. Colourful bougainvillaea and sweet-smelling frangipani. Pleasant restaurant beside the swimming pool.

La Taverna, Jl Danau Tamblingan 29, ☎ (0361) 28 84 97, Fax (0361) 28 71 26. 40rm. ⌾ 🗐 𝄢 ✕ ⚒ 𝒫 cc Hot water. All the rooms are different, tastefully furnished and decorated in the Balinese style. Traditional carved doors, large bowl-shaped bathtubs, plus shells and coral set in the walls of some of the bathrooms. The upstairs rooms are preferable as they are lighter and better ventilated. Magnificent garden with an imposing banyan, frangipani, coconut palms etc. Little Balinese sunshades give a cheerful touch. Pleasant restaurant with a big thatched roof, and pretty swimming pool. A little sandy corner with parasols and deckchairs has been laid out on the seafront. The service is rather haphazard but the place is still charming.

Puri Santrian, Jl Danau Tamblingan, ☎ (0361) 28 80 09, Fax (0361) 28 71 01, santrian@denpasar.wasantara.net.id – 131rm. ⌾ 🗐 𝄢 ✕ ⚒ 𝒫 ✎ cc Hot water. A sober and refined luxury hotel with elegant Balinese architecture. Ecru shades dominate, set off by richly carved and coloured wooden doors and traditional furniture made of wood and rattan. All hidden away in vast grounds with trees and flowers and 2 immense swimming pools. Pleasant seafront with restaurant, deckchairs and parasols.

Segara Village, Jl Segara Ayu, ☎ (0361) 28 84 07, Fax (0361) 28 72 42, segara1@denpasar.wasantara.net.id – 144rm. ⌾ 🗐 𝄢 ✕ ⚒ 𝒫 ⚘ ✎ cc Hot water. The architecture, furnishings and garden are all harmonious, well ventilated and well maintained. The rooms located on 2 floors either give onto a lily pond or the temple. The corridors are peopled with statues of Balinese gods. Many activities for children and adults: billiards, table tennis, cycling, sauna, aerobics, etc.

EATING OUT

Most of the restaurants have similar menus: breakfast, salads and snacks, Indonesian, Balinese and Chinese specialities, pasta and pizza, and Western cuisine. Most of them give onto the main street, Jl Danau Tamblingan, and are therefore unpleasantly noisy. Some stand out through the quality of their food, others for their pleasant settings.

Making the most of Sanur

Basic

👁**Pasar malam Sinduh**, Jl Sinduh (B2).
This is the evening market, which is very
lively from late afternoon on. A score of
little stands set up where you can order
sate, soups, mee or nasi goreng, capcai
and other local dishes, which are prepared in front of you. They also serve cold
drinks and fresh fruit juices. The few vendors still present from the day market
(right at the back) will be delighted to sell
you their last remaining fruits for dessert.
A relaxed stir of excitement reigns against
a background of local popular music. Sitting here on little stools or makeshift
benches, side by side with the locals, is
definitely where you are likely to make
the best contacts with Sanur's inhabitants.

Moderate

Cumi Cumi, Jl Danau Tamblingan 82
(B2). A pleasant setting on a terrace with
a Balinese roof. Classic dishes, both local
and Western.

Warung Aditya, Jl Danau Tamblingan
104 A (B2), ☎ (0361) 28 94 82. An unpretentious little *warung* that opens onto
the street. Good local specialities and a
friendly welcome.

Agung restaurant, Jl Danau Tamblingan
97 (B3), ☎ (0361) 28 80 29. A small
restaurant opening onto the street but
pleasant and well ventilated.

Kalimantan, Jl Pantai Sindhu 11 (B2),
☎ (0361) 28 92 91. In a peaceful little
street leading to the beach. Rustic wooden
tables set in straw huts or under a big
thatched roof. Ideal for lunching without
being hassled by vendors. A few Mexican
specialities liven up the menu.

Nelayan, Jl Danau Tamblingan (B3-B4).
A big covered terrace, well-ventilated and
decorated with plants, set slightly back
from the street. Indonesian and Western
cuisine at good prices.

Tia, Jl Pantai Cemara 38 (B4),
☎ (0361) 28 91 36. A terrace covered by
a big traditional Balinese roof and separated from the street by a garden. Indonesian and Western cuisine and
seafood.

Pantai Cemara, on the seafront near Jl
Pantai Cemara (B4), ☎ (0361) 28 81 53.
A terrace surrounded by small shops. All
sorts of dishes.

Moderate to more select

Warung Bali Sun, Jl Danau Tamblingan
(B3). A small shady terrace on the street.
A bit noisy but good value for money. Lo-
cal specialities and seafood.

Ryoshi, Jl Danau Tamblingan 150 (B3),
☎ (0361) 28 84 73. A small, air-conditioned inside dining room or an outside
terrace. You eat Japanese-style sitting on
cushions on the floor. A few ordinary tables as well. They serve sushi, sashimi,
tempura, soba-udon and other Japanese
delights, including tasty fish. Come early,
the place is popular!

Donald's cafe and restaurant, Jl Danau
Tamblingan (B4), ☎ (0361) 28 94 50. Behind the simple terrace opening onto the
street there is a more elegant dining room
in a garden. A wide range of dishes of all
kinds.

👁**Resto Ming**, Jl Danau Tamblingan
105 (B4), ☎ (0361) 28 19 48 (advisable
to book) [CC] The dining room opens onto
the street and then stretches back inside,
more peacefully, to a straw-roofed area
decorated with plants. It is also a gallery
with paintings, batiks and masks (for sale)
decorating the walls. The pleasant setting
and quality cuisine have made this restaurant a success, which means it is often
full.

Warung Nyoman, Jl Danau Tamblingan
86 (B2), ☎ (0361) 28 87 43 [CC] A covered terrace giving onto the street. Indonesian, Chinese, Italian and Western
cuisine.

Cafe Batu Jimbar, Jl Danau Tamblingan
152 (B3), ☎ (0361) 28 73 74. A pleasant
shady terrace separated from the street by
a curtain of greenery. Very popular, especially for lunch. They serve a variety of
salads as well as good Indonesian dishes
and home-made cakes and pastries. Delicious fresh fruit cocktails.

More select

Abian Boga restaurant, Jl Kesuma
Sari 5 (B4), ☎ (0361) 28 71 74/ 28 78 37.
[CC] Open in the evenings. A big open
dining room in a quiet alleyway leading
to the beach. No menu. You choose a set
meal (Indonesian, Chinese, seafood or
lobster) and they serve an assortment of
ready-prepared dishes. Dance and gamelan performances every evening. Very
touristy but pleasant.

Kul Kul, Jl Danau Tamblingan (B3), ☎ (0361) 28 80 38. 6pm-10pm CC Delightful setting and sophisticated cuisine. You dine in magnificent Balinese pavilions with thatched roofs, decorated with a collection of "kulkul" bells. The Rijstaffel, an assortment of Indonesian specialities, is particularly tasty here. Lovers of seafood or frogs' legs will also be delighted.

Tandjung Sari, Jl Danau Tamblingan (B2-C2), ☎ (0361) 28 84 41 CC Entrance on the street or the beach. The restaurant of one of Sanur's most luxurious hotels is open to non-residents and its prices are affordable. A pleasant setting leading onto the beach plus remarkably well prepared dishes. The Rijstaffel on Saturday evenings gives you a chance to taste an assortment of Indonesian specialities.

GOING OUT, HAVING A DRINK

Most of the restaurants are bars as well. Some also put on performances of Balinese dancing and gamelan concerts or Western music. The programmes are posted-up outside. The night-clubs, which are mainly frequented by a clientele of young Indonesians, are livelier on Saturday nights.

Subec, Jl Danau Tamblingan (B2).

Number One, Jl Danau Tamblingan 138 (B3).

OTHER THINGS TO DO

Diving – Sanur is a good place to start learning to dive. The clubs also organise outings to Bali's best diving spots. Most of the clubs are on the beach or in Jl Bypass. See also p 100.

Bali Crystal Divers, Jl Duyung 25 (B3-B4), Semawang, ☎/Fax (0361) 28 67 37, bcrystal@dps.mega.net.id A very professional team and well-maintained equipment.

Water sports – Parasailing equipment, canoes, glass-bottomed boats, masks and snorkels are available on the seafront and from some hotels.

SHOPPING GUIDE

Shops abound in Jl Danau Tamblingan as well as on the seafront. They all sell more or less the same articles: sarongs, bags, clothing, jewellery, etc. A few shops sell cassettes and CDs at low prices. There are also several photographers.

Bookshops/Newspapers – Many grocer's on the main street sell English-language newspapers. **Toko Buku Kika**, Jl Danau Tamblingan 152 (B3). English-language books and newspapers.

Making the most of Sanur

NUSA LEMBONGAN★★
THE PENIDA ARCHIPELAGO
Small archipelago off southeast Bali
Klungkung district – Map p 350-351 and p 394
Hot dry climate

Not to be missed
Exploring the coral seabed around the islands.
Sunset at Jungutbatu.
The view of the cliffs on the south coast of Nusa Penida.

And remember...
Hire a bicycle to tour Nusa Lembongan.
Avoid flaunting your wealth (jewellery, wads of banknotes, etc)
out of respect for the islands' inhabitants, who are very poor.

Off the southeast coast of Bali, across the Badung Strait, lie three islands encircled by iridescent coral reefs: Nusa Penida and its two minute satellites, Lembongan and Ceningan. Here there are no forests or luxuriant rice fields; the only crops that grow on these limestone plateaux with their arid hills are cassava, sweet potatoes, soya beans, maize and a little tobacco. The traditional housing of makeshift woven bamboo huts with thatched roofs is by far the most common, with corrugated iron not yet having made too many unfortunate inroads.

Because the tourist infrastructure is still very underdeveloped, these islands are not very well known to most visitors, who are content to explore their underwater wealth during luxury day cruises or to surf some of their renowned waves. But they will prove just as much a delight for those fond of bicycling or exploring places miles from anywhere.

Seaweed farming
The inhabitants of these islands, who are considerably poorer than the Balinese, make their living mostly from fishing and, more recently, farming seaweed (*rambut laut*); the dark square patches of seaweed on pale sand immediately catch the eye in the turquoise waters. As soon as the tide starts going out in the lagoon, everyone sets to work harvesting; some work on foot, pushing a bamboo basket sitting on a big rubber ring, whereas others prefer to use a *jukung*, manoeuvring it with a long bamboo pole. On the beaches, in the courtyards and along the roadsides, harmonious carpets of seaweed tinged pink, yellow, green or blue dry in the sun, and everywhere men and women, young and old, bustle about untangling, sorting and washing it. Once sold to a co-operative then exported to Japan or Hong Kong, this seaweed is used in making cosmetics and food products.

Nusa Lembongan★★
About 2km by 4km – Pop 6 500

After a rough crossing on board a crowded *jukung*, it is a pleasure to jump into the warm crystalline waters of **Jungutbatu beach★★**. On arriving straight from the Balinese coast, visitors immediately fall under the spell of the island's ineffable charm.

Nusa Lembongan's seaweed farms, an aquatic mosaic

Y Arthus-Bertrand/Altitude

Here there are no *losmen* touts to welcome new arrivals: the bungalows are concentrated to the north of the beach and visitors are free to choose whichever they want. As you sit on the pale sand or under the coconut palms *(beware of falling coconuts!)*, vendors may come up trying to sell T-shirts, massages or boat trips, but they are still few and far between here.

Reputed for the waves that break on its reefs, Nusa Lembongan attracts large numbers of surfers *(for very experienced surfers only)*. When the breakers swell out beyond the barrier reef, watching the ballet of outlined figures surfing the waves is a fascinating sight.

The **panorama***★★ out beyond the waves takes in all of southeastern Bali from the Bukit Peninsula to Mount Agung. At nightfall the lights start twinkling along the coast and when the moon comes up the line of volcano peaks stands out against the sky.

Exploring the island★★

This is best done by motorbike or bicycle *(check the brakes as some of the hills are steep!)*. Most of the roads are surfaced although there are still some dirt tracks. It is not worth carrying a bottle of water since the numerous stalls along the way offer plenty of opportunities for stopping off to cool down and chat with villagers.

Go through the village of Jungutbatu and follow the road going up towards the southwest. At the village of Lembongan, perched on a hill, take the road going down to the right.

This leads to a delightful little cove of white sand framed by cliffs carved out by erosion. **Mushroom Bay***★★ probably owes its name to the amazing coral formations resembling big mushrooms that emerge here and there. Its turquoise lagoon peopled with myriads of multicoloured fish is just perfect for **exploring the seabed**★★.

Go back up into the centre of Lembongan and take the road on the right leading down to the sea.

Between Nusa Lembongan and its little neighbour, **Nusa Ceningan***, there lies a tiny arm of the sea, a superb checkerboard of turquoise and brown waters on which bobs a flotilla of colourful *jukung (cross the footbridge linking the 2 islands)*. Here, even more than in Lembongan, shouts of "Hello misterrr!" ring out, fingers point at visitors and large smiles light up faces. Sometimes people may stop to ask your name and nationality, or just for the pleasure of chatting; they may even offer to pick a fresh coconut for you to quench your thirst, a kindness that is still disinterested. As the population speaks little English, contact is much easier if you have a few rudiments of *Bahasa Indonesia.*

To return to Jungutbatu, take the surfaced road that goes round the island.

Nusa Penida*
About 20km by 16km – Pop 45 000

Although the biggest of the 3 islands, Nusa Penida has no hotels (with the exception of 2 or 3 basic losmen in Sampalan village). Since regular boat connections with Nusa Lembongan and Bali run only in the mornings, visitors have to charter a boat for the return.

The crossing from Jungutbatu *(about 45min)* takes place at dawn, on board an overcrowded *jukung*. As the frail vessel skirts the Nusa Lembongan mangrove swamps, it is not long before the rising sun starts to light up the coasts of Bali.

All sorts of legends haunt this austere and dreaded island, site of a former penitentiary where the Klungkung kingdom exiled its prisoners, and the refuge of a terrible demon supposed to be at the root of all Bali's ills.

Being difficult to reach, it will enchant all those who like to get off the beaten track. The inhabitants of Nusa Penida do indeed see very few tourists and their attitude – half curious, half shy or even a little frightened – can initially make visitors ill at ease. It is a good idea to ask permission before taking anyone's photo.

When the boat arrives at **Toyapakeh** *bemo* are waiting for the passengers, most of whom are going to do their shopping in **Sampalan* market**, the main village on the island *(in the east)*.

From one coast to the other
The bemo services are very irregular and do not serve the whole island. It is better to hire a motorbike or even a four-wheel drive vehicle (the roads are bumpy), the ideal solution being to take a local driver (the often excessive prices should be bargained down severely).
The finest beaches are on the **east coast*** but the seaweed farms carpeting the lagoon often hinder swimming.
On the right just before Karangsari, a fault in the rock provides the entrance to **Karangsari cave** (Goa Karangsari), a tunnel almost 300m long inhabited by bats *(take a torch)*. It gives onto a beautiful, undulating landscape.

Take the stony dirt track (very uneven after Klumpu but passable by motorbike or four-wheel drive vehicle). You will have to finish on foot with a local child as guide.

The wild, grandiose cliffs of the **south coast**** plunge abruptly into the ocean with, hidden at their feet, a few pretty little **creeks** that are mostly inaccessible. The only way down is by vertiginous wood and bamboo ladders, which, until quite recently, the inhabitants used every day in order to fetch fresh water from the underground springs that gush out of the ground just above sea level. Tanks fed by rainwater have now put an end to those perilous journeys. The most spectacular ladder, a veritable airborne scaffold leaning against the trees growing on the cliff face, is to be found near the village of **Sebuluh**.

Nusa Lembongan

Making the most of Nusa Lembongan

COMING AND GOING

From Sanur – A **public boat service** (jetty near the Grand Bali Beach Hotel) leaves every morning at about 7am for Nusa Lembongan. Passengers and goods are piled in all together and it is not always easy to find a seat. You are guaranteed an exciting atmosphere, particularly as the boat crosses the coral reef! A **Perama** boat also does a round trip every day leaving at about 8am. It is more expensive (although still reasonable) but less heavily laden and has seats, a few life-jackets and tarpaulins to cover luggage. Allow 60-90min for the crossing.

From Padangbai and Kusamba – **Public boat services** leave early in the morning for Nusa Lembongan or Nusa Penida. About 1hr crossing. It is also possible to charter a private boat. In all cases the crossing may be cancelled if the sea is too rough.

For Nusa Penida – A boat leaves from Jungutbatu on Nusa Lembongan about 6am and returns from Toyapakeh about 8am. Allow 45min. It is possible to charter a private boat quite cheaply.

Cruises – Several companies run day cruises on luxury catamarans with various activities and buffet. Prices are high. Most leave from Benoa harbour. **Bali Hai**, ☎ (0361) 72 03 31; **Waka Louka**, ☎ (0361) 26 11 29; **Island Explorer**, ☎ (0361) 28 98 56; **Nusa Lembongan Express**, ☎ (0361) 72 45 45.

ADDRESS BOOK

There is no post office, telephone or bank on the island, so money has to be changed at the **Perama** offices (on Jungutbatu beach), but the rate is very poor.

WHERE TO STAY, EATING OUT

Except for the luxurious Waka Nusa Resort (see below), the only accommodation on the island is in modest bungalows with a somewhat basic level of comfort. Almost all of them serve meals. Electricity comes from a generator between about 5pm and 7am only.

● **Jungutbatu**

Modest

Tarci Bungalo, 4rm. ⌐ 🗙 ✗ ⌂ Two lovely 2-storey bungalows that each sleep up to 4 people. Simple but very pleasant, with verandahs facing the sea. The rooms at the back, which have shared bathroom facilities (not always very clean), are more Spartan.

Bungalo Nusa Lembongan, 8rm. ⌐ 🗙 ✗ ⌂ Lovely 2-storey bungalows for 3 or 4 people with open-air bathrooms. Relatively well spaced out. Those at the front have a view of the sea. Unfortunately the restaurant, which is inside, does not give onto the beach.

Pondok Baruna, 7rm. ⌐ 🗙 ✗ ⌂ This modern building, which lacks charm but is beautifully clean, provides *losmen*-style rooms, all lined up facing the sea.

Ketut's Losmen, 6rm. ⌐ 🗙 ⌂ The bungalows are designed so that everyone can enjoy the sea view; each has 2 bedrooms, 1 on the ground floor and 1 upstairs, plus an open bathroom. The place stands in an attractive little garden and is remarkably well maintained. A charming welcome. The restaurant should be open by the time this guide comes out.

● **Mushroom Beach**

Modest to average

Mushroom Beach Bungalows, ☎ (0812) 390 70 63 – 10rm. ⌐ 🗙 ✗ ⌂ A place that owes its attraction more to its exceptional location than its rooms, which are a bit dilapidated in some cases and tiny in others, although acceptable as far as the most expensive go (with a view of the bay). A pleasant little restaurant looking out over the beach.

Super deluxe

Waka Nusa Resort, ☎ (0361) 72 36 29/72 36 59/72 35 77, Fax (0361) 72 20 77 – 10rm. ⌐ 🗙 ✗ ⌕ ⌂ CC Sober, elegant bungalows (little circular huts with conical thatched roofs and decorated with old photos) scattered over the white sand in the shade of coconut palms. The restaurant and swimming pool take pride of place, the rooms do not give straight onto the beach. Diving club next door.

OTHER THINGS TO DO

Bicycle trips – Bicycles and motorbikes can be hired from some of the *losmen* in Jungutbatu.

Water sports – There is a vast selection: excursions in glass-bottomed boats, fishing trips out to sea, exploring the seabed with mask and snorkel, and surfing (equipment for hire on the spot). Details available at the **Perama** boat jetty or ask in the *losmen*.

Making the most of Nusa Lembongan

UBUD★★
THE CENTRE OF BALI
Gianyar district
25km north of Denpasar – Map p 350-351 and Plan p 400
Pop 8 000 – Pleasant climate, quite cool and rainy

Not to be missed
Watching a dance performance.
Tasting Balinese smoked duck ("bebek betutu").
Wandering in the rice fields around Ubud.
Having a drink in one of the hotels overlooking the Ayung river.

And remember...
Spend several days in the Ubud region so as to discover all its facets.
Shop in the small villages round about rather than in Ubud itself.

Ubud nestles in the heart of the island, spread over gently sloping hills in a green setting that offers a wealth of variety: a harmonious countryside carved out by valleys, gorges and terraced rice fields inhabited by croaking frogs. The town is particularly pleasant because of its mild climate, peaceful atmosphere, sophisticated hotel accommodation and gourmet restaurants, thus making it an ideal place to stay and discover all the richness and complexity of the Balinese culture. It is also the best base camp for exploring the surrounding area, which is packed with temples, ancient remains and arts and crafts centres.

The "real Bali"
Seeing Ubud for the first time – and to a much lesser extent the neighbouring villages it has absorbed in its development – is, however, likely to be disappointing. With its dense traffic, almost uninterrupted rows of shops, travel agencies and art galleries, plus a profusion of hotels and restaurants, the commercial aspect of the tourist boom has not spared Ubud.

But this should not put visitors off! Behind this commercial front there is another, totally different side of Bali to be discovered: men and women for whom life continues in total serenity to the rhythm of ancestral traditions and beliefs. A subtle melody from a gamelan drifting out of a courtyard? With a bit of luck a discreet glance will show you a *legong* rehearsal. A surprising crowd of motorbikes in a small alleyway? The enthusiastic cries going up almost certainly betray a lively cockfight. The insistent beating of gongs and cymbals resonating in the distance is doubtless guiding the steps of some fascinating procession. If dressed in ceremonial outfits, visitors can accompany the Balinese to their temple to watch them worship and make their delicate offerings. A few rudiments of *Bahasa Indonesia* will open the doors of many a home, where an enthusiastic and graceful welcome quickly dispels any feelings of indifference. By keeping away from the main thoroughfares, the hunting ground of tourists come to do their shopping in the heart of the so-called "real Bali", visitors can suddenly find themselves in the midst of rice fields, among country folk bustling about, their backs bent in labour.

The cradle of Balinese arts
The history of the little village of Ubud really started at the end of the 19C, when a series of alliances made with neighbouring kingdoms considerably expanded its lands and the power of its ruler, **Cokorda Gede Agung Sukawati**. This great art

lover welcomed artists and encouraged avant-garde creation. The village rapidly acquired a reputation as a great arts centre and from the 1920s and 1930s on it began to attract the first Western artists. Among these was the German painter **Walter Spies**. Falling under the charm of the place, he settled here and was soon joined by numerous followers. This foreign community helped to turn Ubud and its region into the most active centre for the revival of Balinese arts.

Today all the arts are honoured in Ubud. The town is crowded out with painting and sculpture galleries and there are innumerable performances of music and dance. Although put on exclusively for the tourists, these at least have the merit of perpetuating the island's traditional arts and providing the funds necessary for acquiring costumes and instruments. In particular, the outer courtyard of **Puri Saren** (C2), Ubud's palace, regularly lends its sumptuous setting to good quality performances, with the set formed by the elegant *kori agung* (great gateway) decorated by **I Gusti Nyoman Lempad**. Remarkable performances of **legong** and gamelan are also given in the **Peliatan Palace** (C3) *(2km southeast of Ubud)*.

Walks in and around Ubud

Allow 1 (short) day. For walking in and around Ubud,
buy the map entitled "Bali Path Finder", on sale in the town.

Ubud and its neighbouring villages have now merged into one large, spread-out township. The streets lined with hotels, guesthouses and shops are all centred around two major roads, **Jalan Raya Ubud** (Ubud's main street) and Jalan Wanara Wana, commonly referred to by its English name, **Monkey Forest Road**.

The centre of Ubud★

The nerve centre of Ubud is its **market** (Pasar Ubud) (C2) *(tourist market daily 9am-5pm approximately; food market every 3rd day from dawn)* that occupies a vast concrete structure in the heart of the town. With the tourist boom, many market gardeners

Ready for the ceremony! (near Ubud)

M Lemerle

399

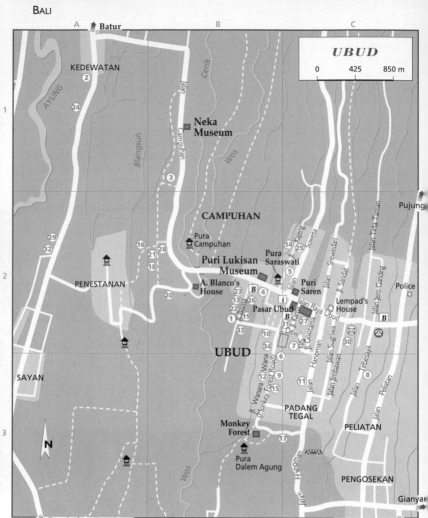

BALI

UBUD

0   425   850 m

HOTELS

Ala's Hibiscus 2 ...... ①	Juwita .... ⑬	🏛 Temple
Amandari .... ②	Kajeng .... ⑭	
Ananda .... ③	Komaneka .... ⑮	Putra Umbara .... ㉔
Anggada .... ④	Kori Agung .... ⑯	Rumah Roda .... ㉕
Arjana .... ⑤	Kubuku .... ⑰	Sama's .... ㉖
Cendana .... ⑥	Londo .... ⑱	Sania's .... ㉗
Dewangga .... ⑦	Nick's .... ⑲	Sari Bamboo .... ㉘
Family .... ⑧	Padma Indah .... ⑳	Sayan Terrace .... ㉙
Gerhana Sari 2 ...... ⑨	Penestanan .... ㉑	Sehati .... ㉚
Indraprastha 2 .... ⑩	Pringga Juwita	Surawan .... ㉛
Jati .... ⑪	Water Garden .... ㉒	Taman Bebek .... ㉜
Jati 3 .... ⑫	Puri Bayu .... ㉓	Villa Cempaka .... ㉝
		Warsi's .... ㉞

have turned their stalls into shops selling clothing, arts and crafts or souvenirs. Nevertheless, at the back of the building the food market continues to be a lively place on every third day, when trucks and *bemo* minibuses pour in from the mountains, overflowing with foodstuffs as colourful as they are appetising. It also houses a few vendors of *sate* and soups, a welcome addition for a quick lunch.

From the crossroads at the corner of the market, take the main street west towards Campuhan.

A large **pool★** covered with lotuses stands in front of the façade of **Pura Saraswati★** (B2), an elegant sanctuary dedicated to the goddess of the arts, learning and wisdom, built in the 1950s under the aegis of Lempad. It provides a most romantic setting for the **Lotus Cafe**, a very pleasant cafe and restaurant opening onto the street (*see page 415, "Eating out"*)

A little further on stands the **Puri Lukisan Museum★** (B2) (*8am-4pm. Fee*). Founded in 1954 on the instigation of the prince Sukawati and the last remaining members of the **Pita Maha** association, this palace (*puri*) of painting (*lukisan*) standing in the middle of a lovely garden holds a miscellaneous collection of works that gives an overview of the major trends in modern Balinese art. It is well worth visiting, even if the exhibition rooms are somewhat old, dismal and badly lit.

Apart from works in the **wayang** style (*see sidebar, p 424*), the main pavilion (*opposite the entrance*) is devoted to the Pita Maha artists. The works on display show a wide overview of the themes and techniques used by the group. Here painting, which was traditionally limited to Hindu mythology and local folklore, has widened its inspiration to secular subjects taken from nature and daily life. The introduction of different bases for the paintings (oil on canvas), as well as new techniques (tempera, ink and watercolour), wide ranges of colours and Western ideas on aesthetics (perspective, chiaroscuro and anatomy) also contributed to the emergence of new trends.

The second building (*to the left of the entrance*) displays the more recent and colourful works by the **Young Artists**, while the room on the right holds temporary exhibitions.

Continue along the main street and cross the suspension bridge over the river Wos.

Campuhan★ (B2)

This hamlet nestling at the confluence of two rivers, in the midst of luxuriant wild vegetation, was from 1930 on a favourite place of residence for numerous foreign artists, among them Bonnet and

A shower of trinkets

P Bénet

Ubud

Pita Maha, the "great vitality"

Under the influence of the European painters who settled in the region of Ubud and Batuan in the 1930s, Balinese painting entered a decisive phase of development. But with the tourist boom and mass demand for cheap works, the artists feared that the commercial element might detract from the quality of their work and corrupt their art. Founded in 1936 around W Spies, R Bonnet, Lempad and Cokorda Sukawati, the Pita Maha association's vocation was to preserve and publicise the work of almost 150 Balinese artists. To do this it organised several exhibitions abroad intended to promote Balinese creation in overseas markets. War and invasion by Japanese troops put an end to the group's activities around 1942.

Spies (his house is now part of the Tjampuhan hotel). In fact some of them still live here today. The public can visit the **house of Antonio Blanco** (B2) *(just on the left after the bridge. 9am-5pm. Fee)*, a Filipino-American painter with a Balinese wife. He exhibits and sells his exuberant works in which women, and in particular his wife, play a major role. The artist sometimes comes to chat with visitors when he feels like it.

Another museum devoted to Balinese pictorial creation is the **Neka Museum** (B1) *(about 1km after the Campuhan bridge. 9am-5pm. Fee)* founded in 1976 by the art collector and dealer, Suteja Neka. It is spacious and well laid-out and has the added advantage of a very lovely setting overlooking a magnificent gorge clad in rice fields. The first building houses classical **wayang** painting followed by works in the **Ubud and Batuan styles**. The second pavilion is devoted to **Arie Smit** and displays canvases by the Dutch painter and by the **Young Artists** *(see p 401)*. A third room holds some beautiful black and white **photographs** by the American Robert Koke, who between 1936 and 1939 immortalised dance scenes and religious ceremonies. There is also a small room devoted to drawings by

Impressionist Bali: a procession through the countryside

M Lemerle

Bali

Lempad, who shows great originality in his treatment of popular Balinese legends and the great Hindu epics. Apart from temporary exhibitions, the last two pavilions present all sorts of contemporary artists, both Indonesian and foreign, whose creations have been inspired by Bali.

Continue west to the T-junction.

The Ayung Gorge**

In the vicinity of **Kedewatan** (A1) and **Sayan** (A2-A3) the scenery becomes superb, with tender green rice fields glinting in the sun, plunging in terraces right down to the winding banks of the **Ayung** *(its tumultuous waters are just perfect for white water rafting)*. To admire this sumptuous **panorama***, of which there is not a hint from the road, visitors should stop for a drink in one of the luxury hotels in the area, such as the Kupu Kupu Barong *(to the north)*, or the Amandari, the Sayan Terrace or the Taman Bebek Villas *(to the south)*.

Monkey Forest (B3)

At Padangtegal, at the southern end of Monkey Forest Road 8am-6pm. Fee. Going south, the main road through the centre of Ubud leads into the heart of a forest peopled with **macaques**. Although it is forbidden to feed these boisterous primates, there is no lack of banana and peanut vendors. However, the monkeys also throw themselves shamelessly on visitors' provisions, so it is essential to keep an eye open. This is also true as far as hats, glasses and cameras go. The monkeys can be so aggressive that the attendants there to ensure visitors' safety are constantly obliged to intervene. A maze of little paths and stairways leads through the forest to **Pura Dalem Agung**, the temple of the dead belonging to the village of **Padangtegal**.

From here, go to Jl Hanoman, turn right and go south for about 1km.

Ubud

Pengosekan (C3)

The artists' community in this village now bears little resemblance to the **co-operative** created in 1969 that helped to build the reputation of its members as painters. Founded on the precept of collective work, the co-operative pooled not only techniques and materials, but also income. Now orientated more towards mass production for export (in particular that of **painted wooden frames**), the group has more or less broken up. To track down fine paintings that are representative of its members' creativity, it is therefore more productive to visit the artists themselves rather than the shops.

The road to Tampaksiring★★

An excursion that can be combined with others around Ubud or continued on to Mount Batur (see p 434).

Take the east road out of Ubud and turn left at the T-junction, where the main street meets the main Denpasar road. By bemo, get off at Tampaksiring, from where it is about a 2km walk, or you can wait for another bemo.

The road *(quite busy)* that climbs up to Mount Batur, to the northeast of Ubud, goes through a delightful scenery of rice fields. There are craftsmen's workshops and tourist shops along it and it also goes through a few major **wood carving** centres such as **Tegallalang** and **Pujung**, where brightly coloured flowers and fruit carved from the especially soft wood of the banana tree cover all the shop frontages.

It is well worth stopping off at **Ceking** *(Kampung Cafe)*, which is halfway between these two villages and filled with carved *garuda* and other exuberant sculptures, to admire the magnificent **panorama★★★** over the terraced rice fields of the **Petanu valley**.

The elixir of immortality?

A popular legend places the origins of Tirta Empul way back during the great battle fought between Indra's divine troops and the demon king Maya Danawa. After declaring war on the gods, the latter succeeded in pushing his adversaries back to a poisoned water source that he had created. Thirsty from the interminable fighting, the divinities drank there and died. Only Indra avoided the trap and, striking the ground violently, he brought forth a spring of "amerta", the elixir of immortality, with which he was able to bring his companions back to life. Thus restored, the celestial army launched an offensive during which Maya Danawa was mortally wounded. The impure blood that flowed from his body as he lay dying became the Petanu river that flows near the temple.

In the centre of Pujung, turn right towards Tampaksiring and then, less than 1km further on, take the road left down to Sebatu.

■ Pura Gunung Kawi★ –

(Not to be confused with the Gunung Kawi archeological site, next page.) 8am-6pm. Fee. The temple sits in a luxuriant **green setting★★** right down in the bottom of a valley, below the road (from which there is the best view). The place is perfectly charming with its *meru* roofs as backdrop, its little pavilions and its altars heaped with offerings. A sacred spring feeds the **baths** where the inhabitants of Sebatu come to purify themselves *(bathers should not be filmed or photographed).*

Continue along the road (to the left on leaving the temple) then follow the signs.

■ Tirta Empul★ – 8am-6pm. Fee. Sarong and sash compulsory *(they can be hired on the spot).* Much frequented by the Balinese, this sanctuary is laid out in three successive courtyards leading to elegant **altars** of carved wood painted in bright colours.

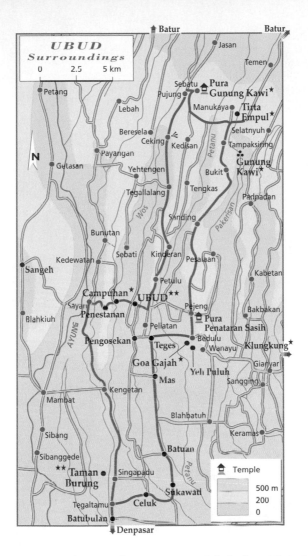

UBUD
Surroundings

0   2.5   5 km

N

Temple

500 m
200
0

Ubud

As in the previous temple, a sacred spring *(tirta empul)* feeds the **public baths**. As it is known for its magical properties, it attracts the population of the whole district. After presenting their offerings to the divinity of the spring, men and women bathe separately in the clear waters of the pools *(photos and filming forbidden)*.

Every year at the full moon in the fourth month of the year, the inhabitants of the neighbouring village of Manukaya also come here to purify a **holy stone**. The inscription on it, which has only recently been deciphered, gives the date of the temple's founding (962 AD) and describes the ritual perpetuated for over 1 000 years. On this occasion the region's villagers form processions around their *barong*, which they symbolically bathe in Indra's holy waters.

Go back up to the crossroads and turn left in the direction of Gianyar-Denpasar for a few hundred metres. A sign on the left indicates the site (car park just after, on the left).

■ **Gunung Kawi**★ – *8am-6pm. Fee. Sarong and sash compulsory. Avoid the hottest part of the day.* A long stairway lined with tourist stalls leads down to the bottom of an enclosed valley and provides a superb **viewpoint**★★ over the rice fields stippled with coconut palms. On the left at the bottom of the steps appear four astounding façades of **funerary temples**★ *(candi)*, carved into the rock-face of a cliff and set in niches almost 7m high. Five other similar structures face them from the other side of the Pakerisan river and a tenth *(more difficult to reach)* is hidden a little further to the south. The inscriptions discovered and deciphered by archeologists have shown them to be royal tombs dating from the 11C. The group of five *candi* is thought to glorify the family of the sovereign **Udayana**, who ruled Bali and East Java at that time. The four others are believed to be dedicated to the chief concubines of Prince **Anak Wungsu**, son of the ruler of Bali.

A little further on to the right, there is also a curious **hermitage** composed of small caves carved out of the rock, probably the remains of cells where the monks retired to meditate *(shoes should be taken off before entering).*

Return to the Tampaksiring road and turn left.

East of Ubud: mysterious remains★
See the map of the region, above.

The region has been inhabited since the Bronze Age (5000-1200 BC) and has an abundance of archeological and historical sites bearing witness to pre-Hinduist, Buddhist and Sivaite civilisations.

■ **Pejeng** – On the left side of the road stands **Pura Penataran Sasih** *(Donation requested. Wear a sarong)*, state temple of the ancient dynasty of Pejeng and famous for its bronze gong, named the **Moon of Pejeng**, hanging high up in a pavilion in the second courtyard. Although visitors cannot get close up, it is still possible to make out its hourglass shape as well as some of the motifs decorating it – geometrical figures and stylised faces

The moon fallen from the heavens
A Balinese legend recounts that the Moon fell from the sky and landed in a tree in Pejeng. It shone so brightly that it impeded the work of a band of thieves who were just about to go into action. As one of them was doing all he could to extinguish it, the Moon fell from the tree and turned into a gong, cracking at its base in the fall. The imprudent thief dropped dead on the spot. Another version recounts that the object was a wheel from the chariot of the goddess of the Moon, or one of her earrings, which fell to earth one night and landed in a tree in Pejeng.

delicately engraved in the metal. At almost 2m high, it is most probably the largest gong in the world cast in a single piece. Its origins, which are thought to go back a millennium, remain uncertain.

Continue along this road to Bedulu, turn right at the crossroads there and follow the signs on the left.

■ **Yeh Puluh** – *8am-6pm approximately. Fee.* Whether coming from the village of Bedulu or via the rice fields *(from Goa Gajah, see below)*, visitors never arrive alone as the local children rush to offer their services as guides in the hope of earning a few

Pura Gunung Kawi, a stone gem set in the greenery

rupiah. They give you a commentary of the remains – an astonishing **frieze*** almost 25m long by 2m high carved out of a section of cliff face – with varying enthusiasm and imagination! In fact the exact meaning of the scenes carved in the rock facing the rice fields, in the middle of nowhere, remains unknown. They were discovered in 1925 and we know only that they are thought to date back to the 14C. **Ganesh** with his elephant's head is easily identifiable but the other figures seem to illustrate scenes from everyday life, particularly hunting, rather than religious subjects, unless they depict episodes from the life of **Krishna**, a reincarnation of Vishnu.

The place also offers a good pretext for a delightful **walk through the rice fields*** to Goa Gajah, still with the local children as guides *(about 30min)*.

Return to the main road and go left.

■ **The Elephant Cave*** (Goa Gajah) – *Approximately 8am-6pm. Fee. Wear a sarong and sash.* The cave discovered in 1923 undoubtedly owes its name to the gaping jaws of the demon standing guard at the entrance, a broad bas-relief which archeologists took for an elephant, its ears merging into a profusion of carved motifs. A simpler explanation is that the place takes its name from the Petanu river flowing nearby, in former times called the Elephant River. The theories are many and varied.

Whatever the explanation, the T-shaped interior does indeed house a **Ganesh**, the Hindu god with an elephant's head, as well as several **linga**, phallic symbols of the god **Siva**. It is thought that the cave was a Buddhist hermitage dating back to the late 11C since the little niches it contains are reminiscent of monks' cells. To the right as you leave you will see a small pavilion holding an old **statue of Hariti**, the Buddhist fertility goddess and protectress of children. The two big **pools** dug in front and fed by **nymphs** bearing waterspouts were excavated in 1954.

The ancient fragments of **carved reliefs** (representing a Buddhist stupa) and the little **cave with a Buddha** (headless!) that locals offer to take visitors to see about fifty metres away through the rice fields, are not really worth the detour. On the other hand, the walk through the rice fields to **Yeh Puluh** *(see above)* is a very pleasant one.

The gods stand guard at crossroads

R Marca

Bali

To the south: the craft villages

*See map p 405. Visitors accompanied by a guide or driver
should be aware that he will receive substantial commission on their purchases.*

The main road running between Ubud and Denpasar goes through a succession of craft villages traditionally specialising in the various crafts of woodworking, stoneworking, silversmithing or goldsmithing, although the divisions between the various types of activities have now become very blurred. Art or business? Balinese craftsmen, long reputed for the quality of their work, have gradually been turning towards mass production to fulfil the growing demands of tourists, even to the extent of exporting all over the world. These two factors are unfortunately tending to make their creations less interesting. Visitors should therefore not be content to just walk along the road with its countless shops that give an impression of vulgar commercialism. It is much more rewarding to explore the adjacent and more peaceful alleyways and to discover, on a doorstep or in some workshop, the dexterity of these craftsmen – sometimes very young children – busy sculpting, carving, polishing and painting, using techniques handed down from father to son.

From Ubud, take the main road to Denpasar. From Goa Gajah, turn left on leaving the car park.

The first village you reach is **Teges**, with its row of picture galleries and some shops selling wood and stone **carvings**. *Turn left towards Denpasar.*

The village of **Mas**, stretching out on either side of the road, is the best-known centre for **woodworking**, with statuettes made of ebony or sweet-smelling sandalwood as well as masks and furniture crammed along the roadside.

Batuan, an artists' village since way back, was in the 1930s the cradle of a new **pictorial style**, characterised more than anything else by an incredible density of highly-detailed motifs in Indian ink which literally "blacken" the canvas. You will also see furniture and amusing objects made of bamboo as well as carved wooden panels.

Not as expensive as Ubud market (provided some hard bargaining is done, all the same!) and much more pleasant, the **market** in **Sukawati** overflows with fabrics, batiks, clothing and diverse craft items. Leather puppets can also be found here since the village is a major island centre for **wayang kulit manufacture**.

The **smiths** in **Celuk** have been devoting themselves to working gold and silver for generations and the jewellery they produce is recognisable by the delicate filigree designs created by using fine metal points.

Just before Denpasar a crowd of stone divinities and demons welcomes visitors to **Batubulan** (literally "moon stone"). Carved out of *paras*, a very soft volcanic tuff, these statues are used to adorn village temples or hotel gardens. The place is also well known for its **barong** dance companies.

To return to Ubud by another route, take the small road that goes off at the Tegaltamu crossroads north of Batubulan.

This road through lovely rice fields and peaceful villages is by no means as busy. Soon there is a sign on the left for **Taman Burung**** (*Singapadu. 9am-6pm. Fee, expensive*), a magnificent **ornithological park** with waterfalls, lotus ponds and tropical trees and flowers. Here visitors can admire innumerable species of birds from all over the world, including multicoloured parrots, elegant birds of paradise, flamingos and pelicans. Just opposite is a **reptile park*** (Rimba Reptil) with incredible specimens of snakes, **tortoises**, lizards, chameleons and **monitor lizards** in an attractive environment that recreates their original habitats of desert, savannah, rain forest, etc.

Ubud

At Sayan, turn right and go through the village of **Penestanan**, crowded with picture galleries. It is here that the **Young Artists** school was born in the 1960s under the leadership of the Dutch painter **Arie Smit**. Armed with canvases and tubes of paint, the village youngsters let their imaginations run riot producing naive, brightly coloured images of their island and everyday life that offered a radical contrast to the more rigid, regulated compositions of traditional painting.

The road then dips into an extremely beautiful **gorge**** overgrown with thick vegetation, before climbing back up to Campuhan (*see above*), where it finally leads into the main street of Ubud at Antonio Blanco's house.

Making the most of Ubud

COMING AND GOING

By shuttle bus – Several daily services between Ubud and the main tourist sites on the island (Kuta, Sanur, Lovina, Candidasa, Padangbai, Kintamani, etc). The *Perama* offices (C3) are in Padang Tegal but all the tourist agencies sell tickets.

By bemo – These minibuses wait in front of Ubud market. To go to the south or west of Bali you have to change at Batubulan; to go east, change at Gianyar.

By taxi – Official taxis, which wait in front of the market, are few and far between, but car drivers are forever offering their services, so it is up to you to negotiate!

GETTING AROUND

On foot – Ideal in the centre of Ubud, where the traffic is sometimes quite heavy, and for window-shopping. Be careful of distances, as the town is more spread out than it seems.

By bicycle – Be aware that the terrain becomes very hilly once you leave the centre of Ubud! Bicycling is nevertheless very pleasant and ideal for medium distances.

By motorbike – A good means of transport if you are used to riding one. Many Balinese offer their services as motorbike taxis – at your own risk!

By car – There are many agencies hiring cars with or without drivers.

By bemo – These mainly run along Jl Raya Ubud and around the market before leaving the town.

ADDRESS BOOK

Tourist information – *Ubud Tourist Information* (B2-C2), Jl Raya Ubud, ☎ (0361) 962 85. Daily 8am-8pm in theory (in practice the opening hours vary). Provides the programme of performances and ceremonies taking place in the area, as well as of organised excursions out of Ubud.

Tourist agencies – There are plenty, especially in Jl Raya and Monkey Forest Road. They provide every kind of tourist service – foreign exchange, organised excursions, shuttle buses, vehicle rental, purchase or confirmation of air tickets, etc – at similar prices.

Bank/Currency exchange – Exchange offices are numerous in Jl Raya and Monkey Forest Road. To withdraw cash with a Visa or MasterCard: *Bank Bali* (B2), Jl Raya Ubud; *Bank Lippo* (C2), Jl Raya Ubud (in the car park beside the market); *BII* (C2), Jl Raya Ubud; *Bank Duta* (C2), Jl Raya Ubud.

Post office – *Main post office* (C2), Jl Jimbawan, Padang Tegal. 8am-2pm; Friday 8am-11am; Saturday 8am-12.30pm; closed Sunday. Poste restante. Internet. Stamps can also be bought and mail posted in the small post offices.

Mailing parcels – Many freight forwarding companies operate out of Ubud. *Nominasi Cargo* (B2-C2), Monkey Forest Road 71, ☎ (0361) 97 50 67. Also provides Wartel and Internet services. *Pandawa Sari Sejati Cargo* (B2-C2), Monkey Forest Road 65, ☎/Fax (0361) 97 56 98.

Telephone – Several **Wartel** telephone offices, especially in Jl Raya and Monkey Forest Road. **Telkom** (C2), Jl Raya (just before the T-junction). Open 24hr a day.

Internet – Ubud is where you will find the most Internet services. You can generally receive e-mail at these addresses as well as faxes.

B@li 3000 (C2), Jl Raya Ubud (a cybercafe serving drinks and cakes); **Trio Business Center** (C2), Jl Raya Ubud; **Balinet** (B3) (open evenings), Monkey Forest Road; **Wartel** (B2-C2), Monkey Forest Road; **Pondok Perak** (C2), alongside the football pitch (it is also a library and restaurant and runs classes in batik and Bahasa Indonesia); **Roda Tourist Service** (B2), Jl Bisma 3; **Prada** (B2), Jl Kajeng 1; **Main post office** (see above).

Car rental – Many local agencies rent cars, with or without drivers, motorbikes and bicycles. Compare prices, insurance contracts and the condition of the vehicles.

Medical services – **Chemist** (Apotek), Monkey Forest Road (opposite Wartel/ Nominasi Cargo) (B2-C2); Jl Raya, just before Ganesha Bookshop (C2)
Ubud Clinic, Jl Raya Ubud, Campuhan, ☎ (0361) 97 49 11.

WHERE TO STAY

● **Ubud centre**

Modest
Arjana, Jl Kajeng 6, ☎ (0361) 97 55 83 – 8rm. ⌗ 🛆 A small family guesthouse set around the family temple. Pretty woven bamboo rooms with open-air bathroom. Simple and clean. Charming welcome.

🐾**Gerhana Sari 2**, Monkey Forest Road, ☎ (0361) 97 53 92 – 2rm. ⌗ 🛆 A small place, simple and charming. Rooms all made of woven bamboo with ikat curtains. Pleasant open-air bathrooms decorated with plants and goldfish. Private terraces looking onto lotuses and rice fields.
Rumah Roda, Jl Kajeng 24, ☎ (0361) 97 54 87 – 5rm. ⌗ 🛆 Pleasant, impeccably clean rooms grouped around the family home. The most recent have an open bathroom. Comfortable bamboo sofas on the terraces.

Kajeng Homestay, Jl Kajeng 29, ☎ (0361) 97 50 18 – 12rm. ⌗ 🛆 Hot water in some rooms. The rooms are on a slope above a river in a natural setting. Room 5 is particularly well located. The older ones could do with a coat of paint.
Surawan House, Jl Karna 89, ☎ (0361) 97 53 07 – 11rm. ⌗ 🛆 ✗ Hot water in the most expensive rooms. The small rooms are simple and clean, set in a garden around the family pavilion. Central and quiet.

Modest to average
Anggada House, Jl Anggada, ☎ (0361) 97 55 52 – 4rm. ⌗ 🛆 Hot water in some rooms. A family guesthouse right in the centre of Ubud but quiet. The terraces of rooms 1 and 4 look out over a river and have a superb view of a gorge. The others are simpler but still clean. Charming welcome.
Jati 3 Bungalows, Jl Monkey Forest (at the end of a little alley, 75m from the street), ☎ (0361) 962 49 – 1rm. ⌗ 🛆 Hot water. Pavilions with 2 little bedrooms set in a pretty garden. A mynah bird welcomes visitors with a "hello" and amuses itself repeating everything that is said! A place that is nevertheless appreciable for its peace and quiet!
Warsi's House, Monkey Forest Road (opposite the football pitch), ☎/Fax (0361) 97 53 11 – 6rm. ⌗ 🛆 Hot water. Quite spacious rooms, prettily decorated, set in a row in front of a little lotus pond. Big terraces. The rooms upstairs have a view of the rice fields.
Sama's Cottages, Jl Bisma, ☎ (0361) 964 81 – 10rm. ⌗ 🛆 Hot water. Pleasant private brick bungalows with thatched roofs, sitting in tiers in a long garden. Most of the terraces look onto each other and so lack privacy. Relaxed atmosphere.
Sania's House, Jl Karna 7, ☎ (0361) 97 55 35 – 15rm. ⌗ 🛆 ⚊ Hot water in some rooms. Private bungalows set in the garden of the family home, around a well appreciated little swimming pool. The number of rooms is constantly being increased and some are a bit close to each other, so you have to choose well!

Average
Ala's Hibiscus 2 Guest House, Jl Bisma (follow the signs through the rice fields; access on foot or by motorbike only),

☎ (0361) 97 65 30 – 5rm. ⚓ 🚫 Hot water. A peaceful place lost in the middle of the rice fields but nevertheless close to the centre. You will hear frogs croaking, and will be looked after by the amiable owner who is gentle, attentive, discreet and efficient. Quite big rooms, on 2 floors, but unfortunately badly soundproofed. Sumptuous breakfasts.

☺**Juwita Inn**, Jl Bisma, ☎ (0361) 97 60 56, Fax (0361) 97 51 62 – 8rm. ⚓ 🚫 Hot water. After an uninspiring car park, Balinese parasols mark the entrance to a magnificent flower-filled garden that is very quiet. Charming private bungalows in white brick with thatched roofs. Although they are a bit close together, each terrace is lent privacy by plants. Bamboo furniture and beautiful Balinese fabrics for curtains and bed covers. Impeccably clean with attentive service.

☺**Kubuku**, Monkey Forest Road (in the south near the junction with Jl Hanoman), ☎ (0361) 97 47 42, Fax (0361) 97 51 20 – 7rm. ⚓ 🚫 ✗ Hot water. Little rooms full of charm in a variety of styles and spread about a lovely flower-filled garden facing rice fields. Those upstairs are more expensive (for the view!). There is also a 2-bedroom house for rent, in its own garden with a carved wooden 4-poster bed for siestas and a Balinese pavilion to use as a living room or for breakfast.

Average to high end

☺**Puri Bayu Guest House**, Jl Bisma, ☎ (0361) 97 47 57, Fax (0361) 97 57 34 – 3rm. ⚓ 🚫 Hot water. A minuscule, good quality family guesthouse that will charm all those wishing to stay with local people but who still enjoy a certain level of comfort. The 2 upstairs rooms look out over the rice fields and provide magnificent views of the sunset. The one downstairs, which has no view, is cheaper. The owner, an art lover, changes the pictures decorating her house as her mood or her guests' tastes dictate. Attentive reception. Perfectly clean and quiet. You are strongly advised to book.

Indraprastha 2 Bungalows, Monkey Forest Road (Gang Beji Jungutan), no telephone yet – 4rm. ⚓ 🚫 Hot water. A recently built house offering irreproachably clean modern rooms furnished with

bamboo and decorated with paintings. The big private terraces look onto a lotus pond and rice fields and provide splendid views of sunset. Excellent value for money.

Dewangga Bungalows, Jl Dewi Sita, ☎ (0361) 963 02 – 9rm. ⚓ 🚫 ✗ cc The least expensive rooms are a bit run-down and close to the street. The bungalows have better soundproofing and amenities plus a pleasant open-air bathroom. Much more expensive are the two 2-storey villas nestling deep in the garden, with a living room and open-air bathtub with hot water. Balinese furniture made of coloured wood. The place is peaceful, surrounded by a spacious garden and small lotus ponds.

Nick's Pension, Monkey Forest Road (Gang Beji Jungutan)/Jl Bisma, ☎/Fax (0361) 97 56 36, ☎ (0361) 962 90 – 22rm. ⚓ 🚫 ✗ 🏊 cc Access from Monkey Forest Road via an alleyway at right angles to the street that goes down towards the river. From Jl Bisma entry is from the restaurant and swimming pool side, in the midst of the rice fields. The cheapest rooms look out over a lovely gorge overgrown with greenery. The most comfortable further up the hill have hot water. A quiet and very pleasant place.

Luxury

Cendana Cottages, Monkey Forest Road, ☎/Fax (0361) 97 32 43 – 16rm. ⚓ 📋 🚫 ✗ 🏊 cc 2-storey brick buildings with carved wooden Balinese doors. Rooms faced in bamboo, with space and luxury depending on category. The standard ones give onto a garden and rice fields, the better ones onto the swimming pool. The place is set well back from the street.

Luxury to super deluxe

Villa Cempaka, Jl Bisma, ☎/Fax (0361) 97 33 12 – 10rm. ⚓ 🚫 🏊 cc Hot water. Comfortable rooms with lovely wooden verandahs. They either give onto a charming garden, or rice fields or the (very small) swimming pool. Good service but still a bit expensive for what is provided.

☺**Pringga Juwita Water Garden Cottages**, Jl Bisma, ☎/Fax (0361) 97 57 34 – 25rm. ⚓ 🚫 🏊 cc Hot water. The deluxe rooms are magnificent private

2-storey pavilions. Downstairs there is a covered terrace providing a comfortably furnished living room, and a sumptuous marble bathroom decorated with plants. The standard rooms are simpler, in wood and bamboo with a pretty terrace. Some, such as room 9, have a lovely view. Those on the ground floor have an open-air bathroom. The place is set in a harmonious garden dotted with small ponds and footbridges. Delightful.

Super deluxe
Komaneka Resort, Monkey Forest Road, ☎ (0361) 97 60 90, Fax (0361) 97 71 40 – 17rm. ⌖▤ 𝄢 ✗⌁ cc Hot water. A hotel with refined luxury. Spacious rooms, elegantly sober (although some may find them a little cold), in which the ecru shades of the fabrics blend with the wooden furniture and marble floors. Japanese-style sliding doors. Pretty terraces, most of which open onto rice fields. The villas have a superb view. An optical illusion gives the impression that the swimming pool flows directly into the gorge below!

● **Padang Tegal**
Modest
Jati Home Stay, Jl Hanoman, ☎ (0361) 97 55 50 – 10rm. ⌖ ⌁ Hot water. A family guesthouse in a particularly good position. The all-bamboo rooms are lined up on 2 floors facing a little rice field. A wide view across the surrounding countryside. An excellent place, well ventilated, quiet and well away from the street.

Average to high end
Sehati Cottages, Jl Jembawan 7, ☎ (0361) 97 54 60 – 6rm. ⌖ ⌁ cc Hot water. Rustic looking wooden chalets with thatched roofs in a lovely wild garden that goes down to the bottom of a gorge. Spacious rooms furnished in bamboo and prettily decorated. A pleasant setting and good value for money.

● **Peliatan**
Modest to average
Family Guest House, Banjar Tebesaya 39, ☎ (0361) 97 40 54 – 10rm. ⌖ ⌁ Hot water in the most expensive rooms. A little guesthouse that lives up to its name! The pavilions are spread out around the family temple in a lovely and totally peaceful garden. The rooms with

hot water are preferable, as they are impeccable and come with pleasant terraces. The one on the lower level, looking out onto a gorge at the back, is particularly pleasant. The others are more basic.

● **Penestanan**
Average
Sari Bamboo Bungalows, ☎ (0361) 97 55 47/97 43 61 – 7rm. ⌖ Hot water. The simplest rooms give onto a small fishpond. A bit further on, standing in a little private garden, are some much more pleasant bungalows with 1 or 2 bedrooms, a kitchenette and a verandah from which there is a fine panorama over the rice fields.

High end
Penestanan Bungalows, ☎ (0361) 56 03/04, Fax (0361) 28 83 41 – 12rm. ⌖ ⌿ ✗ ⌁ Hot water. Bamboo and wood architecture. Comfortable rooms with large terraces but a bit expensive. A pleasant little restaurant with a view of the rice fields.

Super deluxe
Pudma Indah Cottages, ☎/Fax (0361) 97 57 19 – 10rm. ⌖ ⌿ 𝄢 ✗ ⌁ cc Hot water. A lovely series of bungalows scattered about a pretty garden, either around the swimming pool or above the rice fields (lovely view). Big 2-storey rooms with a thatched roof.

● **Campuhan**
Average
Londo Bungalows, ☎ (0361) 97 65 48 – 6rm. ⌖ ⌿ Hot water. Big 2-storey bungalows in the midst of rice fields. Superb rooms with verandahs and bamboo roofs. Pleasant private terrace below. The atmosphere is peaceful and the welcome charming. Accessible on foot or by 2-wheel vehicles only.
Kori Agung Bungalows, ☎ (0361) 97 51 66, Fax (0361) 97 52 98 – 7rm. ⌖ ⌿ Hot water. In 3 houses in the middle of the rice fields. The view from the first house is unfortunately spoilt by the surrounding hotels. The 2 other 2-storey houses are preferable; a little more expensive but in the midst of greenery and with rooms that have big private terraces where you can listen to the ducks and frogs in total peace and quiet. All-bamboo rooms with big bay windows the better to appreciate the scenery. Accessible on foot only.

Bali

Luxury

Ananda Cottages, ☎ (0361) 97 53 76, Fax (0361) 97 53 75 – 45rm. 🍴 ⅍ ✍ ✗ cc Hot water. A pleasant series of rooms looking onto a garden or rice fields. The superior category rooms are spacious and prettily decorated. Covered by a big traditional roof of palm leaves and with bamboo blinds, they have delicious natural ventilation. If opting for the standard category you have to choose well, as some are really small and others a bit close to the road. Most of the ground floor rooms have an open-air bathroom; they can, however, be noisy if there is parquet flooring above.

● Sayan

Luxury

Sayan Terrace, ☎ (0361) 97 43 84, Fax (0361) 97 53 84 – 10rm. 🍴 ⅍ ✗ cc Hot water. Thatched bungalows overlooking the Ayung gorge (extraordinary panorama). Rooms 5 and 6 have the best view, unfortunately slightly spoilt by the recently built Four Seasons hotel. Prices a bit steep given the comfort provided.

Luxury to super deluxe

Taman Bebek Villas, ☎ (0361) 97 53 85, Fax (0361) 97 65 32 – 7rm. 🍴 ⅍ ✍ ✗ cc Hot water. An expensive place but original because of its traditional, country style. All the rooms – mostly actual houses – are different. The wood and bamboo architecture with thatched roofs, plus old objects lend the place character and the feeling of being "at home". The superior category rooms and immense villa suites have kitchenettes, open-air bathrooms and lovely roofed terraces furnished as living rooms. The most expensive – big, private, 2-storey pavilions – have a fabulous view. The garden villas, which are smaller, less interesting and with no view, still have a private garden.

● Kedewatan

Modest

Putra Umbara Home Stay, ☎ (0361) 97 43 01 – 4rm. 🍴 ⅍ A little family place that is beautifully quiet, set well back from the road. The approach is not very inviting but the rooms look out at the back onto lovely rice fields, and you can make out the Ayung gorge in the distance. Basic level of comfort.

Super deluxe

Amandari, ☎ (0361) 97 53 33, Fax (0361) 97 53 35 – 29rm. 🍴 📠 ✍ ✗⅂ cc Hot water. Perhaps the loveliest hotel on Bali with its combination of charm, elegance, luxury and discretion. Each pavilion sits in a private garden and some even have their own swimming pool. You never tire of the panorama over the rice fields and the Ayung gorge. The restaurant is sophisticated and the service very personalised, attentive and thoughtful. The staff seem to be used to visits from curious visitors as they will happily indicate the best viewpoint (see p 403, "Sayan").

EATING OUT

Ubud is famous for its gastronomy. Here you will find all sorts of cuisine at all sorts of prices. The local speciality of duck braised in a banana leaf ("bebek betutu"), which has to be ordered the day before, is a real delight!

● Ubud centre

Basic

Ibu Oka, Jl Suweta (opposite the Royal Palace) (C2). Lunchtimes only. Very popular with the Balinese. Visitors eat like them, using the right hand while sitting on the floor under the "bale". Just one dish, a "babi guling" of sucking pig with crisp, glazed skin and melt-in-the-mouth meat accompanied by rice, vegetables and spicy sauce. Do not be surprised if instead of change you are handed some bananas home-smoked in their skins – much better than rupiah! Delicious food and friendly staff.

Arie's Warung, Monkey Forest Road/Jl Dewi Sita (alongside the football pitch) (C2). A charming little family place. Good grilled chicken and excellent bananas with honey and coconut. Also worth tasting is the black rice pudding. The Balinese duck (which must be ordered the day before) is particularly succulent here!

Gusti's cafe, Jl Sriwedari 2 (C2), ☎ (0361) 97 47 34. An unpretentious little family place. 2 terraces upstairs on a quiet street. Good Indonesian dishes and charming welcome.

Oka's Warung, Jl Kajeng 2 (C2). Very unpredictable opening hours. Just 4 tables on a terrace beside a quiet street, where you can enjoy delicious local specialities lovingly prepared and served.

Balina Lagoon, Jl Kajeng 10 (C2). A long, narrow terrace on a peaceful alleyway. Family cuisine, Indonesian or Chinese, that is tasty and nicely served.

Basic to moderate

Bamboo, Jl Dewi Sita (C2), ☎ (0361) 97 53 07. A restaurant that opens onto the street (the terrace upstairs is preferable as it is less noisy). Good Balinese specialities (tuna in particular). The Western cuisine is not quite as successful. There is a relaxed, friendly atmosphere.

Apa Kabar, Jl Dewi Sita (C2), ☎ (0361) 97 71 96. A very simple little terrace on the street. It serves mainly Italian specialities such as delicious grilled aubergine canapés, good pasta and pizzas. (Note that as the oven for the pizzas is not on the spot, there is at least an hour's wait!).

Moderate to more select

🍴**Bumbu**, Jl Suweta 1 (opposite the Royal Palace) (C2), ☎ (0361) 97 42 17. A delicious Indian restaurant which also serves a few Balinese and Thai dishes. Set in greenery, well protected from the street. Try the "thalis", exquisite assortments that enable you to taste several specialities at once (including a highly flavoured dhal that is not to be missed!). Let yourself be tempted by a delicate lassi with cucumber and cumin, which goes wonderfully with this refined cuisine, and finish off with a cardamom ice-cream with rose petals. Your taste buds will never forget it!

🍴**Casa Luna**, Jl Raya (B2), ☎ (0361) 97 74 09. A dining room sheltering under a big palm roof or, on the lower floor, a terrace overlooking a beautiful gorge overgrown with bamboos. An original and varied menu combining local and Western ingredients. A wide choice of salads, bread and home-made cakes and pastries. They even serve good espresso and cappuccino coffee! Indifferent service. Films are shown in the evenings in a separate room.

Miro's, main street/Jl Bisma (B2), ☎ (0361) 963 14 A pretty terrace, either open-air or straw-roofed, buried in a magnificent flower-filled garden. A good choice of sandwiches with different types of bread plus refreshing salads. Also pizzas, Balinese dishes and a variety of teas and coffees.

Cafe Bali, Jl Monkey Forest (B2-C2), ☎ (0361) 97 55 40. A beautiful traditional Balinese house with a double roof opening onto rice fields and away from the street. Quiet and well ventilated. All sorts of dishes. Steak and chicken of all types, fish and seafood, as well as pasta and pizzas, plus all the Chinese and Indonesian classics.

Thai, Jl Monkey Forest (B3), ☎ (0361) 97 74 84. Thai cuisine, as the name suggests! You eat sitting on cushions in little wooden shelters. An intimate and charming setting lit by candles in the evenings.

🍴**Ryoshi**, Jl Raya Ubud (B2), ☎ (0361) 97 63 62. Japanese restaurant. An inside dining room with gentle air conditioning where you eat Japanese-style sitting on cushions on the floor. A few ordinary tables as well. They serve sushi, sashimi, tempura, soba-udon and other delights. The fish is deliciously fresh, tender and tasty. Come early, the place is popular!

More sophisticated

🍴**Cafe Lotus**, Jl Raya (B2), ☎ (0361) 97 56 60. The setting alone makes it worth coming here for a drink: pretty tables around a big lotus pond with Pura Taman Saraswati as a backdrop. A gamelan orchestra generally completes this idyllic picture and in addition the food is rather good.

Kafe Batan Waru, Jl Dewi Sita (C2), ☎ (0361) 97 75 28. Bar and restaurant opening onto the street. Pleasant setting although somewhat noisy. Delicious curries and salads.

Tutmak, Jl Dewi Sita (C2), ☎ (0361) 97 57 54. A terrace on the street or a room set back from it with seating on cushions or at tables, as you prefer. Delicious cappuccino coffee with cinnamon and a large choice of home-baked cakes and pastries. Also good Indonesian and Western dishes. Service is slow and indifferent.

🍴**Cafe Wayan**, Jl Monkey Forest (B3), ☎ (0361) 97 54 47. The low or normal tables are spread out in a beautiful garden away from the street, under big thatched roofs or more intimate little straw ones. Generous servings of nicely prepared Indonesian specialities. Theme menus on certain days and traditional Balinese buffets on Sunday evenings. It is also a cake shop. Attentive service.

Making the most of Ubud

● **Padang Tegal**

Basic

Masakan Padang Simpang Tigo, Monkey Forest Road (near the junction with Jl Hanoman) (C3). An inside dining room with no particular charm but it is here that you can taste the best Padang food (see p 76).

Bali Buddha, Jl Jimbawan (opposite the post office) (C2). A small place with a very relaxed atmosphere where you can enjoy salads, good cakes and pastries and some organic produce accompanied by original fruit juices. Ideal for snacks during the day.

Moderate

Kubuku, Monkey Forest Road (near the junction with Jl Hanoman) (B3-C3), ☎ (0361) 97 47 42. Vegetarian restaurant. Bamboo-roofed pavilions where diners sit on mats and cushions to admire the sunset over the rice fields. A gamelan performs some evenings. On the menu: pea or pumpkin soup, salads, jackfruit curry with coconut milk, plus a few original cakes.

More select

Darimana, Monkey Forest Road (B3-C3), ☎ (0361) 97 57 15. This gives onto rice fields where the Balinese hunt frogs at nightfall. The upstairs dining room is more pleasant but you eat seated on cushions on the floor. Rather French-influenced cuisine cooked to varying degrees of success. The menu offers magret of duck with peaches, gratin Dauphinois, lamb cutlets, steak with pepper or Roquefort sauce, etc. Very expensive French wine or cheaper Californian.

Bebek Bengil (Dirty Duck Diner), Jl Hanoman (C3), ☎ (0361) 97 54 89 [CC] Under a big Balinese straw roof, open to the street on one side and looking onto rice fields and lotuses on the other. A pleasant setting where you can enjoy an original, flavoursome cuisine that draws its inspiration from a variety of sources. Try the house speciality of crunchy duck with Indonesian spices, or Balinese duck smoked and full of flavour. The place has had an excellent reputation for a long time but it unfortunately seems to be resting on its laurels.

HAVING A DRINK

Evenings are quiet in Ubud although most of the restaurants are also bars. Some of them show films in the evenings around 7pm. These are often mediocre, big-success American movies but the programme also has some nice surprises. Some places also put on concerts. Posters in the street advertise what is on.

Cafe Exiles, Pengosekan (opposite the Kokokan Hotel) (C3). The only place in the region where there is dancing to a real group, on Saturday evenings only and until about midnight! Very pleasant setting and good music. The place is mostly frequented by Western expatriates and Indonesians. A warm, friendly atmosphere.

Jazz Cafe, Jl Sukma 2, Padang Tegal (C2), ☎ (0361) 97 65 94. This bar and restaurant regularly hosts music groups, mainly jazz. Look for the posters in the streets in Ubud.

Kupu Kupu Barong (beyond A1). It is worth having a drink on the restaurant terrace to enjoy the panoramic view (see above, "Ayung Gorge"). Expensive!

OTHER THINGS TO DO

Music and dance – Numerous performances of music and dance are given every evening in Ubud or in the surrounding villages. For performances taking place outside of Ubud, transport is generally provided and included in the price of the ticket. The programme is available from the tourist office, which also sells tickets. These can also be bought in the street, at tourist agencies or on the spot at the last minute.

Massage – The following 3 massage parlours (there are others) offer a full range of beauty care and massage. Allow yourself to be tempted by a "mandi susu" (milk bath) or a "mandi lulur" (traditional herbal bath) for guaranteed relaxation and well-being! **Nur Salon** (C3), Jl Hanoman 28, Padang Tegal, ☎ (0361) 97 53 52. **Trinadi Salon** (B2), Jl Bisma 69, ☎ (0361) 97 79 34. 9am-8pm. **Milano Salon** (B2-C2), Monkey Forest Road (just after the football pitch on the south side), ☎ (0361) 964 88.

Raditya (C2-C3), Jl Jimbawan, Padang Tegal. This little place is much more traditional than the ones mentioned above. It proposes real therapeutic massage and, in particular, acupressure and reflexology.

Cultural activities – Ubud and its surrounding area are crammed with places where you can learn Balinese arts. *Pakudui Foundation*, Pakudui Tegallalang, ☎ (0361) 90 12 34/90 10 27, Fax (0361) 90 18 59. Classes in Balinese wood and stone carving, painting and dance. Serious but friendly instruction in a very pleasant setting. *Ganesha Bookshop* (C2), Jl Raya Ubud, ☎ (0361) 963 59: classes in Balinese gamelan. *Banjar Kalah* (C3), Peliatan, ☎ (0361) 963 67: making wayang kulit (shadow theatre puppets). *Pondok Perak*, see "Internet", p 411. Classes in Bahasa Indonesia and batik.

SHOPPING GUIDE

Arts and crafts – Ubud and its region are a treasure trove for arts and crafts lovers. There are so many shops and galleries that it is impossible to single any out. Although most of them sell sarongs, clothing, jewellery and souvenirs, often of a rather mediocre quality (as in the markets), if you hunt around you can also find more original or more finely-worked products.

Bookshops/Newspapers – Several bookshops in Jl Raya stock a good selection of books on and maps of Bali and the other islands in the archipelago. They also sell English-language newspapers, which can be bought from street vendors for a few rupiah more (you have to bargain). *Ary's Book Shop* (B2), Jl Raya Ubud [CC] A good selection of newspapers, magazines and books. *Ganesha Bookshop* (C2), Jl Raya Ubud.

Photography – Film for prints, slides and (sometimes) camcorders is on sale more or less everywhere. There are several laboratories that develop photos in 1hr (prints only); not expensive but not very good quality.

Cassettes and CDs – Many shops, mainly in Monkey Forest Road and Jl Raya, sell cassettes and CDs of local and international music at very good prices. The sound of gamelan or popular music will lead you to them.

Miscellaneous – *Remaja II* (B2), Jl Raya Ubud. A supermarket stocking just about all the everyday articles you may need (toiletries, foodstuffs, etc).

Making the most of Ubud

ON THE SLOPES OF MOUNT AGUNG★★

THE TEMPLE OF BESAKIH
Karangasem district – Map p 350-351 and p 423
Cool, misty climate higher up

Not to be missed
The panoramic view from the top of Besakih.
The small roads round about.

And remember...
Visit Besakih in the morning, before the crowds and mist arrive.
Hire a vehicle, as public transport is very unreliable.

Gunung Agung, the highest peak in Bali at 3 014m (since its last eruption), is the most feared and at the same time the most venerated of the volcanoes, with every island temple possessing a shrine dedicated to its spirit. According to legend it came into being when the mythical **Mount Meru** (Mahameru), the Hindu's original axis

P Bénet

Bali

mundi, was split in two, the other half forming Mount Batur. Created by the gods to serve as their throne, the volcano symbolises the "navel of the world", the centre of the Balinese universe occupying a fundamental place in the island's cosmogony and spiritual life. This means that directions, which are so important on Bali, are often given with reference to Mount Agung *(see sidebar, p 355)* and it is on these scarred slopes furrowed by time and eruptions that the most holy of Balinese temples stands, Pura Besakih.

From the central crossroads in Klungkung take Jl Gajah Mada to Besakih (about 22km; 30min). Bemos run to the temple but they stop early in the afternoon.

On the switchback road up, it is worth stopping at **Bukit Jambul** to admire the superb **panorama**** over rice fields and clove trees. In fine weather the view extends as far as the sea.

Lunch can be eaten here in one of the tourist restaurants mainly frequented by groups. At lunchtime every day they serve copious buffets (in the moderate to more select category). After lunch, continue along the same road then bear right at Menanga, a short distance beyond Rendang.

Ceremony at Besakih

Besakih,
the Mother Temple**
(Pura Besakih)
8am-6pm. Fee. Allow about 45min.
A (hired) sarong is compulsory if you have bare legs.

Spread over the lower slopes of Gunung Agung at an altitude of almost 1 000m, Bali's Mother Temple fully justifies the use of superlatives: it is the largest, the oldest, the holiest and the most venerated of all the

The wrath of the gods
On 8 March 1963, when all the Balinese were preparing to celebrate Eka Dasa Rudra, the island's most important purification ritual, Mount Agung suddenly came to life after slumbering for over six centuries (since 1350). Grumblings had announced its coming wrath a few days previously but were taken as a favourable omen. Alas, the volcano suddenly started spitting out clouds of smoke that were visible as far away as Java, while torrents of lava and molten rock flowed down its slopes burying all the villages round about. The cataclysm claimed almost 2 000 lives. A carpet of opaque ash covered the whole island, and the torrential rains that followed the eruption destroyed all the crops. The only place that was spared was Besakih sanctuary. A sign from the gods? The catastrophe was interpreted as a divine punishment, and the population had to wait until a propitious day in 1979 before the ceremony could be held again, this time without tragedy.

On the slopes of Mount Agung

temples on the island. Its origins are still uncertain but 11C inscriptions indicate that rituals in honour of the volcano's all-powerful god took place here before the Hinduist era. In the 15C Besakih became the official temple of the **Gelgel dynasty**, and it was here that the deified ancestors of the royal family were venerated. The temple was destroyed by an earthquake in 1917 then rebuilt, before being miraculously spared by the terrible eruption of Gunung Agung in 1963.

More than just a temple, Besakih is in fact a huge complex comprising a score of sanctuaries. A long ramp lined with souvenir stalls leads from the car park to the gates of the main temple. As visitors walk up it, they are assailed by hordes of vendors (a chance to taste the region's delicious fruits – and to bargain more than ever!) and real or supposed guides attempt to sell their services. Apart from this rather tiresome harassment, visiting Besakih may be a disappointment as only pilgrims are allowed to enter the enclosures holding the sanctuaries, which in addition have retained few of their original elements.

A sanctuary in constant celebration

The complex is nevertheless extremely impressive. Every day intense activity reigns in the maze of courtyards and altars. The Balinese come to collect holy water for the rituals they perform in their villages, to make offerings to some local divinity or to complete the long series of funerary rites following the cremation of a relation. But a visit to the sanctuary takes on a totally different dimension when one of the 70-odd annual **ceremonies*****, which attract thousands of pilgrims from all over the island, is taking place. Every temple in the complex respects its own calendar, with the **odalan** (anniversary festival) of each one being celebrated every 210 days. Even more grandiose are the **Panca Wali Krama** purifying festivals, which take place about every 10 years. Lastly, at the beginning of each century, the most impressive ceremony of all takes place, **Eka Dasa Rudra**.

R Marca

Going to the temple

The three major temples at Besakih venerate the Hindu trinity, with the largest, **Pura Penataran Agung** *(in the centre)*, dedicated to Siva. From over the wall surrounding it, visitors can contemplate its *meru*, its *bale* and its altars loaded with offerings, as well as the triple **lotus throne** *(padmasana trisakti)* in the second courtyard, for the use of the divine trio. Further over to the left stands **Pura Batu Madeg** (the temple of the standing stone), dedicated to Vishnu, and on the right **Pura Kangin Kreteg** (the temple of the east of the bridge) honours Brahma. Steps lead up alongside the successive courtyards laid out on terraces down Agung's slopes. Only rarely can the volcano's summit, always lost in cloud, be glimpsed, but from a little higher up and slightly to the right, there is the loveliest **panorama**** over the site – an elegant forest of *meru* swathed in the mist – and in the distance the green hills slope down to the dark blue sea.

Climbing Mount Agung★★
(Gunung Agung)

The climb is a very difficult one and is forbidden during certain religious ceremonies. It should be tackled during the dry season, preferably between July and October, in clear weather and if possible on a night with a full moon. A guide is essential (they can be hired at Besakih, Selat or Tirtagangga). Leave very early (3-4am) so as to reach the summit before the clouds. Wear good non-slip walking shoes (it is very rough, slippery walking) and take some kind of protection against cold and rain, a powerful torch, a lot of water and energy-giving foods.

The climb can be made either from **Besakih** or from the village of Selat. Although the route from the temple is tougher (*a 2 200m difference in altitude; allow 6hr going up and 4-5hr to come down*), it goes right up to the top of the crater, to the highest part of its rim. In clear weather climbers' efforts are well rewarded by a grandiose 360° **panorama★★★** going beyond the spectacular volcanic slopes and taking in a large part of the island.

From **Selat** the path is shorter and a little easier (*allow 3-4hr going up and 3hr to come down. Climbers should register with the police in Selat before leaving and on returning*), but it leads up to the lower edge of the crater rim from which the **view★★** is unfortunately obstructed by the higher part. It is nevertheless a magical view that opens out onto the landscapes of southern and eastern Bali that were modelled by the lava flows of 1963.

On returning to Menanga, turn left to Rendang, where you then turn left towards Amlapura.

Outings around Mount Agung

The road to Selat★★
From Rendang to Amlapura a small and little-used road goes around Mount Agung halfway up its slopes and through a succession of villages lost in the countryside, in the midst of rice fields and **plantations of salak** (a fruit with a firm white flesh, distinguishable by its brown "snakeskin"), reputed to be the best in Indonesia. In good weather it affords some sumptuous **viewpoints★★★**.

A short distance beyond Duda take the right-hand fork.

This slight detour leads to the village of **Putung**, an open window onto a delightful **panorama★★** to the south, which stretches as far as the sea and, in clear weather, even allows a glimpse of the coasts of Nusa Penida.

This road then continues east to Amlapura (see p 427). If you prefer to go back down to Klungkung in order to follow the coast (see p 423), turn round and, just after Duda, take the left turn to Sidemen.

The road to Sidemen★★
The little road (*rather poor condition; allow 1hr*) that goes through the village of Sidemen provides another delightful outing. It meanders through undulating countryside interspersed with deep ravines, with magnificent **viewpoints★★★** over the rice fields in the valley, the high point being at **Sidemen** itself. All along the road back to Klungkung carpets of cloves drying in the sun exude their delicate fragrance.

EAST BALI★★
FROM KLUNGKUNG TO TULAMBEN
Klungkung and Karangasem districts
Map p 350-351
Tour of about 90km (allow at least 2 days)

Not to be missed
Swimming at Pantai Kecil, a pretty beach near Padangbai.
The rice fields along the road to Tirtagangga.
Diving down to the wreck of the "Liberty" at Tulamben.

And remember...
Plan to stop the night on the way so as to make the most of the region.

Both reassuring and frightening, **Mount Agung** watches, omnipresent, over the whole of East Bali. The vast mass of its hollowed-out peak rises up 3 014m, completely overwhelming **Mount Seraya** (1 175m), its little brother forming the eastern tip of the island. The entire region seems to be in the power of these mountains of fire. The terrible eruption in 1963 *(see sidebar, p 419)*, when Agung's divine wrath devastated all of East Bali and isolated it from the rest of the island, has left its mark on the landscape forever by shaping the relief into steep crags. It has also provided a most fertile soil, for on these torrents of lava frozen in time, nature has reclaimed its rights, little by little colonising the beds of rivers that in former years rushed down from the heights. As the road continues eastward it hesitates constantly between sea and mountains, past and present. For a time it winds from beach to beach through peaceful seaside resorts, before plunging further on into hillsides sculpted by tiers of rice fields or offering views of forgotten villages and the remains of ancient royal cities lying at the bottom of valleys.

■ **Klungkung★** (Semarapura) — *Klungkung, where this tour starts, was renamed Semarapura in 1992 but the Balinese still prefer to call it by its old name. Allow 1hr.*
When in 1710 the Gelgel dynasty transferred its capital to Klungkung, a true golden age began for the little town. Even though the kingdom itself was already in decline, the court of Klungkung established itself as a worthy heir to the rulers of Gelgel and their commitment to the arts *(see p 352)*.
Of its prestigious cultural aura the town has unfortunately conserved very little, since the Dutch almost totally destroyed it in 1908. A provincial little township with about 16 000 inhabitants, today's Klungkung reveals nothing of that tragic episode. Only a stone monument erected in the centre of the town offers a reminder of the bloody **puputan** to which the raja called his subjects, a collective suicide that marked the end of the very last independent kingdom on Bali.

The Royal Palace★ (Puri Semara Pura)
Entrance opposite the car park, in Jl Puputan, next to the town's big central crossroads. 8am-6pm. Fee. The palace built in 1710, when the Gelgel dynasty settled in Klungkung, was almost entirely destroyed by Dutch troops in 1908. The only surviving original element is the south door, **Pemedal Agung★**, which is magnificently ornamented. But the buildings that have been restored are just as worth looking at. In the middle of a waterlily pond, spanned by a lovely stone footbridge lined with guardian statues, stands the majestic **floating pavilion★★** (Bale Kambang), a place of leisure for members

of the court. The high roof has a superb **painted ceiling**** in the *wayang* style of Kamasan *(see below, sidebar)*. The extremely realistic scenes inspired by everyday Balinese life illustrate legendary stories.

It was in the **law pavilion*** (Bale Kerta Gosa) *(on the corner of the palace)* that the most delicate affairs, presided over by the *pedanda* – high priests of the Brahman caste – were heard, those to which a solution had not been found at village level. By contemplating the **ceiling**** in the courtroom, also adorned with classical Kamasan paintings, the accused could meditate on the clement paradise reserved for the innocent – or the terrible punishments awaiting the guilty. Under the Dutch occupation justice continued to be meted out here.

Despite major restoration work carried out over the last few decades by artists from the neighbouring village of Kamasan *(see below)*, the paintings in the two pavilions are suffering from damp. The rather quaint little palace **museum** is not of any great interest.

A more interesting visit is to the **market**, held every third day in a covered gallery opposite the palace entrance *(behind the car park)*. There are some lovely **fabrics** to be found here.

The "wayang" style of Kamasan

It is the figures' resemblance to the puppets in the Javanese shadow theatre that earned the Kamasan pictorial style its name, although the three-quarters portrayal (of head and body, full-face, with legs in profile), which gives the characters their movement, is in fact considered to be inspired by the Majapahit style. Works are created as a collective, often family, activity with each person taking part at some stage. But a master supervises the creation, to which he puts the first and last touches. On a canvas that has previously been boiled, starched and polished, the artist starts by tracing out a light sketch in Indian ink. Then comes the colouring, in which red, yellow and brown dominate (chemical dyes are now tending to replace natural pigments). Apart from astrological calendars, the classic themes generally involve the Hindu epics of the Ramayana and the Mahabharata.

The paintings in Klungkung law courts

E. Planchard/DIAF

Turn right on leaving the law courts and go down Jl Puputan. Turn left as you leave the town, a few hundred metres further on.

■ **Kamasan** – The inhabitants of this peaceful village, descendants of the Gelgel court painters, perpetuate the style created by their ancestors, so it was naturally they who were called on to restore the damaged ceilings in Klungkung palace. Visitors can observe the painters' painstaking work when wandering through the courtyards and workshops. With the tourist boom this creativity is tending to turn towards mass production of a lower quality, for export or for sale in the region's shops, but a few fine pieces can still be found here and there.

Between the sea and the hills
From Klungkung the road east joins the coast at Kusamba.

■ **Kusamba** – *Go down a little alleyway on the right to reach the beach.* This peaceful fishing village on the edge of a wide swathe of black sand still harvests salt using age-old methods *(see sidebar, p 428)*. Very early some mornings the **fleet of jukung★★**, a superb line-up of prows with their colourful figureheads pointing out to sea, can be seen getting ready to leave from in front of the thatched-roof huts scattered along the beach. They sail slowly away towards the fishing waters, sometimes crossing the rough Badung Strait to supply the inhabitants of Nusa Penida with fish, rice and fruit.

■ **The Bat Cave** (Goa Lawah) – *Shortly beyond Kusamba, on the left of the coast road (signposted). Fee. Hire of sashes compulsory.* As with many temples on Bali, Goa Lawah has its sacred animals, considered its guardians. Here they are bats, thousands of them, hanging upside down from the walls of a natural cavity above little offerings altars. This cave, which symbolises the mountain, takes on considerable importance during the purification rituals that follow cremations, and legend recounts that a long tunnel links it to the Mother Temple of Besakih. But what with harassment from pedlars plus the sickly smell and high-pitched cries of the bats, the place is not really very enticing!

About 5km further on, turn right off the main road onto a smaller one

■ **Padangbai★** – Nestling in the curve of a little bay encircled by hills, this fishing village is also one of the most important ports of transit in Bali, with the ferries for Lombok leaving from here *(see p 430)*. Although tourist structures are now starting to develop, the place has preserved its charm and the people are extremely pleasant. The **beach**, which is crowded with *prahu* and polluted by the harbour, does not really lend itself to swimming but its liveliness makes it pleasant all the same. As dawn breaks and the fishermen return, it is transformed into a real fish auction, a good opportunity to enjoy some grilled octopus or tuna in one of the *warung* round about. It is also very easy to find a boat to go exploring the splendid **sea bed★★** in this area, particularly around **Pura Jepun** and **Blue Lagoon**, or to go to Nusa Lembongan and Nusa Penida *(see p 396)*.

From the ferry jetty take the road going up to the right of the harbour. After 100m a stony track goes off to the left (in front of the Ayodya Bookshop).

Once past the hill *(15min walk)* the track reaches **Pantai Kecil★★** (little beach), a charming creek with white sand and turquoise waters encircled by black rocks *(beware of the currents).*

On returning to the main road, turn right a few kilometres further on at the Bulina Royal Bali sign.

East Bali

■ Balina Beach – Another beach, more sand, but this time grey. Although eaten away by erosion like neighbouring Candidasa *(see below)*, it still provides the village of **Buitan** and its few hotels with a peaceful and pleasant setting.

As you approach Candidasa, take the road going up left after a small bridge.

■ Tenganan – *9am-5pm. Fee.* Behind its stone walls the village of Tenganan is home to a **Bali Aga community** *(see p 354)*, descendants of the island's original population who inhabited it during the pre-Hindu era. This village is the oldest on Bali. The organisation, traditions and rituals of this archaic micro-society are unique and unchanging: the 300-odd inhabitants of Tenganan, all born in the village, must marry among themselves or be banished! Their *adat* (customary law) is said to have been dictated by the god Indra, the legendary founder of the village.

This minority, which remained cut off from the outside world for a long time, is now exploiting the tourist bonanza resulting from its cultural individualism. The **houses** lined up facing each other on either side of the village's main street are all built to the same plan and all house shops. But it is still interesting to enter one of them in order to get an idea of what the inside is like, as well as to admire the patient work of the women, busy weaving the **double ikat** *(kamben geringsing)*, which is only produced here. The Bali Aga attribute protective and healing powers to these admirable fabrics, and indeed for a long time they were used throughout the island during rites of passage (tooth filing, cremation, etc). To make them, each thread in both warp and weft is dyed with meticulous care according to the final motifs desired (floral or geometric) and then skilfully woven so that the colours match up. It is easy to understand that making a simple sarong can take several years and the delicacy of the work is reflected in the price. Visitors should be careful too, as the ikats sold in Tenganan, although very decorative, are not all authentic *geringsing*, far from it. The community also perpetuates various ancestral **ritual festivals**** *(for the dates consult the calendar of Bali events, published by the tourist offices)*. Among the most spectacular is the **Perang Pandan**, a battle that pits men armed with prickly pandanus leaves against each other, egged on by the percussions of the *selunding* gamelan (composed of bronze slats fixed on to strips of leather). These instruments also provide the rhythms for the **rejang**, a delightful and very slow offerings dance in which young girls draped in silk and wearing crowns of gold flowers wave long colourful scarves. During the festival of **Usaba Sambah**, the women are swung through the air, several metres up, while sitting on wooden structures turned by two men. Spectacular!

A providential stench

Legend recounts that the inhabitants of Tenganan acquired their vast territory (14C) through subterfuge. One day the powerful king Dalem Beda Ulu lost his favourite steed. The villagers went out looking for the horse and after a long search at last found it dead. As a reward for their services, the Bali Aga asked the king to give them all the lands over which the smell of the corpse had spread. An envoy from the king went out to determine the area accompanied by the head of the village. Together they covered great distances but, curiously enough, wherever they went the pestilent smell persisted. After several days Beda Ulu's exhausted envoy decided to give the villagers all those stinking lands and the Bali Aga's leader was at last able to extract the piece of unsavoury meat from under his clothes where he had hidden it!

■ Candidasa – Developed during the 1980s in order to take the pressure off South Bali, this seaside resort stretches almost 3km on either side of the main road running alongside the sea. The production of lime for building the hotels has unfortunately led to excessive exploitation of the coral

and signed the beach's death warrant: as the waves are no longer broken by the reef, they have gradually swept the sand away and the concrete dykes built all along the coastline have not succeeded in halting the erosion. So between its very busy road and its almost non-existent beach, Candidasa is notably lacking in charm. Only the part of it further to the east, where a little bit of beach still subsists at low tide, is still pleasant. Boats can be hired to go and explore the **sea-bed**★ around the neighbouring islets (Mimpang, Tepekong and Biaha).

Continue along the main road.

■ **Amlapura** (Karangasem) – It is difficult to imagine that this sleepy little town with its provincial atmosphere was the capital of the most powerful kingdom on Bali. After breaking allegiance with the Gelgel dynasty in the late 17C, Karangasem submitted to the Dutch in 1895 and embarked on its golden age. But Mount Agung scarcely left it time to blossom. After the 1963 eruption the town was renamed Amlapura so as to divert the wrath of the gods, which does not stop the Balinese from continuing to call it by its former name most of the time.

Turn right where the road from Candidasa comes in. After the bridge, follow the signs to "terminal" on the left, then right and right again (the one-way streets make it necessary to make a detour).

Of all the town's palaces – where members of the royal family still live – only **Puri Agung** (or Puri Kanginan) is open to the public (*Jl Teuku Umar/Jl Gajah Mada. 8am-6pm. Fee*). Built in the late 19C, this is an eclectic mixture of architectural and decorative elements. It includes Balinese features (pavilions, carvings and statues), European ones (the **London bale** with a verandah and furniture that bears the crest of the British royal family), and Chinese ones (carved doors and other decorations). The whole place is badly maintained, which gives it an overall feeling of emptiness and abandon.

Continue straight on along this street (the name changes). It soon leaves the town to the south (towards Seraya), through a pretty landscape of rice fields (about 5km).

■ **Ujung** – On the left of the road stand a few ruins looking out over a lake. This is all that is left of the sumptuous **Ujung Water Palace**★ (Puri Taman Ujung), which the last ruler of Karangasem had built in 1921. Unfortunately the complex was seriously damaged by the eruption of Mount Agung in 1963 and then by an earthquake in 1979. The palace, a superb pleasure garden used for receptions and relaxation, comprised several pavilions as well as ponds with fountains.

Bali

Beyond Ujung the road continues along the coast, skirting **Mount Seraya** to Amed, winding along the volcano's slopes. What with the arid hillsides and the wild coast looking out to the open sea, it affords some splendid **panoramas★★** but unfortunately the road is very bad and narrow (*travel by motorbike or four-wheel drive vehicle with good tyres and shock absorbers! 25km; allow 2hr*).

From Ujung it is better to return to Amlapura, a safer road which in addition makes it possible to visit Tirtagangga (go back through Amlapura and turn left at the monument, then take the Singaraja-Denpasar road on the right after the bridge).

■ **Tirtagangga★** – Sitting on a hillside lost in the middle of rice fields, this peaceful village has a pretty **Water Palace★** (Tirta Ayu) built, like the one in Ujung, by the last ruler of Karangasem (*8am-5pm. Fee*). Dating from 1947, it was also considerably damaged by the 1963 eruption but has since benefited from much restoration work. The royal baths, big pools fed with spring water by stone monsters, are laid out in a harmonious setting. Visitors can cool off in them but the moss covering the walls and the shallowness of the water do not make them very attractive for swimming.

Once through the village, the road winds between the hills with the bends here and there opening onto magnificent landscapes of **terraced rice fields★★★** (on the right hand side of the road just beyond Tirtagangga and then a few kilometres further on, near the village of **Abang** in particular), before going back down again towards the sea.

Turn right at Culik (there are signs to the hotels).

■ **Amed★★** – On approaching the village the countryside becomes flatter, although still dominated by the pale green of the rice fields. Beyond Amed the road (*in a bad state*) follows the coast, undulating along the flanks of Mount Seraya and in and out of the indentations in the coastline, where there are a few fishing hamlets: **Jemeluk**, **Bunutan**, **Lipah**, **Selang**, etc. The landscape then becomes more arid and turns to yellow. On the shore, the colourful hulls of colonies of *prahu* stand out against black sand or pebbles, awaiting dusk before sailing out to sea, while laughing children play hide-and-seek behind the **salt marshes**. In the early morning the triangular sails billowing in the wind reappear on the horizon and the women crowd down to the beach to unload the catch.

Sea crystals

During the dry season the villagers devote their time to the salt harvest. Damp sand is taken from the sea and set to drain in conical baskets placed above bamboo tanks. The water thus collected contains a high concentration of salt. It is then poured into hollowed-out palm trunks cut in half lengthways, which are lined up on the beach. After a few days in the sun, the water evaporates leaving a deposit of crystallised salt which is then scraped off and sold in the market.

The easternmost part of the island, still preserved from mass tourism despite hotels going up everywhere, has conserved all its charm along with an end-of-the-world atmosphere of peace and quiet that gives an idea of what Bali used to be like. Long may it last! This means visitors can explore the superb **coral reefs★★** in the vicinity undisturbed (*most hotels hire out masks and snorkels*).

P Bénet

Amed, between volcano and ocean

The incredible fate of the "Liberty"
During the Second World War, in 1942, a Japanese submarine torpedoed an American cargo ship that was cruising off the Balinese coast. The vessel ran aground on Tulamben beach during a vain attempt to tow it into the port of Singaraja to recover its cargo. But in 1963 the eruption of Mount Agung and the torrents of lava that flowed down its slopes provoked a terrible tidal wave that pushed the cargo ship back out to sea. It hit a reef and sank not far from the coast, in a few metres of water. Forgotten by everyone, the wreck – over 100m long! – was rediscovered by divers about ten years ago. Since then its extraordinary coral and colonies of fish have turned it into a favourite spot for all who love exploring the sea-bed.

Return to Culik and take the main road to the right for 9km.

■ **Tulamben –** Long ignored by tourists and Balinese alike, this ordinary grey pebble beach has recently become one of the island's main **diving spots**. Very close to the shore lies the **wreck of the "Liberty" cargo ship*****, where myriads of multicoloured fish have taken up residence and dance a stunning ballet among the coral. But the place has now acquired such a reputation that it is better to stay the night on the spot so as to dive early in the morning and thus avoid meeting more tourists than fish in the waters!

You can return to Amlapura and from there take the pretty Selat road (see p 421) to Rendang. Otherwise you can continue northwards along the coast, through the desolate eastern landscapes marked by Agung's eruption.

Making the most of East Bali

COMING AND GOING/ GETTING AROUND

By shuttle bus – Daily services to Padangbai, Candidasa, Tirtagangga and Tulamben from the main tourist resorts (Kuta, Sanur, Ubud, and Lovina).

By bemo/By bus – From Batubulan bus station there are frequent departures for Klungkung, Candidasa and Amlapura. Buses going to Singaraja serve Tirtagangga, Culik and Tulamben.

By car – The main road (Denpasar-Amlapura) is good but the secondary roads are often in a much worse state of repair.

By ferry – 6 ferries shuttle between Padangbai (Bali) and Lembar (Lombok). The crossing takes 4-5hr. Departures both ways every 90min from midnight on. The agencies offer all-in transport of ferry plus minibus on arrival and departure.
Mabua's agency, ☎ (0361) 723 70 (Bali), ☎ (0364) 811 95 (Lombok).

ADDRESS BOOK

Bank/Currency exchange – There are exchange offices in Padangbai and Candidasa. For the moment it is not possible to withdraw cash with a credit card anywhere.

Post office – There are post offices in Padangbai (near the jetty), Candidasa (on the main street) and Amlapura.

Telephone – There are **Wartel** centres in Padangbai (in the street leading to the jetty), Candidasa (near the Kubu Bali Bungalows) and Amlapura (Jl Ngurah Rai). Amed and Tulamben do not yet have telephone lines.

Travel agencies – There are several in Padangbai (on the seafront) and Candidasa (on the main road). They often serve as exchange offices and laundries, sell shuttle bus tickets and organise excursions. Most of the hotels provide the same services.

Car rental – Cars, motorbikes and bicycles can be hired in Candidasa.

WHERE TO STAY
• Padangbai
Stay as far away as possible from the ferry terminal, as the loudspeakers announce boats day and night and there is a tremendous amount of activity virtually all the time. The places below are all in Jl Silayukti (the street running along the beach to the east of the jetty), slightly set back from the street in sparse gardens.

Modest
Kerti Beach Inn, ☎ (0363) 413 91 – 12rm. ⌁ ⤫ The cheapest rooms are really very basic but you can opt for a 2-storey bungalow with thatched roof, built along the lines of the old Balinese rice stores. Simple but pleasant.

Padang Bai Beach Inn, ☎ (0363) 414 39 – 25rm. ⌁ ⤫ ✗ Same description as above but this guesthouse also has a few more modern rooms for those who do not like rusticity.

Luxury
Hotel Puri Rai, ☎ (0363) 418 56, ☎/Fax (0363) 413 86 – 34rm. ⌁ 🍽 ✗ Hot water. Padangbai's luxury hotel. It has comfortable modern rooms on 2 floors but is totally lacking in charm.

• Balina Beach
Luxury to super deluxe
Balina Beach Resort, ☎ (0363) 410 02, Fax (0363) 410 01 – 42rm. ⌁ 🍽 ✗ ⤫ ⚇ cc Hot water. Adjacent diving club. Small palm-roofed rooms spread around a pretty garden that opens onto the beach. Avoid those at the back which are cramped and have no view. The place is charming and the welcome friendly. Overpriced but negotiable.

Super deluxe
The Serail, ☎ (0361) 97 59 63, Fax (0361) 97 59 68 – 58rm. ⌁ 🍽 ℘ TV ✗ ⤫ ⚇ cc Hot water. Several thatched buildings surround a vast garden with coconut palms and an enormous swimming pool. Peaceful and well ventilated. Although elegant, the rooms are a little lacking in warmth.

• Candidasa
Modest
Flamboyant Bungalows – 12rm. ⌁ ⤫ ⚇ Access from the main road along a little alleyway going down to the sea. A row

of thatched bamboo bungalows a reasonable distance from each other. Simple but clean and quiet.

Modest to average
Hotel Genggong, ☎ (0363) 411 05 – 12rm. ⌁ ⤫ ⚇ The rather sparsely furnished rooms are on 2 floors in a garden facing the sea. The upstairs ones are preferable. Pleasant little straw huts in which to have a drink and admire the sunset. A real beach and a fine view out over the islands.

Ida's Home Stay, ☎/Fax (0363) 410 96 – 6rm. ⌁ ⤫ ⚇ The bungalows are all different and stand facing the sea in a vast, well-ventilated garden. Some have 2 floors, sometimes with a verandah upstairs. The owner, who is passionately fond of antiques, aims to preserve a traditional Balinese feel. He has even moved a house from a neighbouring village and rebuilt it in the garden. All the rooms are inspired by the local architecture and are built entirely of natural materials. Amiable welcome.

Puri Pudak Bungalows, ☎ (0363) 419 78 – 8rm. ⌁ ⤫ Hot water. Thatched bamboo bungalows in a row along a little alley leading to the sea. Clean and functional.

Kelapa Mas Home Stay, ☎ (0363) 419 47 – 24rm. ⌁ 🍽 / ⤫ ✗ A lovely series of rooms at varying prices. 8 different rates depending on comfort and view. The cheapest are basic and open onto the garden. The more comfortable ones have an open-air bathroom with hot water and face the sea. Unfortunately the restaurant gives onto the street.

Luxury
Ida Beach Village, Desa Samuh, ☎ (0363) 411 18/19, Fax (0363) 410 41 – 17rm. ⌁ 🍽 / ⤫ ℘ ✗ ⚇ ⚇ cc Hot water. Private little houses, impeccably clean and quite spacious, surrounded by a low brick wall. Some have a small verandah, upstairs under a thatched roof. The place is a little cramped but the privacy of each room is preserved. From the restaurant terrace there is a beautiful view over the sea and the islands. A stairway goes directly down into the water.

Kubu Bali Bungalows, ☎ (0363) 415 32/412 56, Fax (0363) 415 31 – 20rm. ⌁ 🍽 ⤫ ℘ ✗ ⚇ cc Hot water. This ho-

Making the most of East Bali

tel built in an extremely beautiful location offers luxury thatched bungalows staggered up the hillside and well spaced out from each other. The ones higher up are further from the road and enjoy a more open view of the sea – they are of course the most expensive but the decoration may not be to everyone's taste. Open-air bathrooms. Small fish ponds, lotus flowers and statues decorate the garden.

• Tirtagangga

Modest to average

Prima Bamboos Home Stay, ☎ (0363) 213 16, Fax (0363) 210 44 – 8rm. ⌖⌁ ✕ Acceptable rooms but no more than that. The more expensive, recent, ones are roomier and more comfortable. A magnificent view over the rice fields, and the road below. Even if you are not staying here, it is worth visiting for the view. Very cheap restaurant.

Tirta Ayu Bungalow, in the grounds of the Water Palace, ☎ (0363) 216 97 – 4rm. ⌖⌁ ✕ Small private bungalows (2 categories of rooms), a little basic for the price, located behind the restaurant overlooking the royal baths. A little more expensive than the previous entry. Pleasant, peaceful restaurant.

Average to high end

Puri Sawah Bungalows, ☎ (0363) 218 47, Fax (0363) 219 39 – 4rm. ⌖⌁ ✕ Hot water in some rooms. A charming place overlooking the rice fields. Nicely appointed double or family rooms. The downstairs ones have open bathrooms. A delightful garden and pleasant little restaurant. Sometimes noisy because of the road nearby.

• Amed

Modest

Vienna Beach Bungalows, Lipah – 10rm. ⌖⌁ ✕ Simple but acceptable rooms, all in bamboo on 2 floors facing the sea. The downstairs ones have an open-air bathroom. Little restaurant facing the beach. Full board only.

Modest to average

Good Karma Bungalows, Selang – 17rm. ⌖ ✕ ⌁ Private palm and wood bungalows with pleasant open-air bathrooms in a row facing the beach. Various prices depending on size and comfort. Charming terraces with bamboo furniture

where it is pleasant to read or have a siesta. Good restaurant with a very convivial atmosphere. If the place is full up when visitors arrive, the owner generally suggests 1 of the 2 neighbouring bungalsows (just behind); these are very recent, impeccably clean and have an open-air bathroom (with Turkish-style WC).

Kusumajaya Beach Inn, Jemeluk – 8rm. ⌖⌁ ✕ ⌁ Small private white-brick bungalows with open-air bathrooms. They are set in a line but quite well spaced out, between the road and the beach. Restaurant opening onto the sea. A friendly place.

High end to luxury

Coral View Villas, Lipah, ☎/Fax (0361) 43 12 73, Fax (0363) 210 44 – 19rm. ⌖ 🖥 / ⌁ ✕ ⌁ ⌁ CC Grey stone pavilions with thatched roofs and Balinese doors, scattered around a lovely garden. Restaurant on the beach.

Hidden Paradise Cottages, Lipah, ☎/Fax (0361) 43 12 73, Fax (0363) 210 44 – 16rm. ⌖ 🖥 / ⌁ ✕ ⌁ ⌁ CC Not far from the one above and under the same management. These bungalows are set in a well-maintained garden and have pleasant bathrooms with open roofs and plants. Restaurant on the beach. Adjacent diving school. Several rates depending on comfort.

• Tulamben

All the hotels have their own diving clubs and hire out masks and snorkels (check the state of the equipment carefully). They often give special prices for divers.

Modest

Paradise Palm Beach Bungalows, ☎/Fax (0363) 410 52 – 20rm. ⌖⌁ ✕ A series of rooms that are rather close together but set in a beautiful garden. Restaurant with a view of the sea. A good place for Tulamben.

Modest to average

Bali Coral Bungalows – 10rm. ⌖⌁ ✕ ⌁ Thatched bungalows on different levels, facing the sea but mostly lacking a view. The rooms are pleasant, as is the restaurant giving onto the sea.

High end

Bali Coral Bungalows – 10rm. ⌖ 🖥 ✕ ⌁ Hot water. Same description as above.

High end to luxury
Paradise Palm Beach Bungalows,
☎/Fax (0363) 410 52 – 22rm. 🛏 🍽 ✗
Hot water. Same description as above.

Super deluxe
Mimpi Resort, ☎ (0361) 70 10 70,
Fax (0361) 70 10 74/(0363) 21 939,
☎/Fax (0363) 216 42 – 30rm. 🛏 🍽 🏊
🏊 ✗ ⚓ ⚓ CC Hot water. This luxurious hotel offers good all-in "room + diving" rates for enthusiasts. Lovely rooms,
mostly small and sober, with fabulous
garden bathrooms. The cheapest are,
however, rather badly positioned.

EATING OUT

● **Padangbai**
Along the beach are several *warung* serving Indonesian dishes and good grilled
fish. Many of the *losmen* have a small adjoining restaurant.

● **Candidasa**
Most of the restaurants are on the road,
which is very busy. Those in the hotels on
the seafront are preferable.

Moderate to more select
Chez Lilly, main road. This restaurant,
prettily decorated with old black and
white photos of Bali, offers an original
menu on which "gratin Dauphinois" and
home-made quiche sit happily beside
"sayur papaya" and Balinese smoked
salmon. Just like many of its neighbours,
it shows films every evening from
7.30pm, when it then becomes very difficult to hear yourself speak. A good place
nonetheless.

TJ's Cafe, main road, ☎ (0363) 415 40.
Dishes from different countries, mainly
Tex-Mex, for those tiring of Indonesian
cuisine. Unfortunately a bit noisy.

Pandan Restaurant, in the hotel of the
same name, ☎ (0363) 415 41. Pleasant
terrace looking peacefully onto the sea.
The delicious Balinese buffets organised
on some evenings enable visitors to taste
an assortment of local specialities. On
other days there is a choice between Indonesian or Chinese dishes or seafood, all
well prepared.

Pandan Harum, main road. Balinese
dance performances take place on Tuesdays and Fridays from 9pm.

● **Tirtagangga**
Avoid the little warung near the palace as
cars park in front and souvenir sellers do
the rounds. The *losmen* restaurants (see
above, "Where to stay") are preferable as
they are cheaper, quieter and have a view
of the rice fields.

● **Balina Beach**
Apart from the hotel restaurants there are
2 small **warung**, friendly, good and inexpensive, in the street running between the
main road and the sea.

● **Amed**
Apart from the hotels there are a few pleas-
ant restaurants at **Lipah**, near the Hidden
Paradise and Coral View bungalows.

Making the most of East Bali

MOUNT BATUR★★★
(GUNUNG BATUR)
Bangli district
About 70km north of Denpasar – Map p 350-351
Cool cloudy climate

Not to be missed
The view from Penelokan over the caldera.
Sunrise from the top of the volcano.

And remember...
Leave early in the morning before the clouds block the view.
Take a jumper if spending the night at the lakeside.
Take a lot of water and a headlamp torch when climbing the volcano.

Whether visitors are content with a short excursion to admire the truly magnificent panorama over the caldera, opt for a boat outing on the lake inside the caldera or tackle the climb up the volcano and a tour of its still-smoking craters, Mount Batur leaves everyone with vivid memories as this is without a doubt the most fairy-tale location in all Bali. Innumerable roads lead up to it, winding through a fresh, cool region of fertile volcanic soil covered in luxuriant high-altitude vegetation. The striking landscape, sculpted by the wrath of this "mountain of fire" and lying unsuspected until the last minute, suddenly opens before the eyes – an invitation to contemplation and to enjoy some unusual walks.

On the way to Mount Batur★

There are many roads leading to Mount Batur, some of them very lovely, so the ideal solution is to take one road there and a different one back. The 3 routes we suggest all lead to the village of Penelokan, on the edge of Batur's caldera. Allow about 1hr for the journey there.

As the road climbs up into higher ground, the rice paddies give way to market gardens (maize, cabbage, ginger, cloves, coffee, tobacco and citrus fruits). Banana trees and coconut palms become scarcer, replaced by brilliant red poinsettias, all sorts of crotons and, higher up again, tufts of bamboo and tree ferns.

Via Tampaksiring★★
Leave from Bedulu. The Tampaksiring road, the most common route, goes through some lovely scenery of **terraced rice fields★★** in superb little valleys with tiered slopes where the bright green sets off the scarlet leaves of the first poinsettias (*See also p 404*).

Via Bangli★
Leave from Peteluan, just beyond Gianyar on the road to Klungkung. This other quite popular route goes through **Bangli**, the former capital of the Gelgel dynasty and a pleasant, well kept provincial township with trees and flowers.

Here visitors can stop off to see the very lovely **Pura Kehen★★**, the state temple of the ancient kingdom of Bangli, where its rulers were crowned (*go north through the town. Beside a statue a sign indicates "PR Kehen", 200m to the right. Fee*). The building rises in eight terraced levels out of a sumptuous natural landscape. **Statues of elephants** greet you at the bottom of the steps. Higher up, the finely worked entrance gateway leads to a magnificent **banyan★** tree in which a *bale kulkul* (*see p 357*) is perched. You then enter the first courtyard where some of the walls are inlaid with **Chinese**

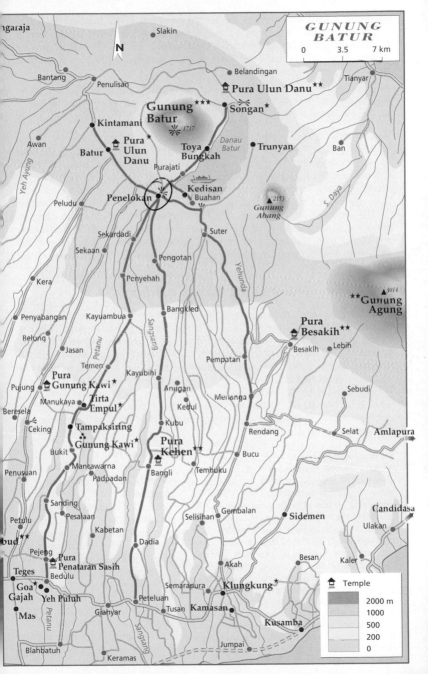

porcelain. Various **altars** occupy the second courtyard, which honours the ancestors of the kingdom's last dynasty. Then follows the third courtyard with its elegant row of **meru**. The highest and most holy is dedicated to the god of fire, while another prettily carved altar portrays the **three thrones** dedicated to the Hindu trinity of Brahma, Siva and Vishnu.

To go straight to Penelokan, return to the road through Bangli and continue north. It is also possible to join the Rendang road (see below). From Bangli or Klungkung, follow the road to Besakih, then to Kintamani.

Via Rendang★★

In the village of Suter, which is on the way, locals may try to sell entry tickets for the Batur site; they are the same price here as in Penelokan. Not as busy as the two previous routes, this one goes through peaceful villages forgotten by tourists and affords exceptionally beautiful **landscapes★★** which make the changes in vegetation even more enjoyable. During the last part of the journey, after a series of bends, you can first see the outline of Mount Agung, then that of **Mount Abang**. After the village of **Suter**, the road climbs through the heart of a dense **forest** where the air is noticeably cooler; then, on a bend in the road, the **view★★★** suddenly opens up over Lake Batur: you have reached the edge of the caldera. *Penelokan is a little further to the right along the road.*

The Mount Batur caldera★★★

A breathtaking sight! In the centre of the caldera, a gigantic rocky arena 13km in diameter, sits Mount Batur (1 717m), a sombre cone from which a cloud of smoke rises ceaselessly. On its desolate slopes the various generations of lava flows have formed subtle shadings of brown hues. The vegetation has already started recolonising these, sketching swathes of green velvet that add even more to the splendour of the decor. To the east, the flanks of **Mount Abang** (2 153m) plunge abruptly into the bluish, mirror-like waters of the lake. A little further over on the horizon *(towards the east)*, when the clouds are not hiding it, the majestic outline of **Mount Agung** (3 014m) stands out against the azure blue, just behind the first two peaks.

Birth of a caldera

Around 30 000 years ago a 3 000m volcano awoke in an eruption of unimaginable violence throwing out tonnes of ash and lava. When the underlying pocket of magma had emptied, the summit of the volcano collapsed in on itself, creating a caldera in its place, a wide cauldron with vertiginous walls. Almost 10 000 years later a new eruption gave birth to a secondary volcano, Mount Batur, while at its feet the caldera filled up with water to form a lake. Since its appearance Mount Batur has erupted several times, the last being in 1997, and is still active. Lava flows and projections of ash, scoria and stone have shaped its slopes and formed new cones, which indicate fresh eruptions to come. And yet in the villages that have flourished at its feet, life continues, carefree, taking advantage of the soil's fertility.

Penelokan

Fee (see above, "Via Rendang"). With its extraordinary **panorama★★★** of the caldera (weather permitting), Penelokan is one of Bali's major tourist stopovers. Surrounded by a plethora of excursion coaches, visitors are assailed by a crowd of the most tenacious vendors selling sarongs, souvenirs and regional fruit, before they have even had time to take in the scenery! Those who feel hassled by this should continue on to Kintamani, a little further west, where in theory things are a little quieter *(see also p 441, "Eating out").*

At the Puri Sanjiaya restaurant, a steep winding road goes down into the caldera to the village of **Kedisan** (*about 10min*). Here there is accommodation (*see p 440*) and visitors can set off on the climb up the volcano, although it is better to go on to **Toya Bungkah** (*see below*), which is more pleasant.

On the lake
The jetty is at Kedisan, 100m to the right
of where the road comes in from Penelokan. Allow 90min-2hr.

The classic boat trip takes you to the village and cemetery of **Trunyan** then on to **Air Panas** (Toya Bungkah), where you may disembark if you do not want to return to Kedisan. However, in order to avoid the tourist trap and the organised racket that is rife in Trunyan (*see below*), it is better to be content with a simple trip on the lake. This gives you the opportunity to admire in peace and quiet the fishermen in their makeshift canoes dug out of tree trunks, an oar tucked under one arm and a line held in the other hand.

■ **Trunyan** – The **Bali Aga** community of Trunyan (*see p 354*) lives in self-sufficiency, isolated on a narrow strip of land on the eastern shore of the lake. Visitors are not allowed to see much of the village, whose inhabitants are not very welcoming to strangers. The only tourist attraction is a visit to the **cemetery** (Kuban), which is not particularly cheerful, since the Aga follow an archaic funerary ritual and do not cremate their dead but leave the bodies to decompose in the open air. The local population now exploits to commercial ends the curiosity awakened by these funerary traditions, by arranging the skeletons to dramatic effect. Those fond of macabre sights should be aware that donations are sought most insistently!

Once back in Kedisan, a bumpy little road winding through the fallen volcanic rocks goes round the western side of the lake.

■ **Toya Bungkah** – *13km from Kedisan. Fee, even if not bathing.* This hamlet owes its nickname, **Air Panas**, to the hot volcanic springs that flow out at the water's edge (*behind the Amertha restaurant*). Despite the cool air and beautiful setting, the little bathing area full of rubbish is not really very inviting for a swim.

Continue north along the (bad) road to Songan (about 15-20min from Toya Bungkah by car). Go through the village.

■ **Songan**★ – This picturesque little village at the northern end of the lake has a very pretty temple enhanced by its majestic setting. Right at the end of the road, the multiple-roofed **meru** of **Pura Ulun Danu**★★ stand out against the foot of the caldera's fern-clad rock-face.

From here it is possible, weather permitting, to climb up onto the rim of the caldera (*quite an easy 15-20min walk*). The **viewpoint**★★★ looks out over Lake Batur on one side and the east coast of Bali on the other, with the omnipresent outline of Mount Agung as a backdrop.

Climbing the volcano★★★

Allow about 3hr walking for the return trip by the shortest route, which is tiring but not particularly difficult. It is essential to take a torch (if leaving in the dark), a lot of water (1-2 litres per person depending on the length of the excursion) and good non-slip walking shoes (preferably high cut as the terrain is sandy and steep in places so there are numerous opportunities for twisting ankles!). A warm garment is also necessary as it is cold on top.

Mount Batur

As soon as you arrive in Penelokan, you will be approached by guides. You are strongly recommended to hire one to avoid hassle. The fees asked are often exorbitant but severe haggling will bring them down as there is no lack of competition!

To reach the **main crater*** at sunrise it is necessary to leave at 4am *(90min-2hr up, 1hr-90min down; quite easy)*. Once at the summit there is the supreme reward of a most enchanting **panorama***** (unless it is cloudy). The air is pure, the sky still twinkles with stars and a few shooting stars may even make their appearance. The first lamps are being lit in the villages below and in the crater formed in 1917 hot tea or coffee and cold drinks await climbers. The locals even offer to fry eggs on the hot gases seeping from the vents all around! Of course, the efforts of the local women who have brought breakfast up so far have their price, which is only to be expected, but that should not prevent you from bargaining!

As dawn breaks, the outline of Mount Rinjani, then of the coast of the island of Lombok, become visible in the far distance between sea and mist, while in the foreground *(slightly to the right)* the summits of Abang and Agung seem to be superimposed. Far below there may be clouds floating over the lake, softly enveloping its contours. Later in the morning the clouds rise gently up the caldera walls before eventually dispersing. Lastly, the morning sun tinges the little peaks and undulations formed by the lava on Mount Batur's northern slopes with orange. Covered in greenery, these are the territory of a whole colony of wild monkeys.

Those who still have the strength can tour the **secondary craters**** *(5-6hr there and back, including climbing the main crater; quite difficult climbing)* on the way back down. This excursion offers more excitement with the most varied of volcanic landscapes: bare slopes, slippery sands, unstable rocks, acrid sulphurous gases – the volcano

Mount Batur: earth, fire and water

does not make it easy for visitors! The high point comes on reaching the edge of the **last crater*****, formed by the 1997 eruption, where you will see the burning inferno of the mouth, carpeted in multicoloured sulphur deposits, blowing and spitting out red smoke and flames accompanied by impressive rumblings.

On the rim of the caldera⋆

To leave the caldera, return to Kedisan.
From Penelokan, follow the road running northwest along its rim.

■ **Batur** – *The village temple stands on the right just before Kintamani.* The village of Batur originally stood beside the lake, inside the caldera. During the eruption in 1917 the lava came to a miraculous halt at the temple entrance but the 1926 eruption was fatal, destroying the entire village, which was then rebuilt here on the caldera rim, along with its temple. Considered one of the most important sanctuaries in Bali after Besakih, **Pura Ulun Danu Batur⋆** is dedicated to the goddess of Lake Batur, **Ida Betari Dewi Danu**. The lake waters do in fact feed an entire underground network of springs that are used for irrigation and have thus made fertile the vast region to the south of the volcano (Bangli and Gianyar districts). The temple has conserved a few of its original elements spared by the lava, but many of the shrines have not yet been entirely rebuilt. Its elegant **split gateways** open onto vast courtyards from which rise *meru* – the tallest honour the goddess of the lake and the gods of Agung and Batur – and numerous *bale* covered with offerings.

■ **Kintamani** – If you pass through early in the day it is worth having a look at the **market⋆** *(every 3rd day, 5am-10am approximately)*, the biggest in the region. Everything is sold here including anoraks and jumpers. During the fruit season you can taste the delicious *salak*, big green grapefruit, *manggis*, passion fruit and others that grow all around. A real treat!

To go back down to South Bali, return to Penelokan and take one of the routes described above. If you are heading for the north coast, continue north along the caldera to Penulisan. Turn left there at the big stairway going up to the temple and take the winding road that goes down towards Singaraja. This comes out at Kubuktambetan, between Lovina Beach and Singaraja (about 1hr from Kintamani), where it joins the main road along the north coast (see p 445).

Mount Batur

Making the most of Mount Batur

COMING AND GOING

By shuttle bus – Several daily connections from the main tourist resorts (Kuta, Sanur, Ubud, Lovina, etc). The buses go as far as Penelokan or Kintamani. The Gunung Sari restaurant serves as the **Perama** office. Motorbike riders, drivers of private *bemo* minibuses and numerous hotel touts await visitors when the buses arrive and offer to drive them down to the edge of the lake; hard bargaining is in order, or wait for the next public *bemo* (see below).

By bemo – Services to Kintamani via Penelokan from Batubulan, Gianyar or Bangli as well as Singaraja. They are more frequent in the mornings and on market days (every 3rd day). A few regular *bemos* then continue on down to the villages of Kedisan and Toya Bungkah (about 1 per hour, more frequently on market days).

By car/By motorbike – See the main access roads described above.

ADDRESS BOOK

Tourist information – **Yayasa Bintang Danu**, Penelokan (where the road goes down into the caldera), ☎ (0366) 233 70. Daily 9am-3pm. Information about walks and transport in the region. **Jero Wijaya Tourist Service**, Toya Bungkah. Has a map of the volcano and supplies good information about walks.

Bank/Currency exchange – **Bank Rakyat Indonesia**, on the road along the crater rim, a little before Batur temple. Changes cash and travellers' cheques (at a bad rate). **Jero Wijaya Tourist Service**, Toya Bungkah. Same services.

Post office/Telephone – Post office and **Wartel** near the bank. Public coin or card telephones in front of the car park at the entrance to Toya Bungkah village. Telkom cards only work in the Penelokan telephone boxes.

WHERE TO STAY

• Kedisan

Kedisan does not have any really pleasant hotels and suffers from noise from the road. We do however list the village's best hotel for those who wish to spend the night there.

Modest to average
Hotel Segara, ☎ (0366) 511 36, Fax (0366) 512 12 - 40rm. ☏ ⌸ ✗ The rooms are set around a courtyard which also serves as the car park. Minimum comfort for the cheapest (best avoided). All the others are acceptable, with hot water and, depending on price, bathtub, television or American breakfast. The most expensive look onto a little garden.

• Toya Bungkah

All these hotels are much the same (except where indicated) and none is exceptional. In all cases we advise you to check out the state of the bathroom facilities before deciding on a room.

Modest
Under The Volcano I, set back from the road, ☎ (0366) 511 66 – 8rm. ☏ ✗ Small bungalows made of volcanic stone with a Spartan level of comfort. Good restaurant. Their passion fruit juice is delicious!
Under The Volcano II, ☎ (0366) 511 66 – 11rm. ☏ ✗ Much better than its elder brother. The first series of rooms, set along the track, is separated from the lake by a few houses. The second complex of more recent bungalows is on the lakeside. These are undoubtedly the most pleasant in the region. The place is expanding but it is still better to book.
Nyoman Pangus Bungalows, ☎ (0366) 511 67 – 6rm. ☏ ✗ Simple, ordinary rooms. The 2 most recent are a little better. Friendly welcome.
Arlinas, ☎ (0366) 511 65 – 11rm. ☏ ✗ Prices double for the rooms with hot water. A simple, acceptable place but without charm. Performances of "Genjek" dance take place in the restaurant some evenings, in a good-humoured atmosphere that is cheerful and friendly.

Average
Amertha's Home Stay ☏ ✗ Prices double for the rooms that have a hot-water heater. Sparsely furnished rooms but perfectly acceptable, with open-air bathrooms filled with plants. This guesthouse has the only restaurant in the village looking directly onto the lake (barely more expensive than the others).

Average to high end
Lakeside Cottages, ☎ (0366) 512 49/ 512 51, Fax (0366) 512 50 - 10rm. ⚐|✗ cc The superior category rooms are at the end of the track leading to the lake. They are impeccable, quite spacious and have hot water, television and a view of the lake. The other rooms are not so good and are not worth the price.

Luxury
Hotel Puri Bening Hayato, ☎ (0366) 512 34, Fax/☎ (0366) 512 48 – ⚐|✗ This big modern hotel provides spacious rooms that are rather cold but impeccably clean and, for the most expensive, equipped with telephone and television. The bathrooms are fed by natural hot springs. The much cheaper bungalows with terrace and view of the lake only have cold water. Very good price deals during some periods.

EATING OUT

● Penelokan

The obligatory halt for organised tours and day trips for visitors coming just to admire the panorama; Penelokan has countless tourist restaurants offering self-service buffets that are quite expensive and not always very good. It is better to choose one with a terrace with a view as some do not even look out over the volcano!

Moderate
Gunung Sari, **Panca Yoga**, **Puncak Sari**, etc. Along the road to Kintamani, the little terraces of these restaurants are soon visible, sitting just on the edge of the caldera. Simpler and often much better than the ones above, they serve classic Indonesian dishes and sandwiches, plus buffets sometimes (half the price of those in Penelokan). The only inconvenience is the noise from the road but the view helps you forget it.

● Toya Bungkah

Basic to moderate
All the hotels mentioned for this village (see above) have restaurants serving more or less the same dishes at comparable prices. Taste the local speciality of grilled lake fish with a little lemon juice and chopped hot peppers. Delicious!

Making the most of Mount Batur

NORTH BALI★
LOVINA BEACH
Buleleng district
80km north of Denpasar – Map p 350-351 and p 455
Hot, dry climate tempered by the sea breeze

Not to be missed
Sunset on Lovina beach.
Taking a boat trip to see the dolphins and explore the sea-bed.
Visiting the temples on the north coast.

And remember...
Use Lovina as a base for exploring the surrounding region.

Another coast, another side of Bali. Here in the north the mountains reign, plunging steeply and almost directly into the sea, leaving just a narrow coastal plain fringed with black sand beaches, behind which orchards and market gardens take over from rice fields. Less urbanised and still preserved from the tourist invasion, this region is also distinguished by its original artistic traits. These can be seen in the architecture and decoration of the temples as well as in the dynamic local dances (such as the *joged*) and the craftwork, which includes making musical instruments for the gamelan, goldsmithing and, of course, the art of *songket*, those delicate fabrics woven with gold thread.

From north to south and vice versa
Ideally situated on the spice route, **Singaraja**, capital of the kingdom of Buleleng, grew through the centuries into a major trading port attracting merchants from Java, Sulawesi, China and even India and Arabia. An ethnic kaleidoscope that caused mosques, Chinese pagodas, Hindu temples, Buddhist monasteries and churches to exist side by side, some vestiges of which can still be seen today.

An original compass!
Balinese maps are not traditionally orientated according to magnetic north but in relation to the mountains. When you are in the south of the island this is not a problem, since the mountains are in fact to the north. But in the north of the island the situation becomes tricky since the mountains are now to the south! The inhabitants of North Bali in fact see their island upside down, a detail that often leads to confusion. So when asking the way, you should avoid mentioning the points of the compass but rather opt for the term "kaja" ("towards the mountains"). This then creates less risk of heading off in the opposite direction to the one desired!

Singaraja's strategic position did not escape the attention of the Dutch who, following a series of disputes, attacked the kingdom of Buleleng, starting with its capital, which was the first town to fall into the hands of the invader (1849). After being the local raja's capital, in 1855 it became the seat of the colonial government, which from 1882 controlled all the northern part of Bali.

In the early 20C North Bali was still the main point of entry to the island. However, the first tourists to land preferred to leave its colonial and commercial atmosphere for the little villages of Kuta or Sanur, on a quest for the "real" Bali and its peaceful beaches. Today the tide has turned and it is North Bali that attracts all those fleeing the major seaside resorts of the south, looking for peace and quiet and a little more authenticity.

M. Lemerle

A budding fisherman on Lovina Beach

Lovina Beach★

With the tourist boom, the little villages scattered along the coast have spread until they have joined up to form one long seaside resort, Lovina, but despite this expansion the place still has a very pleasant atmosphere, peaceful and casual.

On the shady **beach**★, a long swathe of black sand washed by a calm sea, sits a garland of colourful *jukung* awaiting the following dawn to head out to sea. In front of their makeshift huts fishermen mend their nets while children paddle cheerfully in the water. It is worth exploring the little alleyways running between road and beach, as there is a good chance of coming across an animated game of billiards or an impromptu gamelan rehearsal.

Cetaceans and clown fish

As soon as visitors arrive in Lovina they are inevitably offered a **dolphin tour**★ (*departure at 6am. Go down to the beach a little before or book the previous day at your hotel. Fixed fee. The hotels take a commission*). But the increasing numbers of motorised *prahu* are tending to drive these mammals away. Although numerous some days, they sometimes fail to appear, so the tourists and photographers lying in wait return disappointed! However, if there are no dolphins there is always the consolation of the magnificent **sunrise**★★ over the mountains.

Around 8 or 9am the fishermen drop their passengers back on the beach or they may then take them **snorkelling**★★ (*fixed fee, masks and snorkels provided*). Just a few hundred metres from the coast the coral reefs teem with fascinating multicoloured creatures. There are a few reefs very close to the shore but the water is often cloudy and there is more chance of seeing plastic rubbish than fish.

To increase the chances of seeing dolphins, it is possible to hire the services of a fisherman in the late afternoon, thus catching the animals off their guard as they were only expecting visits in the early morning! And the sunset is by no means inferior to the sunrise either.

East of Lovina★

■ **Singaraja** – Formerly the administrative capital of Bali and now a major university city with more than 95 000 inhabitants, Singaraja does not have a lot to offer apart from dense traffic that includes horse-drawn carriages. Near the silted-up old harbour it has nevertheless conserved a few vestiges from the Dutch era, such as colonial residences and warehouses, mostly in a pitiful state. The contemporary **Gedong Kirtya Historical Library** *(Jl Veteran 20. In theory 8am-2pm; closed Saturday, Sunday and public holidays; in practice very irregular opening times. Fee)* houses a collection of **ancient manuscripts**, mainly holy texts and medical treatises inscribed on *lontar* palm leaves. There is also a very pleasant **night market** *(Jl Durian, between Jl Diponegoro and Jl Imama Bonjol. 5pm-10pm approximately)* where you can enjoy a good *sate* or other Indonesian specialities.

Leave Singaraja by taking Jl Gajah Mada and then follow the road going up to Bedugul for 11km (10-15min to the car park).

■ **Gitgit waterfall**★ (Air Terjun Gitgit) – *8am-6pm. Fee.*
The road winds up the mountain slopes, here and there offering beautiful **views**★★ over terraced rice fields and gorges lost in the dense vegetation. From **Gitgit** take the track leading to the falls *(opposite the Gitgit hotel and restaurant; car park; 10-15min walk)*. Shops line the path right to the end and both coming and going visitors are constantly assailed by vendors trying to sell. But the waterfall is really worth seeing: a curtain of foam cascading down from the top of a rock-face in the midst of greenery. You can have lunch in a *warung* on the opposite bank of the river, which is crossed by a little footbridge.

From there you can continue on to Bedugul and visit the lake region (see p 453). Otherwise return to the north coast and turn right to Sangsit. There is a sign to the temple on the right.

■ **Pura Beji**★★ – *Fee. Sarong and sash compulsory.* This **Subak temple**, typical of the baroque architecture of North Bali with its richly detailed façades portraying terrifying winged creatures, is dedicated to the gods of the rice paddies. The main sanctuary in the inner courtyard, shaded by magnificent frangipani trees, contains numerous small structures for receiving the gods when they come down to earth. These little roofless shrines, which here replace the *meru* of the island's other regions, are also richly carved with floral motifs and demons.

Continue east to a little road going up to the right to Jagaraga (signposted).

■ **Pura Dalem Jagaraga** – *Fee. Sarong and sash compulsory.* This temple, another example of regional architecture although unfortunately less well preserved, has no *meru* but is peopled with numerous statues of terrifying monsters plus amusing bas-reliefs, which offer a complete contrast to the classicism of the South. They include a boat sailing over the waves, a car, a bicycle and even an aeroplane. With a bit of luck there will be some school children to point out these unexpected motifs.

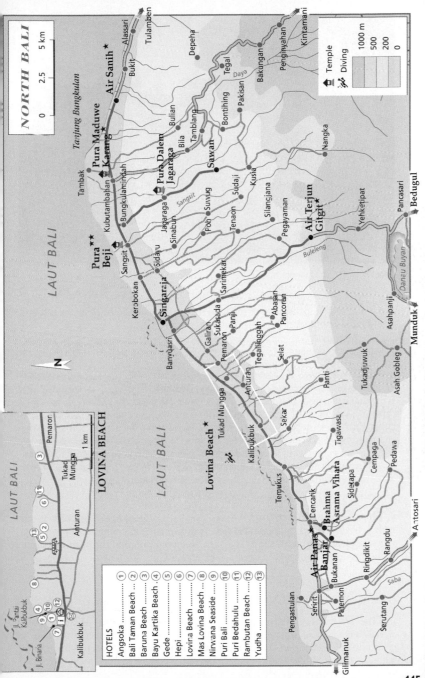

BALI

NORTH BALI

0   2.5   5 km

Temple
Diving

1000 m
500
200
0

LAUT BALI

Tanjung Bungkulan

Tulamben
Alassari
Air Sanih ★
Depeha
Bukit
Kintamani
Penginyahan
Bakungan
Tegal
Daya
Pura Maduwe
Karang ★
Pura Dalem
Jagaraga
Sawan
Tambak
Kubutambahan
Bungkulamindah
Pakisan
Bontihing
Tamblang
Bila
Bulian
Jagaraga
Sinabun
Poh Suwug
Sudaji
Kusia
Nangka
Sangsit
Pura ★★
Beji
Sangsit
Sidayu
Tenaon
Silangjana
Silangjana
Pegayaman
Yehketipat
Pancasari
Bedugul
Kerobokan
Sarimekar
Air Terjun
Gitgit ★
Buleleng
Singaraja
Banyuqasri
Galiran
Sukasada
Panji
Pemaron
Abasan
Pancoran
Selat
Danau Buyan
Asahpanji
Munduk
Tegallinggah
Anturan
Tukad Munga
Panti
Tukadjuwuk
Asah Gobleg
Lovina Beach ★
Kalibukbuk
Sekar
Tigawasa
Cempaga
Pedawa
LAUT BALI
LOVINA BEACH
Tukad Munga
Anturan
Kalibukbuk
Tengukus
Cencrik
Brahma
Asrama Vihara
Sidatapa
Pengastulan
Sririt
Patemon
Bukanan
Ringdikit
Rangdu
Antosari
Serutang
Saba
Gilimanuk

LOVINA BEACH

Jl. Binaria
Jl. Pantai Kalibukbuk
Kalibukbuk
LAUT BALI
Pemaror
Tukad Munga
Anturan
1 km

HOTELS
Angsoka .... ①
Bali Taman Beach .... ②
Baruna Beach .... ③
Bayu Kartika Beach .. ④
Gede .... ⑤
Hepi .... ⑥
Lovira Beach .... ⑦
Mas Lovina Beach .... ⑧
Nirwana Seaside ...... ⑨
Puri Bali .... ⑩
Puri Bedahulu .... ⑪
Rambutan Beach ...... ⑫
Yudha .... ⑬

Air Panas
Banjar ★
445

M Lemerle

Pura Beji: a forest of stone

The road continues on to **Sawan**, a charming village reputed for its gamelan gongs. It is worth asking to visit one of the workshops where skilled blacksmiths cast and beat the red-hot bronze.

Return to the coast road and turn east to Kubutambahan, going a short distance beyond the road to Kintamani.

■ **Pura Maduwe Karang**★ – *The temple stands on the corner of a street leading down to the sea. Fee. Sarong and sash compulsory.* Dedicated to the gods of the earth, this is yet another temple that is striking because of the creativity and originality of its carvings. A plethora of figures drawn from the *Ramayana* epic welcomes you from either side of the steps leading up to it. Split gateways open onto two successive courtyards shaded by frangipani trees. The most surprising **bas-relief**★★ is on the left (children may point it out for you): a man on a bicycle with flowers instead of wheels! Was it carved by one of the first Dutchmen to explore Bali by bicycle or by a Balinese artist who found the sight preposterous? The interpretations vary!

Continue east along the coast road.

■ **The Air Sanih springs**★ – *8am-6pm. Fee and towel hire.* A big pool paved with pebbles and fed by the limpid waters of a mountain spring awaits you for a refreshing halt. Food is available (and even accommodation) in the heart of a beautiful tropical garden that goes down to the sea.

West of Lovina

Go along the coast to Dencarik, where a little road goes up to the monastery.

■ **The Buddhist monastery** (Brahma Asrama Vihara) – *No fee. Dress decently and take your shoes off before entering the rooms.* This monastery occupies a charming site, clinging to the mountainside and looking down over the rice fields with the sea just visible in the distance. The only Buddhist monastery on the island,

Bali

it displays a curious mixture of styles: gilded Buddhas reminiscent of Thailand, offerings and some statues that are typical of Bali plus a stupa that strangely resembles those seen in Nepal, whereas some of the coloured porcelain statues look like nothing less than Virgins of Lourdes.

From the monastery, go back down towards the coast for 1km, then turn left and go through the village. A sign in front of the market indicates the hot springs to the left.

■ **The Banjar hot springs★** (Air Panas Banjar) – *8am-6pm. Fee. Restaurant.* This is a very agreeable spot for lounging around first thing in the morning or after a tiring day of visits and travelling. Several dragons spit warm and slightly sulphurous water into pools set on different levels in a lovely setting of tropical greenery.

Making the most of Lovina Beach

COMING AND GOING

By shuttle bus – Several buses daily to Lovina from the main tourist resorts (Kuta, Sanur, Ubud, Candidasa, Padangbai, etc). The ***Perama*** company offices are on the main road near the village of Anturan but there are numerous other sales outlets so you do not necessarily have to go there.

By bemo/By bus – These are frequent along the north coast's main road and serve all the villages around Lovina. From Singaraja, buses or bemos run to Denpasar, Bedugul, Kintamani, Amlapura (via the east coast) and Gilimanuk. The town has 3 bus stations, ***Banyuasri*** for destinations in the west, ***Penarukan*** for the east and ***Sukasada*** for the south.

By car/By motorbike – On the whole the roads are in a good state of repair and it is easy to find your way.

ADDRESS BOOK

Tourist information – On the main road at Kalibukbuk. 8am-6pm; closed Sunday and public holidays.

Bank/Currency exchange – The exchange offices, which are mainly to be found in Kalibukbuk, accept all main foreign currencies and travellers' cheques (at mediocre rates).

Post office/Telephone – The main post office is in Kalibukbuk on the main road (see plan p 445). ***Wartel***, which is just opposite, also sells stamps and allows you to make international calls.

Internet – ***Spice Dive***, Jl Binaria, Kalibukbuk.

Tourist agencies – These are numerous, especially in Kalibukbuk. They also often serve as currency exchanges and laundries, sell shuttle bus tickets and run excursions. Most of the hotels offer the same services.

Car rental – Motorbikes and cars can be hired in Kalibukbuk.

Medical service – See p 103

WHERE TO STAY

• Kalibukbuk

Modest to average

Angsoka Accommodation, Jl Binaria, ☎ (0362) 418 41, Fax (0362) 410 23 – 38rm. 🚿 ▤ / ✻ ✕ ⛱ CC Hot water in some rooms. A wide range of prices for the small rooms with no charm but an acceptable standard of comfort.

Average

Puri Bali Hotel, Jl Pantai Kalibukbuk, ☎ (0362) 414 85 – 28rm. 🚿 ▤ / ✻ ✕ ⛱ Hot water in some rooms. Acceptable rooms that are fairly well positioned and come at a variety of prices (avoid the cheaper ones, which are rundown). The swimming pool beside the car park is unfortunately not one of the nicest.

Nirwana Seaside Cottages, Jl Binaria, ☎ (0362) 412 88, Fax (0362) 410 90 – 46rm. ⚎🖅 / 🜍 ✕ 🛋 ⚘ cc Hot water. Several rows of attractive thatched bungalows in all styles. Brick or bamboo, 1 or 2 floors, with or without open-air bathrooms – there is something for all tastes and budgets. Direct access to the beach. A pity the staff are not always up to the mark.

Lovina Beach Hotel, Jl Seririt, ☎ (0362) 410 05, Fax (0362) 414 73 – 25rm. ⚎🖅 / 🜍 ✕ 🛋 ⚘ cc Hot water in the most expensive rooms. A simple but reasonable hotel, ideally located on a peaceful beach. Most of the terraces face the sea (avoid the others as they have no view and are close to the road). Pleasant little restaurant giving onto the beach.

Bayu Kartika Beach Bungalows, Jl Pantai, Kalibukbuk, ☎ (0362) 410 55/ 412 19 – 24rm. ⚎🖅 / 🜍 ✕ 🛋 ⚘ The rooms are in a row facing the beach, from which they are separated by a low wall in the case of the cheapest (with cold water) or by a garden in the case of the intermediate category (with hot water and open-air bathroom). Those with air conditioning unfortunately have their backs to the sea.

High end

Rambutan Beach Cottages, Jl Pantai Kalibukbuk, ☎ (0362) 413 88, Fax (0362) 410 57 – 18rm. ⚎🖅 / 🜍 ✕ 🛋 cc A good place 100m from the beach. Little 2-storey brick pavilions with carved stone. Several categories of rooms, with or without hot water, television and air conditioning. The place sits in a lovely garden with play areas laid out for children (swings, slides, sandpit, etc).

Super deluxe

Hotel Mas Lovina Beach, Jl Raya Kalibukbuk, ☎ (0362) 412 37, Fax ☎ (0362) 412 36 – 10rm. ⚎🖅 ✕ 🛋 ⚘ ⚏ cc Luxury small 2-storey houses set in a row in a lovely garden. Each one has 2 bedrooms, a living room and a kitchen, equipped with every modern comfort.

● **Anturan**

Modest

Gede Home Stay Bungalows, ☎ (0362) 415 26 – 9rm. ⚎🜍 ✕ ⚘ Hot water in some rooms. An authentic family guesthouse giving excellent value for money. It will charm those put off by the commercial atmosphere of Kalibukbuk. The rooms are quite simple but impeccably clean, although a little lacking in privacy. Pleasant little terrace restaurant from which you can contemplate the sea and the action on the beach while sipping milk from freshly picked coconuts or enjoying some deliciously prepared fish. The master of the house plays traditional gamelan here every week with his family. He will happily invite visitors to ceremonies in his village and is delighted to talk about his island and show visitors around the area.

● **Tukad Mungga**

Modest

Hepi Bungalows, ☎ (0362) 410 20 – 8rm. ⚎🖅 / 🜍 ✕ 🛋 A cheap hotel just 50m from the beach. White brick bungalows furnished with bamboo, very simple but perfectly adequate with open-air bathrooms decorated with plants. They are set around a spacious garden and a little swimming pool that is unfortunately neglected.

Modest to average

Hotel Yudha, ☎ (0362) 411 83, Fax (0362) 411 60 – 20rm. ⚎ 🖅 / 🜍 ✕ ⚘ Plain simple clean rooms in 2-storey buildings set around a garden. The place is a little cheerless but well located on a peaceful beach. Pleasant restaurant.

High end to luxury

Bali Taman Beach Hotel, ☎ (0362) 411 26, Fax (0362) 418 40 – 30rm. ⚎🖅 / 🜍 ✕ 🛋 ⚘ cc The standard rooms are really basic for the price but they share the hotel's facilities. The air-conditioned rooms have hot water and television. Balinese dance performances are put on some evenings.

● **Pemaron**

Modest to average

Hotel Puri Bedahulu, Pantai Happy, ☎ (0362) 417 31 – 12rm. ⚎🖅 / 🜍 ✕ ⚘ Hot water in some rooms. Small bungalows with carved Balinese doors. The decoration is rather sparse but the standard of comfort is reasonable. The garden is small but luxuriant and gives onto a pleasant beach. Very quiet and good value for money.

High end to luxury

Baruna Beach Cottages, ☎ (0362) 417 45/46, Fax (0362) 412 52 – 38rm. 📺 🍽 / 🏖 ✗ 🛋 🐾 💳 Different rates depending on the comfort and location of rooms. The simplest are really expensive. The most luxurious have air conditioning, hot water and a view of the sea. The medium priced ones have a big open-air bathroom decorated with plants. The place is nevertheless a bit colourless and expensive.

EATING OUT

All the restaurants in Lovina serve fish and seafood as well as classical Indonesian or Western dishes. Except in Kalibukbuk, most of the restaurants are in the hotels and losmen.

• Kalibukbuk

Moderate

Puri Tasik Madu, Jl Seririt, ☎ 413 76. Little restaurant on the beach. Simple and pleasant.

Permata, restaurant adjacent to the Lovina Beach Hotel (see "Where to stay"). A little terrace right on a quiet beach. Friendly reception and unbeatable prices for fairly good food.

Warung Kopi Bali, Jl Binaria. Good Balinese cuisine and charming service.

🍃**Bali Ayu**, seafront (near the Bali Lovina Cottages), ☎ 410 15. A particularly pleasant setting. Open-air terrace giving directly onto the beach. Peaceful and cheap.

Kakatua, Jl Binaria. Serves different dishes from its neighbours: Mexican (nachos, tacos, enchiladas and gazpacho), Thai and Indian specialities in particular.

Semina, Jl Pantai Kalibukbuk. 2 evenings a week this little family restaurant puts on an Indonesian buffet with a Balinese dance performance. Sunday and Wednesday about 7.30pm in theory. A friendly atmosphere.

Warung Gula Bali, Jl Pantai Kalibukbuk. An agreeable little covered terrace giving onto a relatively quiet alleyway. Snacks, salads, Balinese dishes and seafood.

Sea Breeze, seafront (near the dolphin statue), ☎ 411 38. A pretty terrace with a view of the sea. They serve mainly good grilled fish. A little more expensive than the above restaurants.

OTHER THINGS TO DO

Bars/nightclubs – Malibu, main street, Kalibukbuk. A big bar and restaurant; this is THE place for nightlife in Lovina. Films on certain days, and rock, pop or reggae concerts on Saturday and Wednesday evenings.

Diving – Most of the hotels and losmen hire or lend snorkelling equipment (masks, snorkels and flippers).

Spice Dive, Jl Binaria, Kalibukbuk, or main street, Kalibukbuk, ☎ (0362) 413 05. PADI centre. Organises outings to the main diving sites around the island.

SHOPPING GUIDE

Lovina is not the best place for shopping although there are still sarongs, clothing and some arts and crafts to be found, cheap but not always of the best quality.

Making the most of Lovina Beach

AROUND LAKE BRATAN★★
(DANAU BRATAN)
Badung, Buleleng and Tabanan districts
80km round trip – Allow 1-2 days – Map p 350-351
Cool, misty, rainy climate

Not to be missed
Pura Ulun Danu Bratan in the dawn mist.
The Munduk region.

And remember...
Spend the night on the spot or leave very early in the morning to arrive
before the clouds.
Take warm clothes for the evenings.

Escape to the mountains of central Bali. Rice fields have sketched giant stairways down the flanks of volcanoes, mountain rivers have cut gorges overgrown with greenery, and lakes stretch out in the hollows of ancient craters like huge mirrors reflecting all the colours in the sky when the mist finally rises up towards the peaks. Bathed in coolness and generously watered, the fertile slopes are covered with plantations of coffee, cacao, and vanilla and clove trees, which were introduced by the Dutch as an experiment. They still prosper today, side by side with the market garden crops from which the region's inhabitants make their living.

From the south, take the little road that leaves north out of Denpasar. From Ubud take the road to Campuhan and at Sayan turn left at the T-junction. At Kengetan turn right. The road goes through several villages including Mambal then Betang, where you turn right at the T-junction then left just beyond; a sign indicates Sangeh straight ahead, then to the right.

■ **Sangeh, the monkey forest** – *8am-6pm. Fee. Allow 20min.* In the midst of a fine forest of sacred nutmeg trees is a temple covered in moss as if wrapped up in a coat of green velvet. **Pura Bukit Sari**★ and the land around it form the territory of a formidable colony of macaques that are thieving and deliberately aggressive but nonetheless sacred. It is best to be accompanied by an attendant armed with a catapult to act as bodyguard. You should not buy bananas or peanuts, as all the monkeys will immediately rush at you! It is also necessary to keep a close eye on hats, glasses, cameras and wallets, their favourite spoils.

Demon in stone,
demon in fur (Sangeh)

P de Wilde/Hoaqui

An army of monkeys fallen from the heavens
According to a Balinese interpretation of the Ramayana, the macaques living in Sangeh forest were disciples of Hanuman, the commander-in-chief of an army of monkeys and endowed with immense strength as well as the ability to fly through the air. Together the monkeys attempted to kill the demon Ravana by crushing him between the two halves of the mythical Mahameru (the centre of the world according to Hindu mythology), since he could not be slain on earth or in the sky. During the battle, a piece of the mountain fell to earth near Sangeh along with the monkeys still clinging to it!

Bali

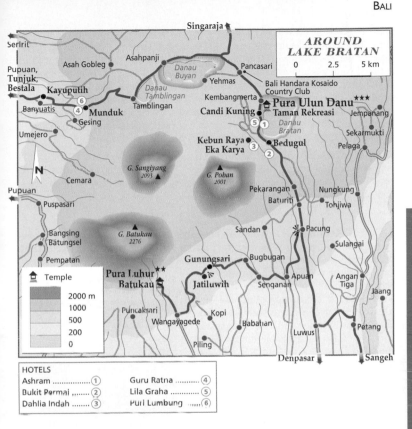

Continue northwards. In the village of Petang turn left towards Bedugul. A small **road**★, in a very bad state in places, winds between narrow escarpments where bamboos, banana trees and ferns intermingle. It comes out at **Luwus**, on the Denpasar-Bedugul-Singaraja road.

In the village of Pacung, turn left at the sign for the Ume Luang restaurant.

■ **The scenic Pacung road**★★ – First it is a good idea to stop at the Ume Luang restaurant *(see p 455, "Eating out")*, if only to appreciate the **view**★★. The road then snakes through the forest. Bamboos sometimes partially block the way but it is always possible to get through.

Go through the village of Apuan and turn right at the market. Soon magnificent **rice fields**★★ appear, swathed in the mist that envelops the mountains or sparkling in the sunlight when a ray pierces through. The loveliest terraced fields are to be seen around the villages of **Gunungsari** and **Jatiluwih**. In fine weather the **panorama**★★★ stretches as far as the south of the island.

Further on, this road joins the one that goes up to the temple of Batukau (see p 360). Otherwise, return to Pacung and take the road left to Bedugul. Pay no attention to the first sign to Bedugul, which indicates the hotel of the same name and not the village.

451

Bali

■ **Bedugul –** At the entrance to the village, on the left, a gateway with a big stone corncob in front marks the entrance to the **Botanical Gardens** (Kebun Raya Eka Karya) *(8am-4.30pm. Fee. Access possible by car or motorbike)*. Although a little too tidy with its surfaced pathways and roundabouts, this is a pleasant place to walk in the coolness of the forest beneath the peaks hidden by mist. The Balinese like to come here to stroll with their families, and have a siesta or a picnic, and the village youngsters take over the lawns to play football. The plant species, which are mainly imported, may seem banal to Western tourists, with only a few **cacti** in glasshouses, a collection of **orchids** and some traditional **medicinal plants** being worth a closer look.

Return to the road and turn left at the corncob. The **market**★ is also worth a look as it is very colourful, although touristy. It overflows with everything that grows in the region – fruit, vegetables, spices as well as flowers for offerings, roses and orchids – and supplies most of the other markets on Bali.

Continue along the road to Candi Kuning, on the shores of Lake Bratan.

■ **Candi Kuning –** Lake Bratan's big attraction is the **Taman Rekreasi** *(8am-6pm. Fee. Restaurant, see p 455)*, a leisure park for water sports much appreciated by Indonesians and particularly by young Javanese. When not having their caricatures sketched by the portrait artists, they will sometimes ask foreign visitors to pose with them for a souvenir photo with their "English friend"! Motor and rowing boats as well as pedalos are available for a **tour of the lake**.

Pura Ulun Danu Bratan: small stone vessels floating on the lake

A well tended garden opens onto **Pura Ulun Danu Bratan**★★★, a delightful little temple built on two islets with its *meru* reflecting elegantly in the water. Dedicated to the goddess of the lake, **Dewi Danu**, it is venerated by all the villagers living in the region downstream, whose fields are irrigated by the water from the lake.

Not far away stands a curious stone **stupa**★ ornamented with Buddhas.

To fully appreciate all the beauty of the place, it is best to come in the early morning when it is still deserted and silent, without the noise of engines and loudspeakers. As the sun rises opposite the temple, the mist covering the lake starts to drift away, gradually revealing the surrounding mountains. On the ridge a line of trees stands out against the sky, while to the east the summit of Mount Agung timidly emerges. On the lakeside the villagers go about their tasks: a man fishes with a net, another repaints his boat, while the women do the washing or soap their little ones from head to toe.

Continue along the road towards Singaraja. To continue on to the north coast or to Gitgit water-fall (see p 444), go straight on along the pretty winding road that leads to Singaraja. To continue this tour (see below), turn left after Pancasari, at the sign to Selat.

The lake road★

After **Pancasari**, where an imposing split gateway marks the entrance to the **Bali Handara Kosaido Country Club** *(see p 455, "Other things to do")*, a small road along a ridge heads west through fields of flowers. Soon it overlooks the blue waters of **Lake Buyan**, surrounded by market gardens, then those of little **Lake Tamblingan**, just beside it and visible through a row of trees.

Where the road forks, follow the signs to Tamblingan, then to Munduk.

A winding road leads to the village of **Munduk** with its small ageless houses stretching out along the road. A few buildings from the colonial era still remain but unfortunately corrugated iron is making noticeable inroads.

This region, which is targeted by a vast environmental protection programme and is trying to develop ecological tourism, offers some splendid **walking★** *(information from Puri Lumbung Cottages, see p 455, "Where to stay")*. Those fond of "losing" themselves off the beaten track, on foot or by car, should explore the **small byroads★★**

M Lemerle

(the road to Gesing, for example, which turns off left at the next village) through the hills and valleys. In the villages the women can be seen ceaselessly grinding coffee with mortar and pestle while chewing betel, the leaf with blood-red juice that stains the ground. During the harvest season when the pale green of the rice fields turns a golden yellow, bundles of the crop can be seen piled along the roadsides waiting for the workers to carry them to the village on their shoulders. And everywhere a delicate fragrance rises from the carpets of cloves drying in the sun.

Beyond the village of **Kayuputih** (or Banyuatis, as the two roads join up) where a superb **banyan tree** stands guard at the entrance to a temple, the main road goes through magnificent scenery, particularly around **Tunjuk** and **Bestala** where it affords broad **panoramas**** over terraced rice fields bristling here and there with coconut palms.

The road then meets the one to Pupuan. Turn left onto it around a hairpin bend for Antosari, or turn right for Seririt on the north coast (see map p 458-459).

Making the most of Lake Bratan

COMING AND GOING

By shuttle bus – Several buses daily to Bedugul or Candi Kuning from the main tourist resorts (Kuta, Sanur, Ubud, Lovina, etc). The *Perama* company is represented by the Ulun Danu restaurant in Candi Kuning.

By bemo – Bemo minibuses run a shuttle service between Denpasar (Ubung station) and Singaraja (Sukasada station). More frequent in the mornings. The little roads with panoramic views described in this tour are rarely served by bemo.

By car/By motorbike – The Denpasar-Bedugul road is good and well signposted, the secondary roads somewhat less.

ADDRESS BOOK

Telephone – *Wartel*, at the entrance to Bedugul village when coming from the south.

WHERE TO STAY

Bedugul and Candi Kuning have a certain number of hotels and losmen, mostly of mediocre quality and overpriced. In addition the service is often quite unfriendly and the food run-of-the-mill (NB, the ho-

tel restaurants generally close very early). But it is nevertheless pleasant to stay a night or two so as to make the most of the region.

● **Bedugul**

Modest

Dahlia Indah, Jl Bulit Catu, ☎ (0368) 212 33 – 20rm. ☈ Hot water. Sparsely furnished rooms but immaculately clean, set in a row in a little garden. There is no restaurant but the hotel is right in the village where there are several warung.

Average

Bukit Permai, on a bend just before the village, ☎ (0368) 214 43, ☎/Fax (0368) 214 45 – 13rm. ☈ ✗ Hot water. Several categories of rooms, big or small, with or without television. Most have quite a good view and a fireplace where a fire can be lit on cool evenings. The cheapest, although a bit rundown, have the advantage of being quieter.

● **Candi Kuning**

Modest to average

Ashram, ☎ (0368) 214 50, Fax (0368) 211 01 – 27rm. ☈ ✗ A whole range of prices depending on view and hot water supply. This is the only hotel on the shore of Lake Bratan. Its rooms have little charm but they are clean and staggered up the hillside facing the lake. Breakfast (avoid the pancakes!) can be eaten at the waterside so you have a good view of the sunrise.

Lila Graha Bungalows, ☎ (0368) 214 46 – 15rm. ⁑ ✗ Hot water. Adequate little rooms scattered amongst the greenery and sufficiently well above the road that runs alongside the lake. Pleasant terraces, mostly very private. In the suite (more expensive but also bigger) you can have a wood fire lit.

● Munduk

In the middle of the village a discreet sign on the left indicates these 3 little family guesthouses.

Modest

Guru Ratna Homestay, ☎ (0362) 928 12/925 14 – 3rm. ✗ Monastic rooms but a warm and very attentive welcome. Shared bathroom. Little terrace restaurant for breakfast and dinner only.

Average

Meme Surung and **Mekel Ragi**, ☎ (0362) 928 12 – 4rm. ✗ Rooms with Dutch colonial architecture, a little less austere than the previous entry. Pretty terraces giving onto the family garden where old women prepare offerings while chewing betel. A pleasant little restaurant with a lovely view. The price is still a little high for the level of comfort.

Luxury

⊛**Puri Lumbung Cottages**, above the village, ☎/Fax (0362) 928 10 – 17rm. ⁑ ✗ cc Hot water. Private pavilions designed along the lines of the old Balinese

rice granaries. The wood and bamboo architecture lends a warm, rustic character. The family rooms (twice as expensive) have fireplaces. From the little balconies you can see a few rice fields and in fine weather the panorama stretches as far as Java. A pretty garden and pleasant restaurant. Unfortunately it is all a little cramped. Meditation centre and yoga classes for those interested. Walks in the area can also be organised.

EATING OUT

● Pacung

Moderate to more select

Ume Luang, Jl Pacung, Jatiluwih Baturiti, ☎ (0368) 213 87. Daily 11am-4pm. A panoramic tourist restaurant that serves buffets of Indonesian specialities every lunchtime. Ordinary though reasonable cuisine. As the view is magnificent it is also worth stopping just for a drink.

● Bedugul-Candi Kuning

Basic to moderate

Most of the hotels and losmen mentioned in the "Where to stay" section have adjoining restaurants.

Moderate

Ulun Danu, ☎ (0368) 211 91. Closed evenings. Set in the grounds of the Taman Rekreasi. A wide choice, but of uneven quality.

OTHER THINGS TO DO

Bali Handara Kosaido Country Club, Pancasari, ☎ (0362) 226 46, Fax (0362) 230 48. One of the loveliest golf courses in the world, set in undulating grounds with gardens. Allow US$80-100.

Making the most of Lake Bratan

WEST BALI★
FROM KAPAL TO SERIRIT
Badung, Buleleng and Tabanan districts – Map p 458-459
Tour of about 210km - Allow at least 2 days
Slightly more arid climate than in the rest of the island

Not to be missed
The temples of Mengwi and Batukau.
Exploring the sea-bed around Pulau Menjangan.

And remember...
Avoid the rainy season from December to March.
Leave early for Menjangan and Batukau so as to enjoy the morning light.
Wear long clothing to visit the temples
(otherwise sarongs are available for hire on the spot).

West Bali does not figure on the major tourist routes and thus remains unvisited by the majority of visitors who simply travel through it in order to reach Java. And yet with its wild (but unfortunately dangerous) beaches, its temples with their noble *meru* looking out to sea and its vast forest and marine reserves, it is well worth spending a little time exploring it. Its proximity to Java has turned the area, the least fertile and most sparsely populated part of Bali, into a melting pot of different communities including Muslims from Java, Madura and Sulawesi, Catholic and Protestant Balinese minorities and villagers from the east of the island who took refuge here after Mount Agung's eruption in 1963.

Tanah Lot, a temple on the edge of the world

P. Bénet

456

Sea temples and mountain temples★★

Take the major Denpasar-Gilimanuk road heading towards Tabanan.

■ **Kapal** – *11km north of Denpasar.* A succession of shops selling religious souvenirs welcomes visitors all along the road through the village. Kapal is the ancient capital of the Mengwi kingdom, and has indeed oriented its activities to producing the altars and sculptures that adorn all the family temples on the island. Its inhabitants are happy to show visitors the way to **Pura Sada★**, where a majestic banyan tree stands guard at the entrance, opposite the elegant **split gateway**. Formerly the sanctuary of the Mengwi dynasty, this building is thought to date from the early 13C but the 1917 earthquake caused so much damage that it had to be restored in 1950. The temple's originality lies in its alignment of 64 little brick **altars** in several rows, which were possibly dedicated to the crew belonging to a ruler of the Javanese Majapahit dynasty who was shipwrecked while sailing to Bali. Another unusual feature is that the main altar is not a *meru* with roofs of thatch but a **red brick tower** with eleven tiers, similar to the Javanese *candi (see p 205)*. This could in fact be a royal funerary monument.

Leave Kapal and take the road north to Bedugul. Turn right just beyond the village of Bringkit.

■ **Mengwi** – *About 4km north of Kapal.* Mengwi, the second capital of one of the most powerful kingdoms of Bali up until 1891, when conflicts with neighbouring Badung and Tabanan lead to its downfall, is today no more than a peaceful village. In its centre stands one of the loveliest sanctuaries on the island, **Pura Taman Ayun★★** *(8am-6pm. Fee. Wear a sarong if you have bare legs. Visit in the early morning or late in the day to avoid the tourist coaches).* This state temple belonging to the former dynasty was built in the 17C by the ruler **Cokorda Munggu** when he transferred the seat of his kingdom from Kapal to Mengwi. The long building was restored and extended in 1937 and stands in a pleasant natural setting beside a lotus pond. Only the Balinese are allowed to pass through the great **gateway** leading to the third courtyard, but visitors can walk around the outside and from over the wall see the faithful carrying out their rituals. Right at the back are the **meru**, their slender, elegant outlines standing beside a variety of structures that either serve as altars honouring the royal family's ancestors or portray the holy mountains, Agung, Batur and Batukau. Just like all Balinese temples, Taman Ayun takes on another dimension during ceremonies such as its *odalan*, or anniversary celebration, when lively cockfights take place in the big **pavilion** *(wantilan)* to the right of the central aisle.

Go south from Mengwi (towards Denpasar) and turn right at Bringkit (towards Gilimanuk). About 4km further on, follow the signs to Tanah Lot on the left.

■ **Pura Tanah Lot★★** – *8am-6pm. Fee (the public are not allowed access to the temple itself). Wear a sarong if you have bare legs. It is better to visit during the day so as to avoid the crowds that arrive around 5pm.*

West Bali

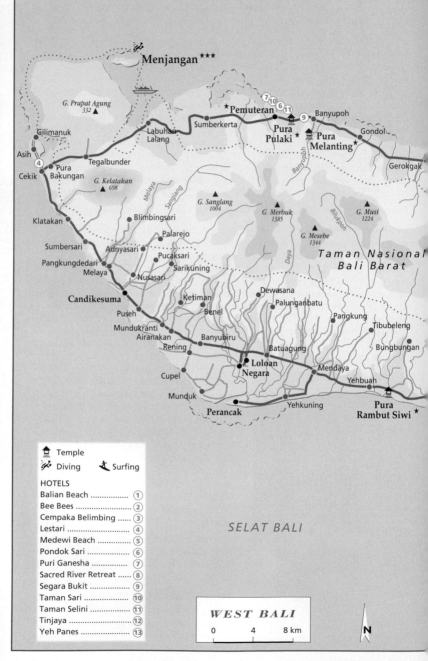

Menjangan ★★★

G. Prapat Agung
332

Gilimanuk
Asih
Cekik
Pura
Bakungan
Tegalbunder
G. Kelatakan
698

Labuhan
Lalang
Sumberkerta
★ Pemuteran
7 10 6 11
9 Banyupoh
Pura
Pulaki ★
Pura
Melanting ★
Gondol
Gerokgak

Banyupoh

Klatakan
Sumbersari
Pangkungdedari
Melaya
Blimbingsari
Palarejo
Adnyasari
Pucaksari
Sarikuning
Nusasari

G. Sanglang
1004
G. Merbuk
1385
G. Mesebe
1344
G. Musi
1224

Taman Nasional
Bali Barat

Candikesuma
Puseh
Mundukranti
Airanakan
Rening
Cupel
Munduk
Perancak
Ketiman
Benel
Banyubiru
Dewasana
Palunganbatu
Batuagung
Loloan
Negara
Yehkuning
Mendaya
Pangkung
Tibubeleng
Bungbungan
Yehbuah
Pura
Rambut Siwi ★

Melaya
Sangiang
Daya
Bilukpoh

SELAT BALI

🏛 Temple
🤿 Diving   🏄 Surfing

HOTELS
Balian Beach .... ①
Bee Bees .... ②
Cempaka Belimbing ...... ③
Lestari .... ④
Medewi Beach .... ⑤
Pondok Sari .... ⑥
Puri Ganesha .... ⑦
Sacred River Retreat ...... ⑧
Segara Bukit .... ⑨
Taman Sari .... ⑩
Taman Selini .... ⑪
Tinjaya .... ⑫
Yeh Panes .... ⑬

WEST BALI
0   4   8 km

N

458

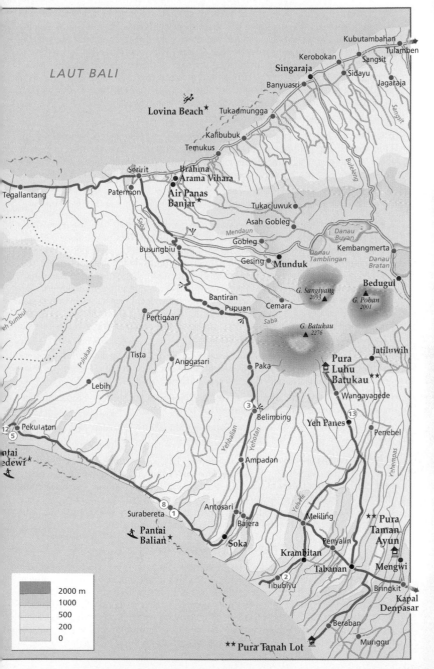

Perched on a black rock encircled by sand, around which the crashing waves swirl at high tide, the temple dedicated to the sea gods seems to be standing there braving the elements. According to legend it was erected in the 16C on the orders of the Javanese priest **Danghyang Nirartha** *(see opposite)*, who was stupefied by the beauty of the site. The small cliff running along the edge of the beach does indeed provide a superb **viewpoint★★★**, particularly at sunset when the black outlines of the *meru* stand out against the enflamed sky. But this is also the time when the tourists pour in, so the place does not escape its share of shops and pedlars.

Return to the Gilimanuk road.

The Tabanan region between Kapal and Antosari is criss-crossed by innumerable little roads leading off the main Denpasar-Gilimanuk road. Take the time to explore them and lose yourself among the villages, in the countryside inland or along the coast. There is some beautiful **scenery★★** to be discovered, in the heart of one of Bali's most prosperous rice-growing regions.

Go west out of Tabanan and take the pretty road right going up to Batukau (indicated by arrows).

■ **Pura Luhu Batukau★★** – *About 20km north of Tabanan. 8am-5pm. Fee. Wear a sarong if you have bare legs.* Clinging to the slopes of the holy Mount Batukau (2 276m), the temple emerges from a luxuriant green setting, a haven of peace and coolness often wrapped in mist. In the midst of tree ferns, crotons, bamboos and banana trees stand sculptures covered in green moss that provide a refuge for an extraordinary colony of **butterflies**. In the main courtyard stand several multiple-roofed **meru** dedicated to the ancestors of the Tabanan dynasty and to local protective divinities such as Maha Dewa, the goddess of the mountain. In the **pool** a short distance away, below, is a little islet bearing two altars, probably in honour of the goddess of Lake Tamblingan and the god of Mount Batukau.

It is possible to continue by taking the little road going off at Wangayagede, a little lower down, and travel through magnificent rice fields to Jatiluwih (see itinerary p 451). Otherwise return down the little road that comes out at Meliling on the main road.

It is worth stopping off halfway down at the **Yeh Panes** hot springs complex to relax in the **warm water swimming pools★★** *(see p 464, "Where to stay")*.

At Meliling go a little way back towards Denpasar, then take the Krambitan road that goes off opposite.

■ **Krambitan** – *About 24km from Batukau.* This sleepy village wakes up every evening for the dance and gamelan **performances** put on for tourists in the ancient palaces of the royal family of Tabanan, **Puri Agung** and **Puri Anyar**. The **calonarang** trances and **tektekan** performances, a noisy procession with big wooden bells and bamboo gamelan, the original aim of which is to chase away evil spirits and bring fertility to the region, attempt to revive vestiges of past grandeur.

The southwest coast★

Between Tabanan and Antosari, the Denpasar-Gilimanuk road winds through rice fields and banana and coconut plantations with the tall outline of Mount Batukau as backdrop. It joins the coast at **Soka**, a pretty bay where you can have lunch looking out over the ocean *(see p 465, "Eating out")*. Then it follows the coastline for miles where you will see vast **beaches of black sand** encumbered with rocks. These are dangerous for swimming as they are pounded by tumultuous waves, but the impressive breakers on the beaches of **Balian★** and **Medewi★** *(see p 464, "Where to stay")* are a paradise for the most daring **surfers**.

Bali

About 7km beyond Medewi beach a sign on the left indicates a little road to the temple, 400m further on.

■ **Pura Rambut Siwi★** – *8am-6pm. Donation. Wear a sarong if you have bare legs.* The temple stands on a fabulously beautiful site, perched on a promontory overlooking the sea in the midst of frangipani trees. Built in the 16C by the Javanese priest **Danghyang Nirartha**, it is said to house a relic of the holy man's hair. The legend tells of him miraculously halting an epidemic that was devastating the region. To the grateful villagers, Nirartha presented a lock of his hair *(rambut)*, which has since continued to be venerated *(siwi)* in the temple. A stairway leads down to the beach where several little caves contain secondary sanctuaries, including the **tiger cave** (where one of Bali's last remaining tigers is supposed to have taken up residence!) and the **temple of the holy spring**.

Continue along the main road for about 8km and turn left just before leaving Mendaya (before the bridge over the river). Allow another 10-15min to Perancak.

■ **Perancak** – Sitting in isolation at the mouth of a sea inlet, this little village wakes up in late afternoon when the **fishing boats leave★★** and the mountains and coconut palms stand silhouetted against the rays of the setting sun. If you follow the sound of music floating out from transistor radios, you will be able to watch these superb **multicoloured boats★★** and their crews getting ready to sail out to sea for the night. A sight not to be missed!

Return to the main road. If you do not wish to retrace your steps, you can return to the main road via some rather bad tracks that wind through the rice fields.

■ **Negara** – The name of this little town, the seat of the ancient kingdom of Jembrana, is known more than anything else for its **buffalo races** *(mekepung)*, which in theory take place in the surrounding area between August and November *(information available on the spot or in Denpasar tourist office)*. These races, probably originally brought over from the island of Madura *(see p 328)*, are associated with traditional rites to honour agricultural divinities and attract their favours for the coming harvest. The event takes the form of a competition between sumptuously harnessed buffaloes pulling little two-wheeled carts in pairs. In addition to their speed, the driver's style and the beauty of the harness are also taken into consideration in deciding on the winners.

The Negara region is also famous for its surprising **musical tournaments** in which impressive orchestras of giant instruments made of brightly painted bamboo *(jegog mebarung)* or, more rarely, oversized drums *(kendang mebarung)* that may be up to one metre across and two or three metres high, compete with each other. The result is so powerful that the very air vibrates for kilometres around!

Perancak: the fishermen's flamboyant departure

R Marca

You can make a detour through **Loloan**, a village located about 1km from the centre of town (*ask the locals to show you the way*), where in the 17C a Muslim community of Bugis sailors settled. This little outing will plunge you into a totally different atmosphere in which mosques replace temples and women are veiled. There are also some remaining **traditional houses** on stilts to be seen, often very dilapidated.

Continue towards Gilimanuk.

Halfway between Negara and Gilimanuk, the great bay of **Candikesuma** with its swathe of black sand fringed with coconut palms is worth a mention, for it is the only beach where it is not dangerous to swim.

The West Bali National Park★★
(Taman Nasional Bali Barat)

Fee and compulsory guide. It is better to go to the office at Labuhan Lalang (7am-2pm), about 10km east of Gilimanuk, as it distinctly more efficient than the one at Cekik. It is better to organise an outing the day before so as to set out when it is still cool. Various possibilities are available, from a short 2hr walk to a 2-day hiking trip with tents and sleeping-bags provided. It is as well to know, however, that a short walk is not sufficient to explore the interesting parts.

The national park covers almost 80 000sqkm, or virtually all of the entire mountain region of West Bali. The eastern part is worked for its forest resources whereas the west remains wild, being officially devoted to the preservation of rare species. The park also covers some few thousand hectares of sea-bed around Pulau Menjangan.

Forest walks
The forest that covers the mountain slopes up to a height of 1 500m has many facets. The south side of the massif, exposed to the rains, is covered in dense tropical vegetation that remains green all year round. The less damp north side is the domain of deciduous trees, whereas mangroves have taken over the shores of the island's westernmost tip, although various species of palm tree are also found.

In this maze of greenery live some rare animals and birds such as the **Bali starling** (on the island of Menjangan), the island's only endemic species. A programme has been implemented to attempt to save the bird, of which only a few specimens survive. The last remaining **Bali tigers** are also said to have taken refuge in the park, although none have been seen for several decades now. On the other hand, you are more likely to spot deer and monkeys, iguanas, antelopes or even leopards, as well as a multitude of birds.

The Pulau Menjangan Maritime Park★★★
7am-2pm (visibility is best between 10am and 12noon). Boats leave from Labuhan Lalang (allow 30min). Fee and compulsory guide. Hire of masks, snorkels and flippers on the spot. It is possible to buy provisions and lunch near the jetty. For scuba diving go to the diving clubs in the hotels in Pemuteran (see p 465, "Where to stay") or Lovina (see p 447).

Visitors can go around the island but it is under the water that the real show takes place. Once equipped with masks and flippers, you dive into a fairytale polychrome aquarium – all the richest fauna in Bali seems to have gathered together in these coral reefs. Following the delicate outline of the butterfly fish, listening to the parrot fish nibbling the coral, playing with the wriggly little clown fish in the clumps of sea anemones – it is a question of where to look next! More mind-blowing sensations are to be experienced by scrutinising the deepest parts where rays, turtles, sharks and other "big fish" can sometimes be spotted.

The northwest coast*

Like a monotonous asphalt ribbon, the coast road goes through a succession of small villages where temples and mosques alternate. Here it seems that each family cultivates its own little plot of vines spiked with coconut palms, banana trees, mango trees and bamboos. When in season, the flamboyant trees touch up the picture in bright shades of yellow and red, whereas the peaks in the national park, hidden in everthreatening clouds, watch over the deserted beaches stretching out along the coast.

Follow the coast road east.

■ **Pemuteran*** – The big, shady, sandy cove that forms Pemuteran beach is a pleasant place to stay and it is here that the most agreeable hotels in West Bali are to be found, making it an ideal base for exploring the wealth of Pulau Menjangan.

■ **Pura Pulaki*** – *On the right hand side of the road.* The pretty grey stone temple climbing up the mountainside, thought to have been built by the Javanese priest **Danghyang Nirartha** *(see p 461)*, has a splendid **view*** out over the ocean. But you should watch out for the monkeys that inhabit the sanctuary as they will steal glasses, hats or cameras with amazing dexterity!

Continue along the coast road and turn right at the sign to the temple (PR = pura).

A charming little road lined with flamboyant trees and vines leads to **Pura Melanting***, 2km from the main road. In this peaceful environment, at the foot of a mountain covered in luxuriant vegetation, the temple emerges from among the flowers. A fine stairway flanked by *naga* (mythological serpents) and stylised lotus flowers leads to the entrance gateway. The sanctuary courtyards, unfortunately badly maintained, are of no particular interest.

From Seririt you can continue along the north coast to Lovina and Singaraja (see p 444) or return south along the route described below, and so reach the lake region by taking the road to Munduk (see p 453).

Returning south along the Pupuan road**

54km from Seririt to Antosari. Allow 90min-2hr. From Seririt a road climbs up towards the mountains through a magnificent scenery of **terraced rice fields***, particularly after Pupuan, before heading down to the south of the island where it comes out at Antosari on the main Denpasar-Gilimanuk road.

West Bali

Making the most of West Bali

COMING AND GOING

By car – The only way to explore this region freely. The roads are good and it is quite easy to find your way around.

By bemo – Between Denpasar (Ubung station) and Gilimanuk, *bemo* minibuses serve Kapal, Kediri, Tambanan, Kerambitan, Batukau and Tanah Lot. Services are less frequent along the Gilimanuk-Singaraja road. NB, services generally stop quite early in the afternoon and they are much less frequent along small roads than on the main coast road.

By bus – Buses and more direct and faster shuttle buses link Denpasar and Lovina with Gilimanuk. It is possible to get off along the way.

WHERE TO STAY

● Penatahan

Luxury

Yeh Panes Natural Hot Spring and Spa, Jl Batukau, ☎ (0361) 26 23 56, ☎/Fax (0361) 75 24 11 – 16rm. ⌁ ▤ ⌖ Hot water. Lovely, comfortable rooms on different levels, in the midst of coconut palms. They are nicely spaced out, giving total peace and quiet. It is also possible to enjoy the hot spring without staying here. There are 9 pools of hot water carved out of the rock, as well as a big, refreshing swimming pool.

● Tibubiyu

Average

Bee Bees, 4km from Kerambitan, ☎/Fax (0361) 23 60 21 – 5rm. ⌁ ⌖ ✗ Rustic all-bamboo bungalows with 2 upstairs bedrooms and an open-air bathroom decorated with plants. Meals are taken facing the rice fields. Positively heavenly peace: a 10min walk from Pasut's wild beach (beware of waves and currents as swimming is dangerous).

● Balian beach

Average

Balian Beach Bungalows, ☎/Fax (0361) 81 30 17, bobbali@denpasar.wasantara.net.id – 10rm. ⌁ ⌖ ✗ cc A peaceful place in the midst of coconut palms, looking out over rice fields, the river mouth and the ocean (about 300m away). All the rooms are different and more or less well positioned and appointed. Room 8 has the best view plus a charming open-air bathroom. Swimming is dangerous but surfing is possible. It is better to bathe in the river below (except after heavy rain, so ask first). Swimming pool on its way.

High end

Sacred River Retreat, ☎/Fax (0361) 73 09 04 – 15rm. ⌁ ⌖ ✗ ⌖ cc Small private bungalows in a rustic style with verandah and hidden in greenery. Big Jacuzzi and little swimming pool. A new-age ambience for those interested in yoga, meditation, massage and transcendental seminars.

● Medewi beach

Modest

Tinjaya Bungalows, ☎ (0365) 429 45 – 8rm. ⌁ ⌖ ⌖ Basic all-bamboo rooms with Turkish-style toilets. Comfort is minimal but the setting is pleasant, on a beach covered with prahu boats. There are also more comfortable rooms but at twice the price and close to the very busy main road.

Luxury

Medewi Beach Cottages, ☎ (0365) 400 29/400 30, Fax (0365) 415 55/ 400 34 – 28rm. ⌁ ▤ / ⌖ ⌀ ⏹ ✗ ⌖ ⌖ cc Hot water and air conditioning in the most expensive rooms. Avoid the standard ones (in the Modest category) which are cheerless and right on the road. The others do not have much charm but give onto the garden, the swimming pool or the sea.

● Cekik

Modest to average

Lestari Homestay, Jl Raya Gilimanuk, ☎ (365) 615 04 – 15rm. ⌁ ▤ / ⌖ ✗ This is the best place in Gilimanuk (for want of any other!). It has no charm but is clean. Some rooms have an open-air bathroom and television. 5 different rates. The most expensive have air conditioning and hot water. The cheapest are Spartan.

● Pemuteran

High end to luxury

Pondok Sari Beach Bungalows, ☎/Fax (0362) 923 37 – 22rm. ⌁ ▤ / ⌖

✗ ⚶ cc Hot water in the air-conditioned rooms. Lovely bungalows furnished in bamboo and decorated with ikats. Charming open-air bathrooms. Diving club adjacent to the hotel.

Luxury

⚶**Taman Sari Bali**, ☏ (0362) 926 23/ (0361) 28 80 96/28 68 79, Fax (0361) 28 62 97 – 29rm. ⚟ 🍽 / ⤨ ✗ ⚶ cc Hot water in the air-conditioned rooms. Thatched bungalows scattered about a vast garden, with pretty open-air bathrooms. Pleasant restaurant giving onto the beach and diving club adjacent to the hotel. Another excellent hotel but more expensive than the previous entry. There will soon be a swimming pool.

Super deluxe

⚶**Puri Ganesha Villas**, ☏ (0361) 26 16 10, Fax (0361) 26 16 11, ☏/Fax (0362) 934 33 – 4rm. ⚟ 🍽 ⤨ ℘ ✗ ⤸ ⚶ cc Sumptuous thatched villas, each with a big living room, kitchen, 2 bedrooms, a superb open-air bathroom and a private swimming pool. The hostess designed the architecture and the interior decoration herself down to the smallest detail and the result is very successful. Personalised reception and flavourful cuisine served on request and according to what you feel like. In addition, the villas stand just opposite the loveliest part of the sea bed around Pemuteran. Negotiable prices.

● **Banyupoh**

Average

Segara Bukit Cottages – 9rm. ⚟ ⤨ ✗ ⚶ Rooms lined up facing a garden that is still rather bare, between the road and the sea. Reasonable but with no great charm. Pleasant little restaurant facing a beach of black sand.

● **Belimbing**

Luxury

Cempaka Belimbing Guest Villas, ☏ (0361) 75 31 74/75 15 17, Fax (0361) 75 27 77 / 75 75 86 – 6rm. ⚟ ⤨ ℘ tv ✗ ⤸ cc Hot water. The first hotel here and the most recent in the region has comfortable private bungalows on a slope above the rice fields, in an enchantingly peaceful setting. The Cambodja room is the most charming, the others being generally a little cold. Interesting walks are organised around the villages and spice plantations in the vicinity.

EATING OUT

Virtually all the hotels mentioned above have restaurants open to everyone.

● **Soka**

Moderate

Soka Indah Restaurant. Closed evenings. Lunch is served in little pavilions on the beach facing the wild ocean.

● **Medewi**

Basic to moderate

The unpretentious little restaurant facing the beach is ideal for watching the surfers dance over the waves. The food is, however, better at the place below.

Kafe Mai Malu, Jl Pantai Medewi (the street that goes from the main road to the beach). Unexciting setting and location. Salads plus classic Indonesian and Chinese dishes, all of acceptable quality.

● **Belimbing**

Moderate to more select

Cafe Belimbing, on the road to Pupuan. Closed evenings. A terrace looking out over the road and the terraced rice fields. The noise is compensated for by the splendid view and the quality of the cuisine. Delicious curry.

Making the most of West Bali

In a Sasak village (Sade), conversation between two elders

P Bénet

LOMBOK

Moving from Bali to Lombok means moving into a different world: the southern zone of the Indonesian archipelago begins on the eastern side of the famous "Wallace Line" *(see p 16)*, characterised by a different type of natural environment. After the gentle harmony of Bali, the landscapes of Lombok strike one as highly distinctive. The "chilli" island – its name in Indonesian – looks wilder and tougher, in a word, more highly spiced.

It is also varied. Indeed, there is nothing in common between the crops of the **central plain**, with its heavy rainfall, and the **southern hillsides** clad in dry savannah and scrub. You see the ochre shades of the latter again on the northern flank of **Mount Rinjani**, while on the south of the volcano green rice fields have been carved out in terraces like giant steps. A few idyllic sites are strung out along the southern coastline, including beaches of white sand and deep bays with turquoise water covering shimmering corals – a gallery of images to observe from the top of the volcano, spanning one of the richest panoramic views of the whole archipelago.

These landscapes do, however, have something in common – a hot climate, very hot indeed during the dry season (May to October). The only cool zone is on the upper slopes of Mount Rinjani, with its crest lost in the clouds at an altitude of 3 726m. Rinjani is a holy mountain, a god of stone and ash from which Lombok derives its fertility but also its problems.

In both its landscapes and its different people, the island is a treasure for the traveller in search of authenticity. True, it attracts increasing numbers of visitors and its hotel infrastructure has expanded considerably *(see p 475-476, "Making the most of Mataram")*. But you only need to step off the beaten track to discover a unique culture that combines Islam and animist traditions. And it is not unusual for a tourist passing through a village to attract a crowd and be given noisy greetings of "Hello, misterrr!"

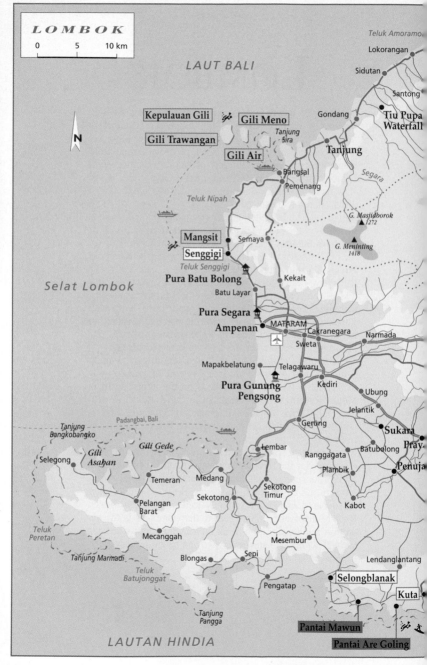

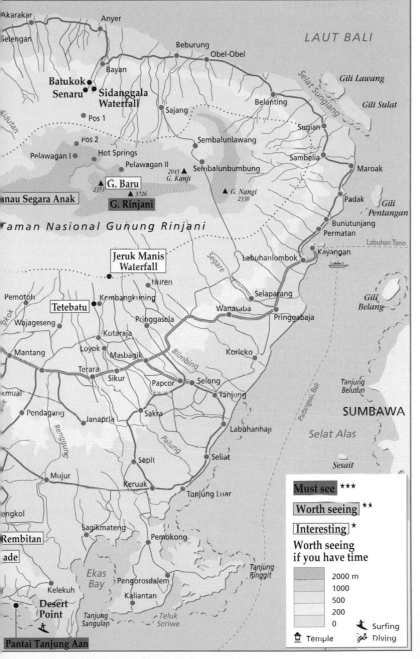

LAUT BALI

Akarakar
Anyer
Selengan
Beburung
Obel-Obel
Bayan
Gili Lawang
Batukok
Senaru
Sidanggala
Waterfall
Gili Sulat
Belanting
Pos 1
Sajang
Sugian
Pos 2
Sembalunlawang
Sambelia
Pelawagan I
Hot Springs
Maroak
Pelawagan II
2045 ▲
G. Kanji
Sembalunbumbung
Padak
anau Segara Anak
▲ 2351
G. Baru
▲ 3726
G. Rinjani
▲ G. Nangi
2330
Gili
Pentangan
Taman Nasional Gunung Rinjani
Bunutunjang
Permatan
Labuhan Tano
Jeruk Manis
Waterfall
Segare
Labuhanlombok
Kayangan
Duren
Pemotoh
Kembangkuning
Selaparang
Gili
Belang
Tetebatu
Pringgasela
Wanasaba
Pringgabaja
Wajageseng
Kotaraja
Mantang
Loyok
Masbagik
Korleko
Blimbing
Terara
Sikur
Papcor
Selong
kmual
Pendagang
Janaprla
Sakra
Tanjung
Tanjung
Belusun
SUMBAWA
Labuhanhaji
Selat Alas
Mujur
Sepit
Seliat
Keruak
Sesait
engkol
Tanjung Luar
Sagikmateng
Pemokong
Rembitan
ade
Tanjung
Ringgit
Ekas
Bay
Kelekuh
Pengorosdalem
Desert
Point
Kaliantan
Tanjung
Sangulan
Teluk
Seriwe
Pantai Tanjung Aan

Must see ★★★
Worth seeing ★★
Interesting ★
Worth seeing
if you have time

2000 m
1000
500
200
0

⚓ Surfing

⛩ Temple   🏊 Diving

The first settlers

The earliest human colonisation of Lombok (and of Sumbawa) probably dates back 30 000 or even 50 000 years. The oldest traces of settlement, however, date only from the 4th millennium, when a group of Austronesians (see p 31) set sail from the Philippines via Sulawesi. They were to become Lombok's first true community, ancestors of the **Sasak**. These animist farmers, faithful to their ancestor worship, developed livestock breeding and pottery. Between 500 and 300 BC the **Dongson civilisation** expanded in its turn in the archipelago (see p 31), as far as Timor, bringing with it the art of making bronze.

The pre-Islamic history of Lombok has not yet been written. However, through the 14C Javanese account in *Negara Kertagama*, we know that for a time the island came under the yoke of minor Sasak kings whose authority barely exceeded a few villages. The exception was **Selaparang**, whose authority extended over the whole of the east of the island.

From Islam to independence

Matters changed with the appearance of Islam, imported from Java in the early 16C. The new religion swiftly evolved into a syncretic form with elements of Hinduism and animism. This "oriental style" of Islam was barely affected when **Muslims from Makassar** (Sulawesi) settled in the east of the island in the following century.

The Balinese conquest – During the same period, however, the Balinese invaded the west coast, where their influence had already been felt for a long time. They were quick to push towards the east and, in 1678, they even succeeded in overthrowing the kingdom of Selaparang. However, the colonisation of the eastern part of the island was not complete until after the victory of **Mataram**, in 1838, nearly two hundred years later! This very slow conquest perhaps explains why Balinese influences, apart from farming with irrigation, were to remain limited to the west of the island.

Islam "Sasak style"

Although most Sasaks are now Muslim, their Islam is coloured by animist traditions. Nearly 250 000 of them are "Wetu Telu", faithful to the original belief in their ancestors and in nature, and followers of a very temperate form of Islam. They respect the "threefold" principle of obedience to God, to the village chief and to their parents, but they are not required to pray five times a day, and observe a very relaxed form of Ramadan. The gateway to Islam in Lombok, Bayan (in the north of the island) has remained the centre of their culture. However, their form of belief is diminishing in the face of hostility from the government, which does not recognise them, and from orthodox Muslims who, having tried to convert them (1927-33), turned instead to persecuting them (1965). Today there are few Wetu Telu who proclaim their faith and, since the faith does not accept the membership of other Muslims, it seems condemned to disappear sooner or later.

The Batavian era – In 1894, under the pretext of helping the Sasaks, whose relationship with the Balinese was always stormy, the Dutch invaded Lombok. Routed once, they returned to eliminate Mataram and loot the palace of Cakra; a bitter battle in which hundreds of Balinese lost their lives. The new occupying forces exploited the island and, despite the spread of irrigation systems, the rapidly expanding population sank into destitution.

In Lombok the attempted *coup d'état* in 1965 took the form of severe repression that ended in the massacre of the island's Chinese and Communists. This tragic episode was intensified a year later by a fresh period of famine, the result of poor harvests.

Today, Lombok, which with Sumbawa constitutes the province of West Nusa Tenggara, has recovered a degree of prosperity through its fishing and agriculture (rice, tobacco, soya, coffee, onions, pimentos and spices), activities that still employ most of the population. Above all, the tourist industry is expanding year by year, and the island is opening up to the outside world, and exporting its handicrafts. But is the Sasak culture, still highly traditional, truly ready to face this new challenge?

A Sasak-dominated island

Compared to other islands, such as Java or Sulawesi, the population of Lombok (2.4 million) is relatively homogeneous: the **Sasaks** themselves make up nearly 90% of the population, with Hindu **Balinese** (in the west) constituting the most substantial minority (9%). The remainder of the population consists of urban groups – **Chinese**, **Arab** and **Javanese** – while the small **Bugis** and **Sumbawanese** communities are concentrated on the east coast.

The average density (over 500 inhabitants per square kilometre) hides very substantial geographical disparities: although it reaches peaks in the central plain, the south is almost empty. This extreme imbalance poses serious problems for the population on the plain in terms of supplies and hygiene, resulting in Lombok holding the national record for infant mortality.

A unique range of arts and crafts

Lombok is famous for its arts and crafts, the ancestral inheritance of the Sasaks. The ikats in particular are remarkable for the diversity of their designs and the brilliance of their colours, even though the use of natural thread and colourings has almost vanished in recent years in favour of synthetic materials (*see p 66 and sidebar, p 494*). Another flagship of local arts and crafts is **pottery**, which is highly valued for its plain and elegant lines, even though the low-temperature manufacturing process makes the pieces fragile. **Basketry** and wickerwork are equally impressive (beautiful round birdcages are an island speciality), as is work in **wood** and **bamboo**, which is varied and delicate, such as the **lacquer ware of Sayang Sayang** with its shimmering colours.

Island dances

Although Sasak arts and crafts demonstrate great originality, other artistic forms have borrowed heavily from neighbouring islands. The influence of Java and Bali in particular is strongly evident in the **performing arts** through the **gamelan** (*gamelan oncer* or *kendang belek*), which accompanies singing, theatrical performances and above all the famous **tari oncer**, in which two percussionists mime a warlike confrontation.

During your travels you may have the chance to see a **Sasak tembang** performance, a form of sung poetry, or a cupak **grantang**, a very ancient Hindu dance (of surprising sensuality for a nation professing the Muslim faith!) featuring the Javanese hero Panji.

The **Arab and Malaysian cultures** have mainly influenced the religious arts. Although the repertoire is still inspired by the traditional gamelan, the island's bronze instruments have been banished in favour of the Middle-Eastern rebab. Similarly, the Sasak shadow theatre, the **wayang sasak** – derived from the Javanese *wayang kulit* –, has Amir Hamza, uncle of the Prophet Muhammad, as its hero.

Lombok

THE MATARAM CONURBATION
Capital of West Nusa Tenggara Province
Map p 468-469 – Pop 250 000
Hot dry climate (rainy season from November to March)

Not to be missed
The old quarter of Ampenan and the fishing boats setting out to sea.

And remember...
Stroll about in Ampenan, but do not linger in the rest of the
conurbation, which offers little of interest.
Avoid using a middleman to find a hotel
or to hire a vehicle (except at your hotel).

The provincial capital of Mataram now consists of a substantial conurbation that includes the neighbouring towns of Ampenan, Cakranegara and Sweta. It stretches 10km from east to west, with its soulless buildings lined up along an apparently endless avenue, changing name and appearance with the districts that it slices through. From the little fishing port of Ampenan – the only true point of interest in the conurbation –, Jalan Pejanggik plunges into the heart of Mataram, a grid of dreary streets lined with administrative buildings and prosperous villas. Then it passes through Cakranegara, Lombok's main commercial centre, with several weaving workshops, before it reaches Sweta, formerly the island's main bus terminus.

Ampenan (A1-A2)
*Allow around 2hr, on foot and by bemo. The junction of Saleh Sungkar,
Koperasi and Yos Sudarso is a good departure point for exploring the old quarter.*

What was once Lombok's main port is today no more than a small peaceful town with pretty Dutch, Arab and Chinese houses, where life comes to a halt at the hottest time of day. If you can resist the call of a siesta, set off on foot to explore

Ampenan beach: colourful prahu boats and oil tanks

M. S. Yamashita/Rapho

Lombok

the lanes of the **Arab and Chinese quarters** (A1), still safe from concrete, where you can see descendants of Chinese and Arabs with light-coloured eyes, evidence of a past when the port drew in traders from the ends of the earth. To the west, little **Jalan Koperasi** has a variety of stalls, antique dealers and *warung* strung out along it. As you pass, your eye is caught by a small **Chinese temple** and the faded façades of deserted warehouses.

After 300m, the street ends at the **beach**, a desolate strip of sand dominated to the right by the great storage tanks of Pertamina, the national oil company. To the left, *prahus* are lined up with their prows facing the sea, ready to depart, while their captains play dominoes and wait for the heat to subside. The sight of this **multicoloured fleet*** putting to sea, with Mount Agung, on Bali, as backdrop, is superb.

From here, take a bemo to Mataram, get out opposite the Natour Hotel and walk up Jl Pajajaran for about 500m. This will save you a very long detour.

The best way to explore the cultural riches of Lombok and Sumbawa is to visit the little **Nusa Tenggara Ethnographic Museum** (Museum Negeri Propinsi Nusa Tenggara Barat) (A2) (*Jl Panji Tilar, 8am-4pm; closed Monday, fee, allow 30min*). Beyond the hall of fossils and stuffed animals you will find all sorts of handicrafts – sculptures, Chinese porcelain, basketwork, wooden chests, Sasak ikats and Sumbawa *songkets* (embroideries with gold or silver thread), as well as a beautiful collection of **Dongson and Hindu bronzes**. Don't miss the **jewellery and gold plate**** (dishes, kris, etc), the highlight of the museum.

Continue eastwards across Mataram. At the junction of Jl Bung Hatta (north) and Bung Karno (south), you reach Cakranegara. Jl Prjanggik now becomes Jl Selaparang.

Cakranegara (C2-D2)
Allow around 2hr, by bemo.

Encouraged by its very active Chinese community the commercial vocation of "Cakra" (pronounced "Chakra") is very much in evidence. Shops selling clothes or electronics, car dealers and cassette sellers jostle each other for space all along the main avenue, alongside a number of workshops weaving ikats. This is where you should go to find the finest sarongs (*see "Making the most of Mataram"*).

The only remaining trace of the Balinese princes' former capital, **Pura Meru** (C1) (1720) is Lombok's largest Hindu temple (*Jl Selaparang, donation at the entrance*). Devoted to the *tri loka*, the trinity of Siva-Vishnu-Brahma, the sanctuary has three elegant **meru**. On the other side of the avenue is the royal palace and its garden, the **Puri Mayura** (C1) ("Water Palace"), protected by a red brick wall. In the middle of a large pool crushed by the heat stands the **Bale Kambang** pavilion, the seat of the former court of justice (1744), at which the lords of Bali assembled. In 1894 this was the site of a pyrrhic victory when the Balinese defeated the Dutch.

You leave the conurbation of Mataram by bus from the **Bertais** terminus (D2), which has replaced the **Sweta** terminus (*4km east of Cakranegara, by bemo*). The **Sweta textiles market*** has followed suite and now occupies a large concrete building close to the new terminus. Still very lively and overflowing with fabrics, local handicrafts, fruit and spices, this provides the opportunity for a whole-hearted plunge into crowds, scents and colours.

Around Mataram

From Mataram you can escape eastwards to explore some sacred sites hidden in the countryside. There is the **Lingsar Temple** (Pura Lingsar, beyond D1) (*2km northeast of Cakranegara, along Jl Gora*), the main place of worship for the **Wetu Telu** Muslims (*see*

The Mataram conurbation

Lombok

G. Guérard

Cakranegara, the peaceful Puri Mayura

sidebar, p 470), and also for Hindus who celebrate *Pujawali* here, a rice festival in honour of Batara, the god of Mount Rinjani.

From here you can continue to the **Hindu temple of Suranadi** (beyond D2), (*4km northeast of Sweta, along Jl Sandubaya*). As one of the island's most sacred sanctuaries it draws pilgrims from all over Lombok. In a charming garden, a spring fed by water from the slopes of Rinjani keeps the pools full.

To the east, visit **Narmada** (*10km from Sweta, along Jl Sandubaya*), where in 1805 the king of Mataram ordered the construction of the **Kasala Temple** (Pura Kasala) (beyond D2). When he became too old to climb Rinjani – the sacred mountain – the king decided to build a replica of it on a human scale, a little sanctuary with its own pool.

Lastly, if you have the time, make a final expedition to the south (*7km from Mataram, along Jl Gajah Mada*) to **Gunung Pengsong Temple** (beyond B3) perched on a rocky hillside (*reached by a flight of 236 steps!*). This is worth the trip above all for the fine **panorama★** from the site over the central plain and the volcano. Dedicated to Dewi Sri, the goddess of rice, this Balinese sanctuary comes to life at every harvest for the ritual sacrifice of a buffalo. When they are not accompanying the rare tourists to the summit, the local boys spend their time firing stones from their catapults at the monkeys!

Making the most of Mataram

COMING AND GOING

By air – Selaparang airport (B1) is 4km north of Ampenan. Several connecting flights daily to and from Bali, virtually the only available route for Java or Sulawesi. Flights to the east (Sumbawa, Flores, Timor and Sumba) are offered by Merpati.

By boat – 6 ferries run between Padangbai (Bali) and Lembar (Lombok). The crossing lasts between 4 and 5hr, with departures in both directions every 90min, from midnight. Travel agents can arrange transport to include boat and minibus for departures and arrivals.

A speedboat offers two crossings a day (2hr30min) between Benoa (Bali) and Lembar, but it costs almost as much as flying. **Mabua's** Agency, ☎ (0364) 811 95 (Lombok), ☎ (0361) 723 70 (Bali).

By bus – Lombok's main terminal is at Bertais.

By minibus – At Lembar, you will be assailed by *bemo* touts for Mataram (22km) or Senggigi. To avoid any cheating, take one that already has passengers, or travel in a group.

By car – In theory, vehicles hired in Bali should have a permit to be taken off the island. At Padangbai, people will offer to arrange this for you, for a price, of course.

GETTING AROUND

By bemo – The main form of public transport, *bemos* use all the major thoroughfares. Be warned, one-way streets occasionally mean considerable detours.

By taxi – Taxi Lombok, ☎ (0364) 270 00;
Lendang Express, ☎ (0364) 246 88.

By cidomo – A small horse-drawn two-wheeled buggy. If you are not in a hurry!

By motorbike – Ask for information at your hotel.

Car rental – The rates are higher than in Bali, but this is very convenient for getting around town and going to Senggigi. Bargain, and make sure you get an exact price for accidental damage excess. **Oriental** (or **Pak Hommy**), Jl Selaparang, Gang Kepundung II/4 (C2), ☎ and Fax (0364)

312 08. Somewhat difficult to find, but the prices are fair. ("Jimny", for two, or four people squeezed in, or "Kijang Super", more comfortable). **Rinjani**, Jl Bung Karno 6B (B2-C2), in front of the Granada Hotel, ☎ (0364) 322 59.

ADDRESS BOOK

Tourist information – Jl Langko 70, Mataram (A1). Monday-Thursday, 7am-2pm, Friday 7-11am, Saturday 7am-12noon. Reasonably well supplied. It offers brochures in English, and maps.

Bank/Currency exchange – Plenty of banks and ATM cash dispensers, but try to change your currency before you reach Lombok, where the rates are unfavourable. You will also find exchange places in the **Cilinaya** commercial centre (C2).

Bank Duta, Jl Pejanggik 6/ (C2). ATM and exchange desk until 3pm.

Bank BCA (C2), next door to the above. ATM and exchange desk in the mornings.

Post office/Telephone – You will find a telephone agency and post office opposite the tourist office (A1). The town also has numerous Wartel, mainly in Jl Cokroaminoto (B1-B2). **Main Post office**, Jl Sriwijaya (B2), Mataram.

Airline companies – Bourag, Selaparang Hotel, Jl Pejanggik 4 (C2), Cakranegara, ☎ (0364) 273 33;
Garuda, Lombok Raya Hotel (C2), Jl Panca Usaha 11, Cakranegara, ☎ (0364) 379 50;
Merpati, Jl Selaparang 10 (C2), Cakranegara, ☎ (0364) 367 45.

WHERE TO STAY

Staying overnight here has no advantage unless you are en route for Sumbawa and Flores.

Modest

Triguna, Jl Koperasi 78, Ampenan, ☎ (0364) 317 05. 📖 ✗ Low price, well-placed and pleasant, with verandah and garden. For anyone preparing to climb Rinjani, the hotel is a mine of information. If it is full, try the other hotels in the street, all in the same category. Hire of motorbikes and cars.

Suradipa Homestay, Jl Cokroaminoto, gang Macan VII n° 4, Mataram, ☎ (0364) 245 76 ⚐ 🍴 ✕ A place for seasoned travellers, where you can find books to consult and access to the Internet.

Average

Natour (Wisma Melati), Jl Yos Sudarso 4, Ampenan, ☎ (0364) 237 80 – 24rm. ⚐ 🗏 ✕ Quiet, well located (near the tourist office), with a garden. The rooms are comfortable but a little expensive. Don't hesitate to bargain.

Granada, Jl Bung Karno, Mataram, ☎ (0364) 360 15 – 100rm. ⚐🗏 📺 🏊 CC A charming establishment: the building is elegant and the aviary in the garden adds an exotic note. The rooms are impeccable.

EATING OUT

● Ampenan

Basic to moderate

Jl Koperasi is full of small cheap restaurants, including the **Rainbow** (A1), towards the beach. Simple cuisine. The owner, a reggae fan, hires out cars and gives interesting information about Lombok.

Betawi, Jl Yos Sudarso 152 (A1), ☎ (0364) 236 09. 8am-11pm. The restaurant is well ventilated, but you may prefer the terrace, even though it overlooks a somewhat noisy crossroads. Indonesian and Western cuisine, with French baguettes, and yoghurts.

Pondok Ampenan, Jl Yos Sudarso 194 (A1), on the beach, ☎ (0364) 343 53. 9am-1am; closed on Monday. Established in a former 19C bank with high ceilings and a beautiful verandah overlooking the sea. It offers Indonesian cooking, seafood and salads. Groups play music at weekends.

● Cakranegara

Try the confectionery and local specialities in the **New Mirasa** cake-shop, Jl A A Gede Ngurah (C2), near the market. You will not know what to buy, so will have to experiment.

OTHER THINGS TO DO

Travel agency – Perama Travel Club, Jl Pejanggik 66 (C2), Mataram, ☎ (0364) 359 28. Offers car hire (a little expensive), bus transport and tours to Lombok and Sumbawa.

Horse racing – Selagalas Stadium, 2km northeast of Cakranegara, towards Lilir. A thrilling event that always has a tremendous atmosphere. Sunday, particularly in August and December.

SHOPPING GUIDE

Market – In **Bertais** (D2), you can find a wide selection of Sasak handicrafts and fabrics (although most of the ikats come from the factories in Jepara, in Java). Remember that the sight of a tourist tends to put prices up: bargain firmly – divide by two to begin with, or even by three, and don't give way!

Shopping centres – Cilinaya Shopping Center, Jl Pejanggik (C2), Mataram. **Cakra Plaza**, Jl Pejanggik, Cakranegara.

Antiques, handicrafts – In Ampenan, Jl Saleh Sungkar (A1) is full of small shops selling wooden items and basketry. At **Citra**, Jl Yos Sudarso 129 (A1), you will also find beautiful objects characteristic of Lombok.

A large shop offering craft items: **Rungkang Jangkuk** in Sayang Sayang (C1), to the north of Cakranegara.

You can also make a visit to **Gunung Sari** (5km north of Mataram), a village that specialises in wood and leather. The advantage is that articles cost less here than in the shops in Mataram and Senggigi.

Ikats – Slamet Riyadi Weaving, Jl Tenun (C2), Cakranegara.

Sari Kusuma (C2), Jl Selaparang 45, Cakranegara.

Rinjani Hand Woven, Jl Pejanggik (B2), Mataram, sells ikats of all types, with designs that draw on the archipelago's varied styles.

Lombok

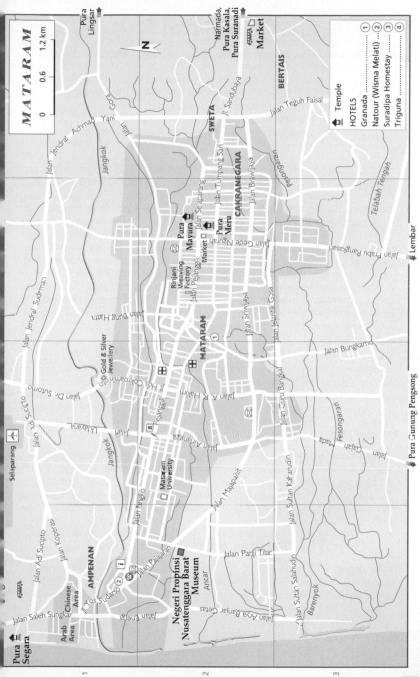

MATARAM

0   0.6   1.2 km

Temple 🏛

HOTELS
Granada .... ①
Natour (Wisma Melati) .... ②
Suradipa Homestay ...... ③
Triguna .... ④

Pura Lingsar

Narmada, Pura Kasala, Pura Suranadi
Market

SWETA

BERTAIS

Jalan Teguh Faisal

CAKRANEGARA

Jalan Tumpang Sari

Jalan Seraparang

Jalan Brawijaya

Jalan Gede Ngurah

Market

Pura Meru

Pura Mayura

Rinjani Weaving Factory

Jalan Pejanggik

Telabah Tengah

Pesongaran

Jalan Prabu Rangkasah

← Lembar

Jalan Sriwijaya

Jalan Jelntik Gosa

Jalan Bung Hatta

MATARAM ①

Gold & Silver Jewellery

Jl. Hos Cokroaminoto

Jalan A. R. Hakim

Jalan Bungkarno

Jalan Guru Bangkal

Pura Gunung Pengsong →

Jalan Pancak

Jalan Airlangga

Jalan Udayana

Jalan Dr. Sutomo

Jalan Jendral Sudirman

Jalan Jendral Achmad Yani

Jalan Gora

N

Jangkok

Jangkok

Pesongaran

Jalan Gajah Mada

Jalan Majapahit

Jalan Sultan Kaludin

Mataram University

B

Jalan Pingko

Jalan Panjang

AMPENAN

Jalan Adi Sucipto

Jalan Koperasi

Chinese Area

Arab Area

Jalan Saleh Sungkar

Pura Segara 🏛

← Selaparang ✈

Jl. Yos Sudarso

Jalan Energi

Jalan Pejajaran

Ancar

②

i

Negeri Propinsi Nusatenggara Barat Museum

Jalan Panji Tilar

Jalan Arya Banjar Getas

Jalan Sultan Salahudin

Barenyck

Jl. Sandubaya

477

SENGGIGI★

10km north of Ampenan – Map p 468-469 and p 480
Rainy season from November to March, hot and dry for the rest of the year

Not to be missed
The wild landscapes along the road from Mangsit to Tanjung.

And remember...
It is best to book in advance in the high season.
Choose a hotel to the north, towards Mangsit, to avoid the crowds.
To tour the north of the island, hire a car and avoid the rainy season.

Hillsides plunging to the sea, crescents of fine sand ringed with coconut palms, dazzling crowds of *prahus* setting off to fish, sunset over Bali – the west coast of Lombok has some idyllic sights and spots. Promoters and developers have been quick to grasp the profits that they can make from the area, particularly as it is so near Mataram airport, and everything is done to attract visitors. Several dozen hotels are flourishing where, even fifteen years ago, there was nothing but a few isolated fishing villages. To the north of Ampenan, the resort town of Senggigi stretches out for 10km, and has the island's largest concentration of tourist facilities. Don't worry, however, you are well away from Kuta Bali and, apart from the new shopping centre, a sort of incongruous pastel-coloured hacienda, most of the hotels with their thatched bungalow accommodation set in the greenery do not intrude excessively into the landscape. As you travel north, beyond Bangsal, you gradually find yourself in wilder countryside that extends to the dry majestic slopes of Mount Rinjani.

From Ampenan to Senggigi

Soon after Ampenan the road passes a **popular market** (*on the corner of the Ampenan road and Jl Adi Sucipto*) where you can experience your first Sasak aromas and atmosphere. Further on (*1km to the north*), you pass an amazing **Chinese cemetery** on the left where the tombs, constructed in cement, are entirely covered in coloured ceramics. Just behind it the *meru* of a Balinese temple, **Pura Segara**, stand facing the sea close to the remains of a Muslim cemetery.

■ **Pura Batu Bolong** – *Shortly before Senggigi (1km to the south); variable hours; donation*. Do not miss this other Hindu sanctuary, perched on a narrow rocky promontory reaching out into the sea. Its name – *batu* ("rock") and *bolong* ("hole") – refers to the cleft that splits it in two. From here the **panoramic view**★★ over Bali is magnificent. In the old days people truly knew how to choose the best sites for meditation. Fortunately the tradition of despatching virgins as food for the sharks has disappeared!

The beaches on the west coast★

■ **Senggigi** – *10km north of Ampenan*. There is a change of atmosphere a few hundred metres further on, as you come to the island's largest seaside resort. Souvenir shops, restaurants and nightclubs have invaded the town, and the fishermen have

The beach at Senggigi, white sand and coconut palms

packed their bags, giving way to the somewhat persistent beach traders. In the evening the bars and discos attract a crowd of tourists and Indonesians, as well as a number of prostitutes and other characters willing to be friendly – for a fee. But the sand is incomparably fine, the water warm and clear, and the **sea-bed** rich in corals and fish, even if they do not match those of the Gili Islands. Senggigi is also an excellent departure point for a trip to the Gilis (as well as for **Bangsal**, which faces the islands across the sea, 23km to the north).

Cramped between the sea and the western bastions of Rinjani, which prevent any settlement inland, the coast road winds on through coconut groves and rice fields, with fine **viewpoints★** here and there.

■ **Mangsit★★** – Further north, Mangsit appears as a haven of peace, and the landscape here has retained all its charm. Hotels are far fewer and the **road to Bangsal★★** affords a whole series of wild, breathtakingly beautiful bays, alternating with little fishing hamlets caught between the white sand and the clumps of coconut palms. Sadly, the developers are starting to move in.

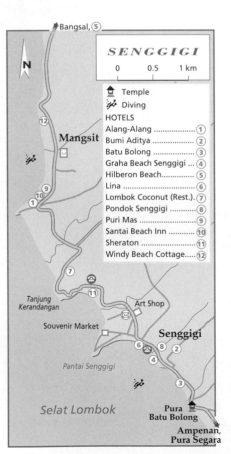

In Pemenang, a road to the left leads to Bangsal jetty for trips to the Gili Islands. If you have your own car, you can go off on a trip along the north coast via Anyer to the eastern shore. This is one of Lombok's most desert-like and arid regions, with some wonderful landscapes – but note that beyond Pemenang the road is in bad condition.

The northern road★

If you reach **Tanjung** (*10km northeast of Bangsal*) on a Sunday, pause a while to watch the animated **livestock market**.

Beyond **Gondang**, the landscape, suddenly very dry, is dominated by the imposing bulk of Rinjani, with its bare slopes descending gently to the sea. A track leads to the beautiful **Tiu Pupas falls**, a few kilometres inland. Beyond here, you will reach the dry land of the windward sides of the volcano, a rough and desert-like landscape; it could be the end of the world.

Making the most of Senggigi

COMING AND GOING

By bemo – The large hotels offer a shuttle service to the airport and the Lembar jetty. You can also charter a bemo if you want to travel direct to Lembar.

By taxi – See "Making the most of Mataram" p 475 or enquire in the hotels.

GETTING AROUND THE WEST COAST

By bemo – Undoubtedly the simplest and cheapest way.

Car and motorbike rental – From local agents or your hotel.

ADDRESS BOOK

Most of the shops, restaurants, travel agencies and other services (car hire, supermarkets, Wartel, post office and banks) are grouped together south of the point on which stands the Senggigi Beach Hotel. The hotels are strung out for 10km along the coast

Bank/Currency exchange – Rates in Senggigi are roughly the same as in Mataram. The **BNI** near the supermarket, has an automatic ATM cash dispenser and accepts travellers' cheques made out in dollars.

Post office/Telephone – Post office and **Wartel** near the supermarket.

Internet – **Bulan Cybercafe**, opposite the Bayan Restaurant. Daily, 9am-9pm.

Medical service – At the Senggigi Beach Hotel (near the souvenir market), an English-speaking doctor is available for consultation, daily from 5pm, ☏(0370) 932 10.

WHERE TO STAY

Hotels in Senggigi tend to lie in the up-market range. It is difficult to suggest a choice – places change and proliferate. The selection here is given from south to north. Try Mangsit as well, particularly if you are looking for peace and quiet.

Modest to average
Bumi Aditya, ☏ (0370) 938 62. ✈ ✗ ⌕ Set back from the beach, behind the Melati Dua. Small bamboo bungalows in a garden, clean and cheap.

Pondok Senggigi, on the way into Senggigi, ☏ (0370) 932 73. ✈ ✗ ⌕ Often full. This renovated hotel now offers rooms with air conditioning and private bathrooms, as well as other cheaper rooms without bathrooms. The bar has music groups (noisy).

High end
Batu Bolong, on the way into Senggigi, near the Dynasty restaurant, ☏ (0370) 930 65 – 30rm. ⌕ ✈ ☰ ✗ A stand-by hotel, clean but with no great charm. Hire of motorbikes and cars, diving and water-skiing.

Lina, ☏ (0370) 932 37 – 12rm. ⌕ ☰ ⌀ ✗ ⌕ Fairly central location. Simple rooms, with hot water. Be careful, the price does not include breakfast.

Luxury
Graha Beach Senggigi, ☏ (0370) 931 01, Fax (0370) 934 00 – 39rm. ⌕ ☰ ⌀ ▭ ✗ ⌕ ⌕ ⌘ Luxury that is somewhat garish and expensive, but reductions of up to 50% are often available. Breakfast included. Karaoke and swimming pool (with a 90m-long slide). Two good Chinese restaurants (go for the one by the sea, more welcoming). Fresh fish served.

Sheraton, ☏ (0370) 933 33, Fax (0370) 931 40 – 154rm. ⌕ ☰ ⌀ ✗ ⌕ ⌕ ⌀ ⌘ ⌘ A great ocean liner of a place with good architecture – but it is valued particularly for its many services: shops, bookshop and sports centre. Very expensive.

EATING OUT

Senggigi has few *warung* and most of the restaurants belong to the hotels. For seafood, take a look in the freezer or, better still, in the fish tank if there is one (more expensive, but much better). Suggestions from south to north:

Moderate to more select
Wayan, on the way into Senggigi, ☏ (0370) 930 98. 8.30am-11pm. Although it lacks the charm of the Bali establishment of the same name, the site is pleasant and the menu quite varied.

Dynasty, near the above, ☏ (0370) 933 13 ⌘ 4pm-12midnight. The terraced restaurant overlooks the sea. As it is popular with groups, it may be noisy but the menu is varied and the quality is good. Indonesian, Chinese, Italian dishes and seafood (crayfish and fresh fish).

Sun Shine, ☎ (0364) 932 32 [cc] 8am-10pm. Lombok specialities, soups, salads, crayfish and fish from the tank. The reception is fairly impersonal and the background music may be irritating, but the cuisine is good and some tables overlook the beach.

Kartika, ☎ (0370) 032 28 Right in the centre. The restaurant is not glamorous but the Chinese cuisine and the seafood (from the tank) are excellent.

Lombok Coconut, at Kerandangan, on the way out of Senggigi, ☎ (0370) 931 95. Open in the evenings only. A beautiful open split-level restaurant, set against the hillside, with welcoming decor (wooden furnishings, with bamboo roof and floor-tiles). Seafood, grilled chicken and cakes are on offer. Avoid the cocktails, they are heavily diluted with water.

Alang-Alang, in Mangsit, see the hotel of the same name. 7am-11pm. Good Indonesian and Italian food, and seafood dishes. A pity that the service is somewhat slow.

GOING OUT, HAVING A DRINK

Bars/nightclubs – There is no shortage of choice, and they are all very lively in season. The **Pondok Senggigi** and the **Marina Pub** regularly engage local musicians (who mainly play international standards).

OTHER THINGS TO DO

Excursions – **CCT Lombok**, ☎ (0370) 368 59. Tours and buses for Bali, Komodo and Flores.

Sun Shine, near the restaurant of the same name, ☎ (0364) 930 29. Tours to the Gili Islands, Kuta and Tetebatu.

PT Cinta Lombok Lestari, ☎ (0370) 935 61. Car rental, and tours. Fairly expensive.

Diving – Go for a specialised agent, for high-quality service. Their prices are much of a muchness but do not hesitate to compare quotes.

Albatross, ☎ (0370) 933 99. An agent that does business with the Sheraton, for beginners or experienced divers. The qualified instructors prepare people for the PADI certificate. Sale and hire of equipment.

Baruna, Senggigi Beach Hotel, ☎ (0370) 932 10. The instructors are qualified. For beginners or experienced divers. Also hires out windsurfing boards.

SHOPPING GUIDE

Shopping centres – You can find everything at **Senggigi Abadi** or **Pacific Supermarket**: books, postcards, telephone cards, photographic material, and clothes. 9am-9pm.

Handicrafts, antiques – **Pamour Art Gallery**, opposite the post office. Furniture and furnishings made of wood, both antique and new. Expensive but good quality.

Bahri-Shop, Pasar Seni. They also have a shop in Cakranegara.

Galeri Nao, Meninting, on the Senggigi road. A furnishing shop run by a Frenchwoman.

Photography – **Indra**, near the supermarket. You can have films developed here, and buy Kodak and Fuji films.

Making the most of Mangsit

WHERE TO STAY AND EATING OUT

Much quieter, Mangsit will delight travellers in search of a little more solitude. You eat in the hotels, as each one has its own restaurant.

Average

Santai Beach Inn, ☎ (0370) 930 38 – 10rm. ⚐ ✗ ☼ A small group of pretty bamboo bungalows, with a friendly pseudo-communal atmosphere: you eat together and you write down your drinks. Avoid the cheapest rooms, which have no ventilation (hot as a furnace!).

Windy Beach Cottage, beyond the Holiday Inn, ☎ (0370) 931 91, Fax (0370) 931 93 – 14rm. ⚐ ☴ ✗ ☼ cc Charming bamboo bungalows in a garden shaded by coconut palms, beside the sea. The breakfasts are excellent. Shame that the restaurant is more ordinary. Hire of masks and snorkels.

High end to luxury

Puri Mas, ☎ (0370) 930 23 – 14rm. ⚐ ☴ ✗ ☼ ☼ cc Very pleasant place consisting of small bungalows scattered in a garden. Depending on price, the rooms may or may not have hot water and air conditioning.

Alang-Alang, ☎ (0370) 935 18 – 17rm. ⚐ ▤ ✆ ✗ ☼ ☼ cc A group of charming bungalows, with open-air bathrooms, standing in a beautiful tropical garden with a pleasant swimming pool. Good value for money.

Hilberon Beach Hotel, ☎ (0370) 938 98, Fax (0370) 932 52 – 25rm. ⚐ ▤ ✆ TV ✗ ☼ ☼ cc Set in a vast park of 2.5ha. Family bungalows measuring 70sqm with marble floors. The hotel runs a free shuttle service three times a day to Senggigi and offers reductions of up to 50%.

Making the most of Mangsit

Graceful "prahu"

R. Marca

THE GILI ISLANDS**

On the northeast tip of Lombok
Between 8 and 16km off the coast of Bangsal –Map p 468-469
Pop 2 000

Not to be missed
The sea-bed, among the most beautiful in Indonesia.

And remember...
In summer the hotels are often full.
Beware of theft from rooms and on the beach.
If you visit Gili Meno, take anti-malarial treatment.

A short hop from Cape Sira **(Tanjung Sira)**, the northwest tip of Lombok, the little group of the Gili Islands (Gili means "island" in Sasak) spreads out in three banks of sand covered with coconuts or pines, where no motorised vehicles are allowed. White sand beaches, clear waters full of fish, depths of shimmering corals – these islands have become a haven for those who love **diving**, or who just want to relax. The Gilis are in fact among Indonesia's most famous places, and you may be lucky enough to see turtles, rays and even sharks (no danger). So, on with your snorkels, unless you prefer deep-sea fishing or the very animated night-life.

Guitars and snorkels

You will not be alone, particularly in high season. The mass of *losmen*, restaurants and night-clubs all over the islands attract a motley crowd, including local young people, who arrive with their guitars slung over their shoulders. In their wake there may also be a few less friendly spirits with their eyes open for neglected bags. No need to be paranoid, but be aware.

Tourism, a new source of income for the islands, is now more valuable than fishing, coconuts or tapioca. The substantial development now poses serious problems for the water supply, and the growing number of divers also endangers the coral. Divers treading on it are destroying the reefs, which will take years to grow back – take care to avoid causing damage.

Three different islands, three different atmospheres

An island to suit everyone. Take your pick, depending on what you are looking for: comfort and leisure, peace and quiet, or hectic night-life.

Gili Air**

The island nearest to the coast (*8km as the crow flies*) is certainly the one that offers the best compromise in terms of tourist facilities and tourist numbers. You can easily choose between an isolated retreat and the **southern or eastern shores**, which have the island's heaviest concentration of *losmen* and restaurants. Most of them are set back from the beach, among the coconut palms. No hardship staying here...

Gili Meno**

The quietest of the three islands, a delight for those who want to idle about undisturbed. Here, coconut palms give way to pine trees and the sand is even finer than on Gili Air. The hotels and restaurants (a little more expensive than elsewhere) are mainly grouped on the east coast. The best sites for **snorkelling** are in the northeast and the south. The only cloud on the horizon is that although the human population

Gili Air: a thread of sand between sky and sea

is sparse, the mosquito population is dense – the result of the small inland lake that is probably the cause of the outbreaks of malaria. It is therefore essential to take the appropriate precautions.

Gili Trawangan★★

There is a complete change of atmosphere on Trawangan, the largest of the three islands (2km by 3km), the most touristy and the liveliest. If you want peace and quiet go to another island! Trawangan is the place for night revellers: no sooner has the sun gone down than the bars and restaurants open up to music groups, and video images light up the walls. In the high season, in particular, the island is a hangout for anyone looking for fun, ending the evening on the beach with a new found friend, watching the mass of stars sparkling overhead.

Most of the facilities are clustered on the **southeast coast**, ideal for swimming and for **snorkelling★**. Unfortunately, since the devastating fire in 1993, concrete has replaced bamboo and the location has lost much of its charm. The more isolated **northeast coast★** also has the island's most beautiful **beach★** opposite **superb coral reefs★**. And the west coast is one of the most romantic places at **sunset**.

Making the most of the Gili Islands

COMING AND GOING

By boat – Bangsal jetty is 23km from Senggigi and 40km from Ampenan (32km by the inland route, via Kekait). Access by *bemo* as far as Pemenang, then by horse-drawn carriage. Tickets are sold at the window, departures 6am-5pm when the boat is full (charters available). Crossing time to Gili Air: 20min; Gili Meno: 30min; Gili Trawangan: 45min.

GETTING AROUND

By cidomo – In the absence of all motorised vehicles, the only form of public transport is the horse-drawn buggy.

By bicycle – Bicycles can be hired on Gili Trawangan (near the jetty).

ADDRESS BOOK

Bank/Currency exchange – No bank – but exchange facilities on all the islands.

Worth avoiding, however, because of the rates.

Post office/Telephone – Telephones are rare on the islands, and most hotels do not have one. Only Gili Air is rather better equipped: you will find a telephone at the Coconut Restaurant and at the Gili Indah. On Gili Meno, there is a Wartel near the Kontiki. There is also a Wartel on Trawangan, near the jetty.

WHERE TO STAY

Most of the *losmen* (guesthouses) are of the same standard, clean and reasonably inexpensive (Gili Meno is the most expensive island), but prices double in the high season. Life is changing fast in the Gilis, and word-of-mouth information from other travellers is the best way to find what you want.

● Gili Air
Modest
Nusa Tiga, to the right of the jetty – 8rm. ✎ ✗ The wooden huts are scattered across a garden slightly back from the beach. The rooms are rustic but clean, with mosquito nets. Breakfast included.
Nina (or Corner), beyond the above – 12rm. ✎ ✗ ⚘ This is only mentioned in order to warn against it: the price is set at $10 a room (!), and what is more the cleanliness is doubtful.
Gita Gili, beyond the former – 7rm. ✎ ✗ ⚘ The slightly more expensive equivalent of the Nusa Tiga.

Average
Gili Indah Cottages, to the left of the jetty, ☎ (0370) 363 41 – 35rm. ✎ ✗ ⚘ The largest hotel on the island. A little expensive, but worth it, even though some of the bungalows are somewhat dark.
Hotel Gili Air, on the northern tip of the island, ☎ (0370) 344 35 – 26rm. ✎ ✗ ⚘ Superb bungalows on the sea front. The deluxe rooms have air conditioning. Negotiate the price. The restaurant menu offers Italian and Indonesian food.
Fantastic Cottage, near the northern point – 6rm. ✎ ✗ ⚘ Family atmosphere. Clean, quiet bungalows. Breakfast included.

● Gili Meno
Modest
Janur Indah, to the right of the jetty – 6rm. ✎ ✗ ⚘ The bamboo bungalows face the sea. Clean and comfortable, but fairly expensive (breakfast included).
Kontiki, in the south of the island – 15rm. ✗ ⚘ The new bungalows, built of concrete with thatched roofs, have a private bathroom. The older wooden ones are simpler but face the sea. The restaurant, on the beach, is excellent – the ideal place to enjoy fresh fish.

Average to high end
Casablanca, 100m to the right of the jetty, ☎ (0370) 338 47, Fax (0370) 934 82 – 15rm. ✎ ✗ ⚏ Set back from the beach, in a flower garden with a small swimming pool. Fan or air conditioning in the rooms. The hotel is high-priced for its category, but try some hard bargaining. Breakfast included.
Gazebo Meno, 150m to the left of the jetty, ☎ (0370) 357 95 – 10rm. ✎ ▤ ⊼ ✗ ⚘ ㏄ The rooms, in bungalows set among pine-trees, are decorated with coconut wood and have a small sitting area. They have definite charm and you will enjoy the quiet.

Luxury
Bougainville Resort, on the southwest tip of the island – 10rm. ⊼ ✗ ⚏ ⚘ This latest addition offers magnificent colonial-style bungalows with high ceilings and large beds with mosquito nets.

● Gili Trawangan
Modest to average
Fantasi, to the left of the jetty – ✎ ✗ This recent hotel is clean and comfortable and is good value for the price.
Pak Majid, left of the jetty ✎ ⊼ ✗ ⚘ Right in the middle of the guesthouses facing the sea. This is one of the island's oldest *losmen*, without great character, but the rooms are clean and the staff friendly.
Pondok Santi, on the southern tip of the island ✎ ⊼ ✗ ⚘ A quiet, comfortable place, surrounded by coconut palms. Charming, even though the beach is not the most beautiful here.
Sunset, southwest coast – 10rm. ✎ ✗ ⚘ A quiet, isolated place, with a warm welcome, perfect for watching the sun go down over Bali (from the verandah). Bungalows with mosquito nets.

Lombok

Nusa Tiga I and ***Coral Beach***, on the northern tip. Two isolated *losmen* for travellers who prefer solitude, but the upkeep leaves something to be desired.

Luxury

Vila Ombak, to the south, ☎/ Fax (370) 220 93 – 24rm. ⌧ 🏊 ✕ 🕭 cc
The island's first luxury hotel, set apart from the *losmen*, is a success. Its bungalows, built of concrete with thatched roofs, are tucked away in a pretty garden. Some rooms have air conditioning. The terrace and the open-air bathroom are very pleasant. Shuttle service to Mataram airport (expensive, but very fast: 45min).

EATING OUT

Most of the restaurants belong to hotels. They serve Indonesian and Western dishes, as well as excellent seafood.

Moderate

• **Gili Meno**

Brenda's Place, left of the jetty. The seafront restaurant of the Malia's Child Bungalow. Delicious pizzas.

• **Gili Trawangan**

Borobudur, near the jetty. Seafood served in a pleasant setting.

Vila Ombak, see under the hotel of the same name. An enormous restaurant overlooking the sea, with a bamboo roof. You can also have your meals on the beach. Indonesian and Italian cuisine, and seafood.

GOING OUT, HAVING A DRINK

Bar – Gili Trawangan is undoubtedly the perfect place to meet people and go out in the evenings. The main restaurants also have a bar and show video films. Styles evolve rapidly and it is not easy to indicate a preference. Make your mind up depending on the decor, atmosphere and music.

OTHER THINGS TO DO

Diving – The best period is the dry season, when the water is at its clearest. You will find agents on all the islands, offering tours and hire of equipment.

Making the most of the Gili Islands

Nothing can beat the "dolkar" for exploring the Gili Islands

MOUNT RINJANI★★★
(GUNUNG RINJANI)
Lombok's highest point (3 726m) – Map p 468-469
Ascent on foot, 4 days (including 1 day for the return)
Temperature on the heights: between 18 and 22°C, down to 0°C at the summit

Not to be missed
The Pekelem pilgrimage, during the full moon in October and November.
Swimming in the hot springs near the lake.

And remember...
Good physical fitness is essential. Arrange your climb for the dry season
(May to October). During the rainy season the ground is very slippery
and visibility severely reduced.
Take a guide and plan carefully to take the necessary equipment and food.
Respect the environment and take everything back with you.

R. Helmi/Altitude

Lombok

Take a trip up Rinjani, the highest volcano in Indonesia after Mount Kerici (Sumatra, 3 805m), and one of the most beautiful in the archipelago. Crossing the tropical forest, climbing down into the heart of the crater, camping beside the lake with the stars reflected in the water, the last assault through a lunar chaos of ashes and stones – and finally the spectacular view from the summit. This is a climb you will never forget.

For the Sasaks and Balinese of Lombok – Hindus – Rinjani is a holy mountain, the setting for **Pekelem**, a great pilgrimage during the full moon in October and November. The faithful go in a procession to the lakeshore and throw in offerings, pray for the rains to come, and collect water. Vulcanologists keep a careful eye on the volcano, which is still active: it last ejected its ashes over the whole island in 1994. Classified as a national park, the Rinjani massif is also the last refuge for Lombok's wild animals and flora, a sanctuary that is sadly threatened by the expansion of tourism and poaching.

In the Rinjani crater

Climbing the holy mountain

Take the road from Anyer, the main town on the north coast, to Bayan (10km to the south), from where you reach Batukok and Senaru, departure points for expeditions.

Before reaching Senaru and beginning the climb up the volcano, stop off at **Batukok** (or Batu Koq) to see the **Sidanggala falls** nearby, springing out of the greenery *(30min on foot from the village; certain stretches go underground)*. When you reach **Setnaru**, take a stroll round the village. It is typical of Sasak settlements with **traditional houses** with their bamboo walls and thatched roofs standing inside a fragile wooden enclosure.

The day before the climb you should go to bed early as trekking expeditions set off very early in the morning. Depending on your fitness and the time available, you can either do a simple there-and-back to the edge of the crater *(open-air camp on site)* – in itself a substantial goal for a walk – or descend into the caldera, beside the lake that has formed there *(allow 2 days in this case, with 1 night by the lake)*. The most athletic visitors will continue right up to the top *(around 4 days' walking)*.

You can also climb Rinjani from the east, starting from **Sembalunlawang** (1 200m). It takes 8hr to reach the **Pelawangan II** pass on the rim of the caldera, then another 3hr for the summit. This path is much less used, but most of the climb is done in full sun without the protective shade of the trees.

Mount Rinjani

■ First day: towards the crater – From Senaru **(Pos I)**, the path plunges into the heart of the still-silent forest. You walk for three hours, as the plants and trees gradually awaken to the sound of creatures of every kind. Then you reach **Pos II**, a little shelter halfway up, at a height of 1 570m. As you continue further up *(90min)*, you reach base camp, **Pos III** (2 300m), a shelter with rudimentary facilities where you can stay overnight. *(If it is not too late in the day, you can also push on as far as the lake, a further 4hr walk from here.)*

■ Second day: down to the lake – The first objective next day *(get up 2hr before dawn)* is the **Pelawangan I** landmark on the crater rim, at a height of 2 634m. As you climb, the tropical forest gradually thins and makes way for clumps of increasingly sparse pines, and then the formless confusion of rocks. The thrilling sight of the **caldera★★★** appears at the last moment: a vast cauldron measuring 6km by 8km, with sides 500m high. At the bottom, **Lake Segara Anak** ("child of the sea") is a blue-green crescent with a milky veil of mist. An impressive volcanic cone, still smoking, rears up from the centre: this is **Mount Baru★** (2 658 m), which formed in 1942. Beyond it, the sea is visible in the distance, across an extraordinary **panorama★★★** (which, in clear weather, stretches as far as Bali and Sumbawa).
Climb down to the lake along a narrow path that winds across the mountainside *(allow 2hr of careful walking)*. When you reach the lake (2 100m), walk round it to the left *(for about 30min)*, to the **hot springs**, the final destination for the day. Pitch your tent close by, and take advantage of the springs for a swim – a wonderfully relaxing treat. The much cooler waters of the lake are full of fish, attracting fishermen from whom you may be able to buy a carp, to be eaten grilled, by the shore.

■ Third day: up to the summit – *To reach the summit at dawn, before clouds cover the sky, set out at 1am (you should allow 5hr steady climbing).* The path goes close to the hot springs then climbs up to the right. A guard rail is helpful at the beginning of the climb, but on the ridge, progress across ash and rocky pebbles is exhausting *(take care, the ground is steep and slippery)*.
Finally, the summit, battered by a chilling cold wind. But the 360-degree **view★★★** is astounding: the whole of Lombok lies at your feet, a great stone ship floating on the ocean. Opposite, in clear weather, it is possible to see neighbouring islands that appear to be within touching distance: Bali and Mount Agung, 110km to the west, and Mount Tambora, which dominates Sumbawa, 170km to the east. On the other side, scored with deep ravines, the sides of the volcano plunge down to the plain. And, lying 1 700m below, the caldera gapes like an open mouth. Magical.

The return, along the same path, requires a further night beside the lake. Here you can enjoy a well-deserved rest before the next day's long march (4th day: climb back up to the ridge of the caldera, then descend to Batukok).

Making the most of Mount Rinjani

COMING AND GOING

By bus and minibus – A few buses run from Sweta to Bayan (3hr). Departure early in the morning. You will generally need to change in Pemenang or in Anyer. From here, continue by *bemo* to Batukok or Senaru. Be careful: for the return trip, the last *bemo* leaves Senaru at 4pm.

WHERE TO STAY, EATING OUT

To be ready to leave at dawn, spend the night at Batukok or, better, at Senaru, the nearest village to the departure point. The *losmen* here have Spartan facilities, but the welcome is warm and the food fortifying.

Modest

Pondok Baru Bakti, Batukok – 7rm ✕ A small hotel with simple facilities (a few of the rooms have a private bathroom), but run with care by a teacher who helps walkers.

Pondok Senaru, Senaru – 6rm ⌂| ✕ Comfortable rooms and a restaurant with a view. Equipment for hire.

Bale Bayan, Senaru – 7rm ⌂| ✕ Bedrooms with open-air bathrooms. The welcoming and efficient staff can offer help to find porters and guides.

EXCURSIONS

Note that rates at the agencies in Mataram and Senggigi are very high.

Perama, Jl Pejanggik 66, Mataram, ☎ (0364) 227 64, Fax (0364) 233 68.

Satriavi, Jl Pejanggik 17, Mataram, ☎ (0364) 217 88, Fax (0364) 217 07.

Wisma Triguna, Jl Adi Sucipto 76, Ampenan, ☎ (0364) 217 05.

If you are travelling alone, hire porters and a guide for safety and to make your expedition more enjoyable. Food and cigarettes (for everyone) will be charged to you in addition to the negotiated rate.

Equipment – A torch with a back-up supply of fresh batteries, a knife, matches, spare clothing, a cotton or wool sweater, a waterproof jacket, sturdy walking shoes, and binoculars. In Batukok you can hire a camping stove, saucepan, duvet and tent. On the other hand, do most of your food buying in Mataram and top it up as you go. Food requirements: 1-2 litres of water per person per day, chocolate, coffee, eggs, sugar, biscuits, bread, "indomie" (instant soup with noodles and vegetables) or nasi goreng (prepared at the *losmen*). The lake water is drinkable, once it has been boiled or treated.

Making the most of Mount Rinjani

TETEBATU★
THE CRAFT VILLAGES
Map p 468-469
One-day tour – 20km, departure from Tetebatu

Not to be missed
The Jeruk Manis waterfall.
The craft villages.
And remember...
Avoid the rainy season.
Keep your mosquito repellent close to hand!

The southern slopes of Mount Rinjani have a much less tormented appearance than the northern flanks. The very heavy rainfall and the fertility of the soil, enriched with the volcanic ash, have created a rich land where rice, maize, onions and tobacco grow. Still untouched by mass tourism, this area will often offer you the opportunity to meet Sasak people and find out about their culture: their way of life, feast-days, and above all their craftsmanship. Therefore, as a foreigner, expect to be treated with great curiosity.

Tetebatu★

50km from Mataram (Bertais). Clinging to the slopes of Rinjani (at a height of 550m), Tetebatu is a charming sight with its houses scattered among the terraced rice fields. This is to some extent the Ubud of Lombok, with a more modest style. It has a mild climate and few tourists, and you will not be harassed by the usual street vendors. In short, this is a place where it's easy to relax and do nothing, except perhaps watch the Sasaks going about their business, tending to the fields and their craft workshops.

From Tetebatu, a lovely walk brings you to the **Jeruk Manis waterfall**★ *(6km north-east of Tetebatu; 2hr30min to get there, and the same to return along a different track)*, hidden in the heart of a tropical forest that is home to troops of black monkeys. You can reach the falls via rice fields, an opportunity to see some superb panoramic **views**★★. Peasants busy planting out, cutting or gathering the rice, groups of women carrying water on their heads, little children playing with kites while their older brothers and sisters return from school – everyone stops to greet you, or simply to watch the unexpected sight of a tourist doing his utmost not to slip into one of the rice fields! If you are less energetic, you can reach the waterfall by car, via **Pondok Bulan**, to the east of the village of **Kembangkuning**, and then along an open footpath *(30min on foot)*. 50m high, the waterfall springs out of the luxuriant foliage and plunges into a small rocky pool. This is the moment to bring out your swimming costume!

From village to village
Allow a half-day from Tetebatu. Don't hesitate to call on the services of a guide (enquire at your losmen)

It is as if some superior authority had overseen a wise division of labour as almost every village in the area has specialised in a specific craft. Even though tourism is tending to modify production, the processes for making the handicrafts have scarcely changed and tradition remains very much alive.

In the shadow of Rinjani: the rice fields of Tetebatu

Eurasia Press/DIAF

Ikat weaving

A women's prerogative, the work of weaving Sasak ikats follows an ancestral technique. Resting against a wooden pole that supports her back and is also used to stretch the threads, the worker becomes as one with her loom, working at it for hours at a time, sitting on the ground on her doorstep or in the shade of an awning.

The hamlet of **Loyok**, for example, 1km south of **Kotaraja** *(or 4km from Tetebatu)*, is known for its basketwork and the weaving of mats from bamboo fibres, work carried on in the home.

Rungkang, 1km away to the east, is the centre for **black clay pottery**, one of the island's great specialities. Don't hesitate to explore one of the village workshops, piled up with items wrapped in plaited bamboo fibre.

To the northwest *(2.5km)* is **Pringgasela**, one of Lombok's most famous **centres for weaving** ikats.

The tour ends at **Masbagik**, on the main road *(6km east of Rungkang)*, a large town known for its **pottery** and **ceramics**. The workshops lie on the edge of the town, to the east.

Heading east, the road leads to the sea at **Labuhanlombok**, the port of embarkation for Sumbawa, and offers no interest unless you intend to continue to the islands of eastern Indonesia. The Bugis people who live here are a reminder of the period when the region came under the control of the Celebes (the former name for Sulawesi).

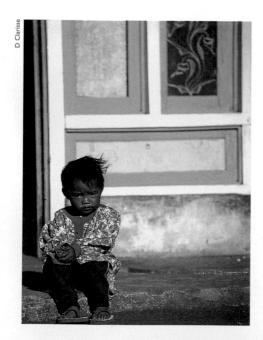

D Clarisse

Making the most of Tetebatu

COMING AND GOING

By bus and bemo – To reach Tetebatu, take a bus from Masbagik to Bertais (90min) and get off at Paokmotong. From there, take an "ojek" (motorbike-taxi) or a *bemo* to the village (10km; 30min).

GETTING AROUND

By cidomo – As a change from the ubiquitous *bemo*, you can take a "cidomo" (small horse-drawn buggy), ideal for short journeys.

Motorbike rental – At the **Mentariku** and **Cendrawasi** *losmen*.

Car rental – At the **Mentariku**.

ADDRESS BOOK

Post/Telephone – Wartel and post office on the main road, near Masbagik.

WHERE TO STAY

Tetebatu has some charming *losmen*, with fairly basic but adequate facilities. Other more attractive establishments can be found in the rice fields near the neighbouring village of Kembangkuning (on leaving Tetebatu, 1km before the Soedjon Hotel, take the right fork). Since the climate here is mild, you will need neither air conditioning nor a fan.

Modest

Pondok Bulan, in Kembangkuning (turn right before Tetebatu) – 7rm. ✗ The rooms, with white-painted brick walls, are small but impeccable and look out onto the rice fields. Take care, some of them do not have a private bathroom. Warm welcome. Guide services available.

Cendrawasi, in Kembangkuning, facing the Pondok Bulan – 4rm. ☝ ✗ Red brick bungalows with thatched roofs. The restaurant is a small rotunda where you eat sitting on mats, admiring the rice fields and Mount Rinjani. Hire of motorbikes.

Haikiki, in Kembangkuning – 6rm. ☝ ✗ Small rustic bungalows in Sasak style, in a delightful setting. The restaurant, set on piles, overlooks a rice field. Try the curried chicken or the "urap urap", an excellent and fairly spicy vegetable salad.

Mentariku, in Benteng, 3km beyond Kembangkuning – 8rm. ☝ ✗ Well tucked away, but with an outstanding view over rice fields and Rinjani. A pity that the rooms are so small and poorly kept. However, the lunch is to be recommended. Hire of motorbikes and cars.

Average

Soedjono, in Tetebatu, at the end of the road, ☎ (0370) 221 59 – 33rm. ☝ ✗ ⚊ Established in the former home of a Javanese doctor and built during the Dutch period, the hotel has a tropical garden and a spring-water swimming pool (unfortunately somewhat neglected). The restaurant, which features a terrace, serves excellent "ayam opor" (chicken with coconut). Some rooms have hot water. The prices are fair for the standard provided.

EATING OUT

Almost every *losmen* has a restaurant, although the service is often very slow.

Moderate

Green Ory Inn, in Kembangkuning, Tetebatu, before the Pondok Bulan. Standard Western and Indonesian food. Open until 10pm (in theory).

OTHER THINGS TO DO

Walking – Most of the *losmen* will be able to supply a guide to take you to Jeruk Manis waterfall.

Live shows – In August, Ledangnangka is the setting for **ritual Sasak combats** (with bamboo sticks and leather shields). Around here (particularly at Mentariku), you may also occasionally have the chance to watch **traditional dancing**. Enquire at the *losmen*.

SHOPPING GUIDE

Markets – In **Kotaraja**, on Monday and Wednesday mornings. Livestock market in **Selong**, on Mondays.

Crafts – There are a great many ikat stalls in Pringgasela, particularly at the **Dinda Artshop.**

THE ROAD SOUTH★★
KUTA LOMBOK
Tour of 120km from Mataram – 2 days
Map p 468-469 – Accommodation at Kuta

Not to be missed
The Sasak village of Sade.
The beaches at Mawun Are, Goling and Tanjung Aan,
without doubt the most beautiful on the island.

And remember...
The best way to explore the area is to hire a car.
From Mataram to Kuta and back, go via Selongblanak on the way down
and Sade on the way back.

Another side to Lombok is the great overpopulated central plain, which opens out as far as the eye can see as you leave Mataram for the South. There are no major historic sites here, nor monuments to visit – but instead a whole world to observe, entirely regulated by the pattern of work in the rice fields. Women with colourful sarongs, whose inscrutable expressions light up with a smile at the first wave of the hand, flocks of geese strictly supervised by small boys, buffaloes wallowing voluptuously in the mud – the area is a perfect illustration of the stereotypical Asian countryside.

Further south are the grasslands. On these dry slopes, where hills create a barrier protecting the shoreline, are some of the last Sasak villages to have traditional housing. But as you climb, the sun becomes hotter, the villages more rare and, on the other side, a new Lombok appears; undeveloped, divided up by cliffs and luminous beaches with immaculate sand.

The central plain

A Sasak marriage
This is a celebration for the whole village. The bride and groom get ready while a gamelan orchestra of drums and flutes, together with an unexpected Bontempi organ, keeps the crowd happy. With his features outlined in khol and his cheeks rouged, the young man dons a shirt of black velvet embroidered with gold thread, puts on his finest sarong and his orange Nike shoes, and slips the essential kris into his belt. With a thick black chignon adorned with gold jewellery on her head, and her hair extended with black paste over her forehead, the bride keeps her head lowered, her eyes fixed on her sarong. Bride and groom take their place in the procession, men in front and women behind, led by a gamelan that sets out along the road. Then everyone gets into lorries, heading for Praya, where the groom pays his respects to the father of the young woman whom he has abducted a month earlier – and pays him three million rupiah.

A vast flat green expanse, crossed by a thousand watercourses, Lombok's "rice basket" is also one of the islands great Sasak craft centres (even though production here is more tourist-oriented than at Tetebatu). **Praya** (*25km from Mataram*), the main town in the region, forms its heart. There are dozens of villages around it, each one specialising in its own activity. In **Sukarara** (*6km west of Praya*) and its neighbours, black-clad women weave coloured **ikats** on their door-steps, while **Penujak** (*6km south of Praya*) owes its fame to the elegant simplicity of its pottery, which is **hand-polished** and sometimes embellished with geometric motifs.

The south coast★★

From Praya, head south towards Selongblanak (25km), then along the coast to Kuta.

Beyond the plain the hillsides are covered in scrub. As you cross the ridge you have a magnificent **panoramic view★** of the coast. Then the road drops down to **Selongblanak★**, a small fishing village set on a vast curving bank of sand, like a small dot lost in the middle of a page. It is an extraordinarily beautiful bay but is unfortunately threatened by covetous developers who have already bought up 15ha of land from the villagers.

The road then heads east, winding between the hills. After 8km, a small fork to the right leads to **Mawun beach★★**, a superb arc of a bay ringed with white sand. The only building here is a wooden hut that sells drinks and fresh pineapples, refreshment for the few surfers in the area *(beware of pickpockets)*.

Another jewel of sand, **Are Goling beach★★** a few kilometres to the east, is just as lovely as its neighbour *(note: the access track is in poor condition – but you can also reach the beach by boat, from Kuta).*

Kuta★

8km from Mawun. Flanked by blue water and white sand beaches, the little fishing village is on its way to becoming a first-rate tourist destination. For the time being, however, the facilities are still very limited (no shops, no bank) and it has fewer than ten hotels and *losmen* (no-one knows whether the development plan to provide 23 hotels, a golf course and a marina will ever materialise, but a luxurious Novotel has already sprung up out of nowhere). This sudden expansion is naturally affecting the local people's otherwise very modest way of life. The number of street vendors is increasing on the beach but Kuta is nonetheless a pleasant and peaceful stopping-place, which only becomes lively during the **Nyale festival**.

5km east of Kuta, you can sunbathe on one of the two **beaches at Tanjung Aan★**, two strips of sand framed by parched hills. With not even the smallest building visible, there is nothing here but sand, unbelievably white and fine. Around midday it is impossible to set foot on it and everyone heads for the shade.

Kuta, Lombok – the exact opposite of Kuta Bali

A Jongen/Scope

The Road South

497

If you continue for a few more kilometres, to the far end of **Gerupuk Bay**, you reach **Desert Point**, one of Lombok's most famous surfing spots.

Sade and Rembitan★

8km north of Kuta. These two small Sasak villages are among the few to have preserved their wonderful **traditional houses★** with thatched roofs (even the **mosque** is thatched). Built of woven bamboo or palm leaves, each one stands on a metre-high platform of compressed earth, with a stairway carved into it. The living area *(bale tani)* is often linked to a **rice store★** *(lumbung)*, whose strange horseshoe-shaped roof has been adopted as the symbol for Lombok. Despite the incursion of tourism, the local inhabitants still maintain their rural way of life. On the other hand, most of the ikats that they will do their very best to sell you are made elsewhere.

From Sade, return directly to Praya (24km), then Mataram.

A friendly grub

Once a year the nyale (lycidice collaris), a large teredo sea-worm that is eaten raw or grilled, comes to breed close to Kuta beach. A good haul is the sign of an abundant harvest, and the creature is said to have aphrodisiac qualities. According to legend a beautiful princess, Mandalika, sacrificed herself by jumping into the sea, and appears every year in the form of a nyale. The appearance of the nyales is the signal for a great festival during which young Sasak girls and boys compete in water sports and poetic contests ("Pantun"). The festivities, which draw in thousands of people, last for two nights, lighting up Kuta beach with hundreds of bonfires, around which everyone gets to know each other.

Making the most of Kuta Lombok

COMING AND GOING

By bus – There is no regular service between Mataram and the south of the island, but travel agencies in Senggigi and Mataram organise bus transport.

By bemo – To go to Kuta, take a *bemo* in Bertais for Praya (30min), then another to Sengkol (15min), and finally Kuta (30min).

By car – The easiest way is to hire a car in Senggigi or Mataram. The roads are excellent, except for some stretches along the south coast that are not suitable for cars.

GETTING AROUND THE SOUTH

By bemo – Convenient for getting from Kuta to the beach at Tanjung Aan.

Car rental – Bicycles, motorbikes and cars from the *Mata Hari Lombok* losmen, in Kuta.

ADDRESS BOOK

Currency exchange – Enquire at the hotels, but remember that the rates are not advantageous (you will get better rates in Mataram).

Telephone – Public pay phones in Kuta. For your mail, avoid leaving letters with the *losmen* to post – they are not reliable; wait until you get back to Mataram.

WHERE TO STAY, EATING OUT

Apart from the two hotels in the village, the *losmen* in Kuta all offer approximately the same standard of facilities: bamboo bungalows for travellers who are both short of money and undemanding! Choose according to cleanliness, fans and mosquito nets. Breakfast is usually included. They all usually have an open-air restaurant with a view of the beach, and serve Indonesian food.

Modest

Sekar Kuning, ☏ (0370) 548 56, facing the beach – 18rm. ⌐ ✗ ⌐ Rather hot bamboo bungalows (no fan). Mosquito nets. Quiet and welcoming.

Hotel Bungalow Anda, ☏ (0370) 548 36, facing the beach – 16rm. ⌐✗⌐ A little more expensive than the others, for approximately the same standard. Varied cuisine. Popular with surfers.

Rinjani Agung Beach, ☏ (0370) 548 49, facing the beach –21rm. ⌐ ✗ ⌐ The rooms have a fan but the decor is gauche. The "Presidential", with air conditioning and television, is the height of kitsch.

Cockatoo, ☏ (0370) 548 56, facing the beach – 11rm. ⌐✗⌐ Further away from the other *losmen*, clean and quiet. Delightful reception, a pity that the food is so mediocre.

Average

Kuta Indah, west side of the bay, ☏ (0370) 537 81 – 32rm. ⌐ ✗ ⌐ cc Not very well placed. Beyond the wall and barbed wire and the rather cold lobby, the swimming pool in the middle of the garden is pleasant. The rooms are clean and comfortable, some have air conditioning and television. Popular with surfers. Expensive, but try bargaining.

⌐**Mata Hari Lombok**, set back in the village, ☏ (0370) 548 32 – 24rm. ⌐ ✗ The best value for money in Kuta (breakfast not included). Some rooms have air conditioning and hot water but the simplest, with fan, are equally acceptable. Good restaurant and a good range of services. A pity that the reception staff are somewhat offhand.

Luxury

Novotel Mandalika, 2km east of Kuta in an isolated creek, ☏ (0370) 533 33, Fax (0370) 535 55 – 108rm. ⌐ ▤ ⌐ tv ✗ ⌐ ⌐ ⌐ cc This island of luxury is reached along a well-lit two-lane road. The bungalows, with thatched roofs, are very well decorated (bathrooms with natural light). You can do everything here (sports centre, diving, bicycling, shopping), even enjoy a simple salad with excellent bread. All of this, naturally, comes at a price.

GOING OUT, HAVING A DRINK

Bar – Mascot Bar, a bamboo cabin a short way beyond the Rinjani Hotel. Groups play here several times a week.

OTHER THINGS TO DO

Excursions – Enquire at your hotel for deep-sea fishing or a boat-trip to the beaches at Mawun and Are Goling.

Outdoor pursuits – Since Kuta is a famous **surfing site**, you will find everything here that you need for the sport. Hire of equipment at the bamboo cabin near the row of *losmen*.

Festival – Don't miss the Nyale feast, the **Bau Nyale Putri Mandalika**, which takes place in February or March, on the 19th day of the 10th month of the Sasak calendar (see sidebar, above).

Market – Wednesdays and Sundays.

Making the most of Kuta Lombok

Maumere, the market

FLORES

Eastwards from Lombok lies another Indonesia, light-years away from the domesticated green landscapes of Java and Bali. Nature shows a different face here, as harsh as it is strange: giant Tambora with its ever-threatening volcanic rages, valleys narrow as gorges, beaches burning under the sun, dense forests in Manggarai and Ngada, giant lizards on Komodo and the lakes in the craters of Kelimutu with their ever-changing colours. The impression is that the Creator – whoever or whatever this may have been – indulged in every imaginable whim.

And yet far from discouraging mankind, the Lesser Sunda Islands are home to a vast number of micro-cultures that have developed separately, isolated by natural barriers, and have survived away from the agitation of the modern world. Living in close communion with an unforgiving natural world, resistant to compromise, this mosaic of archaic cultures still largely respects animist beliefs, even where Islam or Christian missionaries have left their mark on their land. Beyond the Muslim island of Sumbawa the contrast with the Indonesian West becomes evident. As soon as the traveller approaches the Roman Catholic land of Flores this contrast is obvious everywhere, on the faces of local people with their Melanesian features, on the church façades, in the patterns and colours of the shimmering ikats, and in the extraordinary traditional architecture in the villages where the ancestors are honoured by wood and straw effigies.

For the traveller in search of spectacular landscapes and unusual people, the Lesser Sunda Islands are a sort of final frontier, a string of lands from a different age.

Wooded volcanoes, arid coasts

From Bali to Flores, the group of the Lesser Sunda Islands lies strung out from west to east in a series of volcanic reefs with jagged outlines. Sumbawa, Komodo and Flores make up the eastern section of this arc and lie across the provinces of Nusa Tenggara Barat and Nusa Tenggara Timur. Completing the string of islands in the south are Sumba and Timor, which separate the arc from Australia. There are marked climatic contrasts in the region, with forests and savannah lying close together. An example is the little group of the Komodo islands (340sqkm), sitting in the middle of the Sape Strait between Sumbawa and Flores. With an annual rainfall of only 650mm, they can claim to be the driest part of Indonesia.

Sumbawa and Flores stretch out their long craggy outlines on either side of the strait. Even more elongated than its neighbour, Flores (13 540sqkm) is 350km long, and only has a width of between 15km and 60km (near Maumere and Ruteng respectively). The island consists of a narrow mountain ridge studded with a group of volcanoes. To the west and in the centre of the island, **Inerie** (2 245m) lies close to Poco Ranaka (2 400m), Ebulobo (2 124m) and **Kelimutu** (1 640m), while in the east are Egon (1 703m) and Lewotobi-Lakikali (2 263m, near Larantuka).

Between these fiery mountains there are valleys and basins that are fertile and well watered. Above all the Ruteng area – the "rice store of Flores" – which enjoys an annual rainfall of more than 4 000mm. This contrasts sharply with the east and the northern coast, dry savannah regions with less than 1 000mm of rain.

Restricted by this complex terrain, roads are underdeveloped in Flores. Only the great **Trans-Flores highway** (680km) links the main towns and forms the main communication route; otherwise, there is nothing beyond a few car-worthy roads

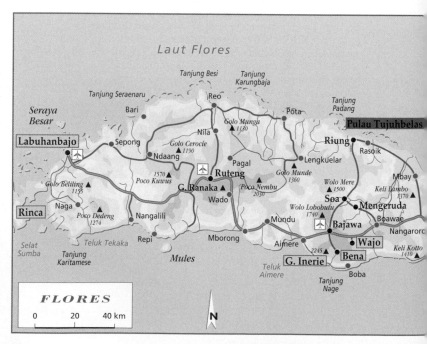

(particularly from Ruteng to Reo and from Bajawa to Riung). And during the rainy season (November – March) it is not unusual for a landslide or collapsed bridge to block the road temporarily.

A widely varied population

With more than 1.2 million inhabitants (in 1990), Flores appears relatively well populated compared to its neighbour Sumbawa (pop 864 000). But hidden in the average density (89 per sqkm) are wide variations. The Maumere region, for example, the driest on the island, is paradoxically over-populated, with more than 600 people per square kilometre, a feature that poses severe ecological problems.

Located in an intermediate region between the **Malaysian world** to the west and the **Melanesian world** of the Papuans of Irian Jaya to the east, the oldest inhabitants of the island have south-Asian features, as well as dark skin and tightly curled hair. Each of these ethnic groups has developed its own language – Manggarai, Ngada, Lio, Ende, Sikka and Lamaholot – all belonging to the great Austronesian group that covers almost all the languages of the Indonesian archipelago. Various neighbours have been added to these ancient peoples down the centuries: **Bugis** and **Makassar** sailors established bridgeheads on the north coast, the **Bima** of Sumbawa settled in the west, descendants of **Arab** traders live in Ende, while Larantuka has a minority group of **Portuguese mixed-race** descendants.

Several phases of settlement

The earliest inhabitants of eastern Indonesia, the Australoid hunter-gatherers seem to have come via the Philippines in the early Paleolithic Age. In 3000 BC, Austronesians from Taiwan in turn migrated to various points on the archipelago,

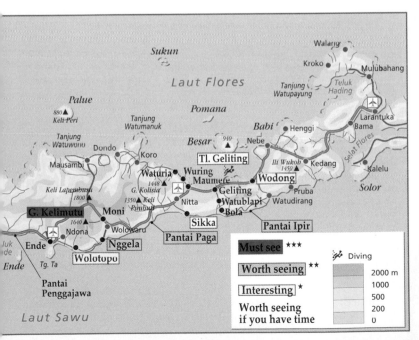

including the Lesser Sunda Islands. Bringing with them rice, bananas and a number of animal species (deer, pigs, dogs, etc), these fearless travellers developed agriculture here.

Proof of the expansion of this brilliant civilisation of Vietnamese origin at the beginning of the modern era can be seen in the testimonies to the Dongson presence, the impressive bronze drums discovered on Sumbawa, Komodo and Alor, together with pirogues and bronze knives found near Ende and Bajawa.

Later, the wealth of Flores (copper, sulphur, coconuts, sea cucumbers, sandalwood, etc) attracted traders from every direction: Javanese from the Majapahit Empire, Chinese (12C), then Arabs and Indians in the 13C.

Yet none of them left a permanent mark on the island. Even the Bugis of the **Gowa sultanate** (Sulawesi), masters of the slave trade in the 15C and 16C, did not impose Islam, and the 17C kingdom of Bima to the west and the principalities of the Moluccas to the east exercised only intermittent control over certain regions of Flores.

Portuguese against Dutch

Although it lacked spices, Flores nonetheless made an early appearance in Portuguese chronicles (1512) written by the Portuguese navigator **Antonio de Breu**. It owed this early fame to its strategic location, between the powerful trading post in **Malacca** (in modern Malaysia) and the island of Timor, rich in sandalwood. The island acquired its name in 1544 when a sea captain cruising off its eastern tip named it the "Cabo das Flores" (Cape of Flowers). In 1566 the **Portuguese** built a fort on the island of Solor (to the east of Flores), and **Dominican** priests soon followed. As zealous evangelists, the latter spread the good word throughout Flores, which in 1599 already had 100 000 Catholics. Having driven off Bugis attacks in 1602, however, the Portuguese were forced to yield to the Dutch, and settled in **Larantuka** in 1613.

An ancestral social structure

Indonesia's eastern islands used to be divided up into small kingdoms, such as Manggarai, ruled by sovereigns of aristocratic parentage, a system known as the "Wau". United through inheritance and task sharing, the basic unit (clan, family or house) renewed its bonds at times of war or natural catastrophe. Despite the upheavals created by the introduction of the colonial system, the social structure of the old Flores has endured, under various forms, through to modern times. The old-time rajahs have thus exchanged their title for that of "kepala desa" (village chief) and are elected by their fellow citizens. Guardian of tradition, the "kolu" still decides on land distribution and organises ceremonies. With the Christianisation of the island, the priest has also become an important figure in the village. Today, however, Indonesian centralisation and the development of tourism are undermining this structure, which is subject to increasingly powerful pressure.

At the same time, in the late 16C they settled in the heart of Flores on the **island of Ende**, the hub of the trade in sandalwood and textiles, where Malay, Chinese and Arab merchants competed with each other. Here too they built a fort, from which they were expelled in 1630 by the local people, who were enraged by scandal involving a priest, the captain of the fort and a local princess. The fugitives took refuge in **Paga** and **Sikka**, where they allied themselves with the **Rajah Dom Alesu Ximenes da Silva**, whom they showered with gifts to

confirm their goodwill. Amazingly, the collection of 70 elephant tusks sealed a bond that was to last until the end of the 19C. The Da Silva line thus ruled over the Sikka region until Indonesia acquired its independence.

In the 17C, however, the **Dutch** successfully confronted the earlier settlers. After the fall of Malacca in 1641 a group of Portuguese fled to the Celebes (Sulawesi), but the loss of **Makassar** in 1667 accelerated their decline. In the same year, the **Treaty of Bonggai** recognised Dutch sovereignty over eastern Sumbawa and Flores, with the exception of Larantuka, Paga and Sikka. Most of the Portuguese colonists and traders from Malacca, Macao and Makassar were thus stranded at Larantuka, where they came to form a mixed-race community, the **Topasses** ("mestizos"), whose descendants still live in the area. Lisbon continued to send missionaries until 1782 and did not give up its claims until 1859 (only East Timor was to remain Portuguese), in return for a promise that the Catholic religion would be maintained there.

The **Dutch East India Company (VOC)**, which at first showed little interest in Flores, did not establish a mission at Ende until 1670. In 1838 an expedition despatched to bring the slave trade to an end destroyed the city, together with a fleet of 50 merchant ships. Later, after the failure of a first exploratory mission into the interior (1890), the Dutch set up a military expedition that achieved little – but left hundreds of dead in its wake. Hampered by the extreme physical barriers on the island, the resistance from local populations never offered a serious threat. In the early 20C the Dutch banished the Catholic king of Larantuka and brought the island under direct control. Once pacification was complete they sent their first mission to Ruteng in 1917, which led up to the complete Christianisation of the island.

A fervent but superficial Catholicism

Although 85% of the population of Flores has been baptised, Catholicism here is strongly impregnated with animist ritual. Be that as it may, the ordination of a priest is always a major event in village life and, in Larantuka, the Easter processions are attended by an enormous crowd every year. The success of Christianity no doubt explains its missionaries' tolerance towards local traditions – which, although they vary considerably from one region to another, all share an element of ancestor worship and homage to the nourishing earth.

Ikat, a major art

Basketwork, craftsmanship and bamboo architecture – proofs of the skills of the Floresians are manifold, and vary with the regions. The **arts of dance and music** should not be forgotten; they are in evidence at many of the feasts and ceremonies (ordination of a priest, inauguration of a house, the reappearance of a spring, marriage, etc).

It is however undoubtedly the art of ikat-weaving that has inspired the greatest amount of literature (see p 66). Although museums and collectors throughout the world have long since bought the finest pieces, at enormous prices, there is still local production of great quality. Natural cotton has now virtually disappeared, replaced by man-made thread; and, although natural colourings are still used in some villages, they are increasingly being replaced by chemical dyes.

Despite these changes, the ikat remains the preferred garment for most of the population, and takes on a variety of ritual and social functions (funerals, marriages and dowries). Each element of the design in effect expresses a magical virtue connected with the various stages of life.

Each region has its own style and technique. In the **Manggarai region** (in the west), in particular, the designs are created by weaving threads of several colours and not by previously dyeing the warp of the fabric. Two main styles co-exist, one representing the Sumbawa tradition, the other from Sulawesi. In the first, red, blue and green predominate, marking out large crosses alternating with grids of fine lines. Dark indigo is used in the second style, distinguished by bands of colour with geometric motifs, sometimes enhanced with secondary patterns.

The dark blue ikats from the isolated regions of the **Ngada region** incorporate simpler geometrical figures – *tumpal* triangles, zigzags and squares. The highly prized **kain kudu** are recognisable by their delicate white horses against a black background, designs that require whole days in the dye-bath, since the fabric is slow to take up the dye. Some have a narrow orange strip that further increases their value.

Although the inhabitants of the **Ende region** wear indigo sarongs for daily use, they have an endless range of ikats, an abundance of warm shades and geometric, animal and floral designs. Outside influences, particularly from *Patola* fabrics of Indian origin are clearly visible.

The **Lio** ikats have a delicate design that combines yellow and brown flowers against a red or dark blue background, with parallel stripes across it. As a concession to modernity, some include aircraft, cars and ships! The same floral themes appear in the thicker ikats from Sikka with a dark background that is sometimes enhanced with red tones.

Lastly, in the traditional **eastern Flores**, where some villages still use natural cotton, each composition is the exclusive preserve of a clan, and there is no question of incorporating the colours of a neighbouring community.

Exploring Flores through its ikats is a fine basis for a tour. Unless you prefer to set out on a volcanic expedition, or simply enjoy the beautiful ribbons of black or white sand fringing the turquoise waters. The choice is wide, quite apart from the mysteries of arid Sumbawa and the legendary Komodo "dragons".

Minor practical suggestions

Travelling in Flores can be wearisome and liable to change because of the state of the roads (allow an average of 30kph). Flying is barely more reliable, as there are few flights, and these are often cancelled. You must therefore have a lot of time at your disposal, and come armed with patience. The island is described here from west to east, but if you want to travel right across Flores you would do better to fly direct to Maumere, and then work your way west by road. It is in fact easier to leave from Labuhanbajo, and waiting there is more agreeable.

Since rates of exchange are poor on Flores, and the use of foreign currencies or Visa cards very unusual, it is better to lay in a supply of rupiah before you set out.

C. Goupi/Scope

THE ISLAND OF SUMBAWA

West Nusa Tenggara Province
75km west of Flores
Rainy season November-March, hot dry climate for the rest of the year.

Not to be missed
Pulau Moyo reserve.
Bima museum.

And remember...
Dress decently to avoid upsetting local sensitivities.

Few tourists visit the magnificent beaches on the south coast, explore Pulau Moyo bird reserve, set out to climb Tambora, visit Bima museum or seek to meet the animist tribes in the mountains. With such a powerful potential, Sumbawa may one day become the new eldorado for tourism in Nusa Tenggara. But at the moment most travellers only stop off briefly on their way to Komodo and Flores, discouraged by the lack of facilities and infrastructure. In addition, the island's population, who are orthodox Muslims (particularly in the east), suffer from an unfortunate reputation for austerity. Yet this is undeserved – you will often be surprised by the warm welcome that awaits you.

An island long ignored

Dominated by **Tambora** (2 851m), a colossal volcano that takes up the whole of a peninsula (in the north), Sumbawa is a mountainous island, a narrow twisting ridge of land. It is 280km long and between 15 and 90km wide (15 600sqkm), with such an irregular shape, marked by a series of deep bays, that it is regarded as two distinct entities: **Sumbawa Besar** in the west, and **Bima** in the east.

On account of this, the two regions have had different histories however far back you look. Even their languages are different: while the inhabitants of the west speak a dialect similar to Sasak, the east has developed a language closer to that of Flores and Sumba. Two islands in one, in effect, which remained ignored for a long period. Sumbawa's eastern geographical position in the Indonesian archipelago has had the effect of keeping it relatively distinct from the influence of the western Hindu kingdoms. The only exception was the (remote) surveillance exercised by the Javanese Majapahit Empire in the 14C. Islam itself only came late to the island (in the 17C), under the encouragement of the Makassars from Sulawesi. This means that native animist communities such as the **Dou Donggo** ("men of the mountains") have been able to maintain a vigorous tradition up to modern times.

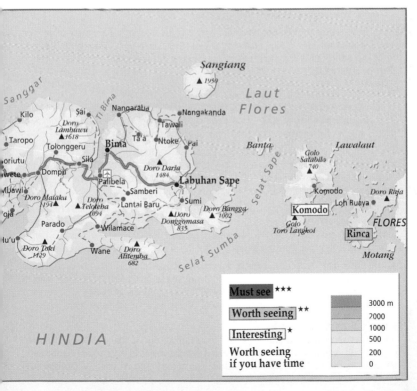

Crossing the island

Allow a day to cross the island, or 2 to 3 days if you are staying on it.

As you approach from Lombok, the arid mountainous landscape of Sumbawa soon becomes visible, the moment the boat nears the coast. Only a few rare villages lost among the heights, small dark marks on the ochre slopes seem to break the monotony of the vast bare expanses.

Sumbawa Besar

When you arrive at Poto Tano, take a bus from the jetty (2hr travelling time). The road winds between sea and mountain. This clean quiet place, the main town in western Sumbawa, stretches out alongside a river, at the foot of a hill. Tourists are rare here, and you can spend a few pleasant days on foot or in a horse-drawn carriage, exploring the streets lined with low buildings.

The former palace of the sultan, **Dalam Loka** *(Jl Batu Pasak, near the market)*, an imposing wooden building set up on piles, gives the impression of a ship that has run aground. Access is along a wide ramp between the two main living areas. Built in 1885, it is an empty shell today and has little of interest for the visitor *(particularly since opening times are uncertain)*.

The sultan's descendants now live in the **Balai Kuning** *(along Jl Wahidin, about 100m away)*, an elegant yellow-walled pavilion designed along the lines of a Dutch mansion *(the tourist office organises visits)*.

From here, return to **Seketeng market** where you can soak up a variety of aromas and colours *(two minutes away, turn left along Jl Urip Sumoharjo)*. Among the stalls of fruit, fish and poultry, women traders give you warm welcoming smiles – through their beauty masks!

Around Sumbawa Besar

When you leave the market, take the Poto road that climbs a small **hill**, from where there is a fine **panoramic view★** over the plain. The bamboo houses have an unexpected touch of modernity with their enormous satellite dishes.

The very picture of "eternal" Sumbawa, the small traditional village of **Poto★** *(12km to the east)* is an opportunity for a glimpse of a wholly different culture. Sitting in the midst of chickens, in the shade of their **houses on piles**, the women quietly weave their **ikats** in time-honoured ancestral tradition.

If you would like a swim, make your way to the **beach at Kencana** *(11km to the west)*. It has no outstanding charms, but you will not find a better one in this area. Or you may prefer to see the **Ai Beling waterfall★** *(36km to the south, take a guide)*, a handsome natural staircase 50m high that springs out in the middle of the undergrowth.

The region's main attraction is **Pulau Moyo★**, an island lying several hundred metres offshore *(take a boat from north of Sumbawa Besar, 90min, to Tanjung Pasir, in the south of Moyo island)*. Its magnificent **white sand beaches★** and **coral reefs★** will perhaps provide it with a prosperous future. Several hotels have already appeared here.

From Sumbawa to Bima

After a series of monotonous hills, the road comes out at the great **bay of Saleh**, dotted with fishing villages and dominated by the majestic outline of **Tambora★★**, far away in the north. Then you continue through the green plain of **Dompu**, the rice-basket of Sumbawa, before reaching Bima.

Bima

Together with its neighbour **Raba**, Bima forms a vast conurbation – but its town planning has managed to keep it to a human scale, without excessively large buildings or roads (it does not even have any traffic lights!).

Established in the former Sultan's Palace (1927), the **Nusa Tenggara Asimbojo Bima Museum*** (daily, 8am-5pm, fee) has unexpectedly rich contents: apart from the collection of **traditional handicrafts** – costumes, baskets and everyday objects – don't miss the

The eruption of Tambora

Less famous than the explosion of Krakatau, the eruption of Tambora is nonetheless considered the most powerful to have occurred in the last 10 000 years, and one of history's most deadly. The volcano exploded in April 1815, hurling 150 cubic kilometres of volcanic material into the atmosphere. Its peak, 4 200m high, became a vast gaping hole, the island was covered in a carpet of ash between 50cm and 1m thick, and Java, 1 300km away, was plunged into darkness for three days. Around 10 000 Sumbawanese died as a result of the explosion, and the subsequent famine caused the death of nearly 65 000 people, 25 000 of them on the neighbouring islands of Bali and Lombok. The effects of the eruption were felt as far away as the Northern Hemisphere, where the summer of 1816 was exceptionally cold. France, for example, recorded the most belated grape harvest for hundreds of years.

treasure room** which has recently opened. It displays magnificent golden kris, and a sumptuously worked betel box. Upstairs, you can also see the former **royal apartments**, in which the only furniture consists of canopied beds.

To see another side of Bima, spend the weekend at **Lewata beach** (3km away, on the airport road), where the Sumbawanese go on family trips to swim, fully clothed – as their religious sensibility requires.

Towards Labuhan Sape

As you leave Bima for Sape, the superb **road**** dips into a valley carpeted with rice fields between the wooded slopes of the **Doro Daria** massif.

Next it reaches **Labuhan Sape**, the embarkation point for Komodo and Flores. Nestling in the curve of a bay where multicoloured **catamarans** are moored, the village with its pretty **houses on piles** stretches along the "main street" that leads to the jetty.

Making the most of the Island of Sumbawa

COMING AND GOING

By air – Sumbawa Besar airport lies 2km south of the town (by bemo or on foot). Merpati serves Denpasar via Mataram, several times a week.

Bima airport, Mohammad Salahuddin, is 20km to the south of the town (by bemo or by chartered minibus). From here Merpati serves Bali, Lombok, Flores, Sumba and Timor.

Airline companies – Note that the travel agencies do not accept credit cards. In Sumbawa Besar: **Merpati**, Jl Diponegoro, ☎ (0371) 214 16.
In Bima: **Merpati**, Jl Soekarno-Hatta 60, ☎ (0374) 426 97.

By sea – From Labuhanlombok to Poto Tano (Sumbawa), ferries between 6am and 8pm (90min).
From Sape, the ferry leaves daily except Sundays for Komodo (5-7hr), then for Labuhanbajo on Flores (total crossing time: 8-10hr). Get there early.

By bus – From Bali or Lombok, you can take a bus direct to Sumbawa Besar, Bima, or even Sape.

GETTING AROUND

By bus – In Sumbawa Besar, the new Sumer Payung terminus (6km west of the town) serves Poto Tano (2hr, 90km). For Bima (7hr, 260km), buses leave in the mornings from the town centre. In Bima, the Dara terminus is on the edge of the town (Jl Terminal Baru).

For Sape, take a minibus from Raba, from the Kumbe terminus (15km east of Bima). Sape terminus is in the town, 4km from the harbour (by *bemo*). Allow 2hr to reach Bima (46km).

By bemo – Practical in the towns, and also convenient for exploring the hinterland.

By lorry – On secondary roads trucks are a regular means of transport. They usually depart from the minibus terminus.

By carriage – Known as a "cidomo" in Sumbawa Besar or a "benhur" in Bima, this traditional means of transport will leave you with unforgettable memories!

Car and motorbike rental – Enquire at hotels and travel agents.

Making the most of Sumbawa Besar

COMING AND GOING

See above, "Making the most of the Island of Sumbawa", under the same heading.

ADDRESS BOOK

Tourist information – *Dinas Pariwisata*, Jl Garuda, Sumbawa Besar, ☎ (0371) 217 14.

Bank/Currency exchange – *Bank Negara Indonesia*, Jl Kartini 10. Currency exchange in the mornings, Monday-Friday. Visa cashpoint.

Post office/Telephone – *Main post office*, Jl Kebayan. Open in the mornings, closed on Sundays. Poste restante. Wartel, Jl Hasanuddin 105. Open 24hr a day.

WHERE TO STAY

Modest
Losmen Saudara, Jl Hasanuddin 50, ☎ (0371) 215 28 – 10rm. The rooms are spacious, but their cleanliness questionable. Some have a private bathroom. Breakfast is not provided.
Dian, Jl Hasanuddin 69, ☎ (0371) 217 08 – 15rm. Cleaner and more recent than the Saudara, it costs very little more.
Dewi, Jl Hasanuddin 60, ☎ (0371) 211 70 – 31rm. ✗ Vast modern building intended to be luxurious but already run-down. Yet comfortable rooms, some with air conditioning and television. Avoid the restaurant.

Average
🏠**Tambora**, Jl Kebayan 2 (towards the airport), ☎ (0371) 215 55, Fax (0371) 226 24 – 49rm. ⊓📖 / 🍴✗ Clean and comfortable, this is the best hotel in town and is also reasonably priced (breakfast included). The very efficient staff can arrange numerous local excursions.

Luxury
🏠**Kencana Beach Cottages**, 11km west of the town (by *bemo*), ☎ (0371) 225 55, Fax (0371) 224 39 – 30rm. ⊓ 📖 / 🍴✗ 🏊 🏐 Small bungalows facing a black sand beach far from the bustle of the town. The owners, who also own the Tambora, intend to open a souvenir shop. Go for the lower-priced rooms, facing the sea, which offer the best value for money.

EATING OUT

Basic
Aneka Rasa Jaya, Jl Hasanuddin 14. This Chinese restaurant also sells groceries. Open until 10pm.
Rumah Makan Ingkang Sae, Jl Hasanuddin 10. The most fashionable restaurant in the town, with karaoke and coloured guitar-shaped neon lights. Try the "sepat" (spicy fish broth).
CV Cirebon, Jl Kebayan 4 (near the Tambora). Javanese and Sundanese cuisine (fried chicken and fried prawns) served in a white-tiled restaurant. Open until 10pm, this hotel-restaurant offers Wartel and car and motorbike hire.

Moderate
Kencana Beach Cottages, (see above). Indonesian, Chinese and Western dishes as well as seafood, served in a very attractive setting near the beach.

OTHER THINGS TO DO

Excursions – The Tambora and Kencana Beach Cottages hotels (see above under "Where to stay") offer fascinating tours in the hinterland, or diving package deals.

Making the most of Bima

COMING AND GOING
See above, "Making the most of the island of Sumbawa", under the same heading.

ADDRESS BOOK
Conveniently, most of the services are concentrated round Sultan Kahanuddin street (banks, hotels, restaurants and shops).

Tourist information – Dinas Pariwisata, Jl Soekarno-Hatta (2km east of the town), ☎ (0374) 443 31.

Bank/Currency exchange – Bank Negara Indonesia, Jl Sultan Hasanuddin. Currency exchange and travellers' cheques. **Bank Danamon**, Jl Sultan Kahanuddin 13. Accepts dollars. The town's only Visa ATM.

Post office/Telephone – Main post office, Jl Sultan Hasanuddin (Monday-Saturday, 8am-2pm). **Wartel**, Jl Lombok. Open 24hr a day.

WHERE TO STAY
Average
Lila Graha, Jl Lombok 20, ☎ (0374) 427 40, Fax (0374) 447 05 – 80rm. ✈ / 🍴 ✕ The hotel is comfortable but could do with some renovation. It offers a wide range of rooms, from the plainest, with shared bathrooms, to the "VIPs", equipped with air conditioning and satellite television. Hire of cars and motorbikes

La'mbitu, Jl Sumbawa 4, ☎ (0374) 422 22, Fax (0374) 410 69 – 26rm. ✈ ✈ / 🍴 🎵 📺 ✕ Very new and perfectly run, the hotel offers good value for money although the rooms are small and have no windows. Satellite television. Hire of cars and motorbikes.

Lawata Beach Hotel, Jl Sultan Salahuddin (5km, on the airport road), ☎ (0374) 436 96, Fax (0374) 436 98 – 38rm. ✈ 📺 ✕ 🏊 🎵 Simple but comfortable bungalows. When the sun is blazing, the site is very refreshing, but the beach is tiny.

EATING OUT
Moderate
Restaurant Lila Graha (see the hotel of the same name). A varied menu (Chinese and Indonesian cuisine, and seafood), for a clientele that is less so (tourists).
Pemuda, Jl Sulawesi 12. Decent but somewhat expensive Chinese cuisine (though everything is relative) and the owner is not particularly friendly.

GOING OUT, HAVING A DRINK
Nightlife in Sumbawa is limited to Bima. A walk round the **night market** (along the alleyway opposite the Lila Graha restaurant) will give you an opportunity to try a "martabak" (a thick pancake with sweet or savoury filling) from a Javanese "kaki lima" (street vendor). You can also have a beer in the illegal bars that open at nightfall along Jl Sultan Kahanuddin.

Making the most of Labuhan Sape

WHERE TO STAY
Modest
Mutiara Beach, at the entrance to the harbour – 20rm. The main advantage of this clean and very simple *losmen* is its location close to the jetty. The bathrooms are shared and breakfast is not included.

EATING OUT
Basic
R.M. Arena, near the jetty. Simple but friendly Javanese restaurant that serves a very varied range of dishes (no alcohol). **Citra Minang**, opposite the Arena. Highly spiced Padang cuisine.

Making the most of Bima

KOMODO★★

ON THE SAPE STRAIT

West Nusa Tenggara Province – Manggarai District
Pop 37 000. – Climate hot and very dry – Map p 509

Not to be missed
The lizards.

And remember...
Never go out on foot without a guide.
In Rinca, wear trousers to avoid being bitten by stinging flies.
When swimming in the sea, watch out for strong currents and sea-urchins.

Komodo is the largest (340sqkm) and the best known of the myriad islands dotted throughout the **Sape Strait**, between Sumbawa and Flores. It is here on these dry volcanic lands, burned by the sun, which seem a thousand miles from all modern civilisation, that the famous **Komodo monitor lizard** has found a suitable refuge. The sight of this monstrous survival from prehistory, evolving in its natural setting, is a unique and never-to-be-forgotten experience.

Apart from a few fishing villages, most of the islands are uninhabited because of the lack of fresh water and the aridity of the soil. But for the passing traveller, these little islands fringed with white sand and bathed in turquoise water are a veritable paradise.

A mysterious reptile

For 25 million years the *Komodo biawak* (or *ora*), named *varanus komodoensis* by scientists, has enjoyed peace and tranquillity on the islands, even though its contemporary the mastodon disappeared long ago. Its origin and survival remain a mystery for paleontologists, who have found a skeleton of what may be its ancestor, 7m long, in Australia.

It was by chance that the Dutch Lieutenant Van Steyn Van Hensbroek discovered the "monster" in 1910, after a crash landing off the coast of Komodo. No one was inclined to believe his account, except another officer who visited the island in 1912 and brought back the skin of a specimen to prove the accuracy of his description. The shock to the scientific community was considerable.

Since then, this prehistoric reptile has been studied at length. Deemed to be the largest lizard in the world – it can reach up to 3m in length – it appears to move its 150kg with difficulty but, once moving, can briefly reach speeds of 30km/h. It is only found on the islands of **Komodo**, **Rinca** and **Gili Motang**, along the south-west and northern coasts of Flores, and in East Sumbawa. Its territory is savannah, but you may see it on the beach or among the mangroves, in search of food. The carnivorous lizard enjoys macaque monkeys, deer, boar and birds. In its search for a balanced diet, however, it does not spurn a few lizards, snakes or eggs, even mosquitoes in times of shortage. Thanks to its very acute sense of smell (its forked tongue operates as a form of radar), it can detect game from kilometres away. The dragon's tail and claws are fearsome weapons and its disjointable jaws, with 26 notched teeth (like the tyrannosaurus!), enable it to eat very large prey – beginning, of course, with the best part, the entrails! To hunt buffalo the lizard is content to bite the animal and thereby inject bacteria that will kill it in a few hours or a few days. It is also a great lover of carrion and on occasions the most powerful males will practice cannibalism. This method of intimidation effectively operates to regulate the density of the population in any area, with the young males being encouraged to seek food and mate elsewhere. The adult giant lizard therefore has no predator other than its own kind – for humans take no interest in a creature whose skin is too thick to be used for handbags or other leather goods. The mating season runs from May to July: then, between July and September, the females lay their eggs in nests dug out on the hillsides. Incubation lasts for nine months and, once born, the young lizards spend their first months in trees, safe from predators. On average, the lizards live for 20 years.

A victim of deforestation, and also of the proliferation of stray dogs that eat their eggs, the species had dropped from 7 200 animals in 1971 to 4 000 by the end of the 1980s. In recent years, however, even though they are still considered to be threatened with extinction, the dragons are enjoying an encouraging expansion.

All kinds of tales circulate about the "dragon" – as the Indonesians like to call it – particularly the story of the Swiss tourist who set out alone on foot a few years ago, and disappeared completely apart from his spectacles and camera. Lizards have also been known to attack inhabitants of the island. In fact the creature is only likely to become a danger to someone who is wounded and on the ground, or in reaction to aggressive behaviour, situations that are therefore to be avoided.

Komodo National Park★★
Allow 1 day. Fee (on arrival), valid for the whole park.
(See also "Making the most of Komodo".)

Recognised as a World Heritage Site by **UNESCO**, the Komodo National Park covers an area of 219 000ha. In addition to Komodo it includes the islands of Rinca and Gili Morang, a large area of the sea and the Mbeliling and Nggorang region on Flores. As you cross the sea through the turquoise water, rounded hillocks of land appear one after another. Bays and capes alternate, as do cliffs, beaches of white sand and

A Komodo "dragon"

A Boutteville

ochre-coloured savannah. Such is the majority of the landscape, which is touched here and there with the bright green of palm trees. Apart from the lizard, you may see water buffalo, macaques, wild horses and deer. And the sea-bed forms the other major attraction of the park, not to be missed.

Sape Strait★★★

The crossing from Flores to Sumbawa is superb. To make the most of it, you could charter a boat for several people for two days. In this way you can visit Komodo or Rinca, enjoy their **beaches of fine sand** in solitude, swim in the clear waters and explore the **seabed★★**, which is outstanding. And in the evening, after enjoying fish fresh out of the sea, you can slide into a peaceful slumber, rocked by the gentle swell of the waves.

Sape Strait is swept by powerful currents that make navigation difficult, but local sailors are very familiar with the region and are well able to sail by night, guided by the stars. You can rely on them to show you the finest places, particularly **Pulau Lawah★**, a little island on the northern tip of Komodo with superb coral reefs, or **Pulau Banta★**, for a final swim before reaching Sape.

The currents also bring vast quantities of nutritional elements out of the depths, which attract **whales**, **dolphins** and many fish. Unfortunately they may be followed on occasion by unscrupulous poachers who do not hesitate to fish with dynamite or cyanide.

The island of Komodo★

In summer the island may have up to a hundred visitors each day, no doubt because it has the largest community of giant lizards (1 700 according to the 1997 census). When you reach the **PHPA camp** (Forest Protection and Environment Conservation Office) at **Loh Liang**, do not be taken aback by a lizard crawling along the beach or dozing in the shade of the bungalows: the first encounter is always the most alarming! Close at hand, the fishing village of **Kampung Komodo** is a pleasant destination for a walk.

Komodo, a fishing village

A Boutteville

Flores

Then set off towards the **natural trench**, which is the special realm of the "dragons". The walk (*2km, best in the morning when the lizards are at their most active*) is done with a guide (set price) who leads the way with a stick, and several dozen tourists. On the edge of the trench a hide enables you to observe the reptiles peacefully. Until 1994 the wardens of the park used to throw them lamb carcasses to amuse the tourists but the practice was abandoned when it was noted that it changed the animals' behaviour. They were becoming used to receiving their handout without having to hunt. Further, the weaker females tended to be excluded from the feast.

If you have the time, take a walk through the **Poreng valley** (*6km from Loh Liang; leave early in the morning, with a guide*). You cannot be quite so sure of seeing lizards, but the landscape is wilder and the tourists less numerous.

The most energetic may push on as far as **Gunung Ara** (538m), from where there is a magnificent **view**** over the archipelago.

Lastly, do not leave the island without enjoying its **diving sites**, including **Pantai Merah***, on the eastern tip of the bay, and **Pulau Lasa***, opposite Kampung Komodo.

The island of Rinca**

You can do the return trip from Labuhanbajo in a day, on a chartered boat, or you can stay on the island.

Although smaller and less touristic than Komodo, Rinca has a more varied range of flora and fauna (except for bird-life), as well as a colony of 1 300 lizards.

Half an hour from the jetty, after walking beside mangroves, you arrive at the **PHPA camp** at **Loh Buaya**. This is where you pay your entrance fee and find a guide.

The lizards that can be seen during your **walk in the savannah**** (2hr), met almost by chance round a bend in the track or in the shade of a tree, make a strong impression. The walk offers other surprises, particularly the **water buffalo** splashing through the mud (*better chances of seeing them in the afternoon, between 3 and 5pm*), or the enchanting rustling of the wind in the branches of the **lontar palms**.

Making the most of Komodo

COMING AND GOING

By sea – You can reach Komodo from Flores or Sumbawa. The journey-time depends on the sea, which is often rough. Chartering a boat at Labuhanbajo (Flores) will free you from being dependent on ferries.

● Komodo

In theory, two ferries offer a shuttle service from Sumbawa and Flores, but on our visit only one was in service and the times had been changed. Arrive early.
From Sape (Sumbawa), departures daily at 4pm, except Mondays (5-7hr).
From Labuhanbajo (Flores), departures daily at 8am, except Tuesday (3-4hr).
Boats cannot land at Komodo and you will be transferred onto a crowded shuttle to Loh Liang, for a small supplement.

● Rinca

For Rinca, you should charter a boat at Labuhanbajo (2hr30min).

WHERE TO STAY, EATING OUT

● Komodo

Modest

PHPA camp, Loh Liang – 35rm. You have the choice between 7 pavilions on piles, with rudimentary facilities, with or without fan and private bathroom. In summer, when the rooms are heavily in demand, you may have to sleep on the concrete floor in the dining room. The electricity supply operates between 6am and 10pm (don't forget a torch). The food is simple but wholesome (breakfast not included).

● Rinca

Modest

PHPA camp, Loh Buaya (30min from the jetty) – 6rm. Wooden cabins with basic facilities, but well maintained. The bathrooms are shared and breakfast is not included, but there are local places where you can eat.

LABUHANBAJO BAY★★
Manggarai District
137km west of Ruteng – Map p 502-503
Pop 3 000 – Climate, hot and dry

Not to be missed
A dive off the islands of Bidadari and Sebolan.
Sunset over the bay.

And remember...
In summer, reserve your room as the hotels are sometimes full.
Take your diving mask and snorkel.

Nestling in the curve of a magnificent bay, the fishing village of Labuhanbajo is one of those peaceful places where you can spend your time doing nothing, apart from watching the coming-and-going of the outrigger sailing boats and the dazzling sunset over the sea. But if you feel tempted to stay longer, it will be above all for the beaches of fine sand and the rich sea-bed around the islets strung out opposite the bay.

Labuhanbajo, the western port of entry on Flores *(although visitors are recommended to start their visit to the island in the east)* is also a good departure point for going to the Komodos. All these advantages have brought the village a substantial tourist boom, and in recent years this has become the main holiday destination on Flores.

Waiting for the fish

Fine sand and lionfish

Allow 2 to 3 days to make the most of the village and the islands.

Depending on whether you arrive from the west (Bali or Lombok), or arrive here at the end of the long journey across Flores, **Labuhanbajo** will either appear as the first stop in truly unfamiliar surroundings or a return to civilisation. At the foot of the hill where houses made of concrete or bamboo can be seen clinging to the slopes, clusters of traditional **Bugis houses** stand with their feet in the water. They line the main street through the village, and now rub shoulders with hotels, restaurants, shops and travel agencies.

Exploring the islands★★★

Most of the agencies in Labuhanbajo offer tours to any destination you choose in the neighbouring islets. They include several stops for diving, and lunch on a white sand beach. Idyllic!

Beneath the turquoise waters of the bay are extraordinarily beautiful **coral reefs★★**, a swirl of colours made up of an exceptional range of **marine life** – lionfish, parrot fish and Napoleon wrasse – which you can easily observe even if you are not an experienced diver. All you need is a mask and snorkel.

It would be impossible to cite all the local **diving spots**. Among the best known are the sites at **Pulau Bidadari★★** and **Pulau Sebolan★★** (*half a day*), while according to enthusiasts, the islands of **Tatawa** and **Sebayur Kecil** are also wonderful.

Around Labuhanbajo

For the idle life, nothing could be better than the **beach at Waecicu** (*5km to the north, 1hr on foot or 20min by boat on the hotel shuttle, which leaves from near the jetty*), a small

C Goupi/Scope

ribbon of sand shielded by a hillside and facing a deserted island. Stay there to see the **sunset★★**, a ball of fire melting into a silky-smooth sea.

From Labuhanbajo you can also set off on a short excursion to the hill at **Batu Cermin**, which is dotted with **caves** with incredible aerial roots growing down through them (*hire a car with a guide. After 4km on the Ruteng road, take a track for 1km; fee*).

Continuing along the Ruteng road you cross a magnificent **mountainous landscape★★**, with a luxuriant green valley (*halfway along, near Limbung*). The winding road affords several superb **views★★** over Labuhanbajo bay before plunging into thick forest.

Labuhanbajo Bay

Making the most of Labuhanbajo

COMING AND GOING

By air – The airport is 2.5km from the town centre (by bemo). **Merpati** is the only airline to serve Labuhanbajo, with departures from Denpasar (4 times a week) and Bima (twice a week).

By boat – The ferry jetty is at the northern end of the village. Departure daily at 8am, except Tuesday for Komodo (3hr) and Sape (8-9hr).

By bus – Departures for **Ruteng** (138km) around 7am and 5pm (4hr). The bus collects you from your hotel but may occasionally spend a very long time waiting for other passengers.
Departure for **Bajawa** at 6.30am (approximately 8hr30min).

GETTING AROUND

On foot – This is the easiest method, since distances in the village are short.

By bemo – Useful for short trips, you can also hire one for the day or half-day.

ADDRESS BOOK

Tourist information – Dinas Pariwisata, in the south of the town, near the Telkom agency, ☎ (0385) 411 71 (7am-3pm; closed at weekends). Offers some good brochures on Flores.

PHPA (Forest Protection and Environment Conservation Office) next to the Tourist information. Brochure on Komodo.

Bank/Currency exchange – Warning, the banks do not accept credit cards.

Bank Rakyat Indonesia, main street. 7.30am-3.30pm; closed for lunch. Accepts dollars and travellers' cheques.

Bank Negara Indonesia, main street. Daily, 7am-3pm. Accepts dollars and travellers' cheques. Reasonably good exchange rates. Negotiate.

Post Office – Main post office, Jl Soekarno-Hatta (near the BRI). Poste restante. Monday-Thursday 7.30am-3pm, Friday 7.30-11am, Saturday 7.30am-1pm.

Telephone – Telkom, on the hillside in the south of the town, near the tourist of-

fice. Open 24hr a day. **Victory Wartel**, main street, near the Gardena Hotel (6am-12 midnight).

Airline company – Merpati, Jl Eltari, on the airport road, ☎ (0385) 411 77. 8am-1pm. Reservations for flights departing from Labuhanbajo only.

Shipping line – Pelni, behind Stella Maria Church, ☎ (0385) 411 06. 8am-5pm; closed on Sundays except when a boat arrives.

WHERE TO STAY

Labuhanbajo offers an excellent range of hotels, at reasonable prices. Most of them are in the main street, and are shown here from south to north for each category.

Modest

Cendana, 4km south of the town, fairly isolated (free shuttle), ☎ (0385) 411 25 – 15rm. ⚑ 🛪 / 🍽 ✗ 🌣 The rooms are large, but the maintenance is less than satisfactory and the vast lobby is quite cold. The friendly staff are casual whatever the circumstances.

Wisata, main road, facing the BNI, ☎ (0385) 410 20 – 23rm. ⚑ 🛪 ✗ The rooms are laid out along a white-tiled corridor without character, but they are comfortable and beautifully kept, and breakfast is included.

Chez Felix, on the hill above the town (take the street near the hospital), ☎ (0385) 410 32 – 10rm. ⚑ 🛪 ✗ The rooms are plain but comfortable, equipped with mosquito nets, and most have a private bathroom (water is rationed in the dry season). After a fairly stiff climb you will be rewarded by the view over the bay and a warm welcome.

Bajo Beach Hotel, main road, just south of the Borobudur restaurant, ☎ (0385) 410 08 – 26rm. ⚑ 🛪 ✗ In the same category as the Wisata, comfortable though somewhat worn. Breakfast (basic) included. The staff are happy to provide information, and offer a wide range of services (bus reservations, tours and car hire).

Gardena Bungalows, main street, 300m south of the jetty, ☎ (0385) 412 58 – 17rm. ⚑ 🛪 ✗ In a garden with trees on the hillside. Small bamboo bungalows provide rustic facilities but are full of charm. The staff are an excellent source of information and can provide numerous services (hire of cars, masks and snorkels).

Waecicu Beach Hotel, 20min north of Labuhanbajo by boat shuttle (reservation opposite the Borobudur restaurant, Fax (0385) 411 04 – 16rm. 🔌 ✕ 🐠 💧 Set in the curve of a small isolated creek, full of charm. The bungalows are lined up facing the beach and are very comfortable (open-air bathrooms). Numerous activities: canoeing, table tennis, walking and diving. The prices, per head and not per room, include three meals.

Average
New Bajo Beach Hotel, 2km south of the town, on the Ruteng road ☎ (0385) 410 47 – 25rm. 🔌 📰 / ☂ ✕ 🐠 You can choose between concrete rooms or quiet and very attractive wooden bungalows facing the beach. But the latter do not lock, and service is particularly slow (breakfast included, but frugal)

EATING OUT

Basic
Warung Arto Moro, main street, 50m beyond the BRI. A wooden hut overlooking the bay, offering simple, cheap but tasty food (vegetables, fried chicken and seafood).

Moderate
Dewata Ayu, main street. European, Indonesian and Chinese cuisine served on a pleasant terrace overlooking the street. The seafood is excellent.

Borobudur, main street, near Dewata Ayu. Also on a terrace. The cuisine is varied (Indonesian, Thai and Western), but the restaurant, a victim of its own success, gives a rather chilly welcome.

Gardena Bungalows, (see above). Chinese and Indonesian cuisine, seafood and pasta.

OTHER THINGS TO DO

Excursions – Plenty of agencies offer tailor-made tours to Komodo and the small islands facing the bay. In the harbour, you can also negotiate directly with the owner of a boat. In all cases, make sure you specify the stops planned and the different services provided (food, masks, snorkels and park entrance).

Mega Buana Bahari, Jl Yos Sudarso 3, ☎ (0385) 412 89. Organises a five-day boat trip to Lombok via Komodo.

Perama, main street, ☎ (0385) 410 58. Offices throughout Nusa Tenggara, offering tours of several days to Flores, Komodo, Sumbawa and Lombok.

PT Wannen Tours & Travel, near the Dewata Ayu restaurant ☎ (0385) 413 48. Tours to Flores and Lombok, or by the day among the islands (diving and visits to the park).

Diving – Waecicu Beach Dive, office in the hotel and in the town centre, ☎ (0385) 411 04/413 44. Qualified instructors (PADI), for beginners or experienced divers. Opportunity to take the certificate.

Grand Komodo Adventure & Diving, Jl P-W Papu, ☎ (0385) 412 77. With its boat perfectly equipped for diving, the agency guarantees reliability.

SHOPPING GUIDE

Shops – You will find plenty of souvenir shops and a few antique dealers, but Labuhanbajo is definitely not the best place in Flores for buying ikats, as the quality is mediocre and the prices are high.

Making the most of Labuhanbajo

RUTENG
THE MANGGARAI REGION
Capital of the Manggarai District
135km from Bajawa – Map p 502-503
Alt 1 100m – Climate, cool

Not to be missed
The rice fields, shaped like a spider's web.
And remember...
Put aside a full day to explore the region.

Ruteng is an inescapable point on the road from Labuhanbajo to Bajawa. It lies at the bottom of a broad mountain valley ringed with volcanoes. Apart from its setting, the town itself has little of interest. If you have the time, set off instead to explore the region with its forests, coffee plantations and terraced rice fields. The area provides a variety of walks and the opportunity to explore the Manggarai region, the home of a unique culture that blends Catholicism and animism.

A brief tour of the town

The football ground, at the junction of Jl Motang Rua and Jl Niaga, marks the town centre.

The capital of the Manggarai region is a large town with scattered buildings that can take pride in having a traffic light – perhaps the only one on the island! Above all it has a **Cathedral**, which rises up like a cardboard cut-out *(at the top of Jalan Sudarso, the main avenue).*

The caci, or fighting Manggarai-style
The people of Manggarai remain deeply devoted to their ancestor worship. They honour them in the "caci", a test of strength and courage that sets the men of two villages against each other. Divided by an invisible barrier, the supporters of the two camps form a circle on the central square, transformed into an arena for the occasion. Each combatant alternatively plays the part of the warrior and that of the buffalo. Armed with a whip, the attacker tries to hit his rival on the arm, the back, even the face, but he has the right to no more than a single blow. Wearing a kind of horned visor, and with a piece of bamboo to represent a tail, the "buffalo" has a shield and a simple stick with which to defend himself. He adopts a casual stance, which he never drops, even when he is struck. But the referee watches, counts the blows and announces the winning village. Sensitive souls should keep away.

Installed in a large cement building, the **market** *(Jl Kartini, 100m east of the football ground)* naturally represents the liveliest part of the town, and the best place to hunt out the sparkling **Manggarai ikats**.

A little further south *(Jl Motang Rua)*, you will see a great thatched roof of a **traditional house** (Rumah Adat). Its round shape, characteristic of the Manggarai region, recalls the pattern of the lingko rice fields.

At the other end of the town *(Jl Mongisidi)*, the disconcerting **wreck of a plane** belonging to the Merpati airline lies in the exact spot where its pilot brought it down in an emergency several years ago.

Ruteng, the "caci" or "buffalo-man" fight

G Guérard

The "rice basket" of Flores

Before leaving Ruteng, climb **Golo Guru** hill *(2km to the north, access by bemo or on foot)*. The road is an unusual **Way of the Cross**, punctuated by statues of Christ that line the route right up to the summit, which is crowned with a small shrine dedicated to the Virgin. From here you have a magnificent **view★** over the town and its surrounding rice fields.

However, the finest **view★★** of the area is from the small **Waebelang hill** *(17km west of Ruteng, near Cancar, by bemo)*, from where you can look out over the **lingko★**, the typically Manggarese rice fields laid out like a spider's web.

The Bajawa road★

Take a bemo as far as Robo (8km east of Ruteng). Ask to be dropped off at the fork of a track that takes you through the woods for 9km. From Ruteng, you can hire a bemo, but the track is impassable after rain.

The highest point in Flores, **Ranaka volcano★** (2 400m) is the destination for one of the most magical **walks** in the area, right through the jungle *(best done in the morning, as the forest wakes up)*. Birds sing amongst giant ferns and orchids. The track leads to a telecommunications station, which was abandoned after the eruption in 1987.

Back on the main road again, continue east to the superb **Ranamese crater lake★** *(23km from Ruteng)*. It lies spread out in the midst of thick jungle, shimmering in the light. Picnic places have been laid out along the shores, making it a pleasant place to relax. In fine weather the sea is visible, far to the south.

Flores

Making the most of Ruteng

COMING AND GOING

By air – The airport is 2km from the town centre (by bemo). **Merpati** provides a weekly connection with Bima (Sumbawa), on Thursday mornings.

By bus – When you arrive in Ruteng the buses take you to your hotel. When you leave, if you use your hotel to buy your ticket, you can ask to be collected.
The terminus lies behind the central market. Departures around 7am and 5pm for Labuhanbajo (4hr), Bajawa (5hr) and Ende (10hr).

GETTING AROUND

By bemo – The most widely available form of transport in Ruteng.

ADDRESS BOOK

Bank/Currency exchange – Bank Negara Indonesia, Jl Yos Sudarso. The best exchange rate in town. Monday–Friday, 7am-3pm (closed for lunch). You can change dollars and travellers' cheques here.

Post office/Telephone – Main post office, Jl Baruk 6 (Monday-Thursday 7.30am-3pm, Friday 7.30-11.30am, Saturday 7.30am-1pm, Sunday 9am-12noon). **Telkom**, Jl Kartini. Open 24hr a day

Airline company – Merpati, Ruteng, Jl Kancil 5 (east of the town centre, near the Kristus Raja Church), ☎ (0385) 211 47.

WHERE TO STAY

Since the climate is fairly cool, it is easy to do without air conditioning in Ruteng. Hot water, on the other hand, becomes a much-appreciated amenity.

Modest

Agung I, Jl Waeces 10 (north of the town), ☎ (0385) 210 80 – 26rm. Laid out along a large dark lobby that leads to a lily pond, the rooms (with or without private bathrooms) are inexpensive but somewhat neglected.

Agung III, Jl Waeces 10, ☎ (0385) 210 80 – 9rm. ☎ ✗ This new hotel built next to Agung I has vast and more comfortable rooms (television with satellite channels), and is good value for the price. Breakfast included.

Average

Hotel Rima, Jl Achmad Yani 14, ☎ (0385) 221 95 – 12rm. ✗ With its chalet style, the latest of Ruteng's hotels is also the most unusual. You are given a warm reception, and the hotel even has a bar. Most of the rooms have bathrooms, and the price includes a substantial breakfast. The only disadvantage is that the site is rather noisy.

Hotel Dahlia, Jl Bhayangkari 18, ☎ (0385) 213 77 – 42rm. This large concrete building, which lacks charm, nonetheless has large comfortable rooms. The simplest rooms share a bathroom, while the most luxurious have hot water and television (running water between 5am and 10pm). It is unfortunate that the service is not up to standard.

Wisma Sindha, Jl Yos Sudarso 26, ☎ (0385) 211 97, Fax (0385) 211 04 – 25rm. ✗ In the same category as the Dahlia, but quieter and more friendly. The hotel has a wide range of rooms, with or without bathrooms and television (satellite channels).

EATING OUT

Moderate

Bambou D'en, Jl Motang Rua 30 (town-centre). A pleasant place with bamboo decor that serves good Indonesian cuisine.

Rima, (see the hotel entry). Apart from the classic "nasi goreng" and grilled chicken, the menu offers a range of dishes. Note that the service is very slow and you would be wise to take a sweater along because the room, open to the outside air, is very chilly.

Merlyn Ruteng, near the Dahlia Hotel. Useful as a stand-by. A small Chinese restaurant with very unexpected satellite television.

OTHER THINGS TO DO

Traditional festivals – In Ruteng and the surrounding villages you can watch a *caci* fight on the national holiday (17 August), or one that has been arranged for a religious or family ceremony (wedding).

THE NGADA REGION★★★
BAJAWA
Capital of the Ngada District
125km from Ende – Map p 502-503
Pop 12 000 – Alt 1 100m – Cool climate

Not to be missed
The villages of Bena, Nage and Langa.
Climbing the Mount Inerie volcano.
And remember...
Take a guide to visit the villages, as they are not always easily accessible.

Overshadowed by volcanoes, hidden in valleys or in the depths of the forest, the Ngada villages bear testimony to the wealth of tradition on Flores. Bajawa, a pleasant mountain town criss-crossed by lanes with low houses, lies in the heart of the region and makes an excellent base camp from which to explore the Ngada lands. It must be hoped that the fragile beauty of the area will survive the invasion of modern life and tourism.

The Ngada, or the memory of the forest
The origins of the Ngada – now numbering around 60 000 – are still fairly obscure, but the use of **standing stones** seems to link this nation with the Dongson culture of Vietnam, which flourished throughout Southeast Asia in the first millennium before the modern era *(see p 31)*. Despite their conversion to Catholicism, introduced in the 1920s, the Ngada remain profoundly attached to their animist beliefs and rituals, based on a complex form of ancestor worship.

Nature, the bastion of national memory, is at the centre of the whole Ngada cosmogony, dominated by Dewa, the god of the sky, and his wife Nitu, goddess of the earth. In this scheme of things the village symbolises the "interior", in contrast with the forest, the "exterior", a world burdened with mysteries and dangers. Inerie, the volcano, represents the sacred mountain.

"Ngadhu" and "bagha", soul of the ancestors
The Ngada villages are all laid out to the same plan: a wide square of beaten earth, surrounded by two rows of houses on small piles, built of wood and bamboo and roofed with thatch. Various buildings stand in the middle of the earth platform – one for each clan – and are the dwellings of the male or female spirits of the founding, protective ancestors.

Flores

The male ancestor of the clan is represented by the **ngadhu**, a carved pole some 3m tall, reminiscent of a parasol: topped with a small conical roof of thatch, the stake is flanked by a pair of arms bearing a spear and a machete. Since each tree has a soul, the Ngada leave it up to the diviner to choose the perfect specimen from the forest to use as a *ngadhu* stake. Removed with its roots, the tree will be covered with a sheet (for it is considered dangerous) before being brought back to the village, along a straight line, to be replanted. This is a moment for special festivities, from which young women are excluded since the tree is believed to be liable to rape them!

Bamboo houses

The Ngada region is full of every kind of bamboo. The largest species, which may reach a height of 30m, provide the main construction material for the houses, each one requiring the felling of some 50 to 60 trunks (Rp5 000 each). Once the work is finished, the house is inaugurated, with the sacrifice of buffaloes and pigs as the high point in the festivities. It is the task of the village diviner to appoint an officiating person to do this, someone whose hand must not shake as it delivers the fatal blow of the machete. After the feast, the horns of the buffaloes are used to decorate the front of the house.

Symbolising the womb, the original mother of all ancestors, the **bhaga** are represented by small square thatched houses. To complete the ensemble, stone steles (*peo*) are driven into the ground round a sacrificial stone.

Lastly, picking up the same symbolism, each house either features a strange warrior figure with spear and machete, like the *ngadhu*, or a miniature hut identical to the *bhaga*.

Bena, a Ngada village

G Guérard

The Ngada Region

Bajawa

Bajawa, the administrative and commercial capital of the region, is a pleasant town, although it has no distinctive features, apart from its lively and colourful **market** (*see "Making the most of Bajawa"*). Its future seems uncertain, since the authorities have decided to move its inhabitants to the north, to the coastal plain of Mbay, a more favourable setting for progress and development.

25km north of Bajawa, on the Riung road (*by bemo*), the little town of **Soa** has a **market** every Wednesday that brings people flocking in from all the local villages. The highlight of this journey, however, is the **hot spring★** (Air Panas) that wells up near the village of **Mengeruda** (*8km from Soa, on the Boawae road; hire a bemo*) in a paradise of greenery. The main pool, in the shade of a spreading fig tree, is so hot that it is a breathless business getting into the water. One can encourage oneself by thinking about a dip in the cooler waters of the little **stream** flowing down below.

On top of Inerie★★ (Gunung Inerie)

It is essential to take a guide. Leave Bajawa at 2.30am. Allow 30min by car to the little hamlet just before Bena, then 4hr on foot for the round trip.

While the climb is not difficult it is demanding because of the excessively straight (and therefore steep) path and the deep layer of ash that slows the pace. When you reach the edge of the **crater★** – a perfect hole 250m deep – follow the ridge (*30min walk*) to the **summit★★** (2 245m). From here you will have a magnificent **view★★** over Bajawa, Bena, **Mount Ebulebo** (2 124m) and, in clear weather, you may even see the island of Sumba, 100km to the south.

From village to village

Allow 2 days. Plenty of bemos serve Langa; but for Bena, Nage and Wajo, it is better to hire one. You can also do the trip on foot, or by truck!

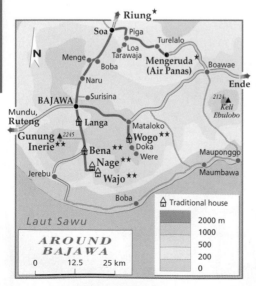

■ **Langa** – *7km southeast of Bajawa*. The first village on the route, Langa is the least typical, although it still has its **ngadhu** and **bhaga**. On market days in Bajawa, the place is virtually empty.

■ **Bena★★** – *16km from Bajawa, donation. After Langa, the track, in increasingly poor condition passes the foot of Mount Inerie. This is without doubt one of the most beautiful villages in the Ngada region. It stands on the neck of a small tree-covered promontory offering a spectacular panoramic view★★★ over the plain and forest that stretch out below. It is true that with the intrusion of*

Flores

tourism, Bena is tending to become a kind of living museum, and the houses round the earth platform have mostly been turned into sales displays for **ikats** (which are still superb, with motifs of horses against a black background). But the inhabitants have fortunately remained faithful to their traditional way of life, and the only concession to modernity appears to be the volleyball pitch next to the **ngadhu***, the **bhaga*** and the **peo** (standing stones).

If you have the time, continue to the south. The track, in poor condition and very steep, takes you through a thick tropical forest.

■ **Nage and Wajo**** – *24km from Bajawa.* Just before you reach Nage, the road crosses a beautiful emerald-green **river***, fed by a **hot spring**. Here you are in the land of *moke*, a palm spirit that is left to ferment in simple bamboo tubes suspended from tree branches. Wherever you look, the **view**** is superb: here and there villages emerge from among the trees, a giant waterfall carves its way through the forest to crash at the foot of Inerie, while to the south the Indian Ocean glints temptingly.

Before you leave the area, make a last stop on the road to Ende. From Bajawa, continue to Mataloko (18km), where you turn right. Then walk for 2km if you have not hired a bemo.

■ **Wogo**** – Still set apart from the modern world and tourism, this large village continues to be self-supporting, providing everything it needs apart from sugar, tobacco, soap, salt and textiles. The picture would be almost idyllic, if it were not for the relative poverty of the inhabitants who find it difficult to meet their major expense, their children's education. Following the traditional layout, two rows of houses stand close together round a wide central space on which stand the **ngadhu** and **bhaga**.

The original village of **Wogo Lama** *(take the road at the end of the earth platform and walk for 15min to a path, on the left)* was abandoned for the present-day site, which was considered more favourable. On the edge of a clump of giant bamboos stands the old square, carpeted with weeds and studded with **megaliths**. From the hamlet below Wogo Lama, you can enjoy a superb **view**** over the luxuriant hillsides where a few buffalo graze, with the tall shape of Ebulobo volcano standing in the background. The village children will be delighted to accompany you to the **hot spring** nearby, from where you can return direct to Wogo *(allow 90min for the whole walk)*.

The Ngada Region

Making the most of Bajawa

COMING AND GOING

By air – The **airport** lies 25km to the north, at Soa (by *bemo*). Merpati runs direct connections with Bima and Ende, but weather conditions may sometimes prevent landings.

By bus – Book through your hotel (warning – the buses are often full).

Watujadi terminus (3km to the east) runs buses to Ende (5hr), Maumere (8hr30min), Labuhanbajo (8hr30in), Ruteng (5hr). Most departures are around 7am.

Ngaru terminus (3km to the north) serves Riung. Early morning departure (2hr30min).

By bemo – **Bemo terminus**, Jl Basuki Rahmat. For the local villages (Langa, Mataloko, Boawae).

By truck – Trucks leave regularly from the *bemo* terminus for Soa, Mataloko and Langa.

GETTING AROUND

On foot – A real pleasure: distances are short and the climate fairly cool.

By bemo – They cover the whole town. A wave of the hand is enough to stop one.

Motorbike and car rental – **Central Motor**, Jl A Yani 58.

ADDRESS BOOK

Tourist information– Dinas Pariwisata, Jl Soekarno-Hatta (Monday-Thursday 7am-2pm, Friday 7-11am, Saturday 7am-12.30pm). Brochures and maps of the area, in English.

Bank/Currency exchange – Bank Negara Indonesia, Jl Pieretandean (Monday-Thursday 7.30am-3pm, Friday 7.30am-2.30pm, Saturday 9am-12noon). Better rates than the BRI. Dollars and travellers' cheques are accepted, but not credit cards.

Bank Rakyat Indonesia, Jl Soekarno-Hatta (Monday-Friday 7.30am-4pm; closed for lunch). Accepts dollars and travellers' cheques, but not credit cards.

Post office/Telephone – Main post office, Jl Soekarno-Hatta (Monday-Thursday, 7.30am-3pm, Friday 7.30-11.30am, Saturday 7.30am-1pm).

Telkom, Jl Soekarno-Hatta, opposite the Bank Rakyat (24hr).

Airline company – Merpati, Jl Pasar Rahmat (near the market), ☎ (0384) 210 51, Fax (0384) 213 53.

WHERE TO STAY

Bajawa has a good range of hotels, most of them offering numerous services (breakfast included, tours, car hire and bus reservations).

Modest

Hotel Anggrek, Jl Let Jend Haryono 9, ☎ (0384) 211 72 – 20rm. ⌨ ✗ The rooms are small but beautifully kept, and offer excellent value for money.

Ariesta, Jl Diponegoro, ☎ (0384) 212 92 – 7rm. ⌨ A pleasant guesthouse set up in a small house with a garden, quiet and clean.

Sunflower, in a lane between Jl A Yani and Jl Pasar Baru – 10rm. ⌨ The rooms are small and rustic, but very inexpensive, and the view of Inerie is incomparable.

Korina, Jl A Yani 81, ☎ (0384) 211 62 – 15rm. ✗ The upkeep of the rooms (plain, some with private bathroom) is fairly basic. All open onto an enormous central hall with an imposing satellite television. Fairly chilly.

Nusantara Hotel, Jl El Tari 10, ☎ (0384) 213 57 – 14rm. ✗ A small unpretentious place, but welcoming and inexpensive. Most of the rooms have a private bathroom.

Elisabeth, Jl Inerie, ☎ (0384) 212 23 – 7rm. A new, quiet and well maintained hotel, although the facilities are somewhat Spartan. Some rooms have private bathrooms.

Average

Losmen Kembang, Jl Martadinata 18 (near the market), ☎ (0384) 210 72 – 10rm. ⌨ The facilities are irreproachable and the reception friendly, but the prices are perhaps a little high.

EATING OUT

Moderate

Camelia, Jl A Yani 82 (opposite the Korina Hotel). The Chinese and Western cuisine is reasonable but unimaginative, and the servings will leave you looking for more. On the other hand, while you are here you can pick up plenty of local information.

Kasih Bahagia, Jl Basuki Rahmat 123, near the market. A small Chinese restaurant, plain and good, offering all kinds of soup, noodles and sate (skewered meat).

Hotel Anggrek (see above). The menu is not very imaginative but the cooking is excellent and, for once, service is swift!

Ganto Garam, Jl Gajah Mada. A restaurant offering Padang cuisine (Sumatra), served according to tradition: a wide selection of dishes (highly seasoned) is set out on your table and you pay only for what you eat. Try the delicious "rendang" (beef in sauce).

OTHER THINGS TO DO

Festivals and ceremonies – Among the Ngada, everything is an excuse for a ceremony: the religious calendar, work in the fields, and the various events of daily life. Ask your hotel about the dates of the festivals.

M'aha Kudus. At Easter (April), men armed with sabres carry a crucifix in procession through the town. This is also the moment for a deer hunt.

Fertility festivals (January) are marked by buffalo sacrifice and singing (around Bajawa).

Paruwitu (October-November), in Soa. Deer hunting and boxing matches.

SHOPPING GUIDE

Market – Bajawa market is particularly lively on Sunday mornings, after Mass. It sells fruit, vegetables, betel, tobacco, glass jewellery and textiles including, naturally, some superb **ikats**.

Antiques and handicrafts – **Bintang Art Shop**, Jl Pasar Inpres (market entrance). A good selection of traditional statues, jewellery and ikats. Note that the finest pieces appear among others of less certain origins, and the prices are high.

A village game of cards

Making the most of Bajawa

PULAU TUJUHBELAS★★★
RIUNG
Ngada District archipelago
70km north of Bajawa – Map p 502-503
Riung: pop 1 500 – Hot climate

Not to be missed
A cruise among the islands.

And remember...
Take anti-malarial treatment.
Warning: Riung has no telephone and the electricity, installed in 1997,
functions only between 6pm and 6am.
For the islands, remember to take protective sun cream and a hat.

Still on the margins of the Flores tourist route, Riung seems likely to have a fine future. A few hundred metres from this peaceful fishing village, the Pulau Tujuhbelas archipelago lies strung out across the turquoise sea, a necklace of deserted islands fringed with white sand and shimmering coral, the setting for some memorable diving. As you arrive from Bajawa, the contrast is marked, for the green landscape of the Ngada region is no more than a distant memory here. Beyond Soa, the road soon opens out onto an enormous basin plateau, at a height of 830m, still enjoying a mild climate, then it drops down again towards the north coast across drier land that affords some fine **views★** over the bay of Riung.

Riung, an oasis in the sea

Riung with its mosaic of houses scattered beneath coconut palms at the foot of a hill scorched by the sun is like an oasis. From a distance there is nothing to reveal the presence of houses, except for the smoke rising above the trees. Here time has settled into an idle calm – there is no commercial district, nor any administrative centre. Most of the houses have no name and even the **harbour**, focal point for all village activity, is really no more than a simple bay without a quay, with a few modest boats tied up. With the **houses set on piles** beside the sea – home to the village's Bugis community – the **mangroves** and the little islets dotted about off-shore, the sea itself looks like a lake, a delightful haven of peace.

The inhabitants of Riung, who are mostly Catholic, have an unusual respect for their animals, from the ordinary stray dog to the local giant lizard. And they give visiting tourists an equally warm reception.

From the top of **Watujapi hill** (*3km from the village, on foot if you do not have your own car*), you will have a rewarding **view★** of Riung Bay and the Pulau Tujuhbelas, before going on to explore them.

The "Seventeen Islands"
*Allow 1 day. The trip to Torong Padang (to see the giant lizards)
should be booked as soon as you reach Riung.*

Contrary to its name, Pulau Tujuhbelas ("Seventeen Islands") actually comprises 23 islands. The name is in fact a reference to the national holiday, 17 August! Despite this, the number of places for diving is sufficiently large to satisfy all underwater

M Jozon/Hoaqui

Pulau Tujuhbelas, an aquatic paradise

Flores

enthusiasts. The wonderfully preserved **coral gardens**** off the islands make up a fantasy land of colour (red, yellow, green and blue) and shape (coral "flowers", basins and plateaux), a superb setting for countless fish, each more colourful than the last *(see plates, p 24-25)*.

As soon as you reach Riung, your main concern will be to find a team and equipment for the next day – a simple task – *(see "Making the most of Riung")*. The programme includes a series of dives with mask and snorkel, and a lunch of grilled fish on a deserted island. What more could you want?

Corals, fish, lizards and giant bats

The day begins with a dive off **Pulau Lainjawa**, then off **Pulau Bakau**, before continuing to **Pulau Rutong**, where you can relax for a while on a magnificent **beach of white sand****.

The trip ends at **Pulau Ontoloe****, the largest island in the group, covered with sparse savannah. A very large colony of **giant bats**, surveyed by a lone eagle often seen flying overhead, has settled in the mangrove swamps that extend to the shore in a labyrinth of roots. The noise of the boats – and the shouts of your guide – will be enough to set off a wave of panic through the colony, and you will see the bats suddenly flying off, covering the sky with a dark sinister cloak. An impressive sight!

If you are fascinated by **giant lizards** (mbu), you can also set up a trip to **Torong Padang**, near **Damu Bay** *(charter a boat, then walk to the watering place)*. A **Japanese ship** sunk during the Second World War is said to lie on the sea-bed here, at a depth of 30m.

Smaller than the Komodo dragons, the local species of lizard can be distinguished by its yellow and black skin, its tapering tail and its long snout. In truth, your chance of seeing one is slight, for they are very timid creatures and capable of scenting you from a distance of 1km. To be more certain of success, the local guides suggest buying a goat carcass, preferably just at the right stage of decay, in order to attract a lizard – if you have the stomach for it.

Making the most of Riung

COMING AND GOING

By bus – You can reserve your bus ticket at most of the hotels, for Bajawa (departures at 7am and 2pm, 2hr30min) and Ende, via Mbay (135km, 5hr, poor road as far as Mbay).

By boat – There are irregular services to Reo and Maumere. You can also charter a boat to Labuhanbajo (16hr).

ADDRESS BOOK

PHPA – Forest Protection and Environment Conservation Office, near the Tamri Beach *losmen*. A good source of information about the region. Go there, if only to see the two large lizards in a cage.

WHERE TO STAY

Tourism in Riung is still in its infancy and on the whole the standard of hotel facilities is fairly mediocre (no en-suite bathrooms). In addition, few of the streets have their names marked; but the village is small and it's not difficult to find your way around.

Modest

Hotel Iklas, Bugis district, near the port – 5rm. An unusual and friendly guesthouse in a Bugis house on piles. The rooms give onto a wide terrace but the facilities and cleanliness are very basic and it is very hot here. Breakfast included.

Homestay Tamri Beach, near the church – 4rm. A small guesthouse with tiny rooms.

Liberty Homestay, near the church – 8rm. An enormous and well-kept house,

with balcony, and a welcoming atmosphere. A pity that the rooms are like ovens.

Madona Homestay, next to the Liberty – 5rm. A style that is definitely in favour in Riung: a family atmosphere, but stifling rooms and rudimentary facilities.

Florida Hotel, 200m south of the above – 10rm. ✗ Better! This offers clean and comfortable rooms, equipped with mosquito nets, some with fans and private bathrooms. The restaurant was being renovated when we visited.

Average

Pondok SVD, on the east side of the town – 11rm. ✗ This belongs to the Ende Catholic mission and is undoubtedly the best in town. The rooms set round a courtyard planted with trees are comfortable and perfectly maintained. You will be warmly welcomed and, if you like, ask for Om Petrus, a masseur beyond compare!

EATING OUT

Rumah Makan Cilegon, near the market. The town's only restaurant offers a good selection of seafood, varying with the day's catch.

OTHER THINGS TO DO

Diving – Nearly all the hotels organise trips to the islands, but the **Florida** and the **Pondok SVD** seem to be the most professional (ask for Pak Sylvester). A diving club has opened recently in Riung; enquire at the Florida Hotel.

ENDE
Headquarters of the Ende District
150km from Maumere – Map p 502-503 and p 542
Pop 66 000 – Hot dry climate

Not to be missed
The view from Nuabosi.
The village of Wolotopo.

And remember...
Hire a car to explore the surroundings.
Allow one day to visit everything, including a trip to the coast.

Standing at the entrance of a narrow peninsula, the largest city in Flores is spread out at the foot of two volcanoes, **Meja** and **Iya**, whose majestic outlines, visible everywhere, provide a wonderfully beautiful setting. The departure point for a visit to Kelimutu (*see p 542*), the town also provides a good base for various colourful excursions to the coast.

Although Flores claims to be more attached to Catholicism than to Islam, it is not unusual to see veiled women in Ende, and the Chinese traders who are active around the port have an extremely varied mixture of beliefs and cultures.

After the terrible earthquake in 1992, which flattened the old harbour, the city experienced fresh difficulties during the riots in 1998. Today, happily, life seems to have settled back to normal.

Exploring the city
Allow 2hr.

Although the new **port of Pelabuhan Ipi** and the airport have been laid out to the east, the liveliest quarter is still the district round the **old harbour**, on the west of the isthmus, the commercial quarter dominated by the **Cathedral**.

200m north of the Cathedral, in Jalan Dewantara, an elegant green and yellow house contains the **Bung Karno Museum** (*8am-12noon; closed on Sundays; donation*), home of the father of Indonesia's independence, who lived here during his years of exile (in the 1930s). Here you can see the little desk where he drew up the famous **Pancasila** that was to become the national creed (*see p 41*).

After the bustle of the **market** (*south of the Cathedral, in Jl Pasar*), you will particularly appreciate the peace and space in the **western bay**, a long ribbon of black sand stretching out opposite **Pulau Ende**. A good opportunity to enjoy the **sunset★** over the little island.

If you like fine views, you should also seek out **Nuabosi hill★** (*9km to the north*), where the panoramic view takes in the whole town and the coast. Strewn with fallen rocks, the road winds up to the top (650m) through plantations of tapioca.

Trips along the coast★

To the west of Ende (*take a bemo from Ndao terminus*), the Bajawa road runs along a vast beach of black sand, 10km long. Then it reaches **Penggajawa beach** (*25km from Ende*) that no doubt owes the surprising blue colour of its pebbles to some celestial whim. Every day five tons of pebbles, looking like giant sweets are gathered up by the villagers (earning Rp500 per kg) to be exported to Japan where they are used as garden decoration.

A Boutteville

Ende, shimmering ikats

Flores

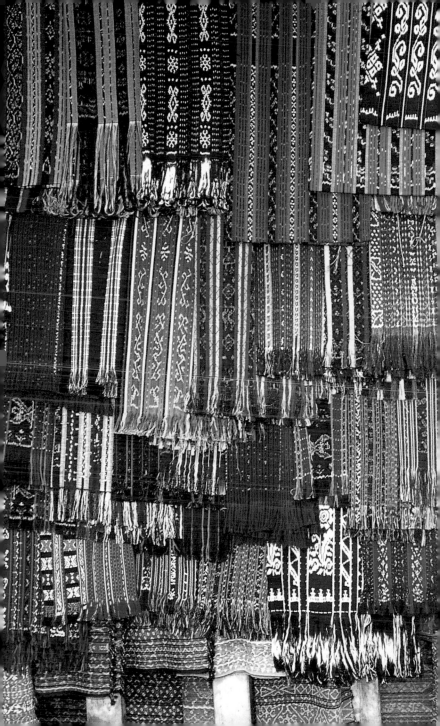

The east coast★

To the east *(take a bemo from Wolowona terminus in Ende)*, there is another beautiful **black-sand beach** where, according to local belief, an evil spirit once settled.

As you round a bend, the village of **Wolotopo**★ *(5km east of Ende)* suddenly comes into sight, overlooking the sea. An enormous **church** with a corrugated iron roof looms over the square in the middle of a cluster of little houses clinging tightly against each other up the hillside. Children will guide you through the maze to the magnificent **long houses**★★ that are typical of the region. The entrance doors are flanked by panels carved with a woman's chest, commemorating the period before and after childbirth.

On the promontory overlooking the village, a little **shrine** houses the body of the legendary warrior Daia. There is a splendid **view**★★ of the bay.

Making the most of Ende

COMING AND GOING

By air – The **airport** is 500m east of the town centre, at the end of Jl Kelimutu. **Merpati** runs direct flights to Bajawa, Bima, Kupang and Labuhanbajo.

By boat – Several **Pelni** boats link Java and Bali with Timor, via Ende and the Sunda Islands.

By bus – Wolowona terminus (5km to the east, by *bemo*) serves the east of Flores. Departures for Moni from 6am to 2pm (2hr). For Maumere, departures from 7am to 5pm (5hr).

Ndao terminus (2km to the north) provides links with the west of the island. Departures for Bajawa between 7am and 5pm (5hr), for Ruteng at 8am (9hr), for Labuhanbajo at 7am (14hr) and for Riung at 7am (5hr).

GETTING AROUND

By bemo – They cover the town until 8pm.

Car and motorbike rental – Telsado, Jl A Yani, (0381) 214 39. Car hire with driver (ask for Amir). **Natura Tourist Transport** (see below).

ADDRESS BOOK

Tourist information – Dina Pariwisata, Jl Yos Sudarso 5, ☎ (0381) 222 17 (Monday-Saturday, 7am-2pm).

Bank/Currency exchange – Bank Negara Indonesia, Jl Gatot Subroto 5 (Monday-Friday 7.30am-3pm, Saturday

9am-12noon). Rates are better than at the BRI. Dollars and travellers' cheques accepted.

Bank Rakyat Indonesia, Jl Yos Sudarso 29, near the Dwi Putra Hotel (Monday-Friday, 8am-3.30pm). Dollars and travellers' cheques accepted.

Post office/Telephone – The **main post office** is in the north of the town, in Jl Sam Ratulangi, but the office in Jalan Dewantara, near the Dwi Putra Hotel, is more practical. **Telkom**, Jl Kelimutu 3 (24hr a day).

Airline company – Merpati, Jl Langka (1km from the town centre), ☎ (0381) 213 55.

Shipping line – Pelni, Jl Kathedral 2, (Monday-Saturday, 8am-12noon and 2-4pm).

Travel agency – Natura Tourist Transport, Jl Pasar 33, ☎ (0381) 213 69. Tours, reservation of tickets and car hire.

WHERE TO STAY

Modest

🏠**Hotel Ikhlas**, Jl Jend. A Yani 92, ☎ (0381) 216 95 – 25rm. ✈ ✗ The Mecca of travellers in Ende deserves its reputation, both for its welcome and for its services (information and currency exchange) and its modest prices. Simple but comfortable rooms, generally with private bathroom.

Nurjaya Hotel, Jl A Yani 20, ☎ (0381) 212 52 – 10rm. A good place for the poverty-stricken traveller, reasonable but rustic. Most of its visitors come from Timor.

Hotel Wisata, Jl Kelimutu 68, ☎ (0381) 222 43 – 18rm. ⌖ / 🍽 Comfortable rooms (most with a private bathroom), but the maintenance is not up to the mark.

Average

Hotel Safari, Jl Jend. A Yani 65, ☎ (0381) 219 97 – 21rm. ⌖ ⌖ / 🍽 ✕ An enormous and pleasant hotel with a courtyard garden, which attracts a mainly Indonesian clientele. The rooms are comfortable but somewhat noisy.

Hotel Dwi Putra, Jl Yos Sudarso 27, ☎ (0381) 216 85 – 35rm. ⌖ ⌖ / 🍽 ✕ A two-storey building in the town centre. Well kept, and good value for money.

Bitta Beach, Jl Gatot Subroto km 3 (near the airport), ☎ (0381) 219 65 – 2rm. ⌖ ⌖ / 🍽 ✕ 🐾 The wooden bungalows facing the bay provide an agreeable alternative.

EATING OUT

Moderate

Istana Bambu, Jl Pasar 39, near the market (8.30am-10pm). A hangout for travellers, serving a good selection of Chinese and Indonesian dishes as well as seafood.

Restaurant Merlin, Jl Gatot Subroto, near the airport (open until 10pm). Excellent Chinese dishes and seafood. The dining room is a bit gloomy, but you are given a charming welcome.

Minang Baru, Jl Soekarno 1. Choose from the dishes set on the table, and only pay for what you eat, according to the Padang (spicy food) tradition.

RM. Ampera, Jl Kelimutu 31. A small Padang restaurant, convenient for a quick meal.

More select

Bitta Beach (see the hotel of the same name). On the beach. Ende's smart restaurant serves excellent seafood and its karaoke makes it the town's only place that stays alive in the evening. Check your bill carefully.

SHOPPING GUIDE

Most of the shops close in the afternoon, from 1pm to 4.30pm. In Jl Pasar, the popular little **Mbongawani market** (fruit, vegetables and fish) is very lively in the mornings.

Ikats – The **ikat market**, on the corner of Jl Pahean and Jl Pasar, has some of the best choice in Flores, at reasonable prices

Peaceful shores
in Flores

R. Marca

Making the most of Ende

KELIMUTU★★★
MONI AND THE LIO REGION★★
Ende District
50km northeast of Ende – Map p 502-503 and p 542
Alt 1 640m – Cool climate

Not to be missed
Sunrise over the volcano.
A visit to the village of Nggela.

And remember...
Avoid the rainy season (November to May), when the colours are less spectacular.
Sleep at Moni to reach Kelimutu as early as possible, before the mist lifts.
Take warm clothing.

With its three lakes of different colours, forming a changing vista of watery stained glass with mist drifting across it, Mount Kelimutu is a natural curiosity. The unique site has been classified a national park, and is surely one of the highlights of a trip to Flores, like Bromo, in Java.

But while in all its magnificence the legendary volcano dwarfs the tortured landscape of the Lio region, the latter has no less enthralling destinations for the walker. From Moni to Nggela, near the shores of the **Savu Sea** (Laut Sawu), a wonderful string of villages with bamboo houses still manages, despite everything, to resist invasion. So, *"Mbana bego"*, ("Have a good journey", in Lio)!

Around Moni

As you leave Ende for Moni and the higher ground, the road crosses a wide gorge that affords views of spectacular **landscapes★★** as you gain height. Down through the years Moni has become the base camp for Kelimutu and as a result small hotels and restaurants line the village's only street. This has created a change in the attitude towards visitors, with commercial gain in mind, a contrast with the warm welcome generally found in Flores. Nonetheless, you can enjoy a very pleasant stay among the mountains and forest.

Although Moni has not retained its traditional houses, the sarong remains the conventional dress for women. When people come out of Mass on Sunday you will see a veritable fashion parade, with the very latest local trends as far as ikats are concerned.

Above the village, a little **waterfall** (Air Terjun) *(10min on foot. On the Kelimutu road, opposite the Sarty restaurant, take the path on the left)* springs out among the trees. There is nothing so reviving as a dip in the pool at its feet, to set you up after a climb up Kelimutu. And you can finish off your recovery session in the stream, fed by **hot springs**.

R. Helmi/Altitude

Kelimutu: the changing colours in the lakes

Flores

The volcano with three lakes***

Every day, around 4am, a truck collects passengers from the various hotels in Moni. Allow 45min for the truck journey, or 4hr on foot. The truck returns at 7am, but you can also choose to return on foot.

From Moni, a tarmac road *(13km)* leads to a small forest track that goes up to the **viewpoint*** *(30min)* on the crater ridge. As you climb the vegetation gives way to a chaotic mass of rock and stone. The eye is first drawn to the outer slopes of the volcano, carpeted with forests, then moves on to **Mount Egon**, to the east, and **Keli Bara** (White Mountain), to the south. Invisible at first in the half-light, the three lakes gradually appear like a mirage as the sun rises. Three spots of colour in a stone setting, 260m below, dominated by the **peak** of the volcano standing on the other side of the twin lakes. Magical!

Like vast cauldrons simmering with some mysterious brew, Kelimutu is surely the work of some supernatural spirit. Local legend offers the proof, seeing in the volcano the dwelling of the god Konderatu and his wife Bobi. The Lio people, who come here regularly with offerings of rice and betel, are convinced that the souls of those who have died young find shelter in **Lake Tiwu Ata Polo** *(on the far right)*, a sheet of water like dark green enamel. The souls of the old are believed to take refuge in the milky blue-green waters of **Tiwu Ata Koofai Nuwamuri** *(on the right)*, and those of thieves and criminals in the dark waters of **Kawah Ata Mbupu** *(on the left)*.

Scientists, however, offer considerably more prosaic explanations for the volcano's eruptions (the most recent was in 1968) and the variations of colour in the lakes, the result of an unstable mixture of acids, sulphur vapours and iron ore. During the 1960s the lakes had extraordinary shades of red, white and blue.

Through the Lio region**
Allow a day.

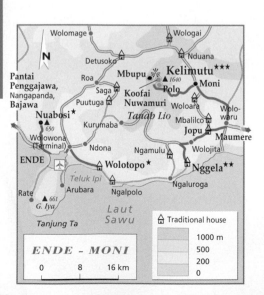

From Moni a few rare bemos go directly to Nggela (28km to the south). The most reliable arrangement is to take a bemo very early in the morning to Wolowaru (13km from Moni) on the Maumere road, then a truck to Nggela (18km by road). You can also do the trip on foot (6-7hr), taking food and drink with you. The easiest solution remains to hire a bemo (90min). On the way out of Moni, in the direction of Maumere, turn right at the first crossroads. From Ende, Nggela is accessible by boat or lorry, but the road is very bad.

From Moni to Nggela, the **road**** zigzags round the foot of Keli Bara, between palms and coconut trees, to the Savu Sea. Before reaching **Jopu** *(15km)*, it goes through some beautiful villages that still have their *rumah adat* ("traditional house"), a superb construction with a pyramidal thatched roof with a small totem pole in front. Here and there, **Christian tombs** decorated with blue ceramics provide an unexpected contrast.

Beyond Jopu, the road crosses Wolojita (6km) before heading due south for Nggela (7km).

Nggela★★

Nestling on the slopes of the majestic Keli Bara, Nggela occupies a superb site, above a coastline fringed with palm trees. In the haphazardly laid out town with a population of 1 300, bamboo and thatch still predominate, although corrugated iron has made an appearance. Here too, substantial concrete **tombs** covered in ceramics, which seem somewhat incongruous, are a reminder that we are in Christian territory. On Sunday – the Lord's day – everyone takes a day off work. The old women chew betel on their doorstep, the men play cards in the shade of a tree, the young men play football in the square, while the women grind rice or weave **ikats★★** (the local ikats are among the finest in Flores). As is the case nearly everywhere else on the island, hand-spun cotton has given way to artificial thread, but the colours are still prepared from roots and leaves. With 2 000 lengths being produced a year, a quarter of which are sold to tourists, ikats represent the basic source of income, ahead of rice, maize, cassava and fishing. Not surprisingly, then, people will make every possible effort to sell them to you.

Kelimutu

Making the most of Moni

COMING AND GOING

By bus – From Ende (Wolowona terminus), a bus runs to Moni (2hr).
From Maumere, buses leave from the west terminus (4hr).
To leave Moni, catch a bus in the main street (note that they are often very crowded).

GETTING AROUND

By bemo – The best form of transport for exploring the local villages.

By lorry – In Moni, advise your hotel the night before if you want to take the truck that leaves for Kelimutu at 4am. The truck returns at 7am, but you can come back on foot if you want to stay longer (2hr30min walking).

ADDRESS BOOK

Telephone – *Wartel*, behind the "Kelimutu" restaurant (open 24hr a day).

WHERE TO STAY

● **Moni**
There are plenty of *losmen* here, but the facilities are very basic (although better places are beginning to appear). They are concentrated along the main street. Breakfast is usually included.
Modest
Palm Homestay, 1km from the market, on the Jopu road (free shuttle for Moni) – 5rm. Charming little bamboo bungalows in the middle of the rice fields. The reception is very friendly and the owner intends to build new bungalows with modern facilities.
Watugana Bungalows, in the centre, near the market – 7rm. Small basic bamboo bungalows, not very well insulated. The owner organises tours in the area.
Amina Moe – 6rm. The atmosphere is friendly and the welcome warm, but the upkeep is not impressive. That said, the prices are absolutely unbeatable.
Mr John – 4rm. Another model of plainness: the bedrooms are laid-out round a room dominated by a large table. That is all there is, but the rooms appear rather better kept than elsewhere.

Wisma Kelimutu – 4rm. A concrete building with very bare rooms (no furniture at all apart from the bed!), but relatively well looked after. In the bathroom, make sure that the water is running.
Pondok Wisata Hidayah, on the way out of Moni, towards Kelimutu – 7rm. Pleasantly located in the middle of rice fields, this well maintained group of little bamboo bungalows is undoubtedly one of the best places to stay in Moni, even though the facilities are modest.
Average
Arwanti Hotel, on the left, near the market – 5rm. Three new and very comfortable rooms have just opened, with bathrooms and small sitting rooms, next to the two older and much more rustic ones.

● **Nggela**
Modest
Homestay Nggela Permai – 3rm. A small hotel with very basic facilities, but which enables you to stay overnight at Nggela. The rooms are equipped with mosquito nets. But note that the service is amazingly slow.

EATING OUT

The food is reasonable in Moni, although the choice is relatively narrow.
Basic - Moderate
Restaurant Kelimutu, 2km from Moni on the Ende road. Standard Indonesian cuisine, but the terrace is very attractive. You will have plenty of time to enjoy it, as the service is very slow.
Arwanti Hotel, (see above). Try the house speciality, "nasi bambu", an excellent rice dish cooked in hollowed out bamboo.
Rona Restaurant & Pub, in the centre, near the church. Meals are taken on a pleasant terrace overlooking the rice fields. The menu is fairly varied (Indonesian and Western dishes), but try the nourishing "nasi rona", a potato stuffed with cheese, vegetables and crackers.

GOING OUT

Live shows – Every evening at 8pm, a traditional dance show is put on in the "rumah adat", the traditional house opposite Moni market.

OTHER THINGS TO DO

Excursions – For a tour of the Lio villages, enquire at the *losmen*.

SHOPPING GUIDE

Ikats – You can make your choice in Moni market or at the fixed stalls beside the road. But it is always more pleasant to buy directly from the weaver, in the surrounding villages and particularly in Nggela.

Nggela, building a house

G Guérard

Making the most of Moni

MAUMERE
THE SIKKA REGION★
Sikka District
150km from Ende – Map p 502-503
Pop 50 000 – Hot dry climate

Not to be missed
A dive in Geliting Bay.
The traditional villages of Bona and Sikka.

And remember...
If you are leaving by air, be sure to reserve your seat as early as possible,
as flights are often full.

After Moni and the green heights of the Lio region, the aridity of the Maumere coastal plain is striking. The town itself has no great interest, like most of the towns in Flores, but its proximity to Kelimutu, the diving sites in Geliting Bay and the fascinating traditional Sikka villages make it one of the leading tourist destinations on the island. Maumere has been the centre of Catholicism in Flores since the arrival of the first Portuguese Dominicans in the 16C and has seen the arrival of many Dutch, German and Spanish missionaries down through the ages. Fervent Christians, the **Sikka** – the local ethnic group – still evoke with emotion the memory of the visit of Pope John Paul II, in 1989. But the great event that has become engraved in all minds remains undoubtedly the tragic earthquake on 12 December 1992. The tremor, 6.8 on the Richter scale, with its epicentre some thirty kilometres offshore, destroyed entire districts and killed 2 500 people, most of whom were swept away by an unprecedented *tsunami*, a giant wave nearly 30m high.

A short tour of the town
Allow 1-2hr, including suburbs.

Maumere is a substantial town with broad streets lined with two-storey concrete buildings creating an unadorned urban style. The crushing heat combines with the absence of interesting features to make it unattractive for a lengthy stay.

It is, however, worth making a brief tour of the **harbour**. Severely hit by the 1992 earthquake, it still has the shells of its devastated warehouses, gaping bleakly towards the sea. But life has returned to normal and the quarter bears testimony to the city's commercial calling, with its export of cacao, cloves and coffee.

Not far away, the **Cathedral** (*Jl Slamet Riyadi*) is undergoing renovation, but you can go into the **neighbouring church**, which is decorated with frescoes illustrating the life of Christ.

Lastly, standing 500m back from the harbour, the **new market** (*Jl Pasar Baru*) marks the town centre, with its shops and hotels.

Make a trip to the western suburbs (*4km from the town centre*) for a fascinating contrast with the Catholic side of Maumere. The Bugis village of **Wuring** respects the precept common to all the villages set up by these Muslim sailors in the Indonesian archipelago: a disorderly assembly of shanties on piles standing directly on the water's edge, surrounding a **mosque** topped with an enormous corrugated iron dome. This matchstick village had to face the tidal wave in 1992.

When the sea retreats at low tide you can see the bare carpet of dead corals that provide foundations for the houses. But the smiles that your visit arouses leave little room for melancholy thoughts of the past.

Maumere,
the Catholic Church

Dominated by the dry slopes of **Mount Kolisia**, the road continues onwards to **Waturia beach** *(16km from Maumere)*, a favourite picnic spot for Maumere's inhabitants at weekends.

Geliting Bay⋆, corals and fine sand
Bemo trip along Geliting Bay. Allow a short day.

Maumere owes its international fame to the superb **coral⋆⋆** that carpets Geliting Bay, a crescent of sand some thirty kilometres to the east of the town. Seriously damaged by the 1992 earthquake, the coral reefs are slowly recovering, to the great delight of divers.

The first stop is **Geliting** *(10km from Maumere)*, a little town whose only attraction is its great Friday **market⋆**, perfect for stocking up with **ikats**.

Waiara *(13km)* has a beautiful black-sand beach fringed with coconut palms and two hotels that specialise in **diving**. You may come here specifically to get acquainted with Napoleon wrasse, manta rays, turtles or angelfish, but you can also admire the scenery as you sit back with your toes in the sand.

At the far end of the bay, **Wodong⋆** (Wairterang) *(28km)* provides a cheaper alternative for a more exotic stay, in bamboo bungalows right on the edge of the beach. The setting, one of the most peaceful imaginable will delight the idle visitor as well as the active type. Apart from climbing **Mount Egon** (1 700m) *(6-7hr on foot; enquire at the hotels)*, a still-active volcano, **diving** is naturally the main attraction. Outings are organised in the bay where a **wreck** lies on the sea-bed, 30m down, as well as to **Pulau Besar**, **Pulau Indah** and **Pulau Babi**, the little string of islands lying out to sea.

From coast to coast★★

Excursion to the south coast. Allow 1 day.

Take a bemo from Maumere as far as Geliting. Next, to reach Bola, it would be best to hire a car because the bemos and trucks only travel south on Fridays. The road is relatively good, apart from a few difficult stretches. Take a supply of cigarettes and pencils.

At Geliting, bear south towards the hills, a tropical garden bursting with palm trees, banana trees, breadfruit trees, tamarinds, mangoes, papayas, guavas, bamboos, banyans and clove trees.

Standing at the entrance to a small pass, the **Catholic mission at Watublapi** *(9km from Geliting)* is famous for its **ikats**. Even if you do not intend to buy any, do not miss the fascinating demonstration that enables you to fully understand the stages involved in making them: spinning the cotton, making the colours with leaves and roots, preparing the designs, dyeing and, lastly, the weaving. A fine **viewpoint★** in the vicinity looks out over the narrowest part of Flores (15km wide), from where you can see both the north and south coasts of the island.

Beyond Watublapi the road soon drops down to the southern shore.

Just before you reach the sea, the bell-tower of a large church with decorative stained-glass windows marks the approach to **Bola** *(6km from Watublapi)*, the Mecca of ikat handicrafts.

Just beyond this the road meets the coast at **Natawatu★**, a peaceful little town with bamboo houses surrounded by coconut palms, stretching along a grey-sand **beach.** The arrival of tourists always produces the same effect: women wrapped in their shimmering ikats, sarong-clad fishermen bearing their catch on their shoulders, and children coming back from school all stop to see you, with a broad smile on their faces.

Heading east, the road runs along the magnificent **coastline★★** with alternating bays and cliffs, to **Ipir beach★★** *(2km from Natawatu)*, which can be seen below with its fine belt of coconut palms. Apart from a few rare fishing cabins, the place is virtually empty.

Continue east for another *14km* to the village of **Habibola** near the large **beach at Doreng★★**, a ribbon of golden sand – rare in this region – 4km long.

Returning westward

Several stopping places lie along the return route to Kelimutu, but you can only enjoy them if you hire a car, since the bus to Moni goes by the direct route.

As you leave Maumere, stop at the **Ledalero Museum** (Blikon Blewet Museum) *(10km from Maumere, by bemo, daily 7am-12.30pm and 3-7pm, fee)*. This is housed in the middle of an enormous seminary among green hills. It shows a wide range of collections put together since the 1960s by Father Piet: traditional jewellery from Timor, magnificent **Dongson bronzes**, basketwork, old photographs and even the tusk of a stegadon (an ancestor of the elephant, dating from the Pleistocene Age). The superb **collection of ikats★** is sadly under lock and key, piled up in a display case.

Sikka★

20km from Maumere, leave the main road, turning left along the small road that descends for 7km to Sikka and the sea (by bemo).

Famous for its **ikats★★** with their varied designs and colours, this large coastal village is an essential stopping point on all tourist tours. The price of this success is that travellers are seen as potential customers here, and immediately surrounded

Flores

by a flock of women determinedly brandishing their goods. Apart from this, the village, nestling at the foot of a cliff and facing a narrow **white-sand beach** enjoys a superb setting.

In the 17C Sikka was one of the earliest Portuguese settlements in Flores – but the **church*** was in fact named after a Norman missionary, **Le Cocq d'Armandville**, and was inaugurated under his auspices in 1899. The walls painted with ikat designs, and the birdsong mingling with the sound of the surf and the wind in the trees all contribute to the romantic atmosphere.

Paga beach**

42km from Maumere, by bus. It is difficult to resist the pleasure of a final stop at this magnificent white-sand beach, a deserted little jewel on the south coast. Only one very attractive wooden *losmen*-restaurant (*see "Making the most of Maumere"*) has been set up here and every morning, in a timeless ritual the women of the neighbouring village, wearing sarongs and carrying rush baskets on their heads, cross the beach to reach the rice fields.

From Paga, if you have the time, make a short excursion to **Lekebai** (*7km east of Paga*). Saturday morning is market-day, when the village families come in from the surrounding area to buy their tobacco, spices, fish, and even dogs, a renowned dish on Flores!

Just before Lekebai an invisible frontier marks the change from the Lio region to the Sikka region. Between gorges and mountains, a few rare rice fields add an unexpected touch of green to the ochre landscape.

Making the most of Maumere

COMING AND GOING

By air – Maumere has the best air communications in Flores. **Wai Oti airport** is 3km to the east of the town (by taxi or *bemo*). You can get a taxi there to go direct to Waiara and Wodong. **Merpati** has flights to Kupang, Bima, Denpasar and Ende.

By boat – Pelni's **KM Awu Voy** links Maumere with Benoa (Bali), Unjung Pandang, Waingapu (Sumba) and Kupang (Timor).

By bus and bemo – The buses have the tiresome habit of crisscrossing the town to look for passengers. You can also arrange to be collected at your hotel.

The **Lokaria terminus** (3km east of the town) serves the eastern end of the island, particularly Geliting, Waiara, Ipir, Wodong and Larantuka (4hr).

The **terminus at Ende** (1.5km southwest of the town) serves Moni (3hr30min),

Ende (5hr, an early morning departure and another late in the afternoon), Sikka and Ledalero.

GETTING AROUND

By bemo – Bemos cover Maumere until 8pm (7pm outside the town).

Motorbike and car rental – There is no official agency. The best solution is to seek advice at your hotel or from a travel agent.

ADDRESS BOOK

Tourist information – Jl Wairklau, ☎ (0382) 216 52 (east of the town). Open in the mornings. Is of little interest.

Bank/Currency exchange – **Bank Negara Indonesia**, Jl Soekarno-Hatta 4 (Monday-Friday 8am-3pm, Saturday 9am-12noon). Dollars and travellers' cheques are accepted.

Bank Danamon, Jl Raya Centis, on the corner of Jl Pasar Baru Barat (Monday-Friday, 8am-2.30pm). Accepts main currencies, and withdrawals can be made at the counter with a credit card.

Bank Rakyat Indonesia, Jl Jend Ahmad Yani (Monday-Thursday 8am-12noon and 1-3pm, Friday 8am-12noon). Accepts main currencies and travellers' cheques.

Post office/Telephone – Main post office, Jl Pos, on the corner of Jl A Yani, near the football ground (Monday-Thursday 8am-2pm, Friday 8am-12noon and 1-2pm, Saturday 8am-2pm). **Telkom**, Jl Soekarno-Hatta 12, near the BNI (open 24hr a day). Facilities to receive fax messages and have them sent to your hotel.

Internet – Comtel, Jl Bandeng 1 (Monday-Saturday 8am-12.30pm / 4-9pm). One of the very few access points in Flores. Warning – the rates are high, since the connection passes via Kupang or Denpasar.

Airline company – Merpati, Jl Raja Don Thomas 19 (8am-8.30pm), ☎ (0382) 213 42.

Shipping line – Pelni, Jl Slamet Riyadi.

Travel agencies – Ramayana Satrya Tours, Jl Jend A Yani, ☎ (0382) 215 91. Tours to Flores and the Komodo islands **Moni Moi Tours**, Jl Jend Sudirman 197, ☎ (0382) 220 26, Fax (0382) 222 72. Organise tours throughout Flores and to Sumbawa, Sumba and the Komodos.

WHERE TO STAY

• Maumere

The hotels in Maumere offer very variable facilities, from sordid dumps to impeccably run establishments. But no matter what the setting, do not expect a palace. Most offer breakfast, but this will often consist of no more than a cup of tea or coffee with a few meagre pieces of toast.

Modest

👜**Senja Wair Bubak**, Jl Komodor Yos Sudarso, ☎ (0382) 214 98 – 10rm. 🍴 The old-fashioned charm of this house and its wallpaper attracts a clientele of travellers. Some of the rooms are air-conditioned. The welcome is friendly and the staff can offer a wide range of services (hire of vehicles, exchange and tours).

Hotel Jaya, Jl Hasanuddin 26, ☎ (0382) 212 92 – 6rm. A place to stay only if you are in a fix, as the rooms are bare and stifling.

Hotel Beng Goan I, Jl Noa Toda, ☎ (0382) 210 41 – 9rm. 🍴 A small and inexpensive hotel that offers good value for money. The rooms lack character but are clean.

Average

Perintis Hotel, Jl Moa Roda, ☎ (0382) 210 41 – 29rm. Another place to use as a stand-by only if the other hotels are full. The rooms (some with private bathrooms and air conditioning) are not as clean as they might be.

Hotel Wini Rai II, Jl Dr Soetomo 7, ☎ (0382) 213 62 – 15rm. 🍴 / 🍽 The latest arrival on the Maumere hotel scene is perfectly kept and has comfortable rooms, with or without private bathrooms.

High end

Permata Sari, Jl Jend Sudirman 49, on the eastern edge of Maumere (at the beginning of the road to the airport), ☎ (0382) 211 71 – 32rm. 🍴 🍽 / 🍽 ✗ 🏊 Located beside the sea, this is one of the most comfortable hotels in Maumere, but is a little out of the way. The bungalows on the beach are better value for money than the rooms in the concrete building, but the latter are larger. Car hire available.

Hotel Maiwali, Jl Raja Don Thomas 40, ☎ (0382) 212 20 – 15rm. 🍴 🍽 / 🍽 The hotel belongs to the Maumere royal family, and is one of the best in town. Nearly all the rooms have a fan or air conditioning and some have the supreme luxury of a bathtub. Breakfast included. In the lobby you can make international telephone calls.

• Waiara beach

High end

Sea World Club, Jl Nai Roa Km 13, ☎ (0382) 215 70 – 48rm. 🍴 🍽 / 🍽 ✗ 🏊 cc Pleasant bamboo bungalows facing the beach. The suites are better value for money than the other rooms. The agency offers tours in the area and diving (see below).

• Wodong (or Wairterang)

Modest

Flores Froggies, 17rm. ✗ ⚲ ◭
Wodong's pioneering *losmen*, opened in 1994 by a French couple. The bamboo bungalows are spread about under the trees, 5m from the beach. Some have a private "mandi". A shame that the ultra-thin walls provide only minimal privacy. The restaurant offers a good selection of seafood and Indonesian dishes, and the breakfast includes French bread! Canoe outings available, and boat hire to explore the islands.

Ankermi, Fax (0382) 211 00 – 11rm. ✗ ⚲ ◭ Charming bamboo bungalows, very well kept, with mosquito nets and, in some, open-air "mandi"! The hotel offers numerous services (bookshop, bar, diving agency, cruises to the islands and walks), the staff are very friendly and the restaurant excellent. What more could you want?

• Paga beach

Modest

Paga Beach Cottage, 10rm. ✗ ⚲
Completely isolated on a dream beach, this rustic little *losmen* promises an unforgettable stay. The bathrooms are open-air and, in the evenings, the lighting consists of oil lamps. The restaurant serves excellent seafood – amazingly expensive, unfortunately.

EATING OUT

Moderate

Sarinah Restaurant, Jl Raja Centis. A good choice of Chinese cuisine and seafood. Air-conditioned restaurant.

Stevani Pub and Restaurant, Jl Raja Cea 1. Seafood, Indonesian and Western cuisine served in attractive bamboo shelters. The karaoke makes this one of the rare places in Maumere that comes alive in the evenings. To be avoided, therefore, if you wish to dine in peace.

Rumah Makan Surya Indah, Jl Raja Centis. Small Padang restaurant open from 7am until 9pm.

Golden Fish, Jl Hasanuddin, on the seafront. Excellent seafood from a tank (fish and crayfish). Air-conditioned restaurant

Rumah Makan Sumber Indah, Jl Raja Centis 31, A vast selection of East Javanese, Chinese, Indonesian and Padang cuisine and seafood.

OTHER THINGS TO DO

Diving – The best season is from April to December. Two agencies organise sea trips, including transport, food and equipment. They also offer tours to Kelimutu and the Maumere region.

Flores Sao Resort, Waiara beach, ☎ (0382) 215 55, Fax (0382) 216 66. The diving club is still active while the eponymous hotel is closed for renovation. Car rental.

Pondok Dunia Laut (Sea Word Club), Waiara beach, ☎ (0382) 215 70. Visa card accepted.

SHOPPING GUIDE

Markets – The old central market was burned down during a riot between Christians and Muslims. The new one is in Jl Pasar Baru Barat.

Ikats – Geliting market (15km east of Maumere), held on Fridays, offers a vast selection of ikats.

Harapan Jaya, Jl Moatoda 19. A wide range of ikats from all over Nusa Tenggara. The prices are not negotiable, and Visa cards are accepted.

Buffalo country – Tana Toraja

SULAWESI

Like a giant octopus surging out of the sea, Sulawesi
stretches its tentacles across an area of more than
190 000sqkm. Its four long peninsulas are washed by the
crystal-clear waters of the seas of the Celebes, Maluku,
Banda and Flores. Coral reefs form a fringe along most of
the coastline, which is carved up into deep gulfs, while a
hundred or more small secondary islets lie further out from
the shore. Its shape is so tortuous that the first explorers
initially assumed that they had reached an archipelago
rather than a single island. In the 16C after running
aground on the north coast, Portuguese sailors named it the
"Puntos dos Celebes" – the "Capes of Ill Fame". The
Celebes appeared under that name on geographers' maps
until Indonesia acquired her independence, when they were
renamed **Sulawesi**, a reference to the metal deposits ("besi")
on the island ("sula"). Shaped by incessant tectonic movement, the island's tortured shape is the result of the collision
between two sections of former continental plates that fused
together several million years ago *(see p 12)*. This titanic
shock gave birth to the abruptly contoured landscapes.
Dominated by high misty land, the narrow **coastal plains**
consist of alternate chalk cliffs and white sandy beaches,
shaded by coconut palms, with peaceful fishing villages
strung out along them. Less hospitable, the interior terrain
rises to a height of more than 500m for most of the island,
reaching a peak at nearly 3 500m. Divided up by gorges in
which rivers have carved themselves routes as short as they
are turbulent, these majestic **mountains** form a jagged frill
round a myriad lakes, some of them in former volcanic
craters. Extinct in the south, the **volcanoes** regularly awake
from their somnolence in the north, where vulcanologists
watch closely over the rages of around a dozen of them.

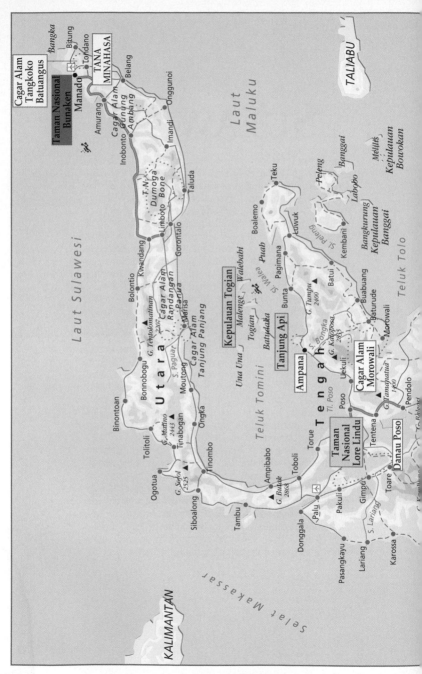

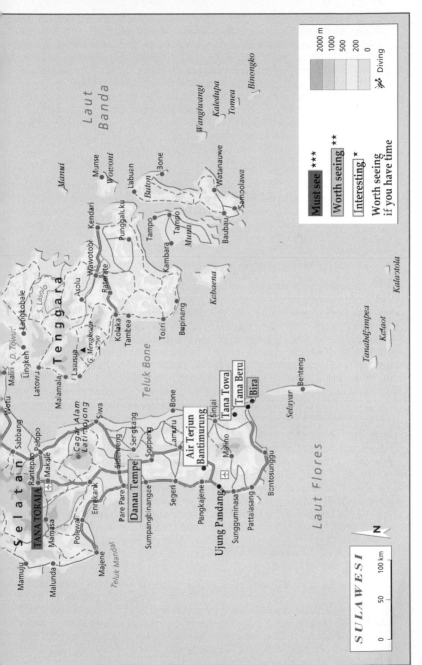

Their devastating eruptions have also fertilised the soil, making the northeastern and southwestern regions the two main **agricultural zones** of the island. Apart from the rice fields – dazzling chequerboards of intense green, or cascades of curving terraces – innumerable plantations of other crops (partly destined for export) complete the picture of agricultural wealth: maize, cassava, vegetables, coffee, cacao, cloves and copra. Everywhere else the forest reigns supreme, an impassable equatorial jungle that together with the island's mountainous landscape makes land communications difficult. Since the late 1980s, however, the **Trans-Sulawesi** highway has covered the 2 000km or so that separate north from south. It is a highly valued link between the four **administrative provinces** of Sulawesi – South, Centre, North and Southeast – which more or less correspond to the island's four peninsulas.

Astride the equator

Lying across the equator, Sulawesi enjoys a relatively stable climate throughout the year, although it varies considerably according to height and exposure to the prevailing winds. It is hot in the coastal areas (average temperature 25°-30°C) and much cooler in the highlands. The dry season runs from April to November in the **southwest** of the island but is much shorter in the **northeast** – August to October. The mountains encourage abundant rainfall, with the rains reaching their maximum in December on the west coast and in May on the east coast.

Unique forms of nature

Although Sulawesi's flora – dominated by the rain forest and by **orchids** – differs very little from what is found on the rest of the Indonesian islands, the fauna is distinguished by its range and rarity. The island's geological origins, its ecological conditions and its relief – substantial natural obstacles to animal migration – explain the presence of so many endemic species. Around a score of them are unfortunately threatened with extinction, the result of deforestation in some areas combined with the misguided introduction of exotic specimens (particularly in the lakes). To see them, you have to plunge into the jungle of great nature reserves where they are now protected, such as the **Lore Lindu** or **Morowali** reserves in the centre, or **Tangkoko Batuangus** in the north.

More than 120 species of **mammal** have been found there, virtually all of them native to the island. During your explorations you may perhaps meet the **anoa**, an aggressive, solitary dwarf buffalo, or the extraordinary **babiroussa** ("horned hog"), with its upper canine teeth growing in a curve above its muzzle to form tusks. Look out also for colonies of monkeys, such as the **black tufted macaque** that moves around in groups leaping from tree to tree. More difficult to track down (for good reason!), the **tarsier** – the smallest primate in the world – is barely 10cm long and weighs barely 100g. Endowed with large round eyes, it is active at night and sleeps by day, hidden in hollow tree-trunks or roots. Another dwarf creature, and also generally nocturnal, the **cuscus** uses its tail like a fifth limb to climb through the trees and seize leaves for food.

There are more than 300 species that make up the rich **bird-life** on the island, over a third of which are found only in Sulawesi. You may perhaps be lucky enough to catch sight of a **hornbill**, a handsome and vividly coloured bird whose outsize beak has a strange red bump. The bird incubates its eggs in the holes of dead trees or in rocks. Then there is the unusual **maleo**, which sets its large eggs to incubate in the heat, hollowing out the ground near a volcano or in sand that is exposed to the sun.

With its 6 000km of coastline and over 110 outlying islands, Sulawesi also has fabulous and internationally famous **submarine fauna**. Large or small, colourful or tasty, an infinite variety of fish populates this watery world, flickering through clusters of corals or gliding though deep abysses: butterfly, parrot, scorpion, lion and clown fish as well as Napoleon wrasse – not to mention sharks, barracuda, rays, snakes and giant turtles.

The island is also outstanding for its myriad insects, amphibians and reptiles, many of them also native to Sulawesi. In particular, it is home to the largest snake in the world, a **python** 10m long!

A much-coveted island

Apart from traces of human occupation dating back to around 30000 BC, and the archeological remains found on the island (megaliths, sarcophagi and stone funeral urns, and later bronze Buddhist and Hindu sculptures dating from the 4C and 5C), there are few traces of Sulawesi's pre-Islamic history.

The rival kingdoms of South Sulawesi

For a long period the island's history was focused on the southern peninsula, which was divided into several rival kingdoms that developed between the 12C and 14C. In the forefront were the powerful Bugis states of Luwu, Bone, Wajo and Soppeng, founded on a commercial economy. **Luwu** greatly dominated the region, but after three armed offensives the troops of **Bone** managed to overthrow it in the 16C.

At the same time the Makassar kingdom of **Gowa** made dazzling progress. Through the interplay of conquests and alliances – particularly with the intrepid "sea gypsies", the **Bajau** – it soon won supremacy over the region and from 1600 controlled the peninsula's southern and western coasts.

Its trade relations with the young Muslim sultanates of northern Java soon brought the kingdom into contact with **Islam**. After the conversion of their king around 1605, the Gowa armies imposed the new "official" religion by force in most of the coastal Bugis states in the south. In 1611 the surrender of **Bone**, Gowa's chief rival, confirmed Makassar hegemony over the peninsula.

Thanks to its large cosmopolitan port, from then on Gowa became the island's most prosperous sultanate. An essential stopping place on the route to the Moluccas, **Makassar** thus rose to the forefront of the international trade in spice, sandalwood, amber, pearls, shark fins and slaves. At the dawn of the 17C Portuguese, Indian, Chinese, Malay and many other merchants came here to barter their manufactured goods for the valuable cloves, nutmeg and other produce.

Overthrowing Gowa

When it came to Makassar in 1609 with the express aim of taking over the spice trade, the **Dutch East India Company** found itself facing powerful opposition. In order to counter Dutch ambitions, the Makassars entered into commercial agreements with other European nations.

But the Dutch had not had their final say: exploiting ill-feeling in the kingdom of Bone, which was humiliated by the defeat inflicted on it by the Gowa forces in 1644, they concluded a treaty with Bone in 1660. The Bugis mobilised a powerful army under the command of Prince **Arung Palakka**. Having sunk some Portuguese ships in Makassar harbour and captured the fort, the Dutch landed with the Bugis fleet in 1666. Nonetheless, it took the coalition a year to force **Sultan Hasanuddin** of Gowa to surrender. In 1667 the two sides concluded the **Peace of Bungaya**, marking the defeat of the Makassars. Under this treaty the Dutch confirmed their control over the town and its harbour, from which they excluded all other foreign traders, thus ensuring their monopoly over Sulawesi's foreign trade. But they had to go on the attack again the next year, to put an end to the Makassar forces that were still holding out. These bitter struggles were to destroy the old city, and yet confirm the prosperity of the harbour. The Dutch handed most of the Makassar dependencies to the **Bone sultanate,** which then extended its supremacy over the major part of the southern peninsula until the death of Arung Palakka in 1696. His reign proved so autocratic, however, that large numbers of Makassars, and also Bugis, fled to other regions. In this way they set up a string of small communities throughout the Indonesian archipelago and the Malay Peninsula, where they even founded fresh dynasties.

The peaceful surrender of North Sulawesi

Although it was equally divided up into **independent states**, North Sulawesi did not suffer the same internal struggles as the south. **Portuguese** merchants set up a trading post in Manado in the 16C, and their missionaries were quick to convert the population to Catholicism. Already settled in their colonies in the Philippines, the **Spanish** landed in their turn, establishing a small fort at Manado in 1617 to supply their Molucca garrisons with rice. The situation changed, however, when they tried to put a half-Spanish king on the throne. The **Dutch East India Company,** which also coveted the site, did not hesitate to answer the call by the Minahasa (the local population), to kick their common enemy out of the peninsula. Anxious to assert their presence in the region, the Dutch built **Fort Amsterdam** in Manado and conquered the **Sangir-Talaud islands** off the north coast. A treaty signed in 1679 confirmed their domination, which was to spread over the Minahasa region for three centuries. Along with its vast programme of conversion to Protestantism, the **Dutch Missionary Society (NZG)** developed a substantial educational system in the 19C, which was to turn the Minahasa into a Christianised, cultured and Westernised elite that would occupy important posts in the colonial administration and army.

A bloody defeat

In order to confirm their sovereignty over the **southern peninsula**, the Dutch were forced to launch several fresh offensives against Bone between 1825 and 1860. In the **north** of the island, total submission was not complete until around 1870. There still remained the highlands of the interior, which the colonial power did not manage to overcome until the first decade of the 20C. Little affected by the Islam that dominated the coastal areas, the people of the **Centre** soon fell prey to the missionaries who explored Lake Poso in 1892 and the Toraja region in 1913. But contact with these remote populations was more difficult: it would take nearly 20 years of patience and perseverance to convert the Toraja.

Throughout the island conquest was achieved through an aggressive military campaign. Bloody guerrilla warfare broke out on all fronts, with the most desperate resistance coming from the **Bugis** of Bone sultanate and the **Makassars** of Gowa in 1905, and also – to a lesser degree – the **Toraja** in the North in 1906.

Having finally crushed all its opponents, the government of the **Dutch Indies** urged them to adopt the new colonial order. While leaving the local chiefs to govern, the Dutch took economic and political control of the island. While it was obtained at a very high price, this victory finally ushered in a long period of **peace** on the island. With the establishment of a centralised **administration** based in Makassar, the colonial era was to be marked above all by the development of a **road network** and an **irrigation system.**

Colours of South Sulawesi: Bugis houses

Sulawesi

Nationalist aspirations

The nationalist movement was born around Manado and Makassar and also expressed itself in occasional outbreaks of direct action, evidence of the population's strong resentment against the Dutch. The sombre interlude in Sulawesi's history of the invasion by **Japanese forces** in 1942 did no more than put the anticolonial efforts on hold, ready to return to activity as soon as the Republic of Indonesia was proclaimed. Named the first republican governor of Sulawesi in 1945, the nationalist Minahasa leader **Sam Ratulangi** (1890-1949) was imprisoned by the Dutch in April 1946. In December 1946 the latter sought to emulate the young republic with a **"State of East Indonesia"**, which they created in Makassar. Their aspiration could not, however, survive the growing mass opposition. Even the terrible massacres that they inflicted could not succeed in stifling the hopes of freedom that finally culminated with the independence of the whole country in 1949.

Regionalism against central power

Between 1950 and 1965 a growing general discontent seized the population of Sulawesi. With expectations disappointed, impatience in the face of the weakness of the Jakarta government, as well as **Sukarno**'s centralising and authoritarian tendencies, a regional reformist movement was soon forced to emerge. This came to a head in 1958 in the north of the island with the **Permesta rebellion.** The official forces responded by shelling Manado, an event that was soon followed by an endless period of armed repression throughout the region. The resistance, however, was not crushed until 1961. Fortunately, the reforms implemented under Suharto's **New Order** were favourable to the local economy and restored peace. This return to calm marked the beginning of expansion in Sulawesi. Cautious at first, more rapid after 1970, it soon allowed the island to welcome its first tourists.

Exploiting natural resources

Apart from tourism, the island's natural resources – land, sea and forest – supply the people of Sulawesi with most of their income. Farming and fishing, in particular, remain largely traditional, generally run on family lines. Despite its wealth of raw materials the island still produces little in the way of manufactured goods, and although it has abundant hidden **mineral deposits**, only the southeastern peninsula's **nickel** mines have really been exploited. As for gold fever, this remains very limited. On the other hand, the export trade in spices and **precious wood**, such as teak and sandalwood, is as successful as it has always been down the centuries.

A mosaic of peoples

Sulawesi's geographical position in the middle of the Indonesian archipelago and its strategic role in the international spice trade have long accustomed the island to foreign contact. With some **13 million inhabitants**, its present-day population is extraordinarily diverse, the result of the waves of migrants through the ages: a mixture of Indian, Chinese, Arab and European influences that have created an incredible ethnic and cultural melting pot.

With its fishermen and hardened sailors – the Bugis fleet is renowned wherever it sails – as well as its farmers, traders and craftsmen, Sulawesi still remains largely oriented towards the sea. Concentrated in the urban and port centres of the coastal regions in the South – home to nearly half the island's population – the principal ethnic groups (Bugis, Makassar and Mandar) adhere to the **Sunni Islam** faith that the Malay traders introduced to South Sulawesi in the 15C. Officially adopted only in the early 17C, today it includes nearly 80% of the inhabitants. It has, however, succeeded in assimilating some of the ancient native beliefs and practices, such as ancestor worship and animist ritual.

The **Christian** (mostly **Protestant**) faith brought in by the Portuguese, Spanish and then above all the Dutch missionaries took root mainly in the mountains of the Toraja region in the South, the highlands in the Centre and the Minahasa territory in the North. Less affected by outside influences, the peoples of the mountains and the dense forests in the Centre and Southeast – a series of often little known minorities – have more easily retained their **animist** traditions. According to their beliefs, a cosmic force animates the universe, and everything has its own resident spirit. Their ritual practices are designed to capture this force, regarded as ensuring happiness, health, prosperity, fertility, etc, on earth.

Grouped in the towns, where it remains very united and enterprising as far as trade and business are concerned, the **Chinese community** – mainly Christian, but also Buddhist and Confucian – represents barely more than 1% of the population. Lastly, within the framework of the governmental **transmigration** plan, certain regions have more recently taken in **Balinese and Javanese minorities.**

Living together peacefully, all these groups speak no fewer than 80 different **languages** and dialects, the leading ones being Makassar, Bugis, Sa'dan Toraja, Minahasa, Mandar and Gorontalo. Most of the island's inhabitants also have at least some idea of *Bahasa Indonesia*, and the youngest among them often speak English.

Whatever the language, you will find hospitality and smiles everywhere – from north to south, from Bugis craftsmen busy building new boats to Minahasa traders delighted to show you the way to the local volcanoes. Drawn by the rich funeral ceremonies in the Toraja region, most visitors allocate only a few days to Sulawesi, ignoring the innumerable treasures of the more remote areas. Hunting them down does of course require a certain amount of time and a thirst for adventure.

Bugis house and...

...Makassar façade

R. Marca

A mosaic of peoples

UJUNG PANDANG
(FORMER MAKASSAR)
Capital of South Sulawesi Province (Sulawesi Selatan)
Map p 454-455 and plan p 569
Pop 1 300 000 – Very hot and humid climate

Not to be missed
A trip by becak to the port of Paotere.
Drinking avocado juice in Pantai Losari at sunset.

And remember…
Use becaks to get around.
Avoid walking about alone at night.
Avoid Sundays, when many of the shops and offices are closed.

A bustling metropolis with never-ending floods of traffic, Ujung Pandang stretches over several kilometres beside the **Strait of Makassar**. Stifling, polluted and noisy, it has little charm for the visitor, who will generally be content to make but a brief stopover here.

As capital of South Sulawesi Province, Ujung Pandang is home to most of the island's administrative offices, trade and industry, while its famous universities also attract large numbers of students from all over the archipelago. As the island's main harbour, it sees a ferment of cosmopolitan visitors in transit, who do much to enliven its night-life, which is not always to be recommended. Endless and rapid expansion together with uncontrolled urban building have entirely stolen the city's character.

Panic aboard!
You may be seized with alarm in the dense and anarchic flood of "pete-pete" buses, motorbikes, cars and spluttering lorries – but do not jump out of your "becak", have confidence in your driver. At every road junction you will be astonished at the driver's skill at getting through the tangle!

Although not at first a very welcoming place, it nonetheless has unsuspected charms, which you may find round the corner in a quiet lane, in an energetic conversation or a frenzied karaoke session. In its intense busyness, it lies naturally open to the visitor's eye: with its sailors and prostitutes, its gangs of street children – musicians, shoe-shine boys or voluble cigarette sellers – its many beggars and also its friendly, helpful inhabitants.

Former Makassar
In the heart of Indonesia, ideally placed on the **spice route** from the Moluccas: its strategic location turned Makassar to trade (in spices, copra, coffee and teak), which was particularly intense in the 15C and 16C. Braving pirates and raging seas, traders ventured forth from China, India, all over Southeast Asia and even from Europe, seeking lucrative business. The town gradually developed round the harbour, and was taken over in 1667 by the **Dutch East India Company**, which set up a trading post. When the country won its independence, the place was renamed **Ujung Pandang**. It has retained its historic vocation as a maritime crossroads and is still one of Indonesia's most active ports.

A tour of the town
Allow half a day. Take care as you walk, the pavements are often very uneven.

Most of the interesting sights and tourist infrastructures are behind the **"Pantai Losari"** (Jalan Penghibur) seafront, on each side of **Fort Rotterdam** (A2), round the large **Karebosi** esplanade (B2) and the **Makassar Mall** (B2-B3).

Fort Rotterdam (Benteng Rotterdam)

Jl Ujung Pandang, on the seafront. 7.30am-6pm. The fort, Ujung Pandang's main historical artefact, owes its name to the Dutch who began reconstructing it around 1667, after they had captured the town. Built in 1545, it was at first part of a stronghold designed to protect the kingdom of Gowa. Despite considerable restoration, the buildings still retain their Flemish architectural style. Around a vast courtyard they house various cultural offices and two museums. In the right wing the **South Sulawesi Province Museum** *(Tuesday-Thursday, 8am-2pm; Friday, 8-10.30am; Saturday-Sunday, 8am-1pm; closed Monday and public holidays; fee)* is devoted to the daily life of the four great ethnic groups of the region. Models of Bugis boats and Toraja houses, farming tools, weaving equipment and traditional costumes make up the bulk of the collections.

Opposite, the **Sulawesi History Museum** *(same visiting conditions)* houses various every-day items and pieces of original craftwork from all over the island. Rundown and with poorly presented exhibits (most of the labels are in Indonesian), these two establishments suffer from a cruel lack of maintenance. They are, however, adequate for a brief introduction to your visit to Sulawesi.

Turn right as you leave the fort, cross over Jl Riburane (a little further along on the right), and then turn left into Jl Sulawesi.

The harbour district

Several **Chinese temples** stand along **Jalan Sulawesi** (A2), particularly near Jalan Serui and Jalan Bali. With a profusion of red lanterns, clouds of incense and an air of silent meditation the quiet atmosphere of the pagodas presents a startling contrast after the calls of the muezzin from the mosque that echo in the distance. A substantial Chinese community prospers in this animated commercial district. It has some picturesque Chinese shops, where the bill is still calculated with the aid of a traditional abacus.

More than a goal in themselves, going to see the Bugis schooners in the old **harbour at Paotere** (beyond B1) makes a pleasant walk *(around 3km north of the town: not to be confused with the modern harbour, which is more central)*. Take a *becak* and explain that you want to lose yourself in the narrow alleyways in the working-class districts, avoiding the direct main roads.

M Lemerle

Ujung Pandang, under the gaze of the wise men in the Chinese temple

Ujung Pandang

South of the fort

Hidden behind the house of the Bundt family, the **C L Bundt orchid garden** (B3) *(Jl Mochtar Lutfi 15; no set hours: knock at the door; entrance free; best flowering period: March-September)* has some unique hybrid species, created through experimental crossbreeding, which have made its name. You will also be shown with pride a rich collection of **shells** *(on sale)*, dusty and badly displayed.

For a pleasant end to the day, take a stroll in the late afternoon along the seafront, **Pantai Losari** *(Jl Penghibur)* (A3-B4). You can have a drink here, or dine watching a magnificent **sunset** *(see also "Eating out", p 567)*.

The surrounding area
Allow half a day.

Go to the central market and take a bemo for Maros. From here, another one will take you to Bantimurung, about 45km northeast of Ujung Pandang (minimum travelling time, 1hr each way). 9am-4pm. Very crowded at weekends. Fee.

This is an ideal excursion to get away from the heat and hurly-burly of the town, where you can have a picnic or a refreshing swim. In the midst of magnificent cliffs shaped like sugar loaves, carpeted with luxuriant vegetation, the **Bantimurung waterfalls** (Air Terjun Bantimurung) cascade harmoniously down onto the eroded rock and form a natural swimming pool. The site is also well known for its butterflies. The British naturalist **Alfred Wallace** *(see p 16)* discovered some rare specimens here in the 19C, which today are becoming rarer.

Making the most of Ujung Pandang

COMING AND GOING

By air – *Hasanuddin* airport lies 23km northeast of the town. Domestic flights from Manado, Tana Toraja, Bali, Java, the Moluccas and Kalimantan. *Malaysia Airline* also provides an international link with Kuala Lumpur, and *Silk Air* with Singapore. The airport has a currency exchange and a cash dispenser (Visa cards and MasterCard). Some hotels and travel agencies are represented here (guides and cars with drivers). *Taxis* are paid in advance (set price) at the counter located at the exit. You can also walk or take a *becak* (three-wheeled cycle rickshaw) as far as the main road (500m), where *pete-pete* minibuses provide a shuttle service to Ujung Pandang (Daya terminus).

By boat –*Sukarno harbour* is central (A1) and receives *Pelni* ships (see address below) from Surabaya (Java), Maumere (Flores), Balikpapan (Kalimantan) and Bima (Sumbawa). For details of connections, get hold of the monthly timetable from a Pelni representative or a travel agency.

By bus – Ujung Pandang is served by numerous companies that link the island's main towns (see under this heading in each chapter). In theory, the *Panaikang* bus station, Jl Urip Sumoharjo (east of the town) serves Rantepao, Sengkang and Palopo; coaches from *Sungguminasa* (6km away, in Jl Bawakaraeng) serve Bulukumba (Bira), Pare Pare and Rantepao; Daya bus station (14km from the centre) serves Rantepao, and *Malengkeri* station, Bulukumba (Bira). To avoid unpleasant surprises, book your places the day before (particularly for the Toraja region), at the bus station or the company's headquarters in the centre. *Litha & Co.*, Jl Gunung Merapi 160, is the most reliable company with the most comfortable buses. *Liman Express*, Jl Laiya 25, is equally recommended.

By pete-pete – The main station for these minibuses is at *Pasar Sentral* (Makassar Mall), Jl Akademis (B2).

GETTING AROUND

On foot – very sprawling, hot and humid, and without pavements in some places, the city does not favour walking.

By becak – The ideal way to get around in town. *Becaks* are ubiquitous and cheap (negotiate the price for the trip before you get in, to make sure).

By taxi – Numerous in the town centre and at the airport. Almost all of them are air-conditioned and equipped with a meter. Your hotel can get one for you.

By pete-pete/mikrolet – These minibuses cover the town and its surroundings. Very cheap, but not always easy to use for the newcomer. Ask the driver or local people to help you find the right vehicle.

ADDRESS BOOK

Tourist information – Jl Pettarani, ☎ (0411) 44 33 55. Far from the centre, it has only a mediocre plan of the town and a few brochures of no great use. The same items are also available in most of the town's hotels and travel agencies.

Bank/Currency exchange – There are numerous banks in Jl Ahmad Yani (A2-B2) and around Makassar Mall (B2). Some banks such as *Danamon* (Jl Ahmad Yani), *RNI* (corner of Jl Ahmad Yani and Jl Sudirman) and *BCA* (Jl Sulawesi) accept withdrawals with Visa card. *BNI*, at the address above, or in Jl Ranggong (A3), changes dollars, as do some of the travel agencies (see below). The airport has a currency exchange and a cash dispenser. You can also change your money at the Limbunan agency (see below) and in most hotels. *American Express*, Jl Sudirman 56 (B4-C4), ☎ (0411) 85 39 06.

Post office – *Main post office (Pos dan Giro)*, Jl Slamet Riyady (A2-A3). Monday-Saturday, 8am-8pm; Sunday and public holidays, 9am-4pm. *Poste restante*. Internet (9am-5pm; closed Sunday and public holidays).

Telephone – Plenty of telephone boxes, coin or card operated, in the street. Many *Wartel* offices for international or reverse charge calls. You will find them particularly in Jl Sulawesi (near Jl Bali) (A2) and

Sulawesi

in Jl Penghibur (at no 42) (A3). For reverse-charge calls, **Home Country Direct** is available in the Legend Hostel (see "Where to stay") and Marannu Hotel (Jl Sultan Hasanuddin) (A3-B3).

Internet – Main post office (see above). **Sena** travel agency, Jl Jampea 1A (A2). **Legend Hostel** (see "Where to stay").

Travel agencies – Numerous. Apart from boat and air tickets (often much cheaper than from the airlines), the agencies offer various tours for exploring the island (or other islands in the archipelago), with or without guides, and cars with drivers. **Limbunan**, Jl Gunung Bawakaraeng 40-42 (C2), ☎ (0411) 31 50 10 / 33 34 44. Probably the agency with the largest range of services. **Mutiara Nusantara**, Jl Gunung Bawakaraeng 121 (beyond C2), ☎ (0411) 32 21 65. **Toraja Nusantara**, Jl Penghibur 10 (A3), ☎ (0411) 32 26 65. **Tunas Indonesia**, Jl H Bau 34 (B4), ☎ (0411) 87 42 55. **Dwi Kartika Travel**, Jl Sulawesi 23 (A2), ☎ (0411) 31 66 78 /32 16 78.

Car rental – In Sulawesi there is no car hire without driver. Check that the price includes petrol, and the meals and overnight accommodation for the driver if you are leaving for more than one day. Enquire at travel agencies or hotels. At the airport and the bus stations you can hire a car with driver, alone or with other passengers.

Airline companies – Travel agents often have tickets at much better prices than those offered by the airlines themselves. **Garuda**, Jl Slamet Riyadi 6 (A2), ☎ (0411) 32 25 43/31 73 50. **Merpati**, Jl Gunung Bawakaraeng 109 (beyond C2), ☎ (0411) 24 11 14/44 24 71. **Bouraq**, Jl Veteran Selatan 1 (beyond C3), ☎ (0411) 45 25 06. **Mandala**, Komp. Latanette Plaza D7, Jl Sungai Saddang, ☎ (0411) 32 42 88. **Silk Air**, in the reception hall of the Makassar Golden Hotel (see "Where to stay"). **Malaysian Airlines**, ground floor of the Marannu Hotel, Jl Sultan Hasanuddin (A3-B3).

Shipping line – Pelni (main office), Jl Sudirman 38 (B3), ☎ (0411) 33 13 93. Daily, 8am-3pm. Boat timetables and tickets are available in travel agencies or direct at the port, Jl Nusantara (A1).

Immigration office – Kantor Imigrasi, corner of Jl Nusantara and Jl Tentera Pelajar (A1).

Medical service – In case of medical problems, check first with your hotel, which will be able to call a doctor. The city has many hospitals, including **Rumah Sakit Umum** (general hospital) to the east of the town, **Rumah Sakit Akademis**, Jl Akademis (B2), **Rumah Sakit Stella Maris**, Jl Penghibur (B4) and **Rumah Sakit Pelamonia**, Jl Sudirman (B3).

WHERE TO STAY

Ujung Pandang is neither restful nor cheap, but you may have to spend a night here to catch a bus, a plane or a boat. None of the hotels is outstanding for its charm, but there are some that are clean and comfortable. All the places listed are in the city centre.

Modest

⌂**Mursalim (Dodo)**, Jl Abdul Kadir, Blok IY 25 (4km south of the city centre), ☎ (0411) 86 39 41/44 35 34 – 2rm. ⫪ Dodo and his charming family will treat you like kings and you will quickly feel at home. Impeccable guestrooms and delicious breakfast, attentive and discreet welcome. A very pleasant way of getting to know the Indonesians on closer terms. Dodo also offers his services as a guide (Ujung Pandang and its surrounding area) and a driver (South Sulawesi).

Legend Hostel, Jl Jampea 5G, ☎ (0411) 32 82 03/04, Fax (0411) 32 68 87, legetata@indosat.net.id – 9rm and a 20-bed dormitory. ☴ Internet access and reverse charge telephone facilities. A type of Youth Hostel and hangout for back-packers from all over the world. Even if you do not stay here, the staff can supply a great deal of information for your travels. Dormitory for the poverty-stricken, or plain and basic rooms with thin partitions and no windows. A pleasant small terrace on the roof. Despite the lack of comfort and the noise of the neighbouring karaoke at night, the place is never empty. A few simple and very mediocre dishes available on the premises.

Modest – average

Pondok Wisata Bontocinde, Jl Sungai Saddang 66, ☎ (0411) 87 12 29/87 47 84 – 31rm. ⫪▤ / ☴ The standard rooms with fan and cold water are small and basic. The better, newer, ones, are equipped with television, telephone, air conditioning and hot water, offering very good value for money. Avoid the rooms facing the street, which are fairly noisy.

Average

@**Pondok Suada Indah**, Jl Hasanuddin 12, ☎ (0411) 31 71 79/31 28 57, Fax (0411) 31 28 56 – 12rm. ⌖▤ ℘ TV Hot water and refrigerator. The rooms are impeccably clean, the superior ones vast and modern, the standard ones smaller and somewhat rundown. Shared terrace and small garden. Excellent value for money.

Hotel Surya Indonesia, Jl Daeng Tompo 3, ☎ (0411) 32 75 68, Fax (0411) 31 14 98 – 31rm. ⌖▤ ℘ TV CC Hot water. Also a very good place for accommodation in this category. Small, comfortable and well kept rooms, including some facing onto a shared balcony.

Hotel Puri Wisata, Jl Sultan Hasanuddin 36-38, ☎ (0411) 32 43 44/32 21 86/31 28 45, Fax (0411) 31 27 83 – 50rm. ⌖▤ ℘ TV ✕ CC Hot water. Pleasant small rooms without great interest. Go for the ones that are laid out on two storeys and set round a type of patio. At all costs avoid the economy ones, which do not have private bathrooms and are basic and gloomy. The restaurant is very depressing!

High end

Celebes Hotel, Jl Hasanuddin 2, ☎ (0411) 32 07 70, Fax (0411) 32 07 69 – 28rm. ⌖▤ ℘ TV ✕ CC Hot water. Modern comfortable hotel, without any special charm. Two price levels, depending on the size of the room.

High end – luxury

Yasmin Hotel, Jl Jampea 5, ☎ (0411) 32 04 24/32 82 57/32 82 58, Fax (0411) 32 82 83 – 83rm. ⌖▤ ℘ TV ✕ CC Comfortable and well-kept rooms, but without character. Rates vary according to size.

Super deluxe

Makassar Golden Hotel, Jl Pasar Ikan 50-52, ☎ (0411) 31 44 08, Fax (0411) 32 09 51, mgh@u.pandang.wasantara. net.id – 60rm. ⌖▤ ℘ TV ✕ ⌗ CC Hot water. A large hotel with interna-

tional facilities, ideally located on the seafront, in the city centre. The expensive, but very attractive private bungalows face the sea. The rooms in the main building – a large modern construction – are more ordinary. Some have a little balcony with sea view, while the cheapest have no windows!

@**Hotel Pantai Gapura**, Jl Pasar Ikan 10, ☎ (0411) 32 57 91, Fax (0411) 31 63 03, hotelpg@upg.mega.net.id – 60rm. ⌖▤ ℘ TV ✕ ⌗ CC Hot water. The standard rooms that lead off from a passageway lack charm, are rather antiquated and do not justify their price! On the other hand, the cottages built on piles by the sea, in Makassar style, are full of character. One of the restaurants is in an old Bugis boat.

EATING OUT

You can venture into the innumerable **warung** in the city, which serve cheap and often good food. Apart from basic Indonesian dishes (nasi and mie goreng), you can eat grilled fish, Chinese cuisine, and Makassar specialities such as "soto Makassar" (spiced broth with buffalo offal). For breakfast, or simply for pleasure, try the local cakes, based on coconut (kelapa), brown sugar (gula mera) or other ingredients.

Basic

@**Pantai Losari**, Jl Penghibur (A3-B4). Every day from 5-6pm, the seafront (between the Makassar Golden and Novotel hotels) turns into a massive night market (until 2am, sometimes later), which the people of Makassar are proud to describe as the "longest table in the world". Dozens of light carts fill the street for more than 1km and cookers begin to smoke. Groups of students, families or solitary sailors crowd round to watch the setting sun as they sip an avocado juice (made with sweetened concentrated milk and chocolate), and eat "nasi goreng", "mie kuah" or "gado-gado". This is an excellent place to practice your rudimentary Bahasa Indonesia. At least go for a stroll here to take in the atmosphere. Do not give in to pleadings by the many child beggars, most of whom work for a "boss". Give them food rather than money. As for the musicians, remember that they will carry on playing until you thank them. If you do not wish to give them a few rupiah, stop them straight away, politely but firmly.

Sari Laut, Jl Pasar Ikan (A3). From 5pm until the early hours of the morning. Located by the sea on a muddy stretch of land, these *warung* (from the street, you will spot the colourfully decorated shellfish tanks) offer excellent fish and seafood, fried or grilled while you watch, accompanied by rice, "sambal" (pimento-based chutney) and lemon. The pimento-spiced prawns are really delicious! Those who do not like seafood can fall back on grilled duck or chicken. The only drinks served are boiled water, orange juice or tea, but you can buy soft drinks or beer from neighbouring stalls. Most of the customers are Indonesians. Note the comment above about beggars and musicians.

Moderate

Kareba, Jl Penghibur 10 (A3), ☎ (0411) 32 60 62. If you are trying to escape the bustle and lack of intimacy in Pantai Losari, take refuge on the terrace of the Kareba, just opposite the seafront. The cuisine is very average but the setting in the open air is pleasant for a drink. Groups come in to play various types of music, every evening from 6pm.

Kios Semarang, Jl Penghibur (A3). A complete change from the above, less hushed and more lively. The restaurant is upstairs, looking onto the street, and is ideally located for making the most of the sunset and watching the life along Pantai Losari. Large choice of noodles and soups, substantial and full of flavour. You can also come here to drink beer. Very varied clientele.

Sri Ratu, Jl Ahmad Yani 21 (B2), ☎ (0411) 32 56 29. Somewhat cold decor yet elegant and relaxed at the same time, and irreproachably clean. You choose a selection of small dishes (various preparations of meat, fish, seafood, vegetables, etc) to assemble your own plateful, with rice. Charming reception.

Ratu Muda, Jl Ranggong 5 (A3-B3), ☎ (0411) 32 79 20. Air-conditioned dining room or small covered terrace. You will be served with tasty specialities from South Sulawesi. Be prepared for a few surprises, as the menu is in Indonesian and the staff do not speak English. The quality of the service, relaxed but efficient and smiling, is fine.

Maxim I, Jl Sulawesi 42 (A2), ☎ (0411) 31 12 81; **Maxim II**, Jl Sulawesi 78, ☎ (0411) 31 59 01/32 23 65. A popular dining room opening onto the street, or a smarter air-conditioned dining room: two options for trying delicious Chinese cuisine. Wide choice. Native diners order an assortment of dishes that they share out with their chopsticks.

More select

Makassar Golden, Jl Penghibur (A3), A large covered terrace, well ventilated, above the water, where diners enjoy a superb view of the lights of Pantai Losari by night. Slightly pretentious, but reasonable cuisine. You can also simply enjoy a drink at sunset.

GOING OUT

If you get on well with the Indonesians, you may be invited to show off your singing talents in one of the city's innumerable **karaoke** establishments. Some may seem a little stiff, such as the large places that are also restaurants (in Jl Penghibur). Others, more popular and smoky, are crowded with a very mixed clientele, sometimes slightly dubious. In all cases, it is an amusing experience.

Kareba, see "Eating out", above.

Zig Zag, Makassar Golden Hotel (see "Where to stay"). The hotel disco hosts a fairly prosperous and cosmopolitan clientele. Formal dress preferred.

SHOPPING GUIDE

Jl Somba Opu (A3), a street parallel with Jl Penghibur, is tempting for window-shopping. Its many small shops primarily sell jewellery (filigree silver or gold), but also handicrafts from the Toraja region and other Indonesian islands. You will also find sarongs and silk clothing here from the Sengkang region, and some Chinese curios.

The **central market** (pasar sentral) (B2) and the **shopping centres** (Matahari and others) offer more ordinary items.

Bookshops – Most of the hotels in the high-end category have a small shop where you can find books and maps of Sulawesi, and occasionally English-language newspapers.

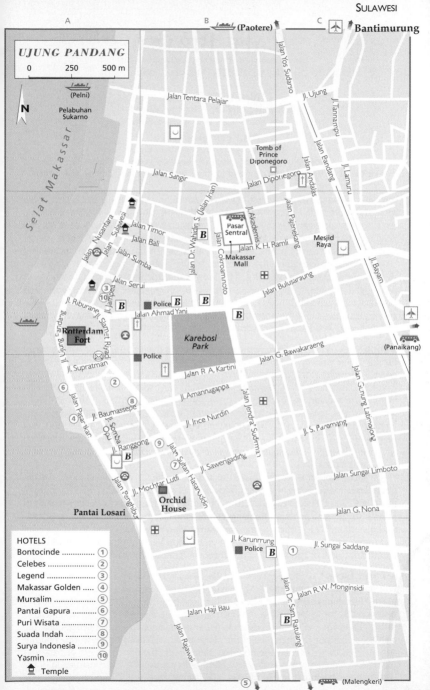

SULAWESI

Bantimurung

(Paotere)

UJUNG PANDANG

0   250   500 m

(Pelni)

N

Pelabuhan
Sukarno

Selat Makassar

Jalan Tentara Pelajar

Jalan Yos Sudarso

Jl. Ujung

Jl. Tannampu

Jalan Bandang

Jl. Lamuru

Jalan Sangir

Tomb of
Prince
Diponegoro

Jalan Diponegoro

Jalan Andalas

Jalan Timor

Jalan Bali

Jalan Sumba

Jalan Nusantara

Jalan Sulawesi

Jalan Dr. Wahidin S. (Jalan Irian)

Jalan Cokroaminoto

Pasar
Sentral

Jl. Akademis

Makassar
Mall

Jalan K. H. Ramli

Jalan Pajenekang

Mesjid
Raya

Jl. Bayam

Jalan Serui

Padjaja Tim

Jl. Riburane

Police

Jalan Ahmad Yani

Jalan Bulusaraung

B

B

B

B

B

Rotterdam
Fort

*Karebosi
Park*

Police

Jalan G. Bawakaraeng

(Panaikang)

Jl. Supratman

Police

Jalan R. A. Kartini

Jalan Gunung Latimojong

Jl. Amannagappa

Jl. Baumassepe

Jl. Somba Opu

Jl. Ince Nurdin

Jalan Jendra' Sudirman

Jl. S. Paromang

Jl. Ranggong

Jalan Sultan Hasanuddin

Jl. Sawerigading

Jalan Sungai Limboto

B

B

Jl. Mochtar Lutfi

Jalan Penghibur

**Orchid
House**

Jalan Pasar Ikar

Jalan G. Nona

Pantai Losari

Jl. Karunrrung

Police

Jl. Sungai Saddang

①

Jalan Haji Bau

Jalan Dr. Sam Ratulangi

Jalan R. W. Monginsidi

B

Jalan Rajawali

⑤

(Malengkeri)

HOTELS

Bontocinde	①
Celebes	②
Legend	③
Makassar Golden	④
Mursalim	⑤
Pantai Gapura	⑥
Puri Wisata	⑦
Suada Indah	⑧
Surya Indonesia	⑨
Yasmin	⑩

🏛 Temple

CAPE BIRA★★
South Sulawesi Province (Sulawesi Selatan)
Map p 554-555 – Hot dry climate

Not to be missed
Bira beach and exploring the sea-bed.
Bugis boats being built at Tana Beru.

And remember...
Spend at least 1 or 2 nights in Bira.
Avoid the weekends, when the beach is very crowded.
Take the coast road on the outward journey, and the Malino road on the return.

The Bira region on the southeast tip of the South Sulawesi peninsula is one of the most arid on the island. As you leave Ujung Pandang along the southern coast, you travel at first through green landscapes punctuated by salt marshes. Rice fields and plantations of banana and coconut palms gradually give way to drier and sparser vegetation where cactus plants are soon visible. Stylish houses on piles, painted in bright colours, stand along the roadside. In the shade of their raised houses the women spend their time weaving. This work supplements the family income from fishing and farming (cashew nuts, cloves, cacao, coffee, maize and hevea trees). The population in general, however, mainly Makassar and Bugis, still looks to the sea: above all it maintains the ancestral tradition of shipbuilding, creating the elegant wooden cargo boats that have haunted the seas for centuries.

■ **Bira**★★ – *200km from Ujung Pandang. See "Coming and going", p 572. Fee.* This peaceful fishing village stretches out for several kilometres before reaching the sea. When you come to the end of the main road you have a feeling of infinite space. To the right (southwest) there is a long **beach**★★ with magnificent white sand, fringed with low cliffs where erosion has carved out caves. At low tide, when the fishermen come with their nets, you can walk to the far end of the beach, a place of utter peace. The crystal clear turquoise water covers exquisite **coral reefs**★★ *(diving, see p 572, and colour plates p 24-25)*. Not far from the shore (particularly opposite the Bira View Inn), you can swim among multicoloured fish and, with a little patience, you will probably see a turtle or sea snake.

Hire a small boat for a trip out to see the **dolphins**, which often appear close to **Cape Lasa** *(dangerous for swimming)*. Apart from the half-starved goats that wander through the village, you will see little apart from butterflies, and untamed monkeys that seem to have made their home on **Puajanggo** hill, to the west. A track *(around 3km)* leads to the summit, which offers a fine **panoramic view**★ over the coast. For a pleasant end to the day, treat yourself to a drink on the Bira View Inn terrace. You will have a front row view of the magnificent **sunset**★★★ igniting the waves.

■ **Tana Beru**★ – *18km west of Bira. Allow 15min by car, 1hr by bemo (irregular service).* Lost among the coconut palms, this charming seaside village is home to one of the main Bugis **shipyards**★ on the island. Behind the houses on their piles, a row of pot-bellied hulls, prows pointed to the open sea, invades the beach for several hundred metres. Following secret methods transmitted from father to son for generations, the craftsmen continue to create one of the oldest traditional fleets in the world. Without any set plan they skilfully assemble the planks with their joints made of bark and rubber and wooden pegs – only a few metal bolts are used in the construction of the largest ships. Ranging from the narrow little fishing *pajala* to the imposing *pinisi* cargo

Timbers rising between sea and sky: a Bugis shipyard (Bira)

ships that weigh nearly 200 tonnes, are more than 30m in length and are designed for the seas of Southeast Asia, the different types of *prahu* are created here by nimble hands, after weeks or months of hard labour. Great ceremonies and animal sacrifice accompany the building of each boat. Concentrated at Tana Beru, shipping work, on a much smaller scale, is also done at **Marumasa** (on the east coast, near Bira harbour).

■ **Tana Towa**★ — *66km north of Bira. Allow 90min by car, 2hr minimum by bemo (they stop on the main road, from where you will have to walk for 15-30min). Guide obligatory. Fee, with obligatory hire of black clothing, and donation to the village chief. No photography allowed of the inside of the houses. Since some members of the community do not have the right to be photographed, seek permission before taking a photograph.*

9km from Kajang, heading inland, Tana Towa (the "old country") is the centre of an isolated ethnic group that still lives according to pre-Islamic traditions. Totally inward looking, this self-governing society is just beginning to open up to the rest of the world. Running water and electricity have not yet come to the village, and the inhabitants continue to practice a self-sufficient economy based on stock rearing and farming. Leading the tribe is the **Amma Towa**, the customary chief whose absolute authority regulates every detail of the inhabitants' life. Everyone has to consult him and obtain his consent before doing anything. A gate marks the entrance to the "town", hidden 1 or 2km from the house where clothing is hired. Along the way you will probably meet a few young girls going to draw water at the well, while the boys take the cows to the river to cool off. Stony tracks lead to the **houses**, built as in the past of untreated timber and covered with a roof of coconut palm thatch. Between the piles of their houses the women weave the community's black clothes. Visitors are requested to present themselves at the **village chief's house** (*rumah Amma Towa*): a good opportunity to see the interior of these normally impenetrable dwellings. After the usual questions (don't worry, your guide will act as interpreter!), you will probably be offered coffee before being discreetly asked for a small donation.

Cape Bira

571

Making the most of Bira

COMING AND GOING

From Ujung Pandang – Leave before 10am, from the Mallengkeri terminus (taxi or *bemo* to get there from the central market). Here you will find either a collective four-wheel drive "kijang" taxi, a bus or a *bemo*, leaving for Bulukumba (3-4hr). There you will need to take another *bemo* to Bira (1hr-1hr30min).

From the north – From the Toraja region, Lake Poso or Lake Tempe, you have to change at Watampone (Bone), where buses, *bemos* or collective "kijang" taxis go to Bulukumba (they usually leave in the morning, when they are full). *Bemos* provide a shuttle service between Bulukumba and Bira.

ADDRESS BOOK

Telephone/Currency exchange – Wartel, ☎ and Fax (0413) 815 15. Variable hours, in theory from 8.30am to 11pm. Local and international calls, fax, currency exchange (does not always have large amounts of currency).

Diving – Bira Diving Resort, at the Bira Beach Hotel, ☎ (0411) 32 75 22 (or at the Wartel, see above). For experienced divers. Check the condition of the equipment.

WHERE TO STAY, EATING OUT

For all the addresses given below you can make your reservations by telephone or fax, through the Bira **Wartel** (see above).

Modest

Riswan Guest House, ☎ (0413) 821 27 – 8rm ⚓ ✗ Unbeatable value for money! Perched high up, this large wooden Bugis-style house provides a magnificent view of the sea from its verandah. Plain but very decent rooms stretch out in a line on the first floor. Shared washing facilities. The whole place is perfectly run. Meals are taken together (full board obligatory). You can take a picnic lunch with you if you do not wish to return for the midday meal. The family welcome is personalised and charming.

Riswan Bungalows, ☎ (0413) 821 27 – 6rm ⚓ The bungalows stand in a row set slightly back from the main street. They

are built of wood and bamboo, with unpretentious facilities (Turkish-style WC) but they are clean and each has its own small terrace.

Pondok Wisata Bagahagia, ☎ (0413) 816 71/816 81/817 01 – 16rm ⚓ More expensive, but somewhat quieter, these Bugis-style bungalows with their pink and sky-blue paintwork lie at right angles to the sea, each with its private terrace. Plain but reasonable.

Average

Bira View Inn, ☎ (0413) 820 43 – 19rm ⚓ ✗ ✗ ✿ An excellent place, ideally located facing the sea. Handsome bungalows on piles, in Bugis style, built of wood, quite simple but comfortable. Their private verandahs open straight onto the sea. A little less expensive but much more ordinary, the standard rooms are hidden at the back. Very pleasant restaurant, on a terrace facing the sea. There is no beach, but you can swim just in front of the hotel, using the ladders installed for the purpose.

Bira Beach Hotel, ☎ (0413) 811 36/ 821 79 – 27rm ⚓ 📧 / ✗ ✗ ✿ 📷 Rather cramped rooms with private terraces, spread round a little garden facing the beach. The least expensive, small and more basic bungalows, lie back from the main street. A satisfactory establishment but without great charm. A pleasant restaurant with sea view. Diving club next door.

Average – High end

Hotel Sapolohe, ☎ (0413) 821 28 – 14rm ⚓ 📧 / ✗ ✗ ✿ 📷 Set slightly back from the beach, with direct access. The large main building on piles, with a green pagoda roof, houses the best rooms. Equipped with air conditioning, televisions and hot water, they open on to a verandah that runs right round the house, but only a few of them enjoy a sea view. The standard rooms (with fan and cold water only) consist of bungalows of woven bamboo with small terraces. They are at the back in a well-kept garden.

Little faces in Tana Towa

M Lemerle

LAKE TEMPE★★
SENGKANG
South Sulawesi Province (Sulawesi Selatan)
Map p 554-555 – Hot and humid climate

Not to be missed
A boat trip on the lake.
And remember...
The rainy season (November-March) is paradoxically the best time
for a visit, as the lake is fuller.
The mornings are the best time to enjoy the bustle on the banks of the river.
Enjoy an outing on the lake in the late afternoon, when the sky catches fire.

From Ujung Pandang, the **road★★** climbing up towards the centre (via Maros) crosses very beautiful landscapes. It winds across green mountain slopes shaped like sugar loaves, before dropping down to rice fields and tobacco plantations. On wedding days the Bugis villages lying along the route come to life in time-honoured fashion with the radiant colours of traditional costumes. A way of brightening your journey, and of forgetting the potholes in the road!

Arrival at Sengkang in the late afternoon is particularly magical: the trees stand out like a Chinese shadow play along the banks of the river against the sky enflamed by the setting sun. Then the outline of the slender minaret appears, lit up from the mosque with green neon lights – the colour of Islam.

A lakeside city★

The charming little town of Sengkang, the former seat of the **Wajo kingdom** that stretched through the centre of the Bugis lands, lies along the banks of the **Walanae**, 5km from Lake Tempe, the source of the river.

On the waters of Lake Tempe

D Clarisse

Sulawesi

Take a stroll round the houses beside the water. You will sometimes have to use narrow bamboo footbridges, in the midst of satellite dishes planted more or less in the water! In the mornings, activity is concentrated on the banks: here, a group of women do their washing, there, a man tinkers with his boat, while further away, a band of giggling children wash themselves from head to foot.

Famous for its **silk weaving** (*sutera*) – made in **Soppeng** and the surrounding area, where you can see silk-worm farms – the town's life is regulated by the steady click of weaving looms. To have a better idea of the work done by the women, who labour at their looms under the family house, go to the north of the town (*3km from the town centre, shortly before the "Selamat jalan kota sutera" sign, a narrow lane leads off the main road to the left. A small sign reads: "170m Wakkelling"*).

On the lake★★★

Motorboat excursions. Rentals through hotels or directly on the river bank, from an owner. Negotiate firmly. Allow 2hr to take in everything. To observe the bird-life as peacefully as possible, try to rent a rowing boat, provided the water is not too rough.

This enormous shallow lake sometimes dries out completely when the rainfall is intermittent. It then becomes an amazing sight: a large bowl carpeted with greenery, and invaded by pedestrians and *bendi* (little local horse-drawn carriages) crossing from one shore to the other! On the other hand, destructive floods may swamp the lakeshore dwellings – even though they are set high on their piles – to a depth of 1m, forcing entire families to take their possessions and swim out with them.

Make the most of the golden light in the late afternoon for a boat trip. As you go up the river to the lake, the narrow boats slice through the water plants that the powerful current pushes around in clumps. At the foot of the houses, fishermen cast their nets with a quick, wide and carefully controlled movement, while others take the air on their verandahs. With a little luck you will stop to fill up at the floating fuel station just before you reach the lake. Here, the picture changes. Far

from opening out to you in a full sweep, the lake reveals itself gradually, in a series of meanders. It is full of unexpected sights: floating fields, moored with the aid of bamboos, alternate with palm groves that emerge from the often rough waters. Here and there a house, also afloat, appears suddenly, its occupants greeting you with warm smiles. More intriguing, you will no doubt pass a few cows grazing peacefully on a carpet of lakeside grass – afloat! The lake is also home to a rich **bird life** (several species of egret, herons, ibis, bitterns, cranes and moorhens), but with the sound of the engine the birds will probably fly off to somewhere quieter.

Lake Tempe

Making the most of Sengkang

COMING AND GOING

From Ujung Pandang – Bus and bemo departures from the Panaikan terminus (192km; allow 5hr travelling time).

From the Toraja region – Bus from Rantepao to Palopo, then bus, bemo or "kijang" from Palopo to Sengkang (6-8hr in all). You can also go via Lawawoi.

From Bira – Bus or bemo from Bulukumba to Bone, then from Bone to Sengkang (6-8hr). Also buses from Pare-Pare.

ADDRESS BOOK

Bank/Currency exchange – *BNI*, Jl Latainrilai (at the crossroads).

Post office/Telephone – *Main post office*, Jl Veteran, northeast of the town. *Wartel*, Jl Emmi Sailan, just across the road from Al Salam 2 Hotel (see "Where to stay"), and Jl Bau Makhmud 26, near the central market.

WHERE TO STAY

Modest

Pondok Eka, Jl Maluku 12, ☎ (0485) 212 96 – 11rm. ☎⌘/✈ A small, simple but well-run hotel. Most of the rooms open onto a large inner courtyard where breakfast is served. Unfortunately television disturbs the peaceful setting – but the welcome is friendly.

Al Salam 2 Hotel, Jl Emmi Saelan 8, ☎ (0485) 212 78, Fax (0485) 218 93 – 28rm. ⌘/✈✗ An unpretentious family hotel. 3 price categories, with the most expensive rooms being three times the price of the cheapest. Air conditioning in the most expensive, shared bathrooms for the cheapest. The whole place is simple and clean, though slightly rundown and without great charm.

Average

Hotel Apada, Jl Nangka 9, ☎/Fax (0485) 210 53 – 19rm. ☎⌘✗ The best hotel in Sengkang, unfortunately located close to the mosque. Attractive wood and shingle buildings with a pretty courtyard and small garden. The rooms, in several two-storey buildings, some with a small balcony or terrace (3 price categories), have nothing outstanding to offer but are clean and cosy. Some have television. The restaurant – undoubtedly the best in the town – sometimes lays on traditional Bugis meals with a dance performance. The owner, a Bugis princess, will talk with great enthusiasm about her region and culture.

EATING OUT

You will find a few very low-priced *warung* along the main street, around the market and the bus station.

Basic

Romantis Rumah Makan, Jl Petterani 2. Classic Indonesian dishes, in a small unpretentious restaurant.

Restoran Tomudy, Jl Andi Oddang 52. Decent cooking in a simple setting.

Moderate

Hotel Apada, the restaurant in the hotel of the same name (see "Where to stay" above).

SHOPPING GUIDE

Toko Sumber Sutera, Jl A Magga Amirullah 140, ☎ (0485) 213 83. A good place to buy sarongs or silk clothes. You will find a wider selection here than elsewhere and, in theory, better quality.

Toko Amina Akil, Jl Wa'na Makka 33, Sempange. Here you can see silk being woven. Limited choice.

R Marca

Sengkang,
checking the nets

THE TORAJA REGION★★★
(TANA TORAJA OR "TATOR")
South Sulawesi Province (Sulawesi Selatan)
Map p 554-555 and p 587 – Average alt 900-1 200m (culminating at 2 369m)
Cool, rainy climate

Not to be missed
Watching funeral ceremonies, between July and September,
the "dry" season, when Torajan emigrants return home for ceremonial occasions.
Bolu buffalo market, the Lemo "tau-tau",
Ke'te Kesu village, and much more...

And remember...
Take suitable clothing for rainy conditions, and stout shoes (for the mud and stones).
Explore a few sites with guides, to benefit from their explanations,
but try to be alone to see a funeral.
No ceremonies take place on Sundays as the day is largely devoted to Mass.

From Ujung Pandang the road runs along the west coast to Pare Pare, then heads inland to wind across hillsides, valleys, mountains and luxuriant green gorges. Try to reach the Toraja region in the golden light that comes before sunset *(if you take the 10am bus you will arrive at the end of the day, at the most beautiful moment)*.

You have left behind the sparkling domes of the Bugis minarets and come to the land of church bell-towers and, here and there, the typically curved Toraja roofs that suddenly appear through the greenery. At the riverside, tiny children wash down their huge buffaloes with the greatest care: very welcome refreshment after a hot day! Back in the village, they will start up a game of *takro* with a rattan fibre ball struck with the foot or the knee, while even smaller children play with hoops made of old bicycle tyres. Not far away, a group of men squat on a doorstep discussing the recent harvest and pass round green bamboo tubes overflowing with frothy *tuak* (palm wine). It will soon be the funeral period and the young people of the family, perhaps government workers in Jakarta, will have just come home with their precious savings to honour an ancestor who died a few years ago.

Sailors from the mountains
Sometimes known as "the mountain race" *(toriaja)*, or "the men of generous hearts" *(toraa* or *toraya)*, the inhabitants of **Tana** (earth, ground) **Toraja** (often shortened to "Tator") occupy the highlands of South Sulawesi. Fleeing the wave of Islamisation along the Celebes coasts, these former sailors (whose exact origins are unknown) withdrew up the course of the **River Sa'dan** to take refuge in the mountains, probably in the 17C. Long turned in on themselves, and on the defensive, they built fortified villages on top of the hills and only moved into the valleys in the early 20C, under the authority of the Dutch.

In this mountainous landscape, farming steep slopes with countless rivers, they devoted themselves to agriculture, carving out magnificent **terraced rice fields** that they irrigated through a skilful network of water channels. Later plantations of **clove trees** and **coffee** were added in colonial times.

Among the 340 000 or so Torajans, scattered across nearly 3 600sqkm (not counting an almost equal number who live on other Indonesian islands), there are those who live in the most remote regions and are little affected by Western influences, and those who live in areas more marked by contact with modern civilisation. These differences can be seen most clearly in the rituals and the use of the Torajan language (*Bahasa Toraja*), which has several regional variants. Around Makale – administrative capital of the region – and Rantepao, in particular, are the **Sa'dan Toraja**. They largely converted to Christianity and were educated by the Dutch missionaries who came to the region early in the 20C. Many of them emigrated subsequently, drawn by the possibility of employment in the large towns. Officially **Christian,** they nonetheless remain faithful to ancient animist traditions, and return home regularly to carry out the major ancestor worship rites of **aluk to dolo**.

A hierarchical society

Torajan society is traditionally divided into three classes. At the top of the ladder the nobility – 10 % of the population – own almost all the land, while 20 % of small landowners constitute the middle class; the remaining 70 %, mostly farm employees and general workers, make up the lower class. It is true that since the early 20C these social patterns have levelled out considerably. This is the result of the Dutch abolishing slavery, the missionaries preaching the equality of man, and the influence of very substantial migration that offered each individual the possibility of gaining wealth. Nonetheless, the ancestral hierarchy is still very much alive and continues to play a decisive role that is particularly visible at funerals.

"Tongkonan", the original houses

Impressive ship-like shapes with their huge elongated roofs, the *tongkonan* houses stud the landscapes of the Toraja region with their strange outlines. Opinions vary as to the origins of their shape. The Torajan roof, a striking construction of overlapping bamboo tiles in staggered rows (increasingly, sadly, being replaced by corrugated iron), looks like a ship's keel to some – an evocation of the ships that brought their ancestors. For others, the shape recalls the curved horns of the buffalo, the most sacred of animals.

Built entirely of wood and bamboo, the houses stand on piles, their façades presenting a multitude of carved and painted designs. A wooden buffalo head is a further decoration on the richest homes, sometimes with a picture of the founding ancestor, and a whole string of pig's jaws! In front of the façade, the pile that supports the projecting roof also holds **buffalo horns** from sacrifices at ancestors' funerals, their number displaying the family's standard of living and social status.

The colours of life

The almost exclusive privilege of the nobility, the decoration of Torajan houses – on the façades of both the house and the rice store – is strikingly beautiful. But over and above any aesthetic qualities it mainly has a strongly symbolic value. Whether it is a circle, triangle, magic bird, ritual object, buffalo or rice plant, each motif bears its own name and meaning. The family generally has images carved of what it aspires to, such as prosperity, fertility and union. The decoration is enhanced by four colours made from natural pigments, also full of meaning. Thus, white evokes peace and equilibrium, purity, and the divine. Yellow stands for human beings and marriage. Red, the colour of blood, signifies war and courage, and black, lastly, designates death and the forces of darkness.

The Toraja region

Sulawesi

Torajan house ("tongkonan") and its matching rice store

Pierced with tiny openings, the main living area is generally divided into three plain dark rooms. Most Torajans are now turning from this to the space and comfort of modern houses. Yet the traditional *tongkonan* where the founding ancestors, their children and grandchildren, were born, still continues to represent the seat of the **family group**. More than merely serving as a straightforward house, it represents in effect the heart of the family, an emblem of the unity and identity of the family community. This community will have a population of several dozen or even several hundred people, scattered more or less everywhere throughout the Indonesian towns and islands. The place of assembly for important discussions and decisions, the *tongkonan* is thus the centre of all religious and family ceremonies, such as funerals, which bring all the members of the family together, including the most distant.

When it comes to (re)constructing the building, the whole family is duty-bound to contribute to the cost and then to the ceremony to consecrate the new house. For this occasion, apart from the ritual sacrifices of chickens or pigs, the **wise man** – holder of the village's oral memory – gives a public account of the family's ancestry. Although the great cost of a *tongkonan* – payable in buffaloes! – long made them the privilege of the aristocrats, the new prosperity of many Torajan emigrants in recent decades is tending to erode the old social hierarchy, extending this privilege to a large number of families.

Lastly, each *tongkonan* has one or more attendant rice stores. Facing north, the houses are laid out facing their **alang**, their inevitable matching stores. Constructed along the same lines as the houses, but smaller, the stores stand on tall piles made of between four and six large palm trunks that are perfectly smooth to prevent rats from climbing up. The rice compartment has a platform where the owners rest and receive friends. In theory only the women are entitled to store the rice in the *alang*, following specific rituals. The strange pieces of bamboo that you will sometimes see on its sides indicate the death of the rice store's owner, or of an important member of the family.

For the gods and for ancestors

The Torajans make a distinction between two types of ceremony. Dedicated to the gods, the **rambu tuka** feasts consist of sacrificial offerings of animals (chickens, pigs or buffaloes). Thus honoured, the gods will accord their goodwill to humans – for the **house** when a *tongkonan* is being built, or for the **crops** at harvest time. With the **to'minaa** (chief priest) officiating, these rituals take place in the morning between 6am and midday, facing the east (the symbolic direction of life). Sometimes there are **traditional dances**, with the rhythm generally being set by a drum. The dances are usually performed by women dressed in bright colours, adorned with pearls, and with the sacred *kris* in their belts. Everyone eats *pa'piong* and sticky rice cooked in bamboo, and *tuak* flows freely.

The **rambu solo** ceremonies, dedicated to the ancestors, are orientated to the west (the direction of the dead), and take place after midday. The most important are the **funerals**, the supreme peak of a Torajan life. For this occasion, the extreme solidarity that binds the members of the family together is visible in all its strength. Everyone contributes to make up the funds needed for the ceremony, which may take place months or even years after the death. During this long period the dead body remains among the family, in the *tongkonan*. Once **embalmed** it is in effect treated as if it were simply a sick person: it is watched over, food is brought at mealtimes and he or she is addressed with the greatest respect. The dead person is not considered as truly dead until after the funeral ceremonies. As soon as the family has gathered enough money, the date is set – after the harvest – and then the preparations begin, with the help of the village people.

Sumptuous funerals

Nowhere else will you see funerals on such a grand scale. The length (between 1 and 7 days) and the magnificence of these costly festivities (the number and type of animals sacrificed may range from a single pig to several dozen pigs and buffaloes!) depend on the social class of the dead person, to whom the family is duty-bound to provide a funeral worthy of his or her rank. The description below is of an intermediate ceremony, lasting over five days.

Buffalo fighting and kick boxing

The general excitement of the final preparations is pierced by sharp squeals: two men are busy cutting **pigs'** throats. As soon as they have been cut up the carcasses go into an enormous pot and the feast begins to simmer. Further away, sturdy **buffaloes** are being prepared for the fight. A funeral song honouring the dead person sometimes serves as a prelude. Then the sounds of the crowd ring across the freshly harvested rice fields. Encouraged by their masters, the beasts size each other up, hesitate, and then attack with vigorous stabs of their horns. Charging their adversary suddenly in a thundering surge across the fields, they sometimes force the spectators to take to their heels and run. Less dangerous but just as violent, **kick boxing** brings courageous young men into combat, emboldened by shouts from the audience. The fighting is aggressive but without animosity.

The Toraja region

M Lemerle

A funeral ceremony: the women's procession

The placing in the coffin

The time comes for the close relatives to bring the body out of the *tongkonan*. It is enclosed in a cylindrical **coffin** and then, with the help of a bamboo stretcher decorated in the same style as the *tongkonan*, it is borne with great pomp to the site of the ceremony. In theory the family then sacrifices a buffalo and some pigs before placing the dead person on the platform built for the purpose.

Greeting the guests

Greeted in specially constructed temporary pavilions – a veritable temporary village made entirely of bamboo, where each person finds a place determined by his or her social status – groups of guests come drifting in. They come to offer a pig, a buffalo, some *tuak* or perhaps, for the city dwellers, sugar and cigarettes. The family will recall these "debts" in order to offer the equivalent on the next occasion. Next comes a solemn, elegant procession: after the men, dressed in black, come the women, wearing large cone-shaped rattan hats, with a little betel bag and a scarf slung over their shoulders. Clad in brightly coloured traditional dress, young girls closely related to the dead person serve cakes and coffee or *tuak* to the guests. Later, and throughout the night (often even the following nights), the men will dance and sing the **Ma'badong**. Forming a circle, tightly packed side by side in the thick smoke of *kretek* cigarettes, they sing the funeral song very quietly, retracing the life of the dead person and, more generally, evoking the cycle of human life.

Puya, kingdom of the dead

Before arriving in "Puya", the soul must give an account of the funeral to the authorities of the afterlife. If the ceremonies were not worthy of the person's social class or in line with tradition, the soul will be condemned to wander. And while waiting for an "ad hoc" ceremony, it will be liable to return and disturb the living, back on earth. On the other hand, if the celebration went well with numerous sacrifices, the soul will bring good fortune to the village and the family. It will then be able to enter the kingdom of the ancestors where – in an illustration of its earthly life – it will regain its personality, its qualities and its social status.

Buffalo sacrifice

The high point of the funeral, the sacrifice of the buffaloes – sacred animals – is intended to allow the soul of the dead to escape, with the animals, to the distant **Puya**. Facing the animal, the executioner raises his carefully sharpened machete and strikes it down with a single conclusive blow. With its throat wide open, spurting out blood, the animal struggles, tries to escape, resists, and then reels. Another blow may hasten its death. In a few minutes all the buffaloes are lying here and there, in the midst of great red pools of blood. The Torajans do not shrink from this macabre spectacle – which may upset the unwary tourist! **Cock fighting** may also follow the sacrifices.

Mankind's sacred ancestor

Seen as an ancestor of humankind, the buffalo is the chosen intermediary between the world of the living and that of the dead. The animal's value depends on the colour of its hide, its stoutness and the length of its horns. For the Torajans, its price – which may reach exorbitant sums – makes it a symbol of their social status. As a result, in order to limit the number of ruinous sacrifices the government now raises a tax on each animal killed. Once the beast has been cut up, the head goes to the "tongkonan" of the dead person and its liver to the house in which he or she was born. The guests receive the other pieces, distributed according to their social rank.

Last voyage

During the final homage to the dead person, the close relatives may give way to moving scenes of distress: embracing the coffin, they utter long groans of lamentation. When the time comes, a group of men suddenly seizes the coffin and begins to run across the fields to the **family tomb**. The procession then winds along in a surprising atmosphere: water and mud are sprinkled and the coffin nearly falls at each change of speed or turn. Everything happens very quickly, amid shouts and laughter. The dead person can finally go to the kingdom of his equals.

The dwellings of the dead

Originally the Torajans laid their dead in an **erong**, a wooden coffin recalling – like the *tongkonan* – the shape of a boat or buffalo horns. It was sheltered in a cave, the richer families choosing to hang the coffins on clifftops.

Today, with the exception of poorer families who are content to use natural cavities, cave tombs **(liang)** are used the most. Dug into the cliff-face, they are set as high as possible, on a part that is steep and difficult to reach, to prevent animals, and above all thieves, from climbing up and taking the precious objects enclosed in the tomb (particularly in the case of high-ranking dead). Considered by the Torajans as their second home – the **"house without smoke"**, as opposed to the hearth of the *tongkonan* – each hereditary mortuary niche provides protection for a family line. Husbands and wives cannot therefore be buried together, unless they dig out another grave for this purpose. As for the children, they can choose whether to be added to the cave of their mother or their father.

The "dead on the balcony"

Like rigid spectators or ghostly protectors, effigies of the dead – or **tau-tau** – appear to watch over the dead, and the living. These strange figures are lined up close to the tombs, sheltered in ledges carved into the cliff-face. Sculpted from **jackfruit timber** for the wealthiest, or from **bamboo** for the others, these costly statues remain the privilege of members of the upper classes, who pay the craftsmen in buffaloes. With their hands outstretched some of the *tau-tau* appear to be waiting for offerings (rice,

The Toraja region

Too short a life

Stillborn babies, or those that die before the appearance of their first tooth, have a special funeral ceremony. In the afternoon, when the sun is sinking in the west (the direction of the dead), the dead child's grandfather or mother places the body upright in a small cavity carved out of a tree-trunk ("liang pia"). Still considered to be pure, the baby will thus continue its life and grow, nourished by the sap of the tree and so return to the original world and also reach "Puya".

tuak, betel or other presents) from their descendants. With the soul of the dead person thus gratified, it is hoped that in return it will bring happiness to the living. Afterwards, a fresh ceremony each year honours the ancestor, whose clothes (and those of his *tau-tau*) are changed. In theory, offerings, animal sacrifices and kick boxing accompany these festivities. Sadly sought out by antique dealers and Western tourists, innumerable original *tau-tau* have been stolen. For this reason, most of those that you will see are simple copies.

Getting on with the Torajans

In order to go (almost) "unnoticed", or at least to avoid blunders that would shock your hosts, it is useful to be aware of a few elementary rules.

In the homes of the inhabitants – If you have a meal or spend the night, take a **gift** (sweets or *kretek*) which you should present to the mistress of the house.

At funerals – To avoid groups of tourists, it is generally sufficient to head off as far as possible away from roads. Contact will be warmer and more spontaneous if you arrive alone, **without a guide**. If you pass people dressed in black or carrying tubes of green bamboo overflowing with froth, they are sure to be preparing for a ceremony in the area. It is often enough to show a lively interest to be invited to join them. Otherwise, you will need to use your tact, your humour and some *Bahasa Indonesia*.

Don't forget that this is a funeral gathering: it is essential to **dress decently** (legs and arms covered, no low-cut necklines), preferably in **black**.

When you are greeted, enquire as to whom (usually a child of the dead person) you should offer your **gift**: it would be proper to give the family sweets or *kretek*. It is

Made of thatch or corrugated iron, the Toraja village lives on

M.-P. Renier/Michelin

Sulawesi

essential to sit in the place you are shown to: each guest in fact is given a **seat** in line with his or her social position. Remember that you risk offending your hosts if you refuse the food and drink that they willingly offer you.

There is no problem with taking a film or **photographs**, provided you remain discreet. Do not get in the way or block people's view, and do not walk about casually without asking permission.

At the sites – However touching the **children** may be, do not give in to the temptation to give them the money or sweets (*gula gula*) that they demand persistently. Lastly, although you will often see happy infants running around the coffins and playing with skulls, remember that to touch the **bones**, the tombs or the *tau-tau* will expose you to the most terrible ill-fortune!

Rantepao
See also the map of the region. 18km from Makale, 340km from Ujung Pandang.
See plan p 590.

Rantepao, the largest town in the Toraja region (population 20 000) lies along the banks of the **Sa'dan**, in a wide valley surrounded by green mountains. With its long main street lined with shops, travel agencies and buses, and its little adjacent lanes studded with hotels and restaurants, the economic and tourist centre of Tana Toraja has no great charm. However, its facilities make it the main place to stay in the area.

Bolu market* (Pasar Bolu)
2km northeast of Rantepao. You will see peasants leading their buffaloes along the roadside, and groups of women carrying enormous baskets on their backs or tubes of green bamboo full of **tuak** (palm wine). Every six days, in a never-ending routine, *bemos* sound their horns at the passers-by, laden with fruit and vegetables, big tins, sacks of rice or chickens, as they flood in to the market. Behind the colourful, aromatic food stalls, the stands of clothes, sarongs and utensils of all kinds, the **livestock market**** takes place in a vast muddy area where quantities of **buffalo** wallow about. They are watered down, brushed and their merits described to potential purchasers, while, further away, strident squeals can be heard from a covered hall, empire of the **pigs**, tied to bamboo posts, waiting to find a buyer.

North of Rantepao**
See the map of the region p 587.

From Bolu terminus take a bemo for Sa'dan or Batutumonga. You will have to walk to reach some of the sites. Most of them are open between 9am and 5pm and charge a fee. Allow 1 day. The distances given below are indicated from Rantepao.

From Pasar Bolu, a beautiful road runs past the rice fields that stretch out beside the River Sa'dan. Around the town of the same name (13km), several traditional villages specialise in **weaving**. Among them is **Ma'limbong***, which also has some very fine **tongkonan****.

Return to the Rantepao road and, shortly before Pangli, take a track that is stony but passable, to the right.

■ **Palawa**** – *10km.* Despite the high-pressure selling with which you will be greeted, this traditional village is worth the trip to see its superb **tongkonan***** with their painted façades, decorated with impressive buffalo horns, lined up facing their **rice stores***. You will no doubt be invited to see the inside of a house, which will turn out to be a shop!

Continue as far as Pangli, where you take the road leading uphill to the right.

The Toraja region

As the road winds it offers some fine **views**★★ of terraced rice fields scattered with large black rocks, remains of volcanic eruptions. At **Deri** *(on the left, below the road)*, rocks hidden among the bamboos provide shelter for **mortuary niches**.

When you get near **Lempo**, coming round a bend *(at the sign indicating Batutumonga 3km away)* there is a superb **panoramic view**★★★ to your right. The 180° view sweeps over the rice fields, steps of tender green or golden yellow according to the season, also dotted with black rocks. A few *tongkonan* roofs emerge in the distance, while Rantepao is visible at the bottom of the valley.

■ **Batutumonga**★ – *20km.* Perched on the foothills of Mount Sesean, this small town is a pleasant stopping place where you can have lunch in relative coolness, facing the **valley of the Sa'dan**★ *(see "Eating out", p 594)*. Bamboos, palm trees and thorn-bushes crowd together on the damp slopes, a good place for some pretty walks in the dry season.

■ **Lokomata**★★ – *26km.* The road continues, lined with **cave tombs**★ on the right and opening onto beautiful landscapes on the left. Suddenly, like a head full of eyes (*mata* means eye), an enormous rock appears with a great quantity of tombs in it (*loko* means cavities). Some of the tombs have carved wooden doors with Torajan motifs. Here and there, photographs and offerings bear witness to ancestor worship.

Beyond this point, the road becomes rough and bemos are very rare. If you want to return on foot, retrace your steps to the track that leads, to the right, to Pana. From here, allow about 1hr on foot to Tikala, where in theory you will find a bemo for Pasar Bolu. By car, return as far as Pangli, and turn right.

■ **Bori**★ – *6km.* You reach the village along a pretty road through the rice fields. Next to the houses, a former **rante**★ (ceremonial area), is visible. It is a small space covered in weeds, and some strange tapering **megaliths**. Used for funeral ceremonies, it was here that buffalo sacrifices used to take place. A stone was set up here for the occasion, its height reflecting the status of the dead person. The tradition has died now, and people are more likely to hang the animal's horns in front of the *tongkonan*. A little higher up behind the *rante*, a few **babies' graves** are hidden in a copse. Bamboo tubes hang from some of the trees, intended to catch the sap of the palm tree, which, after fermentation, will make **tuak**. Twice a day a man climbs up the trunks to collect the precious drink.

South of Rantepao★★

Take a bemo towards Makale and ask the driver to drop you off near the sites that you want to visit (in many cases you will have to continue on foot). Most of them are open from 9am to 5pm and require a fee. Allow 1 day. The distances are shown from Rantepao.

■ **Londa**★★ – *6km. Follow the little track that goes round the site for a better view.* In a very beautiful setting, in the midst of rice fields and clove trees, is an imposing cliff on which you can see, perched at a dizzy height, the **funeral niches** of the local aristocracy, accompanied by some **tau-tau**★ with clothing faded by the sun. Go nearer to see the remains of the **erong**, the strange wooden coffins hanging on ropes below the cliff. Others are hidden in a cave among the bones *(take a powerful torch or hire a lantern at the site).*

Return to the main road, and go left for a short way.

■ **Lemo**★★★ – *11km. Come here if possible in the morning to make the most of the light, preferably very early to avoid tourist coaches.* This is one of the richest sites in the Toraja region. Despite its popularity (you will not be the only person), Lemo has preserved

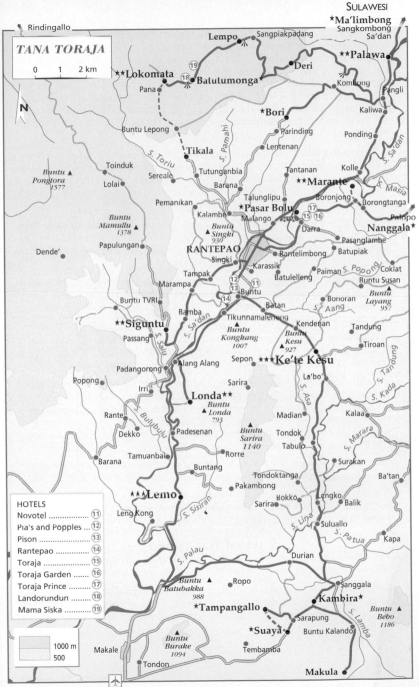

SULAWESI

★Ma'limbong
Sangkombong
Sa'dan

★Rindingallo
Lempo   Sangpiakpadang
★★Lokomata   Balulumonga   Deri   ★★Palawa
Pana   Kombong   Pangli
Buntu Lepong   Kaliwa
Tikala   ★Bori   Ponding
Toinduk   Parinding
Lolai   Tutungenbia   Lentenan   Kolle
Barana   Tantanan   ★★Marante
Pemanikan   Talunglipu   Boronjong   Dorongtanga
Kalambe   ★Pasar Bolu   Palopo
Malango   Darra   Nanggala★
RANTEPAO   Rantelimbong   Pasanglambe   Coklat
Singki   Karassik   Batupiak   Buntu Susan
Tampak   Batulelleng   Paiman
Marampa   Buntu   Bonoran   Aang
Buntu TVRI   Batan   Kendenan   Tandung
★★Siguntu   Tikunnamalenong   ★★★Ke'te Kesu'   Tiroan
Passang   Sepon   La'bo'
Padangorong   Sarira   Kalaa
Popong   Irri   Londa★★   Madian
Rante   Padesenan   Tondok   Surakan
Dekko   Tamuanbai   Rorre   Tabulo   Ba'tan
Barana   Buntang   Tondoktanga   Balik
★★★Lemo   Pakambong   Bokko   Lengko
Leng Kong   Sarira   Suluallo   Kapa
Durian   Sanggala
★Tampangallo   Sarapung   Kambira★
★Suaya   Buntu Kalando
Makale   Tembamba   Makula
Tondon

TANA TORAJA
0   1   2 km

N

Buntu Pongtora 1577
Buntu Mamullu 1378
Dende'
Buntu Singki 930
Buntu Kongkang 1007
Buntu Kesu 927
Buntu Londa 793
Buntu Sarira 1140
Buntu Layang 957
Buntu Batubakka 988
Ropo
Buntu Burake 1094
Buntu Bebo 1186

S. Pamahi
S. Toriu
S. Sa'dan
S. Masia
S. Popong
S. Aang
S. Salu
S. Bulubulu
S. Sisiran
S. Palau
S. Lina
S. Patua
S. Asa
S. Marara
S. Tandung
S. Kada
S. Lamba

HOTELS
Novotel .... ⑪
Pia's and Popples ... ⑫
Pison .... ⑬
Rantepao .... ⑭
Toraja .... ⑮
Toraja Garden .... ⑯
Toraja Prince .... ⑰
Landorundun .... ⑱
Mama Siska .... ⑲

1000 m
500

its magic intact, and you should take your time to look at the site. Apart from the **tongkonan and rice stores★** with their lofty roofs, the site has above all preserved its remarkable **rock tombs**. Dominating the green carpet of rice fields, the cliffs rear up steeply, pierced with innumerable burial places and niches with **tau-tau★★★**. Crowded behind their balustrades, the effigies of the nobility are lined up with dignity in their coloured clothing, their great eyes staring at the visitors who wander below them. The path round the site, lined with souvenir stalls, leads in particular to a *tau-tau* workshop, a commercial establishment, but the work is nonetheless interesting to see.

■ **Tampangallo★** — *24km. Access along an unsurfaced road, then a narrow path through the rice fields.* Hidden in a deep cave, ancient **erong★**, carved in the shape of *tongkonan*, boats or buffaloes, keep company with the remains of skulls and other bones. These abandoned burial places are a strange sight, where local children play hide-and-seek, to the astonishment of the visitors.

■ **Suaya★** — *25km. Access by road. From Tampangallo you can get to the site on foot (1km, muddy track).* This is another rock with resident souls. Above some old royal sarcophagi made of wood, preserved in a dusty display-case, a wall of rock provides support for impressive lines of bleached **tau-tau★★**.

■ **Makula** — *26km.* For a change of atmosphere, take the pretty road that winds through rice fields and forest to the **hot springs** at Makula. You can lounge around in a swimming pool of tepid water and have lunch in a restaurant with a panoramic view *(see "Eating out", p 594)*.

■ **Kambira★** — *24km. Best seen in the afternoon, but watch out for the mosquitoes!* A pleasant track lined with *tongkonan* and shops, leads to the village. Not far away, in the shade of a clump of bamboos, are trees that contain **babies' tombs**.

■ **Ke'te Kesu★★★** — *6km.* From the road, an elegant line of curving roofs stands out above the rice fields. This very touristic village is rather too carefully tended, but it has one of the region's finest groups of traditional **tongkonan★★** and **rice stores★**. Follow the track that begins behind the houses and leads to an escarpment. Here you will see a group of highly coloured **tau-tau★**, set in the shade of a cave before which hang some old **erong★**, forgotten wooden vessels.

Lastly, back in Rantepao, take Jl Merdeka to the left and continue straight ahead and then left beyond the bridge (towards Singki). Look for a small road leading up to the right.

A good excuse for magnificent excursions through the surrounding rice fields, the traditional village of **Siguntu★★** *(6km)* also has some handsome **tongkonan** and **rice stores**. It is a very pleasant place to end the day, when the light is at its best.

East of Rantepao★★

From Bolu terminus take a bemo for Palopo. Most of the sites are open from 9am to 5pm and charge a fee. Allow 2hr for the trip. Distances are indicated from Rantepao.

■ **Marante★★** — *6km. The light is better in the afternoon.* Behind the village dominated by its corrugated iron roofs, a path leads round a cliff where you can see superb groups of wooden **tau-tau★★**, set into the crevices of the rock and dressed in white.

Take the Palopo road, then the smaller one that turns off to the right across the rice fields

M Lemerle

■ **Nanggala**★ – *16km.* A pretty road comes out in the traditional village where former **rice stores**★ stand in a row opposite rundown *tongkonan.* The ferns invading their roofs give them a wild, rather attractive appearance.

If you set out from Tana Toraja for Ujung Pandang, you can enliven your return trip with a walk through the mountains of the **Mamasa region**. This will delight ramblers (*see under "Other things to do" below*).

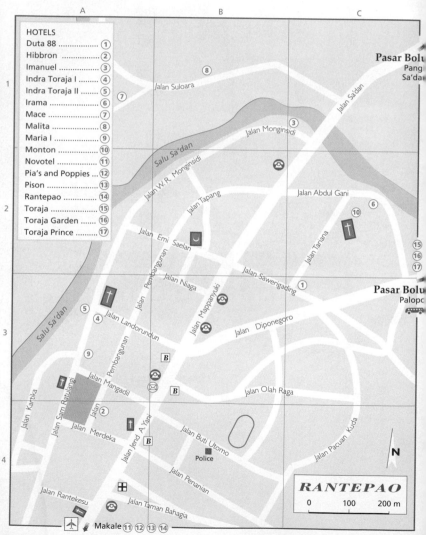

HOTELS

Duta 88	①
Hibbron	②
Imanuel	③
Indra Toraja I	④
Indra Toraja II	⑤
Irama	⑥
Mace	⑦
Malita	⑧
Maria I	⑨
Monton	⑩
Novotel	⑪
Pia's and Poppies	⑫
Pison	⑬
Rantepao	⑭
Toraja	⑮
Toraja Garden	⑯
Toraja Prince	⑰

RANTEPAO

0   100   200 m

N

Making the most of the Toraja region

COMING AND GOING

By air – With the economic crisis, air communications are now only provided once a week (if there are enough passengers) between Ujung Pandang and the Toraja region. **Pongtiku** airport is close to Makale, 23km south of Rantepao. A bus provides a shuttle service between the airport and Rantepao. **Merpati**, Jl Pongtiku 32A, ☎ (0423) 216 15.

By bus – From Ujung Pandang (Panaikang terminus), several coaches run to Rantepao daily. The trip lasts 8hr and can be done by day or by night. Reserve your seats the day before, directly with the bus companies. In Rantepao, these are all in the main street (B2-B3). **Litha** has the best buses, air-conditioned and roomy, with reclining seats and legrests! In principle they drop you off at your hotel (hotel and agency touts who have got on the bus will try to tempt you away). There are also daily connections between Rantepao and Pare Pare (6hr), Palopo (2hr), Pendolo (10hr), Tentena (12hr) and Poso (14hr). See also "Making the most of Lake Poso", p 598.

By car – You can rent a car with driver at the travel agencies in Ujung Pandang or at the airport (see "Making the most of Ujung Pandang", p 565), and at travel agencies in Rantepao (see below).

GETTING AROUND

On foot – Walking is the best way to appreciate the landscape and to reach remote places.

By becak – There are plenty in Rantepao. For short journeys in town.

By bemo – Particularly frequent and crowded on market days, they serve the main villages in the region that lie on tarmac roads. They come and go everywhere in Rantepao, hooting their horns, but their main terminus is in **Bolu**, 2km northeast of the town centre. Ask the driver if he is going in the direction you want, and ask the time of the last *bemo* for the return trip. Remember that the journeys are long and tiring, and that you will not be able to reach remote places.

By motorbike/bicycle – A good way (though sometimes challenging!) to get off the beaten track and travel freely. May be hired in travel agencies in Rantepao and from some hotels or restaurants (collect the night before or early in the morning because the number available is very limited). Before you set out, check the tyres and brakes carefully – the roads in the surrounding areas are steep and bumpy!

By car – The most comfortable way to explore the countryside. Rantepao travel agencies hire out cars with driver.

ADDRESS BOOK – RANTEPAO

Tourist information – The government tourist office appears to have closed down. Enquire instead at travel agencies or your hotel.

Bank/Currency exchange – Several banks and currency exchange offices in Jl Jend A Yani, close to the central crossroads. You can also change money in some hotels. **Abadi** (B3), Jl Jend A Yani 102. Currency exchange office that offers a better rate than the banks. **Danamon Bank** (B3), Jl Jend A Yani. Accepts Visa cards. **BNI** (A4), Jl Jend A Yani. Exchanges main currencies.

Post office – Jl Jend A Yani (B3). Monday-Thursday, 8am-2pm, Friday, 8-11am, Saturday, 8am-1pm; closed Sunday and public holidays. *Poste restante*

Telephone – **Telkom** (B3), Jl Jend A Yani (just beyond the post office). Several *Wartel* along the main street (daily, often up to 11pm).

Travel agencies – Very numerous in Rantepao, they offer similar services at fairly varied prices: walks in the area lasting one or more days, visits to Torajan villages (with funeral ceremony, when possible), hire of bicycles, motorbikes and cars. Most have guides. Check that they are genuine Torajans and will be able to act as interpreters in isolated villages. Remember also that you can very easily visit the Toraja region without a guide. Some reliable addresses: **JET Tourist Service** (B3), Jl Landorundun 1, ☎ (04232) 11 45,

Fax (0423) 232 27. **Celebes Tourist Service** (A3), Jl Mangadil 11, ☎ (0423) 218 13/216 65. **Panorama Indah** (A3), Jl Dr Sam Ratulangi 40, ☎ (0423) 252 76, Fax (0423) 255 22. **Tomindo Tourist Service** (A4), Jl A Yani 75, ☎ (0423) 270 77.

Medical service – The larger hotels will be able to put you in touch with an English-speaking doctor.

Pharmacies, Jl Jend A Yani (just beyond the post office) (B3); Jl Mappanyuki (B2).

WHERE TO STAY

• Rantepao and its surrounding area

Modest

Mace Homestay, Jl Tengko Situru 4, Malango, ☎ (0423) 218 52 – 7rm. ⌁ Hot water in some rooms only. Attractive house surrounded by a garden, in a quiet district, a little out of the centre. Warm and friendly welcome, attentive service. The rooms, plain and clean (some, with Turkish-style WC and a *mandi*, are a bit rundown) open onto the garden at ground level and onto a terrace above. Meals available here if ordered the day before.

Wisma Maria I, Jl Dr Sam Ratulangi 23, ☎ (0423) 211 65 – 23rm. ⌁ Hot water in some rooms. Set in a small garden. Rooms in rows, on two levels, along a shared terrace. The least expensive, at the back, are rather rundown. The others are small but are very clean and comfortable.

Modest - average

Wisma Irama, Jl U Abdul Gani 16, ☎ (0423) 213 71 – 20rm. ⌁ Hot water in the most expensive rooms. A few very low cost rooms lie at the end of the little garden and are simple but clean. Better rooms on the first floor of the main building, opening onto a large, airy and welcoming terrace.

⌂**Wisma Monton**, Jl Abd Gani 14A, ☎/Fax (0423) 216 75, Fax (0423) 216 65 – 19rm. ⌁ Hot water in most of the rooms. A comfortable guesthouse in a quiet little street. Impeccable cleanliness and excellent value for money. The rooms are laid out on three floors (the most expensive ones on the top), opening onto terraces where breakfast is served. Rooms

on the ground floor enjoy the greenery of the garden while those on the top floor (quieter) enjoy magnificent sunsets over the mountains. On Sunday mornings the harmonious singing of Mass can be heard from the church next door. Attentive welcome. The owner here intends to open a little restaurant on the roof, serving Torajan specialities.

Wisma Malita, Jl Suloara 110, ☎ (0423) 210 11 – 29rm. ⌁ ✗ Hot water in some rooms. Located in a quiet district, slightly away from the centre. The rooms are a little rundown but adequate and are laid out on two levels in a pretty garden. Meals can be taken here if ordered in advance.

Wisma Imanuel, Jl W R Monginsidi 16, ☎ (0423) 214 16 – 18rm. ⌁ A family home set back from the street. Most of the rooms face the rear, over a river. The most expensive have hot water and television, the others are more simple. The establishment is laid out on two levels. Charming, generous owners.

Average

⌂**Duta 88 Cottages**, Jl Sawerigading 12, ☎ (0423) 234 77 – 7rm. ⌁ TV Hot water. Private wooden bungalows with terraces, in a style vaguely inspired by "tongkonan", laid out round a rice store in a small garden. The place is somewhat cramped but charming and peaceful. Attentive service.

Hibbron Inn, Jl Pembangunan 27, ☎ (0423) 215 19 – 11rm. ⌁ Hot water in most rooms. A pleasant place, but one that should appear in the "modest" category. Don't hesitate to beat the prices down as they are considerably overvalued! Small unpretentious rooms, laid out round a patio at the back of the house (avoid no 6, in a dark corner). Pretty decor with Torajan panels. Discreet and friendly welcome.

Hotel Pison, Jl Pongtiku II/8, ☎ (0423) 213 44/212 21 – 31rm. ⌁ ✗ CC Hot water. 1km south of the town centre, set back from the main road, in a quiet location. The better rooms, on the upper floor, are simple but faultless and have a small balcony overlooking the countryside. The standard rooms, which are older, face a small garden.

🕷**Pia's and Poppies**, Jl Pongtiku, ☎ (0423) 211 21, Fax (0423) 250 59 – 10rm. 🍴 ✕ Hot water. Facing the Hotel Pison. The furnishings are very varied, with old-fashioned charm, and all the rooms are different. Some have a bathtub hollowed out of the rock. The rooms are laid out along a terrace facing a small lotus pond, with a lovely view over the surrounding countryside. See also "Eating out".

High end
Hotel Rantepao (Rantepao Lodge), Jl Pao Rura, ☎ (0423) 237 17, Fax (0423) 212 48 – 40rm. 🍴 🌴 TV 🛎 CC Hot water. 100m beyond the two entries above, at the end of a small track off the road. The hotel is particularly appreciated for its peace and its swimming pool. The rooms have no great attraction, but they are clean. Best to book in advance, because they often take in groups. An attractive terrace restaurant.

Luxury
Hotel Indra Toraja I, Jl Landorundun 63, ☎ (0423) 211 63/215 83/214 42, Fax (0423) 215 47 – 28rm. 🍴 ✕ CC Hot water. The standard rooms (at ground level) are impeccable but somewhat austere. The dearest (on the first floor) have more decoration and are equipped with telephone and television. The whole place, on two levels, is laid out round a green patio (avoid the few rooms that face the restaurant or the reception area). A restaurant that is airy on the top floor but rather enclosed on the ground floor.

🕷**Hotel Indra Toraja II**, Jl Dr Sam Ratulangi, ☎ (0423) 211 63/215 83/214 42, Fax (0423) 215 47 – 19rm. 🍴 ☎ TV ✕ CC Hot water. Same management as the above, but a more pleasant place. Fine setting. The place is lined with panels of woven bamboo with Torajan designs and is laid out on two levels round a garden patio. The rooms are not especially charming, but are very clean and comfortable. Good restaurant, opening onto the river at the back.

Luxury - super deluxe
Toraja Garden Cottages, on the Palopo road, the extension of Jl Diponegoro, ☎ (0423) 233 36/210 43, Fax (0423) 233 35 – 22rm. 🍴 🌴 � TV ✕ CC Hot water. 3km north of the town centre, a lit-

tle way beyond the market and Bolu terminus. The design of the building, which is entirely made of wood, lends the rooms a note of warmth. They are laid out with their private terraces in a magnificent garden. The swimming pool belonging to the neighbouring hotel is open to clients.
Toraja Cottage, ☎ (0423) 210 89/214 97/214 75/212 68, Fax (0423) 213 69 – 43rm. 🍴 🌴 � TV ✕ 🛎 CC Hot water. Next to the above. Comfortable rooms, with small terraces, on a slight slope in a beautiful garden. Two "tongkonan" house the suites. The hotel often takes in groups

Super deluxe
Toraja Prince Hotel, ☎ (0423) 214 07 /214 30/214 58/214 62, Fax (0423) 213 04 – 60rm. 🍴 🌴 � TV ✕ 🛎 CC Hot water. Just opposite the above. A small lane leads to several buildings, set in a very well kept garden. A verandah with rattan furniture runs the length of the rooms, on two levels. Luxury, comfort and total peace and quiet.

Novotel, Jl Ke'te Kesu, ☎ (0423 211 92/ 270 00, Fax (0423) 216 66, novotor@ upandang.wasantara.net.id – 91rm. 🍴 � TV ✕ 🛎 🍽 CC Hot water. 2km south of the town centre (towards Ke'te Kesu), in open countryside. Large pavilions built on the "tongkonan" model, each one housing a large, 2 large bedrooms, or 4 smaller ones. Attractive interior design, elegant and sober, and private terraces opening onto green countryside.

● **Batutumonga**
Modest
🕷**Mama Siska Homestay** – 17rm. ✕ 10min on foot from the main road, along a track suitable for driving. Real "family" lodgings, so you can immerse yourself in Torajan family life. You will sleep in the family home, or in a bamboo building next to it (mandi and WC in the courtyard). The whole place is very basic, but clean. The welcome from Mama Siska, a powerful personality, is warm and charming and will soon make you forget the lack of facilities. She may ask you if you would like to accompany her to market, to church, or to visit friends. You can talk with her for hours, while you learn about local cuisine, or while you help her hull coffee beans in the courtyard, in front of the "tongkonan". See also "Eating out".

Making the most of Toraja

Landorundun Homestay – 5rm. ☝ Further along the main road. Small, basic rooms set out along a verandah, in a wooden chalet surrounded by an enormous garden. It is possible to have your meals at the place opposite, "Mama Rina".

EATING OUT

Restaurants in the Toraja area will rarely leave you with memories of an unforgettable gastronomic occasion. You will often eat better in the market, in a family home or at ceremonies. Apart from the Indonesian classics (mie and nasi goreng, gado-gado and sate ayam) and a few Western dishes – usually rather mediocre – everyone serves Torajan specialities, which must be ordered several hours in advance. You could try a "pa'piong" (based on chicken, pork or fish, cooked for several hours in a tube of bamboo with coconut milk or pig's blood), accompanied by black rice ("nasi hitam"). During the funeral season (July – September), you can try buffalo meat ("kerbau") but you may be surprised by its very distinctive taste and the fact that it is tough. The "ikan mas", fish from the rice fields, can be delicious. Lastly, don't miss the succulent fresh fruit juices made from "markisa" (passion fruit) or "terung" (a local fruit). You can also feast on the cakes ("kue") based on sticky rice, peanuts or coconut and brown sugar ("gula merah", palm-tree sap). To be enjoyed with black coffee (served with the grounds and very sweet) or "bolok" (or "tuak", palm wine).

• Rantepao

Basic – moderate

Mart's Cafe and Restaurant, Jl Dr Sam Ratulangi 44 **(A3)**, ☎ (0423) 216 92. Closed on Sundays. Set back from the street, in a pleasant little dining room with woven bamboo decor opening onto a small garden. Classic menu and very acceptable cooking. Quiet atmosphere, friendly welcome.

Setia Kawan, Jl Andi Mappanyukki 32 **(B3)**, ☎ (0423) 212 64. A very large enclosed dining room, somewhat chilly. Wide selection of dishes, generous servings and overall good standard.

🐾**Rainbow**, Jl Pembangunan 11A **(A3)**, ☎ (0423) 217 53. A pleasant covered terrace with woven bamboo decor, airy and

quiet, set back from the street. Tasty home cooking. The service is slow. Rooms also available: monastic, but clean.

Lisher, Jl Andi Mappanyukki 107 **(B2)**, ☎ (0423) 213 16. Small terrace giving onto the main street, or a simple inside dining room. Classic Indonesian dishes, or Torajan specialities. The selection is limited but the dishes are well prepared. Friendly service.

Florida, Jl Emi Saelan 25 **(B2)**, ☎ (0423) 210 10. Very ordinary setting and a few tables on a terrace facing the street. Wide range of Indonesian dishes, often well prepared. Charming staff.

Moderate - more select

🐾**Pia's and Poppies**, Jl Pongtiku (beyond A1), ☎ (0423) 211 21. In the hotel of the same name. Agreeable setting, inside or on the terrace. The food here is varied, original and tasty: home made smoked ham marinated in tomatoes, pineapple and mushrooms, pumpkin soup with nutmeg and white wine, eels and all the Torajan specialities.

• Makula

Basic

Sangalla restaurant, ☎ (0423) 241 12. A restful place to stop off during a day's sightseeing or walking. You can also relax in the swimming pool, fed from a natural hot spring. Panoramic view from the terrace. Little choice, but good food, though less distinguished than the setting might imply.

• Batutumonga

Basic

🐾**Mama Siska**, see above, "Where to stay". Whether you arrive hungry after a long walk or simply want to enjoy the hospitality of the establishment between visits, you will always be well nourished in Mama Siska's house. This is not a restaurant, and you will not have a menu to choose from, but you will be given what is simmering on the stove or what can be produced from the ingredients to hand. You will probably be left to pay what you think you should offer.

Mentirotiku, a little further along the road. A covered terrace with a panoramic view, looking out over the whole region. This is a very touristic but pleasant place, although the staff are not particularly friendly. Wide selection of Indonesian, Torajan or Western dishes. The most expensive of Batutumonga's three restaurants.

Mama Rina, a little further away. If the preceding entry appears too crowded or impersonal, this little terrace will offer you a less spectacular view, but more peace and quiet and authenticity. The choice is limited and the cooking offers nothing out of the ordinary.

● **Talunglipu**

Moderate – more select

Island Cafe, 3km north of Rantepao, just beyond Bohu market on the Sa'dan road, ☎ (0423) 235/02/218 64. A pleasant setting, opening onto the rice fields. A tourist establishment, fairly expensive for the region, offering all kinds of dishes, Indonesian, Torajan or Western. Craft gallery next door.

SHOPPING GUIDE

Craftwork/Souvenirs – If you are prepared to work at it, you can pick out some fine pieces of craftwork in the shops along the main street in Rantepao, near the central crossroads (B3). You can find everything here (wooden statuettes, little "tautau", fabrics, ikats, pearl jewellery, etc), of very variable quality. Some objects and fabrics are made in the Toraja region, but many of the items come from other islands. The same applies to the stalls in the villages and tourist sites in the surrounding area.

Photography – Rantepao has a surprising number of photographic shops where you can buy films (check the use-by date) and have films developed (average quality). They are concentrated round the central crossroads.

Miscellaneous – In Rantepao, the *supermarket* (B3) on the main street near the central crossroads is well stocked. *Indra* (A3), corner of Jl Landorundun and Jl Dr Sam Ratulangi. This grocer's and hardware shop sells a bit of everything. This is where you will find the best selection of books and maps on the Toraja region and Sulawesi.

OTHER THINGS TO DO

Rafting – The waters of the Sa'dan and the Maulu are perfect for the sport. Another way to explore the region's beautiful scenery. 1- or 3-day expeditions. Agencies in Rantepao: *Toranggo Buxa (Sobek Expeditions)*, Jl Pongtiku 32A (3km along the Makale road), ☎ (0423) 213 36.

Walking in the Mamasa area – Mountain rambling enthusiasts can leave the Toraja region via the Mamasa area (allow 3hr by *bemo* from Rantepao to Bittuang, then three days' walking from Bittuang to Mamasa, around 65km). From there you can reach Polewali along a nightmarish road, and return to Ujung Pandang along the west coast. This walk can only be done in the dry season, preferably with a guide. If you wish to remain independent, get a map and take advice on weather conditions before you leave, for the rainfall is very high. A few words of Bahasa Indonesia will be very helpful. Accommodation will be with local residents or in very basic *losmen* (at Belau, Ponding, Mawai and Timbaan). Protect yourself from the sun (there is little shade along the path) and take suitable clothing for rain and for warmth – the nights can be very cool! Spend a few days in Mamasa to make the most of the area.

LAKE POSO★
THE CENTRAL ROAD
Central Sulawesi Province (Sulawesi Tengah) – Map p 554-555
Alt 550m – Rainy, fairly cool climate

Not to be missed
Swimming in the lake, off Toinasa beach.
Saluopa Falls.
The megaliths in the Bada valley.
And remember...
Use Tentena as a base for exploring the region.

Still little visited by tourists, the region of Central Sulawesi is well worth exploring. The very tiring road that serves it – the recent **Trans-Sulawesi** linking the island's north and south – has already suffered heavy damage from floods and landslides, frequent occurrences in this rainy region.

You leave the Toraja region along a dizzy road that drops in a series of tight hairpin bends towards the sea, offering magnificent **panoramic views★★** from time to time. It reaches the coast at **Palopo**, the former capital of the powerful kingdom of Luwu, today a well-kept little provincial town with a lively port where the traveller passing through barely lingers.

The vast **Gulf of Bone** stretches out on both sides, fringed with a wide marshy strip with a stifling atmosphere. It has a large number of villages along it, home to a considerable population of fishermen, farmers and traders, mostly Bugis (Muslims). The road runs along the coastal plain, then climbs into the highlands of the interior with their luxuriant vegetation. The **scenery★★** immediately becomes wilder and the road harder, struggling across steep hillsides carved up by deep gorges, with rushing rivers and waterfalls. And everywhere the forest predominates, hiding within it a mosaic of little scattered villages of ethnic communities, many of which were converted to Christianity by Dutch missionaries early in the 20C.

Lake Poso★ (Danau Poso)

Lake Poso lies in the heart of this green landscape, a vast stretch of water 37km by 13km, with fathomless depths. Lying 550m high surrounded by mountains, it enjoys a damp and relatively cool climate that favours crops of all kinds. Contrasting with the dark blue-green ripples on its rough waves is the harmonious gradation of colours in the forests, rice fields and the plantations of cloves and coffee that prosper along its shores and on the surrounding high plains.

■ **Pendolo** – This peaceful village on the south bank offers a refreshing stopping place to rest from the journey. If you are travelling by bus you can spend the night here and wait for the **boat** next day to cross the lake to Tentena (*departure from Pendolo in the morning, from Tentena in the afternoon. Allow 3hr. The crossing is liable to be cancelled if there are too few passengers, or if the lake is too rough*). To continue by car, find out about the condition of the roads round the lake (*seek advice from several sources!*). To the **east**, the trip can be something of a nightmare if the road has not been repaired recently! Furthermore, it has little of interest to offer because hills hide the view. If the track along the **west** of the lake is passable, take it instead. You can take advantage of the opportunity to visit the **Bencea orchid reserve★**, where countless species grow, each more beautifully coloured than the last *(the flowering season normally runs from January to May)*. Just beside the garden a wonderfully pretty little **beach★** awaits you, with golden sand and clear water.

■ **Tentena★** – Lying at the mouth of the River Poso, at the far north of the lake, the village nestles at the foot of green hillsides in a restful setting. It is also the ideal departure point for excursions in the region. Near the covered bridge and the houses on piles you will see traps designed to catch the enormous **eels** (some grow to more than 2m in length and weigh over 20kg!), which may appear on your plate at dinner. The local **caves** are not worth going to see – you would do better to visit the **Saluopa Falls★★** *(12km east of Tentena. Bemos often stop at the Balinese village of Kampung Bali, shortly beyond Tonusu, from where you will then have a walk of about 30-45min. Fee)*. The falls, an elegant curtain of foam, have polished the rock and hollowed out several natural pools lying in steps amidst the thick greenery *(be careful round the falls, the ground is very slippery!)*. As you paddle through the cool crystalline water, note the delicate **butterflies** that flock around the site. A *warung* sells a few snacks and drinks near the entrance. For coffee and roasted peanuts, stop at the wooden house *(500m away)*, where a delightful family will welcome you. Rustic bungalows are expected to be available soon, in a very attractive setting.

Another refreshing dip awaits you at the pretty **Toinasa beach★★** *(see "Siuri Cottages", p 599)*. The waves are wonderful here in the afternoon as they break on the golden sand.

■ **The Lore Lindu National Park★★** – *From Tentena (73km from Gintu), by jeep, on horseback or on foot. It is a difficult walk through the jungle and the mud, with a few watercourses to ford. This is an expedition for the driest months, between June and August. Accommodation is in basic losmen. Take mosquito repellent. Allow at least 5 days for the round trip to make the most of it, and let a guide take care of the practical arrangements (see "Tourist information", p 598).*

Lore Lindu park, the home of a small community that still follows ancestral traditions, lies between Palu and Tentena, a vast domain of 23 000ha containing innumerable treasures both natural and historic.

Indeed, these highlands are home to an **endemic fauna** that is extremely rich. It is the main refuge of the horned hog, the anoa (dwarf buffalo) and Sulawesi macaque monkeys, and it also has a range of rare **birds**.

The ultimate goal of this expedition, however, is above all to visit the remains in the **Bada**, **Besoa** and **Napu valleys**, in the southwest part of the park – the mysterious **megaliths★★** dating from the Bronze Age whose origins and meaning continue to puzzle archeologists. Reservoirs and cisterns, some of them decorated, can be seen concentrated round the villages of **Gintu** and **Doda**, together with some extraordinary statues. Several metres tall, these figures with their primitive lines emerge in the midst of the wilds, hidden in the tall grasses of the plains under the indifferent eyes of the buffaloes that plough the rice fields.

Bada megalith and its warden

R Marca

Lake Poso

■ **Morowali Nature Reserve*** – *A difficult trip, only for the adventurous! To be undertaken during the driest months (June-August). Overnight accommodation in very basic losmen. Take mosquito repellent and let your guide look after practical arrangements (see "Tourist information" below).*

For the bold, and passionate botanist! Set up in 1980 to preserve threatened rare species – both plants and animals – the reserve covers 225 000ha of dense jungle. With patience and a little luck you may catch sight of a horned hog, an *anoa* or perhaps a *maleo* (brush turkey).

From Tentena *(bus or bemo from the bus station)*, a magnificent **road**** winds through the fresh green mountain landscape until it drops down into the harbour town of **Poso** *(allow 2hr)*, in the curve of **Tomini Bay**.

From here, bus or bemo services (from the bus station, frequent departures in the morning, fewer in the afternoon) run along the coast to Ampana (see p 600).

Making the most of Lake Poso

COMING AND GOING

By bus – Several bus companies cover the journey each day between Rantepao and Poso (14hr), via Palopo (2hr). From there, services also run to Ujung Pandang and Sengkang, Pendolo (10hr) and Tentena (12hr). Book the day before with the bus company. The coaches leave in the morning and will generally pick you up at your hotel. The journey is exhausting, with bumpy roads – very bad in places – frequent delays, and buses that are neither air-conditioned nor very comfortable. More reliable and comfortable, coaches belonging to the **Litha** company connect Poso with Ujung Pandang, via Palopo, Pendolo and Tentena, but they do not call at Rantepao. You can join them along the way if you have booked in advance.

By car – Hire a car with a driver to save yourself much of the weariness and the problems of the journey. Enquire at travel agencies or at your hotel.

ADDRESS BOOK

Tourist information – In Tentena, **Natural Cottages** and **Hotel Victory** have good information centres and tourist services: organisation of walking tours lasting several days in the region's nature reserves, local guides, car hire, reservation and confirmation of air and sea tickets, etc.

Bank/Currency exchange – Set out with an adequate supply of rupiah as it is very difficult to change money between Rantepao and Poso. If necessary you can change travellers' cheques and dollars (discouraging rates) in Poso: **BNI**, Jl Yos Sudarso.

Post office/Telephone – Post office in Tentena, near the bridge (east bank). No telephone in Pendolo. Several **Wartel** in Tentena, in the main street.

WHERE TO STAY, EATING OUT

Most of the hotels have a restaurant, and the streets are full of simple **warung**. Among local specialities, try fish from the lake and eels ("sugili") from the river.

● **Pendolo**

Modest

Wisma Victory, Jl Pelabuhan – 9rm. ⚑
✕ The rooms in the main building are basic and fairly rundown. Take a room at the front, more modern, and facing the lake. Meals are served on an attractive terrace overlooking the water. Friendly welcome.

Average

Mulia, Jl Pelabuhan Wisata 1 – 25rm. ⚑
✕ The best place in Pendolo. A few ideally placed bungalows made of woven bamboo and wood open straight onto the beach at the lakeside. The standard rooms, more spacious and comfortable,

and located at the rear in a shady courtyard, are however less pleasing. Restaurant on piles over the lake.

● **Tentena**

All these places are on the east shore.

Modest

Natural Cottages, Jl Jend Ahmat Yani 32, ☎ (0458) 213 11/213 56 – 7rm. ⌂ Simple but spacious, and with a standard of cleanliness that is not always impeccable, the rooms facing the lake, made entirely of wood, have a very attractive terrace. Avoid the little bungalows in the adjacent alleyway, which are noisy and have basic facilities. Good *warung* just opposite.

Pamona Indah Permai Hotel, Jl Yos Sudarso, ☎ (0458) 212 45 – 10rm. ⌂ ✗ Very close to the jetty, the rooms in this soulless hotel are in a row facing onto a verandah that runs right round the building.

Modest – average

Hotel Victory, Jl Diponegoro 18, ☎ (0458) 213 92 – 18rm. ⌂ ✗ A pleasant place, in a quiet location. All the rooms, mostly on the ground floor, open onto a small terrace. The economy and standard rooms are small and basic. Go instead for the "deluxe" or the superior rooms, which are larger and more modern, better equipped and more comfortable. Impeccably clean. Delightful welcome.

Hotel Intim, Jl Yos Sudarso 22, ☎ (0458) 213 45, Fax (0458) 214 88 – 26rm. ⌂ ✗ Hot water (except in the "ekonomi" rooms). The most comfortable hotel in Tentena, recently renovated. Faultless rooms with terrace, overlooking a little garden or the lake (more costly). Avoid the "ekonomi" rooms, which are very basic with shared WC and *mandi*. The restaurant serves excellent food, with a wide selection of dishes. Enclosed dining room or, more intimate and quiet (when the karaoke is not in action!), small terrace near the river. Try the *"woku"* lake eel!

● **Toinasa**

Average

🛏 **Siuri Cottages** – 12rm. ⌂ ✗ 20km southwest of Tentena (better to have your own car, but the hotel is accessible by *bemo* or taxi) Attractive, simple bungalows with terraces, ideally located on the lake shore, beside a real beach of golden sand. Complete peace and quiet.

Making the most of Lake Poso

THE TOGIAN ISLANDS★★
(KEPULAUAN TOGIAN)
Central Sulawesi Province (Sulawesi Tengah)
Map p 554-555 and p 602
Hot and humid climate, moderated by the sea breeze

Not to be missed
Tanjung Api at nightfall.
Exploring the extraordinary coral reefs and their colourful fauna.
Sunset over Kadidiri landing stage.
Strolling round Wakai during the weekly stop of the Poso-Gorontalo ferry.

And remember...
For snorkelling, bring your own mask, snorkel and flippers.
Use plenty of sun protection. Be careful of the corals: don't touch anything
under the water.
Avoid the period from December to February, when the sea can be dangerous.
Bring a torch as the oil lamps are not very bright.

If you are a nature lover and like the sea, have plenty of time and a zest for adventure, are not put off by tricky travelling conditions and do not worry too much about the comfort of where you stay, set off without delay for the remote Togian islands!

Ampana★

Bus or bemo from the coach station in Poso. Frequent departures in the morning, fewer in the afternoon. Allow 5-6hr. The road is often very bad in places as it is regularly swept by rivers in flood.
This peaceful village on the northern coast of Sulawesi's eastern peninsula is also the embarkation port for the Togian Islands. If you are exhausted after the journey, you can relax on the pretty pebble **beach**★ at Marina Cottage *(see p 603)*.
Then, late in the afternoon, negotiate with a local fisherman *(you will pay twice or three times as much if you use a losmen as intermediary!)* for a trip to **Tanjung Api**★★ ("Fire Cape"). The ideal plan is to leave shortly before sunset, to make the most of seeing it from the sea and arrive after nightfall *(allow 2hr for the return trip. Warning: the crossing is sometimes impossible at low tide)*. The water is so clear that you get a perfect view of the **coral reefs** in the lagoon. While the setting sun gradually lights up the waves, you cruise past a series of little coves, at the foot of jungle-covered cliffs that plunge steeply down to the sea. The throbbing of the engine is soon joined by a disturbing symphony of sounds: the lapping of little waves, wild cries echoing through the dark, beating wings whipping through the warm air, and then on the shore, the crunch of your own footsteps. You may suddenly find yourself whispering! Strange flames dart out of the earth and the rock from time to time. If you throw a handful of sand or a few drops of water on them, they just continue. Seeping out from imperceptible cracks, the **natural gas** catches fire as it comes into contact with the air. On the return trip all the elements seem to flare up in a fascinating symbiosis: starry sky with meteorites flashing, clouds of dancing fireflies, and the phosphorescent plankton among the waves. Magical.

From island to island

A group of volcanic islands surrounded by coral reefs rises out of the sea in the middle of the **Gulf of Tomini**. Thickly covered with tropical forest, hundreds of islands and islets emerge from the crystalline water in subtle gradations of blue and green, over which shimmer sumptuous rainbows. Populated with rare species – some of them

Crabs and nuts

Highly prized for the delicacy of their flesh, coconut crabs (a species that has already died out in many of the world's other Islands) are still heavily threatened with extinction. If you are inclined to doubt the theory – that you will no doubt hear – that they climb the coconut palms to cut and open nuts with their large front claws, then it is more probable that coconuts set in front of their retreats will not survive the night there! Now rare, the largest specimens weigh more than 5kg.

native to the region – this impenetrable jungle is home to the Togian macaque, the horned hog, the cuscus, the hornbill and other birds in their thousands. Sometimes impressive **giant black lizards** (*komodo*) venture close to the houses, in search of stray chickens. Less alarming are the entertaining **coconut crabs** that appear in the evenings.

A water paradise

Even more outstanding, the **marine life***** of the Togians lives in the most beautiful seas in Sulawesi, if not in the whole of Indonesia. These islands are the only place where such a wide range of corals can be seen together (200 species!). **Fringing reefs** run along the shoreline, steep **barrier reefs** surround the islands a few kilometres offshore and, further out to sea, two **atolls** contain deep lagoons. Put on mask and flippers and enjoy the inexhaustible sights! From the tiny clownfish flickering through the anemones to the impressive sea cow (though this is undoubtedly more rare), from the fleeting striped snake to the graceful ray, not to mention the alarming sharks and barracuda – a varied assembly of creatures with competing colours spins to infinity among the clumps of coral and sea fans to dazzle you at every turn. As you cruise from island to island, watch the surface of the sea – you may find yourself alongside a colony of **dolphins**. Lastly, at dusk, banks of sparkling flying fish race madly between sea and sky. Soon pale lights appear in the distance where the fishermen in their frail outrigger pirogues are preparing their lanterns and nets for the night.

Modest **villages** set on piles or straight on the ground punctuate the coastline of the largest islands. Immigrants (in particular former Bajau "sea gypsies", now mainly settled, and Bugis sailors) have come to join the indigenous people (such as the

A trip to the Togian Islands (Kadidiri)

M. Lemerle

The Togian Islands

Sulawesi

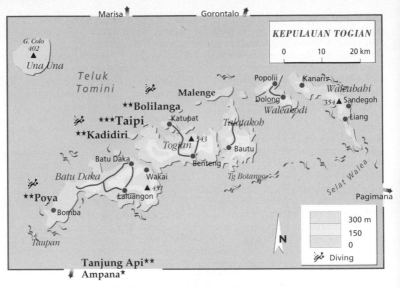

Pamona and the Saluan) who have mixed with the later arrivals to make up an extraordinarily hospitable **population**. Despite the recent expansion in tourism, the **copra** industry and **fishing** (particularly the lucrative trade in sharks' fins, for despatch to China, and pearl oysters) continue to shape the rhythm of daily life.

Wherever you stay you will never be far from the magnificent sea-bed (all the *losmen* have little motorboats available to take you to the finest spots, some of them lying just off the beach, at the foot of your bungalow!). Among the best places are two beaches on the little island of **Poya★★**, visible opposite the village of **Bomba** in southern Batu Daka, the largest island in the group. In the north of the island, the town of **Wakai** comes to life on the days when the weekly ferry to Gorontalo arrives. Not far away, the islands of **Kadidiri★★** and **Taipi★★★** attract the majority of travellers, while further to the east, offshore from the village of **Katupat**, the delightful island of **Bolilanga★★** remains less visited. As for **Malenge**, with its much-vaunted jungle, it is worth knowing that wild life is becoming rare here, and the accommodation is not very attractive.

Making the most of the Togian Islands

COMING AND GOING – GETTING AROUND

From Poso – A weekly boat crosses Tomini Bay, from Poso (in theory, on Monday morning) to Gorontalo (allow 40hr), via Ampana (1 night), Wakai (18hr), Katupat, Malenge and Dolong, the ports in the Togian Islands. It generally leaves again from Gorontalo on Friday evening. The passengers cluster together on the bridge and in the hold among the goods,

in huge discomfort. Arrive early to book the tiny cabin (2 berths) from a member of the crew. It is far from luxurious, but you can at least leave your luggage there and stretch out!

From Ampana – In theory, there is a daily connection with Wakai (5hr). You can ask to get off at Bomba (2-3hr). Some boats go on as far as Katupat (3 times a week). If possible, ask to go on the express boat!

From Pagimana – The port lies 5hr away by bus to the east of Ampana. Ferry to Gorontalo (1 night) every 2 days. Particularly useful in the opposite direction, to avoid waiting for the weekly boat. Warning, it does not stop at the Togian Islands – you must then take the boat from Ampana.

From island to island – The frequency of the service depends on the islands and the season. It is still possible to charter a boat to gain time.

Chartering a boat – Much more expensive, but so much faster! Enquire at Ampana or Wakai harbour, and at the *losmen* in Kadidiri, Taipi or Katupat. To get to North Sulawesi via the Togian Islands, the nearest port is Marisa.

ADDRESS BOOK

Tourist information – Ampana has a small information centre on the Togians (Jl Kartini), but it is run by the largest landowner in the islands and you will always be sent to where the owner has interests. You will often be equally well advised in the *losmen*

Bank/Currency exchange – Take enough rupiah. You can change dollars at Ampana, but at a very poor rate of exchange.

Post office/Telephone – Only at Ampana and Wakai.

WHERE TO STAY, EATING OUT

The infrastructure for accommodation and eating out is in general very rudimentary. The Togian Islands have neither electricity nor running water. Oil lamps are used for lighting, and a *mandi* for washing, with well-water brought each day in a cistern. All the *losmen* offer full board terms. Plenty of fish on the menu.

● **Ampana**

Suggestions below do not give details of the *losmen* in the village itself, which are very basic, noisy and not always clean. It is probably better to take a "bendi" to the place below, further to the east.

Modest

@*Marina Cottage*, Jl Tanjung Api 33, Desa Labuan, ☎ (0458) 212 80 – 10rm. ⌂ 🏖 ✕ 🛥 Simple bungalows, but clean and charming, laid out along a pebble beach. Private terraces facing the sea, and coral close to the shore. Quiet atmosphere, friendly welcome. What more could you ask for?

We could however mention a small restaurant, the *Rumah Makan Mekar*, Jl Kartini 2 (on the corner of the seafront road). A very small place where you can eat delicious grilled fish as well as classic Indonesian dishes.

● **Poya**

Modest

@*Poya Lisa* – 6rm. ✕ 🛥 Attractive traditional bungalows either opening straight onto the beach (a little ribbon of sand on each side of the island) or, more isolated, overlooking the sea. Excellent (and copious) meals; warm, attentive welcome.

Cecilia – 6rm. ✕ 🛥 Just opposite the above. A friendly place to stay, on a little island without a beach. You can, however, swim from the landing stage and you are brilliantly placed for the sunset.

● **Kadidiri**

Three groups of bungalows set out along a delightful sandy beach.

Modest

@*Pondok Lestari* – 8rm. ✕ 🛥 The quietest and most intimate place, where the friendly welcome makes up for the lack of facilities. You can go out with the fisherman who departs with his line ahead of each meal.

Wakai Cottages – 15rm. ✕ 🛥 In the middle of the beach, in the most pleasant site. A few bungalows have a private *mandi*. A younger and more lively place than the one above.

Kadidiri Paradise Bungalows – 25rm. ✕ 🛥 Some of the bungalows have a *mandi* attached, and all have electricity in the evenings (generator). The atmosphere is a bit commercial and impersonal. Diving club (for experienced divers). Check the condition of the equipment.

● **Taipi**

Modest

@*Taipi Beach Bungalows* – 10rm. ✕ 🛥 *Mandi* in the rooms and generator in the evenings. Snorkelling enthusiasts will be delighted by the sea-bed around the tiny island. The meals are sometimes rather unsubstantial.

● **Bolilanga**

Modest

@*Natural Cottage* – 8rm. ✕ 🛥 Spacious bungalows, either on the beach or among the mangroves. Some have a *mandi*. Small beach and friendly family welcome.

Making the most of the Togian Islands

MANADO
THE MINAHASA REGION★
Capital of North Sulawesi Province (Sulawesi Utara)
Map p 607 and plan p 613 – Pop 320 000
Damp, stifling climate in town, cool on the heights.

Not to be missed
Climbing Mahawu volcano.
The "waruga" in Sarangan.
Tasting the lake fish at the "Rumah Makan Danau Tondano".

And remember...
Avoid arriving on a Sunday, when many of the shops and offices are closed.
Rent a car to avoid interminable waits for a bemo.

Tucked into the curve of a wide bay on the Celebes Sea, to the northeast of the narrow peninsula of North Sulawesi, Manado contains all the region's services and administrative offices. Capital of the province, it is also the main urban centre of the Minahasa region, an area that extends across the volcanic slopes of the hinterland. Prosperous and modern, Manado is one of the wealthiest towns in Indonesia, with among the highest rates of literacy, school attendance and health care in the country. Here there are no *becaks*, nor any beggars or street children. Its enterprising inhabitants, who have an unmatched business sense and a feeling for economy, carry on a flourishing trade, particularly with the Moluccas and the Philippines. Between the large shops, the banks and the hotels, the crowded streets buzz with activity. Music, a mark of the warm and outward-looking attitude of the locals, can be heard everywhere, and the smallest *mikrolet* or street vendor seems to be competing to produce the highest volume of sound! It is this cheerful and dynamic atmosphere that gives Manado its charm and interest, offering the traveller a pleasant base from which to explore the surrounding area.

A flourishing harbour
Its strategic position on the **spice route** and the agricultural wealth of the region meant that Manado was coveted by the Europeans at a very early stage. **Portuguese merchants** set up a trading post here in the 16C, and their missionaries were quick to convert the people to Catholicism. Already established in the Philippines, the **Spanish** landed in their turn, for a shorter stay. Supported by the Minahasa, the **Dutch East India Company** soon kicked its European rivals out of the peninsula. In 1679 a treaty acknowledged Dutch domination over the town, which was to last for three centuries. As a result, it was in Manado that the Dutch most obviously exercised their influence. After the Catholics came the Calvinist missionaries, who under-

The "Father of the Minahasa people"
Born in Tondano in 1890, Sam Ratulangi is seen as a national hero. Countless numbers of Manado streets bear his name, countless numbers of statues have been erected in his honour. After a period as a student in Switzerland he returned and founded the Minahasa Independent Protestant Church (KGPM). As the first republican governor of Eastern Indonesia he quickly emerged as the head of the nationalist movement and, during the struggle for independence, his authority encouraged the Minahasa people to support the cause. In the end his militant independence earned him a period of imprisonment under the Dutch in Irian Jaya. On his death in 1949 he was honoured as "the Father of the entire Minahasa nation".

M Lemerle

In the Minahasa countryside

took to reconvert the Minahasa to Protestantism. Educated in mission schools, the latter formed a cultured and Westernised elite that soon took over the higher positions in the colonial administration and armies. This submission brought Manado rapid expansion.

However, the Japanese occupation, beginning in 1942, marked a dark period that ended with the terrible bombardment by the Allies in 1945. A few years later (1958), the town became the centre of the **Permesta rebellion**. In the face of the monopolies of the central power in Jakarta – particularly in the export sector – this reforming movement claimed regional autonomy, bringing down a response in the form of a bombardment of Manado by government forces, followed by a long period of armed repression. Favourable to the local economy, the reforms implemented under Suharto's "New Order" fortunately ended in the restoration of peace and prosperity.

Exploring the town
Plan p 613. Allow half a day.

Manado is very spread out, but most of the offices, shops and restaurants are close together in the city centre, on both sides of **Jalan Sam Ratulangi** (A3-A2-B2), the large thoroughfare that runs parallel to the seafront (Piere Tandean Boulevard). Be careful where you walk, as the pavements are full of dangerous potholes!

To the north, this crowded street leads to the **fish market** (Pasar Ikan) (B1), where activity is at its height at 6am.

Not far away the **Ban Hiang Kiong Temple**★ (B2) (*Jl Panjaitan. Entrance free*) is the main place of worship for Confucian Buddhism, adhered to by the substantial Chinese community established in Manado. Under its pagoda roofs, dragons, lanterns and generous offerings are splendidly coloured in red and gold, bathed in clouds of incense. Find out about feast-days (particularly the Chinese New Year), when the atmosphere of the place changes dramatically.

The only visible theme for the very varied collection of the **North Sulawesi Province Museum** (Museum Negeri Propinsi Sulawesi Utara) (B2-C2) (*Jl W R Supratman 72. Daily, 8am-1pm. Fee*) is local culture and daily life. In the dark and the dust, musical instruments, jewellery, shells and ceremonial dress rub shoulders with *prahu*, carriages, porcelain, models of houses and cooking utensils, with everything described entirely in Indonesian!

Through the Minahasa region★
A one-day tour by car, or short excursions by mikrolet or taxi from Manado or Tomohon.

Leave Manado for the highlands of the Minahasa region, a volcanic land caught between the Celebes Sea and the Maluku Sea. Successive eruptions have created a turbulent landscape here, with highly fertile soil. Pretty roads wind through the hills and across the volcanic slopes, layered with rice fields and market-garden crops, while the dark green forests clothe the steepest hillsides. Above all else the Minahasa region is devoted to agriculture, focusing on export, and is one of the most prosperous areas in Indonesia. Concentrated along the coast, the coconut groves produce **copra**. The main source of wealth, however, apart from nutmeg and coffee, is still **cloves** – exported to Java in enormous quantities to make *kretek* (cigarettes). A trip into these highlands, although so close to the bustle of the city, provides a delightful breath of fresh air and peace. During your explorations, bathed in the delicate aroma from carpets of cloves drying in the sun, you will travel through charming villages that are particularly well kept and full of flowers. With their outstanding good nature, the inhabitants – almost all of them Christian – always appear open and friendly.

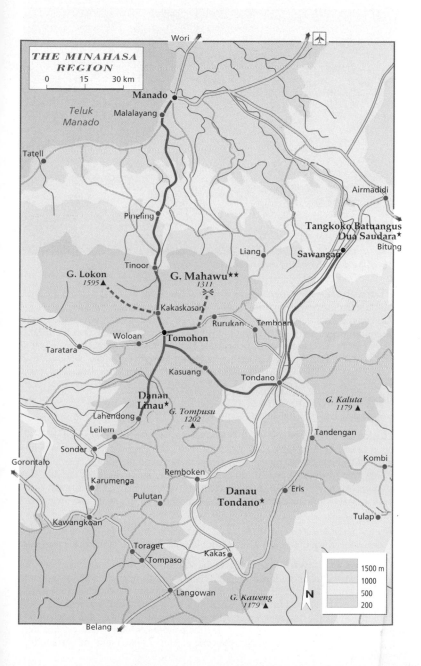

THE MINAHASA
REGION
0   15   30 km

Wori

Manado
Malalayang
Teluk Manado

Tatell

Airmadidi

Pineling

Tangkoko Batuangus
Dua Saudara★
Bitung

Liang

Sawangan

Tinoor

G. Lokon
1595 ▲

G. Mahawu★★
1311

Kakaskasan

Rurukan   Temboan

Woloan   Tomohon

Taratara

Kasuang   Tondano

Danan
Linau★

G. Kaluta
1179 ▲

Lahendong

G. Tompusu
1202
▲

Leilem

Tandengan

Sonder

Kombi

Karumenga   Remboken

Pulutan

Danau
Tondano★

Eris

Kawangkoan

Tulap

Toraget
Tompaso   Kakas

Langowan   G. Kaweng
1179 ▲

Gorontalo

Belang

1500 m
1000
500
200

N

607

M Lemerle

City of the dead: the waruga in Sarangan

■ **Tomohon** – *25km from Manado.* The ideal base from which to explore the area, this little trading town is a pleasant place for a stay, providing a good alternative for those who do not wish to sleep in Manado. You can also obtain information from the **vulcanology centre** on the conditions for climbing the volcanoes in the region. Not far away, at **Kakaskasan II**, behind the Happy Flower Homestay *(see "Where to stay", p 612)*, a footpath leads to the top of **Mount Lokon★** (1 595m) *(2hr to climb up the lava flows. It is best to be accompanied to avoid getting lost).* However, be careful if you climb up, as the last eruption dates back to 1991 and recent forecasts have been threatening.

From Tomohon, follow the main road southwards.

■ **Lake Linau★** (Danau Linau) – *A few hundred metres from the main road, in the village of Lahendong.* A passable road opens onto the lake *(dangerous swimming),* which is enclosed within a fringe of green hills. If you do not mind the sulphurous clouds escaping from the rocks, have a drink at the little restaurant overlooking the site. This is an opportunity to watch the waters changing with the light, going through every shade of green, from pale turquoise to deep emerald. The shores are also inviting for pleasant walks.

Return to Tomohon and take the Tondano road (east). Ask the driver to drop you off at Rurukan, where a footpath begins. Be warned: mikrolet traffic is fairly irregular along the Rurukan road.

■ **Mount Mahawu★★** (Gunung Mahawu) – *Allow 90min-2hr for the round trip (easy walking).* Trudging at first through the fields, then through the stifling damp forest, you will not feel as if you were climbing a volcano. But a spectacular view awaits you at the summit (1 311m), from where you see a magnificent **crater lake★★**, still smoking, where the turquoise waters ringed with yellow give off a bitter smell of sulphur. Walk right round the lake to enjoy the **panoramic view★★** that extends over the sea in the distance and, nearer, the cone of Mount Lokon and the surrounding countryside.

Sulawesi

Continue to Tondano (about 2km from the lake). From here a road runs right along the lakeshore. You can take a mikrolet for Ramboken and get out when you feel like it for a walk.

■ **Lake Tondano★** (Danau Tondano) – *See also below, "Eating out".* Suspended at a height of 600m in the heart of a broad volcanic crater (extinct), the lake lies between a fertile rice-producing plain and a small chain of wooded mountains. Along its winding shores, here and there you will come across floating fields, fishermen's pirogues, pretty houses on piles, and a few villages full of flowers.

From Tondano, take the Monado road to the north that goes through Airmadidi.

■ **Sawangan** – In this little cemetery shaded by frangipanis lie 144 **waruga★★**, strange stone sarcophagi dating from the pre-Christian era. For many centuries the Minahasa would place their dead in these monoliths, more than a metre high, crowned with strangely carved capitals. The body rested there in the foetal position, with jewellery, porcelain and other precious items, which were later looted. Originally located near the village houses, most of the sarcophagi have been placed here out of concern for hygiene and preservation.

■ **Tangkoko Batuangus-Dua Saudara Nature Reserve★** – *Access through the village of Batupitih: by jeep from Girian, just before Bitung coming from Manado. Set out with a guide who will organise your trip and will take care of the (obligatory) permit, and accommodation if necessary. Wear long clothing including socks and cover yourself very thoroughly in mosquito repellent. The forest is teeming with hungry insects and mites that burrow into clothing and cause terrible skin irritation!*

The rainforest on the eastern end of the peninsula, stretching from sea level to altitudes of over 1 000m, is an impassable jungle that the sun's rays can barely pierce. It is home to an outstanding range of **fauna★★★**: **macaques** with black tufts, dwarf squirrels, **cuscus**, *anoa* (rare), **flying lizards**, and countless birds (**hornbills**, **maleo**, sea eagles, frigate birds and parrots). But remember that you will need plenty of patience and luck to see some of the animals. A pair of binoculars is often essential to see the creatures that live high up in the foliage.

Making the most of Manado

COMING AND GOING

By air – The **Sam Ratulangi** airport lies 13km to the northeast of the town. Taxis wait outside it. Another possibility is to take a mikrolet to terminal Paal 2, then another to the city centre. There are several daily flights to Ujung Pandang, 2 weekly flights to Davao, in the Philippines (Bouraq), and 2 more to Singapore (Silk Air). With the economic crisis, connections with Palu and Gorontalo, Biak and Jayapura, have become very irregular, and those with Poso are not available at all.

By boat – The main port is not at Manado itself but at **Bitung** (55km to the east; 1hr). It can take the large **Pelni** ships (see address below) that serve Ujung Pandang, Jakarta and Surabaya (Java), Balikpapan (Kalimantan), and Ternate (Moluccas). For details on connections, get a copy of the monthly timetable from Pelni or a travel agency. Some smaller boats providing connections with Palu, Pare Pare, Sangihe, Ternate, Ambon, etc, arrive direct at **Manado harbour**, Jl Suprapto/Jl Rumambi (B1). The regular crossings to

Sulawesi

the Philippines have stopped. Some cargo boats, however, take passengers (enquire directly in Bitung).

By bus/mikrolet – Manado is well served by road. Buses to Tomohon, Tondano, Sonder, etc, leave throughout the day from the **Karombasan terminus**, at Wanea. For the airport, Bitung and Airmadidi, go to the **Paal II terminus** ("dua"). For Gorontalo, Palu, Kotamabaru and Tanawangko, go to the **Malalayang terminus** (30min from the city centre, to the southwest). The various companies have their offices there. Several bus services run between Gorontalo and Manado every day, departing morning and evening in each direction. Allow 10hr on the road, which is reasonably good overall, with a few stretches in very poor condition. It is more comfortable and quicker to get together (maximum 8 people) to hire a Kijang vehicle (apply at the coach station). The mikrolet terminus (*bemo*) **Pasar 45** ("empat lima"), in the city centre (B2), connects with all these stations.

GETTING AROUND

On foot – Very spread out and stiflingly hot, the city does not encourage walking except for short distances in the city centre.

By taxi – You will find them along the streets, but it is often much more practical to ask your hotel to call one for you. They are usually air-conditioned and have a meter, but you can negotiate a price, for a half-day or a day, depending on the route that you wish to take.

By mikrolet – This is the most widely available form of transport in Manado. They cover the city and its surroundings, more or less regularly (the great drawback is the waiting, sometimes interminable, in the coach stations, since the vehicles do not leave until they are full). The central station is at **Pasar 45** (B2). Very cheap but not always easy to manage for the newcomer. They carry numbers and the destination is shown on the front windscreen, but that is not always helpful! Ask the driver or local people to help you find the right vehicle.

ADDRESS BOOK

Tourist information – North Sulawesi Tourist Office, Jl 17 Agustus (beyond B3), ☎ (0431) 86 49 11. This is out of the way, and not very useful. You will get more information in hotels and travel agencies.

Bank/Currency exchange – The city has a large number of banks, many of which change money or have cash dispensers. Changing money in the hotels is less advantageous. The following places accept Visa cards and MasterCard: **BII** (A2), Jl Sam Ratulangi (separate entrance, Jl Piere Tendean, on the seafront). **Bank Lippo** (B2), corner of Jl Sutomo and Jl Maramis. **Bank BPD**, Jl Sam Ratulangi.

Post office – Main post office (Pos dan Giro), Jl Sam Ratulangi 21 (A2-A3). Monday-Friday, 8am-8pm, Saturday-Sunday, 8am-6pm. Poste restante. Internet (9am-5pm; closed Sundays and public holidays).

Telephone – A few coin or card-operated telephone boxes in the street (particularly in front of the large shops). **Telkom**, Jl Sam Ratulangi 4 (A2), open 24hr a day, international calls. Warning: not all **Wartel** offices offer calls abroad.

Newspapers – The large shops usually sell the "Jakarta Post", as do some of the hotels.

Travel agencies – Apart from airline or boat tickets, many agencies (often much cheaper than the airlines) offer various tour programmes to explore the area, with or without guides, and cars with drivers. They arrange excursions in the Minahasa region (*see p 606*), walking tours in the local Nature Reserves, days of (accompanied) diving – snorkelling or scuba – trips across Sulawesi, etc. **Maya Express**, Jl Sudirman 15, ☎ (0431) 87 01 11. **Vita Tours**, Jl Sam Ratulangi 100 A, ☎ (0431) 85 85 85, Fax (0431) 86 12 51.

Car rental – Cars can only be hired with drivers. Check that the price includes fuel, and the driver's meals and overnight accommodation if you are leaving for several days. Enquire at a travel agency or the reception in your hotel. At the airport and coach stations you may hire a car with a driver, alone or sharing the journey with other passengers.

Airline companies – Remember that travel agencies can offer tickets at reduced rates, often much better value than those available direct from the airlines themselves. **Garuda**, Jl Diponegoro 15 **(B3)**, ☎ (0431) 86 22 42. **Merpati**, Jl Sudirman (beyond C3), ☎ (0431) 86 40 27. **Bouraq**, Jl Sarapung 27B **(B2)**, ☎ (0431) 84 14 70. **Mandala**, Jl Sam Ratulangi 206, ☎ (0431) 85 17 43. **Silk Air**, Jl Sarapung 5, ☎ (0431) 86 37 44.

Shipping line– Pelni, Jl Sam Ratulangi 7 **(A2-B2)**, ☎ (0431) 628 44. Monday-Friday, 8am-2pm. Timetables and boat tickets are also available from travel agencies.

Immigration office – Kantor Imigrasi, Jl 17 Agustus (beyond B3), ☎ (0431) 86 34 91.

Medical service– There is no shortage of **pharmacies**. The following is central and well equipped: Jl Sam Ratulangi 31 **(A3)**, nearly opposite the Matahari shop. Should you fall ill, first tell your hotel, and they will be able to call a doctor. The city has several hospitals, of which the most recommended are the **Pancaran Kasih**, Jl Sam Ratulangi, and the **Rumah Sakit Gunung Maria**, in Malalayang.

WHERE TO STAY

• Manado

Manado is more of a place of transit than one for staying in, but you may have to spend a night here while waiting for a bus, a plane or a boat. The city can also be a useful point of departure to explore the Minahasa region and the island of Bunaken. No one hotel is outstanding for its charm, but some are comfortable and clean. All the places shown here are located in the centre.

Modest

Smiling Hostel, Jl Rumambi 7, ☎ (0431) 86 84 63 – 10rm. ✕ ✕ A place where travellers from all over the world meet and exchange news. Rather like a Youth Hostel, convivial but with basic facilities. Dormitory beds and single or double rooms. You can have breakfast in the little bar on the roof. The staff, young, efficient and very welcoming, will do their best to provide in-

formation, even if you are not staying here. Avoid the rooms facing the harbour and the fish market, as they are very noisy.

Modest – Average

Manado Bersehati Hotel, Jl Jend Sudirman 20, ☎ (0431) 85 50 22, Fax (0431) 85 72 38 – 50rm✕ ▤ / ✕ ✕ Several price categories, from the tiny basic rooms (to be avoided!) with fans and exterior bathrooms, to the air-conditioned rooms with television and hot water, and reasonable comfort. The place is rather cramped, with the rooms on the ground floor arranged round a small inner courtyard, and those upstairs along a narrow corridor.

Hotel Mini Cakalele, Jl Korengkeng 40, ☎ (0431) 85 29 42, Fax (0431) 86 69 48 – 38rm. ✕ ▤ / ✕ A small unpretentious hotel, well located, worth recommending for its "superior" category rooms. Its wide range of prices covers accommodation from rundown little rooms with fan and *mandi* to the most spacious and clean suites equipped with air conditioning, television, telephone and refrigerator. Spread over several levels, most of the rooms look out onto an inner terrace. Unfortunately the neon lighting does not enhance the setting!

Average

Hotel Minahasa, Jl Sam Ratulangi 199, ☎ (0431) 86 25 59, Fax (0431) 86 20 59/85 40 41 – 30rm. ✕ ▤ / ✕ ✕ ᴄᴄ Hot water. An excellent place for Manado, slightly out of the centre but offering very good value for money. The rooms are on two levels, in a green, attractive and quiet setting, behind the main building. All are comfortable and have a private terrace facing the garden. Some have a sea view.

Hotel Regina, Jl Sugiono 1, ☎ (0431) 85 00 90/85 00 91/85 66 55, Fax (0431) 86 77 06 – 33rm. ✕ ▤ ✎ ᴛᴠ Hot water. Modern, comfortable and clean. A good place, even if it is somewhat lacking in warmth and charm.

Average – high end

Hotel New Queen, Jl Wakeke 12-14, ☎ (0431) 85 55 51, Fax (0431) 86 44 40 – 35rm. ✕ ▤ ✎ ᴛᴠ ✕ ᴄᴄ Hot water. An unpretentious hotel, well located,

Making the most of Manado

comfortable and clean. Rooms with carpet and refrigerator, opening onto a corridor or small courtyard garden.

Luxury

Hotel Sahid Kawanua, Jl Sam Ratulangi 1, ☎ (0431) 86 77 77, Fax (0431) 86 52 20 – 100rm. ⌁ 🖃 🖵 ✗ ⌁ cc Hot water. Good quality, pleasant hotel, but wholly without charm. The swimming pool is open to non-residents, who pay for its use

Super deluxe

Novotel, Jl Piere Tendean, ☎ (0431) 85 55 55/85 11 74, Fax (0431) 86 88 88 – 268rm. ⌁ 🖃 ✎ 🖵 ✗ ⌁ ⌁ cc Hot water. A large modern building overlooking the seafront. A luxurious establishment belonging to the famous French chain of hotels, impersonal and unremarkable, yet elegant and very pleasant. A magnificent swimming pool on the 6th floor has been so designed that it appears to plunge directly into the sea.

● **Kakaskasan II (Tomohon)**

Modest

⌂**The Happy Flower Homestay**, 800m from the main road (a track fit for driving begins by the Pniel church (gereja) and leads to the volcano), ☎ (0431) 35 27 87 – 9rm. ✗ A good place, simple but friendly and peaceful, in a pleasant setting. There is a shared bathroom with hot water. Avoid the tiny rooms in the main house, which suffer from the noise of the restaurant and are right in the middle of all the activity. Take the private bungalow instead, with is own bathroom (cold water and Turkish-style WC) and terrace. Another building houses a few rooms with shared bathroom and terrace. More expensive, the pavilion named the "honeymoon suite" (behind the garden), offers a little more space, privacy and comfort (hot shower).

Modest – average

Volcano Resort, opposite the above, ☎ (0431) 35 29 88 – 6rm. ⌁ 🖵 ✗ Hot water. Recently built wooden bungalows, each with 2 bedrooms and private terrace. Set in a large garden, this is an airy and impeccably maintained hotel.

EATING OUT

Manado and its surroundings are teeming with small **warung** (particularly around the "Pasar 45") which, apart from the usual Indonesian dishes, serve grilled fish and surprising Minahasa specialities, such as "kawaok" (forest rat), "rintek wuuk" (dog-meat), or "lawang pangang" (bat stew), all of them highly spiced ("rica")! An opportunity to try out new flavours.

● **Manado**

Basic – moderate

Batavia Restoran, Jl Sam Ratulangi 22A (A2). Large, impeccably clean air-conditioned dining room designed like a cafeteria. You can eat tasty little dishes and all kinds of cakes. Ideal for lunchtime.

Surabaya, Jl Sarapung 33 (B2-B3), ☎ (0431) 86 25 62. The austere façade belies a small unpretentious but pleasant dining room. School children sometimes come here in groups for lunch. Wide choice of well prepared dishes. The television may be off-putting for some.

⌂**Green Garden**, Jl Sam Ratulangi 52 (A3), ☎ (0431) 87 00 89. A good place. An open dining room, set back from the street. A wide range of dishes with noodles or rice. Meat and fish grilled, or in a sauce. Delicious!

Rumah Makan Ria Rio, Jl Sudirman 5 (B2), ☎ (0431) 85 33 13. A small airy dining room, unfortunately dominated by a television set. They serve reasonable fish and seafood.

Moderate – more select

⌂**Sunset Cafe**, Jl Piere Tendean (just opposite the Novotel, to which it belongs) (A2). On the seafront, in an elegant but simple setting. Enclosed dining room but also some terrace tables, pleasant for sipping a drink at sunset. Indonesian, Chinese and Western dishes. The salads are more expensive, but very attractive in the hot weather. You can choose the ingredients and the dressing, concocting them to your liking.

More select

Bahari, Jl Piere Tendean (beyond A3), ☎ (0431) 85 23 98. On the seafront, in an enclosed room. An excellent place for enjoying seafood. There are also Chinese specialities.

● Tinoor

15km from Manado along the Tomohon road, around a dozen restaurants offer traditional Minahasa cuisine. Choose a dining room with a good view.

Basic – moderate

Tamisco, self-service buffet.

Tinoor Jaya, view over Manado. Share an assortment of small dishes to try different specialities.

● Lake Tondano

Basic – Moderate

Rumah Makan Danau Tondano, just before the village of Remboken, on the west shore of the lake, ☎ (0431) 32 11 60. Closed in the evening. A pleasant covered terrace on piles, with a fresh breeze blowing off the water, where you can enjoy excellent lake fish (try the "woku" dish, for instance) and lovely scenery. Attentive staff.

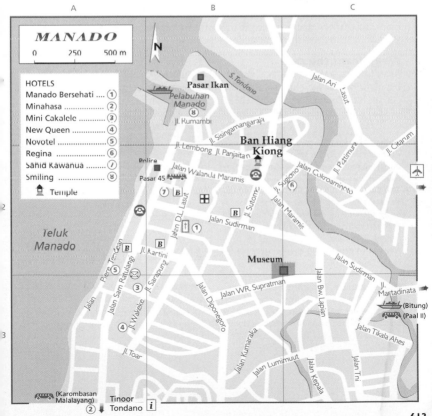

MANADO

0   250   500 m

HOTELS

Manado Bersehati .... ①
Minahasa .... ②
Mini Cakalele .... ③
New Queen .... ④
Novotel .... ⑤
Regina .... ⑥
Sahid Kawanua .... ⑦
Smiling .... ⑧

🏛 Temple

Pasar Ikan

S. Tondano

Jalan Ari

Lasut

Pelabuhan Manado ⑧

Jl. Rumambi

Jl. Sisingamangaraja

Jl. Lembong   Jl. Panjaitan

Ban Hiang Kiong

Jl. Citarum

Jl. Patimura

Police

Jalan Walanda Maramis

Jl. Sugiono

Jalan Cokroaminoto

Pasar 45

⑦ B

Jl. DII Lasut

Jalan Sudirman

B Jl. Sutomo

Jalan Maramis

①

Teluk Manado

B

Jl. Kartini

Piere Tendean

Jalan Sam Ratulangi

⑤

③

Jl. Sarapung

Jl. Wakeke

④

Jl. Toar

Jalan Diponegoro

Jalan WR. Supratman

Museum

Jalan Sudirman

Jalan Bw. Lapian

Jl. Martadinata

(Bitung)

(Paal II)

Jalan Kumaraka

Jalan Lumimuut

Jalan Kepala

Jalan Tikala Ahes

Jalan Tini

(Karombasan Malalayang)

② Tinoor Tondano ℹ

BUNAKEN MARINE RESERVE★★★

North Sulawesi Province (Sulawesi Utara) – Map p 554-555
Pop 2 000 – Hot, dry climate tempered by the sea breeze

Not to be missed
Exploring the sea-bed, snorkelling or scuba diving.

And remember...
For snorkelling, take your own equipment if possible.
Be careful of the corals and don't touch anything under the water.
Avoid the rainy season, above all between December and February,
when the sea is rough.
Visibility is best in September-October.

The Bunaken Marine Reserve is only 8km off Manado, an area of 75 000ha that includes five islands (Bunaken, Siladen, Manado Tua, Montehage and Nain), bordered with mangroves and magnificent coral reefs. The wealth of marine fauna and the diversity of the corals make this an internationally renowned **diving site**. It has no fewer than around twenty spots to explore. There are fringing reefs, but above all steep **submerged cliffs** with **caves** and fascinating crevices that shelter multitudes of fish of every shape and colour. Rays, turtles, barracuda, Napoleon wrasse, dolphins and sharks – all can be seen in these warm clear waters. The place is a paradise for anyone who loves the silent underwater world.

Away from the sea
Apart from its surrounding reefs, **the island of Bunaken★** (Pulau Bunaken) has nothing out of the ordinary to offer in itself. To the southeast the mangroves invade the coast, approaching **Pantai Pangalisang**. The only attractive part of beach is the little ribbon of sand to the south of **Pantai Liang**, on the west coast of the island. Even here, at low tide the coral plateau will force you into a long walk to find enough water to swim. At weekends the inhabitants of Manado flock here by the boatload to have lunch in the surrounding *losmen* or to have family picnics on the beach, where shellfish and coconut sellers look for business.

Pollution alert!
Although the seabed is still splendid, we cannot avoid recognising the damage caused by tourism and also by the local population. You only have to count the number of plastic objects that are thrown overboard in an hour's crossing between Manado and Bunaken to assess the task of consciousness raising that remains to be done! A programme to protect the environment has already been set up, but we are still far from a collective awareness of the problem. The only inescapable obstacle to the development of infrastructures is the crippling lack of fresh water on the island. Let's hope that Bunaken will not turn into a rubbish dump.

A footpath *(be careful of falling coconuts!)* leads to the charming **village of Bunaken**, on the southern tip of the island. Cows, pigs and chickens wander everywhere, and you will meet warm and friendly inhabitants, the fishermen or **copra** producers, who also make a living (increasingly) from tourism.

Making the most of the island of Bunaken

COMING AND GOING

A boat (always crowded and often late) leaves every day from Manado (near the Bersehati market) around 2pm, and returns from Bunaken at 8am. Allow 1hr. You can be dropped off in front of your *losmen*, but unloading merchandise can last for hours. It is better to disembark at the first stop (the village of Bunaken), then walk or charter a small boat. A faster option consists of hiring the services of a private boat (ask diving clubs at your hotel, or one of the fishermen).

ADDRESS BOOK

The island has no currency exchange facilities, no post office and no public telephone, but Manado is only an hour away.

WHERE TO STAY, EATING OUT

Accommodation on the island of Bunaken consists above all of fairly basic bungalows, with *mandi* and Turkish-style WC, and with no running water. All the *losmen* offer full board terms and usually serve good substantial meals, often based on fresh fish. The prices are set per day and per person, full board. Most will hire out masks, flippers and snorkels, not always in very good condition.

• Pantai Liang

Modest
Liang Panorama – 10rm. Bungalows laid out in tiers above the beach. Good view over the sea.
Santika, on the beach – 2rm. ⚐ ✕ 🛝 Small place, friendly welcome.
🏠Tante Nona Cottages – 2rm. ⚐ ✕ 🛝 Overlooking the beach, with a fine view. Friendly warm atmosphere.
Sem Bungalows, on the beach – 4rm. ⚐ ✕ 🛝 Simple and attractive.
Nyiur Melambai, ☎ (0431) 86 90 15 – 4rm. ⚐ ✕ 🛝 Bungalows laid out in tiers above the restaurant. Most have a sea view.
Papa Bua – 8rm. ✕ 🛝 Bungalows with attached or shared *mandi*, spread up the hillside. The hotel is in partnership with the "Froggies" diving club and is popular with divers. Warm welcome.

• Pantai Pangalisang

All these *losmen* are accessible via the beach, or along a path behind it.

Modest
🏠MC Homestay, on the way into the village of Bunaken – 6rm. ⚐ ✕ 🛝 Bun-

galows laid out one above the other, facing the sea. The wooden ones are spacious and pleasant; the others, built of bamboo, are more rustic. Warm welcome.
Lorenso Cottages – 7rm. ⚐ ✕ ✕ 🛝 In a dry garden. Very simple, but pleasant and welcoming.
Daniel's Homestay, ☎ (0431) 81 31 43 – 17rm. ⚐ ✕ 🛝 Bungalows set facing each other, in a sparse garden.

Modest – average
Sea Breeze Bungalows – 20rm. ⚐ ✕ ✕ 🛝 Bungalows spread round a garden, some with sea view. The most expensive, fairly spacious and recently built, are less makeshift than the island average. The others are more Spartan. Very good diving club attached.

Average
Samorina Paradise, facing the jetty – 12rm. ⚐ ✕ 🛝 Hot water. Wooden pavilions, almost luxurious for the island, with a real bathroom! Large private terraces facing a dry garden. The whole place is perfectly kept. Diving club attached.

• Siladen Island

Modest
Martha's Homestay – 5rm. ✕ 🛝 Basic rooms or bungalows. Friendly welcome, but meals somewhat meagre.

OTHER THINGS TO DO

Scuba diving – Most of the diving clubs have their head offices in Manado but you can enquire direct, in Bunaken. They usually offer a package that includes 2 dives, with full equipment, boat, the services of an instructor, and lunch.
Froggies Divers (enquire at the Papa Bua, in Bunaken, or at the Smiling Hostel, Jl Rumambi 7, Manado, ☎ (0431) 824 31 34 78, manado@divefroggies.com A club that is renowned for its reliability and friendly atmosphere. Competent instructors and well-maintained equipment. All levels. PADI lessons.
Indo-Pacific Divers (see the Sea Breeze Bungalows, Bunaken), Jl Piere Tendean 89, Manado, ☎ (0431) 86 11 00/ 85 93 79, Fax (0431) 85 93 68, kudalaut@manado.wasantara.net.id Also well known for its professionalism.
Dive Manado (Bunaken Diver's Lodge, Bunaken), ☎ (0431) 86 52 98 / 82 52 48, Fax (0431) 86 52 98.

NOTES

NOTES

NOTES

NOTES

INDEX

Tana Lot (Pura) (Bali): place or attraction described in the text
Daendels (Herman Willem): individual
Batik: term explained in the text or practical information
Abbreviations:

(Lomb): Lombok	(Suma): Sumatra
(Komo): Komodo	(Sumb): Sumbawa
(Madu): Madura	(Sula): Sulawesi

R

Maps and plans

Manufacture Française des Pneumatiques Michelin
Société en commandite par actions au capital de 2 000 000 000 de francs
Place des Carmes-Déchaux – 63000 Clermont-Ferrand (France)
R.C.S. Clermont-Fd B 855 200 507

© Michelin et Cie, Propriétaires-éditeurs, 2000
Dépôt légal décembre 2000 – ISBN 2-06-855701-0 – ISSN 0763-1383
No part of this publication may be reproduced in any form without
the prior permission of the publisher.
Made in France 11-00/1.1
Compograveur : Nord Compo – Villeneuve d'Ascq
Imprimeur : IME – Baume-les-Dames

Cover photography :
Young girl (P. Benet)
Rice fields, Bali (D. Waugh/Fotogram-Stone)
Klungkung warriors, Bali (E. Planchard/DIAF)

Your opinion matters!

In order to make sure that this collection satisfies the needs of our readers, please help us by completing the following questionnaire with your comments and suggestions and return to:

Michelin Travel Publications   or   **Michelin Travel Publications**
The Edward Hyde Building   P.O. Box 19008
38 Clarendon Road   Greenville, SC 29602-9008
Watford, UK   USA

▪ YOUR HOLIDAYS/VACATIONS:

1. In general, when you go on holiday or vacation, do you tend to travel... (Choose one)
- ☐ Independently, on your own
- ☐ Independently, as a couple
- ☐ With 1 or 2 friends
- ☐ With your family
- ☐ With a group of friends
- ☐ On organised trips

2. How many international holidays or vacations of 1 week or more have you taken in the last 3 years? _____

Last 3 destinations: Month/Year:

_____   _____

_____   _____

_____   _____

3. What do you look for most when planning a holiday or vacation?

	Not at all	*Sometimes*	*Essential*
Somewhere new and exotic	☐	☐	☐
Real experience/meeting people	☐	☐	☐
Experiencing the wildlife/scenery	☐	☐	☐
Cultural insight	☐	☐	☐
Rest & relaxation	☐	☐	☐
Comfort & well-being	☐	☐	☐
Adventure & the unexpected	☐	☐	☐

4. When travelling, do you take a travel guide with you?
☐ Always   ☐ Usually   ☐ Sometimes   ☐ Never

▪ You and the Michelin NEOS guides

5. About your purchase of a NEOS Guide
How long was your holiday where you used the NEOS guide?
How many days? _____
For which country or countries? _____
How long before your departure did you buy it? How many days? _____

6. What made you choose a NEOS Guide?
Highlight everything that applies.
- ☐ Something new and interesting
- ☐ The layout
- ☐ Easy to read format
- ☐ Cultural details
- ☐ Quality of the text
- ☐ Quality of the mapping
- ☐ Practical Information
- ☐ Michelin quality

7. Which sections did you use most during your holiday or vacation?

Score 1-4   *(1 = least used)*   *(4 = most used)*

	1	2	3	4
"Setting the Scene"	☐ 1	☐ 2	☐ 3	☐ 4
"Meeting the People"	☐ 1	☐ 2	☐ 3	☐ 4
"Practical Information"	☐ 1	☐ 2	☐ 3	☐ 4
"Exploring …"	☐ 1	☐ 2	☐ 3	☐ 4

8. How would you rate the following aspects of your NEOS guide?

Score 1-4   *(1 = Poor)*   *(4 = Excellent)*

	1	2	3	4
Cover design	☐ 1	☐ 2	☐ 3	☐ 4
Chapter Order	☐ 1	☐ 2	☐ 3	☐ 4
Layout (photos, diagrams)	☐ 1	☐ 2	☐ 3	☐ 4
Ease of reading (typeface)	☐ 1	☐ 2	☐ 3	☐ 4
Style of writing	☐ 1	☐ 2	☐ 3	☐ 4
Text boxes and stories	☐ 1	☐ 2	☐ 3	☐ 4
Plans & Maps	☐ 1	☐ 2	☐ 3	☐ 4
Star ratings system	☐ 1	☐ 2	☐ 3	☐ 4
Format	☐ 1	☐ 2	☐ 3	☐ 4
Weight	☐ 1	☐ 2	☐ 3	☐ 4
Durability	☐ 1	☐ 2	☐ 3	☐ 4
Price	☐ 1	☐ 2	☐ 3	☐ 4

9. Did you use other travel guides during your trip?   ☐ Yes   ☐ No
If yes, which ones? _____

10. Please give your NEOS guide a rating out of 20: ____/20 (with 20 as top rating)
Would you use a NEOS guide for your next trip?   ☐ Yes   ☐ No
If no, why not? _____
Which other destinations would you like NEOS to cover? _____

11. Any other comments or suggestions: _____

_____

_____

_____

_____

_____

_____

Surname/Last Name: _____ First Name: _____

Address: _____

Age: _____ Sex: ☐ M ☐ F

Profession: _____

Where did you purchase your NEOS Guide: What type of store?
                                    Which country?